Encyclopedia of AMERICAN ECONOMIC HISTORY

Studies of the Principal Movements and Ideas

Glenn Porter, EDITOR
University of Delaware / Eleutherian Mills-Hagley Foundation

Volume II

CHARLES SCRIBNER'S SONS · NEW YORK

Copyright © 1980 Charles Scribner's Sons

Library of Congress Cataloging in Publication Data

Main entry under title:

Encyclopedia of American economic history.
    Includes bibliographies and index.
    1. United States—Economic conditions—Addresses, essays, lectures. I. Porter, Glenn.
HC103.E52   330.9′73   79–4946

ISBN 0-684-16271-7   Set
ISBN 0-684-16510-4   Volume I
ISBN 0-684-16511-2   Volume II
ISBN 0-684-16512-0   Volume III

This book published simultaneously in the
United States of America and in Canada –
Copyright under the Berne Convention

All rights reserved. No part of this book
may be reproduced in any form without the
permission of Charles Scribner's Sons.

1 3 5 7 9 11 13 15 17 19 V/C 20 18 16 14 12 10 8 6 4 2

Printed in the United States of America

Acknowledgment is gratefully made to those publishers and individuals who have permitted the use of the following materials in copyright.

Mergers
Table 1; page 646, "The Decline of the Horizontal Merger, 1926–1964," from C. Eis, "The 1919–1930 Merger Movement in American Industry," *Journal of Law and Economics* 12 (1969), p. 294. Used with permission of *Journal of Law and Economics*.

Government Management of the Economy
Table 1, page 823, "Comparison of Built-in Fiscal Stabilizers with Discretionary Policies in Postwar Recessions and Recoveries," from Wilfred Lewis, *Federal Fiscal Policy in the Postwar Recessions,* copyright © 1962 by the Brookings Institution. Used with permission of the Brookings Institution.

Encyclopedia of
**AMERICAN
ECONOMIC
HISTORY**

Part IV
THE AMERICAN INSTITUTIONAL FRAMEWORK

LAW AND POLITICAL INSTITUTIONS

Harry N. Scheiber

AN economic system necessarily functions within the framework of legal and political institutions. Whether the political order is authoritarian or democratic, law is the product of political processes: through law, society formally invokes government power to establish the rules by which economic activity may be pursued. Thus law defines private rights; it establishes the reach and limits of government power; and it orders and adjusts social relations. Whether the economic system is capitalist, socialist, or mixed, its basic institutions are shaped by law.

Historic economic change, therefore, cannot be analyzed exclusively in terms of supply and demand forces in the marketplace. As Simon Kuznets has written in *Toward a Theory of Economic Growth* (1968), even though the United States historically maintained a large measure of freedom for private property and private enterprise, its historical record

> ... is full of decisions by the state on matters that were vital to economic growth, where a different set of decisions would have meant a different course of economic growth. Every decade marked some [such] decision by the state—on currency, on tariffs, on internal improvements, on land, on labor, on immigration—and each one was reached after explicit discussion in which its importance for the country's economic growth was recognized [p. 108].

Kuznets' emphasis on "explicit discussion" of policy decisions needs qualification, for it seems that certain vital features of the legal order were established and accepted as the result of what James Willard Hurst (in *Law and the Conditions of Freedom in the Nineteenth-Century United States*) has termed "drift and default"—the almost unthinking popular acceptance of certain basic social values and economic policies. These were a matter more of popular faith than of explicit debate and decision: popular faith, for example, in the need for economic growth, in material progress, in releasing private energies and encouraging capitalist entrepreneurship. To be sure, such assumptions did not go unchallenged, for there were times when the society divided bitterly on matters of economic ideology. If there has been a "materialist consensus," there also has always been a strong dissenting tradition in the United States. But faith in economic growth and the positive social value of rising productivity has been the dominant element supporting the uses of law in America.

PRIVATE PROPERTY: A CASE IN POINT

To illustrate the interplay of law and economic change, the question of property rights—a matter that lies at the very heart of the American capitalist system—will be considered. Property is, in the last analysis, a bundle of legal rights, privileges, and immunities. Even if one accepts, for purposes of argument, the notion that American law places extremely high priority on the protection of private persons' rights to their property, one must beware of the seductive corollary assumption that the legal system is therefore only a passive actor in the dynamics of economic change.

Consider the case of Mr. Smith, who owns a tract of land on which he decides to build a sulfur mill. Necessarily this use of Smith's property is going to be a threat to his neighbors because there is going to be an outflow of noxious substances. Hence, the question immediately follows: which way will the law lean? Will it favor Smith's right to use his property for sulfur milling, or will it favor his neighbors' right to protect their property values against the damage that will result from Smith's milling operation? A choice is inescapable. The law must either hedge, and confine Smith's entrepreneurial ambitions, or else stand aside, and permit his neighbors to suffer from them.

Whatever balance the law strikes, government will have intervened by a process of defining property rights. Whether government is in general interventionist or laissez-faire in its preferences is largely irrelevant to this case. The legal order necessarily becomes an active, vital intermediary in the "market relationships" between Smith and his neighbors.

Basic political institutions are going to play a decisive role in determining what policy will be followed. If the political system is under the effective control of sulfur producers or those who identify with them, the law will reflect this balance of political power and will favor Smith. If, on the other hand, the dominant political elements sympathize with Smith's neighbors, their interests will be upheld. The degree to which the political institutions of the society permit mobilization of sentiment on either side, and its translation into real political power, is also of prime importance. If government is so complex, or corrupt, or paralyzed by inertia that one side or the other cannot make its influence felt, then the law may possibly come to a conclusion in this matter that frustrates the majority view, or even the view of the normally dominant political element (whether it is a majority or not).

The case of Smith's sulfur mill is by no means hopelessly divorced from the realities of American law and economy. In fact, it is precisely analogous to confrontations that have taken place in American society from its colonial beginnings to the present. The legal system has constantly been required to make decisions about the abridgment or abolition of established property rights and about the creation of new types of property rights. In effect the law has established economic priorities, and these have changed over time. Moreover, political institutions and the law have functioned in this way fully as much in periods of dominant laissez-faire as they have in periods when government has been characterized by conscious, broad-ranging intervention after extensive "explicit discussion" of alternatives.

THE COLONIAL LEGACIES

Each of the regions that became part of the United States had its own system of law that was the legacy of its colonial era. The principal legacy, of course, was that of English law, which dominated in the British North American colonies and was imaginatively adapted to the American constitutional system after the Revolution. But New York—both in the colonial period and after 1776—also perpetuated some elements of Dutch law that had provided the framework of economic life there in the early seventeenth century. In Florida, Louisiana, and the entire region (except Oregon and Washington) west of the Mississippi, the prevailing tradition was not the law of England (broadly defined as "the common law") but the civil law, which derived from Roman law and was dominant in the nations of western Europe.

France and Spain, and later Mexico, had transferred the civil law to the areas that they controlled in North America. Indeed, even after attaining statehood, Louisiana maintained much of its civil law in effect instead of adopting the common law, as other states did. In California and other states formerly under Spanish and Mexican control, although the common law was largely adopted, certain key elements of civil law were also perpetuated. Thus California courts in the nineteenth century recognized the "pueblo rights" of municipalities that originally had been chartered by Spanish or Mexican authority (rights, for example, to remote sources of water to supply these municipalities and rights of the urban community as a whole to certain common lands within their precincts). They also perpetuated the rule of "community property," which assured wives of a stronger claim to goods owned by the husband than was assured by English law. All the former civil-law jurisdictions also perpetuated, to varying degrees, technical "rules of pleading" that governed procedures in the pursuit of claims in their courts.

Nevertheless, the dominant legal tradition in the United States has been that of English law. Broadly defined, "common law" embraces the

LAW AND POLITICAL INSTITUTIONS

entire body of cumulative judicial decisions and constitutional principles, dating from the Magna Carta (1215), that are the legacy of English jurisprudence. In the English legal tradition, statute laws enacted by Parliament are supreme. But there is a vast range of rules concerning property, estates, family relations, the status of labor, mercantile practices, and other matters that is not strictly governed in detail by statutes. On these matters the courts settle disputes and establish both broad principles of law and detailed procedures for legal action. The body of precedent that results is, in essence, the common law of England. Both in its technical aspects, such as in rules of pleading, and in many vital substantive matters, such as guarantee of trial by jury in criminal cases, the norms of the common law were basically different from those of European civil law.

More narrowly defined, "common law" was a term that applied to the body of precedent and rules that were generated by English royal central courts (King's Bench, Exchequer, Court of Common Pleas). Defined in this narrower way, common law was only one subsystem of English law. At the time the English colonies were being founded in the New World, the legal system of the home country also embodied other important subsystems. First, there was customary law, which prevailed on the manors in the countryside and under which most of the day-to-day affairs of ordinary rural people were adjudicated. Second, equity law, administered by the chancery court, acted on persons rather than things; under it, courts could issue injunctions requiring certain types of private action, failing which imprisonment for contempt could result. Third, there was the law of the church; in the ecclesiastical courts family relations and certain types of estates were governed by rules and procedures often basically different from those of the secular courts. Fourth, a body of law based mainly on civil-law principles, called the law merchant, was enforced by special merchants' courts and governed most of the commercial transactions that transcended merely local trade. (There were also special courts with jurisdiction over merchants in special matters and called piepoudre, originally established on an ad hoc basis to rule on disputes at the fairs where merchants periodically gathered.) Fifth, admiralty law, governing maritime trade and enforcement of the rules of navigation and overseas commerce, was administered by centralized admiralty courts under control of the crown. Apart from all these separate subsystems of the English legal system, there were the overriding elements of statute law, coming from Parliament, and of royal proclamations, emanating from the crown.

The English legal heritage was, then, a complex one. And the American colonies perpetuated this complexity, with each colony developing its unique mix of rules, procedures, and judicial institutions. Each colony, in short, "adapted" English law to its own situation, in its own way.

But if there was abundant diversity, there also were common patterns in basic political structure. Above all, each English colony—whether originally a proprietary colony, a royal colony, or a corporate enterprise under control of a chartered company—eventually won broad powers of self-government. By the end of the seventeenth century, each colony had established an elected legislature, or "assembly," with power to enact statute law controlling most of the important institutions and affairs of everyday life. To be sure, there were bitter conflicts in most of the colonies, pitting the assembly against the proprietors or the crown over the extent to which the rights of self-government should properly reach. Statutes were subject to veto by the appointed governor in each colony; and all colonial legislation was also subject to reversal by the English Privy Council, which served in effect as an appellate court and censorial body beginning in the 1670's. Gradually the assemblies made secure their claim to the "rights and liberties" of Englishmen. As the power of self-government became established, the assemblies won control over internal taxes, vital aspects of property law, the law of estates and descent, law regulating the status of labor (free, indentured, and slave), and commercial law.

All the colonial governments established courts to administer the common law and their own statutes. But only a few colonies, all of them outside New England, established equity courts as well. The English ecclesiastical courts were absent from the American scene entirely, although in New England both religious sanctions and a religious presence in all councils of government were of great importance. In each colony there was an appointed "council," which advised the governor, reviewed legislation enacted by the assembly, and served as a court of appeals.

Each colony adopted its own system of local law. Outside New England there were county justices of the peace, sheriffs, and commissioners empowered to levy local taxes, to lay out roads and highways, to conscript citizens' labor for road work, and the like. These local officials had authority to decree marketing regulations; and they adjudicated day-to-day disputes among the common people, much as the manor courts of England regulated local affairs. In New England authority in local affairs was vested in the township governments. The assemblies granted lands to communities of specifically named "freemen" or "proprietors," who would establish the new settlements. These people were empowered to allot the town land to its inhabitants and "to dispose of all the civil affairs of the Town."

All the people of the town were, under basic Massachusetts law as formalized in *The Book of the General Lawes and Libertyes* (1648), allowed to attend and participate in town meetings; the freemen (those who had voting rights) of each town were given full power "to make such by-laws and constitutions as may concern the welfare of their town . . . not repugnant to the public laws of the country." The General Court (as the Massachusetts assembly was called) also appointed militia officers, justices of the peace, and a constable for each town. The range of what was regarded as the legitimate concern of government became manifest in constables' orders to report on military defense, vagrancy and idleness, crime, commerce and marketplaces, taverns, and the progress of inhabitants in building cottages and putting in improvements. Disputes and lawsuits that could not be settled locally, or that involved the townships and the Indians, were referred to the provincial courts and assembly. In the middle colonies and the South, similar powers were vested in the county commissioners and justices of the peace.

Although the English colonies exercised broad-ranging powers of self-government by 1700, a common element of their respective legal systems was subordination to Parliament and the royal government as the ultimate arbiters of their law. Thus, they were subject to the regulations embodied in the Navigation Acts and other statutes or orders governing basic relations of colonies to the home country. The Navigation Acts regulated trade and shipping—although enforcement of these laws was notoriously difficult, and the colonists blatantly evaded many of them until the 1760's. Parliament also decreed certain broad prohibitions affecting intercolonial commerce, such as the Hat Act (1732) and the Iron Act (1750). The home government provided subsidies for production of indigo, rice, naval stores, and other commodities needed in England; and royal officials controlled the cutting of tall pines needed to build ships for the Royal Navy. Commissioners appointed by the crown and given jurisdiction in the colonial ports collected customs duties and enforced shipping rules. In times of war the home government expected the colonies to muster troops for use in North America and to levy special taxes. And when it was short of sailors, the Royal Navy sent conscription parties, much dreaded, through the colonial port towns to impress seamen.

Apart from being subject in these respects to imperial authority, the colonies had in common a tradition of repeatedly asserting what they termed their "constitutional claims" against England. That is, in formal remonstrances to the English government, but also frequently by overt resistance to royal authority, the colonies contested the claims of England to control what the assemblies viewed as their "internal" affairs. As noted earlier, in some instances the colonists' constitutional claims were founded on the "rights and liberties" of Englishmen. In other instances—especially in cases involving the New England colonies—the Americans founded their claims on astonishingly broad provisions of their original or amended royal charters, which had granted explicit powers of self-government.

Every colony had at least one dramatic confrontation with English imperial authority, either directly or indirectly (in contests with proprietors). In the last quarter of the seventeenth century, these clashes became so frequent that Charles Andrews (in *Colonial Self-Government*) has termed this period "the era of the insurrections." Moreover, from the 1660's until the American Revolution, English efforts to tighten enforcement of the Navigation Acts and to collect the royal customs duties repeatedly triggered colonial responses: customs officers were hauled before colonial courts, or there was mob action and armed violence. Meeting such resistance, royal officials typically drew back from extreme measures for the enforcement of trade regulations. Hence, so far as the trade acts were concerned, "for nearly forty years . . . after 1725 little was done to assert English authority in the colonies or to correct the obvious administrative defects. . . . Prosperity, not glory, was the keystone of Whig thought" that then dominated imperial government (Barrow 1967, p. 113). In sum, salutary neglect was to characterize colonial relations with the home country. When that policy gave way, after 1763, to strict enforcement of the trade laws, the fatal confrontation resulting in the Revolution began.

From the standpoint of the emerging colonial economy, the political structure and the legal institutions of the seventeenth and eighteenth centuries had several important effects. In the first place, many of the constitutional claims and the confrontations they precipitated were closely linked to issues of economic policy. Indeed, the linchpin of controversies that most persistently vexed colonial relations with the home country was English imperial trade policy. The "enumeration" of certain commodities (most notably tobacco) of colonial export—confining them to the English market as the initial destination of shipment; the heavy taxation of foreign commodities imported by the colonies, such as the heavy duties on French and Dutch rum, sugar, and molasses under the 1733 Molasses Act—widely and blatantly evaded by colonial merchants for more than three decades; and restrictions upon shipping and overseas commerce more generally represented a direct and much-resented threat to the American merchants and shippers. Another major irritant in relations with England was Indian policy, with land speculators and small-scale settlers in America pushing actively for an aggressive policy and the British attempting to head off unnecessary conflicts.

Similarly, popular resistance to paying quitrents (annual money payments in perpetuity by private landowners, in lieu of services to a feudal lord) to proprietors in several colonies resulted in political turmoil, challenges to both crown and proprietors' authority, and, in several instances, overt violence. Closely related to quitrents was taxation policy, which affected not only small farmers but also the owners of great landed estates and of plantations in the South. Throughout the eighteenth century, moreover, the power of the colonial governments to issue currency and authorize banking—matters of prime importance to the merchants—caused repeated confrontations with the home country, as the Privy Council vetoed numerous currency laws.

In the second place, the political structure of the colonies gave elite groups in America great leverage in fostering their economic interests. All the governors' councils and, in many colonies, the lower houses of assembly were dominated by the large-scale landowners, the urban merchants, and, in the South, the plantation aristocracy. These men also held the important appointive offices in the provincial executive offices and local governments. As Clarence Ver Steeg observed in *The Formative Years: 1607–1763*: "Whether local government operated in terms of townships, as in New England, or counties, the result was to elevate a group of local gentry who became accustomed to managing local matters" (p. 276). The same was true of the port towns (except Boston), as the leading merchants obtained a virtual monopoly on the membership of lawmaking councils. Thus provincial statute books abounded with laws for inspection of food and other items of trade, public warehousing, legislative apportionment favoring wealthier districts, and similar legislation in defense of important elite-group interests.

Furthermore, domination of public offices by provincial and local oligarchies gave elite groups profitable opportunities to benefit from the largess of the colonial government. Thus, they not only enjoyed salaries or handsome fees for public service; they also were favored when contracts were awarded, especially for supplies in wartime, and they frequently received enormous land grants as special favors from the proprietors or governors. Their control of the political structure in addition permitted these colonial elites to mobilize not only the assemblies but also—if it suited their purposes—considerable popular support, even including support by mobs, when their vital economic interests were threatened by English imperial authorities. Although they were no friends of mass participation in government, the elite groups were always willing to enlist the lower orders in their causes against England; this was, of course, a risky strategy, since mass participation in political processes could easily lead to democratization of institutions. Indeed, by the late 1760's the political dynamics of mass resistance to English authority was bringing about such democratization.

Finally, the political institutions of colonial America had a major impact upon economic development because they afforded great latitude for the shaping of a legal system that reflected (and was responsive to) the needs and aspirations of emergent American capitalism. Because each colony developed its own peculiar mix of legal institutions and substantive policies, there was also a rich diversity of structures and practices.

THINGS DISCARDED, REFORMED, AND ADAPTED

Historians' research on colonial law in America has substantially documented Max Radin's view (in "The Rivalry of Common-Law and Civil-Law Ideas in the American Colonies") that "the common law in the period between 1660 and 1776 certainly made great strides toward the domination of the law of America. But it never quite achieved it. Throughout the colonial period it remained a subsidiary, supplementary law, . . . regarded some times with veneration and at others with suspicion and hostility." For, at best, the heritage of the English courts had to share the arena of power with the colonial charters as basic constitutional documents; with parliamentary statutes, orders in council, and other edicts of the royal government, and local customs and usages (including the decrees of municipal authorities in port towns, the town meetings in New England, and county commissions in the middle and southern colonies); and with the independent decisions of judges who sat in colonial courts. Indeed, it is not too much to say, as George Haskins has argued, that "the law which the settlers brought with them was a curious mixture of religious ideas and of half-remembered customs from other lands" (in Billias, ed., *Law and Authority in Colonial America*, p. 26).

The common law, defined as the embracing traditional heritage of English law, consistently dominated colonial regulation of "private law" —that is, contractual agreements between individuals. Thus, there was little colonial legislation on the rules and procedures of private contract. Technical questions regarding the validity of contracts and the obligations of the parties to them were, typically, settled by colonial judges on the basis of English rules and precedents. It is more accurate to say "English rules and precedents as individual American judges understood them." Especially in the seventeenth century, when law books were seldom available in many American courtrooms, and when colonial decisions were not published, judicial interpretations of the common law undoubtedly varied greatly over time and from one place to another.

Similarly, with tort law—the rules regarding damages to others, including legal assignment of fault and responsibility—the English heritage was variously interpreted. Thus, in some jurisdictions courts applied the common-law rule, holding employers responsible for tortious acts by their workers only when the latter were responding to specific instructions; in other courts a broader standard of employer liability was enforced. Even in criminal law the statutes were often silent on a wide range of specific offenses or simply invoked the law of England, thus leaving it to the courts to impose their diverse versions of English law—or to manufacture variants on old law deemed more appropriate to American society.

In one area of law above all, the colonial legislatures departed significantly from the received English tradition. This was in law pertaining to land and (a closely related matter) the descent of estates. In the home country the land was closely bound by legal rules designed principally to assure stability of tenure—and with it stability of the social status quo—and insofar as English law provided for the transferability of land or changes in the terms of tenure, it was geared to the advantage of the gentry against the interests of the common people who worked the soil. In all the colonies, to varying degrees, "land transactions were converted from status to contract, from a matter of family and birth, to the subject of a free and open market" (Friedman 1973, p. 55). The intricate documentary forms and rules of pleading that made it expensive, in terms of legal costs, as well as a complex affair to transfer land in England were supplanted in the American colonies by relatively simple rules and procedures. More important still, the colonial assemblies and courts stripped all they could of the feudal overlay from English land law, to make land a commodity easily bought and sold in the

LAW AND POLITICAL INSTITUTIONS

marketplace—a commodity obtainable legally on a "free and clear" fee-simple basis, liberated from burdensome obligations and dues owed manorial lords, subject only to money taxes that would be imposed by the elected representatives of the people.

The new status of land as an abundant, transferable commodity was nowhere more evident than in the colonial policies of granting real estate to settlers and entrepreneurs—a vital instrument of government in fostering immigration, the making of new farms, and, more generally, material growth. In both Virginia and Pennsylvania a headright of fifty acres was given to anyone who brought in an immigrant, and indentured servants became entitled to land in their own names on becoming freemen. Throughout British North America the governors and proprietors lavished gigantic grants of land on favored individuals, in payment for public service and in hopes of seeing new lands settled. In New England a different pattern prevailed, with township government serving as the intermediary for disposition of the land and vesting of real property rights to private individuals—but with reservation of "common" land in each town, to be used for the community as a whole. In New England no quitrents or other feudal dues attached to private titles obtained. In the proprietary and royal colonies, quitrents were common; but they were collected only with great difficulty, often resisted by force, and in several colonies rendered practically inoperative.

The tendency everywhere was toward possessive individualism in the institutions of landed property. Once title was settled on a private owner, the common law operated heavily against activities by others (the early-day prototypes of the sulfur miller, Mr. Smith, discussed above) that might damage their property values. William Nelson has described how the common law worked in colonial Massachusetts:

> At the root of the law of land was the common law concept of seisin. The significance of seisin was that it gave legal protection to existing patterns of resource allocation. The basic rule of land law was that "Prior Poss[essio]n" would be deemed "a good Title ag[ains]t him who hath no Title." By so protecting a person who either was in actual possession of land or was otherwise taking profits from it, the law provided stability by giving men the assurance that they could continue to use in the future the land they were using in the present [*Americanization of the Common Law*, pp. 48–49].

Contrary to what would become the dominant tendency in American law in the nineteenth century, the colonial legal system worked to protect vested private rights in landed property. And that, after all, is precisely what one would expect of a legal system produced by (and designed to serve) an emergent American capitalist order based heavily upon agricultural enterprise.

The laws of descent and inheritance—governing what a person legally can do, and cannot do, in disposing of his or her property at death—are a powerful instrument of social control. The rules of a society concerning this matter can go far toward shaping property distribution on either a concentrated or a diffused basis, and toward determining the degree of concentration that will prevail, particularly in landholding. Few legal issues, therefore, were so important as this when the English colonists set about creating the sort of society they wanted to build in the New World. And in few other particulars did their law depart so markedly from the English tradition. In England the prevailing common-law rule was primogeniture, by which at death a man's land passed to the eldest son. (Under dower rules, in the common law, a one-third share of income from the deceased husband's land was reserved to the widow for her lifetime.) Along with entail —the doctrine that restricted descent of inherited landed estates to a single family line— primogeniture long survived in the southern colonies and in New York. But even in the South, where these laws were finally overturned in the Revolutionary period and immediately afterward, the legislatures and courts throughout the eighteenth century made it progressively easier to dock (break) entail restrictions on estates.

In New England, except Rhode Island, and in Pennsylvania, a much clearer break with the English tradition came in the early years of settlement. The model for reforming legislation and judicial innovations elsewhere was Massachusetts. There "gavelkind"—the rule that had prevailed, contrary to general common-law practice, in the county of Kent in England—was early established; by gavelkind, estates of persons dying without wills were divided equally among the sons (the oldest son receiving a double share).

LAW AND POLITICAL INSTITUTIONS

Pressure on other colonies to reshape their laws on the Massachusetts example was great. The reason was only partly humanitarian, a concern for the welfare of younger children; it was also a matter of social policy, a desire to prevent "landed monopoly" and concentrations of wealth that could militate against social mobility and efficient use of resources. And, further, it was partly a matter of competition among the colonies for immigrants. Entail and primogeniture were discouraging new settlement in East Jersey, a critic of the laws of that colony declared in 1683: Reduce men's prospects, by the primogeniture rule, to a life of "miserable and tedious Drudgery" and "their Spirits are spoiled," drained of enterprise. Similarly, a trustee of the Georgia colony observed that because of strict primogeniture and entail, "Inhabitants were daily withdrawing themselves" to make homes in other colonies. "We must change our [laws], or the colony would be entirely abandon'd" (quoted in Morris, *Studies in the History of American Law*, pp. 77, 87).

If American colonial law thus was adapted to the differing social and economic structures of the individual colonies—reformed, to expedite the development of small family farms in the North; and conserved, to accommodate the great plantations of the South—the law was also bent and shaped to the needs of the enterprising merchant class. In one important respect the colonies reformed the law merchant in advance of English practice: in the seventeenth century, Connecticut, Pennsylvania, New York, and several other colonies made it a simple matter to assign debts in the form of negotiable notes not witnessed—thus providing a vital instrument of commerce to the merchants.

More generally the urban merchants were given wide powers by dint of their control of municipal government in the port towns. (Boston was an exception; instead of corporate municipal government, the town was ruled by the traditional New England town meeting. There was direct participation by all residents who chose to attend.) A study by Jon C. Teaford has shown that between 50 and 60 percent of municipal ordinances in selected major towns, in the early eighteenth century, were directly concerned with regulation of trade and markets.

Contrary to the tendency in land law, the trend in municipal commercial regulation was restrictive, representing heavy-handed interference by government. The trading towns regulated prices of bread and other major commodities in trade; they promulgated complex regulations to govern markets and fairs; frequently they restricted entry into certain trades, or even established local monopolies. Weights and measures were standardized, and the city councils regulated apprenticeship in an effort to upgrade quality and make new entry more difficult. The preoccupation with conditions of commerce continued until the late eighteenth century, when pressure for greater freedom from government interference built up against the merchant-oligarchs, and when the city councils turned their attention to provision of social services, safety, and welfare measures.

Regulation of labor was even more heavy-handed, and it reflected the problems of a society that faced chronic labor shortages. Both the colonial assemblies and the municipal councils operated squarely in the tradition of English law, which in that period was geared toward close regulation of apprenticeship, wages, and relations between masters and employees. Paternalism in the form of wage regulation reached its high point in New England during the seventeenth century. Early Massachusetts wage controls concentrated upon the skilled laborers who worked in building trades—an important sector in the economy of a society starting afresh and attracting a steady stream of new immigrants, only a small proportion of whom were skilled construction laborers. Later, Massachusetts specified maximum wages for a broad range of crafts, also devolving upon town officers the power to establish wage controls at the local level.

As John Winthrop admitted, as early as 1640, a colony that controlled workers' wages risked that "they would either remove to other places where they might have more, or else [were] able to live by planting and other employments of their own" (quoted in Morris, *Government and Labor in Early America*, p. 56). Nonetheless, wage controls were imposed (with varying degrees of success), both in New England and elsewhere, well into the early eighteenth century; and they were briefly revived in the period of critical labor shortages during the American Revolution.

Like the law of inheritance, labor law could serve more generally as an instrument of social control and a lever for supporting material growth. The colonies enacted an elaborate set of laws regulating the conditions of labor indenture. Indentured servants, who contracted their labor for a specified number of years, were held strictly to the terms of contracts. In addition to consenting adults who made voluntary indentures, servants in this category included criminals sentenced to indentures by English and colonial courts; poor persons who had become public charges; and orphaned children who were bound as servants by court order. Thus, as Lawrence Friedman has written, the many functions of the indenture system meant it was "a method of organizing labor, of financing immigration, a penal sanction, a way of training the young, a kind of welfare institution" (*A History of American Law*, p. 72).

Closely related to the indenture laws were statutes that pertained to black and Indian slaves. Historians have debated endlessly the question of how the law of slavery emerged, especially when and in what way it became differentiated from the more general labor laws concerning servants. But it is now generally recognized that what, above all, impelled the emergence of a law of slavery was the avarice of southern planters in the tobacco and rice districts. Unable to attract and hold white laborers in sufficient number, they created a law of chattel slavery that could bind nonwhites to perpetual service and that made slaves' children the property of the master. Racial prejudice, the readily accessible African slave trade, and common greed combined to produce black slavery—together with enslavement of Indians—as a separate legal status by the mid-seventeenth century.

Summing up, then, the colonists constructed a legal system—or, more accurately, thirteen legal systems—that constituted a multifaceted heritage for the new nation after 1776. The law of each colony was an amalgam of new doctrines and old. In the staple-producing southern colonies, both the political structure and the law operated to perpetuate a landed oligarchy, on seated estates (protected by entail), with a labor force consisting mainly of slaves. In the middle and New England colonies, departures from both hierarchical political structure and (more especially) English land and inheritance law were more dramatic. There, newly fashioned American law operated to make land a readily salable commodity and to foster a society of family farmers. Township government tended at first to be paternalistic, with communal values and a strong sense of corporative purpose evident. But over time, even in the most conservative areas of New England, privatism and individualism had begun to work major reforms in the law. As Jack P. Greene has written in "Autonomy and Stability . . . ," the quickening pace of commerce, material advancement, and rising population in the eighteenth century undermined the corporate spirit in favor of "social atomism and the behavioral mandates of initiative and autonomy."

Both in the plantation colonies of the South and in the northern colonies with their combination of thriving mercantile centers and agricultural hinterlands, the ruling American elite groups used government and legal institutions to direct the course of development. Often restricted and frustrated by British mercantilist policies, they were in more or less constant tension with England over the question of how far their rights of self-government reached. Once the king's ministers decided in 1763 that the old policy of "salutary neglect" was to be abandoned, with severe new taxes and political controls to be imposed on the American colonies, the dynamics of the Revolution were forcefully set in motion.

THE NEW NATION

The success of the Revolutionary War placed American law on an entirely new foundation. During the war itself the newly formed state governments formally adopted constitutions for themselves, and under the Articles of Confederation the states provided the basis of a federated national government. But in many vital respects the power of Congress and the central government was strictly limited. Thus, although the Continental Congress did negotiate the peace with England and write the basic law for political organization in the West (in the Northwest Ordinance of 1787), there was intense dissatisfaction with its performance.

Conservative propertied elements were especially critical of government under the Articles of Confederation. On the one hand they were alarmed by the direction that affairs were taking in the individual states. Several states adopted laws deemed menacing to private property rights, laws that abrogated the terms of contracts and provided sweeping relief to debtors amid the depression conditions that prevailed in the mid-1780's. Also, by 1786 there were signs of serious social disorder—what George Washington and others deemed a situation close to anarchy—when Shays's Rebellion in Massachusetts and other instances of popular resistance to authority beset the new political order.

On the other hand many political leaders, among them a large segment of the mercantile elite, who found allies among nationalists such as James Madison, were alarmed by the basic weakness of the central government. They feared not only that property rights would not be protected by the states, but also that only a central government empowered to levy taxes directly, to maintain a strong army and navy, to enforce its own laws, and to negotiate from a position of strength with foreign powers could provide the stability and authority necessary for survival of the new nation. Petty commercial rivalries among the states, taking the form of trade restrictions within the national commerce, reinforced the nationalists' determination to produce a stronger union.

The result was the Constitutional Convention and the drafting of a new charter of union, which was submitted to the states in 1787. The Constitution met with bitter opposition. Many state leaders regarded it as an instrument of conservatism, designed to frustrate popular influence in government and to create a central authority capable of crushing states' rights and popular liberties. But the nationalists won the day, and the new government was organized in 1789. Ratification by nine states left the others with no choice but to fall in line.

The Constitution, as it had been designed to do, provided the basis for a central government capable of effective action. So far as economic affairs were concerned, the Constitution vested exclusively in the national government the power to coin money, to regulate commerce among the states, to establish a patent system, and to impose customs duties on imports. Congress was empowered to borrow money on the credit of the United States, establish post offices and post roads, enact uniform naturalization and bankruptcy laws, and frame admiralty laws. Pregnant with implications for the future of the nation, moreover, was a provision enabling Congress "to make all laws which shall be necessary and proper" for exercise of its explicit powers. This last provision became, within a short time, the basis of legitimacy for such measures as the federal chartering of the Bank of the United States; and in future years the Supreme Court would rely heavily on the "necessary and proper" clause to validate a wide range of federal powers.

The Constitution was also an instrument for the limitation of government powers. The states were forbidden to enact ex post facto laws or any laws impairing the obligation of contracts; they could not emit bills of credit or coin money; and their laws affecting foreign commerce were limited strictly to those necessary for "executing . . . inspection laws." Congress, for its part, was prohibited from levying direct taxes except in proportion to the population of the states; and it was required to permit the slave trade to continue until 1808. Moreover, in the Bill of Rights, which took effect in 1791, the Fifth Amendment stated that no person might "be deprived of life, liberty, or property, without due process of law; nor shall private property be taken for public use, without just compensation."

The federal structure of government also served as a limitation upon centralized public power. By assigning responsibility for certain matters to the central government while leaving many other areas of authority to the states, the constitutional system known as "federalism" was relied upon to thwart any effort to establish a new tyranny over the states and the people. In this respect the Founding Fathers planned well, as was proved by the subsequent history of the nation. Not until the Civil War brought profound changes in the Constitution did power become heavily centralized, and not until the Great Depression of the 1930's did American government attain anything like the degree of centralized power that prevails today.

Implicit in the Constitution was a theory of "constitutionalism." Its essential idea was that government—even the power of Congress as the representative body of the people—must not impinge upon certain inalienable rights. Government, in other words, must itself be subject to a rule of law. As a practical matter, both umpiring conflicts between the central government and the states and defining the concrete boundaries of government powers became the responsibility of the judiciary. It fell to the Supreme Court, in the last analysis, to interpret and define the rule of law; this forum was to be the guardian of constitutionalism. Similarly, the judges in state courts became the authoritative sources of doctrine as to the limits of the power of states in areas of law not covered by the Constitution. The doctrines of constitutionalism, embodied in the original Constitution and the Bill of Rights, were designed to protect personal freedom. They were unquestionably designed also to inhibit government from trespassing upon rights of private property that the Founding Fathers held to be equally inalienable.

FEDERALISM AND THE LAW, 1790–1861

Congress quickly moved toward erecting the sort of stronger national government that the Constitution had envisioned. In the 1790's a series of laws was enacted that provided the basis for a central government of "independent energy" (a favorite phrase of that day). A system of federal courts was established, the first Bank of the United States was chartered, the Revolutionary War debts of the states were funded and made the responsibility of the national government, and a system of protective tariffs was instituted. In addition, the early Congresses, dominated by the emergent Federalist party with its close ties to the mercantile community, voted excise taxes to be levied directly upon the people; it passed navigation laws favoring American over foreign shipping interests; and it built a national army and navy.

From the time of Thomas Jefferson's election to the presidency in 1800 until the Civil War, the centralist ideas of the Federalists and their political descendants were generally subordinated to doctrines of limited government. There were important exceptions, to be sure. Notable among them were Jefferson's own aggressive policy resulting in acquisition of the vast Louisiana Territory from France in 1803; the chartering of the Second Bank of the United States in 1816; and President Andrew Jackson's insistence upon the supremacy of federal law when South Carolina sought to mount concerted state resistance to protective tariffs in the nullification crisis of 1831–1832. Moreover, Congress voted limited aid to internal improvements (roads and canal projects) in the early nineteenth century, and it extended land-grant aid to railroad construction in the 1850's. Throughout the pre–Civil War period the national government relentlessly pursued a policy of expansionism—the most dramatic episode in which was the Mexican War (1846) and resultant territorial acquisitions—and the crushing of Indian resistance to expansion of white settlement.

The Supreme Court played a major role in shoring up the foundations of centralized power. It did so, on the one hand, by asserting the exclusive or dominant authority of the central government. In the case of *McCulloch* v. *Maryland* (1819), Chief Justice John Marshall spoke for the court in ruling that the "necessary and proper" clause validated congressional creation of the Bank of the United States even though the Constitution did not explicitly authorize a federal charter for such an institution. And in *Gibbons* v. *Ogden* (1824) the Supreme Court declared that Congress had paramount authority over interstate commerce—thus establishing at least the formal basis for a free internal "common market." The Supreme Court also hewed consistently to the doctrinal theory that the federal courts had the power to decide controversies involving state governments and corporations chartered in other states—or involving corporations of which even a single stockholder was a citizen of another state.

The centralizing doctrines of the Supreme Court were, on the other hand, a matter of curbing certain types of state action. In the Dartmouth College case (1819) the court held that a private-corporation charter was a contract and thus was immune under the Contract Clause of the Constitution from abridgment by later action of a state legislature. In *Bank of Augusta* v. *Earle* (1839) the court under Marshall's successor, Roger B. Taney, ruled that "foreign corporations" (chartered out of state) could do business in other states unless explicitly excluded from doing so by the legislatures of these other states. In other major decisions the court ruled in *Swift* v. *Tyson* (1842) that a federal common law, formulated from precedent by judges, should in certain instances be controlling in the adjudication of commercial transactions; it decided in *Fletcher* v. *Peck* (1810) that once a state had granted lands to a corporation, it could not reverse its action even though fraud had been proven in the original course of legislation; and in the Dred Scott case (1857) it upheld the federal Fugitive Slave Law, for return of escaped slaves, ruling that under federal law a slave was property, not a citizen.

Despite all this, it would be mistaken to conclude that Congress and the Supreme Court had successfully established a highly centralized government during 1790–1861. For, as has already been shown, the range of major congressional legislation was fairly limited. It embraced tariffs, the chartering of the Bank of the United States, regulation of foreign trade and of shipping, control of coinage, management of the national debt, and limited support of internal improvements. (In addition, federal law controlled the disposition of the public lands in the West.) But there was no significant legislation for regulation of business. And national government was frugal and small in administrative scale, so that the taxing and fiscal impacts of federal law were minimal.

The Supreme Court also handed down many important decisions that assured the vitality of the powers of the states. The court in *Willson* v. *Marsh Co.* (1829) ruled that state police powers might be exercised in ways that impinged on interstate commerce so long as Congress had not acted in the matter; and in 1825 it held in *Elmendorf* v. *Taylor* that the state supreme courts had exclusive power to interpret the provisions of their respective state constitutions—an important guarantee of decentralized power that continues to the present day. In the case involving the Charles River Bridge (1837), the Supreme Court held that when new technologies induced the state to undertake internal improvements that threatened older chartered companies, the old charters must be interpreted narrowly, so as to give the states maximum latitude. This decision, Hurst has written, was "the classic statement of policy in favor of freedom for creative change as against unyielding protection for existing commitments" (*Law and the Conditions of Freedom in the Nineteenth-Century United States*, p. 27). In the West River Bridge decision of 1848, the Supreme Court also upheld in sweeping terms the right of the states to use their "eminent domain" powers to take property for public use. And from 1837 to the 1850's, the court even trimmed back its 1824 Commerce Clause ruling, to posit the concept of "concurrent" state and federal powers in laws affecting commerce.

Thus it was with substantial support from the highest federal court—and against a background in which Congress refrained from acting in many areas of policy—that state power flourished from 1790 to 1861. Indeed, the vitality of state power and resultant decentralization well justifies terming these years the period of "dual federalism": the state and national governments, as Scheiber contends in "Federalism and the American Economic Order, 1789–1910," each enjoyed substantial autonomy in separately designated spheres of action.

Dual federalism permitted each state to produce its unique mix of promotional, regulatory, and redistributive policies. Consequently, overall national policy governing economic affairs was an elaborate mosaic of law. As Justice Joseph Story wrote, the jurisprudence of each state differed from the others "in habits, laws, institutions, and principles of decisions." Probably the most important single difference was in the area of labor law: dual federalism permitted the states of the South to perpetuate human bondage in the form of perhaps the most stringent legal variant of chattel slavery known in the Western world. But there were many other important areas of virtually exclusive state law. Among them, notably, were policy regarding corporations, public investment for internal improvements and for the regulation of transportation, and the relations between employer and employee.

Furthermore, each state adopted its own laws of eminent domain, laws of inheritance, family law, and criminal law. Banking rules and practices were principally under the control of the individual states, again with startling variations resulting: some banned banking altogether, others chartered banks very selectively, others had "free banking." Indeed, not only in the area of banking control but also in transportation and corporation law the states exercised exclusive regulatory power; a strong interventionist role for the central government came only with the Civil War with banking, in 1887 with transport, and in 1890 with corporations. Moreover, each state promulgated its own statutory and judicial rules concerning negotiable instruments and other technical features of commercial law—again with resultant variety and often bewildering complexity in the legal environment within which national business operations were conducted. Despite brief episodes of national bankruptcy legislation, for the most part the laws of debt and insolvency were also matters established by the individual states.

Scholars dispute whether this sort of complexity and decentralization of public power inhibited economic growth or, instead, gave private entrepreneurship multiple fields and legal environments in ways that stimulated the process of growth. Whichever is true, there seems little question that dual federalism tended to make it difficult for the public sector to establish effective regulation of emergent business interests such as railroads, the operations of which transcended the geographical reach of state jurisdictions. With public power fragmented and diffused, states were, first of all, often fearful that regulating business too stringently would drive capital and enterprise to other states where laws were more beneficial. And, second, the states found it difficult to impose efficacious regulation when a buoyant, rapidly expanding private sector produced business institutions more extensive in their scope than the states themselves.

PROPERTY AND CONTRACT LAW

Two of the essential institutions of American capitalism were property and contract. In its definition of these institutions, early nineteenth-century American law was set largely by the state judiciaries rather than by the legislatures. Fundamental transformations occurred in both areas of law.

Contract law, in the hands of American state judges, underwent change that reflected the needs of contemporary mercantile capitalism—change that also reflected an antipaternalistic concept of the proper role of government in economic life, as held by judges of the day. In the eighteenth century, courts had held that private contracts should be validated by courts only if (apart from considerations of fraud) their terms were fundamentally "fair." Thus, as Morton Horwitz has written in "The Historical Foundations of Modern Contract Law," the doctrine of the 1700's declared that "when the selling price was greater than the supposed objective value of the thing bought, juries were permitted to reduce the damages." In effect, then, "the community's sense of fairness was often the dominant standard in contracts cases."

But in the nineteenth century, courts moved toward a new theory of contract—gradually at first, but by the 1840's definitively so. Now the doctrine of caveat emptor became enshrined in American law. Under it the parties to a contract were assumed to be acting intelligently and of their own free will. Let the buyer beware! Instead of abstract or community definitions of just price and fairness, the courts allowed the price agreed to in the contract to stand. The new legal doctrine "had a certain Adam Smith severity, a certain flavor of the rugged individual" (Friedman 1973, p. 233).

Because the law of private contracts covers those transactions not embraced by statute law, and because American government before 1861 left so wide an area of economic affairs in the private realm, this period is quite properly termed "the golden age of contract." Still, it is well to recall that the "rugged individuals" who occupied the private sector bought and sold, invested, and collected their profits in a legal environment that also supported them with tariffs, often provided them with government largess in the form of gifts of land, taxed them only lightly, and (in the case of corporations) provided them with valuable special privileges and legal immunities, such as limited liability, that served to hedge risks and reduce their entrepreneurial costs.

The most dramatic confrontation of old values and the new imperatives of dynamic capitalism came in an important area of property law—the law of eminent domain. This was the power of government to take property for its own uses. Universally, in the United States, government was obliged to render money compensation for property thus expropriated. But in fact the American courts validated a startlingly powerful doctrine of eminent domain law. They permitted government not only to take property for building public roads and other public enterprises, but also to authorize private enterprisers to take property for uses that legally were designated as "public" but that in fact were controlled by private companies or individuals. Thus in all states privately owned transport companies gained the power of eminent domain. In most of the industrializing states, the power was also given to mills (at first flour mills, necessary to an agrarian economy, but later to textile mills and other enterprises of an industrial economy).

Antebellum eminent domain law brings one squarely before the example cited earlier, of Mr. Smith's sulfur mill. Not only did the states force private landed property owners to give up their land for use by manufacturing firms, railroads, mining companies, lumber companies, and other types of capitalist enterprises. The states did two things further. First, the legislatures and courts defined "just compensation" in ways that validated takings in which property owners were paid little or nothing for the property they lost by takings—on the ground that the "indirect benefits" of railroads or other enterprises constituted compensation enough. Second, and contrariwise, the courts refused to apply eminent domain analogies to cases in which pollution, water overflow, or other incidental damages caused loss to established property owners. No compensation was required in such instances. In effect, the courts generally relieved new types of private enterprise from the costs that strict liability for incidental damage would have imposed on them. The spillover costs, in effect, were transferred to others.

In this manner, Scheiber argues in "The Road to *Munn*," eminent domain law became a method of establishing economic priorities, depriving certain types of property in order to subsidize the other, favored enterprises indirectly. There was, in other words, no absolute protection of vested rights in property; there could be none, because choices had to be made. And generally the choices fell in a pattern that lent abundant support to new technologies and to material growth. Just as the Charles River Bridge case decision had done, property law in the states favored "dynamic property," which was "an institution of growth," at the expense of "static property" in the form of older vested rights, which was an institution "merely of security" (Hurst 1956, p. 28).

THE MODERN STATE: THE CIVIL WAR AND AFTER

Since the Civil War there has been progressive centralization in American federalism. During the war itself Congress created the underpinnings of a new political economy with the Homestead Act (1862), the National Banking Act (1863), extensive land grants to transcontinental railroads, a protective tariff system of unprecedented bias in favor of American manufacturers (a system that lasted, in its essentials, until 1913), and revision of the tax system to incorporate a much larger element of excise taxes. In 1887 the Interstate Commerce Act brought railroads under national regulation, and three years later the Sherman Act created a federal corporations law.

By the 1890's the central government was playing a major role in conservation and reclamation. Within two decades thereafter, significant federal regulation was being extended over the food and drug industries. Federal criminal laws and "regulatory taxation" were being passed to augment state laws; and a program of federal cash grants-in-aid to states—precursors of "revenue sharing" in the 1970's—had begun. In 1913, moreover, the Federal Reserve system was inaugurated, greatly expanding central control of banking. Also in 1913 the Constitution was amended to authorize imposition of a federal income tax—a vital legal landmark, since so much of the subsequent expansion of the central government depended upon this tax.

The state and local governments also expanded their roles in the economy, undertaking new functions in the field of public services and enlarging their regulatory functions. They continued as well the pre-1861 tradition of promotional legislation designed to foster economic growth. Land grants, cash subsidies, and stock subscriptions went to railroad corporations; the power of eminent domain continued to be devolved liberally upon favored types of enterprise; and corporations received tender attentions from many states, in the form of greater freedom to order their internal management and their finances, tax breaks, and similar privileges and immunities. By the 1870's the states were also moving toward establishment of commissions to regulate railroad rates. Two decades later half the states had placed limits on the use of child labor in industry, and many had enacted laws regulating hours and conditions of labor generally. Sidney Fine has observed: "Although many of the laws were declared unconstitutional and although they were poorly enforced, they nevertheless constituted the real beginning of attempts by the states to improve the competitive position of the working-man" (*Laissez-Faire and the General-Welfare State,* p. 358). Boards of health, factory inspectors, housing inspectors, forest rangers, research-laboratory staffs, and other personnel armed with powers that the states had only seldom exercised in the early nineteenth century, now became fixtures in the state bureaucracies. The total number of state officials and the expenditures of government at the state and local levels rose steadily.

When one looks at the courts in this period, it is obvious that constitutionalism-in-practice often ran sharply counter to legislative trends, yet at other times it reinforced the diverse objectives of state law. The foremost trend in American jurisprudence centered on interpretation of the Fourteenth Amendment. Adopted in 1868 as a piece of Reconstruction reform, this amendment had been designed to guarantee the civil rights of the emancipated blacks. In the language of the amendment, no state might "deprive any person of life, liberty, or property, without due process of law." After corporation lawyers and conservative judges had pressed the courts incessantly to make this a shield of protection for business, they finally succeeded in the 1880's: the Supreme Court officially declared in *Santa Clara County* v. *Railroad* (1886) that "person" was a term that included corporations. Within a few years the court also declared that judges could decide whether state laws regulating wages, working conditions, or business practices were in violation of "due process."

Out of these decisions—which had their counterparts in the state courts—came the new doctrine called "liberty of contract." Like the "right to privacy" honored by the Supreme Court in the 1960's, "liberty of contract" was nowhere to be found in explicit terms in the Constitution. It was derived, as it were, from the general language of that document. And it was applied ruthlessly by the courts to overturn reform legislation enacted by the states. (Indeed, this tendency led Justice Oliver Wendell Holmes, in a famous dissent in *Lochner* v. *New York* [1905], to complain that "the Fourteenth Amendment does not enact Mr. Herbert Spencer's Social Statics. . . . A constitution is not intended to embody a particular economic theory, whether of paternalism . . . or *laissez faire.*") In ensuing years, moreover, the Supreme Court asserted its power to decide whether or not Sherman Antitrust Act prosecutions, or even specific rates set by the Interstate Commerce Commission and state commissions, were "reasonable." The court, in sum, had become a censor of policy as well as of law.

More generally, the Supreme Court and many state judiciaries subscribed to the doctrine of implied limitations. This was the notion that "inalienable rights" included inalienable property rights, and it served as a limit upon the government power to tax as well as to regulate. As the Michigan Supreme Court stated in 1870, in a decision invalidating laws that authorized taxes for public aid to railroads, implied limitations were "as inflexible and absolute" as explicit terms of the Constitution. It is worth noting that this Michigan decision invalidated a law designed to aid business enterprise; and so promotional law, no less than regulatory legislation, could fall victim to judicial conservatism. But it is equally instructive to observe that the Supreme Court overturned this Michigan ruling, declaring that railroads were "public" in their purpose even if private in ownership—and so were eligible for public aid if legislatures wished to grant it.

If the "public purpose" of certain types of enterprise justified government aid, as Scheiber has shown ("Road to *Munn*"), it could also justify government regulation. So the Supreme Court ruled in the famous Granger cases of 1877, when in *Munn* v. *Illinois* and related decisions it invoked an old common-law rule that businesses "affected with a public interest" (as opposed to businesses that were strictly "private") could legitimately be regulated.

The *Munn* doctrine was fated to become, in the hands of an increasingly conservative Supreme Court, an equally effective shield against public regulation for business the court deemed strictly private. And its category of "private" included most manufacturing firms, as it proved. Indeed, until 1938, but particularly in the period

1897–1925, the court repeatedly struck down regulatory laws on the ground that the businesses made subject to regulation were not affected with a public interest.

The Commerce Clause also became a potent weapon in the arsenal of what John Roche has called the doctrines of "entrepreneurial liberty." In the *Wabash, Saint Louis and Pacific Railroad Company* v. *Illinois* decision of 1886, the Supreme Court cut away much of the power it had given the states in *Munn*, by ruling that state railroad regulation could not be used to affect interstate commerce. (This set the stage for enactment in 1887 of the Interstate Commerce Act, which was desired as much by railroad companies wishing to slip from the net of stringent state regulation as it was by reformers.) The Supreme Court also invoked the Commerce Clause frequently, both to invalidate state regulation and to bar certain types of congressional action. The judicial definition of "commerce" also served to narrow the reach of the Sherman Antitrust Act so dramatically as practically to emasculate the law, in *United States* v. *E. C. Knight Company* (1895). This last case was matched in its importance by the *Pollack* v. *Farmers Loan and Trust Company* decision the same year, striking down a federal income tax as a violation of due process—leading to the successful campaign for the income tax amendment to the Constitution; proposed on 12 July 1909 and declared adopted and in effect as the Sixteenth Amendment on 25 February 1913.

Finally, both the federal and the state courts played a leading role in the development of labor law during this period. Federal judges handed down numerous injunctions, the most notable in the Debs case of 1894, during the Pullman strike, which punished union leaders for "conspiracy" and otherwise invoked government powers to cripple striking unions. The state courts also continued, until nearly the end of the century, to apply the "fellow-servant" doctrine, which held an employer blameless for an employee's death or injury if another employee was found partially responsible for the accident. This ruthless artifact of the law of capitalism at its zenith was discarded only when the state legislatures, under pressure from working-class voters and the progressive reform movement, enacted employer liability and workmen's compensation statutes.

DEVELOPMENTAL POLICY AND PROPERTY-LAW INNOVATION

As had been true in the early nineteenth century, so in the post–Civil War era the state courts adapted property law to developmental needs. Thus, vested property rights were abridged in the interest of economic growth. This was especially manifest in the Rocky Mountain and Pacific slope regions. In those areas the process of development was just beginning; the mainstay of the regional economy was extractive industry (agriculture, mining, lumbering); and there were unique regional problems to which the law must adjust: arid land, vast distances, and a mineral treasure located far from populated centers.

Most of the western states declared, in their constitutions or in early statutes, that mining and/or irrigation were "public purpose" activities that justified extraordinary legal support. Therefore irrigators—individual, company, or government-district in organization—and mining companies, and often lumber firms as well, were given the power of eminent domain, to seize private property for building roads and water lines or to sink mines. Constitutional and legislative exemptions, or special treatment in regard to taxation, characterized the laws of several states. The California Supreme Court declared in 1888 that property rights of people whose land was invaded or taken, often at considerable loss to them, had to yield because irrigation was a technology "by which immigration may be stimulated, the taxable property of the state increased, . . . and the comfort and advantage of many thriving communities subserved," all of it redounding to "the common advantage of all the people of the state" (*Turlock District* v. *Williams*, 76 Cal. 360).

In like manner the legislatures and courts shaped or reshaped riparian law, affecting property rights on the banks of flowing streams, to meet the needs of arid areas. In Colorado and other states that followed its example, "appropriation" was the new principle established: first in time, first in right. Elsewhere the lawmakers and courts opted for the older common-law doctrine of riparian rights, which gave every property owner along a stream a claim on the water, subject to "reasonable use" by those located upstream. The justification for such innovations in the law was a pragmatic one. If lacking in formal precedent in English and American water law, one court declared, the appropriation doctrine "is the lineal descendent of the law of necessity" and essential if western "advantages and resources may receive the fullest development for the general welfare" (2 Idaho 750 [1890]; 3 Ariz. 255 [1891]).

While irrigation and eminent-domain law favored enterprises in their promotional phase, the laws of property and torts (damages) were used to favor enterprises in their operational phase. Thus the traditional common-law safeguards of property against invasion or nuisance were in effect suspended, so that mining companies were held free from liability when they caused damage to the land of others; indeed, in California the entire Sacramento basin suffered pollution and flooding for twenty years as the result of mining operations upstream, and the state courts refused to hold miners responsible. (A federal court finally stepped in to halt the damage in 1884.) Nor was this sort of adaptation in nuisance and tort law restricted to the western states. Pennsylvania forced property owners to absorb losses caused by mining operations, on the ground that mining of coal was "a great public industry."

Surprisingly, perhaps, in light of its solicitude for property rights, the Supreme Court upheld all these local variations in property and riparian law. The courts of each state should decide such matters, the Supreme Court declared in 1904, since these local forums could best "appreciate the results upon the growth and prosperity" of their respective states. If we seek consistency in the Supreme Court ruling, it must be in the fact that enterprise, not "static" property, was to receive the beneficent aid of legal and constitutional doctrines.

THE REGULATORY AND WELFARE STATE

This mixed heritage of political institutions and jurisprudence underwent sudden, decisive change during the 1930's, when the Great Depression demanded solutions to unprecedented social problems. Here, in the 1930's, was the watershed of the legal system as it has interacted with society and economy in the present day.

One of the legislative innovations of the New Deal, the National Industrial Recovery Act of 1933, had only a short life. Radical in its premises, implementation, and implications, the NIRA in effect attempted to make most of the modern industrial sector of the economy a managed sector: by industry-wide agreements, given effect by the president (to whom Congress delegated authority), there was to be regulation of wages, prices, and working conditions. The market system was to be rendered largely inoperative. But the Supreme Court struck down the law and, with it, the already faltering apparatus for its administration, in 1935.

Other basic innovations of the New Deal era were destined to shape the basic legal order in ensuing decades. These innovations, the details of which are discussed in other articles in these volumes, included the following:

First, agriculture was successfully made a managed sector in 1933, with federal control of resources in the form of output and acreage allocations for basic (staple) crops, and with government support of prices for farm commodities. Sometimes integrated with this policy, but in other respects incongruously attached to it, were policies for land reclamation, conservation, land retirement, farm-mortgage guarantees, farm credit, temporary immigration of farm labor, and the like.

Second, the New Deal policies of Franklin D. Roosevelt's first two terms, 1933–1941, established the basis for the modern regulatory state in its full scope. Securities markets, the motor-trucking industry, aviation, radio (and later television) broadcasting, and the maritime industries all came under regulation by administrative commissions (modeled on the Interstate Commerce Commission). These agencies were given legislative, judicial, and administrative powers in a hybrid mix that doubtless would have shocked the Founding Fathers had they conceived of such an eventuality in their 1787 Constitutional Convention. The power of these agencies reached to the very heart of the marketplace. In effect they created what Charles Reich has termed a "new property" in the form of franchises, allocated selectively at the discretion of federal officials, to enter certain businesses, to expand or contract services offered to the public, and to charge given prices. The market price mechanism, in sum, was supplanted by government fiat.

Third, the New Deal set up the modern welfare state, especially through its inauguration of the Social Security system in 1935. In addition to marking federal acceptance of responsibility to assure retired and disabled workers at least a small income, Social Security and allied legislation provided for vastly expanded aid to dependent children and—on an enormous scale in the 1930's, culminating with the Works Progress Administration—unemployed workers. On this foundation the welfare state has subsequently expanded to include medical care for the aged (under a program begun in 1965) and federal aid for hospitals and other public facilities.

Fourth, the New Deal—during both the Great Depression and World War II—inaugurated the modern "fiscal state," in which federal taxation and expenditure became a prime mover in the economy, at levels of 25 to 40 percent of gross national product. By 1938, moreover, Roosevelt had become committed to the compensatory spending and countercyclical fiscal policies pioneered by the theorist John Maynard Keynes. The level of emergency expenditures for relief of unemployment and public works in the 1930's made the government role sufficiently large for these policies to become significant. In World War II unprecedentedly high military expenditures carried the new order forward; and since 1945 the combination of a massive peacetime military establishment and the continued rise in federal expenditures for civilian purposes has sustained the new fiscal order.

Finally, the New Deal changed the character of the federal system in fundamental ways. After 1933 real power became definitively centralized. Policy areas formerly reserved to the states became federal government responsibilities; there was a movement toward adoption of minimum national standards, as in federal minimum-wage legislation, from 1938; and, by preempting the income tax so decisively, the federal government effectively placed serious fiscal limits on what the state and local governments might hope to accomplish through autonomous policies and programs. These latter limits were offset, in a fiscal sense, by sharp increases in the 1930's, and again in the period 1964–79, in the level of federal cash grants-in-aid to the states—grants for specific projects such as urban housing or education, grants on a formula basis for broad programs such as hospital construction, and finally, beginning in 1972, revenue sharing on a relatively unrestricted, "no-strings" basis. But with cash grants from the central government came concomitant shifts in the locus of real power. It was Congress that decided what activities of state and local governments would receive aid, and on what terms; it was federal officials who audited state expenditures and imposed controls; it was Washington, not the state capitals, that dispensed power as well as funds.

The new federalism also brought in its train some basic changes in the institutions and behavior of government. Political processes were now characterized by some salient features that had been utterly unknown in an earlier era. Access to government became more complex, for example, as private-interest groups were now affected not only by Congress but also by scores of government agencies, often with fragmented responsibilities; thus only multiple access could provide politically effective access. A new phrase entered the lexicon of politics: "intergovernmental relations." It was a phrase that subsumed more than the new complexities of multiagency activity, grants-in-aid, and federal supervision of state activity. It also subsumed the practical effects of the new centralization of power. These included a "skewing" of state policies, especially in the poorer states, as legislators tended to allocate funds preferentially to programs that qualified for federal matching grants. This was often at the expense of other programs that were equally, or perhaps more, important.

Moreover, the new intergovernmental relations of the revised federalism meant that some government agencies developed a special "clientele" relationship with special-interest groups in the private sector—as the highway administrators did with the construction industry and civil engineers, or as the Department of Agriculture bureaucracy did with the Farm Bureau Federation, representing the middle- and upper-income farmers and their interests. Also part of the new federalism was an unprecedented emphasis upon planning by all levels of government, in response to the requirements of federal grant-in-aid legislation.

The implications of the new federalism were made abundantly clear by Lyndon Johnson during his presidential campaign of 1964. Speaking in Portland, Maine, he discussed the effects on Maine of the area redevelopment, Jobs Training conservation, Small Business Administration,

LAW AND POLITICAL INSTITUTIONS

and antipollution expenditures of the federal government—part of the much wider spectrum of programs that were channeling federal money to the states. He concluded with a reference to the Economic Opportunities Act:

> ... Our poverty program will give a further boost to the great economy of the great State of Maine. The first thing I am going to do when I get to Washington ... is call up Sargent Shriver [then head of the poverty program agency] and tell him to get in touch with Ed Muskie [senator from Maine] and the Governor and tell him to do something about it right here in Maine.

It is difficult to imagine Calvin Coolidge, let alone James Madison, manipulating lines of centralized power in this way, even if they could somehow have succeeded in understanding the vocabulary of the new political language of the mid-1960's.

Since 1969, when Richard Nixon became president, there has been rising concern in national political councils somehow to "return power to the states." But still, it is Congress—with its control of the bulk of all income taxes collected in the economy—that decides how, when, and on what terms.

Meanwhile, yet another feature of the new federalism has come into focus—the concentration of economic power in the private sector to such an extent that in basic respects the largest American corporations, labor unions, and special-interest groups have become actors in the government and political systems that are perhaps fully as important as the state governments. How this giant congeries of private interests can be subjected to the imperatives of a constitutionalism posited on the notion that power must somehow be made accountable, remains one of the most troubling dilemmas of the contemporary legal order.

THE LEGAL SYSTEM AND THE MODERN STATE

The response of the courts to the emergent regulatory and welfare state, and to the new federalism inaugurated in the 1930's, was at first unmitigatedly hostile. The established doctrines that had served to shield business from various types of regulation since the 1880's were invoked by the Supreme Court to wreak havoc on New Deal policies. The doctrine of separation of powers, barring congressional devolution of its own power on the executive branch; the "liberty of contract" idea; the Commerce Clause; due process; and the barriers to government action established under the doctrine of business affected with a public interest—all of these came to the fore in decisions of the Supreme Court in the early 1930's, especially the twin decisions of 1935 and 1936 that struck down the National Industrial Recovery Act and the New Deal's first law for management of agriculture [295 U.S. 495; 297 U.S.1].

But these pillars of judicial conservatism soon fell. Occasionally by gradual erosion, but more often through abrupt judicial about-face, the Supreme Court upheld regulatory, welfare, and reform laws of the New Deal. Judicial policy changed in regard to the legitimate power of the states to regulate wages and working conditions, to give relief to mortgage debtors, to regulate business practices, to establish "milksheds" allocating markets for dairy markets and setting prices, and the like. Also upheld by the courts were state powers to use eminent domain to authorize takings for public housing and parks, and to regulate construction through zoning ordinances and statutes. A massive federal project for regional development, the Tennessee Valley Authority, withstood judicial scrutiny; so did the 1935 National Labor Relations Act. The landmark due-process decisions embodying liberty-of-contract ideas were overturned, and the Supreme Court opened the way for enlarged regulatory powers at all levels of government.

By the mid-1940's the last vestiges of "dual federalism" under the Commerce Clause had been swept away. The Supreme Court in effect abandoned all efforts to stand in the way of congressional regulation of economic activity, only seldom finding segments, usually trivial, of the private sector that were deemed so local as to be outside newly redefined interstate commerce. Opinions of the court celebrated the "federal free trade unit" and inveighed against state laws that discriminated against other states or out-of-state private enterprise, or that threatened to set off "fantastic rivalries and dislocations and reprisals." Instead of drawing firm lines separating state-local from interstate commerce for purposes of ruling on the constitutionality of laws under the police power, since the early 1960's the Supreme Court has consistently resorted to a pragmatic concept of "balancing" the legitimate interests of the states and those of Congress. Moreover, the court has adopted wholesale the doctrine of "preemption," declaring: "When Congress has legislated comprehensively on a given subject, it is presumed to have 'occupied the field' to the exclusion of all incompatible state legislation on the same subject" (Benson 1970, p. 277). Consequently, as Benson has written, "There is the fact of plenary national power over every aspect of interstate commerce. Congress . . . is able to reach into every nook and cranny of the highly interdependent American economic system" (p. 345). Thus liberty of contract and its companion doctrines of an earlier era are laid to rest. And the pragmatic standard under which the Commerce Clause now meets judicial scrutiny is expressed in a Supreme Court decision (*Pike* v. *Bruce Church, Inc.* [1970]), that "the extent of the burden" imposed on commerce by state laws deemed tolerable by the court will depend on the nature of the local interest involved, and on whether it could be promoted as well with a lesser impact on interstate activities.

This sort of judicial pragmatism echoes the phrases by which judges in the nineteenth century justified abandonment of age-old property-law principles to expand the powers of eminent domain or to refashion the law of contracts to meet the needs of a mercantile economy. Similarly, the ideology of "national needs" invoked to justify the new federalism since 1933 parallels the creation of new legal doctrines in an earlier day, to define "public purpose" in taxation or regulatory law. It even echoes the efforts of colonial legislatures and judges to separate what was imperative from what was merely optional in the way of basic doctrines ranging from land and inheritance law to the fundamental liberties of the people.

Law, in sum, has been sometimes formalistic and absolutist; it has sometimes set clear boundaries on state or private action; at other times it has served almost reflexively to ratify the prevailing values and goals of society. For the most part, since 1935 the Supreme Court has accepted the legitimacy of efforts by Congress and the executive branch to develop minimum national standards. In one major area of law—civil rights—the court during the chief justiceship of Earl Warren (1953–1969) moved ahead of Congress and, it is probably fair to say, ahead of public opinion. By insisting that the Fourteenth Amendment required truly equal treatment of all citizens, regardless of race, the Warren court set in motion the successful movement for basic changes in federal law affecting employment practices as well as public expenditures, education, and government personnel policies.

And so, what is the legitimate equipoise, in the classic phrase, between liberty and authority—and, more narrowly, between political principles and economic aspirations—continues to be a central problem in the interplay of law and economy in the United States.

BIBLIOGRAPHY

The Colonial Era

Charles M. Andrews, *Colonial Self-Government, 1652–1689* (New York, 1904), studies constitutional development and colonial conflicts with the home country; and *The Colonial Period of American History*, 4 vols. (New Haven, 1934–1938), is a magisterial survey of colonial institutions and of British mercantilism. Thomas C. Barrow, *Trade and Empire: The British Customs Service in Colonial America, 1660–1775* (Cambridge, Mass., 1967), analyzes British mercantilist and administrative policies—and failures. George A. Billias, ed., *Law and Authority in Colonial America* (Barre, Mass., 1965), contains essays on both general and technical features of colonial law. Beverley W. Bond, *The Quit-Rent System in the American Colonies* (New Haven, 1919), studies land law and its administration, and colonial controversies over quasi-feudal dues. David H. Flaherty, ed., *Essays in the History of Early American Law* (Chapel Hill, N.C., 1969), is an excellent collection of articles from learned journals, with a useful bibliographic introduction. Lawrence M. Friedman, *A History of American Law* (New York, 1973), the best one-volume history of the subject, is especially strong on law and the economy. Jack P. Greene, "Autonomy and Stability: New England and the British Colonial Experience in Early Modern America," in *Journal of Social History*, 7 (1974), is an insightful review essay on studies of colonial communities and the law.

George L. Haskins, *Law and Authority in Early Massachusetts* (New York, 1960), is an imaginative, detailed analysis of the legal system of one colony. Morton Horwitz, "The Transformation in the Conception of Property in American Law, 1780–1860," in *University of Chicago Law Review*, 40 (1973), discusses traditional common-law concepts and their later transformation in American law. Stanley N. Katz, ed., *Colonial America: Essays in Politics and Social Development*, 2nd ed. (Boston, 1971), is a fine selection of scholarly essays. Edmund S. Morgan, *American Slavery, American Freedom: The Ordeal of Colo-*

LAW AND POLITICAL INSTITUTIONS

nial Virginia (New York, 1975), is definitive account of labor problems, slavery, and the idea of liberty in the Virginia colony. Richard B. Morris, *Government and Labor in Early America* (New York, 1946), is a richly documented study of immigration, labor, labor law, and public policy; and *Studies in the History of American Law*, 2nd ed. (Philadelphia, 1959), presents a technical, historical analysis of colonial land law, torts, women's rights, and the common law. William E. Nelson, *Americanization of the Common Law, . . . 1760–1830* (Cambridge, Mass., 1975), studies law and society in Massachusetts. Sumner Chilton Powell, *Puritan Village: The Formation of a New England Town* (Middletown, Conn., 1963), is a richly detailed analysis of Sudbury, Mass., in light of English institutions.

Max Radin, "The Rivalry of Common-Law and Civil-Law Ideas in the American Colonies," in New York University School of Law, *Law, A Century of Progress* (New York, 1937), II, is a technical overview and analysis. Jon C. Teaford, *The Municipal Revolution in America: Origins of Modern Urban Government, 1650–1825* (Chicago, 1975), is an essay on the changing municipal corporation. Clarence L. Ver Steeg, *The Formative Years, 1607–1763* (New York, 1964), presents an interpretive survey of the development of the English colonies. L. Kinvin Wroth and Hiller B. Zobel, eds., *Legal Papers of John Adams*, 3 vols. (Cambridge, Mass., 1965), contains a valuable introduction on the law of the eighteenth century in vol. I.

1790 to the Present

Paul R. Benson, Jr., *The Supreme Court and the Commerce Clause, 1937–1970* (Cambridge, Mass., 1970), presents a constitutional analysis. Thomas C. Cochran, *Business in American Life: A History* (New York, 1972), is an interpretive survey of business institutions in relation to law, values, and social life of the nation. Sidney Fine, *Laissez-Faire and the General-Welfare State: A Study of Conflict in American Thought, 1865–1901* (Ann Arbor, Mich., 1956), the standard study of business thought and public policy, includes a comprehensive survey of the law. Donald Fleming and Bernard Bailyn, eds., *Law in American History* (Boston, 1972), is a collection of articles, including several on law and economy. Tony A. Freyer, "Negotiable Instruments and the Federal Courts in Antebellum America," in *Business History Review*, 50 (Winter 1976), opens up the fascinating history of innovation in American commercial law and shows how the federal judiciary mandated uniformity of law. Lawrence Friedman, *Contract Law in America: A Social and Economic Case Study* (Madison, Wis., 1965), a study of Wisconsin, constitutes the leading history of American contract law; *A History of American Law* (New York, 1973), is the standard one-volume study. Lawrence Friedman and Harry N. Scheiber, eds., *American Law and the Constitutional Order* (Cambridge, Mass., 1978), is an extensive collection of essays on public policy and on law and society, as well as constitutional history more narrowly considered. Louis Hartz, *Economic Policy and Democratic Thought: Pennsylvania, 1776–1860* (Cambridge, Mass., 1948), is one of several available studies of state policy before 1860. Morton Horwitz, *The Transformation of American Law, 1780–1860* (Cambridge, Mass., 1977), contends, although excessively so, that judges' styles of reasoning and decision making shifted profoundly so as to accommodate emergent industrial capitalism.

James Willard Hurst, *Law and the Conditions of Freedom in the Nineteenth-Century United States* (Madison, Wis., 1956), is a classic analysis of law and American society; *Law and Economic Growth: The Legal History of the Lumber Industry in Wisconsin, 1836–1915* (Cambridge, Mass., 1964), is a detailed account of land, corporation, resource-use, conservation, and regulatory law; and *The Legitimacy of the Business Corporation in the Law of the United States, 1780–1970* (Charlottesville, Va., 1970), consists of lectures on the history of federal and state law of corporations. Gabriel Kolko, *The Triumph of Conservatism* (New York, 1963), concerns business support for regulation. Stanley Kutler, *Privilege and Creative Destruction: The Charles River Bridge Case* (Philadelphia, 1971), appraises the pivotal 1837 case on the Contract Clause and the state police powers. R. Alton Lee, *A History of Regulatory Taxation* (Lexington, Ky., 1973), is a survey and analysis. Leonard W. Levy, *The Law of the Commonwealth and Chief Justice Shaw* (Cambridge, Mass., 1957), a brilliant account of Lemuel Shaw's contributions to national and Massachusetts law, has chapters on railroad law and other economic subjects. Charles W. McCurdy, "Justice Field and the Jurisprudence of Government-Business Relations," in *Journal of American History*, 61 (March 1975), is a pathbreaking reinterpretation of constitutional law and business in the late nineteenth century; and "American Law and the Marketing Structure of the Large Corporation, 1875–1890," in *Journal of Economic History*, 38 (Sept. 1978), shows how the litigation sponsored by some large manufacturing corporations led to expansion of the "free market" and curbing of state powers over commerce. Arthur S. Miller, *The Supreme Court and American Capitalism* (New York, 1968), contains essays formulating the concept of the "corporate state" and the "positive state" as they have changed the contemporary meaning of the Constitution.

William E. Nelson, *Americanization of the Common Law: The Impact of Legal Change on Massachusetts Society, 1760–1830* (Cambridge, Mass., 1975), considers how changing judicial styles and doctrines responded to capitalist needs. Douglass C. North and Lance E. Davis, *Institutional Change and American Economic Growth* (Cambridge, 1971), an effort to develop social theory relevant to change in economic institutions, is comprehensive in scope but not reliable on technical questions of law. Arnold M. Paul, *Conservative Crisis and the Rule of Law: Attitudes of Bar and Bench, 1887–1895* (Ithaca, N.Y., 1960), is a telling analysis of how conservative ideas reshaped jurisprudence. Charles Reich, "The New Property," in *Yale Law Journal*, 73 (April 1964), argues that the regulatory and welfare states have created new forms of property in law. John Roche, "Entrepreneurial Liberty and the Commerce Power," in *University of Chicago Law Review*, 30 (Summer 1963), argues that the courts reflexively provided what the business order demanded in Commerce Clause cases; and "Entrepreneurial Liberty and the Fourteenth Amendment," in *Labor History*, 4 (1963), traces the perverse reinterpretation of due process by the late nineteenth-century courts.

Harry N. Scheiber, "The Road to *Munn*," in Donald Fleming and Bernard Bailyn, eds., *Law in American History* (Boston, 1972), studies public-purpose doctrine in eminent-domain and regulatory law to 1877; "Property Law, Expropriation, and Resource Allocation by Government: The U.S., 1789–1910," in *Journal of Economic History*, 33 (1973), is a study of eminent-domain policy and law; "Federalism and the American Economic Order, 1789–1910," in *Law and Society Review*, 10 (Fall 1975), is a monograph on federalism as it affected policy processes and economic institutions; and "Federalism and the Diffusion of Power: Historical and Contemporary Perspectives," in *University of Toledo Law Review*, 9 (Summer 1978), treats economic and social-welfare policies for the post-1910 period. Bernard Schwartz, *The Rights of Property* (New York, 1965), is a comprehensive constitutional analysis and treatise. Benjamin F. Wright, *The Growth of American Constitutional Law* (repr. Chicago, 1967), a concise, lucid account of constitutional law and the Supreme Court, is excellent on contract law and other matters concerning the economy.

[*See also* AMERICAN BUSINESS INSTITUTIONS BEFORE THE RAILROAD; ANTITRUST; COLONIAL ECONOMY; ENTREPRENEURSHIP; GOVERNMENT MANAGEMENT OF THE ECONOMY; LAND POLICIES AND SALES; REGULATORY AGENCIES; SOCIAL WELFARE; *and* STATE AND LOCAL GOVERNMENTS.]

STATE AND LOCAL GOVERNMENTS

Gerald D. Nash

THE ROLE of state and local governments in the American economy since the seventeenth century has constituted one of the most stable elements in the American institutional system. In fact, widespread agreement over the nature of that relationship explains why it has rarely become a divisive public issue. That is particularly striking since the relationship of the federal government to economic growth has been a continuing, volatile, and controversial question. It was an issue at the time of the American Revolution; it was a central problem at the Constitutional Convention; it emerged as a contentious political problem during the first half of the nineteenth century; and during the twentieth century it came to be a central issue in presidential politics from Theodore Roosevelt's New Nationalism to Lyndon B. Johnson's Great Society. And after that the debate did not end.

By contrast, during these same years the role of state and local governments in the economy was rarely subject to controversy. This was indeed a paradox, because their functions were hardly insignificant. Certainly the decisions made by state and local officials were often as controversial as those made on the national level; certainly they affected a large number of individuals. Perhaps the development of a consensus by Americans concerning the role of state and local governments in the economy took the issue out of the arena of political debate. Whatever reasons may help to explain the paradox, the continuity of state and local economic functions stands out as one of the prime characteristics of the historical role of government in the American economy.

State and local governments have played a significant role in the process of American economic development since the founding of the first British colonies in North America. The nature of that relationship varied, but at no time did the functions of state and local governments wither. Indeed, the nature of state and local intervention in the economy reflected much stability even as methods of implementing public policies changed. Thus, both continuity and change have characterized state and local intervention in the economy.

These two factors pervaded the historical development of the role of state and local government in the growth of the economy. During the colonial era (1607–1763) the mercantilist tradition shaped economic policies in America as in England. The Revolutionary era (1763–1789) did not see any immediate changes in the economic functions of state and local governments. But it was paralleled by the publication of Adam Smith's *The Wealth of Nations* in 1776, which inaugurated an economic revolution by emphasizing laissez-faire and individualism in place of the mercantilist emphasis on government intervention and statism. Although Americans did not quickly embrace the newer ideology of laissez-faire, they did begin to modify their once staunchly held mercantilist doctrines.

Thus, during the Revolutionary era, mercantilism was in transition; and in succeeding years, especially in the national era (1789–1860), Americans fashioned an ideology that provided room for selected mercantilist values as well as for individualism. The emphasis of that age was on the encouragement of individuals engaged in economic growth—whether this might be done through particular government policies or by government abstinence. That orientation underwent further modification between 1860 and 1900, an era dominated by the rise of big business. Americans then began to favor more government regulation of economic activities. Yet, when confronted by large corporations of unprecedented size, state and local authorities found themselves unable to implement their regulatory policies effectively, since they lacked the necessary administrative skills. Gradually, and often painfully, as large corporations became more dominant in the twentieth century, governments learned to develop more effective means of implementing public policies, mainly through administrative regulation.

Despite a greatly expanded scope, the nature of state and local economic policies did not change dramatically over the course of more than three centuries. In contrast with the far-reaching changes that characterized the role of the federal government in economic growth during these years, the functions of the states and localities remained remarkably stable. Indeed, the economic role of state and local governments in the United States, as in western Europe, constituted an important, stable element within the institutional framework of American federalism.

THE COLONIAL ERA (1607–1763): MERCANTILISM

From the beginning English settlers in North America expected their governments to play a major role in economic development. This was part of the political heritage that they had brought with them. Throughout seventeenth-century Europe, governments at various levels were actively engaged in directing the economic activities of their citizens. Englishmen, Frenchmen, Dutchmen, and Spaniards alike expected governments to encourage the economic activities of individuals and groups, and to enforce regulations that would be of benefit to the entire community. Although Englishmen also believed that governments should safeguard certain rights of individuals, they felt no qualms about regulating individual behavior for the collective good.

The institutional structure of state and local governments in English North America was profoundly shaped by the ideology of mercantilism. Thomas Muir and other contemporary exponents of mercantilism stated that government had a major responsibility to promote economic growth, but for the benefit of the state rather than for individual citizens. In the attainment of this goal, local governments had as integral a role as central governments. Business and commerce were subject to detailed rules. Local officials, through subsidies and bounties, were to encourage desirable goods or manufactures; by grants of patents or monopolies they were to encourage inventors or tradesmen; through inspection and by enforcing standards of weights and measures, they were to maintain standards of quality. Local governments also had authority to engage in extensive price fixing to protect consumers from gouging. Laborers were subject to intensive regulation: of hours, wages, quality of work, apprenticeship, and employment. Such intensive control of the economy by government would, it was hoped, redound to the benefit of the state and, ultimately, to the welfare of its citizens.

Within this framework of mercantilist ideology, it is not surprising that the colonists felt the need for a concerted effort by governments and individuals to exploit the resources of a vast, virgin continent. Hence they assigned their local and colonial governments major responsibilities for stimulating economic growth. Problems of trade, economic rivalries with neighboring colonies, and the development of manufactures were regarded not as private problems, but as proper subjects for government action.

As early as the seventeenth century, controversies over external trade and commerce led the colonists to endow colonial and local governments with authority to impose tolls and customs duties. Since the colonies were so dependent on the mother country, trade became one of their most vital interests. Hence all of the colonies imposed restrictions on imports and exports. Between 1631 and 1690, for example, seven Virginia laws prohibited the export of hides, in order to encourage domestic shoe manufacturing and tanning. Massachusetts adopted this type of regulation in 1646, as did Maryland in 1685, Pennsylvania in 1700, and New York and North Carolina during the eighteenth century. Colonial governments placed similar restrictions on other needed products, such as wool, iron, and wheat.

Colonial and local authorities also levied import duties as a means of encouraging greater self-sufficiency. Hardly had the first settlers of Massachusetts Bay built their houses when, in

1633, the General Court imposed tariff duties on goods from overseas, including England. Throughout the colonial era many legislatures and counties imposed tariffs on goods from neighboring colonies or communities, in the hope of gaining a favorable trade advantage. In 1715, Maryland absolutely prohibited the importation of competing bread, flour, or beer from Pennsylvania. Lawmakers in Connecticut were more extreme and in 1717 levied a tax on merchandise imported from any other British or foreign colony in North America. During 1721, Massachusetts and New Hampshire engaged in a tariff war in which each imposed retaliatory tariff duties on goods exported by the other. In an effort to promote its own shipbuilding industry, New York in 1734 exempted all vessels built within its borders from the payment of tonnage duties in New York ports.

Some colonies issued patents or monopolies to encourage local enterprise. Monopolies granted to individuals engaged in salt production were common. Massachusetts granted such a privilege to specified individuals in 1646, the same year in which the legislature also issued the first patent awarded in America—to Joseph Jenks, for his model of an improved sawmill machine.

But perhaps the most common form of state and local encouragement of economic enterprise came with the extension of direct subsidies and loans. The Massachusetts General Court in 1637 granted Abraham Shaw the right to take iron ore from the common lands. It stipulated in 1648 that John Winthrop receive three thousand acres of land, on condition that he establish a saltworks that would produce at least one hundred tons of salt annually. This policy was commonly followed from Maine to Georgia. In an early example of federalism, the Massachusetts General Court in 1638 instructed the town of Salem to lend £30 to glass manufacturers and then to deduct this sum from its next tax payments to the General Court. During the seventeenth and eighteenth centuries such loans by New England town governments were frequent. The range of economic enterprises so aided was wide. Rhode Island provided William Borden with a loan of £500 to engage in sailcloth manufacture, and Massachusetts in 1735 lent Joseph Plaisted £800 to further his efforts in potash manufacturing. Every colony paid bounties to producers of goods that were highly desired: flax, hemp, wool, tobacco, silk, and ships. So common was this practice that in 1759 the Virginia legislature created a public corporation solely to encourage manufactures through the award of premiums.

When colonies lacked lands or funds with which to encourage new enterprises, they frequently resorted to the incentive of tax exemption. As early as 1669, Connecticut, in an effort to foster a domestic woolens industry, exempted sheep from taxation. Sometimes colonial legislatures freed particular individuals from taxes. In 1769, for example, New Jersey decreed the Hibernia Iron Works free from taxes for a period of seven years. And, like lawmakers in Virginia and Maryland, the New Jersey legislature exempted mechanics who worked in iron manufacture from militia duty and road taxes for seven-year periods.

When the exertions of individuals seemed inadequate to furnish essential public needs, colonial and local governments were expected to assume such responsibilities. For a time in seventeenth-century Virginia, for example, privately operated tanneries were unable to supply great demand. Thereupon, the legislature in 1661 required counties to establish publicly owned and operated tanneries, and to provide training for shoemakers and tanners. A similar need arose in regard to the weaving of cloth. In 1666, therefore, the Virginia legislature required each county to establish a public loom within two years. In New York and Georgia a dearth of building materials prompted the respective legislatures to create public sawmills. Many towns carried out similar policies within their own jurisdictions. The town officials of Stamford, Connecticut, were hardly unique in the 1640's when they built a publicly owned dam with a nearby mill for public use.

Most of the colonies and their subdivisions established elaborate inspection practices in order to maintain standards of quality with respect to a wide variety of products. Bread, meat, and fish were subject to intensive inspections in most colonies. Local governments often imposed their own specifications and also bore prime responsibility for the administration of such regulations. In addition to foodstuffs, the colonial legislatures stipulated elaborate specifications for export commodities such as timber and naval stores. Possibly the most detailed standards were applied to tobacco by all of the southern colonies and by Connecticut. Usually inspectors were appointed by the governor, although in New England elected town officials carried out the bulk of the inspections.

State and local governments also applied mercantilist regulations to agriculture. In the seventeenth century, Virginia and other southern colonies enacted both rigid crop acreage restrictions and price controls, in particular to foster a profitable export market in tobacco. By the eighteenth century many of these strict regulations were not rigidly enforced, but colonial legislatures still affected agriculture through their land distribution policies. New England colonies commonly made grants to communities or towns. In the middle states and the South, legislatures or proprietors used the headright system, whereby they made grants of varying sizes to individuals or groups.

Laboring men and mechanics were subject to a wide range of colonial and local regulations derived from English practices. These regulations were usually enforced by local courts or county and town officials. They dealt with rules governing apprenticeship, the respective rights of workers and their employers, labor disputes, working conditions, wages, and other contractual arrangements between employers and employees. Since vagrants were often consigned to apprenticeship or indentured servitude, the local courts also exercised wide jurisdiction over unfree labor.

Although financial affairs were largely within the scope of British imperial authorities, colonial and local governments interloped, hoping to foster more rapid economic growth. The shortage of specie in all of the colonies—engendered by an unfavorable trade balance—early led legislatures to experiment with their own remedies. One common policy was to create land banks, publicly owned institutions that issued paper money on the basis of their landholdings. The Massachusetts Land Bank, created in 1714, proved to be one of the most stable. Other colonies that created reasonably successful land banks were Connecticut, Rhode Island, New Hampshire, New York, New Jersey, Pennsylvania, and North Carolina. Such institutions were so effective in expanding the monetary supply of the American colonies that the British Parliament—concerned about inflation—forbade them in the Currency Act of 1749.

Clearly, then, the scope of colonial and local economic policies was wide. On the basis of their mercantilist tradition in Europe, the American colonists endowed their new governments in America with extensive authority to foster economic growth. They promoted a variety of economic pursuits, imposed regulations designed to further economic growth, and undertook public ownership and operation of economic activities considered essential for the public good. The precise impact of all of these measures on economic development may be difficult to gauge. It seems likely that in the seventeenth century—and until the middle of the eighteenth century—the extensive activities of colonial and local governments made a significant contribution to economic development. They hastened the growth of needed crops and manufactures; they helped to develop export markets by the creation and maintenance of standards; they transferred land from the public domain to private ownership; and they relieved the chronic specie shortage in the colonies. Without the aid of colonial and local governments, the task of economic development would have been slower and more difficult.

THE AMERICAN REVOLUTIONARY ERA (1763–1789): MERCANTILISM IN TRANSITION

The era of the American Revolution—whatever changes it brought for the American political system—did not substantially affect the role of state and local governments in economic life. Certainly, Americans in 1776 were not in revolt against mercantilist economic policies. They questioned not so much mercantilism itself as the particular policies that the British government attempted to impose in the decade after 1763. In fashioning their own policies after 1776, Americans retained many of the assumptions, as well as the specific policies, with which they had been familiar as colonists. Only gradually did they begin to question their inheritance.

Certainly the pattern of state and local economic policies did not change appreciably during the American Revolution. In fact, wartime exigencies increased the pace of government intervention in the economy. During the war every

STATE AND LOCAL GOVERNMENTS

state, of necessity, constructed its own saltpeter works. Maryland established a gunlock factory at Frederick, and Virginia built an iron foundry at Westham, near Richmond. Most of the states also assumed major responsibility for road construction—requiring localities to levy the taxes necessary for their maintenance. When not themselves undertaking necessary manufactures, the states sought to encourage private individuals. Legislatures not only offered bounties to iron manufacturers but also held out lucrative war contracts. The foundries built by private entrepreneurs in Springfield, East Bridgewater, and Easton, Massachusetts, for example, were largely spurred by financial assistance from the state government.

The states also played a major role in financing the Revolutionary War. When the Continental Congress issued bills of credit to pay its expenses, it delegated to the states all responsibility for the levying of taxes to raise these sums. Most states refused to collect such taxes. Instead, they issued their own bills of credit, usually against pledges of future tax revenues. Some states also issued treasury notes on which they paid annual interest. But without sound management these state securities—as well as the Continental Congress securities—rapidly depreciated in value.

With the conclusion of the war in 1783, lively debates occurred in most state legislatures concerning the role of government in the economic growth of the new nation. In the absence of a strong central government, the responsibilities of the states were even greater than before the Revolution. Although between 1783 and 1787 sentiment against any form of strong government action was widespread in the debates within states, in practice the pattern of state and local economic activity did not change greatly. But certainly the administration of economic policies became less rigid than it had been under British imperial supervision.

To promote economic recovery after the Revolution, the states drew upon their colonial experience in fashioning legislation during the Confederation. Subsidies and loans to private individuals continued to be common. In 1786, Pennsylvania lent £300, interest-free, for a five-year period to an individual who proposed to manufacture steel. Two years later the legislature paid £100 to John Hague to bring a cotton-carding machine into the state. Massachusetts lent £200 to Robert and Alex Burr to complete models of new machinery for carding and spinning wool and cotton. When states were short of specie, they frequently granted land. North Carolina in 1788 offered five thousand acres to anyone who would set up a successful ironworks. In the next year Massachusetts granted state lands worth £500 to the incorporators of a cotton factory at Beverly. Another promotional policy that continued to be popular was tax exemption. In 1788, North Carolina exempted all lands devoted to iron manufactures from taxes for a ten-year period. New Hampshire exempted oil mills, rod and nail works, and sailcloth factories. And all the states enacted comprehensive import and export duties, designed to discriminate not only against foreign nations but also against each other.

The proliferation of state and local economic regulations in the decade after the Revolution sometimes appeared to retard rather than to foster economic progress. Since state legislatures often enacted economic laws without a clear awareness of the actions taken by their neighbors, many state laws overlapped or even conflicted. In some cases, as in the tariff war between New York and New Jersey, states imposed retaliatory duties on each other in the hope of gaining a competitive advantage. Since inevitable postwar economic readjustments sharpened inflation and unemployment, Americans in the 1780's were caught in economic depression. At the same time the absence of a strong central government authority, such as the British imperial government had provided, left an economic as well as a political vacuum, especially in the dealings between the states and foreign nations.

Such concerns were on the minds of those political leaders who joined in the movement for a constitutional convention. They remembered not only their most recent experiences in the Revolutionary era but also the mercantilist tradition of the British Empire before 1776. And having read deeply in the history of republics both old and new, they sought to draw upon this vast fund of theoretical and practical experience to build a federal system that would be well adapted to the exigencies of their own and future ages.

The product of their labors was the Constitution, which limited the powers of state and local governments. The supreme authority of the new federal government to regulate interstate commerce clearly created a new suprastate entity. And the right of the national government to collect taxes and to assume state debts further enhanced its influence. Other provisions in the Constitution restrained the states from enacting laws that could impede growth of the national economy. These included the provisions allowing Congress sole authority to create and regulate the national monetary system, to coin money, and to prohibit states from issuing bills of credit or from enacting legislation to impair obligation of contracts. Congress also had sole authority to enact uniform bankruptcy legislation, to create a single postal system, and to establish a uniform system of weights and measures. State and local governments, of course, still had a vital economic role and retained broad scope under their police powers. But their role was clearly subsidiary to that of the federal government and to national needs—not wholly unlike the relationship of the colonies under the British Empire.

Thus, by 1789 the economic role of state and local governments had been delimited anew in the federal system established under the Constitution. That new role helped to transform the mercantilist inheritance. The states were particularly circumscribed in the spheres of interstate commerce, monetary affairs, and foreign trade. Nevertheless, states and localities still had broad areas of authority under the police power, delegated authority, or inherent powers. The federal system of 1787 thus introduced a more flexible apportionment of government powers into the American system.

THE NATIONAL ERA (1789–1860): MERCANTILISM AND LAISSEZ-FAIRE

Partly because the values of Americans, and their newly fashioned political system under the Constitution, were conducive to economic growth, the years between 1789 and 1860 were characterized by extraordinary expansion. Americans extended the western boundaries of the nation to the Pacific coast and threw their energies into the first stages of the industrial revolution. The impressive economic development of this period was fueled not only by the energies of millions of new settlers but also by the efforts of governments at all levels. In the process, state and local governments had a pivotal role.

The dimensions of this government activity were determined by historical inheritance as well as by contemporary influences. The assumption that governments had an important role in furthering economic growth did not die with the Revolution, but continued to occupy an important place in American economic thought and practice during the first half of the nineteenth century. Yet the laissez-faire doctrines of Adam Smith were modifying older rigid mercantilist theories. In contrast with mercantilism, which assumed that the state was the dynamic factor in economic development, laissez-faire doctrines focused on the crucial importance of individuals. Thus, during this period, Americans increasingly came to believe that it was the duty of governments to foster the creative energies of individuals and that their collective efforts would ultimately redound to the benefit of society as a whole. Consequently, the adaptation of mercantilist ideas to the doctrines of laissez-faire became an important strand in the ideology of American economic growth.

Yet Americans were above all a practical people, not a nation of ideologues. And so they wedded their ideological assumptions to intensely practical problems that they encountered in the economic exploitation of the continent. The Revolution contributed to a subtle shift of ideologies. And by removing British restrictions against settlement west of the Alleghenies, it precipitated a mass migration west of the Appalachians between 1789 and 1860. That vast population movement created new issues concerning the economic development of the interior of North America.

The role of state and local governments was pivotal in fostering this great surge in economic growth. In addition, governments assumed functions not taken up by individuals or projects too vast for private enterprise. This was true of internal improvements, and the construction of transportation arteries that were a necessary precursor to large-scale economic development of the vast interior of the continent. Americans also expected their governments to provide an institutional environment that would encourage individuals and would stimulate their creative capacities in economic pursuits. Thus governments were expected to create a hospitable legal framework and a stable monetary system. They also carried out a wide range of promotional and regulatory activities, and took a leading part in the distribution of natural resources from the public domain to private individuals. Laissez-faire may have been a popular dogma with some Americans during the first half of the nineteenth century, but its prime goal—maximization of individual freedom (including economic freedom)—would not have been attainable without extensive government activity.

Perhaps few projects so firmly gripped the imagination of this generation of Americans as internal improvements. The years between 1790 and 1830 saw a great road-building boom as turnpikes, through roads, and county roads were built in great profusion. Many of these thoroughfares were built by individuals, with the aid of state and local governments. Through the issuance of charters, states awarded monopoly privileges to entrepreneurs and often contributed needed capital by large purchases of their corporate stock. By 1861 the state of Virginia had expended more than $5 million for roads and bridges, a sum that did not include the substantial financial contributions of the counties. When private enterprise found the challenges too great, state governments undertook major road construction. By 1830, Indiana and South Carolina had built major turnpikes. Road construction, therefore, was a joint effort of private and public enterprise.

Canals and waterways also promised to improve transportation. By their very nature, canals were projects of great magnitude requiring vast capital investments and presenting technical difficulties often beyond the ability of individuals. Americans therefore turned to their state and local governments to assume major responsibilities for canals. New York State set a major precedent in 1817–1825, when it built the Erie Canal at a cost exceeding $7 million. Its immediate success set off a canal craze in the United States, financed largely by state and local governments. Pennsylvania and Ohio built the most elaborate systems, but other states invested large sums as well. Between 1816 and 1840, 3,226 miles of canals were built, most of them with public aid. It has been estimated that the states incurred debts exceeding $60 million for canal construction in the two decades after 1820, half of their total expenditures. This sum did not include smaller amounts spent by the states and counties for improvement of river navigation.

If the canal-building craze abated after 1840, it was largely due to the new interest in railroad construction. Railways were faster, more reliable, more versatile, and, in the long run, cheaper than canals. Like waterways they required a large initial investment, often beyond the competence of private enterprise. Again, Americans turned to their governments for aid. After 1840 state legislatures undertook the promotion of railroads by various means. Corporate charters granted special privileges, including monopolies, grants of eminent domain, or tax exemption. In return, governments retained certain regulatory powers. Moreover, state and local governments provided direct aid. Often they made land grants to railroad corporations, authorized subsidies, bought shares of stock, or made extensive loans.

Between 1838 and 1860 the states borrowed more than $150 million for railroads, and county and city expenditures for the same purpose equaled that impressive sum. In the South more than 55 percent of railroad capital came from the coffers of state and local governments. And where private capitalists were reluctant, states and localities built and operated their own rail lines. Pennsylvania constructed two short railroads, and Virginia and Georgia each built major rail connections. In an effort to surpass some of their trade rivals, city governments also built and operated their own lines. For example, Troy, New York, in 1842 issued $600,000 in bonds to build the Schenectady and Troy Railroad, designed to provide commercial supremacy over Albany.

Between 1789 and 1860 few Americans would have denied that transportation was the key to economic growth. But the task of building a transportation network into the wilderness was clearly beyond the grasp of private individuals. The aid of government on all levels was crucial in this era. This major economic challenge was successfully met largely due to the extensive help provided by state and local governments, which contributed at least half of the capital needed. Internal improvements were a cooperative endeavor between private and public enterprise.

Less dramatically, state and local governments continued to exercise a wide range of functions in business, agriculture, and labor. The power to issue charters of incorporation to business entrepreneurs was of supreme importance. Between 1830 and 1860 the number of incorporations was so large that legislatures ceased to make individual grants. Instead, the states enacted general incorporation laws that granted the privilege to all applicants who could meet certain requirements. Direct aid to business continued to be extended by subsidies, offered during these years for articles as diverse as silk, iron, ships, salt, and rails. Many states—Vermont, New York, and Ohio among them—offered tax exemption as an inducement for manufactures of textiles, glass, and iron. Southern states sometimes offered land grants in addition, to make tax exemption even more attractive.

State and local regulation of business was common during these years. The states continued the colonial practice of providing standards of quality or honest measure for a wide variety of goods. Among products subject to inspection were flour, fish, pork, bread, butter, tobacco, liquors, and gunpowder. Municipal authorities controlled the rates charged by various businesses. Regulation of markets or of draymen's charges was as common in 1860 as in 1815. Gas, water, and ice companies were usually subject to municipal laws that governed rates, safety, and standards of service. States and localities also engaged in extensive licensing of peddlers, brokers, and persons in other occupations.

A similar structure of state and local government policies affected the most important American economic pursuit, agriculture. Every state provided financial support for an agricultural society, for the annual state agricultural fair, and subsidies for county fairs. Most states offered bounties to sustain or to diversify particular types of farming, whether wheat, silk, or sugar beets. As wheat acreage declined in Maine, for example, the legislature in 1837 and 1838 offered bounties for the first twenty bushels produced by individual farmers.

State and local inspectors administered stringent marketing regulations, designed to maintain quality by eliminating inferior products. Mississippi and Georgia conducted extensive inspection of cotton between 1848 and 1860, and every southern state provided for close inspection of tobacco. New York, Ohio, and Kentucky were known for their stringent inspection of meat and flour. Some of the states, including North Carolina, Louisiana, and Virginia, established state-owned warehouses to facilitate effective inspection.

The states expanded their functions in agriculture during these years by becoming increasingly involved in disease control. When Dutch cows introduced pleuropneumonia into Massachusetts in 1859, the state legislature appropriated funds to reimburse owners of affected cattle. In fact, Governor Nathaniel Banks called a special session of the legislature and ordered all sick cattle destroyed or quarantined. Meanwhile, New York State had pioneered in 1853 with the appointment of a state entomologist to aid farmers in their fight against injurious insects. All of the states established geological surveys that, by analyzing soils and mineral resources in particular areas, were directly responsible for guiding potential farmers or miners into unexploited or unpopulated regions.

With the growth of industrialism and a distinct labor force, state and local legislatures and courts adapted laws inherited from a mercantilist age to the new conditions of their own day. In general, legislatures rendered these laws more flexible in regard to indentured servitude, apprenticeship, wages, hours, and working conditions. Chief Justice Lemuel Shaw of Massachusetts, in the landmark case *Commonwealth* v. *Hunt* (1842), affirmed the right of workers to organize into unions in order to engage in strikes against employers. Previously such actions had been illegal as conspiracies under the common law. By endowing workers with greater freedom of action, this decision inaugurated a new phase in the relations between state and local governments and labor.

The states continued to be closely involved in the national banking system. When capital was scarce, Americans often turned to their state governments to take up the slack. In the South and West especially, states created their own banks to relieve a chronic credit shortage. One of the most stable public institutions was the Bank of South Carolina, operating between 1812 and 1868. The State Bank of Indiana could match its record, but state banks in Alabama, Kentucky, Mississippi, and Illinois were poorly managed and eventually failed.

STATE AND LOCAL GOVERNMENTS

When not engaged in banking directly, the states regulated private bankers to ensure the flow of capital into new enterprises. Between 1789 and 1838 state corporate charters for banks were special legislative acts that stipulated explicit requirements concerning reserves, issuance of bank notes, and capital requirements. As the number of private banks increased, the states adopted general banking legislation. The New York Free Banking Act of 1838 was one of the most admired of these laws. It offered banking privileges to any group of individuals who could meet specified conditions. To safeguard bank notes, the act required banks to deposit bonds with the state controller, thus creating a safety fund. Banks that did not redeem their notes in specie were required to pay annual interest charges of 14 percent to note holders.

Between 1789 and 1860 thirteen coastal states became a continental industrial power. This dramatic change was accomplished through a common effort of private and public enterprise. Governments provided the institutional framework that stimulated individuals to direct their energies into economic development and, through an intricate framework of promotional and regulatory policies, fostered the momentum of growth. Moreover, in critical areas of the economy in which shortage of capital funds threatened to delay development, governments stepped in to fill the vacuum. This was true in transportation and finance. It has been estimated that state and local governments provided approximately half of the capital invested in new enterprises between 1789 and 1860. Obviously, then, this was not primarily an age of laissez-faire, but a period in which laissez-faire doctrines were adapted to mercantilist practices.

THE ERA OF BIG BUSINESS (1860–1900): LEGISLATIVE REGULATION

About the middle of the nineteenth century, the economic role of state and local governments was modified by the increasing momentum of industrialization. The Civil War hastened the growth of some manufactures while retarding that of others. But despite fluctuations in economic development, by 1894 the United States emerged as the leading manufacturing nation in the world. The rhetoric accompanying this change, especially social Darwinism, increasingly came to stress laissez-faire rather than government intervention in the economy. Yet the traditions of state and local government activity were too deeply ingrained in the American system to succumb to mere rhetoric.

Thus, between 1860 and 1900 state and local governments continued to exercise significant functions in many areas of the economy. Yet legislatures found effective implementation of their policies increasingly difficult. The complexities of an industrial society often vitiated legislative intentions, because many new industrial problems were of national rather than local scope. Moreover, powerful new business groups exerted extraordinary influence on state and local governments. Another source of frustration to many officials was their lack of technical or specialized skills needed in an industrial society. Amid such major changes, new economic needs tended to expand the functions of state and local authorities more than in previous years.

The continued growth of commerce and manufacturing created many strains for state and local governments. Especially difficult was implementation of controls over corporations. Despite frequent demands for federal laws, incorporation continued to be primarily a responsibility of the states. Some, like New Jersey and Delaware, provided for special ease of incorporation to attract as many businesses as possible. But since corporations were their creatures, legislatures attempted to impose regulations on them to prevent abuses. By 1880 many states required detailed annual reports, prohibited excessive levying of assessments on stockholders, limited issues of stock, and regulated the appointment of directors. In most instances administration of such provisions was extremely lax. Corporations proliferated much faster than the ability of state governments to control them.

By 1880 the abuses of certain types of corporations had become so serious that most state legislatures enacted more stringent regulatory measures. The frauds and other irregularities by state-chartered banks led more than two dozen states to create state banking commissions. Their responsibilities included periodic inspection of bank statements to ascertain financial conditions and investigation of dishonesty, fraud, or questionable banking practices. These agencies provided continual state supervision. Similar regulations accompanied the growth of insurance companies. By 1880 more than thirty states had created state boards of insurance commissioners (sometimes a single commissioner) who had authority to inspect the books of these corporations and to evaluate their assets. Moreover, they had broad powers over business practices and investigated complaints from policyholders.

One of the prime concerns of state and local governments during this period was effective regulation of railroads. As problems of railway construction gave way to problems of operation after 1870, new issues were created. Excessive rates, discrimination in rates or service, stock watering, and dishonest business practices were only a few of the complaints that turned public admiration of railroads into bitterness and hatred. A veritable ground swell of public opinion led state legislatures to expand their regulatory activities. Massachusetts led the way when in 1869 it created a board of railroad commissioners that, under Charles Francis Adams, Jr., sought to use publicity as a device to control the carriers. The middle western states imposed more stringent rules in the Granger laws between 1869 and 1874. They created railroad commissions with powers to regulate rates, short- and long-haul charges, and standards of service, and decreed the abolition of rebates or other forms of discrimination. By 1900 every state had created such an agency with similar powers. But these public agencies found it very difficult to carry out their legislative mandates. The magnitude of the expanding railroad network, increasingly complex technical problems, and sometimes active opposition made effective enforcement difficult.

During this period, municipalities enacted similar regulations covering railways and harbors under their jurisdiction, particularly covering the rapidly expanding street railway systems being built in most larger cities. As municipalities issued charters for such railways—and other public utilities such as water, gas, electric, sewage, and telephone companies—they included regulation of routes, rates, and standards of service.

The need for new services in an era of industrialization led state and local governments to continue public ownership and operation. As private companies rapidly expanded the railroad network, so state and local governments strained to construct roads and highways to connect localities with rail lines. Although road building had not been a major responsibility of state and local governments at the beginning of the nineteenth century, between 1860 and 1900 public, rather than private, enterprise assumed virtually sole authority for this vital function. Since many states had been burdened with heavy debts in the two decades after the Civil War, the road-building function devolved largely upon city and county governments.

As in earlier years, state and local governments continued to play a significant role in agriculture and the extractive industries. Many of the farmer's problems during this period stemmed from the shift from self-sufficient to commercial agriculture. For millions of American farmers this transition was painful and led them to turn to their state and local governments for help with new problems of production, marketing, and processing. Increased scientific knowledge about plant and animal diseases led most states and some counties to appoint special officials or agencies to develop effective control programs. State legislatures continued to use bounties to encourage certain crops—including wheat, silk, wine grapes, and hemp—and a wide variety of other products.

As agriculture became more specialized, state legislatures created new agencies to provide aid. California, for example, created separate state boards of horticulture, viticulture, and silk culture, and a state veterinarian; and other states established comparable bodies. These state officials usually were active in disease control and in research (besides the work of agricultural colleges and experiment stations). They also sought to improve techniques of production and distribution, and engaged in educational activities. Many states in the Middle West and in the South built state-owned warehouses and grain elevators to facilitate marketing of crops. They also expanded crop inspection programs to assure the maintenance of minimum quality standards with a view toward making marketing more efficient.

Land distribution continued to be a vital state function during this period. As a result of various federal land acts, between 1860 and 1900 the states had more than 72 million acres to distribute. Each of the states maintained a land office to dispose of its public lands. In general, state administration often violated legislative intent to distribute small tracts to independent farmers. Distribution was very lax and usually allowed speculators to amass vast tracts of land.

Without great success, state and local governments sought to slow the rapid depletion of natural resources. In the West, states established new agencies, such as that of the state engineers, with the task of developing plans for the more efficient use and allocation of water. States also authorized the creation of special local districts for irrigation, reclamation, or drainage to cope with such problems at the grass-roots level. All of the states established fish and game commissions, which began programs to replenish depleted wildlife and attempted to curb the high rate of kill by requiring licenses and by developing regulations for hunters and fishermen. Similarly, most states created forestry commissions that undertook reforestation of denuded areas and stipulated regulations for timber cutting and fire control on state lands.

As the number of wage earners and factory workers increased sharply during this period, the responsibilities of state and local governments in labor relations increased as well. State legislatures enacted laws to ensure safer working conditions. The proliferation of state laws concerning labor made their administration more difficult. By 1880 more than twenty states had created the post of state labor commissioner, the holder of which had responsibility for the execution of labor statutes. The commissioners collected information concerning workers and wages, and made some efforts in factory inspection. But most of these officials lacked staffs large enough to render their work effective. State labor regulation was more evident in legislative intent than in administrative execution.

During the era of big business, then, state and local governments continued to play a significant role in the economy even though laissez-faire doctrines were espoused by contemporaries. In contrast with the first half of the nineteenth century, private enterprise took the major investment risks during this period. But this was due to the changing role of government, from promoter to regulator. And although state and local governments discovered that they lacked the administrative skills to implement their policies effectively, they laid the foundations for more comprehensive public regulation in the twentieth century. By 1900 their role in the economy had become highly institutionalized.

THE INDUSTRIAL ERA (1900–1975): ADMINISTRATIVE REGULATION

The emergence of the United States as an industrial civilization after 1900 left its mark on government. As industrialization created manifold new problems, an increasing number of Americans looked to government—rather than private individuals or voluntary groups—for remedies. Moreover, since many of the new problems seemed national rather than local in scope, the federal government assumed increasingly greater responsibilities. In the partnership among the national, state, and local governments, the national government was beginning to assume a more dominant role than in previous years.

This shift in political power became clearly discernible in the Progressive era (1900–1917) and continued at an accelerated pace thereafter. Although governments at all levels increased their economic activities, the expanding power of the national government was most striking. This was largely because a majority of Americans came to believe, with Theodore Roosevelt, that only big government could meet the challenges of big business.

The role of state and local governments in the economy did not undergo significant changes during the twentieth century. More characteristic was the extension of policies that they had inaugurated during the nineteenth century and the development of more effective administration. To lawmakers in the Progressive era, such reform could often be summarized in the word "efficiency." That was the dogma that grew out of the scientific management movement, which was embraced by businessmen, labor and farm leaders, scientists, intellectuals, reformers, and government officials. The culmination of their efforts with respect to state and local government came in 1911 with President William Howard Taft's appointment of the Commission on Efficiency and Economy in Government. This body made recommendations for reforms that provided the foundation for administrative reorganization in more than thirty states between 1915 and 1940.

One of the key measures proposed by reformers was the creation of administrative commissions staffed by experts. This proposal was prompted by the example of business corporations, which were governed by a board of directors that supervised a staff of specialists and professional managers. The commission form of regulation came to be a prime characteristic of state and local governments between 1900 and 1975, and was extended to a broad range of economic activities.

As state and local governments created bureaucracies to administer their manifold functions, they improved the effectiveness of their administration. The creation of commissions increased government efficiency in the regulation of business, as it became increasingly complex and specialized. In some areas state governments utilized commissions to enforce the extremely detailed regulation of industries that were considered of particular importance. This was true, for example, of the burgeoning oil industry in Oklahoma and Texas, where state agencies controlled not only drilling practices but also daily production quotas.

Government ownership and operation were less common than regulation. Nevertheless some states, including North Dakota, owned and operated banks, insurance companies, and grain elevators. State ownership of port facilities existed in New York, Alabama, Georgia, Louisiana, and California. More common was municipal ownership and operation of public utilities and airports.

Administrative regulation also pervaded state and local agricultural policies. Most states expanded their existing regulatory programs to include new crops. And, paralleling a trend in other spheres of public policy, the states consolidated dozens of separate agencies into centralized departments of agriculture.

Similar expansion and centralization characterized state labor policies during the period. At the behest of progressive reformers, state legislators enacted laws stipulating minimum wages, maximum hours, workmen's compensation, restriction of child labor, and safe working conditions. But execution of these laws varied greatly. Massachusetts and New York were among the most proficient and came to be models. They established centralized state bureaus or departments of labor that coordinated the enforcement of hundreds of diverse labor regulations for which the states had come to assume responsibility.

The Great Depression brought state and local governments to one of the most severe crises in their history. As tax revenues and income fell, many states and localities found themselves in, or on the verge of, bankruptcy. Thousands of local government units fruitlessly attempted to cope with the problems of unemployment and economic recovery. But the depression was national in scope, and the states and localities felt powerless to deal with it effectively. Americans expected their national government to assume that responsibility. The states and localities thus emerged from the Great Depression greatly shaken. They had not outlived their usefulness—as some critics charged—but their economic role had definitely become subordinate to that of the national government.

Yet the quiet but still significant role of state and local governments in the economy during this period should not be dismissed too easily. They had assumed significant functions in the national economic life that most Americans now took for granted. Amid much of the political acrimony over the New Deal in the 1930's, virtually no criticism was directed toward the structure of state and local economic regulation. Perhaps because it had become largely institutionalized, it occasioned far less public debate than the proper economic role of the national government.

Although by 1945 state and local governments seemed greatly overshadowed by the continuing ascendancy of the federal government, the proliferation of their activities continued at an increased pace during the next three decades. With the growth of a technologically oriented society, Americans demanded increasing intervention by governments at all levels to ensure economic stability. Although the extraordinary expansion of federal power aroused much debate, the unobtrusive role of state and local entities was no less significant in the bureaucratization of society that was taking place. Large-scale organizations staffed by technicians and professional managers became characteristic of American political and economic life.

The impact of state and local governments on the twentieth-century economy was considerable. Their total expenditures constituted a significant proportion of the gross national product (GNP) and clearly affected monetary and fiscal policies of the federal government. In view of their great expansion, they became one of the largest employers in the nation. At a time when service industries produced an increasingly larger share of the GNP, states and localities accounted for a substantial percentage of income of this sector.

State and local finances reflected these trends. In 1940 the states and localities expended $5 billion; in 1960, $31 billion; and in 1975, $221 billion. A part of this increase was, of course, due to inflation. But the percentage of state and local government expenditures in the GNP also rose, from 7.8 percent in 1940 to 10.4 percent in 1960 and to approximately 12 percent in 1975. State and local debts reflected this enormous expansion of services. In 1940 state and local debts totaled $20 billion; in 1960, $77 billion; and in 1975 the estimates ranged at about $100 billion. These statistics reflected no new departures in the structure of state and local economic regulation, but they did reveal an enormous expansion of functions and services and an enormous growth of their bureaucracy.

In 1929 state and local government employees totaled 2,532,000; in 1940, 3,206,000; in 1950, 4,285,000; in 1960, 6,387,000; and in 1975, 12,096,000. By contrast federal government employees numbered 580,000 in 1929; 1,042,000 in 1940; 2,117,000 in 1950; 2,421,000 in 1960; and an estimated 2,890,000 in 1975. Clearly the activities of state and local governments bore directly on the fiscal policies of the nation and constituted a significant source of employment.

CONCLUSION: THE AMERICAN SYSTEM

The institutional relationships between government and the economy in the United States evolved into a system that embraced national, state, and local governments. But while the proper functions of the federal government were an object of continual controversy and dispute from the founding of the nation to the twentieth century, the economic role of state and local governments did not become a public issue. Certainly, by 1900, Americans had developed a consensus on this question that largely took it out of the realm of heated conflict. The significance of an institutional framework conducive to economic development was hardly appreciated until the second half of the twentieth century. At that time the failure of many less developed countries to industrialize rapidly was found to be rooted not merely in the lack of technical skills, but also in cultural values and political institutions that hampered economic change. In contrast, the federal system in the United States was geared to accelerated economic growth.

As the economic role of state and local governments crystallized in the late nineteenth century, their functions were broad but fell into four recognizable categories. The ultimate purpose of these manifold activities was to foster economic development while maintaining a measure of social and political stability. Hence, promotion became one of the most important functions of state and local governments, from the colonial era to the late twentieth century. Direct aid offered by state and local governments in the form of subsidies, gifts, loans, grants of special privilege, and tax exemption was common. Public bodies joined private enterprise through purchases of corporate securities. In the colonial era governments granted monopolies, trademarks, or patents, functions assumed by the national government under the Constitution. Another vital form of promotion was the creation of a legal framework by the states and localities within which economic enterprise could flourish. Laws providing for incorporation, and for the conditions under which private enterprise could operate, have had a far-reaching impact on the economic structure of the nation. Similarly, laws governing the making of contracts have conditioned the business environment of the United States. And bankruptcy legislation has provided a framework of expectations for entrepreneurs in which they are willing to risk capital and energy for new projects.

To a considerable degree the regulatory policies of the states and localities have been forged to control or remove obstacles to economic growth. This pattern was remarkably consistent from the seventeenth to the twentieth century. Throughout this period state and local bodies used fiscal measures, whether taxes or the control of interest rates, to regulate economic practices. Lawmakers, courts, and executive officials conceived of these not merely as revenue-producing measures, but also as techniques designed to stimulate or encourage economic activity. A similar goal prompted public policymakers to create and maintain standards that were applied to agricultural commodities and manufactured goods. They also administered restrictions or prohibitions of behavior that was conceived as impeding economic development. By the twentieth century the states and localities made extensive use of their licensing powers to regulate entrance into scores of professions, as well as into various businesses and forms of transportation.

Although promotion and regulation were the most distinctive features of state and local economic policies, they also included public ownership and operation. Where local or regional conditions warranted it, the states—but more often municipalities, counties, or special districts—provided essential services. These included public utilities, transportation systems, banks, warehouses, and a great variety of enterprises. Ironically, the many critics of government ownership and operation usually focused on the activities of the federal government, but hardly ever on those of the states and localities. This occurred despite the fact that the total impact of state and local economic enterprises was hardly less significant than that of the national government.

Educational and research activities of the states and localities have contributed significantly to economic growth. Until the middle of the twentieth century, educational functions were largely in the domain of state and local officials; thereafter the federal government began to assume greater responsibility. Education was pursued not only through the public schools but also by various demonstration agencies, whether state agricultural fairs in the nineteenth century or industrial trade fairs in succeeding years. The states also made important contributions through their research activities. Geological surveys, agricultural colleges, conservation agencies, and scientific research laboratories were among the many agencies created by the states and localities to stimulate growth in diverse spheres of the economy. Research and education, therefore, in addition to public ownership and operation, and promotion and regulation, have been the dominant areas of state and local intervention in the economy.

The economic functions of state and local governments have become one of the most stable elements in the American institutional system. While the nature and the functions of the federal government underwent great changes over the years, the structure and functions of state and local governments remained far more stable. Founded in a mercantilistic age, modified by doctrines of laissez-faire, and hewn out of the practical experience of successive generations of Americans, the role of state and local governments had become increasingly institutionalized by the end of the nineteenth century. The American experience was not entirely unique among industrialized societies. Historical development of west European nations revealed similar tendencies. Despite cataclysmic changes in French central government after the Revolution, local government provided stability and continuity amid great changes. The German experience was similar. So in the United States, as technology wrought great disruptive changes, the economic policies of state and local governments provided an element of continuity and economic —as well as social and political—stability.

BIBLIOGRAPHY

Hugh G. J. Aitken, ed., *The State and Economic Growth* (New York, 1959), ch. 1, by Henry W. Broude, provides a brief general overview of the subject. Stuart Bruchey, *The Roots of American Economic Growth, 1607–1861: An Essay in Social Causation* (New York, 1965), a brief survey of the American economy, includes consideration of government activities. Guy S. Callender, "The Early Transportation and Banking Enterprises of the States in Relation to the Growth of Corporations," in *Quarterly Journal of Economics,* 17 (1902), is a classic account that is still instructive. Paul W. Gates, *The Farmer's Age: Agriculture, 1815–1860* (New York, 1960), vol. 3 of *Economic History of the United States,* an impressive work of synthesis, gives special attention to government relations with agriculture. Carter Goodrich, *Government Promotion of Canals and Railroads 1800–1890* (New York, 1960), is an excellent, detailed study of the role of state and local governments in the internal improvements movement. Bray Hammond, *Banks and Politics in America, from the Revolution to the Civil War* (Princeton, 1957), a major work, touches on state and local

STATE AND LOCAL GOVERNMENTS

banking policies. Oscar Handlin and Mary Flug Handlin, *Commonwealth: A Study of the Role of Government in the American Economy; Massachusetts, 1774–1860* (Cambridge, Mass., 1947), is an informative analysis with prime emphasis on ideology. Louis Hartz, *Economic Policy and Democratic Thought: Pennsylvania, 1776–1860* (Cambridge, Mass., 1948), a suggestive book about public economic policies in a major state, stresses the interplay of ideas and legislation. Milton S. Heath, *Constructive Liberalism: The Role of the State in Economic Development in Georgia to 1860* (Cambridge, Mass., 1954), an illuminating volume, reveals elements of continuity in state and local policies.

James W. Hurst, *Law and the Conditions of Freedom in the Nineteenth Century United States* (Madison, Wis., 1956), a profound book, provides the legal, institutional, and philosophical context necessary to an understanding of the role of state and local government. Edward C. Kirkland, *American Economic History After 1860* (New York, 1971), a selective bibliography, also contains references to state and local government policies. Robert A. Lively, "The American System: A Review Article," in *Business History Review*, 29 (1955), is a brilliant evaluation of the literature on government's role in the economy. Richard B. Morris, *Government and Labor in Early America* (New York, 1946), an exhaustive study, is illuminating for labor relations and provides insights into the broader range of colonial local economic regulation. Gerald D. Nash, *State Government and Economic Development: A History of Administrative Policies in California, 1849–1933* (Berkeley, 1964), is a detailed analysis of government activities in a western state. Curtis P. Nettels, *The Emergence of a National Economy, 1775–1815* (New York, 1962), vol. 2 of *Economic History of the United States*, is a useful work of synthesis although it gives only passing attention to government policies. James N. Primm, *Economic Policy in the Development of a Western State: Missouri, 1820–1860* (Cambridge, Mass., 1954), is a brief survey of the government's role in the economy of Missouri. George R. Taylor, *The Transportation Revolution, 1815–1860* (New York, 1951), vol. 4 of *Economic History of the United States*, is a superb survey that gives special attention to public policies; and *American Economic History to 1860* (New York, 1970), a useful general bibliography, also contains references to government relations.

[*See also* AGRICULTURE; AGRICULTURE IN THE NORTH AND WEST; AGRICULTURE IN THE SOUTH; AMERICAN BUSINESS INSTITUTIONS BEFORE THE RAILROAD; ANTITRUST; BUREAUCRACY; COLONIAL ECONOMY; DOMESTIC TRADE AND REGIONAL SPECIALIZATION; ECONOMIC GROWTH; ECONOMIC THOUGHT; ECONOMY FROM THE REVOLUTION TO 1815; ECONOMY FROM 1815 TO 1865; ECONOMY FROM RECONSTRUCTION TO 1914; ECONOMY SINCE 1914; EDUCATION; ENTREPRENEURSHIP; THE EUROPEAN BACKGROUND; GOVERNMENT MANAGEMENT OF THE ECONOMY; INSURANCE; LABOR ORGANIZATIONS; LAND POLICIES AND SALES; LAW AND POLITICAL INSTITUTIONS; MANUFACTURING; REGULATORY AGENCIES; SAVINGS AND INVESTMENT; SCIENCE; TARIFFS; TAXATION; TRANSPORTATION; *and* WESTWARD MOVEMENT.]

LABOR ORGANIZATIONS

Melvyn Dubofsky

AS long as humans have lived and worked together, they have associated in various forms of organizations for social companionship, cooperative endeavor, and economic security. Such organizations have altered in structure and composition as historical changes have transformed the modes of production and the social relations resulting from these organizations. Among the youngest of such human institutions historically have been labor organizations, a form of association that did not develop until the emergence of marketplace capitalism and the wage-labor relationship became manifest in the eighteenth and nineteenth centuries. As men and also women found themselves in a common predicament, subject to the vicissitudes of an impersonal market and to the demands of employers whose wages determined their level of living, they formed labor organizations to gain fellowship, security, and an improved standard of living. This article will examine, in brief compass, the persistence and change in United States labor organizations from the colonial era to the present, and how the structure, practice, and goals of such organizations have reflected changes in the external social and economic environment.

THE COLONIAL ERA TO 1843

For the first two and a half centuries of their existence, the European settlements on the North American continent were primarily rural. Indeed, at the dawn of the nineteenth century, approximately 90 percent of United States inhabitants lived in the countryside and, except for slaves, on scattered farms. With the vast bulk of the population deriving its subsistence directly or indirectly from the land and widely distributed about the countryside in separate household units, little reason existed for the emergence of labor organizations.

By the mid-eighteenth century, however, a substantial number of people lived in seaboard cities that compared in population with typical European urban communities. Such colonial cities as Philadelphia, New York, Boston, Charleston, and Baltimore ranked among the larger population centers in the British Empire and included large numbers of men and women who sustained themselves by labor. Two primary forms of work characterized the colonial labor force. One set of workers functioned within the traditional universe of artisan production. Divided into masters, who controlled the trade; journeymen, who assisted the masters; and apprentices, legally bound to masters from whom they learned the secrets of the craft, these workers labored under a nonwage system. Masters earned their incomes on the basis of the difference in the cost of the product they produced and the price for which they sold it; journeymen shared a portion of that income; and apprentices ordinarily received room and board. The second set of workers provided the seaboard cities with casual labor. They loaded and unloaded ships, carted merchandise to and from the docks, and engaged in various heavy manual jobs. Paid wages by the day and employed only irregularly, these workers formed an exceedingly casual, transient, and volatile mass.

Owing to the irregularity of their employment and the volatility of their membership, the mass of day-wage laborers could neither associate collectively nor form labor organizations. Workers in the traditional artisanal trades were better situated to act collectively, and they did try in many instances to establish European-style craft guilds in the New World. But a system already declining in eighteenth-century Britain could scarcely be replicated across the Atlantic, where few master craftsmen were themselves products of a traditional apprenticeship-journeyman training and where rapid population change and relatively weak government made the enforcement of guild regulations impracticable. Masters and journeymen might form benevolent associations to assist each other in case of injury, illness, or death; but they failed to establish guilds capable of regulating production standards, prices, and apprenticeships. For colonial American workers, whether artisans or day laborers, labor organization was largely absent.

The ferment associated with the American Revolution, however much it affected the consciousness of laborers and artisans, produced no permanent, stable labor organizations. Urban laborers and mechanics (another term commonly used to describe artisans) joined the colonial mobs that attacked British agents, enforced trade boycotts, and sustained the revolutionary cause. They also sympathized with the revolutionaries, who favored more democratic and egalitarian practices, in contrast with the system of aristocracy and deference associated with British rulers and American Loyalists. But organizations created by workers to control wages, working conditions, and job security were not a part of the revolutionary ferment.

Beginning in the 1790's labor organizations began to emerge in the United States. From 1790 to 1815 urban population grew more rapidly than did rural population, and as cities grew, the pace of economic activity quickened. Enterprising merchants sought to satisfy a larger consumer market and hence intensified price competition. Distinctions began to arise between wholesale and retail trade, direct production for a consumer and indirect production for a wholesaler or retailer. The drive for greater productivity at lower cost precipitated an attack on the traditional system of artisan production, the employment of women and children in place of higher-cost, more skilled men, and the spread of the wage-labor relationship. Some masters in effect became employers; others, probably a larger number, functioned as hired employees although they still owned the actual tools of production. With the collapse of the customary lines that separated masters, journeymen, and apprentices—never firm in the New World—labor exploitation grew more common. In response, journeymen and former masters, if not yet a proletariat stripped of the tools of production, united in collective associations to protect their standards and values.

Philadelphia shoemakers were the first group of urban workers to organize collectively, establishing their first labor organization in 1792 and two years later achieving stability as the Federal Society of Journeymen Cordwainers, an association that endured until 1806. In 1794 printers in New York City formed the Typographical Society of New York, which survived for ten years; and between 1800 and 1805 cordwainers, printers, and other craftsmen in Boston, Baltimore, and Pittsburgh organized similar unions. At first, most of these early labor associations invited masters as well as journeymen to join. But as wholesale and retail trade grew and the gap between journeymen and masters widened, the unions closed their membership rolls to employers. For example, in 1817 the New York Society of Printers resolved that "the interests of journeymen are separate and in some respects opposite to that of employers."

These early labor organizations adopted many practices later associated with the term "business unionism." They sought to protect their members against the dilution of craft standards, increase their income, shorten hours, and improve working conditions through agreements with employers. Early unions also served as benevolent societies, levying dues in order to assist members in case of illness, death, or unemployment. To achieve their objectives the craft unions bound their members to strict rules and regulations, compelled members to abide by organization wage and work standards, and demanded that members labor only alongside other unionists. Through the closed shop and the strike, when necessary, the craftsmen sought to act collectively.

Although the early unions sought aims familiar to modern trade unionists, they practiced a singular form of bargaining. Rather than sit across a table from their employers and discuss the terms and conditions of employment, the craftsmen simply drew up a list of their demands, posted it publicly, and waited for the employer to accept or reject it. Acceptance would produce a settlement; rejection, a strike. The craftsmen also refused to bargain about wages, insisting instead that they should receive a fair price for their product, not a wage for their labor. In no sense were these first-generation American trade unionists proletarians, and so in their bargaining they sought to legitimate their status as respectable, independent producers whose labor power could not be bought and sold on the open market. Urban growth and economic change may have compelled craftsmen to act collectively in order to defend their role and status in society, but from 1792 to 1816 (indeed, for several decades afterward as well) they demanded respect as producers who possessed the tools (as well as the skills) of their trade rather than as wageworkers.

Legal restraints and an economic depression following the War of 1812 doomed the first trade unions. Many employers refused to deal collectively with their workers and went to court to seek relief against trade unionism. Just as the first stable labor organization originated in Philadelphia among cordwainers, so one of the most important early nineteenth-century cases in labor law affected the city's shoemakers. The shoe manufacturers of Philadelphia asked a local judge to declare the collective action of their employees to maintain wage rates and a closed shop to be an illegal restraint of trade under the common law. In what became known as the Philadelphia Cordwainers' Conspiracy Case, the court ruled in 1805 that individual shoemakers could refuse to work for wages they deemed too low or to work with nonunion members; but if two or more cordwainers jointly acted in that manner, such action was indeed an illegal restraint of trade subject to judicial interdiction and punishment. In effect, the Philadelphia decision rendered collective efforts to establish wages, working conditions, and rules illegal. Under its terms unions could continue their voluntary, fraternal, and benevolent functions; but they could not compel employers to respect union standards.

What legal restraints began, economic decline finished. The depression that struck the nation between 1816 and 1820 made labor superfluous, bankrupted union treasuries, and led union members to desert their organizations in order to find employment, whatever the standards and conditions of work. Of the many craft unions that flowered in urban America between 1792 and 1812, none remained by 1820.

Economic growth and change in the structure of the marketplace during the 1820's precipitated a second flowering of labor organization. With the opening of the Erie Canal in 1825, connecting the Atlantic seaboard with the Great Lakes, the spread of improved turnpikes across the Northeast, and the general use of steamboats on eastern and western waterways, the national economy boomed and manufacturers, wholesalers, and retailers competed for customers in a widened market. Factory and other forms of modern industrial production expanded in parts of New England and the Hudson and Delaware river valleys alongside the older, more traditional forms of artisan manufacture. As merchants and manufacturers competed for customers in an increasingly integrated economy, they strove to cut costs and prices. In the textile factories of Fall River and Lowell, Massachusetts, women and children provided a source of low-cost labor. Elsewhere, employers eager to reduce their costs of production diluted the skills of craftsmen by subdividing the process of manufacture into specialized but simple processes that could easily be learned without the time and expense of formal apprenticeship systems. Again, as skills were diluted, female and child labor could be substituted for that of more costly male craftsmen.

American economic development during the 1820's proved the truth of Adam Smith's dictum that the extent of the market governs the division of labor. As transport innovations widened the market, employers increasingly undermined customary artisan practices, assaulted the apprentice-journeyman system of training, and, when possible, hired the cheapest, least skilled sources of labor.

The combination of economic growth, on the one hand, and an employer assault on traditional work structures and practices, on the other, caused craftsmen again to unite for collective action. Buoyed by the return of prosperity and a rising demand for their labor, hatters, carpenters, house painters, stonecutters, weavers, cabinetmakers, cordwainers, printers, and even some factory hands formed trade unions. And to win their goals, they acted aggressively. In 1824 craftsmen in New York City, Philadelphia, and Baltimore struck to demand higher wages and shorter hours. The following year six hundred Boston carpenters left work in the peak spring season to obtain a ten-hour day in place of the customary sunrise-to-sunset work schedule.

In many respects the labor organizations of the 1820's were like their predecessors. By and large they were composed of artisans, skilled craftsmen who still possessed the tools of production and demanded a price for their product, not a wage for their labor. Benevolent and fraternal functions proved as vital to union existence as ever. And collective bargaining still proceeded more by ultimatum than by negotiation, with the closed shop and the strike remaining the two most effective instruments of union power. Like the pre-1816 organizations, the labor unions of the 1820's were basically local in character and composition. Organizations of carpenters and printers did not establish links between different cities, and within the same cities diverse crafts seldom acted or joined together. Finally, labor organizations were still extremely vulnerable to legal restraints and fluctuations in the national economy, as revealed by a decline in their number and strength in the late 1820's, when several unfavorable judicial decisions and an economic downturn occurred simultaneously.

Between roughly 1827 and 1833, collective working-class action added a new dimension. Hitherto essentially fraternal and economic in behavior and exclusive in character, labor organizations became increasingly political in focus and more inclusive in composition. Again Philadelphia workingmen pioneered in developing new forms of collective labor action. In 1827 working-class leaders in that city formed the Mechanics' Union of Trade Associations (MUTA), an organization that combined fifteen local craft unions and functioned until 1831. A year later, in the summer of 1828, the MUTA founded the first labor party in the United States. From Philadelphia the working-class political movement spread in all directions: cities in western Pennsylvania, Ohio, New Jersey, New York, Delaware, and New England witnessed the emergence of local labor parties. All told, between 1828 and 1834 independent labor parties emerged in sixty-one different urban areas and published nearly fifty labor newspapers. In all cases the political associations, unlike the craft organizations, sought to unite local workers across the lines of trade and skill, for effective political action required solidarity, not exclusiveness.

But the leadership of the labor parties resembled that of the craft unions. Most of the political spokesmen for labor emerged from the skilled artisan class and remained dedicated to preserving the honored, independent status of the traditional craftsman. In their political programs the labor parties assaulted special privilege, artificially created class distinctions, and an emergent American financial-commercial aristocracy. They demanded free public education; the abolition of imprisonment for debt, compulsory militia service, and chartered monopolies; and laws to ensure that workers received their wages. In other words, they desired the repeal of laws that apparently favored the well-born over the poor and that threatened the integrity and independence of the artisan. In politics, as in economics, the organized workers of early nineteenth-century America struggled to defend their customary status as equal citizens in a democratic republic, beholden to no one for employment, income, and existence. Respectability and personal independence were the sine qua non of collective working-class action throughout the first half of the nineteenth century.

When working-class politics declined as a consequence of factionalism and Democratic and Whig party manipulation, workers naturally resorted to trade union action. Economic change and growth during the early 1830's encouraged the turn to economic action. After 1834 prices soared ahead of wages, the cost of living skyrocketed, and many workers felt their standard of living threatened. Moreover, the trend begun in the 1820's toward specialization of labor, breakdown of apprenticeship and craft rules, and the use of cheaper female and child labor intensified. Buffeted by price inflation, on the one hand, and by new work methods, on the other, thousands of laborers looked to trade unionism for relief.

By 1836 more than fifty local unions had been formed in both New York and Philadelphia, and comparable numbers existed in smaller cities. For the first time, moreover, factory workers and women began to form labor organizations. Estimates, admittedly crude, suggest that total union membership in the period grew from 26,000 to 300,000. New York alone, it has been said, claimed 11,500 organized workers, almost two-thirds of the labor force in the city. Trade unionism also spread from the Atlantic seaboard to the new cities of the interior: Buffalo, St. Louis, Cleveland, and Louisville, among others. Many craft unionists now extended aid to factory workers, and men encouraged women to join labor organizations. The new solidarity and militancy produced more than 168 recorded strikes between 1833 and 1837, including a walkout by Lowell mill girls in 1834 to protest a wage cut, and a strike the following year by male and female factory hands in Paterson, New Jersey.

Whereas workers had hitherto formed citywide organizations primarily to engage in political action, after 1833 citywide trade union movements developed. The first citywide association of trade unions was founded at New York in 1833, and the form spread to Baltimore, Philadelphia, Washington, and Boston. The founders and leaders of the citywide labor associations met in March 1834, at the invitation of the New York central organization, and founded the first American national labor federation, the National Trades Union. The National Trades Union held conventions in 1835 and 1836 in an effort to offer labor leaders a sense of common purpose and the promise of external support for their local struggles. Some craft unionists, such as the cordwainers and the printers, also tried to move from local to national organizations. Improvements in transportation and communications had intensified competition in product and labor markets, and trade unionists intended to protect themselves by forming national organizations with the power to set uniform wages and work standards.

The labor movement that flourished in Jacksonian America signified the first effort to build a movement that cut across skill, sex, and geographical lines. Although still led primarily by traditional artisans who preferred to think of themselves as independent producers rather than dependent wageworkers, the Jacksonian labor movement nevertheless sought to come to grips with a society in the process of industrializing, in which customary work practices were disappearing and in which a substantial proportion of the labor force, especially women, had no choice but to accept their role as dependent wage earners with nothing to sell but their labor power. Typically human in looking to the past to legitimate their behavior in the present, artisan labor leaders honestly tried to build an inclusive working-class movement capable of defending the worker's place in a rapidly industrializing, capitalist marketplace society.

Once again economic depression shattered labor organization in the United States. The depression of 1837–1843, the most severe in the first half of the nineteenth century, obliterated the Jacksonian labor movement and its commitment to labor solidarity. Economic privation and insecurity stimulated ethnic and religious rivalries, and workers hitherto united against their employers now divided among themselves as Protestants versus Catholics, American-born versus Irish immigrants, and whites versus blacks.

PRECURSORS OF THE MODERN LABOR MOVEMENT, 1843–1881

A new wave of economic growth and urban expansion beginning in the mid-1840's stimulated the reemergence of the American labor movement. Between 1840 and 1860 the number of wageworkers more than tripled, reaching 3.5 million by the latter year. More than 150,000 men, women, and children labored in textile factories, which on the average employed seventy workers per establishment. Another 147,000 toiled in the coal and metals mines, and more than 35,000 on the spreading railroad network. By 1860 nearly 15 percent of the northern population was classified as wage earners, and in the most industrialized state, Massachusetts, 21 percent of the population were wage earners.

Immigration added substantially to the ranks of wage laborers. During the 1840's more than 1.7 million immigrants came to the United States, and in the following decade almost 2.6 million Europeans arrived. Settling largely in the cities, the immigrants composed a substantial proportion of the labor force. By 1860 the foreign-born population was 48 percent of the total in New York City, 50 percent in Chicago and Pittsburgh, and 60 percent in St. Louis. Largely Irish, German, or British in origin, the immigrants, especially the German and British, exerted singular influence on the formation of trade unionism in the United States.

Economic growth and the creation of a more integrated national transportation and communications network further widened the gap

LABOR ORGANIZATIONS

between employer and worker, and undermined the traditional work habits and rewards of artisans. Once again, as prosperity and rising productivity increased the demand for labor, workers formed trade unions to protect their customary work practices and their standard of living. Also as in the past, skilled craftsmen led in the formation of trade unionism and founded the more stable and successful labor organizations.

By the early 1850's local craft unions had reemerged in most of the building and service trades, such as carpentry, bricklaying, painting, printing, tailoring, baking, and hotel and restaurant service. Composed almost entirely of skilled artisans, these exclusive organizations developed strict apprenticeship codes, substantial initiation fees, uniform wage standards, and strike funds. In order to protect members against nonunion labor, the locals of the same craft pooled information about employment opportunities and scabs (nonunion workers or, more typically, strikebreakers), and they issued traveling cards to members seeking employment in a different city. The craft unions also continued to bargain with employers in the traditional manner, publicly posting their demands and threatening to strike if employers did not meet them.

By the mid-1850's trade unionism began to appear among the more skilled workers in the industrial sector of the economy. British immigrant workers employed in the Fall River, Massachusetts, textile mills organized the Mule Spinners' Association, and fellow immigrants in the shoe-manufacturing towns to the north, also having served in English trade unions before emigrating, organized unions among Lynn and Natick shoeworkers. Former British Chartists founded short-lived miners' unions in the anthracite region of Pennsylvania, and in 1861, Daniel Weaver, a former Chartist, organized the American Miners' Association, perhaps the first American industrial union encompassing the entire labor force of a trade. During the 1850's skilled puddlers, heaters, rollers, and molders in the expanding iron mills and foundries also formed unions.

Just as labor organizations spread from the community-based, traditional building and service trades to the national-market-oriented industrial sector of the economy, so local craft unions combined in the 1850's to form national trade unions. The printers began the trend toward national unionism at a convention in New York City in December 1850 that was attended by delegates from New York, New Jersey, Pennsylvania, Maryland, and Kentucky. The product of their meeting, the National Typographical Union, held its first national convention in May 1852. At that meeting it resolved to limit the number of apprentices in the trade, set a five-year minimum term for all apprentices, raise a strike fund to assist locals in distress, issue traveling cards to all members seeking work out of town, and circulate the names of "disgraced" members who had accepted jobs beneath union standards. Nine other important national unions —of plumbers, hatters, cigar makers, mule spinners, and cordwainers, among others—were organized between 1853 and 1860, and sought to implement union rules and standards comparable with those set by the printers.

Except for the National Typographical Union, the Machinists' and Blacksmiths' National Union (founded 1859), and the National Molders' Union (founded 1859), most national trade unions proved ineffective and unstable. Meeting once a year only to pass platitudinous resolutions, the bulk of the national trade unions lacked the resources to survive the vicissitudes of the economy. The slightest setback to the national economy crippled these feeble unions, and the severe economic decline that began in 1857 even destroyed the blacksmiths' and machinists' and the molders' unions. Only three national trade unions—the printers', the hat finishers', and the stonecutters'—survived the depression of 1857.

The revival of the economy in 1860 produced a new wave of working-class protest and labor organization. Especially significant for the future was the rebirth of unionism among the shoeworkers, traditionally pioneers in the labor movement. But the reemergence of trade unionism in the shoe industry differed significantly from past patterns. Whereas cordwainers' labor organizations had previously united highly skilled craftsmen who labored in small shops, the 1859–1860 revival of unionism among New England shoeworkers involved factory hands who ran machines and allied men and women. Centered in Lynn, Massachusetts, where British immigrant workers took the lead in building trade unions, the shoeworkers' movement spread to other New England towns and precipitated one of the largest and longest strikes in antebellum American history. From late February to early April 1860, more than twenty thousand New England shoeworkers struck against a wage cut instituted by their employers. The strike involved novice factory hands and traditional cordwainers transformed by economic change into machine operators, male and female workers, adults and children. The size and militancy of the strike led many employers to rescind wage cuts, though few recognized trade unionism, and it presaged the emergence of a militant labor movement among industrial workers during and after the Civil War.

The Civil War stimulated trade union growth, as workers threatened by a substantial rise in the cost of living took advantage of the tight wartime labor market to reorganize unions that had collapsed after the 1857 depression and to strengthen unions that had survived it. By 1864 an estimated two hundred thousand workers, concentrated in New York, Massachusetts, and Pennsylvania, were organized into trade unions. By then, also, the predominant form of labor organization had become the national trade union, twelve of which had been formed by 1866 and twenty more in the next five years. By 1870 thirty-two national trade unions, encompassing the largest and most skilled trades, functioned throughout the nation; and, as was customary, they were led and composed in the main by the more highly skilled workers.

Three of the national trade unions—the International Typographical Union (printers), the Iron Molders' International Union, and the Knights of St. Crispin (shoemakers)—exemplified the tactics, the values, and the strengths and weaknesses of the workers who organized them. The printers pioneered in establishing the characteristics most common to successful trade unions. Control of the organization became centralized in a general executive board consisting of well-paid national officials with substantial expense accounts and office staffs; the union levied relatively high dues in order to amass strike funds and disburse welfare benefits to its members; in return for strike payments and welfare benefits, local unions surrendered the right to call strikes to national officers. Finally, because the printing trades operated primarily in a local market situation and competition was more common between workers than employers, the union issued traveling cards that promoted craft solidarity and curtailed scabbing.

The molders were perhaps the first stable, effective union to appear in a characteristic factory milieu, iron manufacture and fabrication. Reorganized in 1863 largely through the efforts of William Sylvis, the most famous labor leader of the Civil War era, the Iron Molders' International Union, like the International Typographical Union, subjected local unions to national authority, outlawed unauthorized local strikes, issued national membership cards, raised dues, and established a strike and welfare fund controlled by the national officers. Sylvis practically tripled the number of locals and members in his union, and under his leadership the iron molders engaged in several protracted strikes against large employers.

The Knights of St. Crispin was the largest trade union of the Civil War era, reaching a peak membership of about fifty thousand between 1870 and 1872. Although led by the more skilled workers in the shoe industry, many of whom had served an apprenticeship in a small artisan shop, the Knights sought to organize all workers in the industry regardless of skill or sex. The union attempted to gain control of machine production, not abolish it; it preferred to coexist with new factory methods of shoe production, provided that union members operated the machines at union wage rates. The Knights demanded citywide wage rates, advocated an amalgamated craft form of organization that encompassed all workers in the trade, developed a staff of salaried professional officers, and sought arbitration of grievances between employees and employers. All these practices, wrote a historian of the Crispins, "are signs of a group well advanced in learning how to defend the workers' status in industry."

Once again, as labor flexed its muscles and national trade unions grew apace, a demand arose for the creation of a national federation of trade unions. At a convention in Baltimore in 1866 attended by representatives of national trade unions, eight-hour leagues, and reform societies, the National Labor Union (NLU) was formed. After William Sylvis' election to its presidency in 1868, the NLU became the primary political arm of organized labor. It established a labor lobby in Washington, promoted an eight-hour day for all federal workers and similar legislation in the states, and various other labor and welfare reforms. The NLU also supported the claims of female workers by demanding equal pay for equal work; and it refused to draw a color line in the organization, resolving at its 1869 convention that "the National Labor Union knows no north, no south, no east, no west, neither color nor sex on the question of the rights of labor, and urges our colored fellow workers to form organizations . . . and send their delegates from every state in the union to the next congress."

Because its structure and functions led it to stress political action, the NLU became involved in a number of highly charged and divisive political questions. Deprived of Sylvis' firm leadership by his untimely death in 1869, the NLU soon split over the proper position to take on issues of monetary reform, third-party political action, and women's rights. As reformers fought over these questions, many of the trade unionists left the organization, following the example of the International Typographical Union delegates, who had concluded after the 1870 NLU convention that "they failed to discover anything in the proceedings that entitle the Congress to representatives from a purely trade organization." In the words of Norman Ware, the NLU by 1872 had been "taken over by labor leaders without organizations, politicians without parties, women without husbands, and cranks, visionaries, and agitators without jobs." By then, however, the entire Civil War–era labor movement, the national trade unions included, stood on the brink of collapse.

As the NLU split internally and its trade union affiliates drifted away, many of the larger national trade unions, particularly the iron molders and the Crispins, suffered defeats in struggles with employers. And just at the moment that the unions met increased resistance from employers, depression struck the national economy in 1873, persisting until 1878 in what was the worst economic collapse of the century. As factories closed and workers lost their jobs, the labor movement weakened. The NLU completely disappeared, as did almost all of the thirty-two national trade unions that had been formed between 1862 and 1870. Employers forced workers to choose between unions and jobs, and most workers made the natural choice in the circumstances. Those unions that survived the depression of the 1870's, such as the International Typographical Union and the Cigar Makers International Union, did so in a gravely weakened state, reduced to a loyal core membership and bare treasuries. Once again, depression spelled disaster for the American labor movement.

CREATING A STABLE LABOR MOVEMENT, 1881–1933

For more than ten years after the beginning of the depression of the 1870's, the labor movement in the United States barely existed. None of the substantial national trade unions that had flourished between 1862 and 1872 wielded much economic power, and no new national labor center emerged to replace the moribund National Labor Union.

Meantime, the American economy grew and changed. Further improvements and innovations in transportation and communications created a more integrated national market in which economic competition intensified. During the 1880's and 1890's such large enterprises as Carnegie Steel, Standard Oil, McCormick Harvester, and G. Swift and Company reshaped the face of business. Competing in a national market, operating plants in several locations, and diluting traditional artisan skills through technology and managerial innovation, these large firms sought absolute mastery of their work forces. American businessmen, struggling for survival and stability in an intensely competitive milieu, sought security through power.

Workers, too, responded to a rapidly changing social and economic environment. Like businessmen, they sought to understand the forces reshaping their lives and, through organization, to control them. The result was an efflorescence of working-class organization in the mid-1880's and a surge of working-class militancy customarily characterized as the "Great Upheaval" of 1886, which was associated with a national movement for the eight-hour day, an unprecedented outbreak of strikes, and a labor organization, the Noble and Holy Order of the Knights of Labor. About the latter an editorialist wrote: "Never in all history has there been such a spectacle as the march of the Order of the Knights of

LABOR ORGANIZATIONS

Labor. . . . It is an organization in whose hands now rests the destinies of the Republic. . . . It has demonstrated the overmastering power of a national combination among workingmen."

What occasioned such praise and such anxiety? Why did a national labor organization appear so powerful for the first time in United States history? How did it succeed, by 1886, in recruiting between seven hundred thousand and eight hundred thousand workers, approximately 10 percent of the nonagricultural labor force? Who were the Knights of Labor, and what did they seek?

Briefly, the Knights of Labor originated in Philadelphia in 1869 as a small craft union of garment cutters that copied the rituals and secrecy of the then popular fraternal societies. Before 1873 it scarcely extended beyond the Philadelphia-Camden, New Jersey, conurbation. But, unlike most other labor organizations, it survived the depression of the 1870's. With the return of prosperity after 1878, the Knights became the natural beneficiary of a revived desire for organization among workers. At a convention held in Pennsylvania in 1878, the organization launched itself as a national labor center and elected officers. Three years later, in order to appeal to Roman Catholic workers, who constituted a rising proportion of the American labor force, the Knights eliminated their secret oaths and rituals and went completely public. That same year Terence V. Powderly, a machinist, trade unionist, orator, and mayor of Scranton, Pennsylvania, became grand master workman (chief executive officer) of the Knights of Labor. Under Powderly's leadership the organization grew steadily but slowly until suddenly, between 1885 and 1886, it soared from roughly 112,000 to 730,000 members, a rate of growth so rapid and unsettling that Powderly ordered his organizers temporarily to stop enrolling new members.

The enormous growth of the Knights seemed more fortuitous than planned. Indeed, the event that precipitated the sudden surge in membership between the summers of 1885 and 1886— a successful strike by an affiliate of the order against the southwestern railroad network of Jay Gould—was neither authorized nor sanctioned by Powderly and his fellow executive officers. But the apparent success of the Knights in defeating a major railroad caused workers by the hundreds of thousands to look to the organization for leadership, action, and security.

The Knights represented a significant transformation in national labor organization, not only in terms of the rapidity of its growth and its success in battle against a major railroad, but also in its structure, composition, and goals. Unlike previous labor organizations that were composed almost entirely of skilled artisans and that focused largely on craft-oriented activities, the Knights welcomed all workers, regardless of skill, sex, or race, and promoted a form of labor solidarity intended to transcend customary craft loyalties. It recruited members from the more modern sectors of the economy that functioned in competitive national product and service markets, such as railroad workers, coal miners, textile employees, glassmakers, iron puddlers, and molders. Although the Knights made room for national trade unions within the organization, its leaders preferred members to participate in local and district assemblies where workers from different trades and industries joined together to promote working-class solidarity. Committed, as its 1884 national convention resolved, "to a radical change in the existing industrial system," the attitude of the Knights toward the existing order was "necessarily one of war."

To achieve its goals, the organization had to attract an inclusive membership, one built on a common social brotherhood that cut across lines of occupation, nationality, religion, race, and sex. A new, cooperative society would never emerge through the actions of separate craft unions dedicated to defending and advancing the interests of their members within individual trades and industries. In that sense the Knights, like the NLU before it, was primarily an educational and agitational institution that transcended the interests of sectoral trade unions and practiced the principle that "an injury to one is the concern of all." As long as trade unions respected the basic principles and objectives of the Knights they functioned effectively within the organization.

The Knights of Labor collapsed as rapidly as it rose. By midsummer 1887, its membership had fallen by more than half; by 1890 it was reduced to one hundred thousand members; and by the mid-1890's it was moribund. How does one explain the swift descent of the organization?

For the Knights of Labor, failure was nearly as

fortuitous as success had been. Just as an unplanned strike against the Gould railroads catapulted the Knights to prominence, so a subsequent unsuccessful walkout against the same railroads in 1886 precipitated a membership decline. Simultaneously, although Powderly condemned the anarchism associated with the notorious Chicago Haymarket riot of May 1886 and dissociated the Knights from the national eight-hour-day movement endorsed by the trade unions, conservatives held his organization responsible for radicalism, and many workers blamed it for the failure of the eight-hour movement. In other words, just as association with success, however unjustified, had stimulated growth, so association with failure induced decline.

Most simply, the reach of the Knights exceeded its grasp. The task of the organization, as defined in 1884, was enormous; the strength of its enemy, capitalism, was waxing. Faced by the determined opposition of employers, the Knights failed to practice the solidarity that it preached. Seeking, in the words of the historian of the organization, Norman Ware, "to teach the American wage-earner that he was a wage-earner first and a bricklayer, carpenter, miner, shoemaker after; that he was a wage-earner first and a Catholic, Protestant, Jew, white, black, Democrat, Republican after . . . meant that the Order was teaching something that was not so in the hope that sometime it would be." Unfortunately for the Knights, that time was not the 1880's, and the organization lost its appeal, members, and influence.

The failure of the Knights of Labor did not leave American workers bereft of organization. Several of the national trade assemblies that functioned within the Knights survived quite well outside as national trade unions, and other national trade unions that either survived the depression of the 1870's or reorganized afterward flourished as the Knights declined. Indeed, in the same year (1886) that the Knights peaked and then declined, the national trade unions, at a convention in Columbus, Ohio, organized their own labor center, the American Federation of Labor (AFL). Once before, in 1881, the trade unions had tried to establish a federation among themselves known as the Federation of Organized Trades and Labor Unions of the United States and Canada. But this federation accomplished little and functioned for five years in the shadow of the larger, more influential Knights of Labor.

Reconstituted as the American Federation of Labor, the national trade unions that had failed to establish a labor center in 1881 succeeded in 1886. Indeed, for the next half-century the AFL functioned as the only stable and effective labor organization that represented the interests of more than a single trade or industry. Structurally not vastly different from the Knights of Labor, the AFL followed two organizational principles quite distinct from past labor practice: exclusive jurisdiction and union autonomy. Both principles flowed from the fact that the AFL had no individual members; a worker belonged to the AFL by virtue of membership in a national trade union, and hence it was the national unions that wielded effective power in the organization. Exclusive jurisdiction sanctioned the principle that only one union might organize workers in a given trade or industry; the worst sin a trade union could commit was to organize workers in the jurisdiction of another union and practice "dual unionism." Union autonomy recognized the intrinsic power of AFL affiliates and the inability of the central organization to interfere in the practices and policies of its affiliates. Where the Knights of Labor sought to implement a uniform policy for all its members, the AFL relied on the voluntary cooperation of its affiliates.

The early history of the AFL can be divided into two periods: the years from 1886 to 1897, when its existence was perilous and its policies and practices had not yet hardened into dogma; and the years from 1898 to 1919, when the organization and its affiliates flourished and their principles became sanctified as the only legitimate form of trade union practice.

During its earliest years the AFL lived from hand to mouth. Its first president, Samuel Gompers (the only chief executive the organization had between 1886 and 1925, except for the year 1895), inherited an empty treasury and an eight-by-ten-foot office furnished with a child's desk, crates, and boxes. For his first four months in office, Gompers received no salary; nevertheless he persisted in his mission of building an effective national labor center, and the AFL began to grow steadily if slowly. By 1892 the number of national trade unions affiliated with the AFL had grown from thirteen to forty, although most were small and in dire financial condition. Membership statistics for the organization were totally unreliable; for example, in 1890 total membership was as high as 630,000 or as low as 225,000, depending on which set of figures one accepted. After the depression of 1893, membership fluctuated more wildly, and AFL statistics became even less reliable. In 1897, at the end of the depression, the AFL, after a decade of existence, claimed 447,000 members, far less than the peak membership of the Knights in 1886.

The national trade unions affiliated with the AFL scarcely did better. In 1886 the Amalgamated Association of Iron, Steel, and Tin Workers may have been the largest and most powerful trade union in the AFL; six years later, after the Homestead steel strike of 1892, it was a whipped and declining organization. Marginally more successful than the Amalgamated Association, the other trade unions staggered from crisis to crisis between 1886 and 1897. None represented as many as one-third of the workers in its trade, and together they claimed less than 5 percent of American wageworkers, the vast majority of them organized on the fringes of the national economy. The dominant sector of the economy, exemplified by the emerging mass-production industries, remained impenetrable to trade unionism. As Friedrich Engels observed in 1892, "Organized labor in America still occupies an aristocratic position and wherever possible leaves the ordinarily badly paid occupations to the immigrants, only a small portion of whom enter the aristocratic trade unions."

The early AFL unions were also ambivalent about the mission of the labor movement. They could not decide whether unions existed primarily to serve the narrow immediate material interests of their members or whether they should act primarily as educational and agitational institutions that taught their members about the superiority of a noncapitalist, nonexploitative economic system. Advocates of "business unionism," a system that stressed sectoral craft interests (such as exclusive jurisdiction), clashed persistently with the advocates of "reform unionism," who continued to demand working-class solidarity. Led by Samuel Gompers, whose rhetoric from 1886 to 1895 sounded the tocsin of class war, the AFL, at times, seemed more committed to eradicating capitalism than to making its peace with the dominant social and economic system.

After 1897 the AFL and its affiliates became less ambivalent about their mission and more successful in carrying it out. Between 1897 and 1904 union membership rose from 447,000 to 2,073,000. (See table 1.) The end of the depression and a surge in economic growth, which laid the foundation for union advances, also enabled trade unions to win substantial material gains for their members. An 1897 strike in the bituminous coal industry was followed the next year by an agreement between the union (United Mine Workers of America [UMW]) and the operators that stabilized labor relations in western Pennsylvania, Ohio, Indiana, and Illinois, provided union security, and established the eight-hour day. The agreement brought twenty-five years of labor stability to northern soft-coal mining and strength to the UMW, which grew from fourteen thousand members in 1897 to more than three hundred thousand by 1914, making it the nation's largest trade union. Between 1898 and 1908 the International Typographical Union won the eight-hour day for nearly all union printers, and in 1900 the International Association of Machinists secured a nine-hour day from the National Metal Trades Association. The railroad brotherhoods, representing the more skilled railway workers, obtained substantial material gains from employers and legislative protection from Congress. And in New York, Chicago, and San Francisco, the local building trades unions combined economic and political influence to build powerful and often corrupt labor empires.

An employers' antiunion drive beginning in 1904 and an economic recession in 1908–1909 retarded the growth of trade unionism. Between 1909 and 1913, however, another seven hundred thousand workers entered the ranks of organized labor, including many minimally skilled immigrant workers concentrated in the garment trades. After another setback, owing to economic depression from 1913 to 1915, organized labor surged ahead from 1916 through 1920 as World War I tightened the labor market and created a favorable milieu for union organizers. By 1 January 1919, trade union membership had passed the three-million level, and by the end of the year unions claimed more than five million members, or almost 20 percent of the labor force, the highest proportion yet achieved in American history.

In this era of union success and growth, the AFL and its affiliates perfected the policies and

LABOR ORGANIZATIONS

TABLE 1

Labor Union Membership, by Affiliation, 1897–1934 (includes Canadian members of labor unions with headquarters in United States)

Year	Total Union Membership (1,000) BLS	Total Union Membership (1,000) Wolman	AFL Number of Affiliated Unions, BLS	AFL Total Membership (1,000) BLS	AFL Total Membership (1,000) Wolman	Independent or Unaffiliated Unions, Total Membership (1,000), Wolman
1934	3,249	3,671	109	2,608	3,030	641
1933	2,857	3,048	108	2,127	2,318	730
1932	3,226	3,191	106	2,532	2,497	694
1931	3,526	3,379	105	2,890	2,743	636
1930	3,632	3,416	104	2,961	2,745	671
1929	3,625	3,461	105	2,934	2,770	691
1928	3,567	3,480	107	2,896	2,809	671
1927	3,600	3,546	106	2,813	2,759	787
1926	3,592	3,502	107	2,804	2,715	788
1925	3,566	3,519	107	2,877	2,831	689
1924	3,549	3,536	107	2,866	2,853	683
1923	3,629	3,622	108	2,926	2,919	703
1922	3,950	4,027	112	3,196	3,273	754
1921	4,722	4,781	110	3,907	3,967	815
1920	5,034	5,048	110	4,079	4,093	955
1919	4,046	4,125	111	3,260	3,339	786
1918	3,368	3,467	111	2,726	2,825	642
1917	2,976	3,061	111	2,371	2,457	605
1916	2,722	2,773	111	2,073	2,124	649

Year	Total Union Membership (1,000) BLS	Total Union Membership (1,000) Wolman	AFL Number of Affiliated Unions, BLS	AFL Total Membership (1,000) BLS	AFL Total Membership (1,000) Wolman	Independent or Unaffiliated Unions, Total Membership (1,000), Wolman
1915	2,560	2,583	110	1,946	1,968	614
1914	2,647	2,687	110	2,021	2,061	626
1913	2,661	2,716	111	1,996	2,051	665
1912	2,405	2,452	112	1,770	1,818	635
1911	2,318	2,343	115	1,762	1,787	556
1910	2,116	2,140	120	1,562	1,587	554
1909	1,965	2,006	119	1,483	1,524	482
1908	2,092	2,131	116	1,587	1,625	505
1907	2,077	2,080	117	1,539	1,542	538
1906	1,892	1,907	119	1,454	1,469	438
1905	1,918	2,022	118	1,494	1,598	424
1904	2,067	2,073	120	1,676	1,682	391
1903	1,824	1,914	113	1,466	1,556	358
1902	1,335	1,376	97	1,024	1,065	311
1901	1,058	1,125	87	788	854	270
1900	791	868	82	548	625	243
1899	550	611	73	349	410	201
1898	467	501	67	278	312	189
1897	440	447	58	265	272	175

Source: U.S. Bureau of the Census, *Historical Statistics of the United States, Colonial Times to 1957* (Washington, D.C., 1960), p. 97.

practices associated with the term "pure and simple unionism" (also "business unionism"). First and foremost was the acceptance of industrial capitalism, or the bargain made by trade unionism with employers. In return for allowing trade unions to achieve material gains for their members, employers received a pledge from labor leaders to respect capitalism and to honor the union contract even when it conflicted with the principle of working-class solidarity. Simultaneously, labor leaders rejected both partisan political action and advice from intellectuals and middle-class reformers. Unions instead practiced what Selig Perlman characterized as "job consciousness." All union policies had one objective: to defend the integrity and security of the worker's job. The typical labor union restricted membership, attempted to ration job opportunities by controlling the pace of production, and negotiated closed-shop contracts (which denied employment to nonunion members). The ability of a union to achieve these goals determined its success or failure.

By World War I "voluntarism" had become the dominant doctrine among unions affiliated with the AFL. The concept flowed from the rudimentary principle that workers must defend their own interests in society, that to look to politics or the state for salvation was to court failure. Union stability derived from power, and power in turn came from organizational self-sufficiency. Hence the worker's most vital needs—job security, unemployment relief, sickness and death benefits—must be provided by the union, not the state. Government benefits, union leaders reasoned, would dilute the workers' loyalty to the union. "Some men," observed Gompers, "unconsciously and with the best of intentions get to rivet chains on their wrists." In Gompers' hyperbole, government welfare programs would institute "the beginning of an era, and a long era, of industrial slavery." That sentiment was shared by most leaders of AFL affiliates.

The above practices and principles made "business unionism" the dominant aspect of union behavior. Labor leaders, like their twentieth-century corporate counterparts, sought to build more perfect organizations in which the rank and file obediently followed the orders of professional, well-paid officials. National union officers struggled ceaselessly to discipline disorderly or rebellious regional and local affiliates. Whenever the principle of union democracy and rank-and-file participation conflicted with union stability and leadership security, democracy gave way to union autocracy. Indeed, it was often the case that the more successful unions became in serving their members' material interests, the less the membership shaped and determined union policy.

Despite the relative success of the AFL and its affiliates from 1897 to 1919, they proved unable to organize the great mass of American workers and failed abysmally in the dominant sectors of the economy, especially such mass-production industries as steel, meat-packing, autos, rubber, and electrical goods. Moreover, modern technology and large-scale industry rendered craft unionism and exclusive jurisdiction obsolete, as the inability of the AFL to organize the undifferentiated mass of semiskilled workers proved. Craft unionism may have been a practical response to mid-nineteenth-century conditions of work and perhaps still functioned well for workers in the more traditional, skilled crafts, but it offered scant benefits to the millions of machine operators in basic industry.

More militant trade unionists of socialist and syndicalist inclinations therefore demanded that labor aggressively organize mass-production workers and place them in industrial unions that united laborers rather than divided them by craft. For much of the period 1900–1916, socialists exerted considerable influence inside the AFL and received nearly one-third of the delegate votes at the 1911 AFL convention. In such unions as the United Mine Workers, the International Association of Machinists, the United Brewery Workers, and the Ladies' Garment Workers, among the largest AFL affiliates, socialists either were leaders or exerted significant influence. Largely in response to pressure from such left-wing affiliates that demanded the implementation of industrial unionism, the AFL between 1905 and 1914 established several subsidiary organizations intended to eliminate artificial distinctions among crafts that had been diluted by technology. As an alternative to industrial unionism, the AFL offered its socialist militants building trades, metal trades, and mining trades departments, which were designed to encourage solidarity among related crafts without diluting traditional grants of exclusive jurisdiction.

LABOR ORGANIZATIONS

Such concessions to industrial unionism failed to promote organization in the mass-production industries and scarcely satisfied labor leftists. Yet political socialists could neither gain dominance in the AFL nor shape its policies to their liking. They had no alternative to the dominant pattern of American trade unionism.

Syndicalists tried to offer workers an alternative to AFL-style trade unionism. In June 1905 a small band of leftists committed to organizing the mass of less-skilled workers met in Chicago and formed the Industrial Workers of the World (IWW), better known as the Wobblies. These labor radicals intended to build an organization that would organize workers along industrial, not craft, lines and that would wage unrelenting class war against capitalism. Eugene Debs, one of the delegates, expressed the prevailing sentiment: "The choice is between the A. F. of L. and capitalism on one side and the industrial workers and socialism on the other."

For its first five years, the IWW was crippled by sectarian struggles between revolutionary and reformist socialists, "pure and simple" industrial unionists and revolutionary unionists, advocates of political action and their critics. Within four years of its founding, all that remained of the organization was a dedicated core united in its rejection of business unionism and political action, and committed primarily to direct action by workers at the point of production.

Over the next seven years this small core of radicals built the most feared left-wing labor organization in American history. Appealing to immigrants, nonwhite workers, restless migrants—a volatile, explosive mixture—the Wobblies led violent industrial conflicts in McKees Rock, Pennsylvania (1909), Lawrence, Massachusetts (1912), Paterson, New Jersey (1913), the Mesabi Range (1916), the Louisiana piny woods (1911–1913), the California hop fields and orchards (1913–1917), the wheat fields of the Midwest (1915–1918), the forests of the Pacific Northwest (1913–1918), and the copper mines of the mountain states (1917–1919). Although Wobblies failed to build a mass membership or to organize a stable industrial union, they did influence two to three million workers who passed through the IWW ranks and millions more subject to its influence.

At its acme from 1915 to 1917, the IWW symbolized more than industrial unionism. It exemplified those labor radicals who conceived of an ideal society in which workers, through direct action at the point of production, could seize the industries of the nation and administer them by and for the working class, without political parties or the state as intermediaries. The poor and the exploited, Wobblies preached, must organize themselves to achieve power, which alone could liberate them. Convinced that traditional craft unionism and parliamentary socialism alike had failed to emancipate workers from industrial thralldom, American Wobblies, like British, French, and Italian syndicalists of the same period, taught that workers could build a perfect society through mass strikes that would culminate in a general strike paralyzing society and proving the supremacy of the working class.

World War I provided the IWW with the opportunity to widen its appeal and also ensured its collapse. As Wobblies became involved during 1917 and 1918 in strikes that threatened the war effort, state and federal authorities reacted. They treated the IWW as an illegal, subversive organization and by 1919, through vigilante, military, and judicial repression, had decimated the Wobblies.

The collapse of the IWW presaged the fate of the AFL in the postwar decade. In 1919, at the peak of its power and size, the AFL and its affiliates became involved in an unprecedented wave of strikes. More than four million workers engaged in industrial conflicts in 1919 alone, strikes that included a citywide general strike in Seattle in February, a Boston police strike in September, a national steel strike involving 350,000 workers from September through February 1920, and a nationwide soft-coal strike in October and November. The ubiquity of industrial conflict raised the specter of Bolshevik revolution in the United States, and employers and public authorities sought to reassert order and stability. The Seattle and Boston police and national steel strikes were crushed, and the coal miners were ordered back to work by the federal government. The 1919 strike wave ended the advance of the AFL and organized labor. For three more years, until 1922, unions and their members acted militantly, but in the latter year national coal and railroad strikes brought disaster to the labor movement. Thereafter, until the coming of the New Deal in 1933, organized labor declined.

LABOR ORGANIZATIONS

During the peak of the prosperity decade, from 1923 to 1929, the unions not only failed to add new members, but total union membership declined from 3,662,000 to 3,461,000, or 11 to 12 percent of the nonagricultural labor force, the lowest level since before the war. Even more revealing were the trade unions that endured the worst losses; among the sufferers were those organizations most likely to include less-skilled workers, laborers in basic industries, militants, and radicals. The United Mine Workers fell from about 500,000 members in 1923 to 200,000 in 1929; union membership in the metals and machinery trades (mostly among the International Association of Machinists) dropped from 859,000 in 1920 to 211,000 in 1929. The transportation industries lost 400,000 members, and the clothing trades suffered a fall from 374,000 to 218,000 members. Only the building trades unions experienced a substantial increase in membership, because their strength centered in an industry least susceptible to modern methods of production and having the most traditionally trained and structured work force.

Nothing that the AFL did during the 1920's added to its advantage. Pursuing a policy that might best be characterized as strategic retreat, its leaders, first Samuel Gompers and, after Gompers' death in December 1924, William Green, offered to collaborate with employers in implementing scientific management and industrial efficiency; they repudiated domestic radicalism, criticized overseas leftists, extolled the virtues of voluntarism, and flirted with the American Legion and federal military. The labor leaders whom he met in the Detroit area impressed the young minister and reformer Reinhold Niebuhr "as having about the same amount of daring and imagination as a group of village bankers."

Neither class collaboration nor patriotic pronunciamentos gained members for the AFL. The American Legion and the military extended invitations to AFL leaders to address their members but did nothing to promote trade unionism. Employers in the basic industries scorned the AFL and instituted scientific management, personnel relations, welfare capitalism, and the nonunion open shop. And workers seemed to prefer the premium wages, clean cafeterias, sanitary washrooms, company picnics, annual bonuses, and pension plans provided by their paternalistic employers to the benefits promised by trade unions.

No substantial left-wing alternative to the AFL existed during the 1920's. American socialism was moribund and the IWW equally impotent. Communists sought to stir militancy among workers but succeeded mostly in stimulating sectarian labor struggles. In 1920, William Z. Foster, the leading trade union communist, established the Trade Union Educational League (TUEL) to promote radicalism among workers and to bore from within existing AFL unions. The TUEL proved more notable for its rhetoric than for its successes. After eight years of meager results and in response to a new line in communist policy that called for unremitting struggle against social democrats and class collaborationist trade unionists instead of the popular front, Foster in 1928 transformed the TUEL into the Trade Union Unity League (TUUL) in an effort to build alternative unions outside the AFL and to practice dual unionism. The TUUL proved no more successful than the TUEL.

When the Great Depression struck in 1929, the American labor movement was in no position to protect workers. Weakened during a decade of prosperity, the AFL and its affiliates further declined in a time of economic adversity as unemployment soared by 1933 to 25.2 percent of the civilian labor force and 37.6 percent of nonfarm workers. (See table 2.) Between 1929 and 1933 total union membership fell from 3,625,000 to 2,857,000, the lowest level since 1916. Reduced to perhaps 100,000 dues-paying members, the United Mine Workers lost all its contracts with employers and tore itself apart in an internecine union struggle in the Illinois coalfields. The International Ladies' Garment Workers' Union survived the depression initially by obtaining a cash loan from the Lehman Brothers banking firm. Nothing about the American labor movement in 1932–1933 seemed to contradict the prophecy made by Professor George E. Barnett in December 1932, in his presidential address to the American Economic Association: "I see no reason to believe that American trade unionism will so revolutionize itself within a short period as to become in the next decade a more potent social influence than it has been in the past decade."

LABOR ORGANIZATIONS

TABLE 2
Labor Union Membership and Membership as Percent of Nonagricultural Employment: 1930–1956
(in thousands)

Year	Total Union Membership	Nonagricultural Employment Total	Membership as Percent of Total	Year	Total Union Membership	Nonagricultural Employment Total	Membership as Percent of Total
1956	18,477	51,878	33.7	1942	10,762	39,779	26.1
1955	17,749	50,056	33.6	1941	10,489	36,220	28.2
1954	17,955	48,431	35.1				
1953	17,860	49,681	34.1	1940	8,944	32,058	27.2
1952	16,750	48,303	32.9	1939	8,980	30,311	28.9
1951	16,750	47,347	33.7	1938	8,265	28,902	27.8
				1937	7,218	30,718	22.8
1950	15,000	44,738	31.9	1936	4,164	28,802	13.8
1949	15,000	43,315	33.0				
1948	15,000	44,448	32.2	1935	3,728	26,792	13.4
1947	15,414	43,462	34.0	1934	3,249	25,699	12.0
1946	14,974	41,287	34.9	1933	2,857	23,466	11.5
				1932	3,226	23,377	13.0
1945	14,796	40,037	35.8	1931	3,526	26,383	12.5
1944	14,621	41,534	34.1	1930	3,632	29,143	11.7
1943	13,642	42,106	31.4				

Source: U.S. Bureau of the Census, *Historical Statistics . . .*, p. 98.

CREATING A MASS LABOR MOVEMENT, 1933–1946

In less than a year Barnett's prophecy proved false. The coming to office of President Franklin D. Roosevelt in March 1933 and the implementation of the New Deal liberated organized labor from a decade of lethargy. The most important early New Deal legislative act, the National Industrial Recovery Act (NIRA), included Section 7(a), a clause that guaranteed workers the right to join trade unions of their choice and to bargain collectively with employers. The federal government had sanctioned the right of labor to organize.

The more astute and daring labor leaders immediately capitalized on the new situation. John L. Lewis of the United Mine Workers spent what remained of the paltry UMW treasury to dispatch organizers to the coalfields. Preaching the gospel according to the New Deal and the UMW, Lewis' organizers had succeeded by midsummer 1933 in enrolling most coal miners in the UMW; indeed, in many cases the miners seemed to organize themselves. And in September 1933, again with the assistance of federal officials, Lewis gained for his union the first agreement with coal operators that covered the coalfields of southern Appalachia as well as of the North and the West. In less than a year the UMW had grown from less than one hundred thousand dues-paying members to between three hundred thousand and four hundred thousand. At the same time David Dubinsky rebuilt the International Ladies' Garment Workers' Union, and Sidney Hillman revitalized the Amalgamated Clothing Workers of America.

By 1934 labor unrest and trade unionism spread across the American landscape. In that year there were more strikes involving more workers than in any year since 1919. In Toledo, Minneapolis, and San Francisco factory workers, teamsters, and waterfront hands fought pitched battles with police and soldiers. In the spring and summer more than 350,000 textile workers went out on strike, and national strikes threatened to paralyze the auto and steel industries until the Roosevelt administration arranged compromise settlements.

Yet the 1934 labor turmoil failed to produce lasting gains for the labor movement. Employers fought back vigorously, and the federal government seemed more solicitous of industrialists than of labor leaders. More important, the AFL refused to push an aggressive organizing campaign among mass-production workers. Most of its leaders were more concerned with protecting their craft union fiefdoms than with extending unionism among the unorganized. They worried about how to divide jurisdiction among mass-production workers in industries where no precise craft or skill lines separated employees. To workers who thought in mass terms and preferred industrial unions, the AFL offered the prospect of eventually being divided among separate craft unions in which the less-skilled workers would be treated as second-class citizens. To workers eager to test their strength in strikes against employers, the AFL counseled moderation and accommodation with employers. By the end of 1934, the AFL seemed to have squandered an unsurpassed opportunity to increase the size and influence of the labor movement.

But some union leaders in the AFL, especially Lewis, Hillman, and Dubinsky, who had already revitalized their own industrial and semi-industrial unions, realized that it was now possible to organize mass-production workers. And in June 1935, when Congress passed the Wagner Labor Relations Act, the situation became even more propitious for the growth of trade unionism. The Wagner Act outlawed company unions, sanctioned majority union representation through federally supervised worker elections, certified union bargaining agents, and required management to bargain with those agents in good faith. It provided machinery to enforce its decisions (the three-member National Labor Relations Board) and thus fully legitimated the right of labor to organize. After the passage of the Wagner Act, the advocates of industrial unionism inside the AFL, led by John L. Lewis, urged more strongly than ever an aggressive organizing campaign in the basic industries.

Yet the majority of AFL leaders still seemed more worried about jurisdictional lines than organizing workers, still seemed more fearful of labor militancy than pleased by the potential of a mass labor movement. During its 1935 convention, AFL delegates voted by a large majority against the principle of industrial unionism for mass-production workers and against an extensive organizing effort among such workers.

A minority refused to accept defeat gracefully or quietly and, led by Lewis, organized itself to promote unionism among mass-production workers. In November 1935, Lewis met at UMW headquarters with eight other labor leaders and they formed the Committee for Industrial Organization (CIO) as a group to promote industrial unionism within the AFL. As conceived by Lewis, the primary mission of the CIO was to organize mass-production workers in such industries as steel, autos, rubber, and electrical goods. His battle cry was organization first, jurisdiction later; the spoils of victory could not be shared before the struggle. Lewis and his associates were eager both to organize workers and to establish industrial unions within the AFL, but they were also willing to act independently if the AFL majority rejected the industrial union way. That is precisely what happened by the end of 1936.

After the AFL Executive Council ordered the CIO to disband in the summer of 1936 and suspended the unions involved when they refused to do so (an action sanctioned by the November 1936 AFL convention), Lewis pursued the independent effort by the CIO to organize the mass-production industries. In June 1936 he established the Steel Workers Organizing Committee (SWOC), staffed it with UMW cadres, and gave it more than $1 million in UMW-CIO funds. From headquarters in Pittsburgh, SWOC spread the message of trade unionism among steelworkers. CIO organizers also proselytized among auto workers in Michigan and rubber workers in Akron, Ohio.

Success blessed the CIO campaign. On 30 December 1936, workers in Flint, Michigan, occupied two General Motors production plants, thus precipitating the great General Motors sit-down strike. For the next six weeks the sit-downers remained inside while Lewis and other CIO leaders negotiated with company and public officials on the outside. On 11 February 1937, General Motors recognized the United Automobile Workers-CIO as the sole bargaining agent for its members and agreed to bargain collectively with it. One bastion of the open shop had fallen. Three weeks later another open-shop fortress fell, this time without a struggle. On 2 March 1937, United States Steel signed a collective bargaining agreement with SWOC-CIO, a step that repudiated a half-century of company antiunionism.

The shock waves from Flint and Pittsburgh reverberated across the nation. When the CIO held its first national meeting in October 1937, it claimed thirty-two affiliates with a membership in excess of four million. Indeed, in one year the CIO had more than doubled the size of the American labor movement and had added more workers than in any other single year in American history. No wonder that, as the first historian of the CIO, Edward Levinson, wrote, "Around mammoth modern mills and at bleak old factories, on ships and on piers, at offices and in public gathering-places, men and women roared, 'C.I.O.! C.I.O.!' Labor was on the march as it had never been before in the history of the Republic."

The CIO not only organized workers where the AFL had failed; it seemed a different sort of organization, a "new unionism." The typical CIO leader was younger and better-educated than his AFL counterpart. He was also more likely to be a militant, a socialist, or a communist. CIO affiliates organized among women workers and non-English-speaking ethnic groups; they also were active in civil rights struggles, and many formed their own civil rights adjuncts. Because nonwhite workers were clustered more in the industries organized by the CIO than in the trades dominated by the AFL, the CIO seemed, for a time, the vanguard for biracial unionism. Also, rather than practicing nonpartisan politics and following the AFL policy of "rewarding your friends and punishing your enemies," the CIO became an active part of the Roosevelt Democratic coalition and in some industrial states and cities became, in effect, the Democratic party.

However different the CIO may have seemed from the AFL, especially after October 1938, when it sealed its divorce from the older group by assuming permanent, independent form as the Congress of Industrial Organizations, its union practices scarcely differed. Most CIO contracts focused on protecting the worker's job security and improving the conditions of his work. The CIO bargained to establish the principle of seniority, equitable grievance procedures, higher wages, shorter hours, and uniform work standards.

That the CIO was less revolutionary or innovative than it had appeared at first was shown after 1937 by the revitalization of the AFL. Challenged by an organized trade union alternative as never before in its history, the AFL reacted with vigor. Seeing that mass-production workers could be organized, AFL affiliates stopped fretting about jurisdictional lines and started enrolling members regardless of skill or trade. Such old-line AFL craft unions as the carpenters, machinists, and teamsters transformed themselves into semi-industrial organizations, hardly different from many CIO unions. Because AFL unions were older and more stable, possessed larger and more experienced staffs of organizers, had substantial treasuries, and seemed more moderate to employers than did CIO unions, the AFL between 1937 and 1940 began to attract many more new members than the CIO. By the end of 1940, AFL membership far surpassed that of the CIO, and its aggressive organizing tactics made possible a total national union membership of 8,410,000 in 1941 (23 percent of all nonagricultural workers), close to two-thirds of whom were in AFL affiliates.

In fact, since its high point in the summer of 1937, the CIO had suffered a series of setbacks. An attempt in 1937 to organize the "Little Steel" companies had been crushed. So, too, had been an effort to organize textile workers by the Textile Workers Organizing Committee (TWOC). And in the auto industry the Ford Motor Company still refused to bargain with the UAW-CIO. On the eve of World War II, the CIO seemed to have lost its momentum.

World War II, however, accomplished for the CIO what World War I had done for the AFL. Even before American involvement, CIO affiliates won contracts from the "Little Steel" companies and Ford Motors. After 7 December 1941, the CIO made greater gains. Sidney Hillman, a CIO leader, became President Roosevelt's primary labor adviser. The "maintenance of membership" principle enunciated by the National War Labor Board in 1942 assured unions of all the membership gains they had made. Once a worker enrolled in a union, it became almost impossible for him to withdraw voluntarily and equally impossible for employers to make

LABOR ORGANIZATIONS

TABLE 3
Union Membership, 1945–1960

		"Real" Membership		Alternate "Real" Membership	
Year	Actual Membership[a]	Civilian Labor Force[b]	Union Membership as Percent of Civilian Labor Force	Nonagricultural Employment[c]	Union Membership as Percent of Nonagricultural Employment
1945	13,379,000	53,860,000	24.8	40,037,000	33.4
1946	13,648,000	57,520,000	23.7	41,287,000	33.1
1947	14,845,000	60,168,000	24.7	43,462,000	34.2
1948	14,916,000	61,442,000	24.3	44,448,000	33.6
1949	14,960,000	62,105,000	24.1	43,315,000	34.5
1950	14,751,000	63,099,000	23.4	44,738,000	33.0
1951	16,211,000	62,884,000	25.8	47,347,000	34.2
1952	16,730,000	62,966,000	26.6	48,303,000	34.6
1953	17,884,000	63,815,000	28.0	49,681,000	36.0
1954	17,757,000	64,468,000	27.5	48,431,000	36.7
1955	17,749,000	65,847,000	27.0	50,056,000	35.5
1956	18,477,000	67,530,000	27.4	51,766,000	35.7
1957	18,430,000	67,946,000	27.1	52,162,000	35.3
1958	18,081,000	68,647,000	26.3	50,543,000	35.8
1959	18,452,000	69,394,000	26.6	51,975,000	35.5
1960	18,607,000	71,056,000	26.2	53,135,000[d]	35.0[d]

Source: Irving Bernstein, "The Growth of American Unions," p. 135.
[a] 1945–1948: Leo Wolman, by correspondence.
1949–1953: Projected from AFL membership.
1954–1958: Bureau of Labor Statistics.
1959–1960: Projected from California membership.
[b] Bureau of the Census.
[c] Bureau of Labor Statistics.
[d] Includes Alaska and Hawaii.

following among such workers. The American Federation of State, County, and Municipal Employees, the Retail Clerks' Union, and the American Federation of Teachers became among the most rapidly growing trade unions. By 1975 talk arose that Albert Shanker, leader of the New York City teachers' union, was a possible successor to the aging George Meany as president of the AFL-CIO. In a sight unfamiliar to many citizens, throughout the 1960's and 1970's schoolteachers, government clerks, and other public employees walked picket lines despite statutes forbidding them to strike. Neither rain, nor snow, nor sleet, nor war might delay the United States mail, but in the spring of 1970 a strike by Post Office employees stopped delivery.

Another long-neglected sector of the labor force emerged from obscurity during the 1960's and sought to organize itself: the farm workers of the West Coast, especially those in California's "factories in the field." Under the leadership of César Chávez, a former farm worker of Mexican-American origin, the farm workers of California in 1962 established the National Farm Workers' Association. Four years later it merged with the AFL-CIO Agricultural Workers' Organizing Committee and became the United Farm Workers' Organizing Committee, now the United Farm Workers of America, an AFL-CIO affiliate. Using the traditional union strike and the less conventional boycott of chain stores by middle-class consumers, Chávez by 1967 won contracts for his union from several California wine producers. As the United Farm Workers proved that agricultural employees could be unionized, the Teamsters' Union, expelled from the AFL-CIO in 1967, entered the countryside to recruit farm workers. Favored by the employers, the Teamsters' Union began to steal members and contracts from the United Farm Workers. By the summer of 1975 Chávez's farm workers and the teamsters were engaged in a full-scale organizing battle on California farms and ranches, the outcome of which was still in doubt by 1979.

As much as the new recruits among white-collar workers and farmhands may have gratified the leaders of the AFL-CIO, they obviously realized that the growth of the labor movement was falling behind the growth of the labor force, and that in 1979 trade unionism represented a smaller proportion of the labor force than it had in 1955. Although George Meany in a 1969 Labor Day interview could take great pride in the growth and successes of the American labor movement since 1933 (a theme he would repeat each Labor Day for the following ten years), trade unionism in America in 1979 seemed incapable of substantial new growth and of offering answers to the unemployment, low wages, and poverty that afflicted many workers. Organized labor during the 1970's, as had been the case during the 1920's, discovered no solution to adversity. One might have predicted, as Barnett did in 1932, that the American labor movement had no future. But, as David Brody noted in an essay written in 1967, one should "not . . . make predictions and . . . avoid being found in error, as is the case with Professor Barnett . . . by future historians."

APPENDIX

TABLE 4
Distribution of Union Membership in the United States by Industry Group, 1939, 1953, 1956, 1958

Industry Group	1939[a] Number	Percent	1953[a] Number	Percent	1956[b] Number	Percent	1958[b] Number	Percent
Total	6,517,700	100.0	16,217,300	100.0	18,104,000	100.0	17,968,000	100.0
Manufacturing	2,299,100	35.3	7,312,800	45.1	8,839,000	48.8	8,359,000	46.5
Nonmanufacturing	4,218,600	64.7	8,904,500	54.9	9,265,000	51.2	9,609,000	53.5
Mining and quarrying	[c]	—	[c]	—	518,000	2.9	622,000	3.5
Contract construction	889,000	13.6	2,197,800	13.6	2,123,000	11.7	2,324,000	12.9
Transportation	[c]	—	[c]	—	2,727,000	15.1	2,712,000	15.1
Telephone and telegraph	[c]	—	[c]	—	428,000	2.4	409,000	2.3
Electric and gas utilities	[c]	—	[c]	—	323,000	1.8	259,000	1.4
Trade	[c]	—	[c]	—	883,000	4.9	852,000	4.7
Finance and insurance	[c]	—	[c]	—	51,000	0.3	104,000	0.6
Service industries	[c]	—	[c]	—	1,222,000	6.7	1,240,000	6.9
Agriculture and fishing	4,400	[d]	8,300	[d]	76,000	0.4	33,000	0.2
Nonmanufacturing (not classifiable)	[c]	—	[c]	—	n.a.	—	19,000	0.1
Government	418,700	6.4	749,600	4.6	915,000	5.1	1,035,000	5.8

Source: Irving Bernstein, "The Growth of American Unions," p. 136.
[a] Troy, *Distribution of Union Membership.*
[b] Bureau of Labor Statistics.
[c] Not comparable.
[d] Less than 1 per cent.

TABLE 5

Union Membership in the United States as a Percent of Nonagricultural Employment by Industry Group, 1939, 1953, 1956, 1958

Industry Group	1939 Membership[a] (000)	1939 Employment[b] (000)	1939 Percent	1953 Membership[a] (000)	1953 Employment[b] (000)	1953 Percent	1956 Membership[c] (000)	1956 Employment[b] (000)	1956 Percent	1958 Membership[c] (000)	1958 Employment[b] (000)	1958 Percent
Total	6,518	30,311	21.5	16,217	49,681	32.6	18,104	51,766	35.0	17,968	50,543	35.5
Manufacturing	2,299	10,078	22.8	7,313	17,238	42.4	8,839	16,903	52.3	8,359	15,468	54.0
Nonmanufacturing	4,219	20,234	20.9	8,905	32,433	27.5	9,265	34,824	26.6	9,609	35,052	27.4
Mining and quarrying	[d]	—	—	[d]	852	—	518	807	64.2	622	721	86.3
Contract construction	889	1,150	77.3	2,198	2,622	83.8	2,123	2,929	72.5	2,324	2,648	87.8
Transportation	[d]	[d]	—	[d]	2,899	—	2,727	2,745	99.3	2,712	2,531	107.2
Telephone and telegraph	[d]	[d]	—	[d]	746	—	428	805	53.2	409	771	53.0
Electric and gas utilities	[d]	[d]	—	[d]	566	—	323	572	56.5	259	579	44.7
Trade	[d]	[d]	—	[d]	10,527	—	883	11,221	7.9	852	11,141	7.6
Finance and insurance	[d]	[d]	—	[d]	2,038	—	51	2,308	0.2	104	2,374	4.4
Service industries	[d]	[d]	—	[d]	5,538	—	1,222	6,160	19.8	1,240	6,395	19.4
Nonmanufacturing (not classifiable)	[d]	n.a.	—	[d]	n.a.	—	n.a.	n.a.	—	19	n.a.	—
Government	419	3,995	10.5	750	6,645	11.3	915	7,277	12.6	1,035	7,893	13.1

Source: Irving Bernstein, "The Growth of American Unions," p. 138.
[a]Troy, *Distribution of Union Membership.*
[b]Bureau of the Census.
[c]Bureau of Labor Statistics.
[d]Not comparable.

LABOR ORGANIZATIONS

TABLE 6
National and International Unions Reporting 100,000 Members or More: 1964 and 1970
(in thousands)

Union	1964	1970	Union	1964	1970	Union	1964	1970
Teamsters (Ind.)	1,507	1,829	Government (AFGE)	139	325	Postal clerks	139	162
Automobile workers (Ind.)	1,168	1,486	Plumbers	256	312	Bakery and confectionery workers	([2])	152
Steelworkers	965	1,200	Electrical (IUE)	271	300	Transport workers	135	150
Electrical (IBEW)	806	922	Musicians	275	300	Firefighters	115	146
Machinists	808	865	Railway and steamship clerks	270	275	Papermakers	133	145
Carpenters	760	820	Transportation	([1])	263	Bricklayers	135	143
Retail clerks	428	605	Rubber workers	165	216	Boilermakers	125	138
Laborers	432	580	Letter carriers	168	215	Transit	133	132
Meat cutters	341	494	Painters	199	210	Printing pressmen	116	128
Hotel and restaurant	445	461	District 50, Allied and technical (Ind.)	210	210	Maintenance of way	121	126
State, county	235	444	Teachers	100	205	Sheet metal workers	117	[3]120
Garment, ladies'	442	442	Pulp, sulphite	176	193	Typographical	113	112
Service employees (SEIU)	320	435	Textile workers	177	178	Chemical (Ind.)	85	101
Communications workers	294	422	Iron workers	143	178	Railway carmen	121	([4])
Engineers, operating	311	393	Oil, chemical workers	162	175	Federal employees (NFFE) (Ind.)	(NA)	100
Clothing workers	377	386	Retail, wholesale	167	175	Railroad trainmen	185	([5])
			Electrical (UE) (Ind.)	165	163	Packinghouse workers	145	([6])

Source: U.S. Department of Commerce, *Statistical Abstract of the United States, 1973*, p. 250; taken from U.S. Bureau of Labor Statistics, *Directory of National and International Labor Unions in the United States, 1965* and *1969*, and *Directory of National Unions and Employee Associations, 1971*.
Note: Data are for unions with headquarters in the United States. All unions not identified as independent (Ind.) are affiliated with the AFL-CIO. Excludes United Mine Workers of America (Ind.), whose membership is believed to be over 100,000.
NA=Not available.
[1]Transportation union formed by merger of four railroad unions in January 1969.
[2]Merger of two unions in December 1969.
[3]Estimate, 1971.
[4]Merged with transportation union in January 1969.
[5]Estimated membership over 100,000. Merged into United Transportation Union in January 1969.
[6]Membership over 100,000; merged with meat cutters.

LABOR ORGANIZATIONS

TABLE 7
Labor Union Membership—Total and Percent of Nonagricultural Employment, States: 1964, 1968, and 1970

State	Total (1,000) 1964	1968	1970	Percent of Nonagricultural Employment 1964	1968[1]	1970	State	Total (1,000) 1964	1968	1970	Percent of Nonagricultural Employment 1964	1968[1]	1970
U.S.	17,188	19,297	19,757	29.5	28.4	27.9	Mont.	62	61	60	35.2	31.3	29.9
							Nebr.[2]	78	79	86	19.2	17.3	17.9
Ala.[2]	158	193	204	18.7	19.9	20.3	Nev.[2]	49	52	66	32.8	29.3	32.8
Alaska	21	27	25	32.1	33.8	27.1	N.H.	42	43	45	20.1	17.1	17.3
Ariz.[2]	71	89	96	18.5	18.8	17.6	N.J.	701	735	768	32.3	29.6	29.5
Ark.[2]	73	97	95	17.0	18.9	17.9	N. Mex.	37	37	43	14.5	13.4	14.8
Calif.	1,857	2,118	2,137	33.3	31.9	30.5	N.Y.	2,453	2,539	2,555	38.5	36.3	35.6
Colo.	128	149	152	22.3	21.9	20.5	N.C.[2]	100	124	137	7.4	7.4	7.8
Conn.	267	275	290	27.0	23.7	24.2	N. Dak.[2]	21	29	28	14.8	18.7	17.2
Del.	41	53	48	24.0	26.2	22.6	Ohio	1,180	1,345	1,413	36.7	35.9	36.3
Fla.[2]	214	279	299	14.0	14.4	13.9							
Ga.[2]	166	239	251	14.0	16.4	16.2	Okla.	94	121	124	15.1	16.6	16.1
							Oreg.	196	213	218	34.2	31.4	30.7
Hawaii	49	70	82	23.6	27.4	28.1	Pa.	1,462	1,585	1,617	38.7	37.2	37.2
Idaho	32	37	38	19.0	19.2	18.5	R.I.	86	83	89	28.3	24.2	26.1
Ill.	1,419	1,538	1,548	38.4	36.0	35.7	S.C.[2]	48	66	81	7.4	8.4	9.6
Ind.	563	653	657	36.4	35.9	35.6	S. Dak.[2]	15	24	21	10.0	14.4	11.9
Iowa[2]	163	183	186	22.6	21.4	21.1	Tenn.[2]	201	246	274	19.2	19.5	20.6
Kans.[2]	109	124	112	18.6	18.5	16.6	Tex.[2]	394	474	523	14.1	13.9	14.4
Ky.	195	235	250	27.0	27.1	27.3	Utah[2]	53	62	75	18.0	18.4	20.9
La.	160	187	193	18.7	18.2	18.4	Vt.	21	29	24	18.7	20.7	16.2
Maine	59	58	61	20.8	17.9	18.4							
Md.[3]	369	429	463	22.9	22.6	23.3	Va.[2]	184	230	245	15.8	16.6	16.7
							Wash.	376	454	434	44.0	41.3	40.0
Mass.	549	562	573	28.0	25.5	25.6	W. Va.	206	213	221	44.7	41.9	43.0
Mich.	1,074	1,068	1,195	42.7	35.9	40.2	Wis.	424	473	482	33.4	32.2	31.4
Minn.	350	375	378	34.0	30.1	28.9	Wyo.[2]	19	20	19	19.4	19.3	17.7
Miss.[2]	62	76	76	13.5	13.9	13.2	Membership						
Mo.	537	584	594	37.9	35.9	35.9	not classified	—	260	108	(x)	(x)	(x)

Source: U.S. Department of Commerce, *Statistical Abstract of the United States, 1973*, p. 250; taken from U.S. Bureau of Labor Statistics, *Directory of National and International Labor Unions in the United States, 1965* and *1969*, and *Directory of National Unions and Employee Associations, 1971*.

Note: Based on reports and estimates for national, international, and local unions directly affiliated with the AFL-CIO, and members in single-firm and local unaffiliated unions. Excludes membership outside the United States and employee associations.

— Represents zero.
X=Not applicable.
[1]Data have been revised to reflect adjustment in nonagricultural employment figures.
[2]State has a right-to-work law.
[3]Includes District of Columbia.

LABOR ORGANIZATIONS

TABLE 8
National and International Unions—Membership: 1940–1970

Item		1940	1950	1955	1960	1964	1965	1968	1970
Unions affiliated with AFL-CIO		147	137	139	134	129	129	126	120
Union membership, total	1,000	8,944	15,000	17,749	18,117	17,976	18,519	20,258	20,752
White-collar membership	1,000	(NA)	(NA)	[1]2,463	2,192	2,585	(NA)	3,176	3,353
Percent of total membership		(NA)	(NA)	[1]13.6	12.2	14.4	(NA)	15.7	16.2
Male	1,000	(NA)	(NA)	(NA)	14,813	14,563	(NA)	16,318	16,470
Female	1,000	(NA)	(NA)	(NA)	3,304	3,413	(NA)	3,940	4,282
Canadian members of U.S. unions	1,000	227	733	947	1,068	1,135	1,220	1,342	1,371
Excluding Canadian members	1,000	8,717	14,267	16,802	17,049	16,841	17,299	18,916	19,381
Membership as percent of—									
Total labor force		15.5	22.0	24.4	23.6	22.2	22.4	23.0	22.6
Employment in nonagr. estab.		26.9	31.5	33.2	31.4	28.9	28.4	27.9	27.4
AFL-CIO	1,000	7,872	12,143	16,062	15,072	15,150	15,604	15,608	15,978
Independent or unaffiliated unions	1,000	1,072	2,600	1,688	3,045	2,825	2,915	4,650	4,773

Source: U.S. Department of Commerce, *Statistical Abstract of the United States, 1973*, p. 249; taken from U.S. Bureau of Labor Statistics, *Handbook of Labor Statistics* (annual), *Directory of National and International Labor Unions in the United States, 1969* and *Directory of National Unions and Employee Associations, 1971*.

Note: Estimates based on average number of dues-paying members of unions with headquarters in the U.S. Certain unions did not report as members persons not required to pay dues, such as apprentices and workers retired, unemployed, in armed forces, or involved in work stoppages. Excludes employee associations, and single-firm and local unaffiliated unions. See also *Historical Statistics, Colonial Times to 1957*, series D 741 and 745.
NA = Not available.
[1] 1956 data.

TABLE 9
National and International Unions—Number and Members, by Industry and Affiliation: 1968 and 1970

	1968 All Unions			1970 All Unions			1970 AFL-CIO Unions		
Industry Group	Number[1]	Members[2] Number (1,000)	Percent	Number[1]	Members[2] Number (1,000)	Percent	Number[1]	Members[2] Number (1,000)	Percent
All unions	189	20,210	100.0	185	20,689	100.0	120	15,916	100.0
Manufacturing	103	9,218	45.6	100	9,173	44.3	70	6,666	41.9
Ordnance and accessories	12	169	0.8	16	157	0.8	9	130	0.8
Food and kindred prod. (incl. beverages)	26	880	4.4	25	906	4.4	17	588	3.7
Tobacco manufactures	8	39	0.2	8	38	0.2	5	37	0.2
Textile mill products	9	191	1.0	10	191	0.9	4	177	1.1
Apparel and related products	13	870	4.3	16	852	4.1	11	836	5.3
Lumber and wood prod., exc. furniture	17	310	1.5	13	215	1.0	8	208	1.3
Furniture and fixtures	15	157	0.8	17	214	1.0	13	187	1.2
Paper and allied products	16	448	2.2	20	453	2.2	12	391	2.5
Printing, publishing, and allied industries	19	375	1.9	18	370	1.8	15	357	2.2
Chemicals and allied products	25	382	1.9	26	361	1.7	19	151	0.9
Petroleum refining and related industries	13	96	0.5	12	80	0.4	7	69	0.4

LABOR ORGANIZATIONS

TABLE 9
National and International Unions—Number and Members, by Industry and Affiliation: 1968 and 1970

	1968			1970					
	All Unions			All Unions			AFL-CIO Unions		
		Members[2]			Members[2]			Members[2]	
Industry Group	Number[1]	Number (1,000)	Percent	Number[1]	Number (1,000)	Percent	Number[1]	Number (1,000)	Percent
All unions	189	20,210	100.0	185	20,689	100.0	120	15,916	100.0
Rubber and miscellaneous plastics products	16	246	1.2	19	272	1.3	13	248	1.6
Leather and leather products	10	131	0.6	13	140	0.7	10	134	0.8
Stone, clay, glass, and concrete products	20	295	1.5	22	284	1.4	17	234	1.5
Primary metals industries	17	773	3.8	16	788	3.8	11	667	4.2
Fabricated metal prod., exc. ordnance, machinery, and transportation equip.	33	543	2.7	33	918	4.4	21	719	4.5
Machinery, except electrical	19	692	3.4	23	550	2.7	16	278	1.7
Electrical machinery equip. and supplies	16	1,014	5.0	19	1,034	5.0	11	793	5.0
Transportation equipment	21	1,333	6.6	21	1,109	5.4	15	291	1.8
Professional, scientific and controlling instr.	12	62	0.3	13	49	0.2	6	21	0.1
Miscellaneous manufacturing industries	36	212	1.0	43	194	0.9	31	147	0.9
Nonmanufacturing	106	8,837	43.7	104	9,198	44.5	73	7,390	46.4
Mining and quarrying (including crude petroleum and natural gas production)	16	342	1.7	15	369	1.8	8	154	1.0
Contract constr. (bldg. and special trade)	26	2,541	12.6	28	2,576	12.5	21	2,476	15.6
Transportation	48	2,503	12.4	44	2,441	11.8	34	1,425	9.0
Telephone and telegraph	8	476	2.4	10	533	2.6	7	483	3.0
Electric, gas, sanitary serv. (incl. water)	15	324	1.6	17	312	1.5	12	268	1.7
Wholesale and retail trade	21	1,392	6.9	24	1,549	7.5	15	1,315	8.3
Finance, insurance, and real estate	5	50	0.2	7	55	0.3	5	51	0.3
Service industries	38	1,093	5.4	48	1,287	6.2	31	1,166	7.3
Agriculture and fishing	5	26	0.1	5	24	0.1	2	4	(z)
Nonmanufacturing, not elsewhere classified	11	90	0.4	11	53	0.3	6	47	0.3
Government	59	2,155	10.7	60	2,318	11.2	34	1,860	11.7
Federal	57	1,351	6.7	56	1,370	6.6	31	927	5.8
State and local	18	804	4.0	19	947	4.6	16	933	5.9

Source: U.S. Department of Commerce, *Statistical Abstract of the United States, 1973*, p. 249; taken from U.S. Bureau of Labor Statistics, *Handbook of Labor Statistics* (annual), *Directory of National and International Labor Unions in the United States, 1969,* and *Directory of National Unions and Employee Associations, 1971.*
Note: See note, table 8. Excludes employee associations and local unions directly affiliated with the AFL-CIO.
Z=Less than 0.05 percent
[1]Nonadditive; many unions have membership in more than one industry group.
[2]Membership computed by applying reported percentages to total membership, including that outside the U.S.

BIBLIOGRAPHY

Irving Bernstein, *The Lean Years: A History of the American Worker, 1920–1933* (Boston, 1960), is a detailed, well-written narrative of the paralysis of the American labor movement from 1920 to 1933; "The Growth of American Unions, 1945–1960," *Labor History,* 2 (Spring 1961), a sanguine statistical analysis of the possibilities and prospects for trade union growth; and *Turbulent Years: A History of the American Worker, 1933–1941* (Boston, 1969), a detailed exploration of the impact of the New Deal on American labor and a celebration of the triumph of the CIO. David Brody, "The Emergence of Mass Production Unionism," in John Braeman et al., *Change and Continuity in Twentieth-Century America: the 1920's* (Columbus, Ohio, 1968), stresses the similarities between the AFL and the CIO. John R. Commons et al., *History of Labor in the*

LABOR ORGANIZATIONS

United States, 4 vols. (New York, 1918–1935), is the classic study of trade unionism in the United States from its origins to 1932. Melvyn Dubofsky, *We Shall Be All: A History of the Industrial Workers of the World* (Chicago, 1969), is an examination of labor radicalism from the 1890's through the 1920's; and *Industrialism and the American Worker, 1865–1920* (New York, 1975), a summary and analysis of both traditional and recent scholarship on the history of labor. Philip S. Foner, *History of the Labor Movement in the United States,* 4 vols. (New York, 1947–1965), a general history comparable with Commons' but written from a Marxist perspective. Walter Galenson, *The CIO Challenge to the AFL: A History of the American Labor Movement, 1935–1941* (Cambridge, Mass., 1960), is an encyclopedic examination of the civil war in American labor in the 1930's.

Joseph Goulden, *Meany: The Unchallenged Strongman of American Labor* (New York, 1972), a lively journalistic biography that covers labor history from the 1930's to 1972. Gerald Grob, *Workers and Utopia: A Study of Ideological Conflict in the American Labor Movement, 1865–1900* (Evanston, Ill., 1961), an examination of the struggle between the Knights of Labor and the AFL, with greater sympathy for the latter organization. Bernard Mandel, *Samuel Gompers* (Yellow Springs, Ohio, 1963), is the most complete biography, although short on analysis, of the longtime AFL president. David Montgomery, *Beyond Equality: Labor and the Radical Republicans, 1862–1872* (New York, 1967), is a brilliant revisionist examination of American labor in the Civil War era. James Oliver Morris, *Conflict Within the AFL: A Study of Craft Versus Industrial Unionism, 1901–1938* (Ithaca, N.Y., 1958), gives a detailed examination of the development of industrial unionism and the origins of the CIO. Edward Pessen, "The Working Men's Movement of the Jacksonian Era," *Mississippi Valley Historical Review,* 43 (December 1956), is an excellent synthesis of literature on the labor movement circa 1820–1850. Frank C. Pierson, *Unions in Postwar America: An Economic Assessment* (New York, 1967), a helpful brief summary of the main lines of trade union development since 1945. Joel Seidman, *American Labor from Defense to Reconversion* (Chicago, 1953), is the indispensable introduction to a study of labor during World War II and immediately afterward. Philip Taft, *The A.F. of L. in the Time of Gompers* (New York, 1957), is a dull, overly detailed institutional history by the official historian of the AFL; and *The A.F. of L. from the Death of Gompers to the Merger* (New York, 1959), a repetition of the basic story, style, and theme of the previous volume. Norman Ware, *The Labor Movement in the United States, 1860–1895* (New York, 1929), though dated, still the most complete and sympathetic history of the Knights of Labor.

[*See also* BUSINESS CYCLES, PANICS, AND DEPRESSIONS; ECONOMY FROM RECONSTRUCTION TO 1914; ECONOMY SINCE 1914; MANUFACTURING; PRODUCTIVITY; PRICES AND WAGES; RISE AND EVOLUTION OF BIG BUSINESS; SERVICE SECTOR; SOCIALISM; *and* WORK.]

SLAVERY

Gerald Gunderson

SLAVERY was a long-established and accepted part of life in the eastern hemisphere. Thus it is understandable that Europeans employed it as an integral part of the development of the New World. In the first two centuries of settlement, the largest colonial effort went into transplanting the sugar industry from the Mediterranean and from nearby Atlantic islands. The largest factor in sugar production was labor, which was supplied by extending the existing trade in black slaves from West Africa across the Atlantic. In the sixteenth century Brazil was the major sugar-producing area—and destination of slaves. This position was taken over by the Caribbean colonies in the seventeenth century. By 1850 perhaps as many as ten million, and certainly more than seven million, black slaves had been shipped west across the Atlantic. Whichever estimate one uses, it was undoubtedly one of the largest movements of people until then.

Beginning in the early seventeenth century a branch of the slave trade was extended north to the area that now comprises the southeastern part of the United States. It was always to remain a relatively small portion of that activity. By 1800, when the trade was nearing its conclusion, only 6 percent of the transported slaves had gone to that destination. The United States, from 1619 on, was outside the mainstream of experience with slavery in other important ways. Only a small fraction of the American slave population was used in sugar production; most worked in tobacco and, later, cotton production. The latter provided a much healthier environment than the tropical sugar establishments for both slaves and free residents.

As a consequence the slave population in the United States increased rapidly, in marked contrast with the rest of the hemisphere, where unhealthy climates and high proportions of males to females usually prevented slaves from maintaining their numbers. In fact, the American slave population increased slightly faster than the free, domestic population of the country, and considerably faster than the free population of Europe. As a result, 36 percent of the slaves living in the western hemisphere in 1825 were in the United States. This was the largest group of slaves in one country at that time, more than that in the second largest holder, Brazil, which had imported more than six times as many. Because of the differences in local conditions, the minority importer became the majority holder.

The difference in the population growth of American slaves carried over to other dimensions. Given their relatively high rate of natural reproduction, the proportion of foreign-born slaves in the United States decreased over time, falling from a level of 80–90 percent prior to 1650 to less than 10 percent after 1830. In fact, in the latter year the proportion of slaves that was native-born actually exceeded the native-born fraction of the free populace. This was, of course, influenced by the prohibition of slave importation after 1808, but a much more important cause was an average increase of at least 3 percent per year in the slave population, which had the effect of doubling the population in less than twenty-five years. (If, for example, one were to start with a population composed entirely of immigrants who had such a rate of increase for fifty years, at least 75 percent of the final population would be native-born in the absence of further immigration.)

In addition, most American slaves were kept in smaller groups and constituted a smaller proportion of the total population than was true of

SLAVERY

slave populations elsewhere in the hemisphere. On sugar or rice plantations, or on the cotton plantations along the Mississippi River, groups of slaves in excess of one hundred were common; but the average figure for the entire South was 10.3 slaves per slave owner in 1860. About 50 percent of the slaves in 1860 were held in groups of twenty or fewer. (These two measures of slave holdings are not, as they might appear, inconsistent. They are the result of a large number of slave owners who had just a few slaves each and a few slaveholders who had large numbers.) About 13 percent were held in groups of five or fewer.

Similarly, in those limited areas cited above, the proportion of slaves in the total population could be quite high—90 percent or even more—but the average level for the South in the nineteenth century was 35–40 percent. In consequence, something like two-thirds of the total slave population lived in areas where they were less than 25 percent of the local population. In other words, American slaves were generally a minority of the population. There are numerous implications that have not yet been fully explored regarding how that situation might affect their experience.

This complex of conditions in the United States was quite different from those usually faced by slaves at other places or at other times. Although other societies considered slavery to be a permanent condition, they usually did not have a slave population that perpetuated itself. Existing slave populations tended to die out, either through low reproduction rates or through emancipation when the slaves were able to purchase their freedom. The former case appears to characterize the experience of other western hemisphere slave populations from 1500 to 1800, while the latter appears to explain experiences in the classical era (in the Roman Empire, for instance). To be sustained, therefore, the slave population required periodic infusions of newcomers, such as those captured in war. In contrast, the American domestic slave population not only was self-perpetuating but also, in the absence of immigration of free citizens, would have increased as a fraction of the population over time. The favorable effect of the American pattern of slave use probably was encouraged by a relative scarcity of labor and by higher average incomes. In any case it produced an experience with slavery that was unusual by historical standards and illuminated the forces at work within slavery.

COLONIAL SLAVERY

The success of American slavery that was evident in the nineteenth century was not nearly as obvious or foreseeable in the seventeenth century. Slavery appeared to get off to a slow start in colonial America and was threatened at first by an alternative system of labor, indentured servants. Free labor from Europe was generally more versatile and skilled, so it is not surprising that American entrepreneurs tried using it first. Indentured servants probably were particularly appealing in the first years of settlement, when experimentation with new crops and production techniques, and adjustment to new climates and markets, placed a strong premium on the resourcefulness of labor. Slavery had a compensating advantage, though: it was cheaper. The slaves came from a society where the alternative uses of labor were not as remunerative as they were in Europe, the source of the indentured servants. As a consequence African slaves were available in America at a lower yearly cost, on average, than European indentured servants. If work routines could be constructed in such a way as to employ less-skilled labor, costs could be reduced.

In the last decades of the seventeenth century, conditions developed that favored slavery as a prime source of labor in the American South. Perhaps these conditions were the result of the standardization of production methods in tobacco and rice. Perhaps it was the acclimatization of the slaves to American conditions. (In 1680 the proportion of domestic-born slaves exceeded 50 percent of the total slave population for the first time.) In any case, the proportion of slaves in the southern economy began to rise, from less than 10 percent in 1680 to almost 40 percent on the eve of the Revolution. This implies a very rapid increase in the total slave population, because the total population of the American South was growing quite rapidly during this period. The number of slaves rose from less than fifteen thousand in 1680 to more than half a million by the Revolution, a more than thirtyfold increase in ninety years (representing

553

an annual population increase of almost 5 percent).

This rapid adoption of slavery in the southern colonies did not carry over to the population north of the Mason-Dixon line. The proportion of slaves in the population of the northern colonies did not rise appreciably above the level of 5 percent or so prevailing in the late seventeenth century. Historians have given considerable attention to this regional contrast without reaching any compelling consensus. Perhaps the most common explanation is that of climatic differences. In the milder southern climates slaves could be employed year-round, whereas—goes the argument—they would still have to be fed, clothed, and housed in the slack winter periods of northern agriculture. By itself this hypothesis is not convincing. There were a number of productive activities available to northern farmers in the winter and, moreover, throughout the eighteenth century northern citizens continued to purchase the services of large numbers of indentured servants who also had to be fed, clothed, and housed year-round.

A second possible explanation was obliquely suggested above. Slaves and indentured servants provided different types of labor services. The South might have had relatively more demand for the type of labor performing unskilled tasks while the North required more skilled, self-directed labor. Again the argument is not fully convincing. The majority of the indentured servants were not skilled craftsmen, and slaveholders discovered that many slaves could absorb extensive training and operate successfully in tasks outside of agriculture. Another possible difference turns on the view held by the public on the ethics of slavery as a public institution. Certainly from the time of the Revolution on, there was growing distaste for local slavery in the northern states. Between 1777 (when Vermont banned slavery) and 1820, slavery north of the Mason-Dixon line was gradually eliminated. It seems unlikely that this disdain for slavery in the North after the Revolution had been sufficiently strong, in the colonial period, to explain the minor role of slavery relative to that in the South. As scholars are wont to say, further work is indicated on this question.

The development of slavery in the southern economy was a sufficiently large change to force some major adjustments upon other aspects of the social organization. For example, the southern colonies understandably borrowed the British legal system as the starting point for their own. The British, though, had never been forced to deal with slavery as a normal, integral part of their affairs, and therefore had never evolved the detailed, ordered system of law necessary for the southern situation. Earlier experiences in the British colonies in the Caribbean were of limited help. Their slave populations were usually concentrated, separate groups, whereas American slaves were more commonly mixed into the regular organization of the society.

In the first half of the seventeenth century, the slaves were simply referred to as "servants"—an existing legal category that included indentured servants. In the course of the century, the terms "black servants" and "servants for life" appeared and continued to be used interchangeably with the now universal expression "slave." At a relatively early date a tacit presumption appears to have emerged that the black "servants" were to be perpetually enslaved, although there was a considerable lag until that consensus could be implemented in the legal code. For much of the seventeenth century, "servants for life" might refer either to slaves or to convicts serving life sentences as indentured servants.

A major problem that illustrates the difficulty of drawing up a legal code for slaves was defining the dividing line between slaves as property and slaves as individuals. When slaves were treated as property, the greater the range of control that the owner was permitted to exercise over the slave, the greater the value of the slave. Yet each right of the owner implied a corresponding reduction of choice for the slave. And it was almost inevitable that a good share of the owner's prerogative would begin to impinge upon what was commonly considered to be the private life of the slave. So, for example, it was in the owner's interest to be able to move the slave from one task or location to another as conditions dictated.

Such adjustments could pull the slave away from family or friends—or private garden plot, for that matter. Thus southern legislatures had to devise laws that kept slave families together, protected them against violence, and safeguarded the property they acquired. There was a very fine line between protecting the slave as an individual and protecting the owner's investment in the slave. Southern authorities worked on that subtle distinction right up to the Civil War and never came close to codifying solutions to all the numerous variations that occurred. As will be shown, a large part of this division was worked out between individual slaves and their owners on the basis of mutual self-interest.

In the first years of the eighteenth century, a careful observer would probably have been able to predict that slavery was going to be a large, permanent part of the southern economy. The number of slaves was increasing rapidly, and southern institutions and social organizations were being modified to include slavery as an omnipresent feature. Two other developments in the course of the eighteenth century made the trend even more evident. In 1732 the British government granted a charter for the colony of Georgia, which was intended to serve the dual function of a protective frontier against the Spanish and Indians to the south and an outlet for English debtors and convicts. To further both of these ends, the administration of the colony prohibited the ownership of black slaves, requiring the use of white indentured servants instead.

This stricture on labor organization soon ran into heated opposition from local planters. They had quickly discovered that they could not pay the going rate on indentured servants and still produce rice and corn cheaply enough to compete with that raised by slave labor elsewhere in the South. By 1750 the trustees of Georgia had been forced to relent on the use of slaves; the colony could not have hoped to develop into anything of consequence without them. The implications for slavery were starkly evident. That form of labor supply had become such an important part of the southern economy that its use overrode considerations of defense and public policy.

Another indication of the pervasive role of slavery in the southern economy appeared in the second half of the eighteenth century. The most valuable export of the colonial South—and of all the American colonies, for that matter—was tobacco. It had been a growth sector in the seventeenth century as new varieties of tobacco and new growing techniques were developed to supply the emerging demands in Europe. In the eighteenth century the expansion of tobacco production slowed down, and other nations such as Turkey and India began to imitate and catch up with the American technology. Not surprisingly, the return on tobacco production declined, as did the earnings on slave labor employed in tobacco farming. Since tobacco planters were the largest employer of slaves in the colonial period, some historians not illogically have drawn the inference that slavery was declining and was retrieved from extinction only by the appearance of cotton at the beginning of the nineteenth century.

Certainly the return on slaves would have been higher had the demand for tobacco been more robust, but the viability of slavery did not depend on a particular crop or group of crops. Although most slaves at any one time were usually concentrated in production of a few crops, slavery ultimately took its value from the return on labor. Given appropriate incentives, that resource had a much wider range of application than tobacco. Slavery provided one form of labor, which in America had always been relatively scarce and was becoming more productive over time. Thus the decline of tobacco did not doom slavery. The general rise in labor productivity in the economy pulled the returns on slaves up with it, enough to more than offset any downward effect that tobacco might have been exerting. Slavery was thus such an integral part of the southern economy that its fate was not tied to any single crop, not even one that dominated the regional economy.

SLAVE PROFITABILITY

The indicator that economic historians have used in recent years to demonstrate that slavery was not declining (along with tobacco) is the average price of slaves. The significance and confidence that scholars now place in this measure might surprise observers who had not followed recent investigations. In the past some scholars took the view that rising prices of slaves indicated overspeculation in slaves and, therefore, dismal prospects for slavery. But that was before the pervasive function of prices in the slave system became generally appreciated. This new perspective concluded the long-standing debate as to whether slavery was profitable and/or overcapitalized while providing a more productive focus to the discussion of the impact of slavery on the economic development of the antebellum South.

The first major breakthrough in understanding the role of slave prices in the slave system occurred in the late 1950's, in the work of Alfred Conrad and John Meyer. They demonstrated that slaves could be considered a business investment. Relative to the costs involved, the returns to slave owners were comparable with those earned on alternative uses of funds. In other words, the excess of revenues over associated expenses from a given slave yielded just about the same return that a slave owner could expect had he invested his resources in land, railroad bonds, or other available opportunities. Conrad and Meyer's initial results have stood the test of subsequent scrutiny quite well. Although some modifications and refinements have been made upon the original calculations, the basic conclusion remains the same. Slavery was profitable. Economic motivation was sufficient to explain the existence of slavery, although other factors could still bear on the choice to hold slaves. And this suggests that there must have been a strong element of economic interest working throughout the operations of the slave system, an implication that should be amply verified in the discussion below.

The finding that slavery was economically profitable immediately discounts two explanations that have frequently accompanied discussion of slavery. One of these is that slavery was less than profitable because southerners were alleged to have kept slaves for noneconomic reasons, such as keeping tight control over the black population in their midst. Conrad and Meyer's calculations indicate that such noneconomic motives were secondary. Slavery provided a means of supervising the behavior of blacks—especially their activities in groups—but it was not the only such means. And if control was the prime objective, slavery by itself was probably a poor means of achieving it. If the return on owning slaves was less than that on alternative investments, slave owners would be under an incentive to sell off their existing chattels and avoid acquiring others. Only a strong sense of social responsibility on the part of potential individual slave owners would cause them to override their self-interest. Since there appeared to be little social exhortation to retain slaves and no lack of willing purchasers, one must conclude that race control was not an important objective of the slave system in the American South. In addition, the South never organized any other comprehensive system to control slaves, as one would have expected if that had been viewed as a serious problem. Even in the late antebellum period, when fears of abolitionist-incited slave insurrections developed, the level of resources devoted to slave patrols was seldom as large as that devoted to police forces in societies without slaves.

Conrad and Meyer's findings also ruled out the possibility that slavery was unprofitable because southerners valued slaves more than their earnings would dictate. A common variant of this argument saw the South using slaves as a type of conspicuous consumption. Slave ownership was reputed to add a dimension of economic and social status that justified paying a premium. In one sense this association between slaves and prestige is understandable. Slave ownership almost always signified an amount of wealth well above average for the time. The price of a slave typically represented ten times the yearly earnings of a free worker.

But while slaves clearly represented sizable wealth, there is no evidence that the owners were paying extra for the associated prestige. Indeed, at the prices that they commanded in the late antebellum period, slaves were too expensive just to place in conspicuous but unproductive locations. If they were employed in what would be termed luxury uses—say, as household servants—they were usually very old or young or, sometimes, handicapped. In other words, they were the ones least costly to take from other uses. In this context it seems significant that it was usually only on larger farms with a large number of slaves that more than one or two were used as household servants: not only would the owner be likely to afford more household help, but there would be more marginal hands to employ. On smaller farms the slaves often worked with the owner in the fields, not exactly an arrangement designed to showcase conspicuous consumption.

Although Conrad and Meyer's results showed that slavery in general was profitable, some of the calculations in specific examples were troublesome. They often indicated that an investment in a particular slave was not at all, or just barely, profitable. Part of the explanation was the usual variability that occurs in most everyday affairs. Not all efforts (particularly investments in slaves) turn out as expected—some are better, some worse, than anticipated. Moreover, even investments that are profitable over the long run can fall short in a particular year. But the factor that made the profitability calculations for slaves even more uncertain than usual was the manner in which the prices of slaves were determined. They always tended to adjust in such a manner that slavery remained profitable, but only just marginally so.

The key to understanding the process is to recognize that the price of a slave was variable and continuously determined (at least in principle) by the attractiveness of slaves relative to other investments. If, for example, the net return on a slave appeared to be lower than that on other investments, potential purchasers would be drawn away from slaves and their price would fall. As the price of slaves fell, the amount earned relative to that price would rise. If the process proceeded long enough, the percentage return would rise to the level of that of comparable investments. An analogous process would occur if the returns on slaves were higher than those on competitive investments. Investors would shift toward acquiring these attractive assets, but in the process they would bid up the prices of those assets until the rate of return on them was pushed down to that of comparable investments. The latter process indicates why historians have never been able to find instances where slavery was exceptionally profitable. As soon as such circumstances began to develop, the self-interest of potential investors would reduce the returns back to the normal level.

This mechanism of price formation also explains the long-term upward trend in slave prices. As a general rule labor in the American economy has become more productive over time. This is primarily the result of improved technology and better training (and much less a consequence of how ambitious the workers are). The productivity of slaves appears to have increased in a parallel fashion. As a consequence potential owners would experience rising incomes from investments in slaves and—assuming that the percentage return on alternative investments did not rise as rapidly—bid up their prices until that extra return was fully incorporated.

The rise in slave prices over time illustrates why slavery was profitable. The returns from the ownership of a slave above and beyond the expenses of maintenance were positive. And those expenses included not only current costs but also the longer-term expenses of raising young slaves to the age at which they began to pay their own way. (In the rural antebellum South, which had low living costs and numerous opportunities to use different skills, that crossover point was relatively young, perhaps eight to ten years of age.) Consequently, slavery was not only profitable, in that it paid to use the existing slave population, but also was viable for the long term because it paid to support and encourage subsequent generations of slaves.

This last point bears directly on the contention, once frequently heard, that the Civil War was not necessary to eliminate slavery, because it would have died out on its own. By excluding outside political or legal pressures, "on its own" meant, in effect, predominantly economic forces. For slavery to die out, it would cease to be viable, which is to say that the earnings from slaves would fall below the level necessary to support them over a lifetime. In such circumstances one would expect the price of slaves to fall and, when slavery ceased to be viable, reach zero. At such a point slaves would be given away to any taker or, since there would be no reason for others to want slaves, simply freed and turned out on their own.

This scenario is far removed from what seemed to be the case just prior to the Civil War. The price of slaves appeared to increase as before. Granted, the South was to face some difficult adjustments ahead, whether or not the Civil War occurred. In the antebellum period the South had been in the fortunate position of specializing in a few staples, particularly cotton, that were growth sectors at that time. In the latter half of the nineteenth century, the inevitable slackening of demand occurred, intensified by the lack of alternative opportunities within the region. For both whites and blacks, whether the latter were free or slave, it meant a slowdown in the growth of income, not total collapse of existing opportunities. The "self-destruction thesis" regarding slavery would have required not only total collapse but also a nearly complete impossibility of shifting slaves to other activities. The position is certainly based on a very naive approach to human behavior. The best indication we have of the prospects of slavery in the absence of the Civil War or other major constraints is the estimate by Robert Fogel and Stanley Engerman. They project that, by 1890, there would have been an increase in the average price of slaves of more than 50 percent over the 1860 level.

The economic conditions reflected in the rising prices of slaves over time also were evident within the structure of slave prices. The correlation of prices to age is an obvious example. For a given type of slave labor, prices rose with age up to some point in early adulthood, then decreased. The result was a modified bell-shaped curve in which the slope in the later years was more gradual than in the earlier years. This particular configuration was a direct indication of the present value of all future earnings for a given slave at each age. At birth a slave had the prospect of a full lifetime of earnings. That income, though, would have to be heavily discounted by the length of time the owner would have to wait for it, by the costs of maintaining and training the child, and by the risks of death or injury. As the child matured, he or she would become more experienced and productive, and there would be less time until earnings would begin to accrue to the owner. The price of the slave would rise as these forces continued to increase his or her productivity with age. At some point, typically in the late twenties for a field hand, the effect of aging and the reduction in the remaining lifetime would offset the gains from training and experience. At that time the price of the slave would reach a maximum level, then decline.

The ranges at the ends of the age-price curve provide some interesting clues about the environment facing a typical slave. First, newborn babies commanded a positive price. Southern laws and the self-interest of the owners dictated that an infant would not be sold if its mother was capable of caring for it. In the case of orphans there was an opportunity for price to register their expected value. The existence of a price was a reflection of the viability of slavery in the antebellum South. It was worthwhile for slave owners to acquire young slaves because, even after including the expenses of supporting them through the first unremunerative years, their yield was still positive.

Even though it was prompted mainly by the self-interest of the owners, the positive price for infants had a humane influence on the slaves. It paid owners to provide good care and generally guard the well-being of young slaves. On larger plantations that usually meant some form of daycare center staffed by older women. On farms with fewer slaves, it often meant some release time for mothers with young children, especially regularly scheduled breaks for nursing mothers. Expectant mothers also received special consideration. The reduction in their work load generally went beyond the physical dictates of pregnancy, taking on the dimension of a reward for childbearing.

Slave owners took other, more indirect steps to encourage an expansion of the slave population. Even though southern law did not recognize slave marriages, masters commonly sought to solemnify and encourage permanent nuclear families. The owners appeared to recognize that this environment of social stability and solicitude provided the best encouragement for long-run population growth. Slave histories have contained frequent references to "slave breeding," which is to say that slave owners deliberately manipulated the private lives of their chattels to increase their reproduction. But even given the numerous extant records on American slavery, no such instances have been verified. And that appears understandable when one recognizes that direct interference in the personal lives of the slaves would almost certainly have been counterproductive. Rather, slave owners seem to have sensed that a passive policy of supporting what they thought to be a normal social environment was the most productive practice.

At the other end of the age-price curve, older slaves also commanded a positive price, in most cases right up to the point where they faced imminent death. Again, the pattern was the result of the self-interest of the slave owners. Most older slaves, even when enfeebled or handicapped, could work at some task that produced at least enough to cover the cost of their maintenance. Thus owners had reason to retain and sustain their older slaves. As a result the American slave society had a dimension missing from many other slave experiences, particularly those elsewhere in the western hemisphere. The older slaves provided extended family structures and a continuity of experience that increased the stability and depth of the slave community.

SLAVERY

The economic element so obvious in the price-by-age pattern of slavery also made its influence evident in other aspects of slave pricing. At a given age male slaves generally commanded higher prices than females because the former had an advantage in the heavy work in fields and mills that constituted a large share of slave assignments. For slaves employed in the fields, males typically commanded a premium of 20 to 25 percent at age twenty-five. There was one significant exception to this pattern. Until they reached their late teens, female slaves commanded a price as high as, if not higher than, that of males. This difference reflected the additional income that young females would soon be providing through childbearing. This income, added to that from normal field tasks, continued until the females were in their thirties, but most of this effect on the price of the slave had already been incorporated prior to age thirty. This premium for childbearing is, of course, the next logical adaptation to the positive price of slave infants.

Slave prices also incorporated the special attributes of individual slaves. Liabilities to productive activity were reflected in reductions from the prevailing price for given categories of slaves. The handicapped, sickly, and drunkards were exchanged at large discounts (50 percent or so was not uncommon) from the usual price. (Southern laws, which regulated and recorded slave sales in a manner much like modern real estate transactions, required the seller to reveal any of a specified list of known vices or liabilities at the time of sale. Failure to do so was grounds for invalidating the sale.) Special skills of individual slaves also were incorporated into their prices. The craftsmen, such as carpenters, blacksmiths, coopers, and wheelwrights, commanded substantial premiums. That made it advantageous for owners to encourage their slaves to acquire such skills; such training of course entailed expenses, usually in the form of an apprenticeship. Consequently the age-price curve of skilled slaves had a shape different from that of unskilled workers. Although the prices of skilled slaves reached a higher level, the peak of the curve occurred at a later age. In addition, prices of (future) skilled slaves were often lower than those of the unskilled in their earlier years because much of their time was spent in training rather than in immediately remunerative work.

The lives of skilled slaves differed from those of the unskilled in several other important aspects. By virtue of their specialization they often served a wider clientele than just the home farm. In addition, their work was not suited to the close supervision and crew organization that characterized the life of the majority of slaves who worked in the fields. As a result skilled slaves usually had much more freedom than field hands, and that became an important incentive within the slave system. Not only was having a skill a way for slaves to gain more personal freedom within the slave system; it was also the main avenue by which they might obtain freedom. The usual pattern was for skilled, trusted slaves to be set up as independent contractors by their owners, frequently in a large southern city. The slaves could then purchase themselves (their freedom) out of earnings, or sometimes they were given freedom in the owner's will. Understandably, skilled crafts positions were readily sought by slaves, and owners were able to use such opportunities to provide a strong incentive for performance by the slaves and to reward the most productive.

The pervasiveness of economic forces in slavery that is evident in price patterns extended to other areas as well. Slaves proved to be sufficiently adaptable to be useful in urban and industrial employment, and the number holding such jobs appears to have been sensitive to the relative expense of existing alternatives. Similarly, differences in prices appear to have directed the relocation of slaves that occurred in the antebellum period. Around 1800 the majority of slaves were engaged in tobacco production not far from Chesapeake Bay. By 1860 almost 75 percent of the slaves were employed in cotton production. (This characterization about specialization should be qualified. Because cotton had varying labor requirements over the course of the year, the slaves on cotton plantations actually spent a good portion of their time in other types of work.) Cotton production was concentrated in a belt running across the lower South from South Carolina to eastern Texas.

This shift in production activity was a response to the change in the economic opportunities of the antebellum South resulting from the rapid growth in the demand for cotton, which made the returns to resources in that sector more attractive. To slaveholders this was signified by higher prices for slaves in the lower South than in the tobacco-growing areas of the upper South. The resulting incentive was to shift slaves to the developing cotton areas. But the human element—the fuzzy line between slaves as property and slaves as individuals—made the resource transfer much more complicated than usual. Moving slaves out of an area almost inevitably severed some of their connections with friends and relations. This was likely to be most pronounced in the case of a single slave, who would be a complete stranger in the new area.

This effect could be mitigated by relocating an established group of slaves, thereby maintaining nuclear families as well as keeping many relatives and friends together. This raised the cost of relocation. When an entire plantation was moved—the typical practice—it involved selling the old farm, moving the entire plantation population with baggage and equipment, and, often, clearing land and creating a new plantation in an unfamiliar area. Nevertheless, it was the means whereby the vast majority of slaves was taken to the lower South, 84 percent by the best estimate. It also explains why the difference in prices between slaves in the old and the new parts of the South remained so large throughout the antebellum period. The costs that could result from disrupting the social relations of the slaves were greater. Only the relatively expensive procedure of moving entire groups intact could avoid that expensive disruption.

The pattern of prices and associated practices in slavery that have been described were only high points of what was a very large, highly developed system. The institution of slavery was remarkable—if not always admired. This is made even more apparent when one considers the diverse and complex forces that slavery had to accommodate. Above all, slavery was a property right. But it was applied to the most varied and adaptable of all resources, people. In addition, these resources had interests of their own, so that they could adjust and learn over time. In the first half of the nineteenth century, there was no other economic institution that rivaled it for sophistication. That period marked the beginnings of national commodity markets, such as those for cotton and wheat. Although these markets developed prices for various qualities and future deliveries, they had nothing like the multiple dimensions of prices evident in slavery. In fact, there still is not a system of explicit prices for labor that rivals the comprehensiveness of that of slavery. In recent years economists have devoted considerable study to what they term "human capital"—that is, optimal investments in the education and skills of people. In their search for examples or verification of human capital models, American slavery has proved to be one of the most comprehensive examples.

To someone who has not followed the recent scholarship on slavery, some of the above generalizations must come as a surprise. Although scholars in this area would probably disagree with some of the adjectives employed, most would conclude that slavery was profitable, viable, and strongly shaped by economic forces. This advance frequently has been obscured by a well-publicized controversy over another aspect of slavery, its effect on the well-being of the slaves themselves. This controversy was raised to the level of a large, spirited debate by the publication of Fogel and Engerman's *Time on the Cross* (1974). Part of the book, which provided a great amount of empirical support for the emerging view of the economic nature of slavery, appeared without much challenge. But the sections that argued that slaves were able to obtain good levels of economic well-being and freedom despite slavery were met with heated objections.

The heart of Fogel and Engerman's thesis is that the self-interest of both the slave and the slave owner made certain kinds of mutual accommodation attractive. In order to enlist the slave's cooperation in production, the owner found it worthwhile to create a series of positive incentives—in contrast with the negative incentives, such as whippings, emphasized by traditional accounts. The availability of incentives raised the real income of slaves by augmenting their supplies of food, housing, money, and free time. It also created a hierarchy within which conscientious and talented slaves could be promoted to positions offering greater freedom and income. Hardly any scholar would deny that some of these positive incentives were at work in the antebellum South. The debate centers on the relative size of the rewards. Fogel and Engerman have taken the position that the economic gains from the slave system overall were large and that the share of that output going to the slaves was sufficiently large to make their real income not too far below that of free citizens.

Discussion on this question has not yet reached anything like a consensus because the evidence is not entirely clear-cut. Unlike the case of slave prices, where the records are abundant and the pattern quite clear, there are no comprehensive measures of slave well-being. Until such indexes are available, scholars are free to follow their usual practice in such a situation: advocating the position that most closely fits their own predilections.

While slavery was generally prospering in the antebellum South, one of its essential underpinnings was being eroded elsewhere and would eventually cause the entire institution to collapse. Being a property right, slavery required the protection of the legal system and, because the United States operated under representative governments, ultimately the approval of the populace. Although slavery still commanded the support of a majority of the voters in the slaveholding states as of 1860, support elsewhere had turned to hostility. By 1820 most of the northern states had enacted programs that curtailed local slavery and made its demise inevitable. A similar trend was occurring elsewhere in the hemisphere at about the same time. The major European powers prohibited the transatlantic slave trade and enforced its cessation, then freed the slaves in their own colonies. Other states in the western hemisphere also moved against slavery, so that by 1860 the only areas outside the American South to allow slaves were Brazil and some of the Caribbean islands. In the 1830's the first outside efforts aimed at abolishing southern slavery began. The Liberty party organized antislavery interests in the northern states in 1839. These interests, growing with time, fused with the more broadly based Free-Soil party in 1848. By the 1850's the Republican party represented a clear stand against slavery by a major portion of the population. Its victory in 1860 enlisted the powers of the federal government against slavery.

The South was growing more isolated in its defense of slavery, and by 1860 the future looked increasingly dismal. Yet as of that date the South had nearly $4 billion of wealth in slaves, so a very aggrandized defense of its position appeared warranted. Of all the slave areas in the western hemisphere, it was the only one to resort to armed resistance to protect its investment. Ironically, it was the economic success of American slavery that prompted such a drastic defense and, as a result, such a sudden demise.

BIBLIOGRAPHY

Yoram Barzel, "An Economic Analysis of Slavery," in *Journal of Law and Economics*, 20 (April 1977), is a conceptual explanation of the existence of slavery. John Blassingame, *The Slave Community* (New York, 1972), gives a social history from the vantage of a slave. Alfred H. Conrad and John R. Meyer, "The Economics of Slavery in the Ante Bellum South," in *Journal of Political Economy*, 66 (April 1958), is the seminal work on the economics of slavery. Paul A. David, Herbert G. Gutman, Richard Sutch, Peter Temin, and Gavin Wright, *Reckoning With Slavery* (New York, 1976), has the best of the economic historians' doubts about *Time on the Cross*. David B. Davis, *The Problem of Slavery in Western Culture* (Ithaca, N.Y., 1966), seeks the reasons for the demise of slavery in the modern world. Stanley Engerman, "Some Considerations Relating to Property Rights in Man," in *Journal of Economic History*, 33 (March 1973), discusses slavery as a property right. Robert W. Fogel and Stanley L. Engerman, *Time on the Cross: The Economics of American Negro Slavery* (Boston, 1974), is a widely disputed, but clearly the leading, statement of the economic nature of slavery. Claudia Goldin, "The Economics of Emancipation," in *Journal of Economic History*, 33 (March 1973), gives the incentives at work in emancipation; and *Urban Slavery in the American South, 1820–1860* (Chicago, 1976), shows how urban slavery responds to economic incentives.

Lewis Cecil Gray, *History of Agriculture in the Southern United States to 1860* (Washington, D.C., 1933), is an old but still useful account of American slavery. Ralph Gray and Betty Woods, "The Transition From Indentured to Involuntary Servitude in Colonial Georgia," in *Explorations in Economic History*, 13 (October 1976), discusses how slavery became irresistible in the colonial South. Gerald Gunderson, "The Origin of the American Civil War," in *Journal of Economic History*, 34 (December 1974), discusses how vested interests in slavery might have contributed to the Civil War; and *A New Economic History of America* (New York, 1976), is an economist's view of the economic environment of slavery. William N. Parker, ed., *The Structure of the Cotton Economy of the Antebellum South* (Washington, D.C., 1970), gives important reports on the antebellum economy. Richard H. Sewell, *Ballots for Freedom, Antislavery Politics in the United States, 1837–1860* (New York, 1976), discusses the rise of political antislavery in the North. Kenneth M. Stampp, *The Peculiar Institution: Slavery in the Antebellum South* (New York, 1956), is a still useful account of slavery. Robert S. Starobin, *Industrial Slavery in the Old South* (New York, 1970), maintains that slavery adapted well to industry. Gary M. Walton, ed., "Symposium on *Time on the Cross*," in *Explorations in Economic History*, 12 (Oct. 1975), is a collection of sophisticated critiques of *Time on the Cross*. Gavin Wright, *The Political Economy of the Cotton South* (New York, 1978), uses modern analytic methods to examine the nineteenth-century South.

[*See also* AGRICULTURE IN THE SOUTH; BLACKS; COLONIAL ECONOMY; ECONOMY FROM THE REVOLUTION TO 1815; ECONOMY FROM 1815 TO 1865; FOREIGN TRADE; LAW AND POLITICAL INSTITUTIONS; POPULATION; *and* WORK.]

FARMERS' MOVEMENTS

Theodore Saloutos

ALTHOUGH farmer protests of a local character emerged in the colonial period and on a statewide basis after the American Revolution, broad-based farmers' movements spearheaded primarily by general farmers' organizations and their political offshoots appeared for the first time in the Middle West and the South after the Civil War. The American farmers were slower than the wage earners in organizing for action on a national or sectional basis. This was because the agricultural revolution reached the United States after instead of before the industrial revolution, because of divergent commodity interests, and because the effects of the spread of commercial farming, market-related problems, and technology were felt later. The farmers also were handicapped because they were spread over a wider geographic area, harder to reach for organization purposes, too individualistic and conservative in outlook, and slower to recognize the possible benefits of organized action.

Small and medium-size farmers experienced great difficulty in adapting themselves to highly organized methods of production and distribution. A combination of contributing causes—such as the unwise land policies of the federal government, poor management, bad weather, crop failures, one-crop farming, glutted markets, and the inability to adapt to changing market demand—made farming less profitable, if not downright unprofitable. But the farmers chose to believe they had become the victims of the railroads, the bankers, the middlemen, and the large corporations. They had placed great hopes on the railroads, but they did not receive the higher prices for their products and the good service they had expected; they blamed the bankers and their allies for the lack of capital and credit, the large corporations for placing them at a competitive disadvantage in buying and selling, and an unfair system of taxation that exacted too much from them and too little from the owners of intangibles and the wealthy. In later years the farmers' protests focused more on the disparities in the prices they received for their products and the prices they paid for the goods and services they bought. They were convinced that as an occupational group they were losing the competitive struggle with other groups in the economy.

The life span of the farmers' organizations has varied. The first and the longest-lived is the Grange, the beginnings of which date to 1867. The second oldest is the Farmers' Educational and Cooperative Union, better known as the National Farmers' Union (NFU), which was organized in 1902. The youngest and most influential of the contemporary organizations is the American Farm Bureau Federation (AFBF), founded at Chicago in November 1919.

The goals of the farmers' organizations were to make farming sufficiently attractive and rewarding for the farmers and their children to want to remain in agriculture by giving them greater returns for their efforts, improving the quality of farm life, and upgrading farming as an occupation by placing it on a level comparable with that of industry, business, and the professions. The organizations would accomplish this by getting higher prices for agricultural products, liberal credit facilities, better service and lower rates from the railroads, equitable tax loads, and diversified production. In politics they would seek the regulation of the railroads, the bankers, the middlemen, and their allies. They also would broaden the political base of American society through the direct election of United States senators and the adoption of the Australian ballot and of initiative and referendum.

FARMERS' MOVEMENTS

THE GRANGE

The Grange at first was intended to be a loose organization that would bring together the farmers of the South and the North in a social and fraternal organization that would help to heal the wounds of the Civil War. These early thoughts of reconciling the formerly warring sections of the country soon gave way to a demand for an organization for the social, cultural, and educational uplift of the farmers. Before the depression of the 1870's affected agriculture, the Grange joined the growing campaign to regulate the railroads, the first large corporations.

Scholars have challenged the thesis that the Grangers in the Middle West inspired the initial drive to regulate the railroads at the state level. Granted that the small shippers, town merchants, and other members of the business community were active participants in the crusade—in some instances more so than the farmers—and that the so-called Granger laws were crude, hastily drawn, ineffective, and in need of drastic modification or repeal, the fact still remains that the protests of the farmers—Grangers and non-Grangers alike—were vigorous, constant, and heated. Society at the time was predominantly rural, the values of the towns and many of the larger cities were rural values, and the interests of the small businessmen, mercantile firms, and other nonfarm groups were not very far removed from what the farmers believed were their best interests. The farmers were needed allies, if not necessarily always the leaders, in the drive for regulatory action. The more conservative leaders in later years were embarrassed by the Grangers' role in trying to regulate the railroads, but they could not deny what the Grange had done.

Pressure for cooperative action at the business level had become great within the Grange by 1874; the principle of "buying together, selling together, and in general acting together for mutual protection, as the occasion may require" had become a leading objective. Efforts were made at the local level "to bring producers and consumers, farmers and manufacturers, into the most direct and friendly relations . . . possible." Cooperative stores sought to lessen retail margins and to effect economies in purchasing; farmer-owned grain elevators and livestock shipping associations attempted to decrease marketing costs and give the farmers a larger share of the consumer's dollar. Although these and other ventures, such as Granger attempts to manufacture farm machinery and implements, sewing machines, wagons, and other farmer needs, were unsuccessful, the farmers' mutual life insurance companies enjoyed remarkable success from the start. By 1880 nearly all cooperative efforts had failed, except fire insurance companies, the business exchanges, and agencies for the pooling of orders to buy in bulk. These failures hurt the reputation of the order, especially in the Middle West, where it had acquired a large following.

Efforts were made to lighten the tax burden of the landowning farmers, to acquire a more abundant supply of farm labor, to lower tariffs on goods that farmers needed, and to collect accurate statistical data to assist farmers in planting and marketing. Some local Granges even sought a curtailment in the production of cotton as a means of influencing prices.

Critics also complained that agricultural colleges spent too much time and money on academic offerings that turned farm youth away from the farms. They sought the separation of these agricultural colleges from universities, hoping that such separation would give the colleges greater freedom to teach courses that were more practical for farm youth. College administrations and curricula in Ohio, California, and other states were investigated; and during their first flush of enthusiasm for educational reform, Granger schools were organized in some states.

The Grangers also sought to promote a better life for the farmer and his family. Social gatherings were welcome in a day when rural telephones, free mail deliveries, and good highways were unknown. The wives and daughters found the picnics, barbecues, and other social activities joyful and relaxing. Since the ranks of the Grange were open to women on the same basis as to men, the order might also be considered a pioneer in women's rights.

The Grange began to decline during the mid-1870's because of: unwise recruiting methods that brought into the organization farmer and nonfarmer members who were ill-informed about its objectives; poor business management; failure to deliver the benefits that many had expected from membership; the depression of the 1870's; internal dissension; and a decline in the payment of dues. At its peak the Grange claimed about 800,000 members. Attempts to revive the Grange during the 1880's and 1890's brought great disillusionment to those who still hoped the order would regain its earlier prominence. The largest concentration of Grange membership after 1900 was in the states east of the Mississippi River and in the Far West.

In substance, the Grange pioneered in the attempt to instill into the farmers an appreciation of the importance of organized action. It stressed the need for the teaching of a practical, vocational type of agriculture to young people in the agricultural colleges, advocated cooperative marketing and purchasing, sought the social and cultural advancement of the farmers, and served as a model for such contemporary organizations as the Agricultural Wheel, the Louisiana Farmers' Union, the Farmers' Alliance, and the National Farmers' Union.

Often referred to as a rural Masonic order, the Grange enjoyed a long life because of the prestige it had acquired through the years and still maintains today, the appeal it had to the better-established family-oriented farmers who prized the social and cultural opportunities it offered, the reputation it earned as a stabilizing influence in rural life, and the frequent recognition it received from the federal government.

THE FARMERS' ALLIANCE AND THE POPULISTS

The Farmers' Alliance, which did not enjoy the long life of the Grange, achieved its peak membership and activities in the late 1880's and early 1890's, likewise in the South and the Middle West. Having little that was original in its objectives and devoid of the ritualistic appeal of the Grange, it appealed to small white farmers who felt menaced by the encroachments of industry on rural society, the seizure of public lands by the large corporations, the investments of foreign syndicates in America, and the dangers—real or imagined—posed by the arrival of immigrants who threatened to convert the United States into the "cesspool of Europe." Basically, the Farmers' Alliance was a conservative organization with leaders who believed that the problems generated by industrial capitalism could be resolved within the political and economic framework of the existing system.

The early history of the Farmers' Alliance, unlike that of the Grange, is complex. Three different organizations, national in name only, bore the Farmers' Alliance label: the Southern Farmers' Alliance, the National Farmers' Alliance, and the Colored Farmers' National Alliance and Cooperative Union. All three were antimonopolistic in philosophy and paid tribute to the virtues of an agricultural, as opposed to an industrial, society.

The Southern Farmers' Alliance came into existence after the Texas Farmers' Alliance merged with the Louisiana Farmers' Union to form the National Farmers' Alliance and Cooperative Union (NFA&CU). In 1888 the NFA&CU united with the Agricultural Wheel to form the National Farmers' Alliance and Laborers' Union (NFA&LU); the next year the NFA&LU adopted the name National Farmers' Alliance and Industrial Union (NFA&IU). The National Farmers' Alliance, also known as the Northern or Northwestern Alliance (and the smaller of the two alliances), made an unsuccessful effort to bring all the alliances into one organization. The Colored Farmers' National Alliance and Cooperative Union (CFNA&CU), on the other hand, came into being because of the liberal charter-issuing practices of the Northern Farmers' Alliance, not because the Southern Alliance members wanted to organize the black farmers. Once organized, the CFNA&CU, owing to geographic and economic considerations, became loosely identified with the Southern Alliance.

Especially qualified for membership in the Southern Farmers' Alliance were "honest-to-goodness dirt farmers"; rural preachers, teachers, doctors, and mechanics who toiled for a living; and farm editors who knew "the blessings of a healthy agriculture." Those disqualified from membership included

> ... merchants, merchants' clerks, or anyone who owns an interest in drygoods, hardware, furniture, drugstore, or any other mercantile business, unless said member is selected to take charge of a Co-operative Farmers' and Laborers' Union store; no lawyers who have a license to practice law in a county, district or supreme court; no one who owns stock in any National, State, or other banking association [Saloutos and Hicks 1960, p. 75].

FARMERS' MOVEMENTS

Reliable membership figures are unavailable or fragmentary. The Southern Farmers' Alliance claimed in 1888 that it had 419 county units, 9,629 suballiances, 362,970 members (of whom 42,496 were women), and 350 organizers. Early in 1889 it claimed some 12,000 suballiances and 700,000 members; and in 1890 its membership was put at three million. Accurate information on the social and economic status of the farmers joining the Southern Farmers' Alliance is unavailable, but the presumption is that most of them were small producers in the lower income brackets. Membership in the Northern Farmers' Alliance was smaller than in its southern counterpart and probably never reached more than 200,000 or 300,000.

The organization of the Colored Farmers' National Alliance in Houston County, Texas, in 1886 was inspired by Milton George, publisher of the *Western Rural* and driving force behind the Northern Alliance; but the task of organizing the blacks into a separate and secret order was assumed by R. M. Humphrey, a white clergyman who was a former missionary. Organizing the blacks was received as a sort of second emancipation in some quarters and with outright resistance and horror in others. The Southern Farmers' Alliance resolved in 1888 that the white alliances should bar blacks from membership and that the blacks should bar whites from membership in their organization, but it left the enforcement of this decision in the hands of the individual state organizations. In late 1890 the Colored Farmers' National Alliance claimed 1.2 million members, some 700,000 of them males, in all states of the South and in some border states of the North.

The Southern Farmers' Alliance fought an uphill battle in trying to build its marketing and purchasing agencies. These agencies needed capital and credit, good business managers, and a backlog of experience to guide them during their first years. Besides being exposed to prosecution under the antitrust laws, they were hampered by the hostility of farmers who had lost money in earlier ventures, internal dissension, the opposition of town merchants and wholesalers who feared that the success of the farmers would drive them out of business, and the apprehensions of a general public that was frightened by labor disturbances and the cries of socialism (and could be aroused to combat the legitimate needs of the farmers).

Meanwhile, agitation for political action began to grow. Many argued that a program chiefly of an economic character in a period when politics was becoming a primary vehicle for reform was both inadequate and unrealistic. Obtaining equality in Congress and in state legislative bodies was just as important as obtaining equality in the marketplace, and the farmers were obligated to share in the shaping of public policy.

The political agrarians developed a twofold strategy: one, to make the farmers believe they had been betrayed, had had their rights trampled on, and had had their dignity as human beings insulted; and two, to drive home the argument that the government was dominated by lawyers who represented corporations, railroads, bankers, middlemen, insurance firms, and other groups that viewed the farmers as legitimate prey. Only when farmers elected farmers or public officials who were sympathetic to their needs would Congress pass laws that farmers could accept as being in their best interests. The more militant Alliance members distrusted the Republicans and Democrats, and wanted a new political party.

The Populist party, which was organized in Cincinnati in May 1891, had the support of farmers, free-silver advocates, former Greenbackers, disciples of Henry George and Edward Bellamy, labor leaders, and other reformers who wanted to wrest control of the government from the special interests and return it to the people, where it belonged. Populist spokesmen believed that a platform seeking the free and unlimited coinage of silver, an increase in the amount of money in circulation, a graduated income tax, the secret ballot, the direct election of United States senators, a shorter workday, and greater recognition for women would help accomplish this.

Although the election of 1892 gave the Populists encouragement, it was evident that the party was likely to remain a sectional party at best. Half the votes received by James Baird Weaver, the Populist presidential candidate in 1892, came from the Rocky Mountain and Far West states because of the special interest the voters in these states had in silver, and not because of any broad commitment to Populism. The vote for the Populist slates in the South was small, and even smaller in the states east of the Mississippi River. Populist failures in the eastern half of the United States may be attributed to the facts that agriculture in that part of the country was more diversified, instead of the one-crop variety found in the South (cotton) or Middle West (wheat)—the farmers therefore lacked a common commodity interest around which to organize—and that the eastern farmers suffered from the expansion of agriculture into the West, where production was cheaper.

The farmers failed to give the Populist party the support that the Populists hoped for in 1896. Farmers who believed in free silver but had doubts about the Populist party had the option of voting for William Jennings Bryan, the standard-bearer of both the Populist and the Democratic parties, on the Democratic ticket, which many did; but Bryan still lost. Sectional differences and conflicting commodity interests—wheat versus cotton—made it difficult to weld the farmers into an effective political organization. Nor were the reactions of the wage earners, organized and unorganized, conducive to the formation of an effective farmer-labor alliance. The wage earners wanted higher wages, lower prices, and better working conditions as soon as possible. Why should they campaign for the free and unlimited coinage of silver when that inevitably meant higher prices for the food they bought?

Many farmers had been taught that free silver would bring them higher farm prices, lower interest rates, and a greater ability to discharge their debts, but free silver went down to defeat in 1896. The Republicans believed that protection for industry was more important than free silver, and the Republican tradition was still strong in the agricultural West. Financial, commercial, and industrial interests with international affiliations were opposed to free silver at a time when the leading European nations were on a gold basis. The rise in farm prices beginning in 1897 also eliminated one of the forces that had given the farmers some cohesiveness.

THE FARMERS' UNION AND THE EQUITY

As a remedy for low prices, curtailing the size of the crop and withholding a portion of it from the market attracted some attention during the first decade of the twentieth century, as it had during the 1890's. Renewed encouragement was given this effort by the American Society of Equity (ASE), founded at Indianapolis, Indiana, in 1902 and by the National Farmers' Union (NFU), also founded in 1902 (in Point, Texas). The NFU and the ASE had two things in common: both emerged in a period of rising farm prices; and both sought to raise prices, at least in the initial stages, through the restriction of production and the withholding of crops from market.

In the beginning the NFU gained most of its members in the cotton belt, while the ASE, after enjoying temporary success in the tobacco fields of Kentucky and Tennessee, gained a firmer footing in Wisconsin, Minnesota, North Dakota, South Dakota, and Montana. The NFU experienced a period of rapid growth after the formation of the national union in 1905 and in 1910 claimed a membership of three million—a rather dubious claim. Determined efforts were made in 1906, 1907, 1908, and later years to raise cotton prices by restricting the cotton acreage and withholding a portion of the crop from market. Local warehouses were established to store the cotton being held by the farmers. Group buying and selling, better farming, and getting farmers to produce more of the things they needed on the farm (and thus not to rely as heavily on the merchants for these needs) were encouraged. Better rural schools, the establishment of an NFU university, the restriction of immigration from southern and eastern Europe, Africa, and Asia, the protection of the farmers from false advertising, the enactment of a parcel post law, and the creation of a Division of Markets in the United States Department of Agriculture also were sought.

The demise of the NFU in the South had causes quite similar to those that brought about the decline of the Grange and Farmers' Alliance: rank opportunism on the part of some leaders; the lack of a common bond of interest between the more and less substantial farmers; poor business management; and general dissatisfaction with the accomplishments of the organization. The acreage-curtailment and crop-withholding efforts of the NFU seemed to benefit farmers who did not curtail their production and withhold their crops from market more than those who did, and poor management of the business associations and rapid expansion brought disastrous consequences.

As a rival the ASE never equaled the NSU in membership, in the scope of its activities, or in longevity. The first serious efforts to put the ASE program into action occurred in the tobacco fields of Kentucky and western Tennessee. But a land tenure system that made it difficult for tenant farmers to join the campaign, the slow, lethargic, and indifferent farmers, the opposition of the "tobacco trust," and the continued need for financial assistance posed numerous problems. The unwillingness of many tobacco farmers to eliminate a portion of their crop in 1907–1908 brought retaliation, coercion, and violence. Most of the burley crop was eliminated and higher prices were obtained in the marketplace, but at too high a cost in terms of personal hardship and terror. Most growers were therefore reluctant to participate in future campaigns to raise prices.

Longer-lived were the accomplishments of the ASE in Wisconsin, where by 1920 it claimed an estimated membership of 40,000 and the distinction of having become the largest farmers' organization in the state. Working closely in many rural communities with the followers of Senator Robert M. La Follette, the Scandinavians, and other sympathizers, the ASE in Wisconsin pioneered in establishing local livestock cooperative marketing associations, helping organize the small cheese producers to sell their product, passing legislation to protect cooperatives from prosecution under the antitrust laws, and having a constructive influence on the organized farmers of the state. A politically ambitious president of the state society and an equally ambitious group anxious to promote cooperative buying and selling on a mass basis helped bring about its downfall.

Even more significant was the pioneering work of the Equity Cooperative Exchange (ECE), an independent subdivision of the ASE, on the terminal grain market of Minneapolis. Organized in 1908 and working primarily among the spring wheat growers of Minnesota, North Dakota, South Dakota, and Montana, the ECE believed that cooperative marketing of grain on a local basis could not prevent abuses on the all-important terminal market. The ECE began an aggressive bid for the support of the spring wheat growers in 1912 and encountered the hostility of the Minneapolis Chamber of Commerce, the leaders of which feared the growth of the cooperative grain marketing movement. Later the ECE lent its support to the campaign to build a state-owned terminal elevator in North Dakota. The defeat of this proposal helped prepare the stage for the appearance of the Nonpartisan League, a political movement of serious dimensions.

Although the appearance of the Nonpartisan League (NPL) in 1915 relegated the ECE to a position of secondary importance among the farmers in the region, some of the ECE leaders were active in the formative stages of the NPL. The growing wartime demands for wheat and the adoption of a more decentralized system of marketing helped the ECE become an important terminal marketing agency in the years immediately after World War I. Unfortunately, unwise expansion, the drop in wheat prices in the early 1920's, a management that was better equipped to fight the "grain trust" than to conduct a successful grain business in a period of declining prices and mounting indebtedness, and bitter infighting contributed to its decline, its eventual placement in the hands of receivers, and finally the transfer of its remaining assets to the business affiliates of the Farmers' Union in the Northwest.

The NPL owed much of its early growth to the preliminary work in North Dakota of the Socialist party, which had been trying to organize the farmers of the state, as had the ECE. The actions of the party were based on the theory that cooperative marketing would never bring about the defeat of the "grain and milling trust" that farmers believed was responsible for the low prices they received. The only answer to their dilemma was the construction of state-owned industries that the farmers controlled. Employing an artful group of radical writers and thinkers capable of finding a least common denominator among their readers and listeners, using few themes, and repeating them untiringly, NPL leaders advised the farmers to operate through the dominant political parties and do anything else that would further the cause.

A slate of candidates for state offices was nominated, mostly on the Republican ticket, in the spring of 1916, and in the fall elections every elective state office, except one, was won by the NPL-endorsed candidates. Three others who believed in state-owned utilities were sent to the North Dakota State Supreme Court. As a result of the 1916 elections, the NPL had control of every branch of the state government except the senate. Despite this success it was not until 1919 that the industrial program of the NPL was finally approved by the North Dakota legislature. It provided for an industrial commission to head the state-owned industries, the organization of the Bank of North Dakota, the construction of a state-owned mill and elevator, and cheaper homes for farmers and workers.

This major NPL victory was followed by vigorous criticism of the state industrial program from within the NPL itself as well as from without, and finally the holding of a special election in 1921 that brought about the recall of Governor Lynn J. Frazier and Attorney General William Frederick Lemke, and passage of the control of the all-important industrial commission into the hands of the opposition. Moderate and conservative elements viewed the NPL program for state-owned industries as the American version of the Soviet experiment and as a warning to do something about the mounting unrest among the farmers of the country.

THE AMERICAN FARM BUREAU FEDERATION

Earlier efforts to consolidate the activities of competing farm groups into one coordinating agency that would speak for all farmers were repeated with the formation of both the Farmers' National Headquarters and the National Board of Farm Organizations, but proved ineffective. Most farmers were unaffiliated at the time, the rural population of the country was declining, agriculture was receiving a dwindling share of the national income, the cooperative movement at the local level was thriving and a need was felt for the coordination of these local associations into state and even national organizations, and above all else something had to be done to counteract the social and industrial unrest that was plaguing the country. The American Farm Bureau Federation (AFBF), created at Chicago in 1919, appeared to many to be the kind of organization capable of providing the leadership needed to carry the farmers through the troublous postwar years.

The county farm bureaus in the early years had been committed in theory to the principle of bigger and better production. Philosophically, the work of the county agents was a part of the efforts of Seaman A. Knapp, who in the first decade of the twentieth century tried to help the farmers of the South combat the boll weevil and solve some of the problems of production. In the North and West, where more farmers owned their farms, agriculture was more diversified, tenant farming by blacks was unknown, and some of the most pressing needs were for more efficient methods of distribution and production, the county agents assumed a more independent course. Financial assistance was given the county agents by some of the states, the counties, and private business groups, but the passage of the Smith-Lever Act in 1914 placed rural extension work and the county agents, whose task was to disseminate agricultural knowledge, on a firmer and more permanent footing.

The preamble of the AFBF constitution stated that the object of the organization was "to correlate and strengthen the farm bureaus of the several states and to promote, protect, and represent the business, social, economic, and educational interests of the farmers of the nation." Differences soon emerged over whether the AFBF was to help the farmers by consolidating their cooperative marketing activities or whether it would confine itself to educational activities.

Cooperative marketing, especially of grain and livestock on a large-scale basis, assumed a very prominent part of AFBF activities from 1920 to 1924. Amid differences over the role and influence that marketing groups outside the AFBF were going to have and the course that the marketing programs were going to take, the organization of the short-lived United States Grain Growers Incorporated was announced. Poor management, controversy over policy, intrigue, and opposition soon brought about its failure.

Efforts to launch a large-scale livestock marketing association under AFBF auspices also stirred up controversy and dissatisfaction between growers in the "corn/hog belt" and range states on matters relating to the relationships of

FARMERS' MOVEMENTS

the newly formed group to the existing livestock associations and the general farmers' organizations.

By 1924 AFBF leaders expressed a preference for the McNary-Haugen plan, which sought to narrow the disparity created by the low prices the farmers received for what they sold and the high prices they paid for the goods and services they bought. The leaders now believed that McNary-Haugen provided a more realistic approach to the problems of the farmers, who had become the victims of unfair trade practices, marketing agreements, discriminatory tariffs, embargoes, and other business activities. Although two non-farmers, George N. Peek and Hugh S. Johnson, who had seen their farm machinery business wither away in the postwar depression, had popularized the ideas that agriculture was entitled to as much protection from foreign competition as industry was and that farmers had to have a "fair exchange value" for their products if they were to survive, it was the AFBF, the Grange, and the Farmers' Union that spearheaded the drive for the enactment of the McNary-Haugen plan into law.

Despite warnings from the farmers' lobby, the frequent conferences, the public pronouncements, and the threats of impending disaster if the farmers failed to receive the necessary protection, President Calvin Coolidge vetoed the McNary-Haugen bill twice after it had been passed by the House and the Senate. Secretary of Agriculture William M. Jardine defended the existing protective tariff system, denied that all tariffs discriminated against the farmers, urged the modification of those that did, and endorsed large-scale cooperative marketing and the establishment of a federal farm board.

The AFBF, the Grange, and the Farmers' Union (the "big three"), embittered by the defeat of McNary-Haugen and the export debenture plans—the latter a simplified version of the former, sponsored by the Grange—issued a declaration after the election of Herbert Hoover as president stating what they believed were the essentials of any workable farm program: it had to provide for an effective tariff on agricultural products, for production and surplus controls, and for farmer ownership of the agricultural machinery established by the federal government.

FARMER ORGANIZATIONS AND THE FARM BOARD

The general farmer organizations and lesser farm groups were consulted in the selection of personnel for the Farm Board authorized by the Agricultural Marketing Act of 1929, which provided for a revolving fund of $500 million to encourage large-scale cooperative marketing associations and stabilization operations. The appointment of Alexander Legge, president of the International Harvester Corporation, as chairman of the Farm Board drew fire because of his big-business ties. None of the Farm Board appointees were ranking officers of the AFBF, the Grange, or the Farmers' Union, but most had been or were identified with prominent cooperative associations or agriculture. The "big three" were represented at meetings that resulted in the formation of the Farmers' National Grain Corporation, the American Cotton Cooperative Association, and the National Livestock Marketing Association under the sponsorship of the Farm Board.

Opinion within the general farmer organizations on the Farm Board changed from what it had been in 1928–1929. Sam Thompson, the national president of the AFBF and formerly an outspoken advocate of the McNary-Haugen plan, in 1930 urged county farm bureaus to unite against those forces that sought to abolish the Farm Board. After some midwestern Grangers asked that the Farm Board be discontinued because it brought few tangible benefits to the farmers, the national master announced that the Grange would cease its criticisms until Congress convened the following year. The differences within the Farmers' Union were even greater. John A. Simpson and the anti–Farm Board faction within the NFU gained control of the national organization in 1930 and continued their attacks on the Farm Board, while the pro–Farm Board faction, which was in control of some of the state unions, designated Charles E. Huff, the deposed national president, as its official spokesman and served notice on the anti–Farm Board faction that it would not tolerate interference with the marketing machinery. Shortly thereafter Huff became president of the Farmers' National Grain Corporation, and the marketing activities of the pro–Farm Board group within the Farmers' Union acquired new life.

FARMERS' MOVEMENTS

Despite Farm Board efforts to stem the tide of declining prices, huge surpluses of wheat and cotton kept accumulating and farm prices kept falling. Early in 1932 the heads of the "big three" drafted a platform that they said they endorsed, but by the end of the year the AFBF, the Grange, and the Farmers' Union were campaigning for their own programs. The Grange once more advanced the export debenture plan; the AFBF, the equalization fee; and the Simpson-headed NFU, "cost of production plus a reasonable profit" and the remonetization of silver.

THE FARM STRIKE

The "farm strike" or Farm Holiday Movement, as it was officially known, represented a militant reaction by members of the Iowa Farmers' Union to the Farm Board and the anticipated New Deal farm program. It was headed by Milo Reno and militant members of the Farmers' Union who wanted "cost of production plus a reasonable profit" for the farmers. These and other efforts, using first peaceful persuasion and then violence, dramatized the plight of the farmers but did not resolve their problems. Growing opposition to the farm strike, sagging interest among the strikers, passage of the Agricultural Adjustment Act (AAA) in the spring of 1933, and fear that the launching of a national strike at a time when the AAA was struggling to get off the ground was likely to create more ill will than goodwill for the farmers resulted in postponement of the strike and the adoption of a "wait-and-see" policy.

FARMER ORGANIZATIONS AND THE NEW DEAL

Parity, the chief aim of the AFBF and the other farmer organizations that supported the AAA, was a modernized version of "making the tariff on agriculture effective" and "achieving equality for the farmers." Parity sought a better balance among agriculture, industry, and labor in the marketplace. In theory, parity aimed to bring to the farmers a purchasing power equivalent to that which they enjoyed in 1909–1914, when the prices they received for their goods were believed to have been in better balance with the prices of the goods and services they bought. AFBF claims to have originated the parity concept and the processing tax were exaggerated, but it did support the concepts during the Farm Board years, as did other farm groups. Most credit for seeking to achieve this price balance goes to Milburn L. Wilson, a former professor of agricultural economics at Montana State College who worked indefatigably for the Domestic Allotment Plan in the pre–New Deal days.

The criticism of organized labor voiced by the AFBF reflected the thinking of many, if not most, farmers who complained that the wage and hour demands of labor drew many farm workers from the farms into the cities in search of higher wages, made it difficult for farmers to get reliable workers at wages they could afford to pay, increased the prices of the goods and services the farmers bought, and resulted in critical labor stoppages. The AFBF also found fault with the unemployment relief programs and asked that farm labor be exempt from the provisions of the National Labor Relations Act and the Social Security Act.

The AFBF likewise sought a long-range federal land policy that was consistent with the efforts of the New Deal to restrict production and conserve the soil. It opposed the placement of additional lands under cultivation and favored the retirement of marginal lands and the preservation of as much land as possible for use by future generations. It asked that long-range programs be placed under the control of the land-grant colleges and the Extension Service; that lands withdrawn from cultivation be used for public parks, playgrounds, forest rehabilitation, watershed protection, irrigation purposes, grazing, game preserves, and erosion control; and that state and local government units deprived of tax moneys by the withdrawal of land from cultivation be compensated by the federal treasury.

The AFBF also singled out the Farm Security Administration (FSA) for severe criticism because it encouraged production by the "low-and-medium income" farmers and proposed policies counter to AAA objectives. There also were other reasons for opposition: the FSA sought to elevate the status of the blacks in the South; it competed with the Extension Service; and it encouraged the formation of cooperatives that would compete with those already organized.

The growing disenchantment of the AFBF

with the New Deal was worsened in 1936 by the appointment as AAA administrator of Howard R. Tolley, who was less sensitive to political pressures than his predecessor had been, and by the growing tendency of the New Dealers to consult with the more moderate elements within the NFU.

NFU support of the New Deal increased from 1937 on, when the moderates wrested control of the organization from the extremists, who had been as denunciatory of the New Deal as they had been of the Farm Board. The NFU maintained friendly relations with organized labor, was critical of the link between the Extension Service and the AFBF, and supported the FSA, but made no serious effort to organize the farmers in the South during the New Deal, on the ground that it could not compromise its liberalism and remain silent on the race question.

The Grange, more than either the AFBF or the NFU, maintained friendly relations with the federal government from 1933 to 1940 even though it singled out certain phases of the New Deal for criticism. It proclaimed the AAA to be of real benefit to the farmers and asked for amendments to strengthen it; praised the Farm Credit Administration, asked for bipartisan supervision to prevent it from being used for partisan purposes, and urged Congress to give it continued financial support; approved of crop insurance and soil conservation programs but asked that they be kept separate from the program for production control; warmly endorsed the Rural Electrification Administration; and asked for the rigid enforcement of the Taylor Grazing Act, which denied entry to all unreserved and unappropriated lands in the public domain so that operators of family-size farms and resident owners would have priorities in grazing rights over the large, nonresident owners. It also expressed sympathy in the initial stages for the FSA, on the theory that the FSA was designed to aid tenants in genuine need. It later turned against the FSA on the ground that it was becoming a close working ally of the NFU in the way that the Extension Service had become an ally of the AFBF.

The Grange further asked that the Smith-Lever Act be amended to forbid contributions to the Extension Service from private citizens, chambers of commerce, farmer organizations, or comparable groups; to restrict its funding to public sources; and to make its services accessible to all engaged in agricultural pursuits, without regard to farm organization affiliations. Grange opposition to the reciprocal trade treaties was based on the ground that they were more injurious than beneficial to the farmers; and, like the AFBF, the Grange asked organized labor to be more considerate of the special needs of the farmers. The Grange also sought legislation that would make it impossible for aliens ineligible for citizenship to lease or own land under the name of minor children, and pressed for a constitutional amendment that would rescind the citizenship rights gained by birth of children whose parents were ineligible for citizenship.

Governmental policies affecting agriculture during World War II, unlike those during World War I, were directly or indirectly influenced by the major farmer organizations and by groups such as the National Council of Farm Cooperatives and the National Milk Producers Federation.

THE YEARS AFTER WORLD WAR II

Half of the AFBF membership was in the Midwest and one-third in the South when World War II ended. Its leaders believed that most of the basic farm legislation was adequate, that adjustments would have to be made from time to time, and that it was important that the laws be administered properly. In the closing stages of the war, leading agricultural economists and spokesmen for the land-grant colleges and universities questioned the feasibility of continuing support prices based on the parity formula, and as an alternative recommended that prices be allowed to reach a competitive level. After taking note of these criticisms, the AFBF reaffirmed its support of the existing price mechanism until a new, fairer, and more defensible formula than the existing one was developed, and opposed plans for unlimited production.

The AFBF differed with the Department of Agriculture (USDA) over its handling of the direct action programs (that is, the Farm Security Administration), the degree of governmental control it exercised, and the consumer-mindedness it had developed. It wanted the food stamp plan financed from relief rather than agricultural surplus disposal funds. The AFBF was at odds with the AAA over policy when the AFBF and the Extension Service, with whom the AFBF had a close working relationship, were accused of being more concerned with the wealthier farmers than the others, and again when the AFBF sought loan rates higher than the prescribed ones on the accumulations of grains and stock. AFBF plans to decentralize the administration of the agricultural programs and to transfer them out of the USDA never received serious consideration from either the president or Congress.

The Grange sponsored policies comparable with those of the AFBF. Its membership after World War II was placed at about 800,000, the highest it had been in about seventy years; it was largest in the East, Northeast, and Far West, and smallest in the states in which the AFBF was the strongest, except for New York and Ohio. It sought the inclusion of the cost of farm labor in the parity calculations and the substitution of the average of the preceding five or ten years for the 1909–1914 base period. The Grange was more apprehensive of the New Deal social legislation than either the AFBF or the NFU was, less interested in the question of international trade, and in favor of the extension of Social Security coverage to farmers and farm workers. It found unsatisfactory the proposal for free-market prices unsupplemented by government payments to maintain the farmers' income, and continued to press for the separation of the Extension Service from the AFBF.

Meanwhile, the NFU, influenced by a group of younger men headed by James Patton, launched an aggressive but unsuccessful membership drive in the South and introduced changes in the NFU constitution that enabled the organization to function more effectively in shaping national policies. The effectiveness of the NFU in supporting or opposing legislation was due to its cooperation with labor unions, churches, and other social action groups. During the war the NFU supported the use of subsidies instead of urging a rise in price ceilings to prevent increases in living costs, and supported the extension of price controls every time the administration asked for their extension. It endorsed government planning in general, and food and agricultural programs that required large amounts of government direction and control. Unlike the AFBF and the Grange, which usually adopted positions comparable with those of the National Association of Manufacturers, the United States Chamber of Commerce, and other larger employer groups, the NFU supported organized labor in the closing stages of the war and in the period of wage adjustments when controls were dropped.

The AFBF, more than either the Grange or the NFU, expanded its business activities during the war years. Each association affiliated with the AFBF sought a more permanent membership by developing business organizations that would save them more than their annual membership dues, and thus caused them to become more business-oriented than farm-oriented.

The big question in the postwar years was not whether guaranteeing prices to the farmers was an appropriate governmental function, but what the level of the loans and the extent of governmental controls were going to be. Price controls had become the key to the farm programs during those years, not acreage adjustments with price-supporting loans, as had been the case before the war.

Many wartime controls on prices, materials, and manpower were reinstated after the forces of North Korea invaded the Republic of Korea in 1950; this aroused widespread criticism and even evasion, and a number of the controls were discontinued while settlement negotiations were in progress in 1953. Ever since he assumed office in 1947, Allen B. Kline, the president of the AFBF, had been an exponent of flexible price supports for agriculture that would slide up and down in relation to crop supplies.

In the early 1960's the AFBF campaigned vigorously for a return to the free-market system that would determine prices and patterns of farm production. In fact, AFBF leaders thought their ideas were gaining ground in Congress when the election of 1964 brought a landslide victory to Lyndon Johnson, who believed that federal assistance was needed to stabilize agriculture, over Barry Goldwater, whose farm policy views were much closer to those of the AFBF.

The continued growth of the AFBF in the postwar years, its vigorous lobbying activities, and its use of political muscle brought criticism from its traditional rival, the NFU, which favored a continuation of government price supports, and others who claimed that many AFBF members were nonfarmers who joined to obtain cheaper insurance or other bargains that members were entitled to buy from its business affiliates. The *Wall Street Journal* observed in 1967: "Today, the state Farm Bureaus cooperatively or on their own operate 12 life insurance companies with assets of $815 million and $6 billion of insurance in force. They also operate 42 companies that write auto, casualty, fire, crop and other policies and have assets of $380 million. The national Farm Bureau runs a company that writes reinsurance for the state affiliate's insurance companies, it has assets of $20,000,000." Membership in the AFBF in 1974 was almost 2 million, more than half of it in the South.

Although the NFU remained a staunch ally of Democratic administrations and advocated farm subsidies and production controls to maintain farm income, it was displeased with the pronouncements of the Johnson administration that fewer farms were needed to feed the nation and that many farms were unsuccessful operations that could not be sustained adequately even with government subsidies. NFU leaders were apprehensive lest the Johnson administration move closer to the position of the AFBF, which wanted production controls phased out in the name of free enterprise.

In March 1965 the NFU joined the AFBF and the Grange in opposing the United States Supreme Court ruling that required reapportionment of state legislatures on the basis of the "one man, one vote" principle, hoping that the setting aside of this ruling would enable the rural interests to continue to dominate one of the houses in the state legislatures. The AFBF conducted a drive encouraging the state legislatures to petition Congress to call a constitutional convention to draw up an amendment that would set aside the Supreme Court ruling.

The National Farmers' Organization (NFO), a relatively new organization, began in 1955 as a protest movement in the drought-stricken counties of southern Iowa and northern Missouri, where hogs and other commodities were selling at low prices. Operating on the theory that the free-enterprise system had been replaced by a managed economy in which industry and organized labor set their own prices, the NFO believed that unless the farmers and ranchers "unite at least 30% of the production in blocks for collective bargaining," the control of agriculture by a few corporations was inevitable. Enrollment of producers and 30 percent of the production would make it possible, in the opinion of the NFO, to obtain "cost-of-production-plus-a-fair-profit" or to hold essential supplies off the market until this price was met. In 1973 the NFO was recruiting college students who had experience in campus demonstrations, had finished their studies, wanted to become part of an organized effort to bring about changes, and had experience in grain marketing, transportation, and affiliated business enterprises. Part of the NFO strategy was not to release too much information about its membership and marketing activities, on the theory that this was part of the bargaining process. (It then had fifty-four area offices and sixty marketing areas in the country.)

The American Agricultural Movement, a loosely knit group of farmers who organized to protest low farm prices and react to what they believed was neglect of their problems by President James E. Carter and Congress, burst into the limelight in late 1977 by threatening to launch a farm strike if their demands for 100 percent parity were not met. Except for an extraordinary ability to attract the attention of the news media and politicians by organizing farmers to circle their tractors around state capitols and release goats and chickens in the halls of Congress, the American Agricultural Movement by the late 1970's had not come forward with anything new in the way of demands or achievements.

The farmers' organizations, despite their unsuccessful efforts to make farming more profitable for the smaller farmers and to stem the flow of people from the farms into the cities, served as spokesmen for those who chose to follow their leadership. Although over the years they waged numerous battles on behalf of what they believed were the legitimate needs and interests of the farmers, and helped to realize such objectives as more liberal credit facilities, support for cooperative marketing, regulatory and price legislation of various sorts, none—with the exception of the short-lived Southern Tenant Farmers' Union—made any attempt to represent the small tenant farmers and the sharecroppers. The AFBF reputedly served the interests of the more successful and better-placed farmers, more so than either the Grange or the NFU; although the Grange had more in common with the AFBF than did the NFU, support for which was confined largely to the Great Plains states. The declining importance of the farm population in American society has had an adverse effect, and organizations such as the AFBF have spread activities such as insurance and other programs to include nonfarmers.

General farmers' organizations, congressmen, and others sympathetic with agriculture were less influential after World War II than they had been before. Agriculture will remain an indispensable source of food and raw materials in the foreseeable future, but politically it also has become relatively less important than industry in American society. The pressing problems after World War II were world peace, military policy, housing, full employment, civil rights, the regulation of industrial and commercial relations, energy, and inflation—not agriculture. The growing concern with famine in overpopulated and underdeveloped nations may trigger a renewed interest in the American farmer and his problems. Even though the farmers continued to exert an influence considerably beyond their numbers after World War II, it is unlikely that their numbers will increase sufficiently in the immediate future to give them and their organizations the preeminence they enjoyed in former years, when the farmers constituted a sizable part of the American population.

BIBLIOGRAPHY

Gladys L. Baker, *The County Agent* (Chicago, 1939), is an illuminating study from the perspective of a student of administration. William J. Block, *The Separation of the Farm Bureau and the Extension Service* (Urbana, Ill., 1960), gives a scholarly treatment of a highly controversial subject. Murray R. Benedict, *Farm Policies of the United States, 1790–1950* (New York, 1953), contains a chapter on farmer organizations from 1870 to 1920, as seen by a farm economist. George Brandsberg, *The Two Sides in NFO's Battle* (Ames, Iowa, 1964), treats antecedents of the NFO, the reasons for its rise, the people behind it, the issues, and the controversies. Solon J. Buck, *The Granger Movement: A Study of Agricultural Organization and Its Political, Economic, and Social Manifestations, 1870–1880* (Cambridge, Mass., 1913), is a standard study of the Grange in its formative years. Christiana M. Campbell, *The Farm Bureau and the New Deal* (Urbana, Ill., 1962), is a useful study of the AFBF despite serious omissions. John A. Crampton, *The National Farmers' Union: Ideology of a Pressure Group* (Lincoln, Neb., 1965), provides a sociological approach from the vantage point of the national organization rather than that of the farmer. Henry C. Dethloff, comp., *A List of References for the History of the Farmers' Alliance and the Populist Party* (Davis, Calif., 1973), is an exhaustive bibliography. Gilbert Fite, *George N. Peek and the Fight for Farm Parity* (Norman, Okla., 1954), studies the man and the groups that joined him in the campaign for the McNary-Haugen plan. Lawrence Goodwyn, *Democratic Promise; The Populist Movement in America* (New York, 1976), although weak in economic analysis, is written with a journalistic flair; southern, if not Texan, in orientation. Donald H. Grubbs, *Cry From the Cotton: The Southern Tenant Farmers' Union and the New Deal* (Chapel Hill, N.C., 1971), gives a sympathetic treatment of the STFU that is critical of the landlords and the administration. John D. Hicks, *The Populist Revolt* (Minneapolis, 1931), is still the best single volume on the subject.

Robert Lee Hunt, *A History of Farmer Movements in the Southwest, 1873–1925* (College Station, Tex., 1935), has details unavailable elsewhere. Orville M. Kile, *The Farm Bureau Through Three Decades* (Baltimore, 1948), is a sympathetic treatment by a former executive. Wesley C. McCune, *The Farm Bloc* (Garden City, N.Y., 1943), offers good journalistic insights into farmer politics during New Deal and early World War II years. Robert C. McMath, Jr., *Populist Vanguard: A History of the Southern Farmers' Alliance Vanguard* (Chapel Hill, N.C., 1975), is a handy reference and thorough on the subject. Roscoe C. Martin, *The People's Party in Texas: A Study in Third Party Politics* (Austin, Tex., 1933), gives a penetrating interdisciplinary study of the Populist party in Texas. George H. Miller, *Railroads and the Granger Laws* (Madison, Wis., 1971), is more on railroads than on Grangers, but useful. Robert L. Morlan, *Political Prairie Fire: The Nonpartisan League, 1915–1922* (Minneapolis, 1955), is general and descriptive, but covers critical years. Denton E. Morrison, ed., *Farmers' Organizations and Movements: Research Needs and a Bibliography of the U.S. and Canada*, Michigan Agricultural Experiment Station Research Bulletin 24 (East Lansing, Mich., 1970)—the title provides an accurate description of the contents. Dennis Sven Nordin, *A Preliminary List of References for the History of the Granger Movement* (Davis, Calif., 1967), is a useful list; and *Rich Harvest: A History of the Grange, 1867–1900* (Jackson, Miss., 1974), stresses social, cultural, and educational features.

Walter T. Nugent, *The Tolerant Populists: Kansas, Populism and Nativism* (Chicago, 1963), is an in-depth study of populism in Kansas that finds little evidence of anti-Semitism. Stanley B. Persons, *The Populist Context: Rural Versus Urban Power on a Great Plains Frontier* (Westport, Conn., 1973), recounts the conflict of interests and values between farmers and villagers. Theodore Saloutos, "The American Farm Bureau Federation and Farm Policy, 1933–1945," in *Southwestern Social Science Quarterly,* 28 (March 1948), focuses on prime issues of concern to AFBF at federal level. Theodore Saloutos and John D. Hicks, *Agricultural Discontent in the Middle West, 1900–1939* (Madison, Wis., 1951), emphasizes the role of the farmer organizations; and *Farmer Movements in the South, 1865–1933* (Berkeley, Calif., 1960), the only volume on the subject dealing with the South, has social and economic emphasis. Fred A. Shannon, *American Farmers' Movements* (Princeton, 1957), is a documentary treatment with introductory statements. John L. Shover, *Cornbelt Rebellion: The Farmers' Holiday Association* (Urbana, Ill., 1965), is a comprehensive account of a militant episode. Carl C. Taylor, *The Farmers' Movement, 1620–1920* (New York, 1953), is a general survey by a pioneer rural sociologist. Edward Wiest, *Agricultural Organization in the United States* (Lexington, Ky., 1923), is ponderous and old, but still useful for the earlier years.

[See also AGRICULTURE; AGRICULTURE IN THE NORTH AND WEST; AGRICULTURE IN THE SOUTH; ECONOMY FROM RECONSTRUCTION TO 1914; ECONOMY SINCE 1914; LAND POLICIES AND SALES; *and* WESTWARD MOVEMENT.]

WESTWARD MOVEMENT

Martin Ridge

IN 1790, shortly after the adoption of the Constitution, the population of the United States numbered almost 4,000,000. Of these, 750,000 were nonwhite, most of whom were of African ancestry and lived in bondage. Of the white population, the largest number were descendants of settlers who came from the British Isles, although Dutch and German elements were significant. Americans were healthy and essentially young; the median age of white males was slightly less than sixteen. Primarily agricultural —scarcely 5 percent of the population lived in urban centers (towns with 2,500 or more persons)—the population lived along the coast in the tier of states from Georgia to Maine.

At the time of the Revolution, the movement of Americans westward had been frustrated for almost half a century, first by the French and Spanish, and later by English colonial policy, especially by the Proclamation Line of 1763, which was intended to restrict settlement to regions east of the Appalachian Mountains. But the Indian wars, the fur trade, and the keen interest of Virginia and Pennsylvania land speculators, who had eagerly petitioned the English crown for vast tracts of land in the trans-Appalachian West, paved the way for the rapid settlement of Kentucky, Tennessee, and Ohio. During the French and Indian War (1754–1763), roads had been cut through the wilderness from central Pennsylvania and Maryland to Fort Pitt (later Pittsburgh); but even earlier, adventurers and restless hunters in search of cheap fur had worked their way through the Cumberland Mountains into Kentucky. Indian traders from the Carolina colonies had found trails into western Georgia and even Alabama. The Wilderness Road, marked in 1775 by Daniel Boone for his employer Richard Henderson, chief promoter of the Transylvania Company, passed through the Cumberland Gap. These roads of course were little more than trails, and traffic over them tested the mettle of even the hardiest settler. Nevertheless, once the French had been driven from North America, Pennsylvania businessmen hauled goods by pack train to Pittsburgh, built boats, floated goods down the Ohio River, and opened stores in Indiana and Illinois. Jewish and Scotch-Irish merchants were eager competitors for the Indian trade. Thus, the routes to the West had been clearly marked by the close of the Revolution.

OHIO AND MISSISSIPPI FRONTIER

At the end of the Revolution, the trans-Appalachian West was also opened for land speculation and contests over landownership. As the various states argued over their rights to western lands, their citizens staked claims. To restore some degree of order after the states yielded their interests to the central government, Congress enacted the Ordinances of 1785 and 1787. The Ordinance of 1787—the Northwest Ordinance—established a pattern of territorial government that would assure stability. The Ordinance of 1785—a land ordinance—called for the survey of the public lands of the Old Northwest before they were sold. It mandated the creation of townships six miles square, which in turn would be divided into sections of 640 acres, and the sale of land in section-size plots at a minimum price of $1 per acre. Although these terms were hardly intended for the average farmer— $640 was an almost prohibitive price and 640 acres was probably ten times the size of the average farm in the North—the scheme offered the promise of orderly land distribution. Frontier settlers virtually ignored the federal land sales; they simply took over unoccupied land as squatters, in advance of the township ranges, or bought land on the installment plan from investors. These investors had purchased huge tracts directly from the government at discount prices, using Revolutionary War currencies that had depreciated in value or military land scrip that had been awarded to soldiers and then sold at reduced prices.

This land policy proved unworkable. Congress enacted the Land Law of 1800 so that land could be bought in parcels as small as 320 acres, but this was reduced in 1804 to parcels of 160 acres, and again in 1817 to 80 acres. The price of land in 1800 was $2.00 per acre but land could be purchased on credit with as little as 25 percent down. The contracts called for payment within four years. Rural bankruptcies during the panic of 1819 forced an abandonment of this liberal land policy. In 1820, Congress enacted what became the basic land law of the United States. The price of land was set at $1.25 per acre, and land was sold in parcels of eighty acres with cash payment required. Investment in large tracts of land was not ended by this law, but a family farm unit, viable for the early nineteenth century, was established. In the South, which had slaves and a plantation economy, large tracts were assembled; but even there the average farmer usually worked a small parcel. Furthermore, pioneer farmers continued to take up unsurveyed land and improve it until an investor bought them out or until they saved enough to make a modest purchase.

The family farm was the main source of capital accumulation in the West. Trees felled, underbrush cleared, lands planted, houses and barns built, and increased livestock inventories represented savings. The growth rate was low, and it was offset by soil depletion. The pioneer farmer in the westward movement rarely had access to the best information about land management, technological changes, better grains, or improved livestock. But he did not lag too far behind, and he did take advantage of the fertility of the virgin soil. The yields of corn and wheat—the major grains of the Middle West—were little better than those in Pennsylvania and New York, but the yield per man-hour of work per acre was higher.

The tide of emigrants that swept across the Appalachians began slowly and grew to a torrent. In 1800 perhaps as many as 400,000 persons lived in the region; by 1810 the number reached 1,000,000. Many of these virtually impoverished farmers supplemented their diets and enriched their pocketbooks by hunting and trapping. Distant from transportation, they lived at a bare subsistence level, unable to export their meager production or to buy manufactured goods from the East. Good-sized cities and towns were developing, almost all of them located to serve as markets or commercial centers. Louisville, St. Louis, and Nashville boasted one thousand inhabitants each in 1810. New Orleans was a metropolis with almost twenty-five thousand persons, and Pittsburgh, Lexington, and Cincinnati, although having fewer than five thousand persons each, were becoming important.

The use of the steamboat in the West, first demonstrated effectively by the *New Orleans* in 1811–1812 when it steamed from Pittsburgh to New Orleans, brought a gradual end to the economic isolation of western settlers. The capacity to ship goods both up and down the Mississippi and Ohio rivers greatly enhanced the economic well-being of western farmers who had previously been totally dependent on flatboats to export bulk products. Those who produced wheat, tobacco, pork, and hemp had been at a disadvantage because they paid high prices to import as well as to export. Steam-driven vessels lowered both costs and gave these farmers a favorable trade balance. The opportunity to ship bulk products, which had been almost impossible to move, encouraged farmers to shift from subsistence to commercial planting. Farms remained self-sufficient, but they became increasingly related to staple production.

The steamboat was a vital agency of interregional transportation until 1850, but turnpikes and canals also served to extend the limited economic activities of settlers who lived far from navigable rivers. The Erie Canal, the most successful venture of its kind, not only reduced freight rates dramatically after it opened in 1825 but also offered the farmers of the Great Lakes region an excellent outlet for bulk goods. Interregional trade between the Middle West and the East, formerly much restricted, increased markedly. The Erie Canal also channeled a new

WESTWARD MOVEMENT

wave of emigrants into the heart of the continent. Its success provoked a canal-building craze. Canal costs undoubtedly helped to deepen the problems of the panic of 1837, because midwestern states were left with huge debts when the canals failed. European investors were appalled when the states defaulted on canal bonds. Yet the transportation system that had been created certainly raised the personal income of western farmers and merchants. Even though economic growth lagged during depressions, exports via the Erie Canal rose steadily, as did those that went down the Ohio and Mississippi rivers. The Ohio and Mississippi traffic tended to double each decade before the Civil War.

The population of Ohio, Indiana, Illinois, Wisconsin, and Michigan reached four and a half million by 1850. And comparable growth occurred in Kentucky, Tennessee, Alabama, Mississippi, and Louisiana, including a substantial slave population—more than one million—that moved into the region. Tobacco was an important crop in Kentucky and Tennessee, but it was cotton culture that led to the advance of the southern frontier. It would undoubtedly have been otherwise had Eli Whitney not in 1793 invented a simple cotton gin that could extract the seed from a hardy strain of cotton that flourished on land far from the coast. Abundant, cheap land and slave labor, which permitted cotton production, prompted a land rush into Alabama and Mississippi that neither tobacco nor corn could have induced. Wheat, which required a cooler climate, did not fare well in the South. The westward movement was, then, spurred by one commodity that fit the environment, brought high returns, and was compatible with the labor system. The southern movement was a direct result of technological progress.

Therefore, although the first farmers to settle in the South raised corn and small grains, their later counterparts turned to cotton production as soon as adequate transportation was available. The return on the investment was so great that eastern planters sometimes bought out pioneer settlers, or even bought raw land, and moved entire plantations to the West. They attempted to reproduce the system of cotton production and plantation life that they had known in the East. Because the demand for cotton seemed elastic, cultivation spread into Texas and Arkansas. In 1816, New Orleans marketed less than 50,000 bales of cotton; by 1840 the number reached 900,000.

TRANS-MISSISSIPPI WEST

Although the migration of easterners and Europeans into the Great Lakes states and the South accelerated in the 1850's, with the coming of the railroads the pioneer stage in large measure had passed. The birthrate in eastern Ohio and other settled regions was declining. Some well-established farmers began to sell their lands and seek newer holdings farther west. The development of the reaper (1831), thresher (1830's), and seed drill (1840's) made the relatively rock-free lands of the prairie that were earlier considered unproductive more appealing, and the limited amount of cheap raw land in the older states encouraged emigration by the poorly situated as well as by newcomers looking for a place to start. The presence of good transportation also stimulated interest in the virgin lands beyond the Mississippi River. No one denied that economic opportunity still existed in both the Great Lakes and Gulf states, but the region was "filled in." The basic factors that encouraged migration were present: new lands were close at hand, wage differentials in the West were genuine, there were fewer neighbors and less competition, and a settler could seek a society of his own preference. These were the basic economic reasons for emigration.

A large portion of the trans-Mississippi West had been acquired by the United States in 1803. In the years that followed, army officers explored the region. Meriwether Lewis and William Clark blazed a trail up the Missouri River to Oregon (1806), and reported on the land and its promise. Zebulon Pike, fresh from a quest for the headwaters of the Mississippi River (1805–1806), searched the area between the Arkansas and Red rivers; pushed on to Colorado, where he tried to climb the mountain that bears his name; and was taken prisoner by the Spanish when he ventured into New Mexico (1806–1807). Stephen Long followed the Platte River and explored the high plains (1819–1820). His depressing report, which labeled the plains "the Great American Desert," had a profoundly negative impact on settlement. The cost of these expeditions was regarded as a legitimate investment by a generation of Americans eager for knowledge of economic opportunity.

The most successful explorers were often unsung and unknown hunters and fur merchants who, driven by dreams of huge profits, searched every quarter of the West. For more than a century before Lewis and Clark, French and Spanish traders had exploited the lower portions of western rivers; but the Lewis and Clark expedition aroused the American interest in the fur trade. After studying the market on the upper Missouri and Yellowstone rivers from 1806 to 1808, St. Louis traders formed the Saint Louis Missouri Fur Company in 1809. Undercapitalized—unable to sustain poor fur harvests and serious Indian depredations—the company soon retreated from the northern Rocky Mountains. Far more ambitious, the American Fur Company, established by John Jacob Astor in 1808, planned to establish its headquarters at the mouth of the Columbia River in Oregon, where, through a series of posts, it would dominate the collection of furs and then ship them to China in American vessels. The Astorians successfully built their post on the Columbia and even stumbled on South Pass—the best route through the Rocky Mountains—but the War of 1812 ended their promising venture. Fearful that the British would destroy their fragile post, Astor's partners sold out to the North West Company of Canada, for less than $60,000.

By 1824 the Hudson's Bay Company, which had merged with the North West Company in 1821, began to monopolize the trade in the region. Forts were erected, brigades of traders scoured California and Utah for furs, and ships plied the coastal waters, virtually stripping the area of fur. Dr. John McLoughlin, who directed the activities of the company, made its post on the Columbia River, Fort Vancouver, a thriving center. Cattle were brought from California, pigs from Hawaii, and sheep from the East, and retired and idle fur men turned to husbandry. Foodstuffs were sold to the Russians in Alaska, and Oregon salmon appeared in European markets.

While McLoughlin won control of the Columbia trade, a group of Americans exploited the rich fur reserves of the central Rocky Mountains. Unlike the Canadians, who used forts and brigades of traders to overawe the Indians, the Americans lived among the Indians and gathered once a year for a trading fair or "rendezvous," when merchants from St. Louis would come to the mountains. Indians joined whites to barter the catch for supplies, liquor, and a few days of "rip roaring debauchery." Competition was keen, and profits ranged as high as 2,000 percent for the Rocky Mountain Fur Company, as much-sought-after beaver skins—used to make hats—were traded away. By the 1840's, when the Hudson's Bay Company invaded the territory, the supply of beaver pelt was exhausted and the trade was dead.

A few American fur men tried unsuccessfully to oust the Hudson's Bay Company from Oregon, but by the 1840's, American settlements threatened British hegemony in the Northwest. Methodist missionaries, inspired to save the Indians of the Far West, accompanied fur men to Oregon and established a community in the Willamette Valley. Although ineffective as missionaries, they founded and publicized American towns in the region. Before long, companies of American settlers in quest of free land moved along the Oregon Trail. The main route west, the trail—which varied in width from the ruts of a single wagon to a wide swath on the south bank of the Platte River—crossed the mountains at South Pass, turned north to the Snake River, and followed the Snake and the Columbia to Fort Vancouver. Unemployed mountain men frequently guided emigrants along the two-thousand-mile trek to Oregon or, somewhat later, down a cutoff to the south that led to the Sierras and California. Even with the completion of the Union Pacific Railroad after the Civil War, the Oregon Trail remained an important road for emigration.

If fur led the way to Oregon, then cattle, cotton, climate, and especially cheap land—4,428 acres could be bought for as little as $30, payable in four installments—led Americans to Texas. Rambunctious Kentucky and Tennessee farmers vied with Mississippi, Alabama, and Louisiana planters and investors. In 1836 the Americans won their independence from Mexico when that nation, itself newly independent from Spain, tried to abolish slavery and restrict the freewheeling speculative activities of the Americans living in its northern province. The Texans sought annexation to the United States, and only after this was achieved in 1845 did the state begin a healthy economic development.

As Americans searched the Rocky Mountains and beyond for fur and invaded Texas, a handful of adventurous merchants and teamsters opened a trail from Independence, Missouri, across Kansas, Oklahoma, and New Mexico to Santa Fe. They accomplished a goal that Mississippi Valley traders had set more than a century before. Santa Fe, rich in silver and poor in consumer goods, was a small market center. More symbolic than significant or profitable—the trade involved fewer than one hundred individuals and a gross of about $150,000 per year—the Santa Fe Trail teased the American imagination and proved that the route to the Southwest was easy and open. Despite Mexican disapproval, a small colony of Americans settled in Santa Fe.

Texas and New Mexico were not the only Mexican territories that held a challenge to American enterprise. American seamen sailed the waters of the California coast, eyed San Francisco Bay as a port of call for whaling ships, engaged in a lively if sometimes illegal trade in cowhides for the growing leather-goods industry of New England, and smuggled American manufactured goods. Many became residents in the villages on the coast and, like Thomas O. Larkin of Monterey, wrote enthusiastically about California as a place of economic opportunity. By 1840, although the sea trade had slackened, a small number of Americans filtered into California via the Oregon Trail and the California cutoff to take up land.

The decade of the 1840's provides a convenient watershed that divides not only the rate but also the nature of the economic growth of the trans-Mississippi West. The Oregon boundary was settled in 1846, with the British retreating to Vancouver Island and surrendering access to the Washington coast, Seattle harbor, and the vast hinterland to the United States. The spoils of the Mexican War virtually rounded out the southern boundary of the United States, except for the Gadsden Purchase from Mexico in 1853, which was made to provide a low-level route for a southern railroad. The Mormons completed their stations to Salt Lake City. The population of Missouri and Iowa increased sharply, and Iowa became a major producer of grain for export. Even more important, in 1848 gold was discovered in California.

Moreover, the public image of the West changed. Short-grass prairies, flinty mountains, and barren deserts seemed neither valueless nor inhospitable. Before 1840 the region west of the Mississippi River numbered its American population in thousands, virtually all of whom were bunched in the tier of states just west of the river. Perhaps 1 percent of the population of the nation was distributed across the so-called Great American Desert and the Pacific coast. After 1850 the size of the westward migration equaled or exceeded any other movement the nation had known. There can be no doubt that the economic development of the West—the spread of population, the accumulation of capital, and the application of technology—helped to change the economic outlook of Americans and to raise the wage levels of workers living near the newer regions. The status of the small businessman was never higher than it was in the western town or mining camp. The transcontinental railway system and the sophisticated industrial and commercial enterprises that were to emerge with it were still in the offing in 1850. For editors, lawyers, lumbermen, teachers, merchants, physicians, tanners, butchers, and smiths, it was possible to sell one's stock or transport the assets of one's business to the West without fear of outside competition or regulation. Lacking first-rate transportation, each town embraced a host of local monopolies held by every provider of goods or services.

The discovery of gold in California in 1848 was an enormous stimulus to the growth of the western economy. The impact was so great because successful mining operations required substantial inputs of capital, labor, and knowledge, and the immediate rewards could be enormous. Although it is difficult to conceive of the economic history of the West without gold, it can safely be argued that although growth would have been much slower and undoubtedly more orderly without it, the final result would have been essentially the same. The exploitation of base metals such as copper and lead would have sought capital from many of the same sources in Boston, New York, and Chicago, although San Francisco would have played a lesser role. The need for technical knowledge would have forced the innovation or importation of technology that was part of gold and silver mining. The demand for skilled labor would also have drawn hard-rock miners from Cornwall and Germany. Capital and labor, the essentials in the process of economic development, would have moved west anyway, in order to take advantage of other resources.

Most western emigrants moved as individuals or in family groups. There were some significant exceptions, the most important being the Mormon migration to Utah. In its early stages the Church of Jesus Christ of Latter-Day Saints was an economic unit. In fact, without its economic base the social structure of the Mormons would more than likely have proved ineffective. The economic base of a communitarian sect, as Mormon leaders Joseph Smith and Brigham Young recognized, could operate only in quasi isolation. It is worth noting that in Mormonism, a revelatory religion, a large number of the divine expressions received by church leaders dealt in whole or in part with economic matters. Unlike other communitarian experiments in nineteenth-century America, the effort of the Mormons encountered intense hostility. Their exclusivity, economic success, and practice of polygamy drew the wrath of the Protestant citizens of Missouri, Ohio, and Illinois. The assassination in 1844 of Joseph Smith, the founder of the church, led to the abandonment of the Mormon settlement at Nauvoo, Illinois.

The organization of the sect was atypical of community structures on the frontier before the arrival of large corporate ventures, because it stressed conservative values and traditions, emphasized conformity, and, except in its struggle with its harsh physical environment, steadfastly refused to innovate. Because what were frequently seen as virtually "free goods" in the East —water, wood, and arable land—were in critically short supply in the Utah desert, extensive community control was exercised over them.

Comparing Mormon economic practices with those of a large-scale nineteenth-century enterprise is worthwhile. Both recruited capital from the members of the management group in an orderly fashion, sought a disciplined labor force, attempted to control the development of a special environment and resources, and frequently sacrificed short-term returns for long-term expansion to control a marketing region. Both required and developed managerial skill, enterprise, and a quality of leadership during the formative period. During the final years of the century, in both cases individual executive leadership yielded gradually to a committee or a board of directors that had been trained for the task.

Mormon leaders proved more shrewd than most western capitalists. They rarely entered a market without careful planning, and they were not incurable optimists or "plungers," or given to cyclical pessimism. In fact, their caution about expanding into areas where they could not be assured of preeminence led them in 1850 to surrender control of freight transportation to Salt Lake City to outsiders, and made them hesitant about venturing into mining and banking. Their requirement of exclusivity prompted them to move into banking because it was essential to make their community secure. The area of sharpest conflict between Mormon and other western American enterprise rested in each one's perception of resources. Unlike other settlers, the Mormons shunned the ruthless exploitation of natural resources without regard to the future. They attempted to function in a world of renewable resources.

The westward-moving farmers who inched their way across the trans-Mississippi West between 1810 and 1860 were reacting to economic conditions far different from those that had motivated the Mormons. In the South competition from highly efficient slave-owning planters, as well as soil depletion and undercapitalization, prompted some farmers to sell out and move on. Very frequently in both the South and the Middle West, health was a significant expelling factor, not only the health of individuals but also of farm animals. The hog cholera epidemic (1856–1857) in the Ohio Valley was as potent as the "ague," which afflicted people, in persuading individuals to seek a better climate in which to earn a living. Middle western farmers also moved because of competition from lands farther west, and increased taxation seems to have played a part as well. The heavy state debt structure that resulted from borrowing during the canal and turnpike splurges encouraged many farmers to seek new lands in states and territories that were in a more pristine condition.

The lumbermen who opened the pine forests of Michigan, Wisconsin, and Minnesota had different incentives: New England and the Maritime Provinces of Canada no longer offered opportunity commensurate with the effort and investment required. Moreover, the new markets created by the settlement of farmers on the prairies and the establishment of new cities in the Middle West, plus the unusual transportation and power facilities there, proved irresistible. The fact that lumber was virtually a free good on the frontier made profits significant. These same factors proved important half a century later, when Minnesota and Wisconsin lumbermen began to cut in the forests of Oregon and Washington. They had access to capital and technology developed in the Middle West, but the forests of the Northwest required innovation and large-scale investment. By this time timber was regarded as a renewable resource, and forest management became a significant new industry.

For these essentially agricultural groups, the success of which depended on the exploitation of an available resource, the land policy of the government was highly generous. The rights of squatters, long a hotly contested question, were accepted by the Preemption Act of 1841, which provided that the head of a family, a single man over twenty-one years of age, or a widow could file a claim for 160 acres of surveyed public land. For validation of the claim, the most casual evidence was accepted as proof that improvements had been made and a genuine residence established. The Preemption Act did not give land away, but it assured that the earliest pioneer would have a chance to secure land at a minimum price or receive a share of the profits from the improvements. Enacted not so much to encourage the settlement of vacant land before it was surveyed and opened for sale as, ostensibly, to protect the interests of impoverished farmers, the measure proved a boon to both land speculators and pioneer farmers who undertook the risks of being in the vanguard of settlement. Settlers and speculators, before the Preemption Act, staked their claims by forming claim associations. These were mutual protection organizations that allowed for the purchase and sale of claims before clear legal title could be obtained from the federal government. They were willing to enforce these claims by violence and made every effort to control the formal land sales so that only the basic price was bid at each government auction.

Iowa, eastern Nebraska, and Minnesota were settled when preemption was a basic part of the land policy. Cheap land warrants, issued to soldiers as bounties after the Mexican War and valued at $1.25 an acre, were sold for as little as $.50 per acre and were used to buy preempted lands. The only brake on the drive for land engrossment was the lack of adequate transportation. Where the farmer was forced to depend on the freight wagon and the stagecoach, growth was slow; where steamboats could navigate a river, population increased and business boomed. Between 1840 and 1850 the population of Iowa increased to 92,214; and when the railroad reached Iowa in the next decade, the population soared to 674,913. Small towns in Kansas pleaded for craftsmen and businesses of all sorts, because there was a real need for them. But the population growth seems to have been affected by the slavery controversy and the violence that it caused: investors were reluctant to enter Kansas and risk funds. Missourians seeking cheap land, regardless of risks, moved in. Some of them were large-scale farmers. Struggling pioneer farmers held out in eastern Kansas against the blandishments of investors who offered large sums for good land. Perhaps some of these farmers were aware that arable land on the frontier was growing scarce as the line of semiaridity was being approached.

Capital was easy to obtain in the trans-Mississippi West during the 1850's. Most of it was recruited in eastern states for the purchase of land. This not only expedited government sales and contributed to spiraling land prices, but also led to the projecting of new towns as potential rivals of Cincinnati, Chicago, and St. Louis. Money was so abundant that in 1860 a cynic observed that Kansas still did not export enough corn, pork, and hides to pay for the liquor that it consumed; imported capital in the form of loans and gifts made up the balance of payments.

This speculative bubble burst in 1857. Land prices sagged; internal improvements ceased; populations fled eastward. The panic of 1857 brought an end to one of the first rushes for farmland in the trans-Mississippi West. Gold discoveries in Colorado in 1858–1859 exerted a mild influence on settlements in Kansas and Nebraska. Occasionally a prospector's ardor cooled before he reached the goldfields or shortly thereafter, when he learned of the hard work, scanty finds, and precious metal embedded in quartz so hard that machine milling could scarcely extract it. Feeding the prospectors, however, was profitable. Some men settled for ranches and farms on the edge of the plains. Although this land was almost free for the asking, it did require investment capital. A frame house cost $250, breaking the virgin land with plows could cost as much as $3 per acre, and fencing charges could be exorbitant, depending on the proximity of lumber or other materials.

MINING FRONTIER

The economic growth and migration to the West during the Civil War are hard to assess. Mining was, if anything, stimulated by the war. Gold was in short supply and sold at a high premium. It had been found in Gregory Gulch, Colorado, two years before southern guns fired on Fort Sumter. In the better-established mining towns, farmers and townspeople fleeing the guerrilla warfare in Kansas and Missouri mingled with former soldiers and deserters from both sides. Labor was scarce, and no one asked questions. Precious-metal mining had always attracted persons from all strata of society, and mining camp populations proved highly volatile.

During the half-century in which the quest for gold and silver was significant in the West, men from many countries and walks of life attempted to profit in mining camps. Many of them wanted to cash in on the availability of a free resource while enjoying the greatest possible personal freedom in the search for their fortune. The prospector, miner, and mining camp entourage of merchants, engineers, gamblers, and prostitutes readily abandoned one field for another at the first rumor of higher yields at a new strike. Eventually prospectors scanned the topography of every state west of the hundredth meridian, always in search of the mother lode—be it gold, silver, copper, or lead.

Gold was found in California as the United States entered the industrial era. For a generation of Americans convinced that they could better themselves only by taking advantage of each opportunity and functioning in a capital-starved economy, the western mining industry seemed to promise a magnificent chance for success. Initial profits in the goldfields were almost on the basis of luck, an economic arena in which men were equal. In addition, failure was no disgrace; and the mining camp cried out for nearly every skill. Even at rock bottom, day laborers earned three or four times as much as comparable workers in the East.

Small businessmen took great risks in investing in mining areas. By and large the camps grew up in regions where conversion from mining to any other industry was tediously slow or even impossible. Therefore, if the mines did not prove out or the lead time in their development was too great, the merchant slowly succumbed to the credit system that made him a private banker for the field. If the camp did succeed, he alone in the town, besides the proprietors of the mine, had taxable assets, and frequently he alone was left to pay the costs of the social, political, and economic growth of the community, although he was rarely the sole beneficiary.

The American mining experience began when the nation crossed the threshold of industrialism, but the later stages of precious-metal mining belong to the railroad era and the period of urbanization and large-scale industrial growth and consolidation. In fact, precious-metal mining helped to introduce large-scale enterprise to the West. Because gold was often found in quartz, and silver embedded in base-metal ore, the surface wealth that attracted prospectors to a camp was quickly exhausted. The development of a strike required large inputs of capital to purchase milling machinery, meet payrolls, and gather the other resources needed to sustain the mine.

Investors in San Francisco, the metropolitan center behind the far western mining frontier, organized the industry west of Salt Lake City. With fortunes earned initially in the Mother Lode of California and the Comstock Lode of Nevada, where experimentation and innovation frequently meant success, the San Franciscans virtually fixed the technology of their mines and mining practices. From the determination of what was profitable ore to the techniques of setting timbers in shafts and the design of quartz-crushing machinery, Californians made almost no changes after their earliest successes. They did pioneer hydraulic mining, but most of their achievements were based on eastern and European expertise. They made so much money so fast that they turned to nonmining outlets for their investment capital. By the standards of the 1970's, they appear to have been overly optimistic or ill-informed gamblers, but as businessmen in their era they were hardly wild speculators.

The Rocky Mountain mining area functioned with technology tested in Colorado and capital recruited in the Middle West, especially Chicago, where the machines for use in these fields were made. Like their San Francisco counterparts, the major investors in Denver were reluctant to innovate. Once a practice had been proved, designs and technology rarely changed, unless business conditions forced innovations to effect savings.

Western mining camps were essentially company towns, with the exception that they were not intended to be permanent. After the prospectors departed, American miners, unskilled immigrants, and skilled labor from British mines were recruited to work in the deep shafts, so long as yields were high. Many willingly joined labor unions dominated by Cornish immigrants, who fought technological changes and resorted to strikes and violence to preserve their work rules. (Precious-metal miners were not unusual in their reliance on violence; copper miners, lumbermen, and western longshoremen also relied on force in strikes.) Company management regarded mining as a free-enterprise operation and usually disciplined the labor force except in the matter of wages, which tended to remain high even during periods of unemployment. When the returns in a camp began to decline, Chinese workers replaced Caucasians, and human energy and a low standard of living substituted for high-yield ore to keep the mine in operation. Thus, it is little wonder that hostility toward Oriental and Latin American workers plagued the industry.

The successful mining camp displayed few redeeming characteristics. At the flood tide of its prosperity, the workers lived in loft buildings and shacks, even though the town might boast a gaudy hotel or an opera house that could host some of the foremost performers in the world. But surrounding most camps was naked, arid countryside, grassless and devoid of trees (which had been used to timber the mines), while the refuse of the mine and the community, spurning decay, stood as a mute testimonial, not of the abuses of rapid economic growth, but of an absence of public policy based on an awareness of the importance of environment. When the resources were gone, the town was abandoned.

In almost every instance the mining fields developed in regions without existing populations or industry. They required transportation and commercial links with metropolitan centers, and these ties frequently reached over hundreds of miles. For example, San Francisco serviced mines on the Colorado River in Arizona by sail and steam vessels that rounded the tip of Baja California to reach the mouth of the Colorado. Goods were transshipped at the delta, and ore was transported to San Francisco for smelting. The Pikes Peak rush (1859) was supplied by small towns in the Missouri Valley until Denver came to dominate the eastern slopes of the Rockies. Salt Lake City was an exception, in that it was already a minor commercial center before the argonauts on their way west gave its economy a boost; and a brisk trade with the mines on the western slopes of the Rockies and in the interior desert made it a financial center capable of recruiting the capital needed to underwrite a small railway network and a connection with the Union Pacific at Ogden.

The opening of mines was unusual in the westward movement because, during the half-century after the California gold strike, new fields of gold, silver, lead, copper, coal, and iron overlapped each other in development and chronology. The lasting communities grew up around base-metal centers after the 1880's. The coal and iron facilities in Colorado and the copper mines in Montana and Arizona had a more profound impact on migration and settlement than did the scattered gold and silver finds. Even before the shift in emphasis from precious metals to base metals and coal occurred, small farm communities were established on the slopes of the Rocky Mountains. Originally sustained by the products that their farmers sold to miners and other urban consumers, they were only a negligible part of the agricultural growth of the West until the railroad gave them access to national or interregional markets. Water impoundment, irrigation, and the techniques of dry farming encouraged substantially larger harvests and crop diversification.

AGRICULTURAL EXPANSION

The expansion of agriculture was accelerated after the Civil War when farmers occupied more land—225 million acres—than ever before in American history. Kansas added more than 631,000 persons during the 1870's, and Nebraska gained 329,000. More than one million inhabitants of the Old Northwest moved westward to take up lands beyond the Mississippi. Many immigrant groups were lured to the western prairies as "American fever" struck Germany and Scandinavia. Railroads and state immigration agencies publicized lands and arranged for their sale, and transportation was provided. Prices ranged from $2 to $8 per acre, but generous credit terms were available. The railroads, eager to create a clientele and dispose of their lands, subsidized not only transportation but also the education of early settlers. The lines pioneered in demonstrating new grains, livestock, and agricultural technology. The development of "new process" milling in the 1870's opened the western prairies to hard wheat, a reliable and highly profitable crop.

Farming on the prairies was a difficult business, but early profits allowed settlers to escape from their primitive dugouts and sod houses, and to build frame houses. Fuel and wood costs were high, even though the railroad tended to break the monopoly of local merchants. Farmers who raised wheat were rarely able to grow the variety of other crops that made eastern farmers of the same period somewhat self-sufficient. They were almost as dependent on town merchants for consumer goods as town dwellers in the East were. The risks in agriculture compounded as farmers occupied lands in areas of increasing aridity. Droughts, grass fires, locust plagues, and rodents tested the settlers' resilience. High costs of transportation and the setting of grain prices in a world market also made farming hazardous.

Constantly improved technology was critical to the farmer's success. Improvement of the windmill, so that it could survive the high and variable winds of the open prairies, made water from lower water tables readily available. Although the windmill was almost prohibitive in cost, the market for it expanded. With a guaranteed supply of water, raising livestock was less uncertain. The farmer who lived in an area of variable rainfall required deep-furrowing plows and harrows that could break up clods of earth so that moisture would be retained in the soil. Virtually all of the farm machinery invented or developed before the Civil War—seed planters, steel plows, disk harrows, straddle-row cultivators, and threshing machines—were substantially improved by the 1880's. Binders were developed that made grain harvesting faster and easier, but the combine, first used in California in the 1880's, did not reach the prairies until 1900. The mechanization of farming lowered both cost and time of production. From 1830 to 1896, the time spent in producing an acre of wheat fell from sixty-one hours to three hours, and the cost of labor declined from $3.55 an acre to $0.66. Without these gains, farming on the western prairies would have been uneconomical. Little wonder, then, that when farm prices fell, agrarian unrest followed; political movements followed close on this discontent.

Congress enacted a series of generous land laws, beginning with the Homestead Act of 1862. The Homestead Act was based on a noble premise: every American who wanted a farm should have a chance to secure it at almost no cost. This stemmed from the idea that unused land had no value, and that the national wealth would increase if the vacant lands were cultivated. Trading land—an almost free good in the West—so that capital and labor could develop it made sound economic sense at that time. The Homestead Law made 160 acres available to an adult male citizen, for a small fee, after five years of residence on the land. The measure proved unsatisfactory when applied to the semiarid plains, where extensive holdings were necessary for success. Although the Homestead Act failed to provide every American who wanted land with a share of the public domain, it did give some farmers a chance to add to their holdings and make them viable, and others were afforded an opportunity to get land that might otherwise have been denied to them. A series of amendments—the Timber Culture Act of 1873 and the Desert Land Act of 1877—did not make the basic law more effective, although they did allow plains farmers to increase their holdings and ranchers to engross lands at low prices. Although there is evidence of widespread fraud in the operation of the land laws, the acts represented an honest, if ill-informed, effort by Congress to deal with land problems.

The range cattle industry was a unique part of the westward movement of American agriculture. Wild longhorn cattle, brought to America by the Spanish, had long roamed free on the Texas plains because almost no markets existed for them before the Civil War. A few were driven hundreds of miles to eastern markets or shipped as canned beef to the South, but no adequate marketing structure developed before the war. When the war ended, a million head of cattle grazed on the free grass of the public domain, mavericks not claimed or branded by anyone. A few Texans realized that wealth awaited the enterprising individual who would drive herds of cattle to northern markets. Ranchers began rounding up cattle and herding them to railheads in Missouri and Kansas.

The business was haphazardly organized until 1867, when Joseph G. McCoy made formal arrangements with railroads to have cars ready for shipment when cattle were brought to the railroad, built cattle pens, and turned the sleepy little town of Abilene, Kansas, into the first real American cow town. Western railroads, starved for freight, competed for the cattle trade, extending their lines into the Southwest. Since the industry was based on the open range of the public domain—a free good—it spread rapidly through unoccupied federal land. With competitive rail rates, cheap cattle, and free land, profits soared as foreign and domestic investors attempted to capitalize on this special opportunity. By the end of the 1870's, longhorn cows were being bred to prize eastern and imported bulls to improve the herd. A cattle kingdom sprawled from Texas to Montana over land that had once been termed "useless to cultivating man."

Raising cattle on the open range may not have required very much special skill, but the industry was highly complex. It required health and cattle-breeding laws, special railroad cars, effective slaughtering and packing plants, and a complicated marketing and banking structure. Moreover, weather, grass, and competition, as well as quality and demand, influenced price. It could be highly profitable to be a rancher when grass was free and the range understocked. But profits were dearly earned when ranchers had to own land, employ cowboys (who were frequently blacks, Indians, and immigrants), improve herds, battle competitors, pay high interest rates, buy barbed wire and windmills, raise feed grains, and watch the price of livestock in Chicago, where the major packinghouses controlled the stockyards.

TRANSPORTATION

The westward movement was always influenced by available transportation. Before the construction of railroads, the federal government built wagon roads for military and postal services in much of the West. Some of these, like the Mullan Road from Fort Walla Walla, Washington, to Fort Benton, Montana, became emigrant roads, and later the army and the Interior Department built roads explicitly for new settlers. The earliest stage and freight lines, subsidized by the government, relied on many of these routes. Wagons were the mainstays of local and long-distance hauling even after the railroads were built, because many areas in the West were inaccessible or so sparsely settled that railroad construction would have been uneconomical. The teamster was a ubiquitous figure in the West, and the wagon was as indispensable in the nineteenth century as the truck is in the twentieth.

The completion of the transcontinental telegraph in 1861 was a harbinger of modernization. After the Civil War a western railroad system, heavily subsidized with land and cash, was established. The first transcontinental railroad—the Union Pacific–Central Pacific—was completed in 1869. By 1885 four major lines—two northern and two southern—reached from the Mississippi River to the Pacific. Although this early construction far exceeded the economic needs of the nation—in fact, it may have used capital better invested in other parts of the economy—and led to cutthroat competition and financial problems, the roads contributed greatly to western migration. A belt of railroads crossed Minnesota, Iowa, Missouri, and Louisiana, and Nebraska, Kansas, and Texas also were well served. Narrow-gauge lines tapped mining regions in Colorado, and a host of feeder lines were built where markets could be sustained. The roads relied heavily on eastern capital.

Railroads did more than yeoman work in establishing settlements along their rights-of-way. They were more venturesome than most large-scale enterprises because their survival depended on improved service that would guarantee shippers along the right-of-way a competitive position vis-à-vis other producers. In an economic sense the basic interests of shippers and railroads were identical.

WESTWARD MOVEMENT

By 1900, although many residents were leaving the plains and prairie states for the East, a new wave of settlers was preparing to flood the Far West. Oklahoma, New Mexico, and Arizona were not yet states when entrepreneurs began investing heavily in urban real estate in California. By 1912 the last three contiguous continental states had been admitted. Only Alaska and Hawaii remained to be admitted as part of the westward push.

Other economic incentives played a role in bringing people to the twentieth-century West. Health seekers, long among seasonal visitors, became permanent settlers. There was also a steady migration of retired and affluent individuals who wanted a pleasant location. The Southwest, especially California and Arizona, had genuine appeal for these groups. Although a large number of the new westerners came from the eastern seaboard, the largest element still originated in the upper Mississippi Valley and the Great Lakes states. Very few blacks moved west before World War I. Unprecedented demands for food and labor during the war lured thousands of tenant farmers to California and a new life.

This migration was easier because western railroads had been completed and a national highway network was under construction. The Great Depression of the 1930's stimulated a major rearrangement of the American people. The population of California increased by more than one million, and Oregon and Washington also gained from this migration; but the population of some of the mountain, plains, and desert states declined by as much as 10 percent, as the "Dust Bowl" refugees turned to California and the Pacific Northwest. Agricultural successes continued to attract people, but cities in California became the resting place for most emigrants. Major waterpower and reclamation projects made industrial growth and agriculture economically viable. The major dams on the Colorado and Columbia rivers proved to be significant government contributions to the development and attractiveness of the West.

World War II and the "Cold War Era" launched a new wave of emigrants westward. Although the northern plains and prairie states were no longer attractive, California and the Southwest became powerful magnets. The Pacific Northwest also offered jobs and an appealing physical environment. Jobs in aircraft construction, shipbuilding, national defense industries, recreation, electronics, home construction, and food production, as well as a host of other fields, accelerated a persistent trend. Adding to it was a new class of pensioners—Social Security recipients—who sought the warm, dry environment of the Southwest and spawned a major industry—retirement communities—that provided them with services and housing. Retirement villages were an almost entirely new phenomenon.

Although the number of Americans moving west has fluctuated during the nineteenth and twentieth centuries, the reasons for migration remain essentially the same. In fact, the reasons for moving west are the primary reasons for all interregional mobility. The development of comfortable, high-speed transportation has made the whole country accessible. It no longer requires a Daniel Boone to spy out the land, and land investors are still as active as any of the earlier period. Farmland, though, is no longer the attraction that it was when the nation was primarily agricultural. Investors and emigrants, lacking both the skill and the huge sums of money needed for commercial farming, have turned to cities. This has made the wage differential increasingly important, as the new jobs and high salaries of the defense industries of the Far West demonstrated. Yet the changing values of the population have resulted in an increasing number of individuals responding to climate and health factors. For some the society of preference has become critical. The western tilt of the population has slowed, but it has not stopped. By 1980 it was only one aspect of the mobility of a remarkably footloose people.

BIBLIOGRAPHY

The best history of the westward movement is Ray A. Billington, *Westward Expansion*, 4th ed. (New York, 1974). For a documentary treatment of the westward movement, see Martin Ridge and Ray A. Billington, eds., *America's Frontier Story* (New York, 1969). For a useful overview of English frontier policy, see Jack M. Sosin, *Whitehall and the Wilderness: The Middle West in British Colonial Policy, 1760–1775* (Lincoln, Neb., 1961), and Thomas P. Abernethy, *Western Lands and the American Revolution* (New York, 1937). Two volumes that trace the development of the West from the expulsion of the

WESTWARD MOVEMENT

French to the end of the War of 1812 are Jack M. Sosin, *The Revolutionary Frontier, 1763–1783* (New York, 1967), and Reginald Horsman, *The Frontier in the Formative Years, 1783–1815* (New York, 1970). Useful for understanding the West before the Civil War are Paul Wallace Gates, *The Farmer's Age: Agriculture, 1815–1860* (New York, 1960), and George Rogers Taylor, *The Transportation Revolution, 1815–1860* (New York, 1951); but David C. Klingaman and Richard K. Vedder, eds., *Essays in Nineteenth-Century Economic History: The Old Northwest* (Athens, Ohio, 1975) is indispensable, as is Allan G. Bogue, *From Prairie to Corn Belt* (Chicago, 1963). Highly suggested for both its scope and analysis is Malcolm Rohrbough, *The Trans-Appalachian Frontier: People, Society, and Institutions, 1775–1850* (New York, 1978). For one example of how foreign investors played a role in national development, see Dorothy R. Adler, *British Investment in American Railways, 1834–1898* (Charlottesville, Va., 1970). For the government's role in underwriting the transportation system, see Carter Goodrich, *Government Promotion of American Canals and Railroads, 1800–1890* (New York, 1960). A convenient introduction to the opening of the Far West is Ray A. Billington, *The Far Western Frontier, 1830–1860* (New York, 1956).

No single volume provides a complete analysis of exploration or the fur trade, but among the highly useful volumes are William H. Goetzmann, *Exploration and Empire: The Explorer and the Scientist in the Winning of the American West* (New York, 1966); Richard E. Oglesby, *Manuel Lisa and the Opening of the Missouri Fur Trade* (Norman, Okla., 1963); and Paul C. Phillips, *The Fur Trade* (Norman, Okla., 1961). For the American interest in the Pacific Coast, see Norman Graebner, *Empire on the Pacific* (New York, 1955).

The best introduction to Mormon economic thought and action is Leonard J. Arrington, *The Great Basin Kingdom . . . 1830–1900* (Cambridge, Mass., 1958). The standard histories of transportation are William Turrentine Jackson, *Wagon Roads West: A Study of Federal Road Surveys and Construction in the Trans-Mississippi West, 1846–1869* (Berkeley, Calif., 1952), and Oscar O. Winther, *The Transportation Frontier: Trans-Mississippi West, 1865–1900* (New York, 1964). The best treatment of western mining is Rodman W. Paul, *Mining Frontier of the Far West, 1848–1880* (New York, 1963). For a pioneering study of western urbanization, see Lawrence H. Larsen, *The Urban West at the End of the Frontier* (Lawrence, Kans., 1978). Standard treatments of agricultural development may be found in Fred A. Shannon, *The Farmer's Last Frontier: Agriculture, 1860–1897* (New York, 1945), and Gilbert C. Fite, *The Farmers' Frontier, 1865–1900* (New York, 1966). Allan G. Bogue, *Money at Interest: Farm Mortgages on the Middle Border* (Ithaca, N.Y., 1955) is indispensable. The best treatment of the twentieth-century West is Gerald D. Nash, *The American West in the Twentieth Century: A Short History of an Urban Oasis* (Albuquerque, N. Mex., 1977).

[*See also* Agriculture; Agriculture in the North and West; Agriculture in the South; Economy from the Revolution to 1815; Economy from 1815 to 1865; Economy from Reconstruction to 1914; Farmers' Movements; Immigration; Land Policies and Sales; Social Mobility; Transportation; *and* Urbanization.]

LAND POLICIES AND SALES

Allan G. Bogue

ALMOST since the beginning of its national history, the United States government has held large amounts of lands under its direct control and administration. The first accessions of such public lands, or public domain, were obtained from 1781 to 1802 in a series of cessions made to the federal government by states claiming the ownership of lands beyond the Alleghenies under terms of their colonial charters or other official provenance. Table 1 shows the acreage involved in these transfers and in eight other major acquisitions of territory. Texas retained control of the unallocated lands within its state boundaries, the public lands of the Hawaiian Islands became a special case, and other territorial accessions or protectorates acquired after 1890 did not contribute acreage to the original public domain. The United States government recognized the titles bestowed on individuals by the French, Spanish, British, and Mexican governments within the various cessions prior to transfer, subject to verification. By the mid-1970's the federal government retained only minute acreages of public domain in the area donated by the thirteen original states but still held more than seven hundred million acres of public lands, more than half in Alaska and most of the rest in the mountain and Pacific Coast states. Eighty-six percent of the lands of Nevada and 96 percent of the lands of Alaska were still federal property.

Table 2 shows the general disposition of public domain land under nine categories. Although useful, this table is an imprecise and simplified summary of a long and complex story. Category 1, for example, lists the acreage that the United States sold, including preemption purchases, in

TABLE 1
Acquisition of the Public Domain, 1781–1867

	Area (Acres)			
Acquisition	Land	Water	Total	Cost
State cessions (1781–1802)	233,415,680	3,409,920	236,825,600	$ 6,200,000
Louisiana Purchase (1803)[1]	523,446,400	6,465,280	529,911,680	23,213,568
Red River Basin[2]	29,066,880	535,040	29,601,920	
Cession from Spain (1819)	43,342,720	2,801,920	46,144,640	6,674,057
Oregon Compromise (1846)	180,644,480	2,741,760	183,386,240	
Mexican Cession (1848)	334,479,360	4,201,600	338,680,960	16,295,149
Purchase from Texas (1850)	78,842,880	83,840	78,926,720	15,496,448
Gadsden Purchase (1853)	18,961,920	26,880	18,988,800	10,000,000
Alaska Purchase (1867)	362,516,480	12,787,200	375,303,680	7,200,000
Total public domain	1,804,716,800	33,053,440	1,837,770,240	85,079,222

[1]Excludes areas eliminated by Treaty of 1819 with Spain.
[2]Basin of the Red River of the North, south of the forty-ninth parallel.
Source: U.S. Bureau of Land Management, *Public Land Statistics*, (Washington, D.C., 1974), table 2, p. 4.

LAND POLICIES AND SALES

TABLE 2
Disposition of Public Lands, 1781–1974

Type of Disposition	Acres	Percent of Whole
1 Disposition by sale, scrip, etc.	303,500,000	26.5
2 Granted or sold to homesteaders	287,500,000	25.1
3 Granted to states for		
a Support of common schools	77,600,000	6.8
b Reclamation of swampland	64,900,000	5.7
c Construction of railroads	37,100,000	3.2
d Support of miscellaneous institutions[1]	21,700,000	1.9
e Purposes not elsewhere classified[2]	117,500,000	10.3
f Canals and rivers	6,100,000	.53
g Construction of wagon roads	3,400,000	.29
Total granted to states	328,300,000	28.7
4 Granted to railroad corporations	94,300,000	8.2
5 Granted to veterans as military bounties	61,000,000	5.3
6 Confirmed as private land claims	34,000,000	3.0
7 Sold under Timber and Stone Act	13,900,000	1.2
8 Granted or sold under Timber Culture Act	10,900,000	.95
9 Sold under Desert Land Act	10,700,000	.93
Grand total	1,144,100,000	99.58

[1]Universities, hospitals, asylums, and so on.
[2]For construction of various public improvements (individual items not specified in the granting acts), reclamation of desert lands, construction of water reservoirs, and such.
Source: U.S. Bureau of Land Management, *Public Land Statistics, 1974,* table 3, p. 6.

which squatters on federal lands were allowed to buy their claims at the minimum federal price. Such purchases in some respects resembled transfer under the commutation provisions of the Homestead Act (1862), which allowed homesteaders to purchase their claims at the minimum federal sale price instead of fulfilling the residency requirement that would entitle them to receive a patent after the payment of minor fees. The United States issued certificates to various categories of claimants entitling the holder to stated acreages of land when presented at a federal land office (land scrip). The use of scrip is tabulated in category 1, but many states also acquired large amounts of scrip for sale under the provisions of the Land Grant College Act (Morrill Act of 1862), shown in category 3d. Railroad corporations received land under both categories 3b and 4.

Table 2 also does not show the degree to which federal land passed through the hands of intermediaries before reaching the individuals who proposed to grow crops, cut timber, build towns upon it, or extract minerals. Thus, the settler who filed a homestead entry at the appropriate federal land office might cancel that entry for a consideration offered by a latecomer, and this process of "relinquishment" might occur several times on the same land before the settler who actually acquired full title from the United States (the patentee) took possession. The chain of title to a tract within a railroad land grant might run through a state government, the railroad corporation, a subsidiary land company, and an investor, down to a genuine farmer. Nor do the categories of table 2 identify the actual use to which lands were put. Although the Homestead Act was designed to give free land to farmers, entrymen were sometimes lumbermen or miners. Finally, the table tells little of the changing relative importance of various land disposal procedures through time, their incidence in the various regions of the United States, or their impact on the development of the United States. These matters are considered in the following sections.

LAND POLICIES AND SALES

COLONIAL PRECEDENTS

When the members of the Continental Congress began to develop a national policy of public land administration and sales, they could look for precedents in more than 150 years of colonial practice. Since the procedures of the British government had been "haphazard, heterogeneous, planless" (Harris 1953, p. 397), the range of examples was considerable but some generalizations are possible. The natives, it was admitted, enjoyed a right of aboriginal occupancy but not the unrestricted right of disposition implicit in English fee simple title, and the provincial governments ultimately forbade individual colonists to purchase land directly from the natives. In the later years of the colonial period, the imperial government tried to assert supervisory rights over the Indian country and to exclude settlers from that region, thus establishing a precedent for central governance of the back country. The various colonial governments controlled the process of transferring land to individuals within their sovereignties, but there were some regional characteristics observable in their land disposal systems.

In New England the colonial governments developed a system of designating groups of proprietors whose members settled rectangular townships, supervised the internal surveys and distributed the resulting lots to themselves and later comers, and also set aside tracts for the support of education and religion. As the eighteenth century progressed, speculation increasingly entered the New England system, but, according to Charles Grant, land jobbers seldom dominated the settlement process completely. Apparently most of the colonies at some time gave tracts of land of specified size, called headrights, to those who paid their own passage, who completed service under indenture, or who transported impecunious individuals from abroad, on the basis of one plot of land for each such passage. The practice was least common in New England and most prevalent in Virginia and other southern colonies, where it contributed to the development of some large holdings. Cash sales also were common in the southern colonies. Large grants, often to major officials, were particularly frequent in New York. In that colony and in Pennsylvania, settlers purchased their lands to a greater degree than elsewhere. In all of the colonies south of New England, land was often granted subject to quitrents, monetary payments substituted for various personal services originally involved in the tenures of feudal England. Such grants aside, the colonial governments for the most part conveyed land to individuals in allodial tenure, that is, subject only to those rights exercised or retained by the government such as taxation, eminent domain, and the like.

Although some effort to adopt more systematic surveying practices occurred in the middle and southern colonies during the late colonial period, surveying there was generally done under the warrant and metes and bounds method. Under this system the colonial governments authorized purchasers by warrant to have a particular acreage surveyed by using the natural reference points or boundaries deemed most appropriate by the grantee or surveyor, without regard for township boundaries or internal lot lines (as was the case in New England). Overlapping boundaries and islands of unsold land were, therefore, more often found in the middle and southern colonies.

Allocation of land merely on the basis of settlement and improvement, free grants in the interest of frontier defense, and even land grants for the support of higher education were found in some colonies. Given land speculation, overlapping surveys, and impatient settlers, squatter's rights, preemption, and laws of adverse possession (requiring individuals to assert claims to ownership of land within a stated period or see those claims ruled invalid and the land awarded to others who had complied with the law) became part of the colonial land systems.

ORIGINS OF THE FEDERAL LAND SYSTEM: 1785–1800

Although Congress approved a system of government and land sales in the regions north of the Ohio River in 1784, the basic ordinances defining these matters were passed in the following year and in 1787. The ordinance "for ascertaining the mode of disposing of lands in the Western territory" of 1785 described the method of choosing surveyors, their remuneration and methods, and the administration and sale procedures to be followed. Lands were re-

LAND POLICIES AND SALES

served for Canadian and Nova Scotian refugees, three bands of "Christian Indians," and the officers and soldiers of the Virginia revolutionary forces.

The Ordinance of 1785 provided for the survey of seven ranges (east-west) of six-mile-square townships north of the Ohio River, in tiers (north-south) lying south of the "geographer's line" (soon to be surveyed by Thomas Hutchins, geographer of the United States) and running west from the intersection of the western boundary of Pennsylvania with the Ohio River. The townships were to be parceled in thirty-six numbered sections (lots), each one mile square and containing 640 acres. The Board of the Treasury would supervise sales. Lot 16 was reserved for the maintenance of public schools, and the United States also (until 1804) reserved for itself lots 8, 11, 26, and 29, as well as one-third of all gold, silver, lead, and copper mines. Also, the secretary of war might reserve surveyed lands "for the use of the late continental army." The commissioners of the loan offices of the several states were to cry (sell) the remaining surveyed public lands at public vendue (auction), alternate townships being sold whole and the intervening ones by lots. The minimum price was to be $1.00 per acre plus surveying fees, payable in specie (coined money) or Continental paper money.

Many of the provisions of the Ordinance of 1785 were abandoned or changed in the legislation of Congress under the federal Constitution, and from the standpoint of the land seeker, the ordinance provided a land disposal system less generous than much colonial practice. But in recognizing a possessory and purchasable title in the Indian tribes, in stipulating rectangular surveys prior to sale, in providing for public auctions, in establishing a minimum price, and in reserving section 16 for the support of public schools, the Ordinance of 1785 established policies that were continued in the subsequent public land disposal system.

Having approved the Ordinance of 1785, the members of Congress were still willing to deal directly with large purchasers. They soon agreed to sell lands to the Ohio and Scioto Companies, believed by the purchasers to comprise between five and six million acres, and an additional one million acres to John Cleves Symmes and associated New Jersey investors. The rise in the value of federal securities that these groups planned to tender for such lands made it impossible for them to complete the anticipated purchases in full. The Scioto Company foundered, but the other two concerns survived to transfer title of large parts of their purchases to settlers.

CREATION OF A CREDIT SYSTEM: 1800–1820

When the members of the federal Congress made their first major alteration of the land disposal system in 1796, they retained the 640-acre section as the minimum unit of purchase, but the maximum unit of sale was to be the quarter-township. Section purchases were to be available in Cincinnati and Pittsburgh, and purchases of larger units of land were to be made at the seat of the federal government. The minimum price was $2.00 per acre, but the purchaser was provided credit: 5 percent down, 50 percent paid in thirty days, and the remainder paid within a year. There was to be a 5 percent discount on cash transactions.

Congress developed the credit system more fully in the Harrison Land Act of 1800. The minimum price remained at $2.00 per acre, but now payments were spread over four years. Deferred payments carried interest, but the provision of 1796 calling for forfeiture in case of default was eased. The quarter-township units of the Act of 1796 were to be further subdivided into 320-acre units. Four years later Congress reduced the minimum purchase to 160 acres and provided that interest should be charged only on past-due payments.

Within a relatively short time congressmen and government officers became concerned with the delinquencies of credit purchasers. Beginning in 1806 relief acts extended the time during which purchasers in arrears might make payments on acquisitions of a section or less. But prosperity following the War of 1812 stimulated speculation, particularly in Alabama. Land buyers owed the government some $24 million, and many purchasers were delinquent after the contraction of 1819. Congress terminated the credit system in 1820, providing that surveyed public land was to be sold at pub-

LAND POLICIES AND SALES

lic auction, at a minimum cash price of $1.25 per acre. Between 1821 and 1832 Congress passed eleven relief acts giving the delinquent credit buyers assistance in making good their purchases. In the meantime, during the War of 1812 Congress again provided military land bounties for soldiers.

During the credit era Congress developed general policies governing the claims of new states upon the public domain within their boundaries. In 1802 the Ohio Enabling Act set a pattern of pledging acreage to new states: it reaffirmed the reservation of section 16 for public schools, allocated lands adjacent to salt springs to the new state, pledged some sixty thousand acres for the support of institutions of higher learning, and provided 3 percent of the revenues from the sales of Ohio public lands for use in the construction of roads within the new state and 2 percent without. But the federal government retained possession of the unalienated domain within Ohio and exempted the purchasers of federal lands from real estate taxation for five years after title passed.

During the late eighteenth and early nineteenth centuries, the federal government developed long-surviving administrative machinery and practices governing land disposal. Surveyors general replaced the geographer of the United States of the Ordinance of 1785 in supervising deputy surveyors and their crews in the field and in preparing surveying maps (plats) and descriptions of the surveyed lands. Land offices in the western country were placed conveniently adjacent to the public lands at sale. Registers and receivers administered the offices, assisted by clerks and temporary superintendants of public sales. Initially the land office personnel derived their remuneration from fees, but criticism led to a salary system supplemented, in the case of registers and receivers, by a percentage of their office transactions. In 1812 Congress centralized control of the government land business in the General Land Office, a bureau of the Treasury Department administered by a commissioner; the agency was transferred to the new Department of the Interior in 1849. The maintenance of duplicate records in the General Land Office and district land offices laid the foundation for a land disposal system that was administratively effective, although sometimes compromised by dishonest employees.

CASH SALE AND PREEMPTION: 1820–1862

During the period 1820–1862 the United States government continued to sell land at auction to the highest bidder and allowed buyers to acquire offered but unsold land by private entry at the minimum price. The eighty-acre minimum purchase unit specified in the Land Act of 1820 was reduced still further to forty acres. In general the sale prices at auction stayed at or close to the minimum, reflecting collusion among affluent purchasers and the development of intimidating squatters' associations, as well as the value that buyers in general discerned in raw government lands.

The Harrison Land Act of 1800 provided a preemption privilege for a restricted category of purchasers, and various other measures offered preemption rights in specific cases prior to 1820. On occasion Congress granted restricted preemptive rights during the 1820's, and in 1830 it provided a retroactive general preemption law that allowed settlers occupying cultivated holdings on the public lands in 1829 to enter as much as 160 acres at $1.25 per acre before the public land auction, thereby obtaining protection from claim jumpers or unfriendly bidders at the sale. This act expired in one year, but Congress later approved several similar laws before providing a general prospective right of preemption in Clay's Land Distribution Bill of 1841. If they were citizens or were becoming naturalized, all heads of families, single men over twenty-one, and widows might preempt 160 acres of land on the surveyed public domain, provided that they did not already own 320 acres elsewhere or had not abandoned their residence in the same state or territory in order to qualify. The preemptor on surveyed but unoffered lands had to purchase before the land sale; the preemptor on offered lands had to buy his claim within twelve months. During the 1850's preemptions were allowed on unsurveyed lands in California, and the privilege became general in 1862.

Other changes in the land disposal system during this period varied in importance and duration. Congress revised the 3 percent fund for new states to 5 percent during the mid-1830's, but efforts to provide a more generous distribution of land revenues achieved only minor success. When the land sales of the 1830's swelled

LAND POLICIES AND SALES

federal receipts, Congress authorized the deposit of some of the Treasury surplus with the states, and the Distribution-Preemption Act of 1841 provided for the distribution of additional proceeds of public land sales to the states, subject to maintenance of tariff schedules at 20 percent or less. Since the tariff schedules were raised above that level almost immediately, distribution under the Distribution-Preemption Act of 1841 involved only one payment. More significant was the proposal for graduated prices advocated by Thomas Hart Benton and other politicians and publicists. In 1854 the Graduation Act scaled down prices on most offered lands to levels ranging from $1.00 per acre to 12.5 cents for tracts that had stood unsold for thirty years. Congress repealed this measure in 1862, after critics charged that speculators had profited unduly from it.

A system of leasing mineral lands, which originated in the early years of the nation and was applied in the lead region of Missouri, broke down there and, later, in the lead region of Illinois, Iowa, and Wisconsin. It was replaced by a sales policy. Acts of 1847 relevant to the upper Great Lakes region established prices of not less than $5.00 per acre on lead and copper lands, which soon were revised downward to $1.25 per acre. Subsequently the federal government allowed miners to extract the precious metal riches of the Far West without federal regulation between 1849 and the mid-1860's. Much other mineral land passed to the private sector under the operation of the general land statutes.

During this period Congress also used the public domain generously for special purposes. In raising troops for the Mexican War it passed a military land-bounty warrant act in 1847 that was supplemented by laws of 1850, 1852, and 1855. In sum, this legislation provided that all veterans of American wars to that time (or their surviving heirs) who had not previously received a land bounty in the amount of 160 acres of land were entitled to acreage sufficient to make up that amount. Despite some congressional efforts to limit assignment, the veterans frequently sold their warrants to brokers, and such paper could be quite generally acquired at prices below the land office value of $1.25 per acre. In 1824 Congress began to grant land to states in alternate sections along the routes of roads, canals, and river improvements in order to stimulate the construction of such works; the policy was applied to railroad construction as well in 1850. In the same year Congress gave the title of swamplands to the states within which they lay, subject to the requirement that they be drained—a provision that was generally ignored. When it admitted California to statehood, Congress tendered not only section 16 to that state for the support of schools but also section 36, a precedent followed for forty years until even more land was tendered for that purpose. As midcentury approached, the federal legislators discontinued the policy of exempting the purchaser of federal land from taxation for five years.

The town builder moved west with the farmer, and after some early federal efforts to plat and sell town sites, the United States established the policy in 1844 of allowing municipal corporate bodies the right to acquire their town sites by preemptive purchase. Mainly under this law and a more generous statute of 1867, United States authorities transferred some 163,000 acres of land to 474 towns by mid-1883.

THE HOMESTEAD ERA TO THE REVISION ACT OF 1891

There were precedents for a homestead act both in the colonial era and in federal donation laws granting land to early settlers in Florida, Oregon, Washington, and New Mexico. Interest in such a measure grew from the 1830's, both within and outside Congress, and President James Buchanan vetoed a so-called homestead bill providing for five years of residence, improvement, and a purchase price of 25 cents per acre. As approved in 1862, the Homestead Act provided 160-acre holdings on the surveyed public domain for heads of households, Union veterans, and others at least twenty-one years of age (provided that such individuals were citizens or had begun naturalization proceedings and had not borne arms against the Union), subject to the requirement of five years of residence and improvement and the payment of a small filing fee. Homesteaders might commute their entries to cash purchase after six months. For some twenty years most claimants under the Homestead Act could acquire only eighty acres in the alternate sections within railroad land

LAND POLICIES AND SALES

grants belonging to the government, but Union veterans obtained the privilege of a 160-acre homestead in such areas in 1870. Two years later these veterans were allowed to deduct the terms of their service from the five-year residence requirement of 1862, and veterans who earlier had been limited to eighty-acre homesteads obtained additional homestead rights. Legislation of 1866 provided that all public lands in the reconstructed states should be held for homesteading, but as southern pine lands began to attract interest, Congress in 1876 approved the sale of unoffered public domain in the southern states having such land.

The passage of the Homestead Act did not terminate the disposal programs then in force, nor did it inhibit Congress from developing others. Congress continued to allocate lands so as to assist railroad construction until 1870. Particularly during the 1860's, but to some extent thereafter, the government offered land at auction, thus contributing to the supply of offered but unsold government lands available at private entry. In 1862 Congress approved the Land Grant College Act (Morrill Act), allocating public lands or equivalent scrip to each state for the support of colleges of agriculture and mechanical arts, in the amount of thirty thousand acres for each member of the state congressional delegation. Also during this period the United States government continued to offer some Indian lands directly for sale as tribes were moved or their holdings reduced.

One hundred sixty acres or less provided an adequate farm unit in much of the Mississippi Valley during the mid-nineteenth century, but that acreage was frequently insufficient to support the settler who moved after the Civil War into the moisture-deficient regions beyond the ninety-eighth meridian, that is, beyond central Kansas and equivalent regions north and south. Although some homesteaders used both the Preemption Act and the Homestead Act to develop farms, Congress to some degree endeavored during the 1870's to adapt the land disposal system to the environment of the semiarid West. The Timber Culture Acts of 1873 and 1878 allowed settlers to file claims to 160 acres, subject to the requirement that they would plant and raise trees upon substantial portions of their tracts during eight years of development. Under the Desert Land Act of 1877 individuals in most western territories and states might buy 640 acres for the purpose of irrigation agriculture; 25 cents per acre was due at filing and a further payment of $1.00 per acre was due at the end of three years.

Mineral lands policy was further clarified during this era. Legislation of 1864 and 1865 established a minimum price of $20.00 per acre for coal lands, to be sold in units of 160 acres or less, and was further amended in 1873 to allow associations to acquire as much as 640 acres at a price of $10.00 per acre if the land was located more than fifteen miles from a railroad. Acts of 1866, 1870, and 1872 provided for the sale of gold, silver, cinnabar, and copper lode claims at $5.00 per acre and placer locations at $2.50 per acre, with appropriate restrictions on size. Not until the late 1870's did the government begin to develop policy for lands valuable chiefly for their timber. Acts of 1878 allowed settlers in most of the West to use the small amounts of timber needed for their mining or domestic purposes without cost (Timber Cutting Act) or to buy tracts valuable chiefly for timber or stone in acreages of 160 acres or less at a price of $2.50 per acre (Timber and Stone Act).

Efforts in the 1880's to reform the land laws culminated in the General Revision Act of 1891, which included provisions terminating auction and cash sales of public lands with minor exceptions; repealing the Timber Culture Act and the Preemption Act; making the Desert Land Act more restrictive; barring individuals who owned more than 160 acres of land from homesteading; and extending the homesteader's period of required residence prior to commutation to fourteen months. A very important section allowed the president to set aside forest reserves on the public lands.

THE GENERAL REVISION ACT TO THE TAYLOR GRAZING ACT OF 1934

The federal lawmakers increased the acreage of the homestead unit in western Nebraska to 640 acres (Kinkaid Act, 1904) and on the public lands generally to 320 acres in 1909. In 1912 they reduced the settlement period to three years, and in 1916 the Stock Raising Homestead

Act provided a full section for individuals engaged in stock raising.

In the meantime the conservation movement effected a considerable redirection of land disposal policies. While alienation under the homestead laws and some other statutes continued, the conservationists applied reservation and controlled-use policies to various categories of public lands. Presidents Benjamin Harrison, Grover Cleveland, and William McKinley set aside more than forty-six million acres of forest reserves. Theodore Roosevelt raised the amount to more than 194 million acres in 158 reserves, including some lands in Alaska and in private ownership. Legislation under Cleveland allowed the development of forest management policies, and conservationists succeeded in transferring administration of the reserves from the Interior Department to the Forest Service of the Department of Agriculture in 1905. Later legislation (Weeks Act, 1911) allowed the federal government to purchase forest lands of importance in watershed control, thus providing the means for developing forest reserves in longer-settled regions of the country. During this era the conservationists applied the reservation policy to various mineral lands, such as those containing coal, oil, and phosphate deposits, and in 1920 Congress established a general system of exploitation by leasing for such resources. Leasing policies were also developed for waterpower sites on the public lands, under the administration of the Federal Electric Power Commission.

Early federal efforts to assist irrigation development involved passage of the Desert Land Act and the transfer of some irrigable lands to western states (Carey Desert Land Act, 1894); neither policy was highly successful. In 1902 western congressmen, led by Francis G. Newlands, succeeded in passing the Reclamation (or Newlands) Act. Now the revenue from the public lands (except the 5 percent funds) in sixteen western states would provide a reclamation fund for financing the planning, construction, and maintenance of irrigation works under the direction of the secretary of the interior, who might withdraw public lands from general entry for use in irrigation projects. Such lands had to be homesteaded, but charges paid both by homesteaders under the Reclamation Act and by prior residents in the development area were to finance the projects and recharge the fund. The federal reclamation program evolved painfully, and the electric power potential of the reclamation program was not fully exploited until the New Deal era.

By the 1920's the unreserved, unalienated public domain of the contiguous states was mostly rangeland, believed to be damaged by the unsupervised practices of western stockmen. The Taylor Grazing Act of 1934 provided that the unreserved lands in twenty-two western states be withdrawn from entry and, "pending . . . final [federal] disposal," be administered as grazing districts by the Department of the Interior, to a maximum acreage initially of eighty million acres. The Taylor Act did not repeal the homestead laws, the process of withdrawal took time, entries already filed remained in force, and theoretically settlers might still homestead appropriate lands outside the grazing districts. But in effect the law ended the free homestead era in the American West.

Although alienation of federal lands sharply diminished after 1934, limited transfers occurred as old entries were completed and individuals invoked the Desert Land Act, the Mining Act of 1872, and the Small Tract Act (1938), and restricted disposal features of the Taylor Act and its amendments. Community acquisition for recreational and public uses was allowed (1926), and the secretary of the interior's powers of alienation were enlarged temporarily in 1964. But the major federal resource programs now involved the continuing management of national forests (by the Department of Agriculture) and grazing districts, national parks and monuments, wildlife reserves, mineral reserves (including oil rights on the continental shelf), and waterpower sites (by the Department of the Interior). The programs featured multiple-use management, the sustained use of renewable resources, and the controlled use of nonrenewable resources, usually under lease. Symbolically, the General Land Office expired as such in 1946, and its functions were combined with those of the Grazing Service in the Bureau of Land Management. Following the work of the Public Land Law Review Commission during the mid- and late 1960's, Congress approved laws designed to improve the management of the nation's mineral, forest reserve, and Bureau of Land Management lands.

LAND POLICIES AND SALES

FIGURE 1* Original Land Entries, 1800–1934

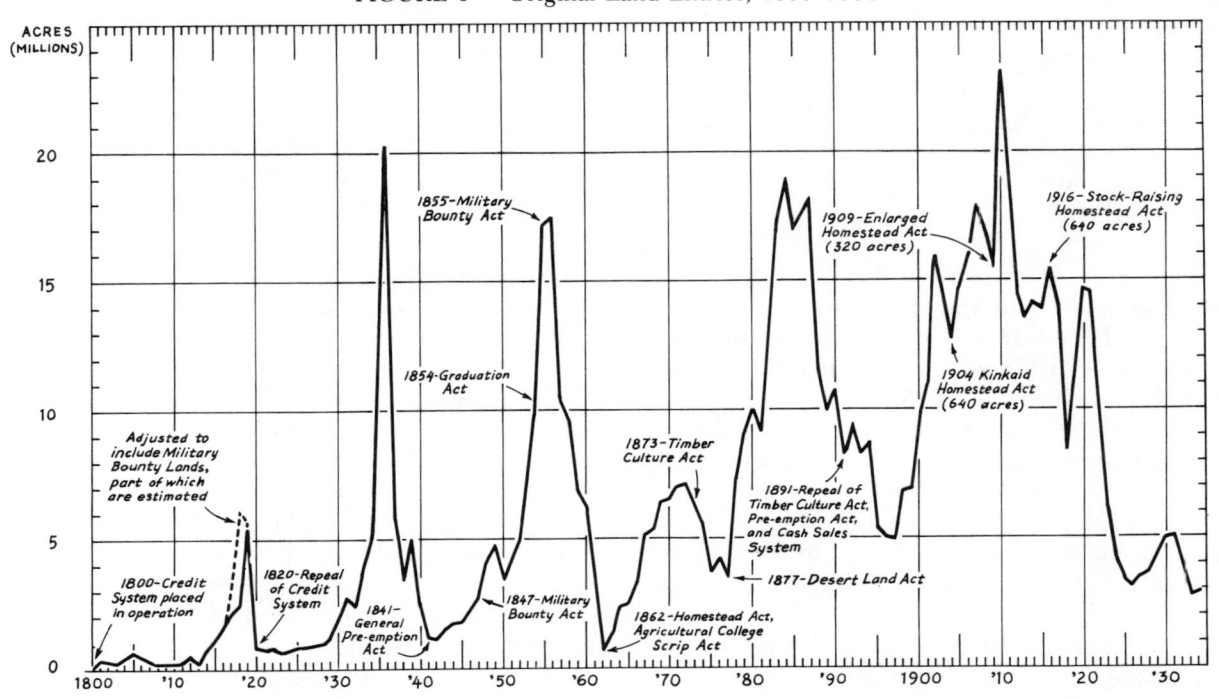

U.S. DEPARTMENT OF AGRICULTURE — BUREAU OF AGRICULTURAL ECONOMICS

Note: In the preparation of this chart all of the original land entries under the various laws were compiled, insofar as this was possible. This chart includes the following types of cash entries: private cash entries, public auction sales, preemption entries, Indian land sales, timber and stone entries under the Act of 1877, mineral-land entries (small), coal-land entries (small), abandoned military reservations, and miscellaneous sales. It also includes entries made with military warrants and various kinds of scrip. Original entries under the Homestead, Timber Culture, and Desert Land acts are included.

It was not possible to secure data concerning all the land entered with scrip and military warrants, the amount not included in the chart being less than 3 million acres, the absence of which does not materially affect the picture here presented.

It should be pointed out that this chart is for original entries. A chart of final entries or one showing the amount of entries going to patent would be substantially different, as a large amount of homestead, timber culture, and desert-land entries never were proved up.

The chart does not include lands granted to railroads or states, nor certain small grants to individuals. Nor does it include Indian land sales prior to 1879 or the sale of Indian allotments at any time.

Source: National Resources Board, *Report of the Land Planning Committee,* part VII (Washington, D.C., 1935), p. 61.

LAND DISPOSAL SUMMARIZED, 1785–1934

It is extremely difficult to estimate precisely the amounts of land transferred to the state and private sectors by the federal government in given years or within restricted time periods. Understandably, the land disposal tabulations maintained by the General Land Office have varied in form through time, and some details of land office accounting are irretrievably lost. Some series may involve double counting. One scholar, therefore, has described the basic data as "confusing, incomplete, or conflicting" (Peffer 1951, p. 353). Moreover, entrymen were more numerous than patentees in cases where land laws specified residence or improvement requirements. The actual process of locating military bounty lands, and state or corporation grant lands, continued long after the original congressional allocation. Some surveyed federal lands, notably the sections in transportation grants, were closed to settlers for varying periods of time, with an attendant impact on regional settlement patterns that is almost incalculable. And in some cases the federal government eventually transferred less acreage to donees than the provisions of special grant legislation actually authorized. Despite such reservations, figure 1 conveys a useful impression of the operation of those federal laws under which individuals obtained unimproved lands directly from the federal government.

If special grants are considered as having been allocated in the year of the enabling legislation and, in general, final patents are counted rather than original entries, the mean annual flow of land from the federal government was probably in the neighborhood of 750,000 acres per annum to 1820, rose to about 8 million acres during the next forty years, increased to perhaps 9.5 million acres per annum in the period 1862–1891, and then declined by some 40 percent until 1934 (if federal lands reserved for special purposes are not included). Four hundred and seventy-four million acres of vacant and unreserved public lands remained in the contiguous states in 1904; and this area had declined to 166 million acres by 1934. By the latter year some 187 million acres of federal lands were reserved or withdrawn for special public purposes, and some 55 million acres of original public domain remained in the possession of native American tribal groups.

TABLE 3
Public Land Sales as Percentage of Total Federal Receipts

Year	Percent	Year	Percent
1801	1.3	1845	6.9
1805	4.0	1850	4.3
1810	7.4	1855	17.6
1815	8.2	1860	3.2
1820	9.1	1865	.3
1825	5.6	1870	.9
1830	9.4	1875	.5
1835	41.7	1880	.3
1840	16.9		

Source: United States Bureau of the Census, *Historical Statistics of the United States* (Washington, D.C., 1960), p. 712, series Y258 and Y263.

Historians have suggested with some justice that the post–Civil War era was a "Great Barbecue," when special interests raided the natural resources of the nation. But rapid disposal characterized the latter part of the antebellum period as well. Nor was the late nineteenth century the era of maximum disposal under the homestead laws, as is sometimes thought. Homesteaders acquired title to 52 million acres through 1891, but to more than 230 million acres subsequently. By comparison, claimants under the Timber Culture Acts patented only 10,866,888 acres.

Table 3 shows that the federal government derived a substantial proportion of federal receipts from the sales of public lands during the early nineteenth century, with that contribution peaking in 1836 (49 percent). Since the federal government transferred large amounts of land to the states, which used it to produce revenue or its equivalent, the data of this table understate the contribution of public land sales to all government receipts.

CHANGE IN THE LAND DISPOSAL SYSTEM

The development of federal land policy was a complex process. In part the federal government responded to obvious problems, such as the need to repay the Revolutionary War debt, to raise troops, and later to husband resources essential to national defense or welfare. But in effecting specific solutions or designing more general policy, lawmakers reflected the perceptions of many constituencies and special interests: veterans, indebted squatters, eastern laborers, railroad corporations, land patent attorneys, land reformers, warrant brokers, town promoters, the National Academy of Sciences, chambers of commerce, conservationists, and many others.

Should the western lands foster a free population of family farmers, or should they become an adjunct to an expansive slave plantation economy? The Civil War answered these questions. Representatives of the original states viewed the public domain as a common fund to be used to benefit their constituents as well as the residents of the new public land regions. But the latter wished to use the public land resources of their regions as they saw fit. Settlers and their advocates wished maximum opportunity to develop farm operations and to benefit from the rise in the price of farmland. Members of the business communities of both East and West wanted maximum opportunity to invest their resources profitably in western development. American political parties mediated among the supplicants and integrated constituency demands into platforms that won national support. Democrats particularly endorsed preemption; the Whigs favored distribution of public lands revenue to the states; the Homestead Law was a Republican triumph. But such was the complexity of national need, resource utilization, and constituency and interest-group pressures that major innovations in land disposal policy often attracted support from both parties.

The Founding Fathers established a system of land disposal that was less generous to the land seeker than much of the colonial precedent had been. The need to retire the debt from the Revolutionary War explains that fact in part, but the minimum sale price prescribed in 1796 was much higher than that set in the Ordinance of 1785 and far above the level suggested by Alexander Hamilton when he was secretary of the Treasury. Nor did Congress allow individual purchasers to obtain land units appropriate for family-size farms until the early nineteenth century. Undoubtedly the lawmakers well understood that their states or constituents still held large tracts of undeveloped land for sale in competition with those in the federal domain. Cheap federal lands in small units might depreciate the price of eastern improved lands, drain off labor from eastern communities, and hasten the development of new states to dilute the power of the older states in Congress.

Initially change in the land system mainly involved making the land offices more accessible, reducing the size of the minimum purchase unit, and providing credit—mere facilitative alterations—as well as establishing the precedent of state grants. Although the Distribution-Preemption Act and the Homestead Act were designed in the interests of family farmers, during the same era Congress allocated large amounts of public lands for developmental purposes in transportation grants and in the swamplands distribution. The retroactive features of the military bounty-warrant legislation of midcentury were in part a response to considerations of equity. But the Congress of that era further developed the welfare and modernizing concerns of their predecessors by making massive additional grants in behalf of education. The growth of so eclectic and developmental a philosophy of public lands management reflected reduction in the national debt, the realization of the tariff and excise potential in a growing and industrializing nation, and an understanding of the importance of the markets and materials provided by the farms, mines, and forests of the West. Amid the complexities of pressures and principles, the lawmakers by the mid-nineteenth century had moved far toward satisfying all major comers. Today the wisdom of their decisions may be tested by cost-benefit analysis, but their calculus was necessarily of a cruder sort.

After settlers reached the moisture-deficient regions, federal lawmakers faced the challenge of making disposal policy conform to the realities of the natural environment as well as to the needs of a growing population in an increasingly complex economic system. Timber culture, encouragement of irrigation, and the increase in the size of the homestead all disappointed their supporters, although each policy contributed to the success of individual settlers.

American land policy changed dramatically during the late nineteenth and early twentieth centuries, but the alterations reflected attitudes that had been developing for some time. Some advocates of the homestead policy faulted other disposal programs, in the belief that the remaining public domain should be reserved for homesteaders. Henry George and other reformers criticized the accumulation of large holdings in California and in the nation generally; land-grant railroads and foreign investors emerged as special culprits in the process. The growth of tenant farming, confirmed by the United States Census of 1880, was distressing in a nation avowedly willing to provide free farms for all able to develop them. Agricultural depressions, persistently recurrent although differing regionally in intensity, encouraged criticism of the land system. Members of the scientific community became critical of the failure of the government to develop a rational forest policy and supported John Wesley Powell's contentions that the land disposal system of the 1870's and 1880's was unsuited to the semiarid West. The diminution of genuine wilderness in America stimulated the emergence of aesthetic conservationists, most notably John Muir. Others realized that the supply of new land that had supported the farm frontier for several centuries was becoming exhausted. All of these elements underlay the change of attitudes and policy during the late nineteenth and early twentieth centuries.

THE HISTORIAN'S VERDICT

Most of the major twentieth-century historians who have described the federal land disposal system have written in the critical tradition of the Progressive era, emphasizing sloppy and fraudulent surveying practices, defaulting land officers, combinations to hold down auction prices, fraudulent entry procedures, illegal occupation of the public domain, plunder of minerals and timber, and failure to adjust the land disposal laws to special environmental conditions or to the needs of particular types of users. They have described the accumulation of large holdings and speculative profits, and the growth of tenancy, to the detriment of independent family farmers. Such large holders retarded regional development, the progressive historians have argued, while, on the other hand, the land-grant railroads failed to meet their statutory obligations or to provide adequate services.

The work of these historians is often impressive, but they did not always weigh the evidence as rigorously as is desirable. The proportion of defective surveys is not known, or the proportion of absconding land officers, or the resultant Treasury losses. Nor is known the extent to which combinations at the auctions affected sales. Investigation of land speculation since the mid-1950's has discredited suggestions that speculators usually either lost money or obtained huge profits. Apparently, long-run returns to investors in land were comparable with those derived from other major types of investment in the same region. Tenancy developed on large holdings during the settlement period, but relatively few farmers rented from the descendants of frontier landlords. Donald L. Winters' regression analysis of tenancy in Iowa (Winters, p. 16) suggests that the relation between modern tenancy and the extent of frontier land speculation there is negligible. The initial sale and survey patterns still influence modern land use and the transportation network, according to Hildegard Johnson, sometimes with deleterious social effects; but generalization on such matters is difficult.

The public lands were a great national asset. Federal policies governing disposal might influence the overall economic development of the country as well as produce redistributive or equity effects. Progressive historians have particularly focused on the latter effects. Since 1960 econometric historians have begun to study the relations between federal land policy and economic development. Because federal land disposal was complex and was only part of the land market, because the federal lands varied greatly in their productive capacity, because some data appropriate to the models in use are not easily marshaled and estimation problems are relatively severe, and because the coverage of such research is incomplete, the findings are as yet largely tentative.

Preliminary results suggest that before the Civil War the demand for government land was closely related to the current prices of major agricultural crops; investors viewed land purchase within the context of the returns from alternative investments; cyclical factors influenced the land market; the government policy of rapid alienation probably fostered the manufacturing sector of the economy but, due to the inelasticity of demand for cotton, rapid alienation of southern lands probably benefited the foreign purchasers of cotton at the expense of Americans (that is, federal revenues generated in the liberal disposal policy were offset by losses in the private sector). This literature suggests that the abundance of land perhaps discouraged soil conservation in the South before the Civil War and trapped underemployed labor on exhausted soils.

Some economic historians have argued that the railroad land-grant program contributed positively to American economic growth in some cases, but one critic regards "the final evaluation of the land grant policy as still open" (Engerman 1972, p. 463). Even more tentatively some suggest that the policy of holding overvalued lands at private entry for long periods of time prior to the passage of the Graduation Act slowed development, as did the tendency of the homestead system to encourage inefficient farmers to take up western lands. Similarly, they argue that retention of the 160-acre homestead unit for a considerable period after settlement reached the moisture-deficient regions also stimulated the inefficient utilization of land resources. In corroboration it has been argued that four original entries and two final homestead entries were required to make a farm in various western states.

In untold numbers of debates in the United States Congress, in the legislative and executive reports of the United States government, and in the publications of several federal commissions (1879, 1903, 1929, 1964), American public servants have struggled to understand, describe, and shape management and disposal policies for the natural resources of the nation. Although the frontier phase of those policies is now past, the magnitude of the mineral, timber, grazing, recreational, and aesthetic resources still to be found in what the Public Land Law Review Commission of 1964 called *One Third of the Nation's Land* guarantees that neither the debates nor the public interest will flag in generations to come.

BIBLIOGRAPHY

Vernon Carstensen, ed., *The Public Lands: Studies in the History of the Public Domain* (Madison, Wis., 1963), the best sampling of the periodical literature on the history of the public domain, includes significant contributions by Thomas LeDuc, Allan G. Bogue, and many others. Stanley L. Engerman, "Some Economic Issues Relating to Railroad Subsidies and the Evaluation of Land Grants," in *Journal of Economic History*, 32 (June 1972), is a thoughtful discussion of the controversial questions involved in determining the entrepreneurial and corporation profits and social benefits accruing from the railroad land-grant policy. Paul W. Gates, *History of Public Land Law Development* (Washington, D.C., 1968), the summation of a lifetime of research on American land policy, largely replaces the earlier surveys by Roy M. Robbins and Benjamin H. Hibbard, and contains a concluding chapter on the history of mineral resource exploitation by Robert W. Swenson, plus a comprehensive bibliography. Charles S. Grant, *Democracy in the Connecticut Frontier Town of Kent* (New York, 1961), includes a useful description of the workings of the Connecticut land disposal system in the mid-eighteenth century. Marshall Harris, *Origin of the Land Tenure System in the United States* (Ames, Iowa, 1953), despite tantalizing omissions and a rather encyclopedic organization, is the best single secondary source of information about the colonial land systems.

Hildegard B. Johnson, *Order Upon the Land* (New York, 1976), an examination by a geographer of the way the United States system of land surveys is reflected in the modern landscape. U.S. Public Land Law Review Commission, *One Third of the Nation's Land: A Report to the President and to the Congress,* (Washington, D.C., 1970), which contains controversial recommendations, is an excellent introduction to the public land issues of the 1960's and 1970's. Richard C. Overton, *Burlington West: A Colonization History of the Burlington Railroad* (Cambridge, Mass., 1941), is an excellent institutional description of the management and settlement of the lands granted to an important midwestern carrier. Peter Passell, *Essays in the Economics of Nineteenth Century American Land Policy* (New York, 1975), illustrates the growing interest of econometric historians in the economic effects of federal land policy. E. Louise Peffer, *The Closing of the Public Domain: Disposal and Reservation Policies, 1900–50* (Stanford, Calif., 1951), the most inclusive monographic treatment of twentieth-century land policy, the coverage of the Taylor Grazing Act and the events preceding the creation of the Bureau of Land Management being particularly useful. Malcolm Rohrbough, *The Land Office Business: The Settlement and Administration of American Public Lands, 1789–1837* (New York, 1968), is a probing and critical analysis of land sale procedures and transactions in the formative years of the national land disposal system. Donald L. Winters, *Farmers Without Farms: Agricultural Tenancy in Nineteenth-Century Iowa* (Westport, Conn., 1978), examines the relation between land disposal and tenure patterns in an important agricultural state.

[See also AGRICULTURE; ECONOMIC GROWTH; ECONOMY FROM THE REVOLUTION TO 1815; ECONOMY FROM 1815 TO 1865; EDUCATION; GOVERNMENT MANAGEMENT OF THE ECONOMY; and WESTWARD MOVEMENT.]

AMERICAN BUSINESS INSTITUTIONS BEFORE THE RAILROAD

Stephen Salsbury

ALTHOUGH the construction and operation of massive railroad systems in the 1840's and 1850's effected radical changes in the nature of American business organization, it was in the prerailroad business era that an important institutional framework was brought into being that is of vital importance to understanding the twentieth-century American economic system. For purposes of analysis, the prerailroad business era may be divided into two parts: the colonial period, extending from the founding of the first colonies in the early seventeenth century to the American Revolution; and the early national period, extending from 1776 to the 1840's. Two intertwined institutions dominated the colonial period: the merchant and the complex credit system that he used. The early national period saw the rise of new forms, one of the most important being the corporation used for organizing banks, transportation enterprises such as turnpikes and canals, and certain industrial ventures such as textile mills. The early national period also saw the beginning of the large-scale factory system.

THE COLONIAL PERIOD

Throughout the colonial period the merchant was the fulcrum on which the American economy turned. The primary economic problem of the British North American colonies was the lack of capital. For this reason the English experience differed radically from that of the Spanish, who in Peru and Mexico found advanced Indian civilizations with large accumulations of gold and silver (specie), commodities that the Europeans used as the basis of their monetary systems. The English, on the other hand, settled lands with no sources of specie, and their colonies had no readily available staple commodity for which they could find a market either in England or on the Continent. To develop their American colonies the English had to furnish vast amounts of capital, which underwrote the transportation of colonists to the New World and supplied them with the tools and farm animals necessary to begin an agricultural system. Capital was also needed to provide for the colonists until the land became productive, a period of at least a year and often much longer. Eventually some English colonies, notably the southern ones (Maryland, Virginia, the Carolinas, and Georgia), came to grow staple crops (tobacco, rice, and indigo) that had ready markets in England and on the Continent. The northern colonies (New Hampshire, Massachusetts, Rhode Island, Connecticut, New York, New Jersey, Pennsylvania, and Delaware) never managed to grow agricultural staples that had a demand either in England or in northern Europe (although grain exports from the middle colonies to non-European destinations eventually would stand as second to tobacco in the value of total commodity exports from the mainland colonies). Nevertheless, the need for capital was every bit as great in the North as in the South. In both cases it was the merchants and the credit system that they administered that supplied this need. Since the mercantile arrangements differed considerably from North to South, each will be considered separately.

AMERICAN BUSINESS INSTITUTIONS BEFORE THE RAILROAD

The Virginia Company. The first English economic venture in North America resulted not from the actions of individual merchant houses, but from the combined efforts of a number of substantial London merchants, who organized a corporation, the Virginia Company of London, in 1606. This company, operating under a royal charter, used what was at that time the most advanced institutional form known. As Wesley Frank Craven has pointed out, the Virginia Company, whatever else it might have been, "was primarily a business organization with large sums of capital invested by adventurers whose chief interest lay in the returns expected from their investment." The company was of the joint-stock variety; its organization had many similarities to the modern corporation. Adventurers purchased shares; and, after the reforms of 1609, they received full power to control the company. They elected a council and designated the treasurer and his assistant as the two chief executive officers of the firm. The council and its officers sat in London and appointed a governor and council to run affairs in Virginia.

The original intention of the London merchants had been that all property in the Virginia Company colony would be owned by the corporation, with labor to be performed by indentured servants. The company would provide the capital necessary to establish the colony, and all of its products would be shipped to England and sold, with the profits being divided among the shareholders. The adventurers expected that their employees would discover gold, silver, and other precious minerals; that they would trade with the Indians for tropical products such as spices, silk, and other valuable commodities; and that a northwest passage opening a new trade route with the Far East would be discovered. Some felt the new colony would become a base from which Spanish shipping could be raided. All of these hopes proved groundless, and after a while it became apparent that if the Virginia Company were to succeed, it would have to turn to agriculture. What was needed was a staple crop that could be profitably exported to England. To do this required a reorientation of the shareholders' expectations, as well as considerable experimentation. In vain the company tried to produce such products as sugar, citrus fruits, and silk. Only after 1614 did tobacco emerge as a profitable staple.

The adventurers were not prepared for this long developmental period. They had expected a return on their capital, at least within seven years. By 1618 the Virginia Company had invested nearly £75,000 but had accumulated debts, not dividends. Therefore, it became impossible to raise funds through the sale of stock even though the colony needed further infusions of capital. To meet this problem, the Company in 1616 turned to a device known as the "magazine," a subsidiary joint-stock venture composed of a group of merchants to whom the main Virginia Company gave a four-year monopoly of the trade of the colony. In this manner merchants were induced to send supplies to Virginia by being allowed to sell the products of the colony and reap the profits from this trade without being responsible for the vast debt of the parent company. With the rise of tobacco, the hopes for the magazine were bright. At the same time the parent company faced a dim future. Production in Virginia shifted from company employees to private planters, many of whom were former indentured servants who had been given land upon the completion of their terms of service. If the Virginia Company of London had any future at all, it was in land. By establishing a thriving agricultural settlement, the firm could sell land; it could also profit from the collection of quitrents, which the company normally assessed at the rate of a shilling per annum per fifty acres, on all land taken up by new settlers. But the debt of the company was so large that it would have taken a mass migration and a long period of years before debts could be retired and profits earned.

Despite bright hopes, the magazine failed because of inexperience and misjudgment on the part of the merchants who controlled it. Although Virginia tobacco fetched enormously high prices when first exported to England, the initial quantities were small and the market was narrow. In response to high prices, tobacco production in Virginia expanded much more rapidly than the market, and the result was a dramatic price decline. The magazine purchased on its own account tobacco from the independent planters, usually by trading supplies for tobacco. The problem was that the magazine representatives in Virginia had English market information that was three or more months out of date. In consequence, the magazine often purchased the crop for more than it could bring in England. In its fourth year of operation the magazine had still not earned a profit, and in 1620 the Virginia Company refused to renew its monopoly. After that, the company made arrangements with individual merchants to supply the colony.

In 1624 the English government decided that the Virginia Company, now bankrupt and deeply divided within its own ranks, could no longer manage its colony. Consequently, King James I revoked the charter, and Virginia became a royal colony. As a profit-making venture, the Virginia Company was an unabashed failure; and much of the difficulty can be traced to the expectations of the adventurers. Thinking in terms of the East India Company experience, they demanded a quick return on their investment. Equally important were defects in the nature of the corporation as an instrument for economic development. English joint-stock companies were in their pioneering stage and had not yet evolved administrative structures capable of managing far-flung ventures. In the beginning, the London Company created a governing council in Virginia in which the lines of authority were not clearly drawn. In this initial council the governor did not have authority superior to the other councillors. It took three years to remedy this defect.

In addition, communication problems made it difficult if not impossible for a policy-making body based in London to maintain effective control over an operation in Virginia. At the best, it took more than three months for a round trip between England and the New World, and even in routine situations control from London would have been difficult. But developing a new agricultural colony was unprecedented in the English experience. By the time London issued orders for carrying out an experiment, months might elapse before it could begin in Virginia. More months or years would pass before an experiment could be evaluated, and then it would be hard to determine whether failure was the result of poor administration in America or because of natural conditions such as climate or soil. Had the Virginia Company had more capital, it might have succeeded; but in an era when a one- or two-year wait for a return on investments was the rule, an enterprise requiring a decade or more of development time had virtually no chance of financial success. It is something of a miracle that the company lasted as long as it did.

Yet it would be an error to regard the Virginia Company as a total failure. Under its administration a permanent colony was established in the New World. Furthermore, tobacco was developed as an important staple, and trade in the commodity started. At the time Virginia became a royal colony, plantations existed in sufficient numbers to sustain a trade organized by more traditional mercantile methods. Without the large infusion of capital by the company, it is doubtful that a commercial colony could have been established on the Chesapeake Bay.

The Merchant in the Southern Colonies. After the collapse of the Virginia Company, individual merchant houses became the dominant business institution in the South. For the first eighty years, or until about 1720, English merchants controlled the trade. Geography helped to determine a trading pattern where towns were not important. Most plantations in Virginia, and later in Maryland, grew up along the shores of the Chesapeake Bay and its tributary rivers. English merchants could send their ships to trade for tobacco directly at the plantation wharves, making the development of towns as commercial centers unnecessary. Learning from the experience of the magazine, the English merchants adopted the consignment system. Under this arrangement a planter could purchase goods (much of the time on credit) at a fixed price by giving their tobacco crop to the merchant, who would credit the planter's account only after the crop had been sold. If the proceeds did not satisfy the planter's debt, the merchant would have first claim on the crop the following year. In this manner, the merchant transferred the risk of falling prices from himself to the planter. Since a planter frequently accumulated a considerable debt—for the purchase of supplies, indentured servants, and, later, slaves—it was often difficult to switch accounts from one merchant to another. This system alienated many planters and brought forth Thomas Jefferson's bitter, but exaggerated, statement in a 1786 letter that "there never was an instance of a man's getting out of debt who was once in the hands of a tobacco merchant & bound to consign his tobacco to him." Jefferson saw the consignment system as

> ...the most delusive of all snares. The merchant feeds the inclination of his customer to be credited till he gets the burthen of debt so increased that he cannot throw it off at once, he then begins to give him less for his tobacco and ends with giving what he pleases for it, which is always so little that though the demands of the customer for necessaries be reduced ever so low in order to get himself out of debt, the merchant lowers his price in the same proportion so as always to keep such a balance against his customer as will oblidge him to continue his assignments of tobacco.

Jacob M. Price has written the most balanced and insightful study of Chesapeake tobacco trade —a commerce that accounted for at least 60 percent of the exports to the United Kingdom of the thirteen mainland colonies on the eve of the American Revolution. Price divides the trading pattern of the colonial Chesapeake into two main periods. The first lasted from the fall of the Virginia Company through the 1720's or 1730's. This was the era of many small commission merchants operating largely from the English ports of London, Bristol, and Liverpool. Although England consumed some of the crop, the reexport trade to the Continent took most of it. As early as 1669 England reexported 50 percent of the tobacco it received; just prior to the Revolution the figure stood at 85 percent. Plantation owners developed a system where each hogshead of tobacco was individually graded according to quality. The English merchants took this product and reconsigned it to what Jacob Price terms a "passive" market run by Dutch merchants in Amsterdam. The tobacco might sit in Holland for many months before it was finally sold to buyers in northern Europe. Thus it could take a year or more before a planter's accounts were finally posted with the proceeds from a sale. This long sale period made English merchants cautious in extending credit to planters. Price blames this institutional arrangement for the stagnation in the growth of tobacco production that occurred between 1700 and 1726.

Price's second era, which lasted to the Revolution, began in the 1720's. France emerged as the single most important purchaser of tobacco, buying more than 20 percent of the crop. Unlike the Dutch market, which was composed of many merchants who dealt in small lots, the French market operated through a government monopoly, assumed by the United General Farms after 1730. The French went to Britain and bought a year's supply at a time. They were interested in quantity rather than quality, and they bypassed the normal commission merchants who dealt in the small lots of finely graded tobacco prepared for the Dutch market.

The large French tobacco purchases coincided with the rise of Scottish merchants based in Glasgow. These commercial houses operated not along the shores of the Chesapeake Bay, but in the interior regions of Virginia and Maryland above the fall line. Instead of trading from ships, they opened branch stores, buying the cheaper tobaccos of the Potomac and James Rivers. It was the Scottish merchants who captured the French business. Operating through British agents, the French made long-term contracts in Scotland. Fearful that war might interrupt a profitable business, the United General Farms contracted in 1744 for the supply of tobacco at a fixed price for a period of six years. The British agents managed to win from the English government assurances that licenses would be granted so that this trade could continue in war as in peace. The Scottish houses behaved quite differently from the English. Because the Scots had contracts at fixed prices, they operated not as commission merchants but purchased tobacco on their own account. Furthermore, their long-term contracts enabled them to adopt a more expansive credit policy. It was the extension of Scottish credit to upland tobacco planters to which Price attributes the rapid and steady growth of American tobacco production that resumed in the late 1720's, after almost three decades of stagnation. Price noted that from about 30 million pounds weight in 1726, annual tobacco production expanded to 50 million pounds in the years 1738 to 1742, "70 million in 1752–1756, and 100 million in 1771–1775" (Price, *Journal of Economic History,* 1964). This growth occurred despite stable or declining prices.

The experiences of both the Chesapeake and the upland tobacco planters illustrate one crucial point: it was mercantile credit that provided the capital that fueled agricultural growth. Without credit, planters could not afford labor (in the form of indentured servants or slaves), tools, and other supplies to enlarge production. The credit policies also explain why large plantations grew at the expense of small farmers. Lewis C. Gray, in his authoritative *History of Agriculture in the Southern United States to 1860* (1933), points out that there were no economies of scale in tobacco farming. Therefore, large planters did not enjoy production advantages over small farmers. It was credit that tipped the balance to the big, well-established planters. With access to credit they could purchase land, slaves, and supplies when small farmers could not. Furthermore, an indentured servant, who had worked faithfully for a large planter and who had built a cordial relationship with him, might at the completion of his term use his relationship with his former employer to establish credit and become a large planter himself. It was the access to credit that was crucial; without it there could be little development.

Merchants from the British Isles dominated the trade of Virginia and Maryland, and prevented the rise of an American merchant class in those colonies. There was one exception to this, the planter-merchant. Almost from the first, men like William Byrd, who were primarily planters, used their superior credit to purchase goods for resale to smaller farmers. These planter-merchants served a particularly useful function by collecting the tobacco of those who were not located near wharves and who lacked ready access to the ships sent to the Chesapeake by the English commission merchants. It should be stressed that these planter-merchants never developed into a full-time business class, nor were they comparable to the sedentary merchants in South Carolina or in the northern colonies.

The Merchant in the Northern Colonies. America's resident merchant class began in the North. Although the first important northern colony, Massachusetts Bay, like Virginia, was founded under a corporate charter, there were few additional similarities. The Massachusetts Bay Colony was a political rather than an economic organization. Its settlement stemmed from the persecution of the Puritans under the Stuart monarchs, culminating in the "Great Migration" between 1630 and 1640. The Great Migration included men of substantial wealth, and the flow of capital that came with them was enough to sustain the colony through the first decade.

The initial merchants in the Bay Colony were of two kinds. The first were settlers who had good connections with the Puritan government of Massachusetts. These men, who often had little previous mercantile experience, were given government licenses to exploit valuable resources such as fur. Typical of these merchants was William Pynchon, who founded Springfield as a trading post in 1635. As fur traders, they flourished as long as their commodity lasted, but most of them quickly turned to noncommercial pursuits when fur became scarce. The second group of merchants usually had backgrounds as small tradesmen in England. In Massachusetts they met incoming boats to purchase commodities brought over by new settlers. This activity enabled newcomers to exchange their capital—brought over in the form of goods—for credits used for the food, livestock, and labor necessary to start farms. Because of this inflow of capital, early Massachusetts merchants did not need to establish connections with their English counterparts.

The Puritan Revolution in England (1642–1648) and the restoration of the Stuart monarchy in 1660 changed the economic position of the Bay Colony. Migration and the inflow of capital slowed. But Massachusetts and the other New England colonies continued to require an ever-increasing infusion of English goods. The problem was, how could this trade be financed? The New England colonies had no gold or silver. They did produce a few minor staples such as furs, naval stores, and, later, whale oil, but these were never enough to settle the English accounts. New England, in common with the mid-Atlantic colonies, never developed an agricultural staple that old England demanded. The northern climate was too much like that of the mother country to produce exotic crops.

The new class of merchants that arose in the North developed complex trading patterns to pay for English imports. Some merchants succeeded through government contracts in the frequent colonial wars with the French. The English usually sent over troops, and those merchants lucky enough to win military-supply contracts normally received drafts payable in England. But it was only those merchants well connected with the colonial governments who received such contracts. The more usual way to earn English credits was through a complicated trading pattern. The idea was to supply New England products and services to regions that had a favorable balance of trade with the mother country and hence credits in London. The North was fortunate in that it had the resources for shipbuilding. Northern merchants quickly underwrote this industry, which gave them the means for carrying out their commerce. Although the nearest region with a favorable English balance was the Chesapeake, New England and mid-Atlantic merchants could not enter this trade because they lacked the commodities that the planters wished to buy.

Thus the North had to look further afield. Some merchants earned credits by sending livestock, grain, and even ice, to the Caribbean. The British colonies there, particularly Barbados, did not produce their own food, yet they had substantial English credits through the sale of sugar. Another important market for American products were the Atlantic islands of Spain and Portugal—especially the Portuguese island of Madeira—which earned English credits through the export of wine. Consequently, the New England merchants supplied the wine islands with fish and barrel staves. Similarly, Portugal and Spain sent England large amounts of port and sherry. To Iberia, Massachusetts sent fish. Once in Spanish or Portuguese territory, American vessels might load a cargo of wine for London; in England it was possible even to sell the ship itself. Other American merchants purchased sugar in the Caribbean and brought it to New England, where it was distilled into rum. They then exported the rum to Africa, where it was exchanged for slaves, which were in turn sent to the Caribbean. When the colony of South Carolina became a major rice producer, northern and Charleston merchants sent that commodity to Iberia and the Mediterranean. Sometimes New England earned specie by illegal trade with Spanish America.

The possibilities for trade were many and varied, but a major goal always remained: to earn credits to pay for a steady flow of English imports. The key factor in the northern economy was the sedentary merchant of the coastal towns, particularly Boston, Newport, New York, Philadelphia, and Charleston. These coastal merchants purchased farm products from their smaller counterparts in the backcountry—from the Dwight family in Springfield, Massachusetts, for example—which they sold abroad, and in return funneled English imported goods, sometimes on credit, to the backcountry stores. Without the seacoast merchants, little economic development could have occurred.

General Characteristics of the Sedentary Merchant. Perhaps the most common way to become a merchant was to have good English connections. Bernard Bailyn observed in his *New England Merchants in the Seventeenth Century* (1955) that at the time of the Restoration in 1660 the original group of indigenous Puritan merchants, of whom Robert Keayne was the most noted, was dying out and being replaced by non-Puritans "leagued" with important English houses, such as Thomas Breedon, Colonel Thomas Temple, and Richard Wharton. At first such men might act as agents for an English house and then, after they had accumulated a reputation and capital, they would establish a business of their own. Even after the Revolution, merchants established themselves in this manner. Stuart Bruchey noted that Robert Oliver, who became the wealthiest merchant in Baltimore during the first decade of the nineteenth century, started in 1783 as an immigrant from Ireland who acted as an American agent for a Belfast house. Another common way of joining the merchant community was through apprenticeship. This was the route taken by Thomas Hancock, who started as an apprentice to Samuel Gerrish, a Boston bookseller, in 1717. By the 1750's Hancock had become one of the largest and most successful of New England businessmen. A final way to become a merchant was through family connections and inheritance. In the late 1750's John Hancock joined his uncle doing office work. In 1764, when Thomas died childless, John inherited the business.

From the foundation of the English colonies to the Revolution, two problems plagued all merchants: the lack of ready money and the small size of the market. Both conditions prevented specialization. Since there were few large towns—in 1760, Philadelphia, the largest American city, had a population of less than 24,000, while the fifth largest city, Newport, Rhode Island, had fewer than 8,000 inhabitants—there was simply not enough business to allow specialization into wholesale or retail stores or into firms that sold a single commodity. The lack of both specie and a banking system posed an even greater obstacle to specialization. Barter was the normal means of exchange. As their customers seldom had money, merchants had to accept what was offered: farm produce, fish, or the products of a local craftsman. Even the House of Hancock, which by the American Revolution was reputed to be the largest mercantile establishment in the thirteen colonies, looked more like a general store than the seat of a great commercial enterprise. After the Revolution, conditions changed. The beginnings of an adequate banking system made barter less necessary, and the rapid growth of urban centers expanded the market. By 1810 there were two cities with populations of more than 50,000 and eleven with more than 10,000 inhabitants. Thus Robert Oliver in Baltimore could specialize as a wholesaler, and Harmon Hendricks of New York City could restrict his interests to the metal trade, especially copper.

It was the commerce with distant places that represented the most difficult challenge to the sedentary merchant. In an era lacking developed commodity markets and without telephones, telegraphs, cables, or radio to transmit information and instructions, information about conditions in other places was always weeks or months out of date. Merchants had to dispatch cargoes without accurate knowledge about the intended markets. Primitive transportation and communication made it impossible for a Boston merchant to retain supervision or control over his shipments, and he had to delegate these functions to others. It was the skill and judgment in delegating authority and control that most often meant commercial success or failure. The most usual solution to this problem was to appoint agents in the various ports of destination who sold merchandise, sometimes diverted ships to alternate ports, and arranged return loads. They usually had complete control over the prices of commodities bought or sold and over the terms of sale as well. Agents hesitated to act if encumbered by rigid instructions. Robert Oliver wrote to a Venetian merchant in 1805, "We have no desire to do commission business unless we can give perfect satisfaction and if you should hereafter think proper to give us any orders, we advise you to state your views and expectations and leave us to judge the propriety of carrying them into effect" (Bruchey, *Robert Oliver: Merchant of Baltimore*, p. 143).

Most merchants wanted to know as much as possible about their agents. Very often they selected relatives for this task. Bernard Bailyn has traced the tangled web of the Hutchinson family of Boston, which rose to prominence after the Restoration. Richard Hutchinson ran a London firm. He dealt with his two brothers, Samuel and Edward, of Boston, who were in partnership with two of Richard's nephews, Elisha and Eliakim. The Boston Hutchinsons conducted their large West Indian trade through Peleg Sanford of Portsmouth, Rhode Island, whose mother was another sister of Richard and who was hence cousin and nephew of the Boston merchants of the family. Peleg sent the West Indian trade to his two brothers, William and Elisha Sanford, who were Barbadian merchants. Over a century and a half later, Robert Oliver appointed his brothers, John and Thomas, to represent him in England and at various European ports. If relatives were not available, then merchants selected agents on the basis of friendship. Nonetheless, a merchant's best asset was his reputation for faithful and honest dealing. People selected those whom they knew the most about and avoided business transactions with unknowns.

Merchants often sent cargoes to ports where no resident agent was available. In these cases, merchants often entrusted their business to a ship captain. Although skilled in navigation, the captains often lacked business sense. Stuart Bruchey quoted Robert Oliver's ill feelings toward Frederick Folger, master of Oliver's schooner, *Wolf*. Said Oliver, "All of his [Folger's] transactions and proceedings were uniformly wrong." Oliver accused Folger of "incapacity, indolence, and irregularity." Lacking faith in a ship captain, a merchant could appoint a supercargo—an officer who traveled aboard ship and had even greater authority than a resident agent. Stuart Bruchey recorded Robert Oliver's instructions to the captain of one of his ships. Wrote Oliver to Captain Beard in 1799, "Obey his [the supercargo's] directions in everything relating to the Ship & Cargo in [the] same manner as you would obey us, if personally present." Merchants used the same criteria—kinship, friendship, and reputation—in appointing supercargoes as they did in selecting agents.

Prior to independence, the sedentary merchants performed the banking function because America lacked a formal banking system and had little or no specie. The chief instrument that they used for this purpose was known as a "bill of exchange." A bill of exchange is comparable to a bank check and came into being in this manner.

AMERICAN BUSINESS INSTITUTIONS BEFORE THE RAILROAD

A Boston merchant might sell fish in Madeira. The purchaser might be a merchant whose primary business was to ship wine to London. He would thereby earn a substantial balance, say £500, with an English merchant. The Bostonian, acting through his supercargo, might not care to buy anything in Madeira. In payment for the fish the Bostonian's agent would take a note for £300 (a bill of exchange) drawn on the London account of the Madeira firm. The ultimate responsibility for this note would reside with the merchant who issued it. In practice this transaction would be comparable to paying a bill by writing a check on a bank account.

Bills of exchange often circulated in place of money. For example, the Boston merchant might buy sugar worth £300 in the Barbados and pay for it with the £300 bill acquired by selling wine in Madeira. In such a transaction the Bostonian or his agent would endorse the bill and thereby assume the responsibility if, for some reason, the note was not honored. Bills of exchange could be used when a person wanted to transfer money from one city to another. Thus a citizen of Massachusetts traveling to England might purchase a bill of exchange from Samuel Hutchinson of Boston drawn on the London firm of Richard Hutchinson. Although bills of exchange reduced the need for barter and eased both trade and travel, they were only as good as the reputation of the merchant who issued them. People always hesitated or refused to take a bill issued by a merchant whom they did not know. Thus bills lacked the ready acceptability of the modern bank note or of specie. This was a serious handicap to trade. But, a bill issued by a merchant of high reputation might circulate far and wide. E. James Ferguson emphasized the importance of reputation in his analysis of Philadelphia merchant Robert Morris' role in the American Revolution. Morris became head of a department of finance established in 1781 by the Continental Congress. At the time, the financial fortunes of the Continental Congress had sunk so low that its obligations were almost worthless. In order to restore government credit, Morris had to sign the government notes himself; and because his reputation stood so high, people readily accepted his notes. Morris explained in a 1784 letter to Charles Pettit that "my personal credit has been substituted for that which the country had lost."

The internal organization of the merchant's business was simple. Even the largest merchants employed only a few assistants, and the records kept were crude. Most colonial merchants did not use double-entry bookkeeping, although the practice gained acceptance toward the American Revolution and after independence achieved wide acceptance. Even so, merchants did not keep accounts that detailed profits and losses on single voyages—in fact, they did not even make annual or periodic summaries of profits and losses. Overall accounts were normally closed when partnerships were terminated. Merchants often mixed personal with business accounts, and they did not pay themselves salaries but withdrew money from the business as they needed it.

Government Regulation and Business Institutions: The Trade and Navigation Acts. Despite assertions to the contrary, it is doubtful that the Acts of Trade and Navigation had much impact on the development of the merchant as a business institution or significantly shaped the flow of trade and credit. The acts had four aspects: first, they required that trade be carried in ships owned and manned by Englishmen (this included colonials as well as those living in the United Kingdom); second, they enumerated certain products (such as tobacco, rice, indigo, hemp, ginger, and furs) that, with some specific exceptions, could be exported only to England; third, they established bounties for the production of scarce resources, such as indigo and naval stores; and finally, they restricted the manufacture of certain commodities in the colonies, such as rolled iron. The regulations concerning ships aided New England merchants, who took advantage of American resources to develop a thriving shipbuilding industry and a significant trade in selling ships in the mother country. Bounties, too, stimulated trade.

Of all aspects of the Acts of Trade and Navigation, enumeration has been the most controversial, since it has been asserted that without it colonial products would have moved in different channels. On closer examination, such arguments are not convincing. For example, when it became clear that trade in an important commodity was unduly hindered, English officials relaxed enumeration. Thus, South Carolina could export rice directly to all European ports south of Cape Finisterre. This built an important trade with Spain, Portugal, and Italy. In most cases trade would have moved through the United Kingdom regardless of enumeration; the pattern of mercantile institutions in the colonial world ensured this. Trade flowed where there was credit, and credit depended on long-term relationships as well as a favorable legal system. In an era when war was almost a constant factor, it was difficult to establish a long-term credit relationship with foreigners. It was for this reason that French purchases of Virginia tobacco flowed through the United Kingdom. Finally, too much has been made of the British regulation that discouraged manufacturing. Colonial America lacked the capital and technology to compete with the British in this sphere. Imperial regulation, therefore, reinforced the mercantile patterns that grew up in the British colonial world.

INSTITUTIONAL CHANGE AFTER THE REVOLUTION

The sedentary merchant continued to be a vital part of the American business scene throughout the nineteenth century. After independence, the merchants took the lead in a number of institutional innovations in banking, transportation, and manufacturing. The new institutions were at first creatures of the merchant community that established them, but by the time of the railroad they were becoming forces in their own right.

The Revival of the Corporation: Banking. With the failure of the Virginia Company, corporations as business organizations ceased to play a role in the English colonies. Part of the reason was that more traditional institutions, such as the sedentary merchant, were adequate to colonial needs. But there was a political reason as well. The English government refused to allow the establishment of banks in America because it feared that the colonial governments might create a paper currency and make it legal tender for the payment of all debts. Should such a currency depreciate in value, it would adversely affect a large number of English creditors. Part of the trouble stemmed from a confusion over the nature of paper money. This should not be surprising. Although the Bank of England was founded in 1694, a century later, in 1794, only four other chartered banks existed in England. Even in the middle of the nineteenth century, Walter Bagehot, the respected and influential editor of the London *Economist,* argued in his book *Lombard Street* (1870) that nineteenth-century British bankers still did not understand banking.

During the era prior to 1776, most American colonies issued some paper money as a result of the four wars with France. War brought on sudden expenditures. There was no specie, and taxes were not adequate for war needs. Massachusetts was the first colony to print paper money; it did so to finance its 1690 expedition against the French. Colonial paper money was not convertible into specie, nor was it ever made legal tender for the payment of English or other debts. The colonies used the paper to pay troops and to buy supplies, and the paper had value because the issuing colonial government accepted it for taxes. Because of the specie shortage the notes often circulated widely and were used to satisfy local debts. Most colonies issued notes conservatively and tried to retire them as they were received for taxes. Therefore, such issues tended to retain their value. The British government was not enthusiastic about colonial paper but allowed it because wartime necessity offered little choice. Finally, after the defeat of France in the French and Indian War (1754–1763), the British government issued the Currency Act of 1764, which prohibited further issues of paper money in the colonies.

Banks were another matter. Merchants constantly sought ways to solve the problems caused by the lack of specie. Some felt that paper money might be created, backed not by gold or silver, but by land. A result was the Massachusetts Land Bank of 1740. The idea was that a person who desired to borrow money could go to the bank and receive notes, giving land as security. The notes of the bank would not be convertible into specie. The land bank, as Bray Hammond has pointed out, was not a wartime measure but, rather, the idea of a number of Boston merchants and wealthy speculators. Some rival merchants organized a bank, the notes of which could supposedly be redeemed in silver at a future date. Other local merchants, as well as the English mercantile community, feared a circulating medium not solidly based on specie. As a result of this opposition, the English Parliament in 1741 extended the Bubble Act of 1720 to

America and thereby suppressed the Massachusetts Land Bank and all other banks as well. England remained steadfast in its opposition to banks in America, and none could be established prior to the Revolution.

The first American bank came out of the chaos of Revolutionary War finance. The Continental Congress, following colonial tradition, tried to finance much of the war through note issues. This policy might have succeeded had the central government had the authority to levy taxes, and if the war had ended rapidly. But neither condition developed, and by 1781 the massive issues of Continental paper had depreciated to the point where it was almost worthless. Robert Morris, as part of his plan to restore the credit of the nation, pushed through Congress in 1781 a bill establishing the Bank of North America, to be located in Philadelphia. Uncertainty about the authority of the government of the Articles of Confederation to issue such a charter caused the bank to seek incorporation in Pennsylvania, and this was accomplished in 1782. Other banks soon followed. Alexander Hamilton wrote the constitution for the Bank of New York, which opened in 1784, but it did not become a corporation until 1791. Massachusetts chartered the Bank of Massachusetts in 1784, and the state-chartered Bank of Maryland opened in 1790. Bray Hammond has calculated that by 1800 twenty-nine banks were in operation, including the federally chartered Bank of the United States (which had been founded in 1791 as one of Alexander Hamilton's financial reforms).

Banks were an important business innovation. Their primary functions were to expand the circulating medium and to enlarge the credit supply of the nation. Although many Americans during the early years of the Republic did not realize it, bank notes were quite different from the paper emitted by the old colonial governments and the Continental Congress. Banks operated as follows. Most received a charter specifying the institution's capital, which was raised through the sale of stock. In theory stock purchasers paid for their shares with a certain percentage of specie. In the case of the first Bank of the United States, for example, one-quarter of the cost of the stock had to be received in specie, and the rest could be paid for in obligations of the federal government. Although many found ways to evade specie payments for their shares, banks nevertheless accumulated a considerable specie stock.

Banks expanded the credit either through the loan of bank notes or of "created" deposits. Bray Hammond has estimated that early banks issued about three or four dollars of bank notes for each dollar of paid-in capital. Herein lay the main difference between a bank note and the paper of the Continental Congress and the old colonial governments. Owners of bank notes had the right to take them to the issuing bank and to exchange them for specie, but the holders of colonial and Continental paper had no such option. In effect a conservatively managed bank took one dollar of specie and expanded the credit supply by creating four dollars in bank notes.

Banks also expanded credit through the use of deposits. From the first they accepted deposits, and it was possible for depositors to withdraw funds by writing checks. It soon became quite common for banks to grant credit in the form of deposits. The holder of such could withdraw funds by check. If the check were deposited in another account, no bank notes would be involved. At the present time there is not adequate data to establish the ratio of deposit loans to bank-note loans; but it is known that as the nineteenth century progressed, deposits became increasingly important.

It was the mercantile community that took the lead in founding the early banks. Merchants purchased most of the stock, dominated the boards of directors, held most of the deposits, and received most of the loans. Indeed, early bankers regarded their institutions as merely an extension of mercantile activity. Banks enabled businessmen to borrow against bills of exchange or to receive loans on commodities. Individual merchants ceased to serve the banking function that they had in the colonial period as chartered banks expanded. Stuart Bruchey noted that by 1800 most Baltimore merchants settled their accounts by checks drawn on bank accounts. This was also the case in the other major cities, but it was not true of the thousands of small towns and villages without banks.

Mercantile control of banks had drawbacks. Merchants thought mostly of short-term loans to support commerce. They opposed long-term loans (secured by such things as real estate) to newly emerging factories, turnpikes, and canals. To support nonmercantile ventures, state legislatures created a number of special-purpose banks. Typical of its type was the Morris Canal and Banking Company (chartered in 1824), which aided New Jersey canal construction. While such special banks often failed both as financial institutions and as internal-improvement companies, by the 1820's bankers began to have wider horizons, and their corporations became an important source of money for factories and internal improvements. Harry Scheiber has analyzed in detail the vital role played by banks in mobilizing capital for the construction of the massive canal system in Ohio, which was started in the late 1820's. Banks also helped early railroads; for example, they supplied as much as one-fifth of the capital for the building of the Boston and Worcester in the 1830's.

In administration, banks did not innovate. While most operated under government charters, such grants were not absolutely necessary. The Bank of Stephen Girard, one of the most important financial concerns in Philadelphia, existed from its founding in 1812 until Girard's death in 1831 without benefit of charter. The main advantage of a charter was the special privileges that it might confer. Congress made both the first and second Banks of the United States official depositories for federal funds. But such favors were not necessary to the creation of large and successful banks, as Stephen Girard proved. As in the case of bills of exchange issued by colonial merchants, bank notes of wealthy, conservatively managed houses could achieve widespread acceptance.

Banks did not develop an administrative structure very different from mercantile houses. With the exception of the two federally chartered Banks of the United States, banks operated from a single location; they were controlled by boards of directors who met together and personally considered each loan application; and bank accounts were restricted to the wealthy and were relatively few. State-chartered banks, therefore, did not require a large staff spread out over a wide geographic area. The informal methods of supervision and control traditionally used in a merchant's countinghouse sufficed well enough for the prerailroad-era banks. Although the two federal banks had branches, they did not innovate. By 1805 the first Bank of the United States had eight branches scattered from Boston to New Orleans; the second bank at its height in 1830 had twenty-five branches. In the case of both banks, a separate board of directors, named by the main office in Philadelphia, managed each branch. Once established, branches had considerable freedom. Indeed they closely resembled allied mercantile houses tied together by kinship and friendship, as were those of the Hutchinson family in the seventeenth century. Poor transportation and communication made a modern administrative system difficult to achieve, even if the managers of the banks had wanted to establish one.

The Adoption of the Corporation: Insurance. In the colonial period insurance, like banking, was predominantly a mercantile function. Merchants engaged in overseas trade needed insurance to reduce the risks associated with ocean shipping. Marine insurance was almost as old as commerce itself and was well-developed in England by the seventeenth century. Prior to 1776 English marine insurance was largely controlled by individuals, not by corporations. In London the center for such activities had become Edward Lloyd's coffeehouse, which was a meeting place for merchants and shipowners. This system spread to America, and in eighteenth-century Philadelphia the London Coffee House served as Lloyd's counterpart. There, merchants met and underwrote the risks of each other's voyages.

After the American Revolution, formally chartered companies began to issue marine insurance. The first general insurance company to be chartered in the United States was the Insurance Company of North America, founded in Philadelphia in 1792 and chartered by Pennsylvania in 1794. Policies issued by the new corporations were backed not by the reputations of merchants who signed underwriting agreements at a coffeehouse, but by substantial amounts of paid-in capital. After 1794 marine insurance firms increased rapidly. Douglass North has estimated that by 1804 the United States had forty companies with a total capital of $10 million.

The United States also developed fire and life insurance companies. The first life insurance firm, the Presbyterian Ministers' Fund of Philadelphia, was organized in 1759, and Morton Keller has noted that the Philadelphia Contributionship for Insuring Houses from Loss by Fire, dating from 1769, was the only chartered private business corporation in colonial America. But life and fire insurance lagged behind marine insurance in importance in the prerailroad era.

Prerailroad banks and insurance companies had many similarities. Both institutions were founded by merchants. Some firms such as the Massachusetts Hospital Life Insurance Company and the Ohio Life Insurance and Trust Company of Cincinnati combined both banking and insurance. Both insurance companies and banks used similar administrative structures. And both types of institutions were important because they mobilized capital and invested it in new enterprises, especially internal improvements such as canals and railroads.

Corporations and Internal Improvements. Corporations were an important factor in many of the internal improvement programs that appeared after the Revolution. The two most significant purposes that they served were conferring the privilege of exercising the right of eminent domain and the mobilization of capital. Canals, turnpikes, and bridges—unlike factories and banks—required the authority to lay out routes over private property. No construction could take place if individual landholders were able to refuse passage or charged exorbitant prices for rights-of-way. Therefore, charters granted to internal improvement firms specified canal or turnpike routes and bridge locations, and provided for eminent-domain procedures to compel landholders to cooperate for the general good.

Corporations also mobilized capital. Most internal improvement undertakings were too large for individuals to finance. For example, the Middlesex Canal of Massachusetts, chartered in 1793 to build a waterway between Boston and the Merrimack River, required $592,000. Turnpikes, while often less costly than canals, were still expensive. The thirty-eight-mile-long Boston and Worcester Turnpike, chartered in 1805 and opened in 1809, cost $150,000. Other New England turnpikes cost in excess of $400,000. Charters for internal improvement companies provided a manner for many individuals to band together and underwrite the projects. Charters usually, but not always, specified the amount of capital to be raised, the value of each share, the amount that had to be subscribed before construction could begin, and provisions for the election by the shareowners of a governing board. Each charter had to be approved by the state legislature and signed by the governor, and no two were exactly alike. While such charters facilitated raising capital, selling shares, especially for the earliest enterprises, was difficult. No stock exchanges existed, nor were there easy methods to bring in foreign capital. In most cases, internal improvement promoters before 1825 tapped local capital, largely that of merchants and artisans who hoped that canals, roads, and bridges would increase their prosperity.

Despite the amount of money involved and the physical size of some of the projects, turnpikes and canals, and the large state projects undertaken in New York, Pennsylvania, Ohio, Indiana, and Illinois, did not bring many administrative innovations. Canals and turnpikes did not employ large staffs, even during construction. The private corporations and later the states hired a small number of engineers who designed the works and supervised construction. The engineers divided a project into many small units that were actually built by local contractors. Thus, large construction companies were not necessary. Nor were vast numbers of employees needed after the projects were finished. Independent operators provided all the vehicles or canalboats. The major responsibilities of the internal improvement companies or boards were merely to collect tolls and to maintain the works. Harry Scheiber estimated that as late as 1858 the massive Ohio Canal system of more than 700 miles had a labor force of only 200 full-time equivalent employees. On the largest works, toll collectors would be numbered in the dozens, and a few repair crews could perform maintenance tasks. Supervision was not difficult and could often be handled on an informal basis, similar to the merchants' supervision of the workers in their countinghouses.

Manufacturing: Agricultural Processing and Crafts. Before the coming of the railroad, corporations played a relatively minor role in manufacturing. In the colonial period two types of manufacturing flourished: agricultural processing and craft production. Agricultural processing normally involved waterpowered mills, particularly sawmills for lumber, and gristmills for grinding grain. After the Revolution, flour milling expanded rapidly, especially in the Middle Atlantic states of Pennsylvania, Delaware, Maryland, and Virginia. These mills benefited from the inventions of Oliver Evans of Delaware, whose

AMERICAN BUSINESS INSTITUTIONS BEFORE THE RAILROAD

improved mill designs quickly spread southward from Wilmington to the increasingly important Baltimore region. By 1800 there were about fifty flour mills within twenty miles of Baltimore. Flour mills were owned by individuals or partnerships and did not use the corporate form. A very large mill represented an investment of $7,000, and it employed no more than thirty people. In such operations, one man could supervise everything, and expansion occurred by plowing profits back into the enterprise. No new managerial or financial forms arose.

In the cities, towns, and villages of the United States before 1850 could be found a large number of craftsmen who produced for local consumption. These included such occupations as coopers, blacksmiths, carriage-makers, furniture and cabinetmakers, silversmiths, tailors, and shoemakers. These craftsmen ran one-man shops or, in the larger places, owned firms that might employ as many as sixty workers. Polly Anne Earl, a student of these craft industries, has emphasized the continuity that existed in them from the early colonial period to the mid-nineteenth century. They did not undergo an "industrial revolution" until the 1870's or later. For example, Earl observed that furniture making in the mid-nineteenth century, even though in 1850 it ranked among the top ten American industries in terms of "value added and aggregate production," had yet to adopt any large-scale use of machinery powered by horses, steam engines, or water. As late as 1860 the important furniture-making center of New Castle County, Delaware, had no powered machinery at all in its furniture shops. Even Cincinnati, which led the United States in the adoption of power for furniture making, reported in 1850 that only "seventeen, of the area's sixty-one furniture firms employed steam, water, or horse power." Even these were small, having an average capital of $19,600 as opposed to about half that amount for those which lacked power-driven machines. These craft shops were family firms or partnerships. They did not need or use an innovation such as the corporation, nor did they develop any special managerial or administrative techniques.

Manufacturing: The Putting-Out System. After the Revolution some types of manufacturing underwent important changes. For the first time, production began for a mass market. This was accomplished in two ways: through the traditional putting-out system, and in factories. The putting-out system had a long history in England, especially in the woolen industry. The merchants were the mainspring of the system. They purchased the raw materials, such as wool, and put it out to craftsmen, such as spinners, weavers, and dyers, who worked in their own homes. The merchants retained ownership of the material through the entire process and took the responsibility for maintaining the flow of production from raw material to finished product, which they sold through their established channels. After the Revolution, New England merchants started large-scale production of boots and shoes and woolen cloth using the putting-out system. And in New York and New England, merchants organized tanning along similar lines. The merchants supplied capital to tanners to establish tanneries and then purchased the hides, which they put out for manufacture into leather.

Manufacturing: The Factory System in Cotton Textiles. The factory system first emerged in cotton textiles. It, too, was a creation of the merchants. The textile revolution came in two stages. The first occurred in Providence, Rhode Island, when the Quaker merchant firm of William Almy and Moses Brown and the English textile mechanic Samuel Slater collaborated in a waterpowered mill to produce yarn. Slater's mill went into operation in 1791. Almy and Brown started a boom in yarn spinning in Rhode Island, Connecticut, and southeastern Massachusetts, but they only partly changed the cotton textile business. The Almy and Brown mill, and those that imitated it, were small in scale, seldom employing as much capital as $50,000. Furthermore, they undertook only one part of the clothmaking process in their factories, the spinning of yarn. The rest of the process—the picking and carding of cotton prior to spinning, the weaving of yarn into cloth, and the dyeing of it—was carried out elsewhere. The Slater-type mills often put out cotton for picking and carding. At first the mills sold yarn to housewives who made their own cotton cloth for home use. After 1810 merchant weavers purchased some of the yarn and manufactured it into cloth using the putting-out system.

The sweeping changes that came over American textile manufacturing during the second stage of the factory system, which started in 1813, owed little to the spinning mills pioneered by Almy and Brown. Between 1800 and 1807, a number of Massachusetts merchants, particularly those in Boston, Newburyport, and Salem, grew rich on trading opportunities provided by the Napoleonic Wars in Europe. After 1807, Jefferson's embargo and the resulting tensions that led to the War of 1812 stopped this trade and created a large pool of unemployed capital. In 1813 a group of Boston merchants, headed by Francis C. Lowell and including Patrick Tracy Jackson, Nathan Appleton, and Israel Thorndike, launched the Boston Manufacturing Company. It was a large-scale venture meant to absorb capital made idle by the downturn in trade after 1807. The Boston Manufacturing Company, located on a falls of the Charles River in Waltham, Massachusetts, employed the corporate form and had an initial capital of $300,000. It used British technology, particularly the power loom that Lowell had observed in the United Kingdom. The Waltham mill, and those patterned after it, performed the entire cloth-making process by machine at a single site. This included picking, carding, spinning, weaving, bleaching, and dyeing. The immediate success of the Boston Manufacturing Company led Lowell and his fellow investors to build a giant cotton mill complex, which set the pattern for the industry during the first half of the nineteenth century.

The major Waltham investors, who became known as the Boston Associates, started their expansion with the purchase of a large tract of land at Pawtucket Falls on the Merrimack River. On this real estate in what became the city of Lowell, Massachusetts, they established the Locks and Canals Company. This corporation had three main functions: to construct a factory to manufacture textile machinery, to build and own in perpetuity a system of locks and canals to develop the property's waterpower, and to lay out specific sites on which new textile mills could be built. Because of their prestige as merchants and their success in textile manufacturing at Waltham, the Boston Associates had access to most of the considerable capital of Boston. They had no need of a stock market to float their shares. The Boston Associates retained control of the Locks and Canals Company, and they incorporated separate firms to build mills on the sites developed by it. The first of these, the Merrimac Manufacturing Company, was one of four new firms at Lowell that by 1828 had a combined capital of $2 million.

The Boston Associates led the development of the cotton textile industry in New England. Using the corporate form, they organized and financed an important number of new factories, but when a new company began to operate profitably, they sold it. In each case, they found willing buyers among people of the same social and economic class—residents of eastern Massachusetts who had made their money in trade or had inherited mercantile fortunes. The purchasers respected the Boston Associates and normally deferred to their judgment in picking factory management. Thus, the Boston Associates, although they sold the textile mills that they had built, actually controlled the businesses through the process of factory-management selection. This method simplified administrative procedures, since it was never necessary to build an administrative structure capable of managing many different factories. And the Associates kept control in still another way. The factories did not have their own sales departments. This function was turned over to an agent, who most often was Nathan Appleton or one of the other Boston Associates. This mercantile control prevented the textile corporations from vertically integrating either backward into the purchase of cotton or forward into the sale of the finished product. In fact, during the prerailroad era the mills neither differentiated their product from that of other mills, nor did they advertise.

The pattern established at Lowell became standard for cotton textiles. The Boston Associates undertook similar industrial development farther down the Merrimack River at Lawrence, Massachusetts; at Chicopee Falls in the Connecticut Valley of Massachusetts; and at Manchester, New Hampshire. Other New England capitalists imitated the Boston Associates and developed factories at such places as Nashua, New Hampshire, and at other sites in New Hampshire, Massachusetts, and Maine.

Manufacturing: Iron. The changes taking place in cotton textiles were not typical of manufacturing during the prerailroad era. More usual were the conditions in ironmaking. This industry had a colonial background with considerable quantities of pig iron being manufactured in small, charcoal-fueled furnaces using Massachusetts and New Jersey bog iron. It was not until after 1810, however, that America began to manufacture pig iron into finished products for new and specialized uses. The steam revolution, which started with stationary steam engines and engines for steamboats, demanded an important new product—boilerplate.

Typical of the firms that began to supply this need was the works established at Coatesville, Pennsylvania, in 1810 as the Brandywine Rolling Mill. Soon after its founding the mill became managed by the Lukens family. Although it was a new mill supplying a product destined for the most advanced part of the American economy, it did not create a new business form. It was a small partnership, with a capital in 1850 of only about $60,000, and seldom employed more than thirty full-time workers. The firm did not integrate either forward or backward. It purchased its pig iron from small nearby bloomeries that smelted ore using charcoal. The Lukens sold their products through agents in major cities such as Boston and Philadelphia. Using crude methods of accounting, more typical of the merchant than of a modern corporation, the Lukens partners did not distinguish between capital expenses and operating costs. In fact, the partners did not separate their personal wealth from that of their firm. Because the works was small, one person could supervise the entire operation on an informal basis. The organization of the Lukens firm typified most manufacturing—including such widely diverse fields as explosives, glassmaking, and copper—prior to 1850.

Changing Institutional Forms: An Assessment. The evolution from an economy dominated by mercantile institutions to one controlled by the large industrial corporation was uneven, slow, and barely under way by the 1850's, when the railroads became a major factor. There are at least three characteristics of the modern industrial enterprise. The first is the factory. The factory system diminished craftsmanship, which, in the words of the English scholar David Pye, is "workmanship using any kind of techniques or apparatus in which the quality of the result is not predetermined, but depends on the judgment, dexterity and care which the maker exercises as he works." In the factory, machines tended by unskilled or semiskilled workers eliminated craftsmen. The factory represented a sizable amount of capital. Alfred D. Chandler, Jr., has suggested that in the 1850's few shops with an investment of less than $50,000 could be considered factories.

A formal accounting system is a second factor that distinguishes the modern industrial enterprise. At the very least, this accounting system separates capital investment from operating expenses, and neither of these is mixed with family or personal accounts.

Finally, the modern industrial corporation is distinguished by its bureaucratic form. Within this structure, management is a specialized unit. As Chandler has pointed out, management coordinates the flow of activity of a firm and allocates its resources. Modern management fixes in writing the structure of a corporation and specifies duties and tasks at every level. It sets job qualifications and makes appointments, not through kinship and friendship, but on the basis of whether or not applicants meet certain fixed standards. Management also establishes methods for periodic and formal evaluations of all aspects of the firm and its personnel.

Measured against these criteria, very few pre-1850 enterprises could be considered "modern." Clearly, early nineteenth-century agricultural processing and craft workshops, engaged in such endeavors as furniture making and carriage making, lacked most elements of modernity. So, too, did manufacturing organized around the putting-out system. Even iron making had few modern characteristics. Although forges used machines, the technology was so undeveloped that even the most skilled iron makers could not guarantee the uniform quality of their product. And like flour milling and craft workshops, iron manufacturing used primitive accounting and managerial techniques; few, if any, separated capital from operating expenses, and none developed an administrative bureaucracy.

Cotton textiles were the most modern part of the manufacturing sector, but even here the mercantile system held sway over large parts of the industry. The small spinning mills, modeled after Almy and Brown's example, probably qualified as factories. The largest of these had capital investments approaching $50,000. And these mills eliminated craftsmanship. Caroline Ware in her *Early New England Cotton Manufacture* reported that by 1800 Almy and Brown employed as machine tenders 100 children between the ages of four and ten. In order to increase efficiency Almy and Brown placed all their spinning machines in a single room, where one adult supervised the children. Yet Almy and Brown did not adopt modern accounting, nor did their operation require a managerial bureaucracy.

The large cotton mills that followed the Waltham precedent were the most nearly modern. They used the corporate form, they kept capital accounts separate from operating expenses, and they carefully costed expense at every level. The Waltham-type mills were unquestionably factories. They employed a capital of between $300,000 and $500,000 and had unskilled labor forces numbering in the hundreds. Despite all this they did not develop a modern system of management. A single executive, called the treasurer, made most of the decisions. Because the Boston mercantile establishment handled the purchasing of raw materials and sales of finished products, the cotton mills did not develop the functional departments that are so characteristic of modern enterprises. The treasurer and his mill superintendent concerned themselves almost entirely with production. And because early mills had a standardized product, there were none of the complex problems occurring in firms that make a varied product line. Furthermore, the Boston Associates blocked the horizontal combination of numerous mill properties. Consequently textile managers were never forced to administer a large number of geographically separated units. In short, the hand of the merchant community remained strongly on cotton textiles and prevented the establishment of a modern managerial system.

Changing Institutional Forms: The Corporation. While the corporation emerged as an important institution in the period after the Revolution, its significance should not be overestimated. Its use was confined largely to banks, insurance companies, and internal improvement projects. Outside of textiles, the corporate form was little used in manufacturing until well after the Civil War. Furthermore, the corporation had mainly legal and financial significance; it did not imply an administrative form. During most of the prerailroad era, corporate charters were granted by specific legislative acts. The concept of incorporation under general laws (that is, allowing individuals to form a company if they followed an established form set down in a general law) did not come about until the 1830's. The Jacksonians regarded general incorporation, which made the form easily and inexpensively available to all, as an antimonopoly reform. George Rogers Taylor has observed that although New York had a limited general incorporation procedure for industrial firms as early as 1811, Connecticut in 1837 passed the first comprehensive general incorporation act. By the 1850's, Taylor notes, most northern states, including Maryland, New Jersey, New York, Pennsylvania, Indiana, and Massachusetts, had such laws. It should be emphasized that general incorporation laws did not aid canals, turnpikes, railroads, or other internal improvement schemes that required such special privileges as eminent domain. For these, special legislative acts were always required.

Limited liability was another concept that only gradually gained favor. Without limited liability corporate stockholders were responsible for all debts of the company; with limited liability they were responsible only to the extent of the assets of the corporation. In the years before 1830 governments could either give limited liability or not; most often they chose not to grant it. Early Massachusetts turnpikes, for example, did not enjoy limited liability; nor did any of the early textile companies. Limited liability, like general incorporation laws, was a Jacksonian reform aimed at reducing the risk of participation for small shareholders. Massachusetts passed the first limited liability act in the United States in 1830, over the strong opposition of the wealthy merchant class. Men like China trader William Sturgis, who as large owners of textile stock had much to gain by limited liability, still looked at things from a merchant's point of view and fought the reform on the ground that it encouraged financial irresponsibility on the part of company managers. By the Civil War many states had joined Massachusetts by passing limited liability acts.

The privileges that corporations enjoyed varied from state to state and from time to time. Many early corporate charters, particularly those of banks, followed the ancient precedent set by the Stuart monarchs and had fixed expiration dates. Gradually, charters came to be granted for unlimited periods. But there were many aspects of corporations that required the development

AMERICAN BUSINESS INSTITUTIONS BEFORE THE RAILROAD

of a new tradition and changes in the legal system. Stuart Bruchey has pointed out that John Marshall's 1819 decision in the *Dartmouth College* case has often been misunderstood. Marshall ruled that a charter was a contract and hence could not be changed by legislative fiat. The major impact of this was to make legislatures more careful in setting the terms for corporations.

More significant was the struggle over vested corporate rights. In 1828 Massachusetts chartered a company to build a free bridge across the Charles River less than 400 yards from an established toll span. The corporation owning the toll bridge charged that the legislature violated their charter by creating a new corporation that would destroy the value of the old. After prolonged litigation, the Supreme Court under Roger Taney ruled in 1837 against the toll bridge, asserting that corporate charters gave no implied rights but only those privileges explicitly conferred by the charter's words. The decision of the Supreme Court in the *Charles River Bridge* case did not prevent states from granting monopoly privileges; indeed, Massachusetts gave the Boston and Worcester Railroad a thirty-year monopoly of rail traffic between its terminal cities. But the decision did restrict corporations from enlarging their power through the doctrine of implied rights. This greatly encouraged the rise of new ventures. But there were many ambiguities in the corporation that were not made clear until well after the beginning of the railroad era. For example, the status of a corporation chartered in one state and doing business and owning property in another remained confused. And the holding company—that is, a corporation created primarily to hold the stock of other corporations—was not invented until the device was needed by the railroads.

The main importance of the corporation was in the mobilization of capital, and corporations brought into being a new institution, the stock exchange, to help distribute capital. The New York exchange opened in 1817. The Boston exchange, largely established to facilitate the transfer of textile stocks, started in 1834. The wealth of corporate experience in banks, turnpikes, canals, and textiles proved immediately useful to railroads, which from the first adopted the corporate form.

CONCLUSION

Throughout the prerailroad era the merchant was the primary business institution. Not only did the merchant organize trade, he started and controlled new ventures in banking, transportation, and manufacturing. In so doing the merchant set in motion forces that would eventually dethrone him with the coming of the railroad.

BIBLIOGRAPHY

Donald R. Adams, Jr., *Finance and Enterprise in Early America: A Study of Stephen Girard's Bank, 1812–1831* (Philadelphia, 1978), contains an excellent analysis of how an important private bank existed in a world of chartered banks. Bernard Bailyn, *The New England Merchants in the Seventeenth Century* (Cambridge, Mass. 1955), is the best overall work on early American merchants. William T. Baxter, *The House of Hancock: Business in Boston, 1724–1775* (Cambridge, Mass. 1945), is a well-written study of one of the most important colonial merchant houses and is especially useful to the beginning student. Stuart W. Bruchey, *The Colonial Merchant: Sources and Readings* (New York, 1966), offers the best introduction to the colonial merchant as an institution; and *The Roots of American Economic Growth 1607–1861* (New York, 1965), gives an excellent short summary of American economic growth to 1860 with the emphasis on institutional change. Alfred D. Chandler, Jr., *The Visible Hand: The Managerial Revolution in American Business* (Cambridge, Mass., 1977), although it is primarily concerned with the railroad era and beyond, nevertheless contains two excellent chapters on the period before the railroad. Chandler's work is the best authority on American business institutions. Wesley Frank Craven, *Dissolution of the Virginia Company: The Failure of a Colonial Experiment* (New York, 1932), is the standard work on the subject. Elmer J. Ferguson, *The Power of the Purse* (Chapel Hill, N.C., 1961), is the best study of the finance of the American Revolution and of the part played by merchants in it.

Carter Goodrich, *Canals and American Economic Development* (New York, 1961), contains excellent chapters on canal enterprises in New Jersey, New York, and Pennsylvania; and *Government Promotion of American Canals and Railroads 1800–1890* (New York, 1960), contains much valuable data on public and private prerailroad canal enterprises. Robert A. East, *Business Enterprise in the American Revolutionary Era* (New York, 1938), is a useful survey. Lucius F. Ellsworth, *Traditionalism and Change: The New York Tanning Industry in the Nineteenth Century* (New York, 1975), has a good description of the institutional arrangements in a key industry during the prerailroad era. Bray Hammond, *Banks and Politics in America, From the Revolution to the Civil War* (Princeton, N. J., 1957), contains a wealth of information on the institutional structure of banking. Lawrence A. Harper, *The English Navigation Laws* (New York, 1939), is the standard work on the subject. James B. Hedges, *The Browns of Providence Plantations*, 2 vols.

AMERICAN BUSINESS INSTITUTIONS BEFORE THE RAILROAD

(Cambridge, Mass., 1952; Providence, 1968), is a detailed study of an important merchant family and early industrialization. Paul F. McGouldrick, *New England Textiles in the Nineteenth Century: Profits and Investment* (Cambridge, Mass., 1968), places more emphasis on the quantitative than on the institutional side of textile investments.

Margaret E. Martin, *Merchants and Trade of the Connecticut River Valley* (Northampton, Mass., 1939), is a superb study of trade and commerce of a less developed inland region as opposed to the dominant coastal cities. Nathan Miller, *The Enterprise of a Free People: Aspects of Economic Development in New York State During the Canal Period, 1792–1838* (Ithaca, N. Y., 1962), is one of the most thoughtful studies of institutions generated by the canal era. Jacob Price, *France and the Chesapeake: A History of the French Tobacco Monopoly 1674–1791 and of Its Relationship to the British and American Tobacco Trade*, 2 vols. (Ann Arbor, Mich., 1973), is the best work on the institutional arrangements of the tobacco trade. Fritz Redlich, *The Molding of American Banking, Men and Ideas*, 2 vols. (New York, 1951), covers the period from 1781 to 1910 and is one of the most thoughtful studies of the banking industry. Stephen Salsbury, *The State, the Investor and the Railroad: The Boston and Albany 1825–1867* (Cambridge, Mass., 1967) has an extensive discussion of the nature of the corporation on the eve of the railroad era. Harry N. Scheiber, *Ohio Canal Era: A Case Study of Government and the Economy, 1820–1861* (Athens, Ohio, 1969), has probably the best overall study of the financing and management of a large canal system in the prerailroad era. Arthur M. Schlesinger, *The Colonial Merchants and the American Revolution 1763–1776* (New York, 1957; first published in 1917), is a standard broad survey of the subject. George Rogers Taylor, *The Transportation Revolution, 1815–1860* (New York, 1951), contains much valuable data on prerailroad business institutions of all kinds. Caroline F. Ware, *The Early New England Cotton Manufacture* (Boston, 1931), is the best overall study of the cotton textile business. Gerald T. White, *A History of the Massachusetts Hospital Life Insurance Company* (Cambridge, Mass., 1955) is an insightful case study of an early insurance firm.

[*See also* CENTRAL BANKING; COLONIAL ECONOMY; ECONOMY FROM THE REVOLUTION TO 1815; ECONOMY FROM 1815 TO 1865; ENTREPRENEURSHIP; EXCHANGES; FINANCIAL INTERMEDIARIES; INSURANCE; MANAGEMENT; MANUFACTURING; MONEY SUPPLY; SAVINGS AND INVESTMENT; *and* TRANSPORTATION.]

RISE AND EVOLUTION OF BIG BUSINESS

Alfred D. Chandler, Jr.

BIG BUSINESS is a term that presents many images—tycoons, financial deals, executive suites, market power, and monopoly. But the term can be defined more precisely. Big businesses have common characteristics that differentiate them from smaller and more traditional business firms. They are large; they are profit-making; and they own and administer a number of separate operating units. A big business may manage several factories, mines, plantations, or sales, buying, or financial offices. Often a single enterprise will include all of these types of units. In such large enterprises each unit has its own manager and its own set of accounts. Each unit could, in theory, operate as an independent business enterprise. In the United States nearly all such multiunit business enterprises have taken the legal form of a corporation, the stock of which is normally held by many scattered owners.

These large, multiunit corporations are administered by a hierarchy of executives. The managers on the lowest level supervise the work of the operating units. Middle managers evaluate the performance of the operating managers and coordinate the flow of materials through the several units of the enterprise. Top managers, in addition to evaluating middle managers, determine policies, define plans, and allocate resources for the enterprise as a whole.

Such multiunit enterprises administered by managerial hierarchies are a product of recent times. Big businesses of this sort did not exist before the 1840's. In the first half of the nineteenth century, the managerial class in the United States was tiny. A small number of managers worked as plantation overseers, textile mill agents, bank cashiers, and ship captains; and the ship captains were more often partners than salaried managers. Rarely did a plantation owner, textile company, or bank hire more than one or two managers. The relationship between owners and managers remained close and personal. In 1840 there were virtually no middle managers in the United States, and nearly all top executives owned the enterprises they managed.

By the 1940's, the multiunit business enterprise with managerial hierarchy had become a powerful and pervasive institution. Its managers made the central decisions concerning current production and distribution and the allocation of resources for future production and distribution. Its appearance changed the structure of many industries and of the economy as a whole, thereby altering the ways of competing in the marketplace. These changes and the growing dependence of small business on the large enterprise brought strong and continuing political protest. The resulting regulatory and antitrust legislation that came in the late nineteenth and early twentieth centuries was aimed primarily at the large, multiunit enterprises. Labor too was deeply affected by the coming of big business. The modern industrial union, the response of labor to the rise of the modern industrial enterprise, soon replaced the craft union as the group most used by wage earners to bargain collectively with management over hours, pay, and conditions of work. Of all the institutional changes that accompanied the transformation of a rural, agrarian, commercial economy into an urban, industrial one, none was more significant than the rise and evolution of big business.

RISE AND EVOLUTION OF BIG BUSINESS

BIG BUSINESS IN TRANSPORTATION AND COMMUNICATION

The large, multiunit enterprise first appeared in the United States in the 1840's. It initially came into being to operate the new forms of transportation and communication—the railroad and the telegraph. The railroads permitted a much faster, more regular, and more reliable movement of goods, passengers, and mail over land than had hitherto been possible. The telegraph permitted almost instantaneous communication over long distances. To supervise their many operating units and to coordinate the high-speed, high-volume flow of freight and messages between these units, railroad and telegraph companies had to invent new administrative and business procedures. The resulting administrative structures became models for the later organization of big businesses involved in the production and distribution of goods. In addition, the unprecedented capital requirements of the railroads led to the growth of the first modern capital markets in the United States.

The railroad and the telegraph differed from earlier forms of transportation and communication in that the rights-of-way and the carrier were owned and operated by the same enterprise. The earlier carriers—the stagecoach, wagon, and canalboat lines, and the oceangoing sailing packets—did not have to build and maintain rights-of-way. On the other hand, the turnpike and canal companies rarely operated the coaches or boats that used their rights-of-way. The carriers were almost always operated by small, personally managed partnerships. Very few such partnerships operated more than a dozen ships or vehicles, and virtually none had the resources to build a turnpike or canal. Because of the large sums of capital involved, these rights-of-way were typically financed by corporations. The incorporation of such enterprises permitted merchants to pool the funds required to improve transportation facilities to and from their cities. Where the cost of construction was particularly high, as with canals, merchants turned to state governments to finance, build, and maintain these facilities.

The maintenance and operation of turnpikes and canals was not a complex task. It was handled easily by a small and relatively unskilled staff. The largest and most successful of the American canals, the Erie, was administered by a state commission made up of five part-time members, a clerk with four assistants, and three or four resident engineers. Each time the political party in power changed, the commission, its staff, and the toll collectors, weighers, and maintenance men on the canal were replaced by appointees of the party taking office. The carriers using the canals and turnpikes continued to be operated by their owners. American businessmen never suggested that these common carriers should be owned and operated by the state or federal government.

In contrast, a railroad owning and maintaining a right-of-way had little choice but to operate the carriers that used it. Trains, passengers, and freight could not be carried safely or efficiently if several companies attempted to move their own trains or freight cars along a single track. Central control was even more necessary for the telegraph than for the railroad. The sending of thousands of messages over hundreds of miles of wire demanded an extremely tight coordination and synchronization of flows. Railroad and telegraph lines were far more complicated to operate than ship, boat, and stagecoach lines, and they required far more costly facilities and equipment. Partly because common carriers had always been privately owned and operated in the United States, and partly because the severe depression of the late 1830's and 1840's discouraged state legislatures from supporting further transportation ventures, the new means of communication and transportation came to be owned and operated by private business enterprise.

Railroads. As the country emerged from the depression of the 1840's, railroad construction began to boom. Between 1848 and the Civil War, the mileage operated rose from less than six thousand to more than thirty thousand miles, and the basic railroad network east of the Mississippi was laid. The operational and financial requirements of constructing and running the new roads brought modern finance and modern management to the United States.

The first order of business for the new railroad enterprises was to obtain the large amounts of money necessary to build and equip their lines. Never before had there been such demand in the United States for funds to build capital facilities. The total expenditure for canals be-

RISE AND EVOLUTION OF BIG BUSINESS

tween 1815 and 1860 was only $188 million, of which 73 percent was supplied by states and municipalities, primarily through the issuance of their own bonds. In contrast, by 1859 investment in privately owned railroads had passed the $1.1 billion mark. Of this amount close to $700 million had been raised in the previous ten years.

The simultaneous construction of so many new railroads caused the institutionalization and centralization of the major national money market in New York City. This centralization of financial activities encouraged the rise of the modern investment banker, who specialized in marketing the securities of the large railroads and in advising and handling the accounts of wealthy individuals who wanted to invest in railroads. In the 1850's the major types of modern financial instruments were perfected: preferred stock and debentures, convertible bonds, and first, second, and third mortgage bonds. Modern speculative techniques—including puts and calls, and buying on margin—also appeared. In the 1850's and 1860's speculators such as Jacob Barker, Daniel Drew, and Jay Gould acquired national notoriety by manipulating the prices of railroad securities.

Once the funds had been obtained and the road constructed, the greatest challenge facing the new railroad companies was that of management. The most pressing need was to create an organizational structure to assure control over operations and to schedule the flows of traffic through the operating units. By the 1850's the largest roads were about five hundred miles long. The basic operating unit was a division of seventy to one hundred miles. Each division had a manager for each of the functional activities involved in the operation of a railroad—movement of trains, movement of traffic, the maintenance of rolling stock and of motive power, the maintenance of way, and the handling of funds. Each manager of a lower-level unit reported to a middle manager in the central office who was responsible for the same function for the road as a whole. These middle managers in turn reported to full-time salaried top managers, including a president, treasurer, and general superintendent, who reviewed the work of the operating division and planned and allocated resources for the enterprise as a whole.

To pinpoint more precisely the authority and responsibility for coordinating the flow of trains and traffic along their tracks, railroad managers began to make a distinction between line and staff officers, a distinction that continued to be widely used by American big businesses. The lower- and middle-level managers in the department responsible for moving trains were placed on the direct line of authority from the president and general manager. Only these officers in the transportation department were empowered to give orders involving the flow of trains, goods, and funds, and those stating when and where rolling stock and facilities were to be serviced and repaired. Staff managers, in contrast, set standards for their shops, repair gangs, and freight and passenger offices, and carried out the specific commands of the line executives as to movement and maintenance.

In administering their enterprises through a departmental structure with line and staff distinctions, the managers became experts at controlling through statistics. All departments sent weekly and monthly reports to the central office. On the basis of these operational statistics and the records of financial transactions, the railroad managers invented many of the basic techniques of modern accounting. Their task was far more complex than that of the managers of even the largest plantations or textile mills. Where the biggest mills carried five or six basic accounts, a railroad often had more than seventy-five. To check these accounts and to see that the large sums of money handled daily by hundreds of employees were properly transferred and accounted for, the railroads hired staffs of internal auditors. From the financial accounts, senior executives worked out sophisticated formulas to determine unit (ton-mile) costs. They also used both cost and operational statistics to evaluate the performance of their subordinates.

The senior executives pioneered, too, in developing schemes to account for depreciation and obsolescence in their multimillion-dollar enterprises. They soon decided that the task of defining depreciation realistically was a hopeless one. Instead, railroad men began to use what became called "replacement accounting," a method by which the maintenance and repair required to keep the facilities in prime condition were charged to operating costs. Since the facilities were theoretically maintained in their original condition, they could properly be listed on the asset side of the balance sheet at original cost.

While perfecting their internal organizations, railroad managers of different companies worked closely together to permit the smooth and swift interchange of through traffic from one line to another. They agreed on a standard gauge, standard couplings, and even a standard time. They perfected such devices as the through bill of lading for the shipment of through traffic; and they set up offices of car accountants that kept track of the cars of their company that were being moved on the lines of other roads and of the "foreign" cars that were being carried on their own lines. By the late 1870's such technological and organizational innovations permitted freight to be moved from one part of the country to another without a single transshipment. Whereas in the 1840's the carrying of goods from Philadelphia to Chicago took at least nine weeks and as many transshipments and transactions, in the 1870's goods went in two or three days and required only one transaction and a single loading and unloading.

Except during the Civil War, railroad construction continued to boom from the late 1840's until the prolonged depression that began in 1873. With the coming of that depression, competition for through traffic replaced operations and finance as the primary concern of railroad executives. The improvements in internal management, the perfecting of techniques for handling through freight, and the continuing construction of new lines resulted in a greatly increased volume of through traffic. As a result, through freight became more important than local traffic as a source of revenue. It increasingly provided the critical margin of profit that permitted a road to pay dividends.

Competition between railroads for through traffic bore little resemblance to traditional competition among many small business firms. Never before had a handful of giant enterprises, each with very high fixed costs, competed for the same trade. In the 1870's, two-thirds of the costs of a railroad remained fixed. Only one-third varied with the rise and fall of traffic. As long as a road was not operating at full capacity, its managers were always tempted to reduce rates to carry any extra traffic that covered variable costs. To retain the traffic lost by such rate cuts, a competing road had to respond by making compara-

ble reductions. Normally the weak roads with lines that were less direct or less adequately constructed or equipped instituted rate reductions. If their action resulted in receivership, they were at a competitive advantage because they no longer had to meet the interest on their bonded debt. Since most American roads were financed by bonds, these charges were high. Therefore most railroad managers and investors believed that the logical outcome of competition for through traffic was bankruptcy for all the competitors involved.

During the years before the depression of the 1870's, railroads had relied on alliances with competing and connecting roads to assure themselves of a continued flow of through traffic along their tracks. The early roads made allies of feeder lines by helping to finance their construction. As the first competing lines went into operation, their managers agreed on a regional rate structure. If the competing roads had difficulty in maintaining that structure, they set up informal traffic or profit pools. By allocating a certain percentage of the traffic or profits from the through traffic to each of the competing lines in the pool, they reduced the incentive to cut rates, since a rate reduction could no longer bring an increase in either traffic or profits.

As the depression of the 1870's deepened and as traffic decreased and competition intensified, these informal alliances fell apart. Railroad men then saw two alternative means to assure a continuing flow of traffic across their lines. One was to build giant "self-sustaining systems," as one railroad president termed them. Such systems would connect the major commercial and manufacturing centers and the timber, mining, and other raw-material-producing areas of a major geographic region. The other was to transform the loose, informal alliances into formal federations with their own administrative organizations to enforce rate and pooling agreements.

Railroad men hesitated to risk the first of these alternatives. The largest roads of the early 1870's were little bigger than those of the 1850's. They were about five hundred miles long. With assets of $20 million to $30 million each and with a working force of about five thousand employees, they were already among the largest business enterprises in the world. Managers feared that roads any larger than these could not be operated efficiently. Investors also were concerned, because a major expansion required the issuance of new stocks and bonds and would, therefore, reduce current dividends. Almost no one believed that there were major economies to be gained by an increase in size, for expansion of track mileage operated required a comparable increase in facilities and personnel. Therefore, the great majority of railroad companies turned to federation.

The largest and most sophisticated of the new railroad federations to appear in the 1870's was the Eastern Trunk Line Association. In 1875 the major east-west lines and their connections made the first attempt to set up an association to administer a rate-maintaining pool. At first this attempt failed because the Baltimore & Ohio (B&O) refused to join; but after a disastrous rate war convinced the B&O to participate, the association finally came into being in 1877. The trunk lines then obtained the services of Albert Fink to manage the cartel. Two years earlier Fink, an experienced and talented railroad manager, had helped to form the Southern Railway and Steamship Association, and had served as its first manager. Upon taking over the Eastern Trunkline Association in 1877, he first reorganized in a more systematic manner the annual meetings or conventions at which the roads agreed on rates and allocations. He then put together an extensive staff to administer the pool. Finally, he appointed a board of arbitration, made up of three railroad experts, to consider and decide on complaints about rates, allocations, and their enforcement. The creation of these legislative, administrative, and judicial bodies, Fink told members of the association, "for the first time established a practical method by which the competitive traffic can be properly managed and controlled." By 1880 similar regional associations had been set up in other parts of the country.

Despite their carefully worked out organizational apparatus, these federations were unable to maintain rates. The pools failed for several reasons. The administration of traffic and, later, money pools proved to be more complex than had been anticipated, and required more men than Fink or his counterparts had at their disposal. The roads continued to quarrel about their allocations and about the rate-making and pooling procedures. Speculators like Jay Gould, who in their manipulations of railroad securities often came to control railroad companies, had little interest in supporting the pools. Indeed, they found the breaking of agreements and the setting off of rate wars an easy way to make and break the prices of railroad stocks and bonds. The greatest obstacle to effective cartelization was the relentless pressure of high fixed costs. To meet these costs, railroad managers were often unable to resist the temptation to subvert the cartel arrangements that they had worked so hard to obtain.

Railroad executives quickly agreed that the only way to make the federations work was to legalize pooling—that is, to secure legislative definition of their cartel arrangements as contracts enforceable in courts of law. They had little success in obtaining such legislation. Farmers and shippers, whose economic well-being depended on transportation costs, were unwilling to give an association the powers of unilaterally determining and maintaining rates, even if a government commission reviewed its decisions. To most Americans not directly concerned with transportation, legalized pooling meant legalized monopoly. As a result, the Interstate Commerce Act of 1887, the first major piece of legislation by the national government to regulate business enterprises and to set up a permanent regulatory commission, specifically forbade pooling.

Well before the passage of the Interstate Commerce Act, most railroad managers and investors had given up pooling. They had already turned, as Fink had predicted they would if the pools failed, to building self-sustaining systems. They had come to agree with Charles E. Perkins, president of the Chicago, Burlington & Quincy, that "each line must own its own feeders." So by leasing, buying, and building, roads operating five hundred miles were soon operating five thousand and even ten thousand miles of track. These systems, with assets ranging from $100 million to $800 million, became—and remained until the twentieth century—by far the largest business enterprises in the world. By 1892, thirty-three railroad systems capitalized at more than $100 million each operated close to 70 percent of the track mileage of the nation and carried an even larger percentage of its traffic.

Since each road wanted its own lines to regional commercial centers and sources of raw materials, system building led to overconstruction of the railroad system and to the bankruptcy of many individual corporations. More railroads were built in the 1880's than in any decade before or since. The 1890's witnessed an unprecedented number of railroad receiverships. By 1895, close to forty thousand miles of track capitalized at more than $2.5 billion were in receivership. It was in financially reorganizing these overextended railroads that the New York investment bankers played their major role in American railroads. The banking house of J. P. Morgan, for example, reorganized the Philadelphia & Reading, the Baltimore & Ohio, the Chesapeake & Ohio, the Santa Fe, the Erie, the Northern Pacific, and the Richmond Terminal (which became the Southern). Morgan and other bankers encouraged the roads to round out their systems and to form "communities of interest" by purchasing each other's stock.

By the middle of the first decade of the twentieth century, the boundaries of the major systems had been defined. They remained much the same until the second third of the century, when the impact of the airplane, automobile, and truck profoundly altered existing patterns and modes of transportation. The completion of the systems and the setting of communities of interest ended incentives for competitive construction and rate cutting. Concurrently, the passage of the Hepburn Act in 1906 gave the Interstate Commerce Commission a stronger say in determining rates. Rate making now became more of a political negotiation involving a railroad, at least two sets of shippers, and the commission. With few strategic decisions to be made about either pricing or expansion, railroad executives, top as well as middle, concentrated almost wholly on day-to-day operations. The administration of the first big business in the nation soon became routinized and bureaucratized.

Other Transportation. The business enterprises that managed other modes of transportation followed the railroad pattern. They were operated by salaried managers who owned little or no stock in the company, who relied on the centralized capital market for funds, and who managed their enterprises through systematic administrative practices and procedures.

In water transportation the railroads became the operators. Nearly all domestic water lines—those operating on rivers, lakes, and canals, and in coastal waters that were reserved for American ships by congressional legislation—were by the end of the nineteenth century owned and managed by railroad systems. The few that remained independent were closely allied to one or two railroad systems. By and large, Americans failed to participate in the development of oceangoing steamship lines.

In urban transportation big business appeared when electricity replaced the horse as the source of motive power. The businessmen who carried out this transformation—Peter A. B. Widener, William L. Elkins, Thomas F. Ryan, and William C. Whitney—made great fortunes. They left operational matters almost entirely to technically trained, salaried managers. Increased costs, demands for costly expansions into the suburbs, and political pressure to maintain low fares caused the founding entrepreneurs to turn the control of their enterprises over to investment bankers, who provided funds for the continuing expansion, and to municipal commissions, which set rates and planned expansion.

Although they were not involved in transportation, the electric power and light companies developed in much the same way as the traction enterprises. That is, they remained local or regional firms. Often they were among the largest business enterprises in the areas they served. Like railroads, they struck many observers as being "natural monopolies"; and rarely did more than one or, at most, two or three of these large enterprises operate in one town, city, or metropolitan area. After the entrepreneurs who formed the enterprises moved out, the professional managers came to share top management decisions with investment bankers and public commissioners.

Communication. In communication big business came as quickly as it did in transportation. The telegraph marched across the continent side by side with the railroad. The railroads found the telegraph essential for their operations, and the telegraph companies found that the railroads provided convenient rights-of-way. Because the telegraph relied wholly on through traffic and required close central control for efficient transmission of messages, it soon came to be operated by a single national enterprise. The telegraph was first used commercially in the late 1840's. By the early 1860's three regional companies operated the network, and in 1866 the three merged to form Western Union. The new consolidated

RISE AND EVOLUTION OF BIG BUSINESS

enterprise operated its thousands of units through a hierarchy of salaried top-, middle-, and lower-level managers. In administering their system they used a line-and-staff organizational structure and accounting procedures very similar to those of the large railroads.

The telephone began to challenge the telegraph only at the end of the century. When it first became commercially practical in the late 1870's, it was used for local calls. Without the technological developments that made possible long-distance or through calls, the telephone network might have been run as were the traction and power and light systems—that is, by many local monopolies. The American Telephone and Telegraph Company (AT&T), by technologically perfecting and operating the "long lines," came to dominate the national telephone system. By controlling through traffic and by assisting in the financing of regional firms, AT&T soon had a near monopoly of the telephone business and became one of the biggest businesses in the country.

Yet the railroads played a much more significant role as pioneers of modern management than did other transportation and communication enterprises. Only Western Union and AT&T were as large as some of the railroad systems (and there were many railroad systems larger than both). Moreover, AT&T and Western Union each handled only one type of traffic: messages or calls. Their traffic problems, like those of traction and utility companies, were far less complicated than those of the major railroad system carrying a vast variety of freight. Therefore, in their financing and operation they learned much more from the railroads than the railroads learned from them.

BIG BUSINESS IN PRODUCTION AND DISTRIBUTION

By making possible unprecedented speed and volume in transportation and communication, the new technologies and the new organizational forms devised to manage them set off a revolution in production and distribution. They encouraged the rapid adoption of new technologies of mass production and new methods of mass marketing. Big business—modern, multi-unit enterprise—quickly appeared where managerial hierarchies were able to coordinate the flow of goods through the processes of production and distribution more speedily and efficiently than was possible through traditional market mechanisms.

The revolution in distribution began as soon as the railroad and telegraph started to move across the country. Before 1840 the merchant and the mercantile partnership had been the primary distributors in the American economy. As the national economy became more productive and began to spread westward across the continent, merchants became increasingly specialized. Instead of handling many products and performing many services, they became importers or exporters or specialized brokers who dealt only in cotton, wheat, dry goods, hardware, or groceries. These merchants also sold increasingly on commission rather than on their account. Nevertheless, their ways of doing business remained traditional. They continued to use the same forms of partnerships, contractual arrangements, and double-entry bookkeeping that Italian merchants had pioneered in the fourteenth century.

Within the historically brief span of two or three decades, the merchant and his traditional ways of business all but disappeared in the sectors where goods were sold in volume. In the marketing of agricultural commodities, the merchant was replaced by the modern commodity dealer, who relied on the railroad (with its through bills of lading and specialized storage facilities), and the new grain, cotton, and other commodity exchanges (where transactions were carried out by telegraph and cable). These dealers purchased directly from many farmers, and sold and shipped the commodities directly to many processors.

In the marketing of manufactured products, the full-line, full-service wholesaler who took title to the goods quickly replaced the commission merchant. Specializing along existing lines —dry goods, hardware, groceries, drugs, wet goods, and the like—the new wholesalers moved massive amounts of merchandise directly from the makers of the finished products to the specialized retailers in the cities or to general stores across the country.

By the 1890's the wholesaler was beginning to lose out to the mass retailer. In the 1860's and 1870's large department stores, which usually began as wholesalers of dry goods or retailers of men's clothing, started to make inroads into the urban markets of the wholesalers. These stores included Macy's, Arnold Constable, and Lord & Taylor in New York; Jordan Marsh, Filene's, and R. H. White in Boston; John Wanamaker, and Strawbridge and Clothier, in Philadelphia; Carson, Pirie, Scott & Company, and Marshall Field, in Chicago; Hutzler in Baltimore; and Woodward and Lothrop in Washington. Then the mail-order houses of Montgomery Ward and Sears, Roebuck began to move into the rural markets. In the meantime, the first chain stores, including F. W. Woolworth and the Great Atlantic & Pacific Tea Company, had grown very large. The major expansion of the chain stores did not come until the twentieth century.

These new mass marketers were big businesses. Their volumes were much higher and their profits much steadier than those of the most successful earlier merchants. They all had comparable internal organizations. Each had buying departments with offices in the leading commercial and manufacturing centers in the United States and in Europe. Companies carrying many lines had a separate buying staff for each line. The "buyers" determined the prices paid, the volume required, and the specifications desired. A sales or operations department handled the advertising, the actual sales, and the delivery of goods to the customer. For the top managers who administered the departments and for the middle managers who coordinated flows, the criterion for successful performance was "stock turn," the number of times during a six-month or year period in which stock was sold and replaced. Increased stock turn meant increased profits, for the same number of employees using the same facilities sold more goods, thus reducing the cost of each individual sale.

Such administrative coordination of flows quickly proved to be more profitable than coordination by traditional market mechanisms. One reason the retailers rapidly increased their share of the market at the expense of the wholesaler was that, through bypassing the wholesaler, they reduced the number of transactions and transshipments, maintained a more direct contact with the market, and scheduled flows more precisely. Dividends from their enterprises made the Filenes, Wanamakers, Fields, Strauses (Macy's), Rosenwalds (Sears), and Hartfords (A&P) among the wealthiest families in the land. Yet their companies kept their prices low enough to bring strident protests from competitors—small retailers and the wholesalers who served them. The first protests that came in the 1890's were against the department stores and soon reached state legislatures in the form of demands for protective legislation. In the first two decades of the twentieth century the protests were turned against the mail-order houses. In the 1920's the chains received the brunt of this political opposition. Nevertheless, the protest and resulting legislation had almost no effect on the continuing growth of the mass retailer.

Nor did comparable protests slow the growth of the modern industrial enterprise—the giant corporation that today epitomizes big business. This type of corporation had its beginnings in the 1880's, when the owners of factories using new mass-production technologies were unable to depend on existing marketers to sell goods in the volume in which they were produced. These new technologies did more than merely replace men with machines. They permitted several processes involved in making and packaging a product to be placed within a single establishment. New continuous, large-batch, and assembling techniques vastly increased the output of a single plant or works. This larger and faster flow (or throughput, as it came to be called) increased productivity and reduced unit costs in the production processes in much the same way that increased stock turn lowered distribution costs.

A faster and larger throughput resulted from both technological and organizational innovation. Technologically, more efficient machinery and equipment, more carefully processed raw materials, and the increased use of energy helped to speed flows, reduce unit costs, and increase productivity. Organizationally, these ends were achieved by improving the design of the factory and the works (a works was a manufacturing establishment with many buildings) and by the adoption of more systematic administrative structures and procedures. Once a major technological or organizational innovation had been perfected, the productivity of enterprises using it continued to improve, though at a slower rate, as workers and managers learned to use the new machines and methods more effectively.

The potential for such technological and organizational improvements was first realized in the refining and distilling industries. The liquid materials and the chemical nature of the processes permitted the rapid development of large-batch and continuous-process techniques. For example, by 1869, only ten years after the discovery of oil at Titusville, Pennsylvania, petroleum was being moved through the refineries automatically, untouched by human hands. Manual labor was needed only for the final packaging. These flows were made possible by improved design of the refinery and by the use of steam power to move the petroleum. Output was further increased by the development of more efficient stills and other equipment and by an intensified use of energy through the adoption of superheated steam and cracking processes. Similar technologies and organizational changes appeared by the 1860's and 1870's in the production of sugar, vegetable oil, beer, and whiskey and other distilled spirits. In the late 1870's and early 1880's comparable mechanical processes were developed almost simultaneously in the production of cigarettes, matches, flour, oatmeal, canned soups and vegetables, soap, and photographic film.

Mass production came more slowly in the metal-making and metalworking industries. There the materials were harder to work with and the processes more complex than in refining and distilling or in the processing of agricultural products. In metal making, the greatest advances came in the speed of production and the output of steel, which was first extensively mass-produced in the United States in the years just after the Civil War, through the adoption of the Bessemer converter. In the 1870's, Andrew Carnegie constructed steel works that incorporated the most recent technological and organizational developments. Carnegie, who had been superintendent of the busiest operating divisions of the Pennsylvania Railroad in the early 1860's, pioneered in transferring accounting and managerial techniques from the railroads to steel production. The speed and volume of the throughput of the Carnegie works were soon the greatest in the world. Such throughput helped Carnegie to gain a fortune comparable with that of John D. Rockefeller, who in 1869 owned the fastest refinery in the West.

In metalworking, particularly in the mass production of machinery, the technological and organizational challenges were even greater than in steel production. Here the basic method of mass production was one of fabricating and assembling interchangeable parts. Such shaping and assembling required the most intricate machines. For this reason the major innovations in the American machine tool industry were those created to shape metal and produce machines. Moreover, the coordination of the flow in the fabricating and assembling of interchangeable parts required more precise scheduling and more careful definition of the worker, as well as more carefully planned location of machines, than did the production processes in other industries. Therefore, modern scientific management, of which Frederick Winslow Taylor was the best-known practitioner, evolved first in the machinery and metalworking industries.

Many of the manufacturers who had adopted the new continuous, large-batch, or assembling processes quickly decided that existing mass marketers could not effectively market and distribute the high volume of their output. These mass producers therefore began to build their own marketing and distributing networks, and then to set up their own buying organizations. The manufacturers who first grew large by this strategy of vertical integration were of three types. They were producers of low-priced, semiperishable packaged products; the makers of perishable products that required quick delivery; and the manufacturers of recently invented machines, such as sewing machines and harvesters, that required specialized marketing services if they were to be sold in volume.

The first set of manufacturers, the mass producers of semiperishable packaged products, included the makers of cigarettes (James B. Duke's American Tobacco), matches (Diamond Match), flour (Pillsbury and Washburn-Crosby), breakfast cereals (Quaker Oats), canned goods (Campbell Soup, Heinz, and Borden's Milk), soap (Procter & Gamble), and photographic equipment (Eastman Kodak). These manufacturers continued to use the wholesaler to distribute the goods to the retailers; but they took over the scheduling of the flows through the wholesalers to the retailers, and they handled the large amount of advertising they believed necessary to assure a continuing demand for their massive output. To be certain of a continuing high-volume flow into their factories, the managers of these enterprises quickly organized extensive purchasing departments to buy, store, and ship raw materials and to schedule their flows into the producing plants.

The other two sets of manufacturers who adopted a strategy of vertical integration in the 1880's dispensed with the wholesaler altogether. The meat-packers (Armour, Swift, Morris, and Cudahy) created national marketing networks with branch offices or "houses" that had refrigerated warehouses and facilities to distribute meat to butchers, grocers, and other retailers. They soon had their own fleets of refrigerated railroad cars and a number of refrigerated ships. To meet the increased demand created by the establishment of the new distribution network, they set up packing plants in towns and cities along the cattle frontier and had their buyers purchase in the stockyards or directly from ranchers. In the same decade brewers selling to the national markets (Pabst, Schlitz, Blatz, and Anheuser-Busch) created a comparable marketing network and somewhat smaller buying ones. In the next decade the forerunners of United Fruit set up a similar organization for the sale of bananas from the Caribbean to American and world markets.

The machinery makers who eliminated the wholesalers did so because those marketers were unable to provide specialized marketing services of demonstration, after-sales service and repair, and consumer credit in a satisfactory manner. Such firms included the makers of sewing machines (Singer), harvesters, reapers, and other complex agricultural machinery (McCormick, Deering, J. I. Case, and John Deere). At first the pioneering firms sold their products through independent distributors. In the late 1870's and early 1880's they reorganized their marketing organizations by replacing the dealers with branch offices headed by salaried managers who supervised a staff that made the sales, provided the necessary services, and monitored the high-volume flow of machines to the territory assigned to that office. The makers of newly invented office machinery (Fairbanks Scales, Remington Typewriter, National Cash Register, A. B. Dick Mimeograph, and Burroughs Adding Machine) created comparable organizations. The makers of newly invented or technologically improved heavy machinery adopted the same strategy and same structure as the producers of light machines. In the 1880's the forerunners of General Electric (Edison General Electric and Thomson-Houston), Westinghouse Electric, Western Electric (makers of telephone equipment), Otis Elevator, Babcock & Wilcox (makers of boilers), and Worthington Pump and Link Belt Machinery built national, and then global, marketing organizations. A little later, chemical enterprises manufacturing mass-produced products that were difficult to store, ship, and use (such as explosives and corrosive acids) set up their own marketing and purchasing networks.

Once the buying and selling organization had been completed, the salaried managers hired, and administrative methods perfected, the first firms to integrate enjoyed a powerful economic advantage. The administrative coordination that they achieved lowered unit costs and gave the pioneers a direct contact with the market. A competitor had to build a comparable national and global organization before it could acquire the volume to reduce its costs to the level of those of the existing enterprise or before it could provide full consumer service. Competitors did appear, but only a very few succeeded in forming comparable integrated firms. The industries in which integrated mass producers operated were dominated by a very few large business enterprises from the moment the new mass-production technologies were applied. They remained highly concentrated industries in which the dominant firms competed in an oligopolistic manner. These industries seldom passed through a period of traditional competition between many small, single-unit family or individual firms.

Also in the 1880's manufacturing enterprises began to take another route to size. This was growth by merger. For some manufacturers mergers were the first step to exploiting the possibilities of mass production and then vertical integration. To many more they were an effective way to control price and production within an industry. Nearly all the early mergers grew out of cartels administered by trade associations.

Formal trade associations to control competition first appeared extensively on a national scale in the early 1870's. These federations were basically the response of manufacturers to the sharp decline in prices that began even before the panic of 1873. This decline reflected an expansion of output that derived from the rapid increase of industrial production made possible by the spread of the factory and the beginnings of mass-production techniques. It also resulted from the monetary policies of the national government, which brought a contraction of the national money supply. Trade associations designed to maintain prices and profits appeared in nearly every American industry. In the hardware industry alone, more than sixty different trade associations managed cartels for as many specialized products.

During the 1880's a few federations formally merged into a single consolidated enterprise. Nearly all such mergers occurred in the refining and distilling industries, where the early application of the new mass-production techniques created a greater excess production than in most other industries and where economies from concentrated production in a few large works could be most readily realized.

To provide a legal vehicle for such mergers, refiners and distillers adopted an old form—the trust—to their needs. The stockholders of many small, single-unit firms turned over their stock to a board of trustees. In return they received trust certificates that promised them an agreed-upon share of the profits of the trust. This legal arrangement permitted the central managing board to do what it could not do in a trade association—directly supervise the management of the constituent units and make investment decisions for the combine as a whole.

All the successful trusts of the 1880's—the oil, cottonseed oil, linseed oil, sugar, whiskey, and lead trusts—consolidated production into a small number of plants. Three of these went even further. The oil, cottonseed oil, and lead trusts (paint was the major product of the last) integrated forward and backward. Of these, the Standard Oil Trust was the pioneer. It was formed in January 1882 by an alliance of refiners headed by John D. Rockefeller's Standard Oil Company of Ohio. Members of that alliance, which had operated one of the most effective cartels in American history, saw the opportunity to further increase their power and their profits by exploiting the economies of concentrated production. Within three years the trust had reduced the number of refineries it operated from fifty-three to twenty-two. By 1885 two-fifths of the world output of petroleum products was being produced by three huge new Standard Oil refineries. The resulting increase in speed and volume of the throughput reduced refining cost from 1.5 cents to 0.5 cents a barrel—far below that of any competing refineries at home or abroad. To market this increased output, in the mid-1880's the trust built its own wholesaling organization in the United States and Europe. In the late 1880's it began to integrate backward, by extracting crude oil in the United States. By 1900, Standard Oil had competition from two other smaller but also integrated oil companies —Tidewater Oil and Pure Oil.

Although only a very few mergers occurred on a national scale in the 1880's, the number grew rapidly in the following decade. One reason was changes in state and national laws. The cartelization of so much of American industry during and after the depression of the 1870's and the economic power that the mass-production technology had given the first trusts brought forth a strong political outcry. States passed laws against cartels and trusts. In 1890, Congress passed the Sherman Antitrust Act, which made illegal "every contract, combination in the form of trust or otherwise, or conspiracy in restraint of trade or commerce."

A few months earlier the New Jersey legislature had passed a general incorporation law of holding companies. Previously a corporation that was to hold stock in other corporations could be chartered only by a special act of the legislature. Under the New Jersey law a charter for a holding company could be obtained merely by filling out forms and paying a modest fee. Since a corporation had a much better established legal standing than a trust, and since corporate shares were more acceptable to investors than were trust certificates, the existing trusts simply transformed themselves into holding companies. Of more significance, because the Sherman Act threatened the legality of the trade associations as well as of the trusts, many of these associations also metamorphosed into holding companies.

The mergers of the 1890's clustered in two time periods. A number took place before mid-1893, when a financial panic and resulting depression put a damper on the promotion and financing of new business venture. As the economy pulled out of the depression in 1897, mergers became extraordinarily popular. Again legal developments played a part. In *United States* v. *E.*

C. Knight (1895) the Supreme Court ruled that the operations of the American Sugar Refining Company, the successor to the sugar trust, did not violate the Sherman Antitrust Act, even though the company refined more than 90 percent of the sugar produced in the United States. In *United States* v. *Trans-Missouri Freight Association* (1897), and in *United States* v. *Addyston Pipe and Steel Company* (1899), the Supreme Court held that any association or federation attempting to control price and output violated the Sherman Antitrust Act. The apparent approval of the holding company and disapproval of the trade association convinced members of most federations that they should merge into consolidated holding companies.

Business reasons were more important than legal ones for the popularity of mergers. The high profits of the integrated enterprises formed in the 1880's and of the early integrated trusts convinced manufacturers of the validity of a strategy of growth through vertical integration. Profit records also impressed investors, who contrasted them with the dismal returns so many railroads were reporting in the mid-1890's. Until then the New York Stock Exchange had listed almost no industrial stocks. Only the securities of transportation and communication enterprises, and those of a few banks and insurance companies, were traded. As prosperity returned in 1897, the demand for industrial securities soared. Manufacturers quickly realized they could exchange the securities of their small, unknown family firms for those of large national holding companies at a highly inflated rate; and financiers were excited by the profits to be made from promoting and financing such mergers.

Thus judicial decisions interacted with the boom in securities prices and the success of the early integrated industrial stocks to set off the first, and probably the most significant, merger movement in American industry. Some mergers were carried out to control competition; others, to gain the profits of the merging procedure itself; and still others, in order to obtain the gains of administrative coordination of high-volume flows through the processes of production and distribution.

Nevertheless, merged enterprises remained profitable over the long term only if they consolidated production and then integrated forward and backward, and only if they used mass-production techniques to produce goods for mass markets. The most successful mergers were those that shifted from a strategy of horizontal combination (that is, of controlling a major share of the output of one basic process of production) to one of vertical integration (that is, controlling the flow of goods through the several processes of production and distribution, from the suppliers of raw materials to the ultimate consumer). And even those firms that made the shift were rarely successful unless the nature of their processes of production and distribution gave them a strong competitive advantage over small, nonintegrated enterprises. Thus, mergers were rarely successful in labor-intensive industries with relatively simple technologies, such as textiles, apparel, leather, woodworking, lumber, and printing; or those for making simple metal products, such as wringers, shears, and bicycles; or, at the other end of the scale, those reaching highly specialized and local markets. Most lasting mergers were in the food, chemical, oil, rubber, glass, metal-making, and machinery industries.

Where the merged firms did integrate and did reap the benefits of administrative coordination, they quickly dominated their industries. In turn, such industries became highly concentrated, as had those in which the integrated enterprise first appeared. The dominating integrated firms competed in the modern oligopolistic manner; that is, they competed more in service (including consumer credit), advertising, product differentiation, and product development than in price.

Where the processes of production were less complex and the speed and volume of the flow of goods slower and smaller, the small, nonintegrated firms were able to compete with the larger integrated ones. Indeed, as the unhappy history of American Woolen and Central Leather companies indicates, size could indeed be a disadvantage. Such industries remained competitive in the more traditional sense. Where manufacturers in such industries produced for mass markets, the larger distribution enterprises, particularly the mass retailers, normally took over the function of coordinating the flow of goods from the processor of raw materials to the ultimate consumer.

Table 1 helps to document these generalizations about the rise of big business in American industry. It includes nearly all American compa-

RISE AND EVOLUTION OF BIG BUSINESS

TABLE 1
Location of the Largest American Industrial Enterprises

Of the 278 American enterprises involved in the production of goods in 1917 and having assets of $20 million or over:

- 30 in mining
- 7   in crude oil
- 5   in agriculture
- 0   in construction
- 236 in manufacturing

Of the 236 manufacturing firms:

171 (72.5 percent) clustered in six two-digit Standard Industrial Classification (SIC) groups
- 39 in primary metals
- 34 in food
- 29 in transportation equipment
- 24 in machinery
- 24 in petroleum
- 21 in chemicals

23 (9.7 percent) scattered in seven groups
- 7 in textiles
- 5 in lumber
- 4 in leather
- 3 in printing and publishing
- 3 in apparel
- 1 in instruments
- 0 in furniture

The remaining forty-two manufacturing firms were in continuous-process and large-batch four-digit SIC industries within the seven remaining groups. In the paper group, the larger firms were clustered in production of newsprint and kraft paper; in stone, glass, and clay, in production of cement and plate glass; in rubber, in production of tires and footwear; in tobacco, in production of cigarettes; in fabricated metals, in production of cans; in electrical machinery, in production of standardized machines; and in miscellaneous, in production of matches. (The most inclusive category in the Standard Industrial Classification of the Census Bureau is a two-digit group. For example, SIC 20 is food and SIC 21 is tobacco. Within the largest categories there are three- and four-digit industries. For example, SIC 206 is sugar refining and 2062 is cane sugar refining.)

nies in 1917 with assets of $20 million or more than were involved in the processes of production (that is, in agriculture, fisheries, construction, and manufacturing). That year is a useful one for analysis. By 1917 the earlier merger movement had shaken down. The mergers that were going to succeed and those that were going to fail had done so. In 1917, the year the United States entered World War I, the economy had not yet felt the full impact of wartime demands.

Table 1 indicates that 236 of the 278 largest producing enterprises in the nation were manufacturers. Of these, by far the greatest number were clustered in the capital-intensive, mass-production industries consisting of enterprises that sold to national and world markets. Less than 10 percent were in labor-intensive, low-technology industries. In 1917 the large firms were still a major force in the food and machine industries, where the giant industrial enterprise had first appeared in the 1880's and 1890's. They were also flourishing in the metal, oil, chemical, rubber, and glass industries, where the volume of output was high and the customers numerous and varied enough to require extensive marketing facilities and careful scheduling of flows. And they appeared and grew as well in new assembling industries like the automobile industry, which required the specialized marketing services of demonstration, repair and servicing, and consumer credit. Thus, 86 percent of all of the producing companies with assets exceeding $20 million and 90 percent of the manufacturing companies had integrated production with distribution.

Many of these American big businesses had already become multinational enterprises. In addition to their overseas marketing and buying networks, they had built manufacturing facilities abroad. In 1914 direct investment abroad by American enterprises amounted to 7 percent of the gross national product (GNP) (precisely the same percentage of GNP directly invested abroad in 1966). Of the forty-two United States corporations listed in Mira Wilkins' *The Emergence of Multinational Enterprise* as having two or more manufacturing establishments abroad, or one plant and one raw-material-producing facility, two-thirds were in the food and machinery industries. The others were all capital-intensive, mass-production enterprises.

By 1917 these large integrated firms had come to dominate the industries most vital to the continuing growth and health of the American economy. And by then their managers had worked out the operating structure and procedures to administer their enterprises. Although the holding company continued to be employed as a legal device in setting up these big businesses, it was used much less for administrative purposes. A few of the largest industrial empires continued to have top management in a parent company supervising, evaluating, and planning for its subsidiaries, but by 1917 approximately 80 percent of the 278 firms listed in table 1 were using the centralized, functionally departmentalized operating structure. All the operating units carrying out a specific function—manufacturing, sales, purchasing, raw-material production, traffic (transportation), and finance were placed in a single department, and each department was usually headed by a vice-president. Those firms with facilities overseas normally had a separate department to supervise and coordinate foreign business. Nearly all of these companies also had smaller departments in the central office to handle the more specialized functions of personnel, legal matters, and research and development.

In carrying out these tasks, middle and top management concentrated on improving the data that flowed into the departmental headquarters and the central office—data that provided a continuing and detailed picture of internal operations and changing external market and financial conditions. As they had done in setting up the departmental structure, the industrial managers adopted railroad procedures to their somewhat differing accounting needs. In financial accounting they made few changes. In capital accounting they moved slowly from replacement to asset accounting. In cost accounting they were more innovative, for costing in production and distribution differed markedly from that in transportation and communication. These managers used the new cost data, particularly the new methods of determining indirect costs, to devise new and more accurate methods of determining rate of return on capital investment. At the same time they pioneered in developing techniques for making market and financial forecasts, on which the current flows and long-term allocations became increasingly based.

By 1917 such decisions about flows and allocations were being made by salaried managers who owned little, if any, stock in the enterprises they managed. From the start the ranks of lower and middle management in these industries were filled almost completely by salaried executives. No family was large enough or talented enough to provide the number of managers required to operate a large, multiunit enterprise. In top management experienced salaried managers often shared decision making with outsiders.

The makeup of top management reflected the route by which the enterprise had grown large. If it had become a big business by carrying out a strategy of vertical integration financed from retained earnings, the founders and their families continued to hold a major share of the capital stock of the firm. In such companies members of these families sat on the board of directors and its major committees. On the other hand, if the enterprise had become big as a result of merger, stock ownership typically was scattered. Not only did the process of merger itself disperse ownership, but the rationalization of facilities and the integration forward and backward that followed such administrative consolidation required the raising of new capital, often acquired by the sale of stock. In such enterprises the bankers and other financiers who had helped to promote and finance the merger often continued to sit on the board. Therefore, at the time of World War I entrepreneurial families, financiers, or their representatives still had some say in the management of American big business.

Nevertheless, their power was essentially negative. Family members or financiers on a board could say no; but unless they were trained and experienced in the affairs of the industry and of the company—that is, unless they were professional managers—they had neither the information nor the experience to propose alternative courses of action.

A board of directors usually met four or five times a year to discuss problems and situations on which the managers had to concentrate daily for months and even years. If these outside directors were unhappy with the performance of their managers, they could hire new managers. Thus, although the American economy had in the early twentieth century some elements of family and financial capitalism, it was already moving toward a system of managerial capitalism.

As the managers grew more influential, they became more professional. As early as the 1880's railroad executives had developed the appurtenances of professionalism. Traffic managers, accounting executives, other functional specialists, and general managers formed their own national societies. Often they had their own specialized journals. By the 1880's executives responsible for construction and maintenance of right of way and equipment were being trained in specialized college and university courses in civil and mechanical engineering.

In the first two decades of the twentieth century, parallel developments occurred in production and distribution. Production engineers, marketers, accountants, and general managers formed their own associations. These societies had their own journals, which managers supplemented by reading such vocational periodicals as *Management and Administration*. At the same time some of the most prestigious institutions of higher learning—Harvard, Dartmouth, the universities of Pennsylvania, Michigan, California, and others—began to provide courses and to set up graduate schools that offered training in functional specialties as well as in general business administration. The schools, the journals, and the societies provided channels through which managers reviewed and discussed common problems and issues. By encouraging such communication and frequent personal contact, they gave the managers a sense of identity. Soon these salaried executives were beginning to see themselves as a group with common outlooks as well as common interests and concerns.

By World War I, therefore, big business had become as central in production and distribution as it had become a generation earlier in transportation and communication. The new mass marketers and the new integrated mass producers supervised current operations, coordinated major flows, and allocated resources for future economic activities in the most important industries. Salaried professionals were taking over the management of major sectors of the American economy from entrepreneurs, families, and financiers. All these trends intensified as the American economy expanded its output and became more urban, more affluent and more technologically advanced in the decades after World War I.

BIG BUSINESS AFTER WORLD WAR I

The rise of big business in the United States was basically an institutional response to the coming of modern technology and the modern mass markets. And the basic reasons that big business continued to grow and become even more dominant were that technology became increasingly more complex and more productive and that markets, except during the Great Depression of the 1930's, continued to expand.

Of these two basic stimulants to the growth of big business, technological innovations had a greater impact on its evolution in transportation and communication than did the expanding markets. In transportation the internal combustion engine—installed in automobiles, trucks, and airplanes—broke the hold of the railroads on overland movement of goods and passengers. In air transport, where precise scheduling and control were operational necessities, a few large, carefully structured big businesses came to dominate. On the ground the operations of truck, bus, and taxi companies required much less precision, less complex equipment, and a smaller capital investment than did the railroads. Smaller enterprises were able to compete effectively with large ones. Therefore, as air transportation became increasingly oligopolistic, ground transportation became more competitive.

In communication the changes were somewhat less dramatic. The telephone replaced the telegraph, but American Telephone & Telegraph continued to operate much as it had earlier in the century. It operated the "long lines" and evaluated the performance (and to some extent planned the growth and allocated the resources) of twenty or more regional companies that it controlled financially.

The coming of radio and television, products of complex sets of technological innovations, created new means of communication and of entertainment. Because of the high capital requirements and complex scheduling needed for national radio and television broadcasting, a few broadcasting networks of great size quickly dominated their industries. They were supplemented by local stations that, like the earlier traction and power and light companies, either had a monopoly in their area or shared it, at the most, with one or two other local enterprises.

In distribution, institutional changes were quite naturally more a response to expanding and changing markets than to new technology. The mass retailers continued to replace the wholesalers, and the retailers continued to expand by adding outlets. The fastest-growing retailers were the chain stores. Existing chains added new outlets and new chains appeared. Particularly significant was the swift growth of food chains and, especially in the years after World War II, the supermarkets. As rural population stopped growing and rural markets declined, the great mail-order houses—Montgomery Ward and Sears, Roebuck—raced between 1925 and 1929 to build national chains of retail stores located in suburbs, towns, and small cities. Urban department stores also began, although not in a concerted way until after World War II, to build new outlets in the suburbs. These changes reflected not only the rapid urbanizing of the nation but also the changes in the ways of living and consumer buying brought by the automobile.

Financial enterprises grew in much the same manner as marketing firms. Just as the building of new outlets permitted the mass retailers to make more intensive use of their central purchasing organization and reduced the unit costs of distribution still further, so banks, brokerage houses, and insurance companies added branches to increase the volume and lower the unit costs of carrying out the basic functions of their enterprises.

The most significant developments in the evolution of big business in the years after World War I were not in marketing, finance, transportation, and communication, but in the large industrial enterprises that integrated mass production with mass marketing. Here both new technology and changing markets had their effect. Both stimulated industrial corporations to increase output of their factories and set up new outlets for their existing product lines, and then to develop new products for new markets. Even before World War I, a number of integrated enterprises began to develop a "full line" of products in order to make more intensive use of their national (and often global) sales networks. Thus, harvester, plow, and tractor enterprises began to produce a wide variety of agricultural implements. Food, drug, and chemical companies developed comparable full lines. Often the managers' desire to use their marketing organization more intensively led to the building of new production and purchasing facilities. For example, after the meat-packers began to use their networks of refrigerated warehouses, cars, and ships to sell and distribute poultry, dairy, and other perishable products, they set up new plants and buying units to purchase and process these products. For the same reasons the marketing of the by-products of production—such as fertilizer and leather in the case of the meat-packers—prompted them to create new marketing units.

After 1920 a few integrated industries began to pursue an explicit strategy of growth diversification into new products for new markets. By 1920 many large integrated enterprises had built extensive research facilities in order to improve current products and processes. Managers began to see the possibility of having their laboratories develop new products, the production and distribution of which could make use of the administrative, technological, and marketing skills of management, as well as of existing facilities.

A pioneer in the new strategy was the Du Pont Company, the leading maker of explosives, which began immediately after World War I to produce a variety of products including paints, celluloid film, chemicals, artificial leather, and artificial fibers. Each new product was based on highly specialized nitrocellulose chemical technology developed to manufacture explosives. Other chemical companies followed suit, basing their diversified product lines on other chemical technologies. In the 1920's the great electrical manufacturers—General Electric and Westinghouse, makers of equipment for producing power, light, and urban transportation—moved into the manufacture of electrical appliances, X-ray equipment, alloys, and radios. A little later General Motors began to make diesel and airplane engines.

By the 1950's the concept of the product cycle had become the basis for a standard strategy of growth for the large industrial enterprises. Companies planned the exploitation of new products in such a way as to obtain a maximum rate of return on capital invested as the new product moved through the cycle from innovation to initial commercialization, to full maturity, and then to obsolescence.

To administer these diversified business enterprises, managers increasingly relied on what came to be called the "multidivisional" structure. In such an organization each autonomous division produced a single line of goods for one major market. Each division had the facilities and personnel required to obtain materials, process them, and market the finished product. Thus the divisions coordinated the flow of goods from the supplier of the raw materials through each step of production and distribution to the final consumer. The divisions were administered by a general office consisting of general executives without responsibilities for day-to-day operations, a wide-ranging advisory staff of specialists, and an equally large financial staff. The tasks of the general office were to evaluate the performance of the divisions, to set basic policies for the corporation as a whole, and to allocate resources for future growth.

The adoption of the diversification strategy and the multidivisional structure helped to institutionalize technological innovation in the American economy. The research departments of large industrial enterprises tested the commercial validity of the new products generated by the central research staff (often based on innovations made outside the firm) and by the operating divisions. The executives in the general office, freed from time-consuming day-to-day operations, determined how the company could most profitably exploit the new product. If they decided that the organization could not effectively process and distribute the product, they licensed it to other firms. If they agreed that the firm could handle the product and that the potential market for it was similar to one in which their enterprise currently sold, they assigned its production and sales to an existing division. If the market was quite different but the product made use of some existing skills and facilities, the top managers set up a new operating division. Through use of such a strategy and such a structure, the diversified industrial organization became the most dynamic form of modern American business enterprise.

The huge expansion of the economy during and after World War II stimulated the growth of all types of big businesses. None flourished more vigorously than the integrated and increasingly diversified industrial enterprise. Gross national product rose from $227.2 billion in 1940 to $309.9 billion in 1947 and to $727.1 billion in 1969. In 1947 the two hundred largest industries in the United States (many of which were not fully diversified or divisionalized) accounted for 30 percent of the value added in manufacturing and 47.2 percent of total corporate manufacturing assets. By 1963, after most of these enterprises had adopted the new strategy and the new structure, the two hundred largest were responsible for 41 percent of the value added and 56.3 percent of assets. By 1968 the latter figure had risen to 60.9 percent.

These industries played the major role in meeting the demand of the federal government for military and other products. As prime contractors during World War II, they not only expanded their output to meet wartime requirements but also supervised and coordinated the work of thousands of subcontractors. In the years of the Cold War, the government continued to require a wide variety of military weapons systems, ranging from aircraft carriers, missiles, and submarines to conventional guns and tanks. It also became a market for highly sophisticated products, such as nuclear reactors for the Atomic Energy Commission and spaceships with all their instrumentation for the National Aeronautics and Space Administration. To serve these markets the companies merely added separate divisions or groups of divisions for nuclear, space, weapons, or government business in general.

In the recent expansion of modern enterprise, foreign markets have been more significant than government purchases. The large integrated food and machinery companies that built their overseas domains before 1914 continued to maintain, and often to expand, them after World War I. During the 1920's a relatively small number of oil, chemical, rubber, and automobile companies followed the pioneering firms abroad. The depression of the 1930's slowed this overseas expansion, and World War II almost stopped it altogether. But in the 1950's and early 1960's, particularly after the formation of the European Common Market, there began a massive drive for foreign markets. Direct American investment in Europe rose from $1.7 billion in 1950 to $24.5 billion in 1970. This second "American challenge" in Europe was spearheaded by the same firms that predominated at home. Two hundred companies accounted for more than half of the direct investment made by American companies abroad. These two hundred were clustered in the capital-intensive, technologically advanced industries. They were integrated, diversified enterprises that had adopted the multidivisional form of organization.

During the 1960's a major variation of the

diversified, multidivisional enterprise appeared, in the form of the conglomerate. Both the strategy and the structure of the conglomerate differed from those of the older, multi-industry, multinational enterprises. The older type of enterprise had grown primarily by internal expansion—that is, by direct investment of plant and personnel in industries related to its original line of products. It moved into markets where the managerial, technological, and marketing skills and resources of its organization gave it a competitive advantage.

The conglomerate, by contrast, expanded entirely by the acquisition of existing enterprises, and not by direct investment in its own plant and personnel; and it often did so in totally unrelated fields. The creators of the first conglomerates embarked on strategies of unrelated acquisition when they realized that their own industries had little potential for continued growth, and when they became aware of the value of a diversified product line and a strategy based on the product cycle. The acquiring firms tended to purchase relatively small enterprises in industries that were not yet concentrated. Because many of these small enterprises had not become wholly managerial, the acquiring firms were in some cases able to provide them with new administrative and operational techniques.

The structure of the new conglomerates reflected their strategies of growth. Their general offices were small and the acquired operating units were permitted more autonomy than the divisions of the larger diversified firm. Yet the major difference in the general office of a conglomerate was not in the size of its financial or legal staff or in the number of general executives, but in the size and function of its advisory staff. The conglomerate had no staff offices for purchasing, traffic, research and development, sales, advertising, or production. The only staff not devoted to purely legal and financial matters was for corporate planning—that is, the formulation of the strategy to be used in investment decisions.

As a result, the conglomerates could concentrate more single-mindedly on making investments in new industries and new markets, and on withdrawing more easily from existing ones than could the older, larger, diversified companies. On the other hand, the conglomerates were far less effective in monitoring and evaluating their divisions and in taking action to improve divisional operating performance. They had neither the manpower nor the skills to nurse sick divisions back to health. Moreover, because conglomerates did not possess centralized research and development facilities or staff expertise concerning complex technology, they were unable to introduce new processes and products regularly and systematically into the economy. The managers of conglomerates became almost pure specialists in the long-term allocation of resources. They differed from the managers of investment banks and mutual funds in that they made direct investments for management of which they were fully responsible, rather than indirect portfolio investments that rarely carried responsibility for operating performance.

Because their functions were limited and because many were formed for speculative and tax gains, conglomerates enjoyed only a brief popularity. During the economic boom of the 1960's many appeared, but in the recession years of the early 1970's few new ones were formed and a number of the existing ones suffered serious financial difficulties. The standard form of big business enterprise in American industry remained the multidivisional enterprise with a large general office oriented to one major technology or set of markets.

THE ASCENDENCY OF THE MANAGER

By the 1960's the manager had triumphed. Although the hundreds of thousands of small firms owned by individuals and families continued to thrive, they were concentrated in the rapidly growing service sector of the economy. Their markets were small and usually local. Many small businesses were suppliers, retailers, and subcontractors for large managerial enterprises.

In the large integrated and diversified industrial enterprises and in the more centralized marketing, service, transportation, and communication enterprises, professional managers completely dominated top as well as middle management. Representatives of founding families, of large investors, or of banking and other financial intermediaries still sat on the boards of these big businesses that had come to control two-thirds of the national manufacturing assets. Yet such outside directors were almost always outnumbered by "inside directors"—that is, by representatives of the managerial hierarchy. Indeed, even the legal fiction of "outside" family or financial control was fast disappearing.

A study made by Robert J. Larner of the two hundred largest nonfinancial enterprises in 1963 revealed that in none of the firms did an individual, family, or group hold more than 80 percent of the stock. In only five of the two hundred did a family or group own as much as 50 percent of the stock. In twenty-six others a family or group had minority control by holding more than 10 percent of the stock (but less than 50 percent) or by using a holding company or other legal device. In 1963, then, 169 (84.5 percent) of the two hundred largest nonfinancial companies were management-controlled. No individual family or group had enough stock to exercise even a veto power over the management decisions. In five of these firms, families did still have influence. They did so not because of the stock they held, but because they were professional, full-time salaried executives. Because big businesses have become responsible for current economic activities and for the allocation of resources for future economic activities in the central sectors of the American economy, and because these big businesses have become manned almost wholly by professional managers, that economy may properly be termed one of managerial capitalism.

BIBLIOGRAPHY

This essay is based on Alfred D. Chandler, Jr., *The Visible Hand: The Rise of Modern Business Enterprise in the United States* (Cambridge, Mass., 1977). The section on the post–World War II multinational and conglomerate enterprises closely follows the references made to such businesses in Alfred D. Chandler, Jr., "Evolution of Enterprise: United States," in Peter Mathias, ed., *The Cambridge Economic History*, vol. 7 (Cambridge, 1976).

Big business in transportation and communication is discussed in John Brooks, *Telephone: The First Hundred Years* (New York, 1976), a history of AT&T that summarizes in a lively style the existing literature on the company's past. Alfred D. Chandler, Jr., *The Railroads, the Nation's First Big Business* (New York, 1965), is a collection of source materials with some analysis that shows how the railroads pioneered in modern finance, management, labor relations, and competition. Thomas C. Cochran, *Railroad Leaders 1845–1890: The Business Mind in Action* (Cambridge, Mass., 1953), is a brilliant study based on the letters of sixty railroad presidents that covers all aspects involved in the building and operation of the nineteenth-century American railroad network. Edward C. Kirkland, *Men, Cities and Transportation: A Study in New England History, 1820–1900* (Cambridge, Mass., 1948), is the best regional history of transportation, which of necessity focuses primarily on the building and operation of the railroad network. John F. Stover, *American Railroads* (Chicago, 1961), is the most useful text on the history of the American railroads. Robert L. Thompson, *Wiring a Continent: The History of the Telegraph Industry in the United States, 1832–1866* (Princeton, 1947), is the one scholarly history of the telegraph industry, (but only up to the creation of Western Union).

Big business in production and distribution is the subject of Harold Barger, *Distribution's Place in the American Economy* (Princeton, 1955), a statistical analysis of the changing channels and flows of the distribution of goods through the economy. Alfred D. Chandler, Jr., and Stephen Salsbury, *Pierre S. du Pont and the Making of the Modern Corporation* (New York, 1971), reviews the achievements of Pierre du Pont in creating two of the most successful integrated mass producers—the Du Pont Company and General Motors Corporation. Alfred S. Eichner, *The Emergence of Oligopoly: Sugar Refining as a Case Study* (Baltimore, 1969), is a first-rate study of the changing market structure and the nature of the business enterprises in a mass-producing, mass-marketing industry. Boris Emmet and John E. Jeuck, *Catalogs and Counters: A History of Sears, Roebuck & Company* (Chicago, 1950), is a fine history, full of detail, of the world's largest mail-order house. Edward C. Kirkland, *Industry Comes of Age: Business, Labor, and Public Policy, 1860–1897* (New York, 1961), provides the most useful detailed background for the rise of big business. Ralph L. Nelson, *Merger Movements in American Industry, 1895–1956* (Princeton, 1959), a statistical work that focuses on the turn-of-the-century merger movement so central to the rise of big business. Glenn Porter and Harold C. Livesay, *Merchants and Manufacturers: Studies in the Changing Structure of Nineteenth Century Marketing* (Baltimore, 1971), is a pioneering study of the changing American marketing and distribution systems that concentrates on the replacement of the traditional merchant by mass-marketing and mass-producing enterprises. Glenn Porter, *The Rise of Big Business, 1860–1910* (New York, 1973), is the best introduction to the topic. Hans B. Thorelli, *The Federal Antitrust Policy* (Baltimore, 1955), a massive study that details the early political and judicial response to the rise of big business, and outlines the resulting legislation. Harold F. Williamson and Arnold R. Daum, *The American Petroleum Industry: The Age of Illumination, 1859–1899* (Evanston, Ill., 1959), describes and analyzes the rise of one of the best-known big businesses—the Standard Oil Company—as it tells the history of all aspects of the oil industry. Harold F. Williamson et al., *The American Petroleum Industry: The Age of Energy, 1899–1959* (Evanston, Ill., 1953), presents the history of both Standard Oil and its many giant competitors up to 1959. Mira Wilkins, *The Emergence of Multinational Enterprise: American Business Abroad from the Colonial Era to 1914* (Cambridge, Mass., 1970), is the standard study of the rise of the American multinational corporation.

On the evolution of big business since World War I, see Robert T. Averitt, *The Dual Economy: The Dynamics of American Industry Structure* (New York, 1968), a study of the interrelationship of the big businesses at the center of the economy and the smaller ones on the periphery. Alfred D. Chandler,

RISE AND EVOLUTION OF BIG BUSINESS

Jr., *Strategy and Structure: Chapters in the History of the Industrial Enterprise* (Cambridge, Mass., 1962), is a study that analyzes the beginnings and spread of the diversified and divisionalized industrial enterprise. John Kenneth Galbraith, *The New Industrial State* (Boston, 1969), an imaginative analysis of the role of the large corporation in the American economy. Michael Gort, *Diversification and Integration in American Industry* (Princeton, 1959), a detailed study of the post-World War II pattern of large-firm diversification and integration. Mira Wilkins, *The Maturing of Multinational Enterprise: American Business Abroad from 1914–1970* (Cambridge, Mass., 1974), is a massive and definitive study.

[*See also* ANTITRUST; COMMUNICATIONS; COMPETITION; ECONOMY FROM 1815 TO 1865; ECONOMY FROM RECONSTRUCTION TO 1914; ECONOMY SINCE 1914; EXCHANGES; LABOR ORGANIZATIONS; MANAGEMENT; MANUFACTURING; MARKETING; MERGERS; MULTINATIONAL ENTERPRISE; *and* TRANSPORTATION.]

MERGERS

Leslie Hannah

MERGERS in business are as old as private enterprise, with inheritance or marriage being the merger "broker" in the early stages of American industrial growth, as in traditional landholding societies. Since the 1880's, the systematic merger of businesses—whether by transfer of assets or exchange of stock, and whether by agreed consolidation or aggressive acquisition—has become an important characteristic of the economy and a crucial factor in the rise of corporate capitalism. The decision to merge is a decision to create one business enterprise where formerly there were two, the relationships of which were coordinated by the market mechanism rather than, as after merger, by administrative fiat. Mergers are therefore an important part of the process through which the coordination of economic activity by the "invisible hand" of competitive forces has been partly replaced by the "visible hand" of management in a more concentrated industrial structure. The historical development of mergers is thus as complex and many-sided as the path of development of the modern business enterprise. This article focuses primarily on mergers in the domestic mining and manufacturing sectors, although mergers have also played an important role in the consolidation of other areas of the economy, and acquisitions abroad have contributed to the spread of corporate power overseas.

THE RECORD OF MERGER ACTIVITY

Fortunately, the early establishment of antitrust law—and the interest that it has generated among professional economists since the 1890's—has left a historical record of merger activity in the American economy that is unparalleled in other Western countries. The statistical record since 1895 is displayed graphically in figure 1, which shows firm disappearances by merger in net terms. (This method standardizes the treatment of consolidations and acquisitions: if one firm acquires another, one firm is said to "disappear"; and if two firms merge to form a third, new corporation, again one firm "disappears.") The statistics for different periods are, unfortunately, not compiled on a consistent basis, as the break in the overlapping years 1919 through 1930 indicates. Moreover, even for series ostensibly compiled by the same method, the quality of reporting of mergers has probably improved over time, so that comparisons between widely separated years are invalid. These statistics should therefore be seen as a general guide to fluctuations of merger activity and not as a precise indicator of the relative intensity of merger waves at widely separated dates.

The major series for 1895–1930 was compiled by R. L. Nelson and C. Eis from the mergers reported in the investment pages of the weekly *Commercial and Financial Chronicle,* and a cutoff point, varying broadly according to the general price level, was employed to exclude the smaller mergers. The cutoff points are not identical for the Nelson (1895–1920) and Eis (1919–1930) series; but as the data for the two overlapping years suggest, the differences are small and the two series may, for present purposes, be assumed to be approximately continuous. From 1919 on, an independent series, compiled initially by W. L. Thorp and continued by the Federal Trade Commission (FTC), is also available. This series employs no cutoff point and thus includes many small mergers; hence no attempt has been made to splice it with the earlier series. While the general level of the Thorp-FTC series is always

MERGERS

FIGURE 1 Firm Disappearances by Merger in American Manufacturing and Mining, 1895–1973

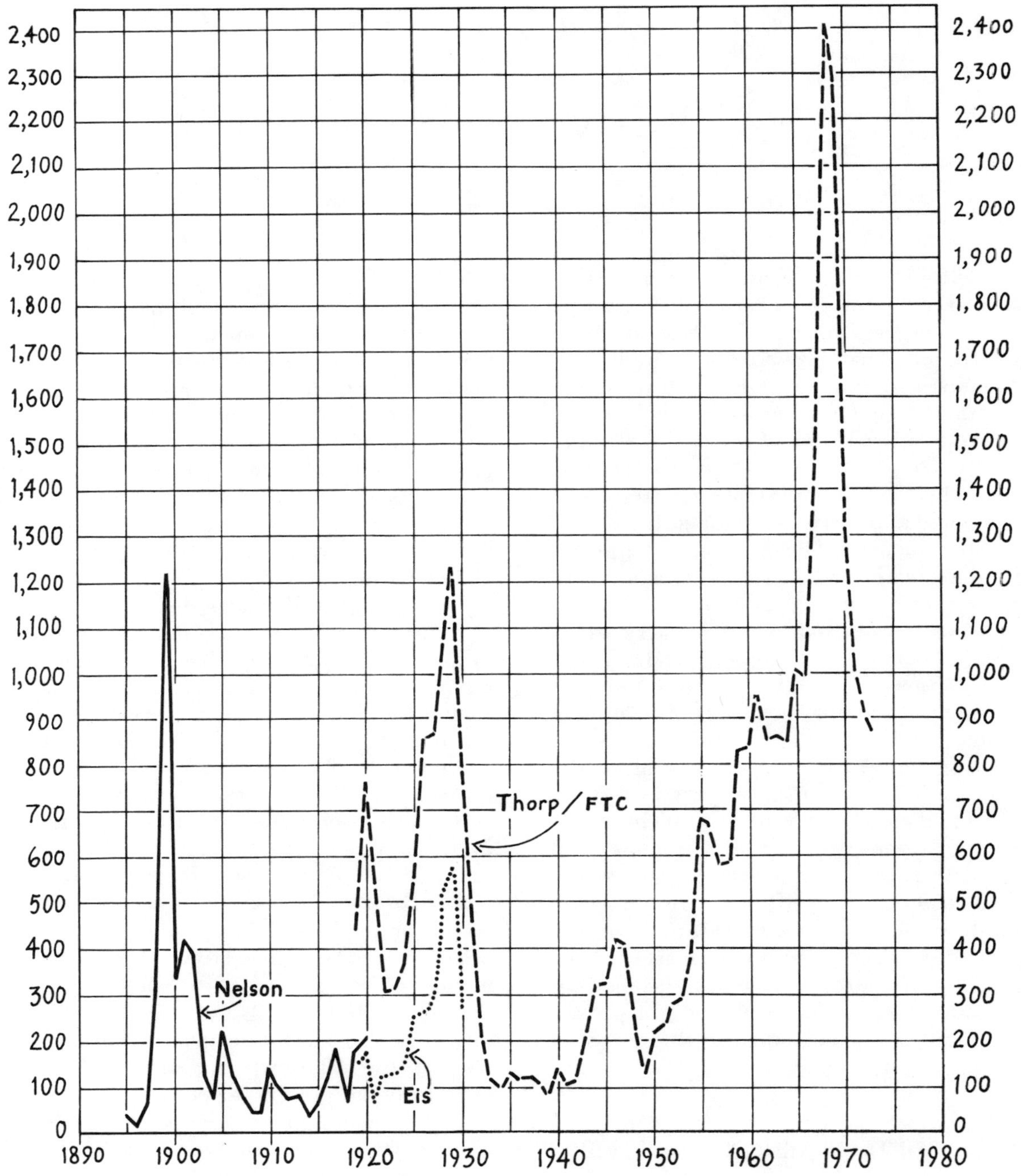

Sources: R. L. Nelson, *Merger Movements in American Industry;* C. Eis, "The 1919–1930 Merger Movement. . ."; W. L. Thorp and W. F. Crowder, *The Structure of Industry;* Federal Trade Commission, *Statistical Report on Mergers and Acquisitions.*

higher, movements in it are closely correlated with those in the Nelson-Eis series. The alternative merger series, based on the values of acquisitions and consolidations, shows greater irregularity than the "firm disappearance" series; but the broad trends in merger activity are very much the same, however they are measured.

The pattern that emerges from figure 1 is one of substantial variation over time, with three periods of intense activity standing out: the turn-of-the-century merger movement, a further wave in the later 1920's, and the postwar wave that reached its height in the 1960's. The designation of the 1960's as a period of intense activity is not implausible to contemporary observers; and that the turn of the century and the 1920's were also crucial periods of such activity is confirmed by a study of the major mergers of sixty-three of the largest manufacturing and mining corporations of 1956. More than half of them experienced their major merger in these two decades: the turn-of-the-century period (1895–1904) accounted for twenty, and the 1920's for a further fifteen. Closer examination of these three periods reveals that the merger movement is far from being a homogeneous historical phenomenon.

THE TURN-OF-THE-CENTURY MERGER MOVEMENT

In the nineteenth century there were many manufacturing industries in which the average size of the firm was large and/or the market structure was oligopolistic, but before 1890 the typical form of management was that of the owner-entrepreneur, the partnership, or the family group. In these circumstances merger occurred only rarely. Such firms did try to control competition through agreements to coordinate output and pricing policies; but such collusion, depending on understandings among many partners, was inherently unstable. From the early 1880's the "trust" form of organization, pioneered by Standard Oil, provided a more stable form of coordination in which corporations placed their securities in the hands of trustees who had powers to coordinate policies in the general interest of the trust partners. This practice enabled firms to circumvent state laws prohibiting holding companies and was adopted in a range of industries, including petroleum, biscuits, explosives, whiskey, leather, salt, and sugar. With the liberalization of the common-law prohibition of holding companies (beginning with the New Jersey incorporation law of 1889), a new form of combination became feasible and most trusts converted to the holding company form. Among those profiting from these new laws was James Buchanan Duke's American Tobacco Company, an 1890 consolidation of five firms. Empire builders such as Duke did not always stop at the legal innovation but also pioneered new administrative methods: within a short time he had developed the integrated, centralized, functionally departmentalized strategy and structure that was to become typical of American corporate capitalism. Additional acquisitions of tobacco companies soon followed this corporation's early success.

Over a wide range of industries, the search for monopoly powers, and for economies of scale and integration, provided the profit incentive for merger. There was a minor merger boomlet in 1888–1893, including the formation in 1892 of General Electric by the consolidation of Thomson-Houston and Edison General Electric (themselves the beneficiaries of earlier mergers). This created (with Westinghouse) the duopoly in many branches of electrical equipment manufacture that still exists. From 1896 the even larger turn-of-the-century merger wave gathered force. In the next ten years there was an unprecedented and permanent change in the structure of American industry, with the one hundred largest corporations increasing their size by a factor of four and gaining control of 40 percent of the national industrial capital. Most of this change was a result of the intense merger activity of 1898–1902, during which 2,653 firms disappeared in mergers. In these years merger capitalizations totaled in excess of $6.3 billion, more than in all the other years recorded before 1914 taken together. Among the market leaders growing by merger were Allis-Chalmers, Anaconda Copper, Corn Products, Du Pont, American Tobacco, U.S. Steel, and American Smelting and Refining. Merger activity occurred in almost every industry and was particularly intense in primary metals, food products, petroleum, chemicals, transportation equipment, fabricated metal products, and bituminous coal; many of these were the industries in which large-scale firms were to retain a competitive advantage for many decades.

The sudden development and widespread influence of this first merger movement has proved to be one of the more difficult problems for its historians to explain. Between 1895 and 1904, 75 percent of firms disappearing were involved in mergers of five or more firms; and it is clear from this dominance of multifirm consolidations, and from their avowed aim of achieving high market shares, that a desire for monopoly control of markets was a major explanation. The American Can merger of 1901, for example, involved 120 firms and claimed a 90 percent market share. And of the ninety-two large mergers studied by J. Moody, he estimated that seventy-eight controlled 50 percent or more of the market; fifty-seven, 60 percent or more; and twenty-six, 80 percent or more. The great majority of mergers were horizontal—that is, between competing firms—and even allowing for some exaggeration in the prospectuses on which many of these estimates were based, it is clear that many resulting firms obtained a significant degree of market control.

Paradoxically, antitrust law developments increased the incentive to monopolize by merger. The Sherman Act (1890) had made cartel agreements and trusts illegal methods of controlling competition, and the *Addyston Pipe* case of 1899 reinforced the legal position by clearly outlawing cartel-type agreements, thus making participation in them a more risky enterprise. At the same time, competitive price-cutting had been intensified in the mid-1890's in many industries facing heavy fixed costs and highly cyclical demand. More generally, the growth of the railroad network—with a mileage increase of 268 percent between 1870 and 1900 and freight rate reductions averaging 60 percent—had increased market sizes and intensified interregional competition. It has been calculated by J. W. Markham that the average manufacturing plant in 1900 served an area more than three times as large as that of a typical plant of 1882. The desirability of reducing domestic competition (and the possibility of achieving high levels of monopoly profits) was significantly enhanced by the reduction in foreign competition implicit in the successive tariff increases imposed between 1883 and 1897. The protection against import competition thus afforded to newly organized monopolies explains in part why the American merger wave was significantly larger than the contemporaneous movement in free-trade Great Britain.

While the desire of businessmen to neutralize competitive forces is an intelligible one, it can hardly provide a convincing explanation of the timing and unprecedented intensity of merger activity in the peak years 1898–1902 and the spread of the merger movement to industries that were not notably affected by increased competitive forces or tariff protection. An important element is the contagious nature of imperfectly competitive market structures: the establishment of monopoly power in one sector can breed monopoly in related areas. The steel industry provides the most striking example of the rapid spread of the merger contagion. In the 1890's a number of dominant steel-producing groups were formed by merger, many of them fully integrated backward into raw material production, and steel users naturally feared that such market power could be used to raise prices. Accordingly, they formed consolidations—including American Tin Plate, American Steel and Wire, National Tube, American Can, and International Harvester—to enhance their bargaining power with the steel producers; and in some cases they began to integrate backward by constructing their own blast furnaces and rolling mills. In retaliation Andrew Carnegie planned to integrate forward and produce finished products in competition with the steel users. The upshot was the billion-dollar merger of 1901, U.S. Steel, bringing together the major fabricating companies and three leading steel companies—Carnegie, Federal, and National—with control of 65 percent of American iron and steel output. Organized by J. P. Morgan and Company, the investment banking firm that had previously coordinated the railway companies by merger, the new firm successfully forestalled the threatened war of competitive integration.

Another important element in the "bunching" of merger activity in the years around the turn of the century was the development of a market in industrial stocks, and particularly the rise to prominence of industrial issues on the New York Stock Exchange. The development of underwriting techniques after 1897 reduced the risks of new issues, and the merger movement and the industrial stock market thereafter developed symbiotically: merger issues deepened the market for industrial stocks, and the success of the stock market contributed to a demand from speculative investors for merger issues. The stocks of some 60 percent of the consolidations of these years were actively traded on the New York Stock Exchange, and a new profession, that of merger promoter, arose to satisfy this demand. It proved to be a lucrative calling, for public flotations created a means of capitalizing the future benefits of a merger—whether from economies of scale or from monopoly power—so that some of it could be appropriated by the promoters. Active promoters could also provide a useful service to owner-managers, as in the case of Charles R. Flint's successful consummation of the U.S. Rubber merger after many months of fruitless effort by industry leaders to come to an agreement. Flint and three other leading promoters were responsible for one-third of the large mergers of these years; a further quarter were arranged by investment bankers (J. P. Morgan and Company taking a leading role), and the remainder by smaller promoters and by industrialists themselves.

The extensive merger activity generated at the turn of the century had an important influence on the development of capitalist enterprise in America, not only quantitatively but also qualitatively. As enterprises grew in size and their stocks were issued to the investing public, the divorce of ownership and control and the creation of a managerial class became a more real possibility and, in some cases, a requirement. Many of the consolidations were professionally rather than entrepreneurially managed, and the social basis of the corporation was thereby gradually but permanently transformed: the personal wealth and credit of an owner-entrepreneur no longer placed an upper limit on the scale of an enterprise.

Yet this transition to new managerial structures was not easily accomplished, and the enlarged corporations did not enjoy uniform success. S. Livermore, for example, estimates that only half of the 328 mergers of 1888–1905 that he examined could be classified as successful. Fifty-three failed shortly after they were formed, and others consistently earned less than the levels of profits originally expected (on the basis of which they had been overcapitalized with watered stock). Decreased market shares for merged companies were widespread in the steel, sugar-refining, agricultural implements, leather, rubber, distilling, and car industries. (G. J. Stigler has shown that this does not necessarily imply failure to maximize stockholder returns; the temporary exploitation of a monopoly, gradually yielding market share to new competitors, may be a profit-maximizing strategy.) Others, including United Shoe Machinery and Eastman Kodak, managed to maintain their market share by enforcing patent protection; still others coerced buyers or suppliers.

The major successes of the merger movement were those that developed a sound strategy—Du Pont, National Cash Register, International Harvester, and Aluminum Company of America—and appropriate managerial structures to run the enlarged enterprise. The clear failures—National Starch, American Bicycle, and U.S. Shipbuilding, among others—were more commonly put together by speculative promoters who lacked any longer-run entrepreneurial rationale for their creations and took no part in postmerger integration and management.

If the turn-of-the-century merger wave had arisen suddenly and proceeded with breakneck speed, it came to an end no less quickly in 1902, and such activity remained at a relatively low level for more than two decades (see figure 1). This was partly due to the exhaustion of merger promotion possibilities after the boom period and partly to the growing investor distrust of the watered stock that had been peddled by some promoters. This became all too evident when earnings failed to match expectations and stock prices collapsed in the "rich man's panic" of 1903. The administration of Theodore Roosevelt attempted to undo some of the more highly concentrated situations created in the early merger wave. The signal was given by the *Northern Securities Company* case of 1904, which dissolved some of J. P. Morgan's railroad consolidations; subsequently Standard Oil was split into thirty-four parts and American Tobacco into sixteen; and International Harvester, Corn Products, and Du Pont were forced to divest themselves of some of their operations. Other firms—including Aluminum Company of America, General Electric, U.S. Steel, and American Sugar Refining—were also under threat, but legal procedures were sufficiently slow to restrict the direct effects of antitrust action to a few corporations, even after the passage of the Clayton Act in 1914.

By 1920, when a pronouncement was finally made in the *U.S. Steel* case, it became clear that the breaking up of mergers would not be enforced by a government that was now willing to recognize the possibility of a "good trust." Yet, despite the unfavorable financial and legal environment in this period, some important mergers were consummated: General Motors, for example, was a merger of Buick, Oldsmobile, and Cadillac (1908) that subsequently acquired seven other automobile producers (including Chevrolet), three truck companies, and eleven parts and accessory companies, just failing in 1908–1909 to acquire Ford as well.

THE 1920'S MERGER MOVEMENT

During World War I and the 1920's the more relaxed public policy toward mergers combined with changes in the market and rising stock prices to produce another large merger wave. After an initial peak in 1920, and a setback in 1921–1922, merger activity continued to rise, reaching a further peak in 1929. Corporate expenditures on mergers ran for most of this period at about one-third of expenditures on new plant and equipment, but at the peak of 1928–1929 the ratio rose to more than two-thirds. Promoters, and particularly investment bankers, again played a major role.

> During 1928 and 1929 some investment houses employed men on commission who did nothing but search for potential mergers. One businessman told me that he regarded it as a loss of standing if he was not approached at least once a week with a merger proposition. A group of businessmen and financiers in discussing this matter in the summer of 1928 agreed that nine out of ten mergers had the investment banker at the core [Thorp 1931, p. 86].

Between 1925 and 1929 the share of the largest one hundred corporations in total manufacturing assets rose by 3.5 percentage points, all except 0.3 point being due to merger. Yet this second great merger movement was less intense than the earlier wave: after allowing for price changes, net values of firm disappearances by merger values in 1926–1930 amounted to only about 60 percent of the level attained at the peak of 1898–1902. (Outside the mining and manufacturing sector there was a contemporaneous merger wave of an unprecedented intensity, for instance, in banking and public utilities.)

The union of many firms into a consolidation with a very high market share, which had been the hallmark of the first merger movement, was relatively rare in the 1920's; this scarcity has led some economists, such as G. J. Stigler, to suggest that the somewhat lackadaisical enforcement of antitrust law could successfully discourage market leaders from merger for monopoly, although mergers among lower-ranking firms continued, thus tending to create an oligopolistic industry structure. Corporations such as U.S. Steel, American Can, and International Harvester, which had been threatened with dissolution by the antitrust authorities, were anxious to erase suspicions of their being "bad trusts" and eschewed acquisitive activity; it is more difficult to accept that there was a significant spin-off deterrent effect on other corporations. For most industrialists, managerial considerations were as important as antitrust laws in discouraging multifirm consolidations: memories of the earlier failures were still clear in the minds of entrepreneurs and stockholders alike. Dominant firms in many industries continued to spend heavily on acquisitions with little regard for the Clayton Act; for the "assets loophole," by which assets could be acquired even though stock could not, provided a ready means of evading the rigors of the law. (In fact, only twenty-nine merger cases were tried under section 7 of the Clayton Act before 1950.)

The view that mergers were beneficial to the economy was commonly held. William J. Donovan, the assistant attorney general in charge of antitrust policy, for example, expressed the view "that consolidations may in some degree correct the evils of destructive competition and that it [the merger movement] represents an effort to adjust the relations between production and consumption, supply and demand" (quoted in Eis 1969, p. 289). Mergers could therefore proceed relatively unmolested. The pattern of gradual, sequential acquisition, which was increasingly favored by businessmen, entailed fewer postmerger strains than the instantaneous creation of a multifirm monopoly by merger, and could be no less successful in building up a large market share. Anaconda and Kennecott, for example, increased their dominance of the copper industry by a series of horizontal and vertical mergers: between 1921 and 1930 the Anaconda market share rose from 9 percent to 20 percent, and the Kennecott share from 2 percent to 27 percent, both of them mainly by acquisition.

Five industries—primary metals, petroleum, food, chemicals, and transportation equipment—that had also been prominent in the earlier merger wave remained the leading merger industries in this second wave, although different firms often were involved. U.S. Steel, for example, experienced a continually declining market share, but, still under the antitrust cloud, it did not attempt to reverse this by acquisitions. Nonetheless, the market shares of its major rivals, Republic, Bethlehem, and Jones and Laughlin, rose as a result of their acquisitions. Even where the antitrust threat was not a major one, oligopoly sometimes resulted: in the cement industry, for example, the market leader, Lehigh, rarely acquired competitors; but several of its lower-ranking rivals came to equal it in size through acquisitions and consolidations. The chemical industry had led the second merger movement: Du Pont diversified within the organic area of the industry so that it became less dependent on its explosives monopoly; Union Carbide consolidated in 1917 (the largest merger since 1901); and in 1920 Allied Chemical and Dye was formed through a consolidation of complementary chemical companies.

The gradual pattern of piecemeal acquisition could be no less powerful than the earlier multifirm consolidations in building up substantial market positions. In the decade after 1924, for example, National Dairy acquired some 340 firms, including 150 direct competitors in ice cream manufacture, 119 competitors in liquid milk, and, in 1929, Kraft-Phoenix cheese, a 1928 merger of the two largest cheese producers with 40 percent of domestic sales. Borden, another dominant food conglomerate, was also a leading acquirer in this period. Other important mergers in the second wave were General Mills, National Steel, United Aircraft, Owens-Illinois, Caterpillar Tractor, and Standard Brands. A significant motive was the desire to exploit a national market through mass advertising and distribution, following the substantial innovations of the radio (with an audience of 40 million by 1928) and of truck transport (3.5 million vehicles registered by 1930).

The combination of a more leisurely, piecemeal pattern of acquisition and longer-run improvements in managerial technique led to a greater incidence of success in the second merger movement than in the first: the number of consolidations collapsing soon after formation were few, and the leading corporations of this period were surer of retaining that status in succeeding decades than their predecessors had been. But the pace of merger activity itself was not so steady: with the stock market crash of 1929–1930, merger activity declined, remaining below the level of the 1920's for two decades. The merger boomlet of the 1940's had little effect on overall industrial concentration, which probably declined between 1930 and 1948. Low levels of merger activity and declining industrial concentration were found in other industrial economies during this period and may have been the result of general slump conditions in the world economy, as depression reduced the size of markets and limited the scope for the division of labor and further economies of scale. Many of the mergers of these years were between small companies and were more a civilized way of transferring management control than a concerted bid for large market shares. J. K. Butters, J. Lintner, and W. L. Cary found that one-tenth by number and one-quarter by value of the mergers of the 1940's were motivated by tax considerations, as owner-entrepreneurs found that with higher wartime tax levels, it was profitable to convert income into capital gains (taxed at a lower rate) by selling out.

THE POSTWAR MERGER WAVE

Throughout the 1950's and 1960's merger activity rose to new peaks, with only a few temporary setbacks to the rising trend. The modern merger boom differed from earlier waves not only in being sustained for a longer period, but also in that merger promoters and investment bankers were less in evidence: managers were now the main instigators of merger activity. In many corporations the executives in charge of acquisitions were among the busiest: acquisition expenditure rose from 5 percent of new corporate investment in the early 1950's to more than 50 percent by the peak of 1968. In that year the two hundred largest corporations alone acquired 1.6 percent of total national manufacturing assets. Between 1947 and 1968 sixteen of the nineteen percentage points of increase in the share of these corporations in total manufacturing assets were attributable to their acquisitions. A sustained period of prosperity and a rising stock market contributed to this extended activity, and although there was a reaction as stock prices fell in the 1970's (see figure 1), it remained to be seen whether this downturn was a temporary setback or the beginning of another long period of low merger activity.

While the merger activity of these years was intense, it is unlikely that the modern merger movement has had as serious an effect on competition as the previous waves, for only a small (and decreasing) proportion of the mergers were horizontal. The 1950 Celler-Kefauver Act, an antimerger amendment to section 7 of the Clayton Act (which plugged the "assets loophole"), was secured after the publication by the FTC of an exaggerated and alarmist report on the impact of the merger boomlet of the 1940's: "Either this country is going down the road to collectivism, or it must stand and fight for competition.... Crucial in that fight must be some effective means of preventing giant corporations from steadily increasing their power at the expense of small business" (Federal Trade Commission 1948, p. 69). Paradoxically, these alarmist comments could more appropriately have been directed at the decades following the Celler-Kefauver amendment rather than those preceding it, but after the amendment both the Department of Justice and the FTC stepped up their activity. By 1965 a total of 173 antimerger complaints had been initiated (a rate fourteen times higher than in previous decades), and more than 80 percent were successful. In 1958, for example, the courts ruled against the horizontal acquisition of Youngstown Steel (market share 4 percent) by Bethlehem Steel (market share 15 percent); and in 1962, in the *Brown Shoe* case, the Supreme Court ruled against a predominantly vertical merger on the ground of its anticompetitive effects. More recently the Department of Justice has published guidelines on the types of mergers that it would challenge; in industries in which the four largest firms had a market share of 75 percent or more, for example, it would challenge an acquiring firm with 10 percent of the market acquiring one with 2 percent or more.

Although large firms continued to make extensive acquisitions, an important change in the pattern of merger activity can be seen in table 1. Conglomerate mergers—in which the partners are neither horizontally related as competitors nor vertically related as suppliers or customers—clearly became the dominant form of merger in the modern wave. Allocation of mergers to particular categories is always somewhat arbitrary—many mergers have horizontal as well as vertical or conglomerate elements—but the broad trends revealed in the table can hardly be the result of capricious classification. In the turn-of-the-century merger wave, horizontal mergers were clearly dominant; by the 1920's, as the table shows, they still accounted for perhaps two-thirds; but by the 1960's they made up only one-eighth of merger activity. This change was certainly in part the result of the antimerger laws, for it is noteworthy that in Europe (where antimerger legislation is weak or nonexistent) overall concentration rose more rapidly than in the

TABLE 1
Decline of the Horizontal Merger, 1926–1964 (percent)

Merger Type	1926–1930	1940–1947	1948–1953	1954–1959	1960–1964
Vertical	4.8	17.0	10.3	13.7	17.0
Horizontal	64.3	} 62.0	31.0	24.8	12.0
Market extension	11.7		6.9	6.4	6.9
Conglomerate, other	19.3	21.0	51.8	55.1	64.1

Source: C. Eis, "The 1919–1930 Merger Movement in American Industry," p. 294.
Note: Column does not equal 100 percent because of rounding errors.

United States during the postwar period, and large horizontal mergers between market leaders remained common.

Yet the trend toward a higher proportion of conglomerate mergers evident in table 1 has been a gradual one, not a sudden change after 1950; this suggests that broader underlying factors have been partly responsible for this change in corporate merger policy. This view is confirmed by comparison with Europe, and particularly the United Kingdom, where there has also been a distinct postwar trend to conglomerate bigness, despite the absence of a strong antimerger law on the Celler-Kefauver model. This seems to be linked with the general development of the science of management and the nature of the modern "visible hand" of the corporation. In the early stages of the corporate economy, management skills were industry- or product-specific, but as functionally specialized techniques have developed and top management—particularly financial management—has become increasingly professionalized, skills have become more easily transferable. Yet a core of specific technical or marketing expertise still indicated the general direction of investment in most cases. In an earlier merger wave Du Pont had diversified by developing its expertise in those areas of the chemical industry in which it already had a comparative advantage, and most modern diversifiers have adopted a similar strategy. White Consolidated Industries, for example, a sewing machine manufacturer facing stagnant markets in the 1950's, acquired other industrial machinery and consumer appliance firms to which it could readily apply its technical management skills; and in 1966, American Brands (formerly American Tobacco), facing the threat of health-hazard publicity in the cigarette market, diversified into packaged food and alcoholic beverages, where its existing core of marketing expertise could be utilized. American Brands and many other firms have exploited their comparative advantage by expanding through acquisitions abroad, where they find relative freedom from antitrust constraints.

At the same time that management skills have become mobile between industries, the divorce of ownership and control has increased managerial incentives to diversify; for while stockholders can spread their risks by holding a diversified portfolio, managers can do so only if their firms expand their line of products. The conglomerate merger is less easy to understand in terms of the usual justifications of economies of scale or the search for monopoly power, but becomes more intelligible in the light of this quest for enhanced managerial security. Recent research has confirmed that managers seek the security of size, rather than enhanced profitability, in growth by merger. Of course the search for profits was not entirely absent from this merger movement and, as with earlier merger booms, a speculative element helped to stimulate activity. Exaggerated expectations resulted in high stock price-earnings ratios for some of the leading "go-go" conglomerates, which made it very cheap for them to offer their own paper securities in payment for acquisitions. As soon as it became obvious that their management skills were not equal to the task of increasing earnings per share on their whole capital as rapidly as their price-earnings ratio suggested, the inevitable collapse came. As a consequence, pure conglomerates like Ling-Temco-Vought saw their stock prices severely depressed and were thus compelled to restrict their acquisition activity.

Such cases captured the public mind and raised doubts about the wisdom of conglomerate diversification, but the widespread diversification of most large corporations remained a permanent legacy of postwar corporate development. Some 80 percent of the largest manufacturing corporations had a significantly diversified product range by 1970, and they have maintained their diversification strategy despite the demise of the "go-go" conglomerates.

THE MOTIVES AND TIMING OF MERGERS

Antitrust lore and economic theory agree in allocating a central place in the motivation of merger to the desire to monopolize. That a monopolistic firm can enhance its profits by restricting output and raising prices is evident, and the extensive market coverages achieved by the turn-of-the-century multifirm consolidations are consistent with the aim of monopolization: the desire to eliminate "free riders" by including as many firms as possible is an intelligible one. In later waves, monopoly was less favored, but the possibility of raising prices through oligopolistic collusion—whether tacit or overt—still provided a powerful incentive to reduce the number of firms through merger. The trend away from horizontal mergers is, moreover, not so conclusive in showing the decline of this motive as it might at first sight appear. Vertical integration with suppliers of raw materials or distributors may confer substantial market control, and a merger that outwardly appears to be conglomerate may nonetheless forestall potential new entry by one partner into the other's market. This possibility has been significantly enhanced by the increasing feasibility of transferring management skills from one industry to another by internally diversifying growth (as is shown, for example, by the new entrants to the copier market that have challenged the Xerox monopoly). Yet, while the market-power motive clearly explains many of the mergers in all three merger waves, it cannot explain their timing, for the motive is presumably always there. What is not clear is why it is manifested in some periods but not in others.

Another major economic motivation for merger, the search for economies of scale, provides a plausible explanation of the explosive growth of merger activity since the end of the nineteenth century. The development of machine technology, of methods of mass production and mass marketing, and of science-based industries was a gradual process, but there seems to be general agreement that it has been particularly rapid in the twentieth century. Again, this gradual evolution can hardly explain the bunching of merger activity in the three movements and its quiescence in the intervening decades. Moreover, it should be noted that many of the new technologies did not require a merger for their realization: Henry Ford was perfectly able to introduce mass production without merger, by building modern plants, gaining access to new economies of scale, and offering consumers better products at lower prices. Indeed, the merging of many small plants cannot by itself create economies of plant size, though of course not all economies of scale are restricted to the level of the plant; from the 1920's especially, economies in marketing and finance have been an important motive behind merger activity. In markets where there were imperfections of competition—and the growth of advertising and of concentration increased the number of such markets—mergers could be prerequisites for investment in plants of optimal scale. The merger of demands was, as it were, necessary where price reductions alone would have been insufficient to win the necessary markets. Economies of scale in research and development have also increased in importance, especially in industries such as chemicals and electrical machinery. Whether merger was either a necessary or a sufficient condition for the achievement of such scale economies is a moot point, but for some corporations merger certainly accelerated their achievement.

If these were the important underlying causes making for larger-scale enterprise and merger activity, the precise timing of merger would seem to have more to do with stock market cycles. The casual impression from our chronological survey is that mergers were closely and positively correlated with stock prices, and this has been confirmed by more precise analysis. Indeed, mergers are more closely related to stock prices than to other variables such as industrial production. In the first wave, for example, mergers subsided as stock prices declined in 1901–1902, although the industrial production index continued to rise. The existence of a causal relationship between stock prices and mergers remains an enigma. Perhaps stock prices and merger activity are expressions of entrepreneurial ebullience, and periods of intense merger activity are merely reflections of the underlying state of business confidence. Most attempts to attach more specific meaning to the correlation have proved inconclusive. It does not seem to be the case that assets are acquired through merger when other profitable investment outlets, such as investment in plant or new equipment, are exhausted. The hypothesis that when share prices are high, the variance of expectations is also high, thus creating opportunities for profitable arbitrage, has so far not been subjected to satisfactory empirical testing.

It seems likely that a difference between the expectations of owner-entrepreneurs and shareholders helped merger activity in times of high share prices. Owner-entrepreneurs usually had more soundly based and more stable expectations about the prospects of their own firms than did investors in the fledgling markets for industrial common stocks. It is thus significant that promoters were most successful in persuading businessmen to sell their businesses to a consolidation (and stockholders were more willing to buy the resulting securities) at times of rising stock prices. More recently, exaggerated price-earnings ratio differentials between acquiring and acquired firms—which may be related to general stock market conditions—have played a similar, though less dominant, role.

WELFARE IMPLICATIONS

If the precise motives for mergers are difficult to pinpoint, the welfare effects are no less so and may of course be very different from those intended. There is a continuing dichotomy between the assumptions behind antitrust policy that mergers create monopolies, restrict output, and raise prices, and the repeated claims of business leaders that they are beneficial to the public. In 1899, when Charles R. Flint, organizer of the U.S. Rubber Company merger, was asked to describe "the benefits of consolidated management," he replied:

> The answer is only difficult because the list is so long. The following are the principal ones: raw material, bought in large quantities, is secured at a lower price; the specialization of manufacture on a large scale, in separate plants, permits the fullest use of specialized machinery and processes, thus decreasing costs; the standard of quality is raised and fixed; the number of styles reduced, and the best standards are adopted; those plants which are best equipped and most advantageously situated are run continuously in preference to those less favored; in case of local strikes or fires, the work goes on elsewhere, thus preventing serious social loss; there is no multiplication of the means of distribution—a better force of salesmen takes the place of a larger number; the same is true of branch stores; terms and conditions of sales become more uniform, and credits through comparisons are more safely granted; the aggregate of stocks carried is greatly reduced, thus saving interest, insurance, storage and shop-wear; greater skill in management accrues to the benefit of the whole, instead of the part; and large advantages are realized from comparative accounting and comparative administration. . . . The grand result is a much lower market price. . . . [quoted in Chandler 1962, pp. 33–34].

Of course, "lower market prices" were not what merger promoters like Flint promised stockholders and managers, and such claims must be examined critically. Many of the benefits cited could in principle be achieved without merger, and others do not necessarily correspond to a social advantage. The greater buying power of a large firm, for example, may enable it to reduce its input costs; but this will not necessarily result in resource savings for the economy as a whole, merely transferring income from raw material producers to manufacturers. It may also confer on the large firm an undesirable and unfair advantage over competitors. Nonetheless, the careful investigations of the strategy and structure of major merged enterprises by A. D. Chandler and A. S. Eichner have shown that longer-run benefits from improved techniques—improvements that were facilitated by the merger movement—were in the long run forthcoming.

Such studies, like business history in general, focus on the successes, while the failures receive less attention. In an examination of mergers this is a severe handicap, for one of the best-attested results of research on mergers over the years is that a high proportion of them fail to reach their objectives. This research has cast serious doubt on the proposition that mergers in general lead to improvements in technique or even to enhanced profitability through monopoly power. Managers, it seems, have a *déformation professionnelle* that leads them to believe they are more capable of exploiting a monopoly position or realizing postmerger economies than in fact they prove to be. There are, of course, problems of defining success: failure to meet the glowing prospectus promises of a promoter may not be failure by reasonable standards; and even where market share declined, as after the U.S. Steel merger, the stockholders were able to realize a substantial gain even from the desultory exploitation of an increasingly threatened monopoly position.

Recent studies measuring the performance of merging firms by the standard of similar firms that do not merge, such as that of Eamon Kelly, have concluded that the stockholders of merging firms were the less successful. In the longer run, failure has been related to the availability of real economies for the merging firms. In the turn-of-the-century movement, for example, mergers in chemicals, primary metals, machinery, transportation equipment, and electrical machinery were, broadly speaking, successful; in the textile and leather industries, on the other hand, a high proportion were failures. It seems reasonable to infer from these examples that success was closely related to the existence of real benefits from increased scale or integration, and that where such benefits did not exist, managerial diseconomies of scale tended to produce bankruptcy or rapidly declining market shares.

Yet, in creating large-scale enterprises, the merger waves contributed to the high levels of concentration that have developed in the American economy since the 1890's. The share of the largest one hundred corporations in manufacturing value added, for example, rose from 21 percent after the first merger wave to 33 percent by the late 1960's. Outside of periods of intense merger activity, on the other hand, concentration has tended to decline, as it probably did, for example, in the first decade of the twentieth century and in the 1930's and 1940's. J. F. Weston and others have suggested that only a limited portion of the growth of large firms can be attributed to mergers, but more recent scholarship has shown that they are the major cause of concentration of market shares in the hands of fewer firms. Weston shows that for eleven out of twenty-five corporations that he examined, the contribution of mergers to increases in their market share was above 100 percent, implying that in the absence of merger, concentration would have declined. On the other hand, it is clear that some corporations have achieved their leading position by internal growth rather than by merger; and it is certainly difficult to believe that even if General Motors had not grown rapidly by merger, the long-run tendency in the automobile industry would have been anything other than that adopted by General Motors: large-scale mass production.

Without mergers, then, the economy would certainly have been less concentrated, but it is not clear that in the longer run it would necessarily have been substantially less concentrated in individual markets. The implications for welfare of high concentration levels remain difficult to assess. Even leaving theoretical considerations of second-best analysis apart, it seems clear that there remain important pressures on management that have supplemented the forces of competition as an incentive to efficiency. Merger in the form of aggressive take-over is one of these: a management underusing its assets may find that its stock price declines, thereby laying it open to takeover. Louis Wolfson's takeover of Montgomery Ward is a case in point, and for large firms this is now a more real stimulus to increased managerial effort than is the threat of bankruptcy. More generally, and in the postwar period especially, competition has been stimulated by tariff reductions under the General Agreement on Tariffs and Trade and the Kennedy Round, and by the growth of competitors abroad, so that American corporations are no longer relatively unchallenged in their home market.

Given the survival of competitive forces, the fact that merging firms are able to maintain their market positions is consistent with the interpretation that they contain significant elements of the "good trust." Indeed, H. Demsetz has shown that the leading corporations in American industry consistently have higher levels of profitability than do smaller firms in the same industry. This suggests that they rely not mainly on their monopoly prices (which would surely be to the advantage of smaller firms in the same industry) but, in part at least, on technical leadership, innovation, and managerial efficiency. It is thus perhaps no accident that, in the 1960's, European governments were encouraging mergers in the hope that this was one way to achieve levels of efficiency comparable with those achieved by the American giants.

BIBLIOGRAPHY

John M. Blair, *Economic Concentration: Structure, Behavior and Public Policy* (New York, 1972), is a useful compilation of case study material arising from antitrust law enforcement, by a committed antitruster. Alfred D. Chandler, *Strategy and Structure: Chapters in the History of the Industrial Enterprise* (Cambridge, Mass., 1962), and *The Visible Hand: The Managerial Revolution in American Business* (Cambridge, Mass., 1977), are the classic studies of the development of the modern American corporation. Harold Demsetz, "Industrial Structure, Market Rivalry and Public Policy," in J. Fred Weston and Stanley I. Ornstein, eds., *The Impact of Large Firms on the U.S. Economy* (Lexington, Mass., 1973), is a stimulating analysis of alternative interpretations of the continued dominance of large firms. Alfred S. Eichner, *The Emergence of Oligopoly* (Baltimore,

1969), is an important case study of the impact of the merger movement on the sugar-refining industry.

Carl Eis, "The 1919–1930 Merger Movement in American Industry," in *Journal of Law and Economics*, 12 (1969), is the standard statistical evaluation of the second merger movement and an evaluation of the impact of antimerger laws. Federal Trade Commission, *Report on the Merger Movement; A Summary Report* (Washington, D.C., 1948), is an alarmist exaggeration of the impact of mergers in the 1940's (cf. Lintner and Butters); *Economic Report on Corporate Mergers* (Washington, D.C., 1969), a more balanced study of the modern merger movement, provides useful assessment of the role of mergers in increasing concentration; and *Statistical Report on Mergers and Acquisitions* (Washington, D.C., annual), is the basic source for modern merger statistics. Michael Gort, "An Economic Disturbance Theory of Mergers," in *Quarterly Journal of Economics*, 83 (Nov. 1969), although a suggestive discussion of the reasons behind cycles in merger activity, is marred by cavalier empirical testing that fails to establish the author's case. Leslie Hannah, *The Rise of the Corporate Economy* (Baltimore, 1976), a comparative study of the British merger waves, suggests that trends attributed by American economists to antimerger laws have occurred in Europe without such laws.

Eamon M. Kelly, *The Profitability of Growth Through Mergers* (State College, Pa., 1967), one of the most carefully conceived studies of the effect of mergers, uses the "matched pairs" technique of comparing merging and nonmerging firms. John Lintner and J. Keith Butters, "Effects of Taxes on Concentration," in Conference of the Universities–National Bureau Committee for Economic Research, *Business Concentration and Price Policy* (Princeton, 1955), reviews the authors' work on tax incentives to merger and the impact of the boomlet of the 1940's on concentration. Shaw Livermore, "The Success of Industrial Mergers," in *Quarterly Journal of Economics*, 50 (Nov. 1935), is the classic study of the failures and successes of the turn-of-the-century merger wave. Jesse W. Markham, "Survey of the Evidence and Findings on Mergers," in Conference of the Universities–National Bureau Committee for Economic Research, *Business Concentration and Price Policy* (Princeton, 1955), is still a stimulating discussion of the evidence, although subsequent scholarship has improved our statistical knowledge and some of the author's generalizations are no longer tenable. John Moody, *The Truth About Trusts* (New York, 1904), is the classic contemporary account. Thomas R. Navin and Marian V. Sears, "The Rise of a Market for Industrial Securities, 1887–1902," in *Business History Review*, 29 (June 1955), is a discussion of the role of promoters and the stock exchange in the early merger waves. Ralph L. Nelson, *Merger Movements in American Industry 1895–1956* (Princeton, 1959), is a major study of mergers through 1920 with a general discussion of the relationship between mergers and the business cycle; and "Business Cycle Factors in the Choice Between Internal and External Growth," in William W. Alberts and Joel E. Segall, eds., *The Corporate Merger* (Chicago, 1966), is another inconclusive attempt to solve the enigma of merger cycles.

George J. Stigler, "Monopoly and Oligopoly by Merger," in *American Economic Review, Papers and Proceedings*, 40 (May 1950), argues, somewhat unconvincingly, that the Clayton Act was the major force behind the creation of oligopolies in the 1920's; "The Statistics of Monopoly and Merger," in *Journal of Political Economy*, 64 (Feb. 1956), is a persuasive argument that Weston underestimates the role of mergers in the growth of large firms; and "The Dominant Firm and the Inverted Umbrella," in *Journal of Law and Economics*, 8 (1965), a demonstration that, despite their declining market share, the U.S. Steel stockholders did well from their investment, is executed with Stigler's customary elegance. Willard L. Thorp, "The Persistence of the Merger Movement," in *American Economic Review, Papers and Proceedings*, 21 (March 1931), is a contemporary view of the second merger wave. Willard L. Thorp and Walter F. Crowder, *The Structure of Industry*, Temporary National Economic Committee Monograph no. 27 (Washington, D.C., 1941), is a wartime report that includes Thorp's statistics on interwar merger activity. John F. Weston, *The Role of Mergers in the Growth of Large Firms* (Berkeley, 1953), is a useful general discussion of mergers, but for more balanced discussion of the subject of the title, see Stigler, "The Statistics of Monopoly and Merger."

[*See also* ANTITRUST; COMPETITION; ENTREPRENEURSHIP; FINANCIAL INTERMEDIARIES; MANAGEMENT; MANUFACTURING; MULTINATIONAL ENTERPRISE; RISE AND EVOLUTION OF BIG BUSINESS; *and* TRANSPORTATION.]

MULTINATIONAL ENTERPRISE

Raymond Vernon and Heidi Wortzel

MULTINATIONAL ENTERPRISE is a term that did not exist until the beginning of the 1960's. Its synonyms—multinational corporation, transnational enterprise, and half a dozen other variants—are just as new. Yet as early as the 1870's a few firms were functioning as multinational enterprises. Within a few decades a score or two of the strongest firms headquartered in the United States had come to look upon their operations in global terms. By that time these firms had established production facilities in foreign countries and were devising their strategies, deploying their resources, and maintaining their day-to-day controls in ways that created continuous operating links between their foreign-based facilities and their producing units in the United States.

By the late 1970's, American firms as a whole valued the stake in their overseas units at more than $150 billion. Practically every one of the two hundred largest firms had established a number of producing subsidiaries on foreign soil, and many were drawing as much as one-third of their total business from activities abroad.

INTERNATIONAL PERSPECTIVES AND NATIONAL INTERESTS

The first indications of American business ambitions to become a force in world markets could be glimpsed during the last decades of the nineteenth century. At that time rabble-rousing politicians and patrician diplomats were promoting overseas extension of the ideology of "manifest destiny" and the image of the United States as a great industrial power. In 1900 the president of the National Association of Manufacturers said, "American manufacturers no longer measure their productive capacity by the consuming power of their home markets; for the world is their market and all the people of the earth are their consumers."

Nevertheless, for all the new sense of daring and destiny found among some enterprises, their foreign establishments were mainly concentrated in a few countries: Canada, Britain, Mexico, and Argentina led the list. In Mexico and Argentina, where investments were principally in mines, oil fields, and agriculture, the sense of right and entitlement was especially strong; the landing of the United States Marines at Vera Cruz in 1914 and the pursuit of Pancho Villa in Chihuahua in 1916 reflected Americans' perception of their nation as an expansive global power.

World War I increased the American sense of right and entitlement to enter foreign markets. The disposition of businessmen to look for opportunities in foreign lands grew stronger. "Manifest destiny" was linked inexorably with the Open Door policy. That concept comprehended the promotion of American exports in China and other foreign markets as well as support for the establishment of American-owned enterprises on foreign soil. One obvious goal in the implementation of the policy was to open the special preserves of the great colonial powers in Africa, the Middle East, and Asia to American businessmen. As part of the new strategy, the government after World War I set about vigorously supporting the entry of the big American oil companies into the Middle East.

The Open Door policy was not an expression of American support for an open international economy; it was simply a policy for achieving equality in foreign lands with the leading colonial powers. Accordingly, the aspirations of large

American enterprises and administrations to penetrate foreign countries did not prevent industry from supporting protectionist policies at home. In debates over the tariff that periodically erupted during the first three decades of the twentieth century, the organizations that represented American industry, such as the National Association of Manufacturers, remained firmly on the side of higher tariffs.

Accordingly, by the 1920's a certain gap seemed to exist between Americans' perceptions of the industrial strength of their country in world markets and the reality of that position. By that time the United States was already the leading industrial power in the world. But its behavior still was that of the uncertain upstart. Its aggressiveness was registered through the Open Door policy; its uncertainty, through a strong policy of protectionism.

The ambivalence in the attitudes and perceptions of American businessmen during that period was registered in other ways as well. By the 1920's American industry had already had a considerable impact on its European competitors, mainly through a stream of successful innovations in machinery, electrical equipment, and automobiles. Nonetheless, American industrialists seemed quite unsure about their long-term competitive strength in most chemicals and drugs, where they still were ruefully acknowledging the leadership of the Germans and the Swiss, and in the more standardized products, such as oil, steel, copper, aluminum, and nitrates, where no major technological differences existed between European and American firms.

In the struggle between daring and caution, caution generally had the upper hand. Fearful of the consequences of an international competitive free-for-all, American businessmen in the 1920's arranged their affairs in international markets in ways that seemed markedly inconsistent with their emphasis on the Open Door. Although they presumably still wanted the option to enter any market that was closed to them, many were prepared to bargain away their right to exercise the option once it had been secured.

During the 1920's and 1930's American businessmen in many industries made agreements with Europeans to restrict international competition. Under these agreements the big firms of the United States and Europe agreed to divide world markets. In oil the agreements took the form of a global "as-is" agreement, under which the leading international oil companies headquartered in the United States, Britain, the Netherlands, and France undertook to freeze their shares of world markets. In electrical machinery the agreements between the leading American and European firms were intended to arrest their incipient penetration of each other's markets and to encourage withdrawal to their home bases; accordingly, in this period General Electric and Westinghouse reversed the expansive trend by selling their European subsidiaries to European producers. In chemicals, lamps, aluminum, pharmaceuticals, and scores of other products, similar arrangements were developed to arrest and reverse the long-run spread of industry.

The structure of these restrictive agreements, or cartels, followed a common pattern. Typically, they sought to reinforce the control of leading firms in their own national markets. Lesser markets that did not have their own large producers were parceled out among the leading firms. British firms usually held sway over the Commonwealth, the continental Europeans over the Continent, and the American firms over the United States and Latin America. Where patents played any role in the industry, the members of the cartel agreed on a division of patents that would reinforce the agreed-upon division of markets. The leader in any market was given control over any patents applicable to that market that were owned by other members of the cartel. Thus each member of the cartel was in a position to apply the restraining power that all the relevant patents in its own market collectively could provide.

Despite the effort and ingenuity invested in the development of these restrictive agreements, they generally proved vulnerable. With the continuous improvement in international transportation and communication, upstart businessmen who were not members of the cartel often managed to intrude into the cartel-controlled areas. The control of the cartels over the American market tended to be particularly uncertain. This was the case partly because of the antitrust laws, the existence of which led American firms to avoid restrictive business practices that were too obvious and explicit. But it was also due to other factors. For one thing, the American economy was very large and the origins of its business class very diverse. The equilibrium of many American industries was often upset by mavericks making a bid to capture a portion of the business and to join the leaders of the particular industry. The American participants, therefore, were relatively unreliable partners in these international agreements because they could not speak with any assurance for the whole of the American economy.

World War II marked a watershed in the development of international restrictive agreements. When the war ended, leading firms in the United States saw little reason, for the time being, to join in restrictive agreements with foreign rivals. For one thing, the legal risks of entering into such agreements had sharply increased for the American participants. A flurry of antitrust cases, launched many years earlier, was finally being brought to completion. Some involved agreements that were international in scope and executed in part on foreign soil. In *United States* v. *Timken Roller Bearing* (1949), Timken Roller Bearing was found guilty of a Sherman Antitrust Act violation for combining with its chief British competitor to form British Timken. That case underlined the point that cartel arrangements that would restrain American foreign commerce could be illegal under American law, even if those arrangements were made on foreign soil. In 1950, Minnesota Mining was found in violation of the Sherman Antitrust Act (*United States* v. *Minnesota Mining*) in connection with an arrangement under which four American firms combined to establish jointly owned factories in Canada, England, and Germany. The same spate of cases found Alcoa (1945), Du Pont (1956), and General Electric (1961) guilty of Sherman Antitrust Act violations.

Another factor that discouraged the recrudescence of the prewar cartels was the fact that industry in Europe and Japan was not in a position to compete effectively with American industry. The war had destroyed many of the industrial plants in those areas, and those that were left had fallen behind American plants in technical capabilities. Accordingly, after World War II "the world is my oyster" reappeared as the prevailing slogan of American-based enterprises. Subsidiaries and affiliates spread rapidly to foreign markets. The headquarters staffs of American-based enterprises found themselves spending large proportions of their time on foreign business.

As the foreign interests of large American enterprises grew, the protectionist cast of business opinion tended to decline. From the viewpoint of any firm that aspired to a global strategy, government restrictions on the movement of goods, capital, or labor were a nuisance. Such measures were not necessarily fatal to the operations of a multinational enterprise, but they did tend to get in the way. By the 1960's protectionism in the American business community became a sentiment confined to special situations and to special sectors of the business leadership.

While businessmen were expanding their international interests and recasting their international ideologies to conform with their interests, labor was responding in predictable ways. From the beginning, organized labor in the United States had leaned to protectionism as a national policy. In 1922, American Federation of Labor president Samuel Gompers reflected the prevailing sentiment when he said: "... we yield not an inch of activity upon any field for the protection and the promotion of the rights and the interests of the working people and the citizenship of our country to any other body on earth." Now and again, to be sure, some labor leaders at the national level had deviated from that sonorous declaration by supporting trade policies that were less chauvinistic and more international in sentiment. But that aberrant tendency was largely confined to individuals at the top of the national labor movement and mainly in periods when the leadership was actively collaborating with the current administration.

In the decade or so immediately following World War II, the propensity of national labor leaders to restrain the protectionist preferences of their members was especially strong. In that period many AFL-CIO officers at national headquarters supported the idea of an open international system. But even then the preference for an open system never had much of a hold on the rank and file. And as American enterprises set up new facilities in foreign locations, many segments of American labor saw the tendency as harmful to their relative position in the economy. The growth of American-based multinational enterprises clearly seemed to benefit managers and stockholders, and it might even benefit the economy as a whole; but, relatively speaking, labor seemed to be profiting least among the affected American interests. The few hundred thousand workers in the headquarters staffs of large corporations whose jobs were tied to foreign business were not closely linked to the labor movement. The more visible and more relevant consequence of the overseas spread of American enterprises, as far as organized labor was concerned, was to create jobs in foreign locations that the domestic economy might have retained. This not only reduced the relative position of labor at home; it also impaired the ability of labor leaders to negotiate effectively with the managers of American enterprises.

Accordingly, the growth and spread of multinational enterprises after World War II eventually produced a marked shift in American politics. Even as management became identified with an open world system, organized labor tended to weaken its ties with international movements and to revert to a stronger and more unqualified support for protectionist policies.

The broad political reactions associated with the growth of multinational enterprises did not fully mirror their economic impact on the American economy. Multinational enterprises cover an enormously diverse set of activities. For instance, those producing high-technology goods, such as drugs and computers, were generating consequences different from those in the more standardized lines of production; and firms in the standardized lines, such as chemicals and aluminum, were moving in ways somewhat different from those that were associated with strong trade names and heavy marketing expenditures. To get a sense of the impact of multinational enterprises upon the American economy, therefore, one has to distinguish among them according to the nature of their business activities.

TECHNOLOGY-BASED PRODUCTS

Multinational enterprises have an especially prominent place in industries that emphasize new products and new processes. In chemicals, drugs, machinery, and instruments, for instance, the leading American producers have an unusually heavy stake in foreign markets, a stake arising out of the innovative character of their products.

The propensity of American industrial innovators to set up foreign production facilities goes back to the beginning of the modern industrial era. By the 1870's the Singer sewing machine, not yet twenty years old, was being produced abroad. By 1900, United Shoe and Westinghouse Air Brake, among others, were producing their equipment in subsidiaries abroad. In 1920, Henry Ford was producing his low-cost, mass-produced automobile in Britain, and was soon followed by General Motors and Chrysler. In the period after World War II the stream of new overseas establishments belonging to American enterprises grew to a flood. By 1980 the foreign affiliates of American firms were producing all manner of advanced products, including nuclear reactors, computers, microcircuits, exotic chemicals, and specialized scientific instruments.

The chain of stimulus and response that produced this pattern of overseas spread by American-based innovating enterprises has not changed significantly over the course of its existence. The tendency of American firms in certain industries to generate a stream of new products and eventually to take them into foreign markets has stemmed from certain distinctive characteristics of the American economy.

Take the structure of costs in the United States. From at least the middle of the nineteenth century, skilled labor was scarce and raw materials were plentiful, as compared with Europe. At the same time, income per capita in the United States was high, measurably higher than the income of most countries in Europe. By the early 1970's, these differences were no longer so apparent. But for most of the intervening decades, the differences were considerable; and being considerable, they stimulated American businessmen to respond to their high labor cost and their high income opportunities rather earlier than their European counterparts. Accordingly, by the time that the national economies in Europe and Japan reached any given income level and any given level of labor cost, American firms already had developed the products appropriate to those conditions. In the industrial products field, for instance, American producers, responding to high labor costs, took an early lead in the development of automatic machinery for the plant and office, and they retained that lead for many decades. In consumer goods American businessmen were stimulated by the high income levels in America to seize the lead in medium-priced automobiles, in consumer durable goods, and in consumer electronics.

Another advantage held by American businessmen in the development of new products was the relative size of the economy. The development and introduction of new products entail a certain amount of risk. If the potential rewards seem large enough, they may be sufficient to offset the risk; large markets, therefore, offer a larger incentive for the introduction of risky new products. In the last few decades that point has developed increasing importance as the cost of industrial innovations has climbed. The development costs of the IBM 360 computer series are reckoned at several billion dollars; the Boeing 747, at $1 billion or so; the breeder nuclear reactor, at about the same amount; and the new generation of Xerox copiers, at nearly the same sum.

The advantages for American-based innovators—and, hence, the handicaps confronting foreign-based innovators—have been palpable in these lines. American-based innovators, if successful in producing a wanted product, can count on confronting a relatively large market. If the government is the main market, as is the case with military goods and space gadgetry, the relatively huge purchasing power of the United States is felt in another context.

Moreover, once American firms had developed an overseas network for their new products, the network enlarged the advantages associated with size. In some important cases no single national market alone—not even the American market—has been big enough to provide adequate promise for the innovating firm. Accordingly, innovating firms have had to count on the export market from the very birth of the product. This condition, for example, faced any firm from the 1950's on that hoped to enter the market for wide-bodied aircraft or nuclear reactors. American firms with international networks could exploit this fact in planning their innovation policies.

One can only speculate how the American economy would have developed if multinational enterprises had not existed in the high-technology field. Businessmen might still have expected to derive some income from their innovations in foreign markets, by way of exports and the licensing of foreign producers. On the whole, however, the likelihood is that industrial innovation in the United States was stimulated somewhat by the existence of multinational enterprises.

MATURE PRODUCTS

The foreign-owned facilities of American-based enterprises are found not only in new, technologically advanced product lines, such as computers and machinery, but also in the long-established product lines such as oil, copper, standard chemicals, and aluminum. The stimuli and responses that have pushed American firms abroad in these industries have included some special elements not found in the technologically advanced products.

First, a question of classification needs to be clarified. The technologically advanced products of one generation often become the mature, standardized products of the next. An American enterprise that plunges into a foreign market on the basis of a unique technological capability soon discovers that foreign rivals are quite capable of matching its performance. The American firm then finds itself in the position of defending markets that it had earlier acquired. All at once its strategic goal is not to exploit a special technological capability but to maintain its position in the market.

When a product has grown mature and its technology has been standardized, it does not take very long for the leaders to recognize that they have a common stake in avoiding any price competition. At that stage, therefore, many of the strategies of the leaders in such products have been directed toward reducing that risk. Some of these strategies have had the effect of inhibiting American firms from developing a multinational network. Other strategies have led to the more rapid development or the extension of such networks.

The international cartel agreements were strategies that discouraged multinational development. But, as some of these illustrations emphasized, potential rivals from different countries sometimes developed joint ventures for the conduct of their foreign business; arrangements of this sort appeared, for instance, in oil, chemicals, and bearings. After World War II the pattern was seen throughout the world aluminum industry, as American firms linked up on foreign soil both with one another and with potential competitors from foreign countries.

Strategies of this sort responded to a basic principle: where an industry consists of a limited number of large firms, any leading firm can reduce its risks in the industry by paralleling the business decisions of the other leaders. Parallel action has the effect of exposing all the leaders to similar market opportunities and product costs; if one of them happens to settle in an especially fast-growing market, the others are there to share its prosperity. And, if all of them settle on an unprofitable location, none is in a position to exploit the error of the others.

Responding to this principle, American firms in standardized lines not only have set up joint ventures with their rivals but also have spread their foreign subsidiaries across the globe in waves of seeming imitation. If one leading firm has set up producing facilities in a given market, there has been a visible tendency for other leading firms in the same line to follow suit.

The efforts of leading firms in standardized products to guard against instability have drawn the American economy into a global network in still another way. With the establishment of American-owned subsidiaries in the markets of Europe and Japan, their leading rivals in those countries found themselves asking how stability could be restored. Agreements that divided world markets on a geographical basis were no longer feasible; too many eggs would need unscrambling in order to effect such a division. Non-American firms that were uneasy over the competitive threat of the Americans could consider a variant on the follow-the-leader principle: the strategy of establishing a producing subsidiary in the American market. Such a subsidiary has various functions. It can monitor the American market for its overseas parent, picking up new developments in product and process that might threaten the equilibrium of the industry in world markets, and it can serve to remind the Americans that if they become too aggressive in the markets of Europe or Japan, there is always the possibility of counteraggression by foreigners in the American market.

In earlier periods of American expansion abroad, European firms had occasionally entered American markets as part of a countering strategy. The decision of Royal Dutch Shell to enter the American market in 1910 had been stimulated by outbreaks of rivalry with Standard Oil in other parts of the world. More recently, Pechiney-Ugine-Kuhlmann, Beechams, and Olivetti entered the American market with a more or less explicit appreciation of the fact that such entry could strengthen their competitive position against the Americans in other markets and restore a certain measure of equilibrium. British Petroleum, Imperial Chemicals, Hoechst, and Badische Anilin are thought to have had something of this sort in mind as they set up or acquired producing facilities in the United States during the 1960's and 1970's.

On the other hand, there were added factors in the 1960's and 1970's that brought the subsidiaries of European and Japanese firms into the United States. Exchange rates between the dollar and other currencies were changing in such a way that production costs in the United States generally declined relative to those in Europe and Japan. Accordingly, the tendency of European- and Japanese-based enterprises to establish facilities in the United States was strengthened further. By the late 1970's the total investment of foreign firms in their American subsidiaries was reported to be in the neighborhood of $35 billion.

As a result of the international moves and countermoves of the leading firms of all nationalities in the standardized product lines, it was hard to think of the American market any longer as if it were a separate national market. American buyers of aluminum, oil, chemicals, automobiles, and other standardized products could look to a number of strong foreign sellers. Meanwhile, American firms drew both their revenues and their strategic cues from markets all over the world. In these products, therefore, the markets of the world had become an oyster shared by producers from many countries.

The increase in the number of sources capable of providing standardized products to most national markets was also raising some questions regarding the stability of such markets in the future. Could a global market structure of this kind be expected to remain stable for very long? If not, would governments seek to restore stability by introducing restrictions on the international movement of such products?

MULTINATIONAL ENTERPRISE

THE TRADE-NAME PRODUCTS

The presence of American industry in the world economy has been epitomized not only by the activities of its technological leaders and of its mass producers of standardized products, but also by the ubiquitousness of its trade brands and trade names. Although trade names such as Singer, Gillette, and Coca-Cola are thoroughly American, they command the loyalty of buyers all over the world. They represent another class of product that first developed a dominant position in the American market, then used that position as a base for penetrating foreign markets. Some of these branded products owe their global coverage mainly to the indefatigable distribution efforts of their owners. Singer's acceptance in Europe, Africa, and Asia, and Gillette's commanding position in the more remote corners of the world, are triumphs of the merchandising art.

But some trade names were literally borne to other countries by the expansive aspects of the American culture. After World War II the movies, song lyrics, army post exchanges, and tourists of the United States bore American products everywhere, creating a ripe opportunity for firms with famous names to exploit the new possibilities.

In some respects the early strength of many trade-name products was based on factors not unlike those of the technology-based products; the uniqueness of their performance accounted for their strength in foreign markets. As a rule, what was unique about their performance was simply their predictability. One Singer sewing machine could be expected to be much like another, as could Gillette blades or Manhattan shirts. In other cases, where the buyer actually thought of the American product as superior, it was hard to say whether the exportation was based on objective qualities or on the fact that the product was American and was strengthened by copious local advertising. In any event, some American products managed to retain their advantage in foreign markets after any technological differentiation from local goods had disappeared. American food products, drugs, cosmetics, and electronics, for instance, have often commanded premium prices even when their technical superiority over local products has been dissipated.

It is hard to estimate the extent to which these American brands in foreign markets suggested the existence of a larger American presence. There is a risk of exaggerating their impact in this respect. For instance, Singer, Hoover, and Coca-Cola are commonly thought by consumers in foreign markets to be local brands, not American products. Moreover, the tendency among American firms to adopt trade names that seem neutral in origin probably dilutes the connection even more; 3M (Minnesota Mining and Manufacturing Company), FMC (Food Machinery Corporation), and ITT (International Telephone and Telegraph Company) illustrate the new breed of trade name.

On the other hand, in some localities, especially in the capital cities of developing countries, the commercial messages of foreign-owned firms on billboards and in newspapers seem overwhelming. The impact of these messages is not easy to evaluate. Among intellectuals and journalists it has clearly added to feelings of hostility already present on other grounds; among local politicians it has sometimes created a political issue considered easy to exploit; among the people at large it appears to have had less impact. All together, American trade names abroad are another witness to the fact that American-based enterprises and the American economy have identified themselves with world markets and a global outlook.

FORCES AND CONSEQUENCES

Although the growth of American-based multinational enterprises is often thought of as a major cause of increased American involvement abroad, it is better seen as a consequence than as a cause. The key factor in the spread of these enterprises during the twentieth century has been the revolutionary change in the means of international transportation and international communication. International cable connections have been vastly extended, international radio communication has been introduced, international air travel has become a commonplace, and international air freight has gained a major foothold.

As has been the case in every other industrial nation, the American economy had been deeply affected by these revolutionary improvements. The impact can be seen in numerous ways. For example, by 1975 about 14 percent of the manufactured goods produced in the United States were exported, as compared with about 9 percent in the early 1970's and 7.5 percent in the early 1960's. The direct investment by Americans in property, plant, and equipment located in foreign countries had risen to constitute more than 20 percent of similar investments in the American economy; the comparable ratio in the early 1960's had been only 12 percent. Other indications of the growing interdependencies between American and foreign economies can be found in data on the use of international communications, international travel, and numerous other statistics.

Some of the consequences of these trends are evident. First, of course, there are the benefits conventionally associated with an increased international division of labor—some reductions in cost and increases in the efficiency of production. In addition, the American economy was tied to an increasing number of foreign markets and of foreign sources for materials; insofar as safety and stability lay in numbers, the position of the United States had been improved. On the other hand, the American economy appeared to be more vulnerable to the shocks and variations originating outside the country. A poor harvest in Argentina, an outbreak of warfare in Africa or Asia, or any other disturbance in the equilibrium of the world markets reverberated more powerfully through the existing mechanisms than had been the case in earlier times. In sum, the United States was gaining some of the advantages of being a part of a global economy and was losing some of the advantages that go with national autonomy.

The intimate links created between the American economy and foreign countries have developed in various ways, not all of them involving the multinational enterprise. Yet the multinational enterprise has played a large part in developing these new interdependencies. Large American firms that have substantial overseas interests account for about one-third of American industry, when measured in terms of output. About 50 percent of the manufacturing exports of the United States are shipped by large multinational enterprises, and about one-third of American imports come through such channels.

Multinational enterprises have provided a major conduit linking the American economy with foreign economies that is unique in many respects. The multinational enterprise has an identity, a strategy, and a set of resources all its own. These must find their tangible expression, in the end, on the soil of a particular nation. But the entity itself straddles the boundaries of the nation-states in which it operates.

The importance of multinational enterprises as channels for the movement of goods and money across the borders of the United States raises the question of whether the capacity of the American government to control what crosses its borders has been impaired. In fact, it was this issue that preoccupied the Church Committee, the Senate subcommittee on multinational corporations in the mid-1970's.

To assess the effects of the multinational enterprise on governmental powers, one has to begin by realizing that in a modern world of easy communication and transportation, goods, money, and ideas can move by many alternative channels. If firms are forbidden by government regulations to export goods, they may still be able to set up plants abroad that can make the goods on foreign soil. If that is forbidden, it may still be possible for such firms to license foreigners to set up such plants in their own markets. And if that too is forbidden, it may be possible for foreign firms to find individuals in the United States capable of setting up such plants. In short, the suspicion of national governments that they may have lost some control over what crosses their borders is not so much the result of the growth of multinational enterprises as the result of increased efficiencies in transportation and communication that offer numerous ways of efficiently penetrating national borders.

Nevertheless, multinational enterprises appear to have greater incentives and greater capabilities than national firms for moving money, goods, people, and ideas across American borders. Accordingly, when the stability of the dollar is threatened, the multinational enterprise is thought to have more options and better facilities for moving its funds out of dollars than does a national firm. When the costs of production rise in the United States, multinational enterprises are thought to have a ready means—readier than national enterprises—for shifting their production facilities to lower-cost areas.

Studies of the behavior of multinational enterprises in moving funds and jobs across international boundaries have usually depicted complex patterns, results that have been used by parties on both sides of the debate to support their contentions. Nevertheless, the potential has been thought to exist even when it has not been realized in practice.

The development of multinational enterprises has also raised the question in the United States and elsewhere of whether the foreign subsidiaries of multinational enterprises are being used abroad as instruments of American government policy. In some situations the tie has been clear enough. From time to time the United States has forbidden American-based enterprises to allow their foreign subsidiaries to ship certain products to Communist countries. Moreover, bizarre episodes such as the efforts by ITT in the early 1970's to overthrow the Allende regime in Chile have raised questions of whether ties of this sort have been even more extensive.

At the same time, fears have been expressed over the possibilities of government influence running in the opposite direction. When other countries have required American-owned subsidiaries on their soil to produce components and supplies for shipment to the parent firms in the United States, the question has been raised of whether foreign countries are manipulating the American economy through these foreign subsidiaries. The question was put in particularly acute form in the oil crisis of 1973, when American-owned Aramco was compelled by King Faisal of Saudi Arabia to cut off shipments of Arabian oil to the United States and the Seventh Fleet.

The difficulty in making any definitive judgment about the effects of the multinational enterprise upon the American economy may be mainly because that question is only a facet of a larger question. With the globe shrinking under the powerful forces of technological change in communication and transportation, all nations find their nationals committing some of their creative abilities and assets to activities located in foreign countries. These commitments may be seen as Trojan horses or as hostages, according to the circumstances. The question for the United States and for other countries is how to benefit from the advantages of their increased interdependence while retaining some of the freedom of action that their national political processes demand. The role of the multinational enterprise can be usefully assessed only with that larger question in mind.

BIBLIOGRAPHY

Marvin D. Bernstein, *The Mexican Mining Industry, 1890–1950* (Albany, N.Y., 1965), is an economic history that enlarges the perspective regarding problems faced by foreign-owned industry in Mexico. Federal Trade Commission, *The International Petroleum Cartel* (Washington, D.C., 1952), is a detailed investigation of the history and practices of the international oil industry. Edward M. Graham, "Oligopolistic Imitation and European Direct Investment in the United States" (D.B.A. dissertation, Harvard Business School, 1974), is an investigation into the behavior of firms in oligopolistic industries, including why major European firms seek direct investment in the United States. H. J. Habakkuk, *American and British Technology in the Nineteenth Century* (Cambridge, 1962), is a historical and theoretical examination of the evolution of nineteenth-century technological developments. Ervin Hexner, *International Cartels* (Chapel Hill, N.C., 1946), is a broad survey of international cartels in the period immediately preceding World War II. Frederick T. Knickerbocker, *Oligopolistic Reaction and Multinational Enterprise* (Boston, 1973), is an inquiry into interactive corporate behavior and a discussion of post–World War II direct foreign investment of American manufacturing industries. Cleona Lewis, *America's Stake in International Investments* (Washington, D.C., 1938), is a comprehensive discussion of the development of investments from 1775 to 1937, as American capital moved abroad and foreign capital entered the United States. Edith T. Penrose, *The Large International Firm in Developing Countries* (Cambridge, Mass., 1969), studies the economics of large international firms through a specific investigation of the petroleum industry.

Nathan Rosenberg, *Technology and American Economic Growth* (New York, 1972), explores the relationship between technological change and the long-term economic growth of the American economy. Frank A. Southard, *American Industry in Europe* (Cambridge, Mass., 1931), is a detailed study of American enterprise in Europe during the first three decades of the twentieth century. George W. Stocking and Myron W. Watkins, *Cartels in Action* (New York, 1946), is a casebook review of the development, methods, and results of international cartels in eight major industries. John M. Stopford and Louis T. Wells, Jr., *Managing the Multinational Enterprise* (New York, 1972), part of Harvard's Multinational Enterprise Project, is an analysis of the structure, strategy, and policies of the multinational enterprise. James I. Sturgeon, *Joint Ventures in the International Petroleum Industry* (Ann Arbor, Mich., 1974), is an empirical examination of joint ventures in the international oil industry, with emphasis on the exploration and drilling phase. Raymond Vernon, *Storm over the Multinationals* (Cambridge, 1977), is an economic and political analysis of the spread of multinational enterprise. Mira Wilkins, *The Emergence of Multinational Enterprise* (Cambridge, Mass., 1970), is a history of American-based multinational enterprise from the colonial period to 1914; and *The Maturing of Multinational Enterprise* (Cambridge, Mass., 1974), the continuation of the earlier book, is an exploration of the development of modern, large-scale multinational business from 1914 to 1970.

[*See also* ANTITRUST; COMPETITION; ECONOMY SINCE 1914; FOREIGN TRADE; LABOR ORGANIZATIONS; MARKETING; ORGANIZED BUSINESS GROUPS; REGULATORY AGENCIES; RISE AND EVOLUTION OF BIG BUSINESS; *and* TARIFFS.]

COMPETITION

Alfred S. Eichner and Davis R. B. Ross

A DISCUSSION of competition in the context of American history poses certain problems. First, the term has only gradually taken on its present connotations. To the extent that Americans prior to the Civil War thought about what would today be labeled "competition," it was probably to take that condition for granted in the same way they took for granted abundant land, equine-based land transportation, and the four seasons of a temperate climate. Second, as Americans became more conscious of competition, it came to mean different things to different groups. For businessmen, it came to mean the opportunity for any individual to start a business of his own. It thus corresponded to what economists term "free entry." For the average citizen, competition came to mean a condition leading to lower prices or, even less sophisticatedly, a condition preventing prices from rising. For the professional economist—once that profession began to emerge in the nineteenth century—competition came to mean a system of social control that obviated the need for direct government intervention. The three meanings of competition can, of course, be linked to one another. Still, they are not the same.

A difficulty with the term is that it is frequently used in an invidious way, to distinguish those types of business behavior deemed to be socially beneficial from those that are not. There are thus two separate aspects to the phenomena classified under the rubric of competition: independent rather than cooperative forms of business behavior, and socially beneficial rather than socially detrimental consequences. The former aspect is, of course, easier to identify than the latter. For this reason, as well as to give the following discussion a more neutral language, the main contrast to be drawn will be between independent and cooperative forms of business behavior.

It is within this conceptual framework that the evolving structure of competition throughout American history will be discussed. The forms of both independent and cooperative behavior on the part of businessmen, it will be argued, have changed as the American economy has moved through three quite distinct stages of industrial structure, corresponding roughly to the development of business institutions. The three distinct stages are (1) an age of imperfect competition, during which the business classes were concerned primarily with the commercial movement of primary products, such as cotton, wheat, and tobacco, and in which the little manufacturing activity that took place relied on handicraft techniques; (2) a "golden age" of competition, following the transportation revolution between 1815 and 1860, during which large numbers of manufacturing industries produced increasingly homogeneous goods; and (3) the modern period, following the corporate revolution at the turn of the century, dominated by large corporations, or megacorps, operating within oligopolistically structured industries. This article will deal with those forces which, both within the economy and emanating from society, have caused the significant shifts from cooperative to independent forms of business behavior and then back again. It will also discuss the concurrent changes in the underlying ethic of cooperation and competition.

COMPETITION

THE AGE OF IMPERFECT COMPETITION

For the colonial merchant and his successor in the Federalist period, the pursuit of personal profit was considered appropriate, indeed even honorific; it was never seen as an end in itself. More important, merchants did not view themselves as competing against one another on the basis of price, with an impersonal market assuring that the greater social interest was being served. Rather, they regarded themselves as members of a mercantile community, bound together in their common interest against a hostile external world. The competitive ethic, which seems ageless from a twentieth-century perspective, had not yet emerged. What prevailed instead was a cooperative ethic, with the norms of the group setting limits on what the individual could do to better his relative position. Some of the conditions that would later contribute to the emergence of the competitive ethic were, of course, already in place. Entry—in fact, multiple reentry—into most economic endeavors was relatively easy. Returns on capital and opportunities for reinvestment were substantial, although far from certain. Government and other institutional restraints on individual behavior were weak. These factors, together with the chronic scarcity of manufactured goods and coin, contributed to the scramble for windfall gains that in turn served to undermine cooperation. Still, it was the cooperative ethic, even among businessmen, that prevailed.

This cooperative ethic derived from four sources. One was the nature of the European colonial expansion. The North American settlements of the English and Dutch were organized either as commercial capitalist ventures or as proprietary grants to individuals. In either case, the colonists were expected to work for the economic benefit of others, whether as servants, as in Lord Baltimore's Maryland, or as subordinate business partners, as in Plymouth Plantation. Whatever their motives for migrating, the first settlers had to conform outwardly to the economic design of London- or Amsterdam-based merchant capitalists. This corporate context, in which individual economic endeavors were given license, left its mark on all that followed. Even after the interest of the absentee capitalists was transferred to the New World because the colonial proprietors were no longer involved, the paramount importance of economic enterprise on behalf of others continued to be recognized.

The cooperative ethic was reinforced by a second factor, the actual conditions of colonial life. The hazards of the environment, in both its animate and its inanimate forms, forced the colonists at each landing during the first three decades of the seventeenth century to choose cooperative social arrangements. These ranged from the corporate communism of the first years at Jamestown and at Plymouth to the later theocratic town governments of the Massachusetts Bay Colony. In each instance, during the first decade or so of settlement, the common need for survival forced individuals to sublimate private desires to larger social objectives.

The third factor fostering the cooperative ethic was religion. Whatever the complex interplay between Protestantism and the rise of capitalism, one should not misunderstand the values that the religions of the day meant to inculcate, nor the seriousness with which these matters were taken. The emphasis on stewardship, social responsibility, and individual spiritual goals found in American Puritanism was fundamental to the cooperative ethic. Although later generations became noticeably more secular in their outlook, there is no evidence that they placed any less emphasis on traditional Calvinist values, such as frugality, self-discipline, and dedication to one's calling.

While the influence exerted by the initial basis for settlement, the dangers of the frontier, and religion waned with time, this was less true of the fourth factor fostering the cooperative ethic— the mercantilist philosophy that the colonists brought with them from the mother country. Indeed, it was mercantilism that, as the framework for economic thought and behavior during the rise of the modern European states in the sixteenth through eighteenth centuries, most directly inspired the colonization of the New World. The keynote of this mercantilist philosophy was a belief in the use of state power to foster the economic interests of the monarch and merchants in concert with one another. If necessary, elaborate regulations were imposed on the merchants to ensure that, in pursuit of individual profit, they did not damage the larger commercial interest of the nation. But just as readily the state, through its monarchical institutions, was

COMPETITION

prepared to intervene on behalf of that national interest when it was opposed by that of some other prince and coterie of urban merchants. The emphasis, as Joseph Schumpeter has noted, was on export monopolism—the ability to control the price in foreign markets so as to enhance the national wealth at the expense of persons living in other countries.

Mercantilism itself derived from a broader view of man and society, especially as understood in Elizabethan England. Man, according to this view, was born degenerate; it was only social institutions such as the state and the church that protected him against himself and his fellow human beings. Still, society could employ man's degenerate nature to serve its own ends. Society needed bread, so it induced some men to become bakers by allowing them to earn profits, perhaps even granting them a monopoly. But because the bakers would naturally try to enhance their own interest at the expense of society, it was necessary to fix bread prices and have inspectors weigh the loaves. Of course, if the bread was sold overseas, that was a different matter. While it might still be necessary to inspect the loaves for quality, there was no longer any need to fix the price. In the overseas market whatever was earned was a pure gain to society. This mercantilist philosophy remained undiminished throughout the colonial period of the United States and well into the Federal era. Adam Smith's attack of it in *The Wealth of Nations* did not appear until 1776, the year of the American Declaration of Independence; it was another generation before Smith's ideas began to have serious influence on American thought.

Until the Jacksonian period, then, it was the cooperative ethic, with its insistence on limits to the pursuit of individual self-interest, that prevailed in the United States. While the four factors listed above go far to explain the development of this ethic, it was in the day-to-day activities of the merchant class that its reality was repeatedly demonstrated and the underlying values reinforced.

Although merchants accounted for less than 3 percent of the population, the merchant—whether in Boston, Newport, Providence, New York, Philadelphia, Baltimore, Charleston, or Savannah—served as the critical link between the largely subsistence, nonmonetary economy of the New World settlements and the greater world-trading network. To the extent that the colonists, and later the citizen farmers of the new republic, were able to produce a marketable surplus, it was the merchant who saw to it that the crops were sold abroad. On the other hand, throughout the colonial and early national period, virtually all manufactured goods were imported from abroad—nails, kettles, Indian trade gewgaws, iron plows, thread, linens, crockery, wine, and fine furniture. Finally, it was the merchant who handled the slave trade, so essential for augmenting the agricultural labor supply.

This complex trade was carried on within the English mercantilist system, characterized by a chronic shortage of coin in the North American colonies and an unfavorable balance of trade, especially for the middle and northern colonies, vis-à-vis the English ports. These two related disabilities forced colonial merchants to scramble for goods that could be gathered from distant ports and "traded up" to meet English import needs. ("Trading up" was the exchange of North American colonial goods generally unwanted in English markets—such as salted fish—for tropical and other products—such as coffee—more in demand in the sophisticated urban economy of the mother country.) New York merchants, for example, could seldom send produce of their own or neighboring colonies directly to London or the other English outports in exchange for manufactured goods. This forced the merchants to develop complicated reexport techniques. They shipped bread, flour, grain, ships, livestock, and salted provisions to the Caribbean and the Carolinas, and flaxseed to Ireland. The sugar, precious woods, and naval stores from the southern ports, and the bills of exchange drawn on London from Irish importers of flaxseed, gave the New York merchant access to English manufactured goods and to such luxury items as wine from Madeira, Funchal, and Tenerife.

Scarcity of coin, dictated by royal policy and the unfavorable balance of trade, forced merchants to rely upon extensive commodity barter. Thus, the physical condition and inherent quality of goods had to be vouched for by the merchant even more than by the producer. For example, Gerald G. Beekman (1719–1797), a New York merchant who specialized in flaxseed for the Irish linen trade, was forced to set up a crude intermediate cleaning process of the flaxseed in New York to ensure that the product associated with his name met Irish flax growers' standards.

Moreover, transactions were completed slowly, since overland, coastal, and ocean transport of the goods often took months. The prolonged duration of individual commercial transactions compounded risks. To move livestock from an interior county of Pennsylvania to the West Indies, for example, exposed that commodity to the possibility of injuries in movement to the port of embarkation and at the time of embarkation and of debarkation, as well as on board ship. Pirates, storms, and navigational errors might result in total loss of the cargo. The merchant—whether he shipped the livestock on his own account or merely acted as factor or on commission for another party—could lose heavily.

Last, the complexity and slow pace of seventeenth- and eighteenth-century commerce discouraged specialization of function. Merchants performed a bewildering variety of business tasks. Gerald Beekman was involved on his own account in the indigo and dry goods trade as well as in flaxseed; he acted on commission for other merchants; he underwrote marine insurance, especially during war years; he invested in shipping, usually as part owner of a particular vessel; he sold goods as a wholesaler; he invested in real estate; he dealt in bills of exchange; he lent money at interest; and he acted as a commissary agent for the troops of the Rhode Island colony engaged in military campaigns along the New York frontier.

Merchants met this business world of delay, uncertainty, and complexity by personalizing their operations. The most obvious and widely used method was to exploit and cultivate ties based on blood, religion, and friendship. Wherever one looks at seventeenth- and eighteenth-century merchant behavior, one finds the pervasive preference for the family as a basis for commercial partnerships, in order to minimize the risks of extending credit, of trading in diverse commodities and ports, and of large-scale shipping ventures. Where no family or other personal ties could be crafted, merchants resorted to other techniques. The partnership was widely used, both as a long-term basis for carrying on commercial activity and, as was more often the case, as a one-time arrangement for a particular voyage. The hazards of overseas trade made it unwise to risk all on any one shipment, and hence merchants usually took different shares on different voyages, depending on whose capital was free at the moment. The fact that one's rivals at one time might well be one's partners on a subsequent venture clearly contributed to the spirit of cooperation among merchants.

That spirit of cooperation was further reinforced by the manner in which the social life of the merchant groups was organized. Most of the colonial commercial centers boasted clubs and trade associations before the Revolution. Even earlier, informal exchange of information concerning commerce took place at the leading taverns and inns. In New York, merchants met both at Fraunces' Tavern and at the Exchange Coffee House. More formal arrangements for social and commercial gatherings emerged in the eighteenth century. Boston merchants established the Society for Encouraging Trade and Commerce in 1761. New York formed a chamber of commerce in 1768, Charleston followed suit in 1773, and Baltimore created a mercantile exchange as a meeting place for buyers and sellers in 1793.

These meeting places and organizations served two additional functions that reflected the cooperative ethic. In New York one of the first tasks that the newly formed chamber of commerce performed in 1768 was the establishment of a commercial arbitration committee to replace the informal, voluntary arrangements previously in effect. The committee met weekly to settle disputes between merchants over such matters as settling of accounts in joint ventures and paying insurance claims. Arbitration was preferred throughout the colonial and early Federalist period. As Robert Oliver, a Baltimore merchant, put it in 1798, arbitration by fellow merchants was "the only fair and speedy mode" of settlement, since legal processes were "very tedious, expensive and the issue extremely uncertain."

Merchants also worked together to influence legislation by municipal, provincial, or imperial bodies affecting trade. Even before the founding of the New York Chamber of Commerce, for example, the merchants of that city had succeeded in persuading the colonial legislature to extend the powers of the New York City Common Council to regulate the quality of flour, meat, fish, lumber, naval stores, bread, casks, and sole leather. After 1768 the chamber of commerce perceived its chief duty to be the insistence that officials enforce these regulations, particularly those governing flour, since the merchants of the city were locked in competition with those of Philadelphia over dominance of that export trade to the West Indies. The outcry raised by resident merchants in the colonial coastal cities after the Sugar Act (1764) and Stamp Act (1765) undoubtedly affected the subsequent repeal of those two measures by Parliament. Less dramatically, North American merchants indirectly affected imperial legislation on such matters as setting bounties for iron and hemp after 1750.

Merchants benefited from other mercantilist regulations that, continuing medieval practices, discouraged entry into their trade by outsiders. Auctions, markets, and fairs, as well as other types of sales, were carefully monitored by authorities, with an eye to protecting local merchants from the "unscrupulous" practices of both itinerant peddlers and potential monopolistic sellers.

One notable feature of the colonial political economy was the survival of the medieval laws prohibiting forestalling, engrossing, and regrating—the trinity of medieval economic sins. Measures designed to prevent any one merchant or group of merchants from cornering the market did not, however, mandate price competition. Indeed, informal understandings as to what constituted a "fair" price, especially when making purchases from the countryside, were the general rule.

The Revolutionary War greatly upset the normal patterns of trade and commerce; and the newly established state governments were only responding to popular pressure when they sought, through increased regulations, to protect the populace from higher prices. Yet the period of war and its aftermath sharply demonstrated that the government was generally powerless in the face of extreme economic dislocation. Prices were scarcely affected by regulation; only trade was slowed down. Not until Great Britain went to war with Napoleonic France in 1798 would the fledgling nation enjoy new prosperity. But this age of sporadic trade, like that of the American war for independence, simply continued the assault on stable trade norms. No less significant as an omen of the threat to the dominance of the merchants was the first stirring of industrial enterprise in the United States, as British manufactured goods, diverted by war from the American market, became scarce. The British punctured the boomlet in 1815 when, after hostilities with France ceased, they unceremoniously dumped their surplus goods at American ports. Yet it was the manufacturing interest that survived this return of British industry to world markets that proved to be the more meaningful portent of the future.

THE GOLDEN AGE OF COMPETITION

The ending of the Napoleonic Wars set in motion a series of interrelated developments that transformed the economic world of the United States. An economy that in 1815 could still be described as agricultural and export-oriented had, by 1873, become industrial and inwardly focused, with business activity increasingly impersonal and specialized. The initial impetus for these changes came from the ripples of the British industrial revolution. The seemingly insatiable demand in England for agricultural raw materials—cotton to feed the textile mills and wheat to feed the mill hands—provided the incentive for bringing the vast trans-Appalachian lands of the United States under cultivation. The construction of canals and then of railroads was intended merely to assure that the harvested surplus reached its commercial outlet. The results went beyond meeting just the British need for basic commodities. An internal market, so essential for industrial development, was also created, since the same canals and railroads that carried agricultural output eastward served just as well to transport manufactured goods westward.

Relying on the tariff when distance alone was insufficient to reserve the market for them, American merchants turned in ever growing numbers to manufacturing, drawing upon Europe for technology and for workers. In the prosperous years between 1845 and 1873, the new manufacturing techniques could barely keep pace with the growth of demand. With the barriers to entry into business still relatively low, a new class of men with origins outside the dominant commercial and landowning classes flocked to take advantage of the burgeoning opportunities, their number creating what would later be regarded as "the golden age" of competition. After 1873, with supply capacity clearly having overtaken demand, this new class found it increasingly difficult to survive in business. The stage was thus set for the corporate revolution at the end of the nineteenth century.

Changes of this magnitude obviously affected the norms of business competition and cooperation. At first the effect was slight, as merchants continued to dominate a business community that was still largely preoccupied with the problems of commerce. As in the colonial period, local loyalties (now attached to the emerging manufacturing and distribution centers of the interior, such as Chicago, St. Louis, and New Orleans, as well as to the older seaboard cities) restricted the full exercise of independent business judgment. Price competition, for example, would be countenanced in "external" markets, but not in local ones. In addition, the obligation to community would be invoked to keep merchants and manufacturers in line. An expression of this urban loyalty can be seen in the following plea of the early 1850's by Job Tyson, urging Philadelphians to regain from New York City their lost prominence in foreign commerce:

> As individuals we are connected with the community in which we live by a thousand ligaments, which none but a sojourner with his property and hopes at a distance can repudiate or sever. The merchant of Philadelphia who employs his capital or shipping in New York, like him who imports his merchandise into that metropolis, acts in forgetfulness of an original duty to himself and his neighbor (Hartz, 1948).

Enlarging the flow of commerce at the expense of some rival city became the primary goal of the merchant groups after 1815. The first consequence was the establishment of a transportation network of rivers, canals, roads, and railroads. New York led the way as it triumphed during the decade after 1815 in its race with Philadelphia for leadership in foreign commerce. It achieved its goal by exploiting its superior position in the so-called cotton triangle—which joined New York as the American entrepôt of trade with the southern cotton ports and English manufacturing centers—and by its timely tapping of a large hinterland market with completion of the Erie Canal in 1825.

As New York swept forward, the merchants of other cities strained to keep abreast. The mercantile community of Philadelphia, caught between Baltimore and New York, persuaded the Pennsylvania legislature to build a canal-inclined railway route to parallel the Erie Canal in New York and to resist completion of water and rail throughways that would improve the access of Baltimore to the western counties of the Keystone State and the growing metropolis of Pittsburgh.

Similar struggles took place in the West. Steam navigation on the inland rivers had brought St. Louis dominance over the Ohio River cities of Cincinnati and Louisville. St. Louis merchants soon discovered that the spread of a transportation network compelled unending vigilance to protect established positions. Overconfident in its reliance on steam navigation of the Mississippi, St. Louis ignored until too late the rail expansion by Chicago into the Old Northwest. After Chicago promoters had completed the Rock Island bridge in 1856 (which spanned the Mississippi, connecting Rock Island, Illinois, with a rail terminal at Davenport, Iowa), the vast corn, hog, lead, and lumber produce of the upper Mississippi flowed increasingly to the shores of Lake Michigan and thence eastward to Atlantic railheads at New York and Philadelphia, instead of down the river to New Orleans via St. Louis. Thus intercity trade rivalries, long a feature of the American economy, were qualitatively altered by technological innovations in internal transportation.

Sedentary merchant activity had marked the pre-1815 period, and commercial rivalries between cities had been relatively genteel affairs. The low-volume, slow-paced, personalized handling of generic products for the domestic market had generated little excitement. Whatever "cutthroat" competition occurred had been restricted to overseas markets, such as beating someone else's vessel to a remote port.

During the 1820's the tempo changed as the internal market grew. Although the intrafamilial pattern of business connections still persisted in some cases, the sheer size of the new nation in both population and geographic extent militated against the predominance of family or coreligionist business relationships. There were too many merchants, too many markets, too many new products, to rely on personal institutions such as family, church, or friendships. The older forms of informal cooperation among merchants in credit checking, for example, increasingly became impersonal with the growth of specialized credit firms.

The specialization of function continued as the complexity of commercial life increased. The limited size of merchant partnerships proved inadequate to cope with the volume of the developing regional and national commerce. As Glenn Porter and Harold Livesay suggest, the reluctance of merchants to abandon older partnership and limited business organizational forms forced them to restrict the scope of their activities by specializing. General merchants became retailers or wholesalers of a single product or group of products, or concentrated their energy and capital on banking, investment, manufacturing, or insurance. This, in turn, led to increased price competition within the newly specialized product lines, since price (along with the quality of service) alone distinguished one seller's offerings from those of another. But the greater specialization on the part of businessmen was not the only factor promoting increased price competition.

The interurban rivalry, spurred by mercantile interests, had produced a transportation network that helped create a domestic market of continental proportions. This tempting prize loosened the ties of the new manufacturing group to the local merchant community and thus relaxed the traditional constraints on independent business behavior. Increasingly, it was the actions of his rivals in distant cities, and not the day-to-day social interaction with other businessmen from the same city, that shaped the behavioral norms of the manufacturer trying to survive in the newly created national, or at least regional, market. Freed from the conservatism of the sedentary merchants, manufacturers plunged into a new competitive order.

During the period of secular prosperity, from 1845 to 1873, the effect of this new freedom was barely discernible. Indeed, the merchants at first continued to dominate the distribution system, using that control to bend the new manufacturing class to their established ways. For example, it was wholesale merchants who, during the panic of 1857, prevailed upon the manufacturers of iron boiler plate along the Schuylkill River to abandon their vows of price maintenance in the face of declining demand. The manufacturers had preferred to shut down their works rather than lower their prices, but the merchants, as providers of credit, insisted that the more traditional mercantile response to a glutted market be followed.

After 1873, as the supply capacity of the new manufacturing industries finally overtook the growing demand and the economy became subject to pronounced cyclical movements, the traditional response to depressed business conditions—the lowering of price—no longer served to bring the desired relief. This was especially true in the high-volume, advanced-technology industries. With such a large proportion of their total costs being relatively fixed in nature, the lowering of price in the face of falling or depressed demand served only to erode whatever equity interests this group of manufacturers might have in their own plants. (That is, the fixed costs soon exceeded earnings, with a consequent decline in value of ownership shares in the enterprise itself.) Tutored by the merchants to lower their prices, yet lacking the cohesion as a national group necessary for limiting the process, those trapped by their investments in these industries found that the unrestrained competition among them threatened to destroy them as a social class. It was at this point, using techniques first employed by the railroads and later by John D. Rockefeller and J. P. Morgan in industry, that manufacturers began evolving a new pattern of cooperative behavior, resulting in what may be termed the "corporate revolution." This development unfolded at the same time that the mercantile community worked to make the markets for the growing agricultural surplus, together with those manufactured products that did not involve high-volume, advanced technology, conform even more closely to the model of "perfect competition."

As early as the completion of the major east-west trunk lines (the Pennsylvania, Baltimore and Ohio, Erie, and New York Central), railroads sought to restrain both price and nonprice competition. The New York Central, the Erie, four western roads, and a Great Lakes steamship company had agreed in 1853 on rates to be charged on western through freight. The following year the general superintendents of the eastern trunk lines met at the St. Nicholas Hotel in New York. They denounced the use of free passes (as a form of unfair nonprice competition) and of commission agents who acted as "runners," presumably attracting business by unethical lures. They also agreed to set up a clearinghouse for rate and other business information, and urged state legislatures to pass laws to uphold the legality of rate contracts. Similar meetings were held among the northwestern roads in October 1854 and among southern companies in March 1855. Tenuous as these agreements were, they were better than nothing, according to John Murray Forbes, president of the Michigan Central Railroad, who observed that his competitors "will cheat but we can stand a great deal of cheating better than competition."

Cooperation was promoted by the newly emerged professional managers of the railroads. Alfred D. Chandler, Jr., lists thirteen professional organizations of railroad men (ranging from the American Society of Railroad Superintendents to the Society of Railroad Comptrollers, Accountants, and Auditors), which by the 1880's bespoke a new type of business group. Previously, as seen during the colonial period, businessmen gathered together as fellow city merchants, usually to promote trade for their urban locality and its trading hinterland. But specialization of function and nationalization of market had made the earlier informal business grouping typified by the chambers of commerce less useful. Now, as in the case of the railroads, businessmen would increasingly meet in national association, with membership defined by function rather than by urban location. On technical matters these professions cooperated readily: Railroad agreements were achieved on standardization of time through the creation of time zones (1883), of gauge (1886), of accounting procedures (1887), and of automatic couplers and air brakes (1893).

But technical cooperation was one thing; agreements on prices or rates, another—especially in the face of falling demand. The depression beginning in 1873 completely undermined voluntary cooperative action on rates. For a decade and more, there followed a period of unrestricted competition in prices and rates that once and for all convinced businessmen that such competition was to be avoided at all cost.

The perils of unrestricted competition brought two responses from rail leaders after 1874. The first was support for government intervention via regulatory commissions—such as the Interstate Commerce Commission (ICC) in 1887. That support, divided and offered somewhat reluctantly at first, became warmer after 1887, when managers saw that the ICC was to be staffed by friendly regulators.

In some ways the railroad managers' second anticompetition tactic was even more important. They sought to expand their lines by merger and by laying more track in order to ensure continuation of their long-term growth. As Chandler shows, the professional railroad managers (in contrast with the owners) were the force behind this tactic—which, by World War I, resulted in an overbuilt railroad network of some 260,000 miles. The main rail companies sought after 1873 to develop "self-sustaining systems" through "inter-territorial strategies." What emerged by 1900 was a series of huge rail systems, physically bloated in size but insulated nonetheless from ruinous rate competition. For railroads, the failure of voluntary cartels and the uncertainties of governmental regulation ultimately led to consolidation. Unrestricted competition, characterized by rate wars, had existed for only a brief period.

The efforts of the railroads to limit competition were emulated in manufacturing—with a lag, and with important differences. John D. Rockefeller led the way. In 1870 the two refineries of the Standard Oil Company in Cleveland accounted for only about 10 percent of the national oil output. Within three years, through the exchange of stock, preferential rail rates, rebates, and other tactics that the Supreme Court would eventually condemn, Rockefeller and his associates had succeeded in extending their control to 90 percent of the industry. The conquest was not a case of megalomania, but the antidote to a condition best described by Rockefeller's biographer, Allan Nevins:

> When competition drove prices below production costs the big firms could not resort to a temporary shutdown. Their overhead, their interest on investment, their charges for maintenance automatically continued. These were heavy costs; to avoid bankruptcy the big establishment was forced to carry on even at a loss, selling at low rates to cover *part* of its expenses.

COMPETITION

It might be forced to do so for years, and come to bankruptcy after all. Thousands would be ruined, tens of thousands thrown out of work. Then the whole cycle would perhaps repeat itself.

Responding to the long-term trend after 1873 of depressed prices, Rockefeller, like the managers of the railroads, first sought to stabilize conditions by working through trade associations (such as the National Refiners' Association) and other cooperative ventures, such as the South Improvement Company. When those schemes failed, he turned to consolidation, via the trust and the holding company. This culminated in the formation of the mammoth Standard Oil (New Jersey) in 1892.

What Rockefeller did in oil, J. P. Morgan performed in steel and Henry O. Havemeyer managed in sugar. A ten-year burst of merger activity beginning in 1895 signaled the end of the brief period of intense rate and price competition among capital-intensive, high-volume industries. The deep insecurities of unrestricted price competition and independent corporate behavior had to be moderated, if not totally eliminated, if the capital invested in those industries was to be protected.

Andrew Carnegie's role in the steel industry illustrates the point. Carnegie was almost obsessed with the need to pare down production costs in order to consolidate the hold that his concern had on the market for steel rails created by the "system building" strategies of the railroads. Carnegie, of course, succeeded superbly in that cost-slashing technique. He rarely turned down the chance to lower production costs, even if it involved a heavy initial investment that would make recently installed equipment obsolete. His success, however, generated continuing insecurity. The more Carnegie's corporation managed to enlarge its hold on the rapidly expanding market for steel rails or railroad bridge supports, the more vulnerable the company became. High-volume, low-unit-cost output required access to correspondingly high-volume, low-cost raw materials and means of transportation. It also required an assured market or, failing that, the ability to maintain prices in the face of falling demand.

Ultimately, to assure access to low-cost raw materials, Carnegie took the step of integrating under one corporate entity the iron ore ranges, the coal and limestone deposits, the Great Lakes steamships, the feeder rail lines, the iron smelters and foundries, and the steel furnaces and rolling mills needed for the production of steel rails. This vertical integration did little to stabilize prices. If anything, by increasing the pressure to maintain high-volume production in order to keep the entire range of facilities operating efficiently, it made the problem worse. Not until J. P. Morgan stepped into the picture and in 1901 merged not only Carnegie's company but also all the other fully integrated steel producers into the giant United States Steel Corporation was the problem of price stabilization finally dealt with effectively. A primary reason for buying out Carnegie was, of course, the desire to be rid of the Scotsman and his penchant for price warfare.

The natural thrust of the corporate revolution was toward monopoly, at least in the technologically advanced, mass-volume sector of manufacturing. Still, two conditions served to prevent that goal from being fully realized. First, the pace of industrial development might be said to have exceeded the capacity of current management resources and organizational forms to keep pace. For example, Standard Oil (New Jersey) managed in effect to monopolize both the eastern petroleum resources of the Appalachian field and the newer ones of the Lima-Indiana field. But even with the inspired legal stratagems of trusts and holding companies, Standard could not keep up with the enormous expansion of oil resources begun when the huge Gulf Coast fields were opened in 1901. By 1911 Standard controlled only 78 percent of the crude oil produced in the Appalachian fields, down from the 92 percent handled in 1880. In significant contrast to 1880, Standard Oil as the industry's largest firm in 1911 controlled only 10 percent of the Gulf Coast, 44 percent of the midcontinent, 83 percent of the Illinois, and 29 percent of the California fields. Its share of refinery capacity had meanwhile slipped from 90–95 percent in 1880 to 64 percent in 1911.

The trend toward monopoly also was blunted by the political reactions to the merger movement. If corporate mergers were often occasioned by businessmen's deepening fears of extinction by ruinous price competition, the mergers themselves evoked a host of fears in others, concerns that often radiated from a heightened consumer awareness. Farmers, emerging as a commercial class, perceived the new business combination as unresponsive to the agricultural producers' need for lower prices of manufactured goods, transportation, and commodity-handling services. Wholesale merchants saw their power over manufacturers being eroded by the coming of the large industrial corporations, which increasingly and successfully sought to bypass merchants in their restless quest for direct access to mass markets. Workers feared that the large combinations would prove to be even less interested in the needs of employees than small businesses had been. And small businessmen, retail merchants, bankers, lawyers, publicists, and other urban professionals added their voices to the growing alarm over the corporate revolution.

This uneasy coalition was translated into political success before World War I by the Populist and Progressive parties. The national administrations of Theodore Roosevelt and of his successors William Howard Taft and Woodrow Wilson proved receptive to the various consumer and "blocked entry" interests. Beginning with Roosevelt's celebrated authorization of antitrust proceedings under the Sherman Act against the Northern Securities Company, leading to the dissolution of that company in 1904, the national government sought to halt the movement toward monopolization. Indictments were sought over the next sixteen years: successfully against Standard Oil (New Jersey) (broken into thirty-four parts in 1911) and the American Tobacco Company (dissolved in 1911 into sixteen parts); with partial success in the cases of International Harvester, Armour, Swift, Corn Products Refining, and E. I. Du Pont, each of which was forced to sell portions of its operations; and unsuccessfully with regard to United States Steel, American Sugar Refining, Aluminum Company of America, and General Electric.

The antimonopoly movement, fueled in part by misplaced nostalgia for a former "golden age" of competition, might well have continued to develop even greater momentum had not World War I intervened. The European war reversed the tide of feeling against big business in the United States. The need to finance and supply the war needs, first of the Anglo-French coalition, then of the United States itself by 1917, made cooperation, not competition, the dominant value. After a slow organizational start, the War Industries Board (WIB), set up in July 1917, began to act vigorously under the chairmanship of Bernard M. Baruch to overcome supply bottlenecks. At one point Baruch threatened the steel industry with government takeover if its leaders failed to agree on set prices. Baruch and his WIB associates persuaded businessmen to effect drastic changes in production, personnel, and pricing policies in order to make the industrial sector efficient in turning out goods. In some cases mergers were encouraged. In other cases the WIB insisted upon cooperation in standardizing output and upon other measures that aided the drive for greater output. All of this contributed significantly to the war effort. Hugh Johnson, one of Baruch's WIB associates, said: "If cooperation can do so much, maybe there is something wrong with the old competitive system."

The war had ended the momentum of the antitrust movement, the last threat to the corporate revolution. It is difficult to see, however, that the movement could have proceeded much further in any event. Monopoly could perhaps be barred, but oligopoly could not be averted. In fact, oligopoly served the needs of business well enough. Control of markets by a few large firms was sufficient to curtail price competition and bar the entry of new firms. At the same time, it did not draw the political wrath that outright monopoly invited.

THE MODERN PERIOD

With the Supreme Court decision in the steel case in 1920 signaling the final political acceptance of the corporate revolution, the American economy soon settled down to a pattern of cooperative and independent business behavior. The most striking feature of the new economic order was the sharp contrast between the technologically advanced industries, organized in large bureaucratic corporations and oligopolistic market structures, and the rest of business enterprise, which still, for the most part, took a proprietary or unincorporated form. Within the former group of industries—universally recognized as constituting the center or "core" of the economy—competition over prices was generally held in check as the interfirm rivalry took new and increasingly more sophisticated forms. Only in those industries that, for one reason or another, had escaped consolidation at the turn of the century was competition over prices still a significant part of the everyday business dynamic, overshadowing other forms of independent business behavior.

But even in the latter sectors of the economy, businessmen sought whatever protection against price competition the shifting political climate and market conditions afforded. Given the new pattern of business behavior, one might expect the competitive ethic that had evolved during the nineteenth century to have undergone drastic change. Yet, for various reasons, Americans—businessmen, consumers, and intellectuals alike—seemed unwilling either to abandon or to modify it. Indeed, the ethic itself was the most significant cultural survival from the earlier, albeit brief, way of doing business—a curiosity seemingly above any and all criticism.

With the economy in 1919 poised between periods of major merger activity, it was finally possible to get a clear picture of the changes wrought by the corporate revolution. These changes were, of course, concentrated within the manufacturing sector. The transportation sector, having experienced the same metamorphosis much earlier, was undergoing a transformation of quite a different sort as a result of increasing regulation by the federal and state governments. Indeed, in 1919 the federal government was debating whether to return the railroads, nationalized as an emergency war measure, to private management. The public utilities sector, still relatively new, would fall increasingly under government regulation in the decades to come. Mining, meanwhile, had become largely the satellite of the manufacturing industries, for which it provided essential material inputs. As for the financial sector, its concentrated nature and key role in the changes taking place in the economy were well known. This left only agriculture, construction, retail and wholesale trade, and services untouched by the corporate revolution—although the rise of Montgomery Ward, Sears Roebuck, A & P, and the other mass retailers was not an insignificant development.

Within manufacturing, Alfred Chandler's data clearly reveal the bifurcation that had occurred. On the one hand there were the major industry groupings—machinery, primary metals, and others—in which 20 percent or more of the value added was accounted for by industries that were clearly oligopolistic in structure. These eight industry groupings, listed in table 1, formed the oligopolistic core of the manufacturing sector. They also accounted for 138 of the 234 manufacturing corporations having $20 million in assets in 1917. On the other hand there were the major industry groupings—furniture, leather, apparel, and others—in which oligopoly had still not made significant inroads. These eleven industry groupings were all that remained of a manufacturing sector in which large numbers of small firms competing independently among themselves had once been the general rule.

Over the next half-century what remained of the nineteenth-century industrial structure shrank even further. By 1917 the large corporation was found in significant numbers within the transportation equipment and chemicals groups; before the end of the next decade, those two types of industries clearly fell within the oligopolistic sector. Other industry groups, or parts of them, made the shift still later. Here William G. Shepherd's data for 1966, somewhat reworked to make them comparable with Chandler's, are instructive. By the latter date only the furniture, leather, lumber, and apparel industry groups were still relatively free of oligopolistic market structures, with printing, textiles, paper, and perhaps even fabricated metals in the marginal category. Despite the secular change in relative proportions, the basic division of the manufacturing sector into oligopolistic and nonoligopolistic components remained.

Outside the oligopolistic core, the pattern of cooperative and independent behavior has changed little from what it was during the heyday of nineteenth-century atomistic competition. Time horizons have remained short, with the emphasis on earning the largest possible return for the individuals directly involved in the ownership and management of the firms. For the most part this has entailed little more than trying to sell as much output as possible at prevailing prices, while keeping costs at a minimum. When the demand has been strong, the decision makers in these industries have not been loath to seek a better price, just as they have not hesitated to cut the price when the demand has been weak. Cooperation, to the extent that it has occurred at

COMPETITION

TABLE 1
Shifts Between Competitive and Oligopolistic Industries, 1919–1966

SIC No.	Industry	Percent of 1966 Value Added in Manufacturing	Percent of Product Value Produced in Oligopolistic Industries 1919	1966
Competitive				
25	Furniture	1.6	0	0
31	Leather	1.0	1	1.4
24	Lumber and wood	1.9	1	2.3
23	Apparel	3.7	1	3.0
22	Textiles	3.2	1	10.6
26	Paper	3.8	2	13.8
Shifted				
34	Fabricated metals	6.4	3	25.0
27	Printing and publishing	5.4	1	45.4
37	Transport equipment	11.8	3	86.7
32	Stone, clay, glass	3.4	5	70.5
28	Chemicals	9.2	9	77.0
Oligopolistic				
35	Machinery	10.9	20	42.6
20	Food	10.1	28	37.0
36	Electrical machinery	9.5	40	50.8
33	Primary metals	8.5	40	74.0
29	Petroleum	1.9	44	86.7
38	Instruments	2.6	48	50.5
30	Rubber	2.5	69	32.4
21	Tobacco	0.8	80	84.6
		98.23		

Sources: 1919 product value based on Chandler, *The Visible Hand,* table E; 1966 product value based on Shepherd, *Market Power and Economic Welfare,* table 7.2. Industries are classified as competitive on the basis of a concentration ratio of 60 percent or better for four-digit industry subgroupings.
Note: Miscellaneous industries, accounting for 1.7 percent of value added in manufacturing in 1966, are excluded.

all, has usually been confined to areas other than price setting.

Two of those areas have been government relations and collective bargaining. In both cases the need for cooperation has been underlined by the changes in political economy associated with the New Deal. Before 1932 the main things sought by small businessmen from government were (1) some toleration of the fledgling trade association movement, especially for its more cartellike aspects; and (2) continuing tariff protection for those industries that could benefit from it. On the labor front small businessmen, like corporate officials, counted on the government to do nothing to aid workers in their struggle to organize. In fact, they expected the power of government to be used to enforce the right of employers to bring in other workers if their laborers went out on strike.

During the Great Depression it became clear that, at least as an emergency measure, the traditional role of the government in the economy would have to be modified. Initially, when the government acted, through the National Industrial Recovery Act (NIRA), to give trade associations the right to enforce price-fixing and other types of cooperative agreements, it seemed the answer to small businessmen's prayers. It was only later, when the downward spiral of prices was finally arrested, that, on the basis of their own calculus, small businessmen finally concluded that the benefits from the extraordinary power they had been given to regulate themselves was not worth the accompanying interference from government officials. The fact that the NIRA codes frequently benefited certain segments of the industry, usually the larger or better-organized ones, at the expense of others added to the discontent. It was hardly surprising that a relatively small kosher poultry business in New York City proved to be the legal undoing of the NIRA when, charged with violating the poultry code, it brought a suit that led the Supreme Court to declare the law itself unconstitutional.

Where possible, the price-stabilizing features not only of the NIRA but also of the Agricultural Adjustment Act (AAA) were salvaged from the wreckage of adverse Supreme Court rulings. The Interstate Oil Compact (1935), by permitting the states to set limits on the amount of oil brought out of the ground (in the name of conservation), preserved for petroleum producers the protection they had previously had under the NIRA. The Robinson-Patman Act (1936), in sanctioning state fair-trade laws, did the same for retailers. Motor carriers found shelter from the gales of competition in an amendment to the Interstate Commerce Commission Act bringing them under the regulatory umbrella of that agency. And the commodity support programs and marketing orders under the revised AAA afforded similar protection to the largest group of small businessmen, American farmers. While not every industry benefited from these and other measures, it was clear, even before World War II, that the relationship between business and government had been fundamentally altered. The struggle with the Axis Powers and the subsequent Cold War experience only confirmed the need for persons in business, small as well as large, to keep a close eye on what was happening in Washington.

Although some companies have preferred an independent approach, whether with their elected representatives on Capitol Hill or with the executive departments at the other end of Pennsylvania Avenue, most firms, especially the smaller ones, have found that only a common lobbying effort is likely to give them an effective voice in the halls of government. The result has been the establishment of one industry trade association after another with offices in Washington and a full-time staff able to maintain continuing and close contacts with key officials. Government relations is not the only area where smaller companies have found themselves forced to join forces with one another as a result of the changes brought about by the New Deal. The Wagner Act (1935), building on Section 7a of the NIRA, put the weight of the government behind the principles of collective bargaining. In the new climate thus created in industrial relations, smaller companies soon realized that they had no chance in negotiations with powerful national trade unions, except by organizing themselves into industry groupings. Yet, as important as these two areas of cooperation have become, they have hardly made any difference in the day-to-day behavior observable in the industries outside the oligopolistic core of the American economy. In these remnants of the more competitive nineteenth-century industrial structure, firms still generally act independently, especially with respect to price setting.

Within the oligopolistic sector, the pattern of cooperation and independent behavior has evolved in new and quite different ways. The recognized interdependence of the large corporations in the industries that form the sector, usually resulting in some form of price leadership, has freed the top management of those companies from any need to concern themselves with sales and prices in the short run, thus enabling them to concentrate instead on long-term investment strategy. Indeed, it is primarily through investment that the contemporary large corporation, or megacorp, competes. In this sense competition can be said to have been raised to a higher plane. Initially competition among large firms centered on the acquisition of raw materials, the establishment of distribution systems, and other forms of vertical integration essential for preserving a firm's relative market share and perhaps even increasing its hold on the industry. Later these competitive strategies declined in importance relative to advertising and other forms of sales promotion, as well as to research and development. Still, the objective has been the same throughout—to protect the share of a growing market controlled by a firm while making it as difficult as possible for new firms to enter the industry.

COMPETITION

Even so, the megacorp found its own fortunes closely linked to those of its industry. Experience soon demonstrated that every industry, no matter how basic to the functioning of the economy it may appear to be, is likely to have its own life cycle of rapid growth, maturity, and decline. To avoid stagnating with the industry that had originally given it its start, the megacorp learned that it had to master the technique of diversification, of expanding into other industries that, while somewhat related technologically, nonetheless offered better prospects of future growth. Alfred Chandler, Jr., and Stephen Salsbury have described the difficulty with which the Du Pont Company, facing an inevitable decline in gunpowder sales after World War I, made the transition to supplying more general chemical products, thereby becoming one of the world's first megacorps with a conscious strategy of diversification. In the period following World War II, the diversification strategy became a more common one for megacorps, the technique being refined so that expansion was no longer limited to industries with a similar technology. Indeed, the culmination to this line of development came with the emergence of the conglomerates in the 1960's—megacorps that had the combined characteristics of a holding company and a miniature planned economy. At the heart of this latest form of business organization was a central staff prepared to commit resources to any industry with above-average growth prospects, by acquiring smaller companies and/or by forming additional quasi-autonomous divisions.

In pursuing their independent investment strategies after World War II, megacorps succeeded in transcending the limits not only of the industries that had originally spawned them but also of the national market in which they had first prospered. Overseas expansion by megacorps had, of course, occurred much earlier. Indeed, the consolidations that took place at the turn of the century often involved companies with substantial operations abroad. Still, the overseas expansion after 1945 was different in two ways—at least in degree. Whereas the primary motivation for operations in other countries had previously been the desire to obtain control over raw materials, now the main objective was to tap the markets created by rising incomes in western Europe and the former British dominions. Moreover, whereas foreign sales previously were largely a spillover from domestic American operations, now sales in overseas markets were made increasingly by subsidiaries. The subsidiaries had their roots firmly in the local economy, except for the business techniques employed, the selection of top management, and perhaps the name.

The process had begun when American firms found the repatriation of earnings blocked by currency restrictions and the Common Market threatening to impose prohibitive tariffs. American firms then decided to build plants in Europe. Later, as the sales there and in other parts of the globe began to rival those in the domestic American market, the overseas divisions began to occupy a more prominent position within the corporate structure. While it is hazardous to project into the future, it would not be surprising if, one day, the American division were to become just one of several regional divisions reporting to the central headquarters of what has become a truly multinational enterprise, one that favors no single national market over another except insofar as it offers differential prospects for growth. This would simply be a replay of what happened during the latter half of the nineteenth century, when the manufacturing firm outgrew its orientation to a particular urban commercial center and became a truly national enterprise.

Even though the American economy continues to be dominated by megacorps that have evolved into conglomerate, multinational enterprises, the intellectual perspective from which these developments are viewed continues to reflect the objective conditions of a bygone era. Economics, the academic discipline most directly concerned, has persisted in specifying models of the economy in which price competition is the operative dynamic. Although it is sometimes grudgingly conceded that markets fall far short of the competitive conditions assumed in the models, this fact is viewed as an imperfection of the real world rather than of the models upon which economists rely. Not being able to specify any effective means of social control over business in the absence of competitive markets, economists have preferred to turn their eyes away from the reality of modern oligopolistic industry. Other social scientists, unsure of their competence to deal with economic phenomena, have so far failed to provide any alternative paradigm. Indeed, they are likely to view the absence

COMPETITION

of price competition with the same misgivings as their colleagues in economics.

With those who specialize in intellectual matters unable to shake off old preconceptions, it is hardly surprising that businessmen and consumers have responded no better to the emergence of the conglomerate, multinational megacorp. For the surviving small businessmen, the megacorp is clearly anticompetitive in the sense that they understand competition: the freedom of any individual to start and prosper in a business of his own. Even though the megacorp has preempted the most profitable lines of business activity, smaller firms regard it ambiguously. In many cases the megacorp is a key customer or supplier of the small businessman. And even when it is not, there is still the hope that some conglomerate, as part of its expansion effort, will buy the small company and thus assure its owners a carefree retirement.

For the managerial group that has supplanted the independent businessmen as the key decision makers within the economy, competition has largely become an argument to be used against any further government encroachment on their powers. Corporate executives insist that despite the changes in their company's size and relative market position, their companies are still controlled by the same market forces as their nineteenth-century predecessors were. It is just that, instead of competing by undercutting the prices of rivals, they now compete by matching the prices of other firms. In any case, it is competition, both the price and nonprice forms, that holds the behavior of the megacorp in check, obviating the need for any outside interference. While the argument runs counter to that of most economists, it nonetheless serves the same purpose—helping to bury the issue of adequate social control over the megacorp.

As for consumers, always a group difficult to organize politically, they have been left especially impotent by the lack of any program that would offer effective recourse against the ability of the megacorp to raise prices continuously and thus perpetuate the wage-price inflationary process that has been so prominent a feature of the post–World War II economy. The dream of a return to a golden age of competition remains unshaken by the continued failure of antitrust policy to make even a modest first step in that direction. If competition is a bitter joke to the small businessmen, and an argument against further government interference to the corporate executive, to the consuming public it is a hope still to be fulfilled, promising deliverance from the continued rise in prices that steadily erodes its standard of living.

Thus, even though the golden age of competition has long since given way to the corporate revolution, the competitive ethic from that earlier era still survives, a cultural relic that gives little evidence of diminishing its hold on the minds of Americans. It is only when that competitive ethic is viewed against the broad sweep of American history that its recentness and, at the same time, its outdatedness become evident.

BIBLIOGRAPHY

Robert G. Albion, *The Rise of New York Port, 1815–1860* (New York, 1939), provides a view of interurban rivalry from the perspective of New York City. Bernard Bailyn, *The New England Merchants in the Seventeenth Century* (Cambridge, Mass., 1955), is the best account of the New England merchants during the early colonial period. Wyatt W. Belcher, *The Economic Rivalry Between St. Louis and Chicago, 1850–1880* (New York, 1947), is a generally overlooked work on interurban rivalry in the Midwest. Carl Bridenbaugh, *Cities in the Wilderness. The First Century of Urban Life in America, 1625–1742* (New York, 1938), gives the view of colonial merchants from an urban perspective. Stuart W. Bruchey, *Robert Oliver, Merchant of Baltimore, 1783–1819* (Baltimore, 1956), is a case study of a leading Maryland merchant, typical of the middle colonies group. Alfred D. Chandler, Jr., *Strategy and Structure: Chapters in the History of Industrial Enterprise* (Cambridge, Mass., 1962), is the work that marks the beginning of the institutional approach to the historical study of the modern corporation; and *The Visible Hand* (Cambridge, Mass., 1977), the latest and most comprehensive study of the emergence of the modern corporation, likely to stand as the definitive work on the subject for years to come. Alfred D. Chandler, Jr., and Stephen Salsbury, *Pierre S. DuPont and the Making of the Modern Corporation* (New York, 1971), a biography that throws important light on the growth of management techniques and the movement toward diversification. Thomas C. Cochran, *Railroad Leaders, 1845–1890. The Business Mind in Action* (Cambridge, Mass., 1953), examines the issues that concerned railroad executives and financiers, based on their own written records.

Donald Dewey, *Monopoly in Economics and Law* (Chicago, 1959), a good survey, with some attention to history, of the antitrust laws. Alfred S. Eichner, *The Emergence of Oligopoly, Sugar Refining as a Case Study* (Baltimore, 1969; Westport, Conn., 1979), an interpretation of the consolidation movement, focuses on the sugar industry and emphasizes the desire to control prices; and *The Megacorp and Oligopoly, Micro*

COMPETITION

Foundations of Macro Dynamics (New York, 1976), a theoretical treatment of the modern corporation, with particular emphasis on its economic role. Louis Galambos, *Competition and Cooperation: The Emergence of a National Trade Association* (Baltimore, 1966), is a valuable study of the efforts to deal with the problems of competition in the textile industry. Virginia D. Harrington, *The New York Merchant on the Eve of the Revolution* (New York, 1935), is a major source of information on merchant behavior in the 1770's. Louis Hartz, *Economic Policy and Democratic Thought: Pennsylvania, 1776–1860* (Cambridge, Mass., 1948), a critical work for understanding the role of the state in early American economic development. Ellis W. Hawley, *The New Deal and the Problem of Monopoly* (Princeton, 1966), the best single study of the policies of the Roosevelt administration toward industrial concentration.

William Letwin, *Law and Economic Policy in America* (New York, 1965), a very useful history of antitrust prosecution during the Progressive era. Harold C. Livesay, *Andrew Carnegie and the Rise of Big Business* (Boston, 1975), the most recent, and best, biography of the steel magnate. Paul McNulty, "Economic Theory and the Meaning of Competition," *Quarterly Journal of Economics*, 82 (Nov. 1968), an essay pointing out that, until relatively recently, competition was simply taken for granted by economists. Richard B. Morris, "Labor and Mercantilism in the Revolutionary Era," in *The Era of the American Revolution*, Richard B. Morris, ed. (New York, 1939), is a useful summary of economic attitudes during the late colonial period. Allan Nevins, *Study in Power. John D. Rockefeller, Industrialist and Philanthropist*, 2 vols. (New York, 1953), is the classic biography of the key figure in the consolidation of the petroleum industry. Norman Pollack, *The Populist Response to Industrial America. Midwestern Populist Thought* (New York, 1962), a sympathetic interpretation of the Populists, emphasizes the reasonableness of their analysis of industrial America. Glenn Porter, *The Rise of Big Business, 1860–1910* (New York, 1973), a good survey and synthesis of the literature on the corporate revolution. Glenn Porter and Harold C. Livesay, *Merchants and Manufacturers: Studies in the Changing Structure of Nineteenth-Century Marketing* (Baltimore, 1971), a singular examination of the merchants' role in the industrialization process.

Joseph A. Schumpeter, *History of Economic Analysis* (New York, 1954), is the most comprehensive survey of economic theory through the ages. William G. Shepherd, *Market Power and Economic Welfare* (New York, 1970), is the best available empirical study of the extent of oligopoly in the contemporary American economy. Robert Sobel, *The Age of Giant Corporations. A Microeconomic History of American Business, 1914–1970* (Westport, Conn., 1972), is a good general survey of twentieth-century developments in connection with the modern corporation. George Rogers Taylor, *The Transportation Revolution, 1815–1860* (New York, 1951), is still the best single account of transportation developments during the first half of the nineteenth century. Robert H. Wiebe, *Businessmen and Reform. A Study of the Progressive Movement* (Cambridge, Mass., 1962), is a view of the Progressive period that stresses the reformist role of businessmen. Mira Wilkins, *The Emergence of Multinational Enterprise: American Business Abroad from the Colonial Era to 1914* (Cambridge, Mass., 1970); and *The Maturing of Multinational Enterprise: American Business Abroad from 1914 to 1970* (Cambridge, Mass., 1974), two volumes constituting the first source to consult on the history of multinational enterprise abroad, virtually the whole literature on the subject.

[*See also* AMERICAN BUSINESS INSTITUTIONS BEFORE THE RAILROAD; ANTITRUST; COLONIAL ECONOMY; ECONOMY FROM THE REVOLUTION TO 1815; ECONOMY FROM 1815 TO 1865; ECONOMY FROM RECONSTRUCTION TO 1914; ECONOMY SINCE 1914; LAW AND POLITICAL INSTITUTIONS; MANAGEMENT; MANUFACTURING; MARKETING; MERGERS; MULTINATIONAL ENTERPRISE; *and* RISE AND EVOLUTION OF BIG BUSINESS.]

ADVERTISING AND PUBLIC RELATIONS

Richard S. Tedlow

ADVERTISING AND PUBLIC RELATIONS are often spoken of as a unit. And, indeed, they have much in common. Both deal with interested communication, and both aim to persuade. Both are strongly associated in the public mind with big business, in the service of which they originated. But both are used by many large American institutions, as well as by some smaller ones, and even by such individuals as politicians and entertainers. In the development of both, relations with the media of mass communications have been of critical importance.

However, the differences between advertising and public relations historically and currently are sufficiently important that they will be considered in separate subsections. A leading marketing scholar, Philip Kotler, has defined advertising as "nonpersonal forms of communication conducted through paid media under clear sponsorship." (This definition is not altogether adequate in that it would seem to preclude public service messages appearing in donated space or time and advertisements placed by "third party" groups that mask the true sponsor. Nevertheless, it will serve as a generalization.) "In ultimate terms," Kotler comments, "advertising is undertaken to increase company sales and/or profits over what they otherwise would be."

Public relations, a term that does not even appear in the index to Kotler's well-known marketing text, may be defined as the controlling of news about an individual or organization by planned and organized effort, through informing and cultivating the press, through the composition of "image" or "institutional" advertisements, and/or through encouraging the corporation itself to alter its policies in accord with perceived public desires. (It should be pointed out that the news that public relations tries to control comprises not only such information as might reflect on the employer's image but also that dealing with his products.) The key clause in the above definition is the latter one. Public relations counselors have traditionally tried to differentiate their work from their less prestigious associates—press and publicity agents—by asserting that they can have genuine impact on the policymaking of a corporation. They have, to use their language, asserted that they work on a "two-way street," aiming their persuasion not only at the public but also, when called for, at their superiors in the organization.

These two definitions highlight the differing concerns of the vocations in question. As a generalization, their relations can be visualized in terms of two overlapping circles: one circle, representing image, is predominantly the concern of public relations; the other, representing sales, is the domain of advertising. Overlap occurs when paid advertising is used for image enhancement.

Although it is more convenient to treat these two vocations independently, there are certain noteworthy similarities. First, no understanding of either field can be achieved if one confines oneself to the business world. Both began as services to the private corporation, but both are now widely employed by nonprofit organizations. To cite just one example, the federal government was in 1977 the twenty-fourth largest national advertiser in America.

The fields must, furthermore, be placed in a cultural context. Advertising copy seeks to strike a "responsive chord" in prospective customers, so social mores obviously constitute an important determinant of the sales appeal. In addition, there are certain basic, ingrained ways of looking at the world that provide an underpinning for these practices. Advertising and public relations are, to state one obvious example, more likely to flourish in a society committed to persuasion, rather than force, as a means of bringing about consensus or change.

ADVERTISING

Prehistory. What is usually regarded as the first printed advertisement in English—a handbill by William Caxton for his *Salisburi pye*—was printed a decade and a half before Columbus' first voyage. Prior to the colonization of America, Britain had become perhaps the world's most advanced nation in advertising. Trade cards and store signs, as well as handbills, had developed as advertising media. In fact, these tools, in addition to pamphleteering and what are now called direct selling and word-of-mouth advertising, played an important role in luring settlers to America. Contemporary observers described London as being papered over with signs declaring the wonders of the New World. So intensive was this effort to "sell" America (by no means the last such endeavor) that Richard Hofstadter has observed that the nation was born amid "one of the first concerted and sustained advertising campaigns in the history of the modern world."

With this background, it is not surprising that advertising took root in the colonies. Newspapers here were edited and published by printers, most of whom were trained in London, to which they continued to look for leadership. Advertisements for a wide number of items, from patent medicines to slaves and indentured servants, were a part of the colonial press from the beginning. Certain leading eighteenth-century figures, especially Benjamin Franklin and the financier Haym Salomon, were among those making advances in advertising copy and graphics.

For the most part the craft lagged behind its counterpart in the mother country. From the point of view of appearance, advertising suffered from the quality of type available. Franklin remarked during the Revolutionary War that "If you should ever have any secrets that you wish to be well kept, get them printed in [the] Papers." As far as copy was concerned, neither the nature of the distribution system nor the fact that scarcity characterized the economy encouraged aggressive selling. Compared to the situation in England, newspaper advertising for patent medicines, for example, has been characterized as "singularly drab." These remedies were usually imported, and the apothecaries who sold them had no proprietary interest.

With certain exceptions, advertising continued to be undeveloped in the early national period. The nature of the mass media and the economy limited its usefulness. Had a reincarnated Johann Gutenberg visited an American printer's shop in 1800, he would not have been much surprised at what he saw. The printing process was still run by manual labor. With maximum effort, handpress operators could produce two hundred impressions per hour on one side of a sheet. Quality paper and type fonts were still in short supply. Some newspapers gave discounts of up to 85 percent to advertisers who published the same insertion, thus requiring no change in type, for a year. Spacious display of any kind was rare. Even with the introduction from 1814 to 1830 of presses that successively vastly increased output, it continued to behoove publishers to stuff as much information as possible onto each page. Advertising as well as editorial matter was shrunk to fit.

The United States in the early nineteenth century was a predominantly rural nation whose farmers, even if not self-sufficient, produced a wider variety of their needs themselves than do modern urban dwellers. When the shopper—the very term seems an anachronism—did pay a visit to a country store, he or she would not be met by shelves full of branded foods or other packaged goods. The retailer was usually able to buy goods of any producer through a wholesaler and then resell what he could. Almost without exception, manufacturers had not integrated forward into marketing, a process that presented enormous problems. The nation was vast and sparsely populated. The primitive transportation network rendered the delivery of goods difficult.

ADVERTISING AND PUBLIC RELATIONS

Knowledge of market conditions was minimal. Seller was linked to buyer by a panoply of middlemen—general merchants, commission merchants, factors, jobbers, agents, and finally the retailers themselves.

It was these middlemen who placed the bulk of the advertising, and their conception of what it could do was limited. In a sense, much advertising of the era was aimed at the goal advocated by modern social critics of the craft. Information was the major purpose. "The name and location of the store, a list of the goods carried in stock, and a brief statement of sales policy were generally given," wrote Lewis Atherton of the pioneer retailer on the middle border. "[B]eyond that the merchant saw little that could be accomplished by means of advertising."

It is this lack of vision that stands as the starkest contrast to advertising practice today. "Promise," Samuel Johnson wrote, "large promise is the soul of an advertisement." America itself had seemed to embody "large promise," and early publicity for it spared no exaggeration. Yet the advertisements internally produced, for the most part, were almost modest. There was little effort to arouse interest, to introduce new products or new uses for existing products, or, in short, to persuade.

Harbingers of changed times were, however, in evidence. The leading product group was patent medicines. By the beginning of the nineteenth century, many nostrums were locally produced rather than imported, and with that pride of ownership came the same boldness of claim characteristic of the Old World. The patent medicine maker was a pathbreaker in the creation of brand loyalty. According to James Harvey Young:

> The big-scale patent medicine maker, during the early decades of the nineteenth century, blazed a merchandising trail. He was the first American manufacturer to seek out a national market. He was the first producer [to go] direct to consumers with a message about the product. He was the first promoter to turn out a multitude of psychological lures by which people might be enticed to buy his wares. While other advertising in the press was drab, his was vivid; while other appeals were straightforward, his were devilishly clever [*The Toadstool Millionaires* (Princeton, 1972), p. 42].

Throughout the nineteenth century the influence of the marketing of patent medication on advertising was simply enormous. This constituted, to say the least, a dubious parentage; for most of these advertisements ran the gamut from the blatantly false to the subtly false. The advertising world has never completely lived down this heritage of untruth.

Two individuals deserve special attention as antebellum precursors of the impending transformation of advertising. One was a media manipulator and the other a media master: Phineas Taylor Barnum and James Gordon Bennett, Sr., respectively.

In the course of his raucous career as the premier nineteenth-century impresario, P. T. Barnum was second to none in attracting attention to his acts, exhibits, and museums, and to himself. He brought showmanship to advertising, announcing with shamelessly boastful hyperbole that what he offered was unique and fascinating beyond measure. He used advertising as a weapon aimed both at potential customers and at detractors. He challenged the public to dismiss the judgments of so-called experts and to determine for themselves whether his exhibits were "real or humbug." Without actually articulating the principle of "Reason Why" advertising, he prefigured Albert Lasker and Rosser Reeves by placing special emphasis on what was unique in his offerings. Although more than willing to lie outright to make his exhibits seem noteworthy, he managed to maneuver his customers into enjoying their amusement even while they were conscious of being deceived. The true secret of his success was that he had an instinctive understanding of the customer's habits and desires. Not only was Barnum an expert advertiser, he was unexcelled at what once was called the publicity stunt but today is often labeled the created, pseudo, or news event. He garnered column upon column of free publicity and should thus be considered a precursor not only of the advertising copywriter but of the public relations agent as well. Barnum was, in a word, a formidable publicist for publicity.

James Gorden Bennett, Sr., another important innovator, did not invent the tools he used. The establishment of the penny press in New York City in September 1833 preceded his *New York Herald* by less than two years, and the concept of using the printed word to speak to the mass public rather than merely to the elite dated at least to Thomas Paine. But Bennett combined what had come before him with a brilliant flair that made him a center of public attention and controversy for decades, and that helped make New York City the American communications capital. Just as Bennett anticipated Joseph Pulitzer with his sensationalism, sports reportage, and stunts, he also presaged modern advertising thought by insisting that advertising should be treated as news. In 1848, at a time when some papers were running the same notice for a year, Bennett initiated the policy of having advertisements rewritten every day. As Bennett's managing editor explained:

> The advertisements of the *Herald* are a feature. They are fresh every day.... On this plan the advertisements form the most interesting and practical "city news." They are the hopes, the thoughts, the joys, the plans, the shames, the losses, the mishaps, the fortunes, the pleasures, the miseries, the politics, and the religion of the people.... What a picture of the metropolis one day's advertisements in the *Herald* presents to mankind!

Another important innovation in the *Herald* was forced upon, rather than begun by, Bennett. Like other newspapermen, Bennett insisted that display in advertising be proscribed. All notices were to appear in agate type (about half the size of the type on this page) and in single columns. The idea, apparently, was that an advertiser should win sales on the basis of what he said rather than how he expressed himself. One advertiser, Robert Bonner, a newspaper publisher himself, got around this rule by buying a full column in which he simply repeated the same message. Indeed, in 1856 Bonner created a sensation by buying a whole page and repeating his message six hundred times.

Thus in the pages of the same paper two important advertising techniques were refined. That they embodied diametrically opposed principles, repetition and variation, well illustrates that advertising is an endeavor in which theory has never sufficiently explained successful practice.

The Great Transformation: 1865–1920. Modern advertising did not mysteriously materialize and force itself upon an unwilling business community. It was made possible by the development of the media of mass communication, and it was made necessary because of greatly improved manufacturing processes that demanded innovation in marketing. In order to understand the development of advertising, one must take into account the environment that enabled it to flourish.

Changes in the factors that had inhibited the development of advertising enabled the vocation to grow toward its modern form in the half-century following the Civil War. At the outset of this period, commercial advertising seems to have been mostly a sideshow to the nation's business, worthy of study more for what it illustrated about social mores than economic conduct. By the dawn of the "New Era," after World War I, advertising had become an integral part of numerous businesses from the local (department stores) to the international (Standard Oil). In 1904 the vocation accounted for 3.4 percent of the gross national product, a level it reached again in 1924 but has never approximated since. Whole new institutions, advertising agencies, had appeared to provide a range of services—from media buying to research to copywriting and illustration—that had been unknown in earlier years. Already, hints of objections from outside the industry to the way it conducted itself, objections that provided a fertile field for the coming of federal regulation, were detectable.

Technological changes during this period transformed the world of print. By the end of the century, Pulitzer and his competitors could distribute daily a half million copies of an eighty-page newspaper. Thanks to telegraphy and the transatlantic cable (1866), newspapers contained up-to-date reports from around the world. In 1870 there were 574 dailies in the United States; in 1920 there were over 2,000. Circulation increased by a factor of almost ten. Rates of literacy were improving, but even immigrants with only a halting command of the language were purchasing English-language papers and periodicals as well as those in their native languages. This appeal was stimulated by the changing appearance of the newspaper itself. Publishers, in a sense, were reaching out to meet the less-than-fluent halfway. They used simple language, large headlines, and copious illustrations. But there was more than this to the popularity of such newspapers as the *New York World*. Cultural considerations contributed to the "mass" character of the mass media in the United States. In an increasingly polyglot nation in which the sense of community was weak, papers and magazines helped teach the customs of the country.

Changes in the transportation system were no less striking than those in communication. The railroads had begun to shrink the continent in the years prior to the Civil War. The railroads themselves became the first major industry to exploit advertising aggressively (and, as we shall see, public relations also). Indirectly they made it possible—indeed, necessary—for other businesses to employ it as well.

The railway web opened up a national market for producers. This magnificent transportation infrastructure helped call into being large-batch and mass-production manufacturing to service newly accessible customers. When coordinated by what Alfred D. Chandler calls "the visible hand" of managerial know-how, these factors enabled corporations to achieve undreamed-of economies of scale and—at least as important, as Chandler has shown—of speed.

The giant firms that entrepreneurs built could be likened to the Roman Empire: there was always trouble on the borders. The Roman solution was also the corporate: annexation. Management reached out to control its environment. Firms integrated backward toward sources of raw material. They attempted to expand horizontally, first through negotiated division of markets and then, when this proved difficult because of antitrust prohibitions and mistrust of fellow executives, through mergers. And they integrated forward to the consumer, arrogating to themselves marketing management formerly controlled by independent distributors.

A fine illustration of these forces at work is the cigarette industry. Prior to the 1880's, the tobacco industry chiefly produced chewing tobacco, snuff, pipe tobacco, cigars, and roll-your-own cigarette tobacco. Producers sold primarily to nearby markets. James Buchanan Duke decided to exploit the possibility for cigarettes, up to then a relatively "exotic" product. He staked the future of his company on the Bonsack machine, which produced 120,000 cigarettes a day and halved the cost per unit. "Output soared," remarks Chandler. "Selling became the challenge." Duke launched the industry on the road to advertising campaigns that took his brands around the nation and the world. While continuing to work through the traditional system, he also established his own far-flung sales force, writing and placing his advertising through agencies and also through his own staff.

With cigarettes and other consumer goods, brand image, brand loyalty, and product differentiation became issues of the first magnitude. In industry after industry, advertising was used to create primary demand (for cigarettes) and then selective demand (for a particular brand). For company after company, it was not production but the search for a market that became the central problem. The great savings engendered by economies of speed in production would be sacrificed if a product merely piled up in warehouses. To solve the technological problems confronting the modern factory was a considerable task; yet no less difficult, if of a different order, were the problems of getting rid of what the factory produced. In the words of Thomas J. Barratt of Pears, "Any fool can make soap. It takes a clever man to sell it."

Developments analogous to those at the national level in manufacturing were taking place in New York, Chicago, Philadelphia, and other growing cities. The very fact that urban areas were expanding was an important stimulus to the increase in consumer goods, for city dwellers tended to buy relatively more than did farmers. Furthermore, population density invited attempts to reach the public through billboards and posters. With the coming of electricity, gigantic advertisements transformed the aspect of the city at night, as the Great White Way and its counterparts came to represent the pace, the allure, and the excitement of modern life.

Just as the railroad had altered relations of time and distance in the nation as a whole, the street railway and later the subway were doing the same in the cities. The urban transportation revolution helped make possible one of the symbols of the modern city, the department store. If the railroads helped businessmen go to their markets, urban transportation brought markets to businessmen. No longer did consumers have to shop within walking distance of their homes. They could now travel to central locations where the large retailer could achieve the same kinds of economies in distribution that manufacturers did in production. High-volume purchases combined with low prices and high-volume sales to enable the department stores to democratize consumption. Velocity of stock turn (economies of speed, once again) was the key to their success. To stimulate this velocity John Wanamaker, Macy's, Marshall Field, and others had to publicize their wares.

The Advertising Industry. The advertising industry slowly developed to serve these manifest needs. Precursors of the advertising agency have been found as early as the 1830's, and in the 1840's the New York City business directory carried a notice for Volney B. Palmer's "coal and advertising" agency. Following the Civil War, more organizations appeared that offered to supervise the placement of advertisements.

These agencies developed randomly, not unlike other nineteenth-century middlemen. In a landmark study of the industry, Ralph M. Hower discerned four stages of development: newspaper agent, space jobber, space wholesaler, and concessionaire. In the first stage, Palmer (and others) solicited advertising orders, delivered the copy, and collected a fee from the publication on whose behalf he acted. As space jobber, the agent worked not for a commission from the publisher but on his own account. He sold space to advertisers on a piecemeal basis and filled the orders by buying space from publications. As a space wholesaler, the agent bought space in large quantities and resold it to advertisers. Finally, as concessionaire, the agent took the wholesaling phase one step further, purchasing all the advertising space in a paper. He developed lists of papers for whom he had, so to speak, the advertising concession, and this list constituted a network for the advertiser seeking wide coverage. The final stage was reached as early as 1867 by Carlton and Smith, a forerunner of one of the largest modern agencies, J. Walter Thompson.

A number of points need to be made about this sequence. First, one should not infer from its apparent neatness that the categorization describes a systematic course of development. As Daniel A. Pope has observed, "the stages often overlapped, and . . . the status and function of the advertising agent was usually quite muddled." It was, indeed, this disorganization caused by the multiplicity of buyers and sellers of space, and imperfect knowledge of changing policies in the market, that generated the need for an agent. Second, it was most unclear precisely for whom the agent was acting. At least one leading figure, George P. Rowell, felt that the agent owed his allegiance to the buyer, the advertiser. Yet he was paid through commission from the publisher. This dual loyalty created an obvious conflict of interst, because the agent seemed to be a party to both sides of a bargain. Third, copywriting—that activity which today is the most visible part of the business—was not a regular service of the agent until the twentieth century. The bulk of the copy written in the nineteenth century was composed by manufacturers and retailers, and the best-known writers were often associated with department stores. But by the turn of the century, the most aggressive agencies, including N. W. Ayer and Son, J. Walter Thompson, and Lord and Thomas, were offering expanded services to their clients. Copywriting was among the most important of these.

It is difficult to discuss the evolution of copywriting because it is relatively easy to find exceptions to rules. Speaking broadly, however, it is not unfair to say that in the two decades or so following 1885, an attitude toward copywriting developed that held that advertisements ought to be more than mere announcements with a disconnected claim to excellence sometimes appended. The increasing number of new products and the competition among branded merchandise called for copy that aggressively sold the product. Persuasion and education became the dual goals, realized by studying the benefits that the product offered and linking them to the needs of the consumer.

Ayer hired its first full-time copywriter in 1891, but it was Albert Davis Lasker at Lord and Thomas who gave the greatest boost to writing as a specialty. Adopting the description of advertising as "salesmanship in print," Lasker spent large sums on writers and thus helped endow their duties with prestige. It was he who popularized the term "Reason Why," by which was meant that an advertisement must provide a specific reason (although perhaps a more accurate description would be "rational-sounding excuse") to make a purchase. Lasker believed that advertising was news, but to gain his approval copy could not merely be a report. It had to have an indefinable something extra: it had to "sing." Through Lasker's agency, from the turn of the century to his retirement in 1942, passed some of the most successful copywriters.

ADVERTISING AND PUBLIC RELATIONS

The advertising agency was positioning itself as a multiservice organization, rather than a middleman, through research as well as writing. Ayer conducted what is usually considered the first systematic market research as part of a successful new business presentation in 1879. By 1910 numerous organizations, including the media, businesses, business schools, and independent research firms as well as agencies, were conducting research projects with methodology borrowed from the social sciences. Psychology received special attention, as advertising men came to realize that it might provide valuable insight into the consumer mentality. In fact the founder of behaviorism in America, John B. Watson, himself went from this discipline into advertising.

As its responsibilities grew more important and more specialized, the advertising world was seeking to establish as firmly as possible its credibility and respectability. This quest can be seen in the new approaches to compensation; in the founding of trade associations, trade journals, and vocational education; and in the changing character of agency clientele.

The ambiguous position of the advertising agent between buyer and seller had engendered a host of purchase and sale arrangements in which the necessity for secrecy fostered manipulation and mistrust. An important builder of the road out of this miasma was N. W. Ayer and Son, which in the late 1870's developed its open contract with a fixed-fee system. This called for the advertiser to pay the agent a commission that was a fixed percentage of the total advertising placed. In 1893, the American Newspaper Publishers' Association (ANPA) resolved to allow a discount of 15 percent on advertising placed through recognized agencies rather than by advertisers themselves. In return the agencies were enjoined from attempting to break the papers' rate structures. Methods of compensation remain a subject of controversy, but both the Ayer and the ANPA systems helped establish a key principle. The advertising agency was working for the advertiser—and for it alone. The solidification of this situation was critical in regularizing agency practice.

Just as voluntary associations have suffused American life in general, as Alexis de Tocqueville observed, so did they develop in the business world. The growth of such associations is an important benchmark in the self-consciousness of a vocation. The first advertising clubs were formed in Chicago in 1894 and in New York in 1896. These seem to have been informal groups that exchanged gossip about the trade. Similar clubs soon sprang up around the nation, many of which were linked in the Associated Advertising Clubs of America (AACA) in 1905. The AACA (which soon substituted "World" for "America" in its name) tried with some success in the years between 1910 and 1920 to put itself forward as the national spokesman for advertising and began its "crusade" for truth in advertising in 1911. Its leadership was instrumental in persuading the Federal Trade Commission in 1915 to support its efforts by declaring false advertising an "unfair method of competition," which the commission was empowered to prohibit. In turning to the federal government, the AACW was acknowledging its inability to expunge the blatant charlatanism that hampered its drive toward respectability. Also unable were succeeding trade groups, the most important of which were the Association of National Advertisers, which became an independent organization in 1915, the American Association of Advertising Agencies, founded two years later, and the Advertising Federation of America, which superseded the AACW in 1929. Nevertheless, these groups have been important as clearinghouses for useful information on various aspects of agency practice and for the establishment of standards against which practice could be measured.

Just as self-respecting vocations have formed trade associations, so they have been served by trade journals. For many years, the most important such advertising publication was *Printers' Ink (PI)*. Founded by George P. Rowell in 1888, *PI* was at first not much more than a house organ singing the praises of Rowell's agency and featuring homilies on the manifold benefits of advertising in general. By 1910, however, it had achieved an independence and breadth of view that rendered an important service to the practitioner. "Its changing perspective—from local to national advertising, from enthusiastic boosterism to restrained advocacy, and from house organ to independent industry spokesman—is both a sign and a cause of the growth of the advertising profession," as Daniel A. Pope has written.

ADVERTISING AND PUBLIC RELATIONS

The development of advertising education was hindered by skepticism within the trade itself. Advertising men, as Pope has noted, held mutually contradictory notions about the explanation for success. On the one hand, they believed that the greats were born and not made; but on the other hand, they believed that long experience was the key. Desire for professional stature, however, combined with the increasing amount of information to be mastered and a growing receptivity to assistance from the scholarly community to produce a more receptive climate. The first course in advertising was taught at New York University in 1905–1906 by an advertising manager at John Wanamaker; others quickly appeared.

The final factor to be considered in the development of the vocational self-awareness of advertising is the changing character of the clientele. In the nineteenth century, the leading national advertiser was the patent medicine manufacturer. By the turn of the century, however, manufacturers of consumer durables and packaged goods were coming to the fore on the national level, as department stores did on the local.

This evolution held noteworthy implications. Patent medicine advertisements were often so false that they were an affront to common sense. They were morally indefensible attempts to exploit suffering. Many of the newer advertisers, on the other hand, offered merchandise that performed legitimate functions and satisfied pressing needs. The opportunity to introduce such new products through advertising's pull rather than distribution's push was most inviting. Yet advertising was hampered by its heritage of untruth.

As agents came to understand that putting the onus of patent medicine hawking behind them might increase their ability to profit from a more respectable clientele, they became more open to efforts for truth in advertising, whether they originated from within the vocation or government. When the advertising professional of 1915 spoke of truth, his meaning should not be confused with that of the modern critic. By truth, he meant the absence of blatant falsehood, not claims that embodied the whole truth or were as true in implication as in assertion.

The climax of the growth of prestige of advertising came with American entry into World War I. Numerous advertising men served on George Creel's Committee on Public Information, carrying, as Creel put it, "the gospel of Americanism to every corner of the globe." The Creel committee was later sharply criticized for the excesses of its propagandizing, but few people doubted its impact. Although some feared its sinister character, everyone seemed to agree about the ability of well-crafted propaganda to change minds and therefore history. Inflated though these notions were, their usefulness in a new client presentation was obvious.

By 1920 advertising had come a long way. From hawking "Hostetter's Bitters," it was now being used to market no less an institution than the United States of America.

The Era of Broadcasting. Since 1920, advertising has grown into a major force in the American economy and society. Although its effects are difficult to predict and to measure, business, government, and nonprofit institutions invested more than forty billion dollars in advertising in 1978. As a percentage of gross national product, advertising is about one point lower than its highs of 1904 and 1924, but the sum in absolute terms is so great that no discussion of American life is complete without recognition of its impact.

In the eighteenth century, as we have seen, American advertising lagged behind that of Britain, and in the nineteenth century important advances occurred both in Britain and in France. In the modern era, however, the United States has been the unquestioned world leader in this vocation. Consumer-product advertising became a signature of American culture. Some foreigners admired it. The English writer Beverley Nichols remarked in 1928, "It is not the Americans who are children. We are children—as far as advertisement is concerned." Nichols marveled at how Americans could endow commonplace products with allure. Others were not so approving. Wrote Sergei Gerasimov in Moscow's *Literary Gazette* in 1949:

> The naked woman's body, like a national trademark, has become the symbol of American commerce. Naked, semi-naked, undressing and dressing women fill not only the films but the pages of magazines advertising food, clothing, automobiles, hotels, refrigerators, chewing gum, and everything which in the opinion of the

businessman would represent the vital interests of the people. The indecency of American advertising is indescribable [Maurice I. Mandell, *Advertising* (Englewood Cliffs, N.J., 1974), p. 65].

Developments in transportation and communication that signaled the rise of modern advertising from the Civil War to 1920 continued to have influence, but, with a single exception, that influence has been more of degree than of kind. In transportation, improvements in shipping and the growth of air and auto travel did not have the basic impact that the railroads did. Nor were the technological improvements in printing and graphic arts revolutionary. The one truly momentous change has been in the development of commercial broadcasting.

Radio between the wars and television after World War II have brought advertising to the public with unprecedented drama and immediacy. Demonstration is what broadcasting could provide in a way that no other medium could. Despite the high cost of television time, it is cheap when compared to the alternative of a corps of door-to-door salesmen blanketing the nation. The importance of demonstration is shown by comparing the introduction of a new product, such as the Polaroid Land camera, in the United States (where commercial television was available) and in France (where, until the late 1960's, it was not). This comparison also helps to explain differences in the distribution systems of the two countries. Polaroid and other firms have been forced to adopt a "push" strategy in situations like the French one: using financial incentives, they have motivated retailers to sell their cameras, because the retailers could show customers how the new product works. In the United States they can use a "pull" strategy, going directly to the consumer and forcing distributors to stock their product because of consumer demand.

Ironically, advertisers and agencies were slow to comprehend what a gift broadcasting was to them. The technological advances prior to World War I that led to radio and television grew out of the tinkerings of amateur experimenters. Except for the military, which was always seeking more direct means for locating ships at sea and soldiers on the battlefield, no one—least of all in the business community—knew what to broadcast or what role broadcasting should fill. When the idea of "ether advertising" was mentioned, it was met with general disfavor as late as 1922. At a radio conference held in Washington, D.C., that year, Secretary of Commerce Herbert Hoover found it "inconceivable that we should allow so great a possibility for service to be drowned in advertising chatter," and there was no public disagreement. Radio was to be the purveyor of information, education, and culture. Through its magic, some hoped, the masses would be uplifted.

Despite what seemed to be a developing consensus for educational and cultural uses of broadcasting, American Telephone and Telegraph (AT&T), which owned a radio station in New York City, decided soon after the conference to inaugurate what it called "toll broadcasting." It would not provide programming but rather rent out its facilities as a sort of "telephone booth of the air" over which, for a price, anyone could address the public about anything.

Advertisers hesitated to grasp this opportunity. The first to experiment with it, however, saw interest in their wares increase sharply. Despite this initial success, advertisers were reluctant to use the kind of hard sell that they had been employing in print for years. Not only had influential people, including the much-admired Hoover, spoken out against commercials, but there was also fear and doubt about how the public itself might respond. Radio executive Edgar Felix wrote in 1927 that the audience "resents the slightest attempt at direct advertising." The sponsor, he added, "does not earn the right to inflict selling propaganda in the midst of a broadcasting entertainment any more than an agreeable weekend guest may suddenly launch into an insurance solicitation at Sunday dinner." This almost prudish attitude extended to the kinds of merchandise that it was acceptable to discuss. Might the audience take offense at the mention of toothpaste, for example, because it was applied to such a personal part of the body?

The problem was that the opportunity to make money collided with what Erik Barnouw has called radio's longing for respectability. The compromise solution was "indirect advertising" through "trade name publicity." Much of the sponsorship—a word that had not yet acquired its present meaning—consisted of product or corporate names attached to performers, such as the A&P Gypsies and the Browning King Orchestra.

This reticence began to break down in the late 1920's, and Albert D. Lasker was instrumental in the change. He wanted to put the same punch in his broadcast advertisements that he used in print. In 1929 he put Pepsodent toothpaste on a nationwide NBC hookup. He had one of his copywriters invent a mysterious name ("irium") for one of its ingredients and had it hawked with the vigor that was making his style famous. The advertisements—and the fact that the program that carried them, "Amos 'n' Andy," was one of the most popular in radio history—helped sales triple within weeks.

The Lasker approach became the preferred method for publicizing products over the air. In the 1930's, advertisers and their agents were the most important determinants of what was broadcast. Advertisers bought entire programs and appended their name to the title both for publicity and as a symbol of proprietorship. Advertising agencies often produced programs for their clients, and it was also quite common for an advertiser's representative to sit in the sponsor's booth during dress rehearsal to make sure all went well. This same kind of control extended to television in the late 1940's and 1950's.

The television quiz show scandals of 1959 and the increasing demand for limited prime time enabled networks to gain power at the expense of the advertising world during the 1960's. Nevertheless, the advertising mentality still suffuses television. The effect on the medium—and through the medium on other social institutions—has been enormous. When television is conceived of as a tool for cultural betterment, its programs are considered its "product." When conceived of as a marketing tool, however, the product becomes not the program but the audience. The customer is the advertiser, and programming becomes, in effect, the manufacturing process used to produce the product. The far-reaching effects of this outlook have extended to entertainment, family life, and politics.

Not only has television been engineered to deliver an audience to an advertiser; that audience must have the proper demographic composition and the program must put it in a receptive state of mind. Many programs, although popular, have been dropped because those who watched them had limited disposable income and because the nature of the program itself belied the simple problem-solution vignette of the thirty- or sixty-second advertising messages that were interspersed throughout it. The structure of sports has also been altered to suit commercial convenience. The "TV time-out" in football and the World Series game scheduled for cold autumn evening hours instead of afternoons are only the most obvious examples.

The most important aspect of the influence of commercial television on family life is through its impact on child rearing. Television seems to exercise a hypnotic effect on children. In the 1970's, the average three- to five-year-old spent fifty-four hours a week viewing television, or about 64 percent of his or her waking hours. By age eighteen, the young adult has watched an average of 24,000 hours of television, twice the amount of time spent in class. Television and, through it, advertising have thus become key educators. Children asked parents for sweets and other gifts before the advent of television, but few companies had door-to-door salesmen soliciting business in the home. The pervasive impact of television has facilitated a quantum leap in the reach of advertising.

The impact of commercial television on politics has been little short of momentous. These changes can be analogized to those in business. Radio and television have both served to short-circuit the traditional political middleman, the party worker. Time and again in the age of broadcasting, dark-horse candidates have been able to appeal directly to the voter. They have thus been able to force themselves on their party by pointing to popularity achieved independently of it. In marketing terms, through news coverage and through purchased time, the politician can develop a "pull" instead of having to rely on a "push" strategy.

Television and advertising have also helped to shape the tone of modern politics. Those who claim that image has become important only with the advent of television lack historical perspective. Image was a critical element in such nineteenth-century campaigns as that for the Illinois senate in 1858 between the Little Giant and the Rail Splitter. And "media advisors" have played a major role in campaigns since at least Andrew Jackson's race for the presidency in 1828.

Nevertheless it does seem that the modern

media environment may be increasing the relative importance of images as opposed to issues in modern politics. First, the reach of television is so great that errors can be seen immediately by almost half the nation. Thus Gerald Ford's remark about freedom in Poland in the 1976 televised debates and the fact that Richard Nixon's makeup was less than ideal in 1960 apparently cost both candidates dearly in tightly contested elections. Second, Americans have become schooled in receiving information in short, colorful spurts, a discovery that the creators of the children's program "Sesame Street" have exploited. These "little stories" often feature information delivered in an appealing, attractive fashion that seems plausible. Such spots may not withstand sustained analysis, but advertisers have come to realize that they will not be subjected to such scrutiny.

A good example of the old and the new styles in conflict was the presidential campaign of 1952. The Democratic candidate, Governor Adlai E. Stevenson of Illinois, tended to give eloquent speeches that he could not or would not trim to suit the demands of television. Dwight D. Eisenhower and the Republicans put their television policy in the hands of the Batten, Barton, Durstine, and Osborn advertising agency and a volunteer from the Ted Bates agency, Rosser Reeves. Together they crafted an innovative videogenic strategy. The speeches that were broadcast were short and simple, and their content was virtually overshadowed by the shots of enthusiastic supporters greeting Ike. In addition, Eisenhower filmed fifty twenty-second commercial spots with dialogue such as:

ANNOUNCER: Eisenhower answers the nation!
CITIZEN: What about the cost of living, General?
IKE: My wife, Mamie, worries about the same thing. I tell her it's our job to change that on November fourth!

Eisenhower himself was heard to sigh, "That an old soldier should come to this," but the approach he authorized was perceived as effective and has since influenced the modern political campaign.

It is not surprising that an institution that has reached as deeply into the fabric of society as has advertising should cause controversy. The debate about the role of advertising in America today can be divided into two categories: social and economic. Raymond A. Bauer and Stephen A. Greyser have shown that despite occasional annoyance, most of the general public does not find advertising to be a pressing social issue. Nevertheless, a highly articulate and growing segment finds its social implications deeply disturbing.

Included among the social issues are the treatment of women and various ethnic groups in advertisements and the impact of advertising on the family. The conscious use of sex to sell dates back at least to the turn of the century. (Some cite the J. Walter Thompson campaign for Woodbury soap—"The Skin You Love To Touch"—as the pioneer.) In the 1960's, feminists began to speak up against what they regarded as the exploitation of women for commercial purposes. No doubt some of them would have agreed with Gerasimov's analysis. The 1960's and 1970's also witnessed a renaissance of ethnic awareness that advertisers have ignored at their peril. Thus in the 1970's a campaign by American Electric Power stigmatizing oil-rich Arab states aroused protests by Arab-Americans, and objections were made by Chinese-Americans to Yves Saint-Laurent's Opium fragrance advertisements and by Mexican-Americans to the Frito *bandito*.

A vigorous and effective lobby has also arisen in opposition to television advertising directed at children. Spearheaded by Peggy Charren, who along with other concerned Boston-area parents founded Action for Children's Television in 1968, this group has held that television advertisements aimed at children are inherently deceptive because their targets are incapable of comprehending the difference between commercial and program content. But the real engine behind their complaints is not this fairly technical objection. It is, rather, that market relations should not be permitted to invade the sanctity of the family as television advertising enables them to do. Pressure from people holding these views has been a major factor in prompting the Federal Trade Commission to conduct hearings aimed at determining how "kid vid" should be regulated.

Objections of a more general nature have been voiced over the past six decades by intellectuals, who have attacked both the content and the method of advertising. In a 1951 *Fortune* article, Bernard De Voto cited advertising to explain

ADVERTISING AND PUBLIC RELATIONS

"Why Professors Are Suspicious of Business." Corporations, he asserted, have appealed for judgment "in a torrent of mendacity, imbecility, and bilge." Otis Pease believes that advertising has served to "circumvent . . . rational thought" in a society that depends upon a rational, responsible citizenry. Many others hold that it induces people to purchase things they neither need nor want.

Advertising spokesmen have been aggressive in their own defense. "The American people like advertising and respond to it," declared the Advertising Federation of America at their 1936 convention. "They like its emotional appeal. It suits their temperament, is cheerful and optimistic. It gives to common things of the market a subjective value which goes beyond mere use. It helps people enjoy life. . . ." With World War II and the Cold War, partisans of advertising chose to regard "commercialization," which their critics used as an epithet, as a compliment instead. The "familiar clarions of commerce," wrote one, "are actually the last long line of free enterprise."

The actual effect of advertising on free enterprise has been a matter of some dispute among economists. Does advertising, for example, result in higher prices? It costs money and someone has to pay for it. Or does it lower prices? By increasing sales, it allows companies to achieve economies of scale. Does advertising, by making possible brand proliferation and product differentiation, function as a barrier to the entry of new firms into a market sufficient to constitute a violation of the antitrust laws?

These questions are of more than academic interest to the advertising world. In 1972 the Federal Trade Commission brought an antitrust suit against the leading producers of ready-to-eat breakfast cereals. In this case, still in litigation in 1979, the FTC alleges that the industry is a "shared monopoly." It has been able to charge "supercompetitive" prices because of cleverly constructed barriers to entry, erected with the aid of intensive advertising. If the commission should win, some observers believe that the role of advertising in modern marketing will be significantly altered.

Thus, as has happened with the social issues, the debate over the economic role of advertising has become a focus of concern for public policymakers in Washington. In the 1970's the economic and social controversies about the practice were translated into legal and regulatory actions to an unprecedented degree. The future of advertising will perhaps be in large part determined by their outcome.

PUBLIC RELATIONS

Prehistory. The rise of public relations is commonly attributed to a change in attitude by the business community toward the public. The archetypal businessman of the Gilded Age is said to have been William H. Vanderbilt, who, when badgered by a reporter about public service, allegedly snapped, "The public be damned!" In contrast, the modern businessman is asserted to be far more desirous of public approbation and has adopted as his motto "The public be pleased." This modern businessman needed public relations advisers to help him project a favorable image to the public. In fact, the development of this vocation is far more complex. As with advertising, it must be understood in a broad cultural context.

Like advertising, public relations has deep roots in American culture. Benjamin Franklin was sharply aware of the necessity for the public man to mold a persona acceptable to his peers in what was, even in the eighteenth century, a middle-class nation. Early in life, he adopted the "habit of expressing myself as terms of modest diffidence. . . . This habit, I believe, has been of great advantage to me when I have had occasion to inculcate my opinions." In a society in which upward mobility was possible to an extent unknown in the Old World, Franklin emphasized the need to look good. His autobiography contains many remarks about personal appearance, and, in a justly famous passage, he explains,

> In order to secure my character as a tradesman, I took care not only to be in *reality* industrious and frugal, but to avoid all appearance to the contrary. I drest plainly; I was seen at no places of idle diversion. I never went out a fishing or shooting; a book, indeed, sometimes debauch'd me from my work, but that was seldom, snug, and gave no scandal; and, to show that I was not above my business, I sometimes brought home the paper I purchas'd at the stores thro the streets on a wheelbarrow.

ADVERTISING AND PUBLIC RELATIONS

Reality was not good enough; appearance was necessary as well, for the public had to be convinced. The most celebrated American boasted of trimming his sails to the prejudices of anonymous men. He understood instinctively that in a democratic society, the locus of power lay with public opinion. In a nation that valued equality, no powerful person could afford to flaunt his position. As Hans Speier observed, public opinion in America would not permit the ostentatious enjoyment of power, because its enjoyment suggested its abuse.

Antebellum America was rife with precursors of the modern public relations attitude. An example is a type that may be indigenous to the United States: the booster. This new species, *Businessman americanus,* based his career upon developing towns by selecting a site and then trying to attract settlers, merchants, railroads, and so on. His loyalties were intense but volatile, and the success of his venture depended upon his ability to persuade others that it would succeed. To that end, the newspaper editors whose publications seemed miraculously to spring up in the midst of these myriad villages were not above, in Daniel J. Boorstin's words, "represent[ing] things that had not yet gone through the formality of taking place."

Despite its characterization as the "public-be-damned" era, the years between the Civil War and the turn of the century saw big businessmen showing heightened respect for the power of public opinion. Public enthusiasm for great business enterprises such as the railroads was an important element in their success. But social approval was important for personal as well as professional reasons. Like any other group, businessmen lived in society and were democratic enough to thirst for the approval of those around them. The effect of unpopularity on morale is illustrated by these observations from an executive of Standard Oil, probably the most maligned corporation in the Age of Enterprise:

> We are quoted as the representation of all that is evil, hard-hearted, oppressive, cruel, (we think unjustly,) but men look askance at us. We are pointed at with contempt. . . . None of us would choose such a reputation. We all desire a place in the good will, honor and affection of honorable men [Ralph Hidy and Muriel Hidy, *Pioneering in Big Business* (New York, 1955) pp. 214–215].

Businessmen also showed their respect for public opinion by their approach to journalism. First, they began to purchase newspapers. "Papers on the financial rocks," according to Bernard Weisberger, "had a way of drifting into portfolios of big time investors, who recognized the utility of having press spokesmen on their side." Second, in the late 1860's corporations began to hire press agents, whose duty it was to bring to the attention of newspapers those stories that the company felt were both favorable and newsworthy. In 1884, a newspaper trade journal observed that any organization that advertised would also have a man "working the press" for free publicity. The railroads pioneered in this practice.

The most important characteristic of public relations–type activity before the turn of the century was its haphazard nature. Some businessmen, especially in large firms that dealt with the general public, such as the railroads, sensed the need for caution in matters that might have impact on corporate reputation. Few, however, had their companies systematically provide that care.

The Progressive Period. We have seen how the development of the mass media around 1900 provided opportunities for businessmen as advertisers. The media were also producing a problem for them in the realm of public reputation: the content of the media was often antibusiness. Indeed, exposé journalism in popularly priced magazines caught fire in the early years of this century. Between 1903 and 1912, almost two thousand muckraking articles appeared in these magazines, generously buttressed by editorials and cartoons, and the public devoured the revelations. To be sure, not all the muckrakers were antibusiness, but enough were to disturb the astute executive.

Some scholars have pointed to muckraking as the explanation for the rise of public relations. Unquestionably it played a part, but other factors are at least as important. Chief among these were developments within the business world.

Corporations were growing at an unprecedented rate at the turn of the century. Between 1895 and 1905, three hundred separate firms were disappearing through mergers every year. The managers of these giant companies were learning that bigness resulted in problems different not only in degree but in kind from those confronting the small entrepreneur. No longer were the key decisions about a local plant being made by a manager living in the plant community. No longer did the manager know all his employees by name, nor was he necessarily on intimate terms with the civic leaders of the town. He may not even have known the doctors, the lawyers, and, most important for our purposes, the newspaper editors. Yet there was a manifest need to stay on good terms with local opinion leaders.

These years saw a massive effort to rationalize business management. Nowhere was this effort more strenuous than in the search for answers to the much discussed "human problem." Industrialists were learning that they had to understand the living world that their factories contained. Taylorism, industrial psychology, and various measures under the general heading of welfare capitalism were being developed at this time to assist them. Industrialists were also straining to form a new relationship with the world that contained their factories. The transformation in advertising, as we have seen, was part of this trend. So was the development of public relations.

The distinguishing characteristics of modern corporate public relations are, first, that it is a planned and organized functional activity within the corporation; and, second, that the directors of this function have the ear of corporate decision makers and may influence policy. Both characteristics can be traced to this era.

The two companies that led the way in organizing public relations were the American Telephone and Telegraph Company and the Pennsylvania Railroad. Both employed large numbers of persons and dealt directly with the public, and both boasted shrewd leadership.

At AT&T, Theodore Newton Vail moved to combat the unpopularity aroused by what some felt were the harsh methods the company used to eliminate the competition of local telephone companies and the brusque manner of some of its operators. He made an effort to be personally available to reporters, and in 1908 he hired as an assistant James T. Ellsworth, a specialist in press relations. Vail's program of "publicity and full disclosure" for corporate activity helped establish a more favorable public attitude. AT&T pioneered in the use of institutional advertising to attract favorable attention to its conduct. The company recognized the importance of reputation because its existence as a sanctioned monopoly depended upon a benevolent public policy.

The Pennsylvania Railroad was the nation's acknowledged leader in its field, and when its president hired a public relations man, also in 1908, the world took notice. The man in question was Ivy Ledbetter Lee, who is deservedly known as the father of his vocation. Lee set about transforming the company's traditional policy of secrecy. Instead of trying to cover up news of an accident, for example, Lee arranged for reporters to travel to the scene at the railroad's expense and then provided opportunities for photography and information gathering. He understood that rumors would often be more damaging than the truth and that the company had a better chance of manipulating coverage by working with the press than by fighting it.

Lee soon opened his own consulting firm and numbered among his clients in the next quarter-century many of the nation's biggest businesses. He performed a critical service for the vocation by helping to make it respectable. Prior to his advent, public relations men were considered little more than press agents. They were often associated with the entertainment world, and they seemed more than a little buffoonish. Lee showed that they could be well-heeled, well-dressed, and well-mannered, and that when properly employed they could indeed help corporations. He also showed that the richest and most powerful men in the nation would take at least one of their number quite seriously.

Toward a Definition of the Vocation: 1920–1940. Public relations emerged from World War I with an enhanced prestige for the same reasons that advertising did. It is erroneous, however, to think of the two as similar in other ways. For much of the two decades under discussion here, practitioners in the two fields considered themselves adversaries. Advertising men were suspicious about precisely what public relations was. What did it mean when Ivy Lee claimed to "[interpret] the Pennsylvania Railroad to the public and the public to the Pennsylvania Railroad"? Was he a bona fide policymaker or just a well-dressed "space grabbing" publicity man?

Most advertising people suspected the latter. They often expressed their hostility in moral terms. The basic difference between their vocation and "publicity," they asserted, was that the sponsor and purpose of what they had to say were clearly declared, while the publicity man tried to manipulate events to attract attention for free. "The man who is hired," observed an advertising partisan,

> ... to use his specialized training as a writer, as an artist and as a judge of good typography to present the merits of a definite product over the signature of the manufacturer or seller of that product, and solely inside of advertising space which had been bought and paid for by that manufacturer or merchant, is certainly enacting an open role which is very different from that of the man who remains behind the scenes and manipulates various stage devices for purposes best known to himself and those who employ him ["Through Many Windows," *Advertising and Selling*, clipping in the papers of Edward L. Bernays].

As long as seller sought buyer, the role of the advertising man would at least be tolerated. "But with his public relations cousin, that super-off-stage person who juggles with the League of Nations in one hand and with millinery and cosmetics in the other, I fear the accountability is different." Such a man was "useful whenever ... manipulation is needed to accomplish an end that cannot be disclosed."

Behind this rhetoric were hard facts. If the public relations man were primarily concerned with product publicity, he was in direct competition with the advertising agent for the corporate-promotion dollar.

Integrity and economics also fueled the opposition of newspapers to the growth of public relations. Describing this "menace to journalism" in 1921, R. C. E. Brown wrote that potential reporters who chose to make a career in public relations were forsaking a noble craft in favor of special pleading. Brown foresaw "the growth of a race of mere retailers of ready-made intelligence, and the turning of the newspaper more and more to distribution, less of news than to what somebody wishes to be considered news." To a degree greater even than during the political-party press of the early nineteenth century, the American newspaper was "taking things at second-hand and allowing artificially stimulated sentiment to appear as the expression of natural public opinion." To the reply of the public relations man that he provided positive news that offset the journalist's natural inclination to accentuate the negative, Brown argued that "news that is too retiring to meet the reporter unchaperoned by the press agent ... is too good to be true." The only remedy, he observed in a refrain often to be repeated, was a boycott: "Nothing but the absolute refusal to recognize the press agent, or to publish news that is not prepared by the editorial staff."

Although publishers were mightily exercised over the way corporations and independent agencies were hiring their reporters away at higher salaries, they were even more worried by the financial threat. Public relations, which they insisted on referring to derisively as press-agentry, might so reduce their income from advertising that they would go out of business. According to one estimate, if the press agent could deliver equal lineage to an advertisement at one-third the cost of paid space, advertising would end and with it newspaper revenue and reader confidence. The free publicity problem "goes more thoroughly into the guts of the newspaper business than anything else," the 1927 convention of the American Newspaper Publishers' Association was told. "There is no subject closer to our belts than this one." The ANPA accordingly decided to expand its anti–press agent crusade, adopting a proposal to set up a monitoring service to warn papers of press agent activity. At the bottom of its bulletins appeared in boldface type the question: "WHY DON'T THEY PAY THE PUBLISHERS FOR IT?"

Important developments in public relations during these decades served better to establish the vocation's parameters and eventually resulted in a muting of the tension among these occupations, although, especially in the case of journalism, that tension has never disappeared completely.

Ivy Lee continued his leadership. It was he to whom businessmen would turn first when they wanted public relations help. Although he succeeded in practice, he was less than adept at theory, which was important if his vocation was to survive as an independent service. He gave a number of speeches and produced two books on the topic of opinion formation and manipulation; but these efforts, as even he sensed, were not intellectually satisfying. He was unsure whether emotion or reason was paramount in determining attitudes. He was not at home with the title "public relations man," and after twenty-five years in the business confessed that he had "never been able to find a satisfactory phrase to describe what I do."

Noteworthy contributions toward increasing the status of public relations were made in the 1920's by Edward L. Bernays. A nephew of Sigmund Freud, Bernays had had experience as a Broadway press agent before joining the Committee on Public Information. He enjoyed his work but longed to endow it with greater prestige. In this cause he coined the term "public relations counsel." The last word was consciously borrowed from the law and was aimed at endowing the vocation with a professional status that sharply differentiated it from press-agentry and publicity. Bernays insisted that the public relations man must operate on a "two-way street": he must have influence on corporate policy beyond press relations alone. The counselor helps, wrote Bernays, "mold the actions of his client as well as to mold public opinion."

Bernays developed a theory that the public was essentially emotional in its judgments. He advised that to effect attitude change this bias had to be taken into account. He was also instrumental in refining what he called the "created event" (which an earlier generation labeled "publicity stunt"). This entailed attracting attention not by paying for space but by creating a situation so out of the ordinary that reporters had to cover it as news. In the process, they publicized Bernays' client.

By the 1930's Bernays had begun to work for important executives and he would continue to do so until his semiretirement in the 1960's. In a sense, his most successful client was public relations itself. Probably the nation's best-known living public relations man, he indefatigably boosted his trade and, by doing so, boosted himself as well. By the 1950's, he had become the acknowledged "window on the world" of public relations.

Ironically, Bernays always had a rather ambiguous relationship to the other leaders of the vocation. He did not join their clubs and associations, and for their part they tended to view him as too flamboyant and perhaps too politically liberal really to fit in.

A contemporary of Bernays who was very much an insider in the vocation was Arthur W. Page. A former magazine editor, Page became the director of public relations of AT&T in 1927 and began to streamline its operations. Although independent counselors often talked of policy influence, it was Page and others who had positions within corporations themselves who may well have had greater influence in making the practice a recognized and respected staff function.

Page worked vigorously not only to get information out but to get outside information into corporate leadership. In this effort he made extensive use of public-opinion surveys, which appear to have been important factors in corporate deliberations. During Page's tenure, which lasted until 1947, AT&T probably learned more about its customers' wishes than any other large company in America. And it acted on this information.

Transition. The Great Depression was a watershed in the positioning of public relations within the corporate and trade-association communications portfolio. During the 1930's, image problems were not restricted to individual firms but afflicted the American business system as a whole. A president took office in 1933 who not only eschewed the homilies to corporate America so common from national leaders in the 1920's, but who was actually perceived as being antibusiness. Franklin D. Roosevelt, a superb exploiter of communications despite the editorial opposition he incurred, seemed to many executives to be usurping what they regarded as their rightful position as national leaders. In order to counteract this situation, individual businesses, trade associations, and general business groups such as the National Association of Manufacturers (NAM) launched "campaigns of education" unprecedented in size to "sell the American way of life to the American people." These campaigns were intended to convince Americans that society should not substitute Roosevelt and the New Deal for traditional business leadership.

The NAM was preeminent in this effort. Hard-hit in membership and finances by the depression, the NAM found in public relations a raison d'être. It became not only a crusader for the point of view of conservative big businessmen, it also educated the executives of smaller firms in the method and necessity of persuasion. For public relations men themselves, it became a clearinghouse of information, and the annual public relations conventions that it sponsored in the 1940's probably facilitated the search for clients.

Under the impact of the Great Depression and with the encouragement of organizations such as the NAM, the practice of public relations began decisively to concern itself more with image management than with free product publicity. It must be noted that product publicity continued to be a major concern of the vocation, a concern that spread to radio, and, after 1950, to television, in addition to the press. But as a generalization it is not unfair to say that the most important corporate public relations work has, at least since the 1930's, dealt with the image of a company as an institution.

This emphasis facilitated a more congenial relationship with the advertising world. Public relations managers have often found themselves recommending that their firm make public-policy statements through paid advertising. Thus public relations began to stimulate advertising rather than to circumvent it.

Relations with newspapers and other media were also smoothed by the discovery that public relations could and did generate revenue. Of course, the problem of planted information did not end with product publicity. A corporation could still seek to inspire favorable stories about itself as an institution, and this practice has posed a continuing dilemma for journalistic integrity.

Yet the media have reached a more successful modus vivendi with this situation than R. C. E. Brown would have predicted. Brown's model newspaper, which printed only information that its reporters gathered independently, is impractical if the newspaper seeks to cover not a single industry or group but the whole range of world events for a general readership. Such a paper needs help from news sources, and when that help is provided with integrity the paper can benefit.

To the Present. Public relations activity has increased during such times as the Great Depression when business has been under broad attack. That public relations has not, however, been solely a reply to such attacks but also a response to inherent organizational demands is shown by the fact that the vocation has persisted—and indeed flourished—despite an improved atmosphere for business. Thus, during the 1940's, when American productivity was hailed as creating an "arsenal of democracy," and during the 1950's, when business leadership was widely praised, public relations activity increased.

During this period, noteworthy steps were taken toward putting the panoply of professionalism in place. From a number of dinner clubs (analogues to the early advertising clubs) and other fledgling associations, the Public Relations Society of America (PRSA) was formed in 1948. The PRSA has grown into an important service organization. It has adopted a code of ethics and taken disciplinary measures against member agencies that have violated it. It maintains a staff that, among other duties, dispenses funds for the study of public relations and provides information about the field. It also supervises the publication of two trade journals. Like its equivalent in advertising, the PRSA has not and probably will not take the step from service organization to policymaker. Its membership is too limited and the effects of its censure too uncertain. Like advertising, public relations has become an indispensable function for large organizations outside the business world, including labor unions, nonprofit organizations, and government agencies, and for politicians.

Unions have often fought battles of persuasion with corporations. The job of the union public relations man is facilitated by his opportunity to paint a picture of "the masses" versus "the interest." Yet he has also suffered under burdens that seem heavier than those of his adversary. By the late 1930's, some unions seemed to be growing more powerful and less democratic than the public wanted. During World War II, when big business was accumulating image capital that it lived off for years, John L. Lewis was calling strikes.

By and large, unions were slower than management in developing a national public relations apparatus and less efficient in handling local news. Many newspapers have maintained a staunchly antiunion tradition, and unions have had less money than corporations to buy advertising space or time. Moreover, some union leaders have questioned the efficacy of a favorable public reputation, regarding their membership as not their primary but their sole constituency. They have decided that a reputation for responsiveness to reason could actually damage their appeal within those unions whose membership might prefer fighters.

It is difficult to say how many public relations specialists work for the federal government, because the Gillett Amendment passed in 1913 prohibits such employment without specific appropriations. This requirement was imposed by congressmen who feared, not without reason, that agencies would dispense partisan publicity. Nevertheless, the public relations function in federal agencies has grown dramatically. The estimated number of practitioners in Washington was about three hundred in the late 1930's; the *Wall Street Journal* put their number at nineteen thousand in 1979.

It is the use of public relations in politics rather than in administrative agencies that has attracted the most attention on the public-policy level. Some public relations firms, such as Whitaker and Baxter in California, have specialized in election campaigns. It and others have put themselves at the disposal both of politicians and of special-interest groups supporting or opposing public questions on the ballot. Some scholars have seen public relations as a new kind of lobbying. Instead of, or in addition to, buttonholing representatives in legislative halls, this tactic calls for the creation of (or at least the creation of the appearance of) broad public support for the measure in question. The hope is that the representative will read the apparent signs of public opinion and act accordingly.

Like advertising, public relations has always been controversial. And, like advertising, controversy has greatly intensified when the practice made the leap from business to politics.

CONCLUSION

Advertising and public relations have both encountered severe criticism from the articulate public. In a brief but thought-provoking critique, David M. Potter rightly remarks that the impact of advertising far transcends economics. It is a prime agent of education in an affluent society. Yet it eschews the moral burden of the traditional educational institutions:

> Certainly it marks a profound social change that this new institution for shaping human standards should be directed, not, as are the school and the church, to the inculcation of beliefs or attitudes that are held to be of social value, but rather to the stimulation or even the exploitation of materialistic drives and emulative anxieties and then to the validation, the sanctioning, and the standardization of these drives and anxieties as accepted criteria of social value [*People of Plenty* (Chicago, 1958), p. 188].

Others have focused on what they believe to be the mendacity of much advertising. Robert L. Heilbroner says that it teaches children that adults are willing to lie for money. John Kenneth Galbraith calls it "organized public bamboozlement."

Untruthfulness has also been a charge leveled at public relations. Indeed the vocation's founder, Ivy Lee, was labeled a "paid liar" during the Ludlow coal mine strike of 1914. A disaffected counselor in the 1950's remarked that the true progenitors of his craft were the Sophists, who for a price would make the worse argument appear the better. Thoughtful counselors have been deeply disturbed by this problem. "To what extent," asked David Finn in the *Harvard Business Review* in 1959, "does a business have a responsibility to tell the truth to the public—about prices, labor policies, and so forth—and to what extent can it afford to dissimulate?" His reply: "In public relations, truth is a hard word." Indeed, counselors have often been more concerned with "creating the impression of truth" than with the genuine article.

Some critics have seen both vocations as effective and insidious methods of social control, which may eventually subvert the democratic polity. Indeed both have been used for the explicit purposes of control. In 1937, at the height of labor-management conflict, *Printers' Ink* asserted that although many manufacturers seemed to think that advertising was of no account as an antistrike weapon, if they would invest just "one-tenth of the money in advertising preparation that they apparently were quite willing to invest in labor spies, tear gas, and other methods, which have proved worse than useless, they will stand a far better chance of winning public support than is possible under present circumstances."

Victory over the unions, rather than rational

dialogue, was the goal of this conception of corporate communications. Nevertheless, the suggestion was being made that talk would be more efficacious than violence in settling disputes. Even if what was said was lacking in integrity (to put it mildly), the use of argument seems a step in the right direction. As Marvin Meyers said in another context, "With talk begins responsibility."

In the last analysis, persuasion is what advertising and public relations are all about. There are many reasons to be dissatisfied with the content of the persuasive messages churned out under their auspices. Yet societies must be organized in some way, and it would seem that persuasion is a not uncongenial method. Advertising and public relations have not subverted democracy. Perhaps we should look at them as part of the price we pay to live in a pluralistic nation with large organizations that search for order not through force but through freely given consent.

BIBLIOGRAPHY

On advertising, see Lewis Atherton, "The Pioneer Merchant in Mid-America," in *The University of Missouri Studies*, 14 (1 April 1939), which sheds some light on nineteenth-century advertising on the middle border. Erik Barnouw, *A History of Broadcasting in the United States*, 3 vols. (New York, 1966–1970), is a beautifully crafted history, with clear and astute coverage of advertising; and *The Sponsor* (New York, 1978), makes even more explicit Barnouw's critique of the role of advertising in radio and television. Daniel J. Boorstin, *The Americans: The Colonial Experience* (New York, 1958), *The Americans: The National Experience* (New York, 1965), and *The Americans: The Democratic Experience* (New York, 1974), is a brilliant and beguiling award-winning trilogy that contains many enlightening comments on advertising and a most helpful bibliography. Merle Curti, "The Changing Concept of 'Human Nature' in the Literature of American Advertising," in *Business History Review*, 41 (Winter 1967), is a meticulous study by an important historian. Neil Harris, *Humbug* (Boston, 1973), is a very useful biography of P. T. Barnum. Ralph M. Hower, *The History of an Advertising Agency: N. W. Ayer and Son at Work*, rev. ed. (Cambridge, Mass., 1949), is a fine monograph based on original sources. Philip Kotler, *Marketing Management* (Englewood Cliffs, N.J., 1976), is a respected general textbook. Otis A. Pease, *The Responsibilities of American Advertising* (New Haven, Conn., 1958), surveys the social role of advertising from 1920 to 1940. Daniel A. Pope, "The Development of National Advertising, 1865–1920" (Ph.D. dissertation, Columbia University, 1973), is comprehensive and indispensable. Richard S. Tedlow, "From Competitor to Consumer: The Changing Focus of Federal Regulation of Advertising," in *Business History Review* (forthcoming), concentrates on the first quarter-century (1914–1938) of the Federal Trade Commission. Bernard A. Weisberger, *The American Newspaperman* (Chicago, 1961), is brief and useful.

On public relations, see Daniel J. Boorstin, *The Image, or What Happened to the American Dream* (New York, 1962), which is an interesting if occasionally petulant essay on those aspects of our culture which have contributed to public relations–mindedness. Scott M. Cutlip and Allen H. Center, *Effective Public Relations*, 4th ed. (Englewood Cliffs, N.J., 1971), is a textbook that not only provides "how-to" information but also presents in accessible fashion much background material. Richard S. Tedlow, *Keeping the Corporate Image: Public Relations and Business, 1900–1950* (Greenwich, Conn., 1979), is a survey of the growth of corporate public relations, with some observations on public relations among labor unions and in politics as well.

[*See also* COMMUNICATIONS; LABOR ORGANIZATIONS; MANAGEMENT; MARKETING; ORGANIZED BUSINESS GROUPS; *and* RISE AND EVOLUTION OF BIG BUSINESS.]

EXCHANGES

Robert Sobel

SECURITIES and commodity exchanges were direct outgrowths of markets. Although sometimes used interchangeably, "exchanges" and "markets" refer to different kinds of institutions. Markets are places where goods and services are purchased and sold, often on an occasional basis, and lack written rules and regulations or an organization to enforce them. Such markets existed in Mesopotamia five thousand years ago. What today would be recognized as bills of exchange were traded in the Greek city-states and in Rome. Commodities transactions took place at medieval trade fairs, and in the seventeenth century every major European city had several such centers.

ORIGINS OF THE MODERN EXCHANGE

What generally is considered to be the first modern exchange, or organized market, was organized at Amsterdam in 1602. Little is known of its workings, but it did emerge from a securities market. Apparently several leaders of this market, feeling the need for stricter rules governing both brokers and securities, wrote a constitution, established an administration, and later constructed an edifice to house the trading. This pattern was followed by most later exchanges. Thus it was, for example, that the out-of-doors traders in Paris organized the Bourse in 1726. At that time the London merchants gathered at Jonathan's Coffee House in Change Alley to transact business in shares. In 1773 they came together to form a London exchange. Like the Amsterdam Exchange, those in Paris and London had constitutions, regulations under which brokers could be admitted, sets of rules, schedules of fees, and methods by which securities could be listed for trading. Those brokers who would not accept this discipline were excluded, and those who remained agreed to favor one another in dealings. In effect, a guild of brokers controlled the exchange, excluding unacceptable securities and men.

The American colonial economy was crude and did not require exchanges, so none existed. But the first organized market—a place where sedentary merchants would spend an hour or so a day to discuss enterprises, and perhaps buy and sell bankers' instruments—appeared at Philadelphia in 1746. Eight years later several of these merchants met in the London Coffee House in Philadelphia to organize the Board of Brokers, which was really a guild. In 1781 the Bank of North America was incorporated at Philadelphia, and its shares entered the market. Few were traded at first, but it appeared evident that other banks and insurance companies would be organized, and that markets might be needed for their shares. The Philadelphia Board of Brokers therefore expanded the scope of their market, and in 1800 drew up regulations and a constitution, and elected one of their number, Matthew McConnell, as their first president. In this manner they organized the Philadelphia Stock Exchange, the oldest in America.

The Bank of the United States was opened in December 1791, also at Philadelphia, and its shares entered the market. Although the Philadelphians traded in these shares, most of the trading activity was centered in New York. There —as in Philadelphia, Boston, and other cities— bankers and merchants had long dealt in financial paper. By the 1790's they offered bank stocks as well, and some speculative fever developed. As business increased, many of the brokers (a part-time occupation in this period) gathered on Wall Street in New York City to buy and sell shares for themselves and their clients. In addition, several of the more enterprising brokers organized regularly scheduled auctions, at which sellers could deposit their shares and buyers would come to bid, with the auctioneer taking an agreed-upon fee for each transaction. The brokers competed with one another for business and, in the process, cut commission charges. Business continued to be brisk despite a speculative panic in April 1792. New banks and insurance companies were organized and their securities traded on Wall Street, and various state bonds also found buyers there.

By early May two aspects of the market had become evident to the major New York brokers. First, the auction was more efficient than individual trading, for it had become troublesome for sellers to seek buyers and vice versa. Second, something had to be done to end rate cutting, for profits were declining.

On 17 May 1792, twenty-four prominent brokers gathered to organize what in effect was to be a guild of stockbrokers. They signed what came to be known as the Buttonwood Agreement (because it was said to have been signed under a buttonwood tree), in which they agreed to trade only with one another and exclude outsiders, and to set commissions at a floor of .25 percent. A central auction was scheduled at the Tontine Coffee House on Wall Street, admission to which the members purchased through a subscription of $200 apiece.

This arrangement continued for twenty-two years, during which time the members developed a list of regularly traded securities (thirty stocks, bonds, and government obligations were listed in 1812) and developed means by which outsiders could obtain "seats" and members could transfer and sell their shares in the exchange. The members strove to win new business by offering better prices to buyers and sellers than did the Philadelphia Exchange and exchanges in other cities. The New York brokers tried to sell shares in a given company to their clients at a lower price and buy at a higher one than could be obtained elsewhere. In addition, they worked to broaden the list, so as to have a wide variety of securities with an assured supply and demand.

While competing with the Philadelphians, the members of the Tontine also competed with outside New York traders who had not joined the organization. But even had the New York traders combined, they would have lacked the power and prestige of the Philadelphians, who by then already had a regular exchange. The presence of the Bank of the United States in that city gave credence to its claim to be the financial capital of the nation.

The Wall Street brokers felt that one of the reasons for the success of Philadelphia was its exchange. So in 1817 they sent one of their number to that city to study the situation and report back. In March the New York brokers organized a true exchange of their own, complete with constitution and bylaws. Called the New York Stock and Exchange Board, it initially had eight firms and nineteen brokers. The New York Board held daily sessions, centered around the morning auction. The members spent their afternoons elsewhere, since business was not sufficient to occupy any of them on a full-time basis. In 1817 securities were owned and dealt in by a very small minority of Americans.

THE PRIMACY OF WALL STREET

The contest between Philadelphia and New York was resolved in the 1830's, when President Andrew Jackson sided with the New York bankers in their contest against the Bank of the United States. In addition, the completion of the Erie Canal in 1825 had enhanced the economic position of New York, and its banking community was more aggressive than that in Philadelphia in seeking new business. In Boston brokers transformed their market into an exchange in 1834, and for a while they hoped to mount a challenge to the New Yorkers. But the New England city lacked the capital and experience for such ambitions; it remained a market for local securities and followed New York in setting the prices for government bonds and bills. Other cities organized exchanges, most of them modeled on the New York Board. They concentrated on local issues and on serving investors and speculators who wanted the convenience of a nearby broker.

The local exchanges remained viable so long as communications were poor and interest in securities low. With the introduction of the telegraph in 1844 and the establishment of branch offices by the brokerages, they either disappeared or declined, and small local brokerages sought affiliation with larger Wall Street houses. Regional economic booms encouraged the establishment of several exchanges—the California gold rush (1849) gave birth to a handful of mining exchanges, the Pennsylvania petroleum boom in the 1860's did the same in that state, and there were several mining exchanges in Nevada after the Comstock Lode was uncovered in 1859. But the best of the boom stocks were traded in New York as well as locally. This was particularly true for those out-of-state companies financed by New York banks, which insisted upon having trading centered in their own city, not for reasons of civic pride but so as to monitor their activities. Generally speaking, the millionaires who emerged from the California and Nevada mining camps and the Pennsylvania oil fields made their fortunes from exploration, production, and the selling of supplies. With only a handful of exceptions, those who made large amounts of money from securities transactions in the mines and oil wells were New Yorkers or those who dealt at the New York Board or the outdoor market.

The 1850's were a boom period for America. Railroads and industrial corporations were organized at a rapid rate, and their securities were traded on Wall Street. This boom created three problems for the Stock and Exchange Board. First and least important were the attempts by rival exchanges in other cities to profit from the boom and thus to challenge the New York Board for supremacy. The Philadelphia Exchange experienced a revival in this period, and the Boston Exchange expanded its stock list. But the banking-exchange complex in Manhattan was able to repel these threats, knowing that the capital requirements of the new corporations could be met only in New York.

The second problem concerned standards for listing securities. If the New York Board was to win investor confidence, standards would have to be raised—for both securities and members. Investors and speculators in other cities would have to be convinced that acceptance on the list constituted a form of certification, that the New York Board did not deal in shoddy stocks. In addition, out-of-town investors had to be assured that the board members were honest men, far more so than those who were not members of the board. Raising standards was no simple matter. Each time that they were raised, nonmembers organized rival exchanges and some members—in contravention of rules—sneaked off to transact business at them. Then, when standards were lowered to kill the rivals, trading volume increased but the poorer reputation of the New York Board frightened away some customers. The question of standards would perplex exchange leaders for more than a century.

Finally, there was the matter of trading methods. By the 1850's the New York Board had two auctions, one in the morning and one in the afternoon. Between auctions the members would trade among themselves and conduct other business—or perhaps go to a rival exchange. Volume was rising, straining the auction system, for a member would hardly stay in the room for an hour or more awaiting the call of a stock in which he had an interest. It made more sense to deal for the stock outside the auction, even in the street itself, for individuals who wanted to buy and sell were always available there. In the late 1850's the outside continuous market and the indoor auction market coexisted, although it was evident even then that the outside market had decided advantages.

These three problems—competition from other cities, conflicts with rival markets in New York, and flaws in the trading methods—were, and still are, the major problems facing organized exchanges. To these a fourth was added in the twentieth century—relations with governmental agencies, especially those at the federal level.

As the New York Board grew in power, it attracted much public attention. Many Americans considered it and other exchanges to be nothing more than glorified gaming rooms. There was an element of chance, to be sure, but there was also a growing realization that exchanges filled a definite and important economic function. The publicity given to prices helped to enlarge the market for stocks and bonds. Furthermore, the exchange structure provided liquidity—the holder of a stock or bond knew he could sell it, if and when he desired to do so. Because of this he was more willing to own such paper than might otherwise have been the case. Newly formed companies could turn to the exchange for assistance. They would sell their stock, either privately or through an investment bank, and then hope that it would come to be accepted for listing at an exchange. Such listing would provide publicity for the security and would assure potential buyers that it had passed certain tests and was of a higher quality than issues traded off the exchange. Potential purchasers assumed risks in the knowledge that liquidity existed should they want to sell.

In the colonial and early national periods, when joint stock companies backed single voyages and went out of operation when the voyage was over, markets and exchanges might not have been needed. But in the age of the corporation, which continued to operate until destroyed by bankruptcy or taken over by another entity, liquidity was a prime requisite. This was the function of the New York Board and other exchanges —to provide liquidity and to certify the men and securities under their aegis.

PROSPERITY AND REBIRTH

In 1857 there was a financial panic, but recovery from it was rapid, so that stock prices were high and activity brisk on the eve of the Civil War. The war precipitated a major boom on Wall Street and in other financial centers. Huge profits earned by railroads and industrial corporations made their stocks more attractive, and so they rose in price. The flotation of new securities and the rapid increase in the amount of government paper available heightened the speculative fever that usually accompanies major wars. In addition the federal government printed fiat money—greenbacks—that by law was legal tender (currency which had to be accepted in payment for debts). The flight from greenbacks resulted in the organization of a gold exchange in New York, where gold was sold for greenbacks and vice versa, the price depending more upon the expectation of a Union or Confederate victory than upon any other single factor. For the duration of the war, this was the most active exchange in the city, and trading continued even after President Abraham Lincoln attempted to close it.

Volume was high at both the Stock and Exchange Board and the old outdoor market. But the demand for action resulted in the formation of new exchanges, which fell into two categories. The first comprised exchanges designed to complement the New York Board, to offer facilities when those of the major market were not available. Several were open only in the evenings, while others traded securities between the auctions. By 1864 there were at least three round-the-clock exchanges; they resembled floating crap games because they transferred locations regularly so as to avoid police raids. The second group competed with the New York Board, by admitting men and securities considered inferior by the major market. One new exchange, the Open Board of Stock Brokers, eliminated the auctions completely and featured continuous trading. It was open both to members and to individuals who paid a daily admission fee. The brokers would mill about, as they did in the open-air market, seeking others who were interested in the same stocks as they were, and then trying to deal with them.

This was an important innovation, for in time the brokers came to know where each "crowd" was located and would gravitate there when hoping to purchase or sell a particular security. By itself this was not unusual; the floor of the London Exchange had been organized that way. Before the end of the Civil War, however, the men of the Open Board developed a new institution, the specialist system. This was a decided improvement on all previous trading methods, combining as it did the best features of the auction and continuous trading.

The specialist was a broker who remained in one location on the floor, prepared to buy and sell shares in specific securities. He existed to service those brokers who came in with orders from the general public as well as members who wanted to speculate for their own accounts. In the beginning, at least, the specialists engaged in speculation on their own; but as time passed, they found they could do much better by providing this service. The structure existed in embryo at the Open Board. The specialist system was informal, but all members knew of its existence. In practice they would head for the specialist in the stock they wanted to buy or sell, ask him for the prices at which he would buy and sell the stock, and then, if the price seemed right, make their deal. There was no single auction at the Open Board, for the specialist system made it unnecessary. Rather, each specialist performed some of the duties of the auctioneer, but on a continuous basis.

Toward the end of the Civil War the Stock and Exchange Board, the Open Board, and the Gold Exchange were three of more than twenty exchanges in New York. Other cities witnessed a similar expansion of exchange facilities to service growing speculative demands. It is impossible to calculate the exact number of organized and unorganized markets and exchanges during this period (some lasted only a short time and left no records), but the total was well over one hundred. Some of the California exchanges that specialized in mining shares, such as the San Francisco Stock and Exchange Board (founded in 1862) did a larger volume of trading than any exchange in New York.

This hectic activity died down after the war, and most of the exchanges went out of business. The New York Stock Exchange (NYSE)—the name taken in 1863 by the Stock and Exchange Board—did all in its power to eliminate those that survived. Still, the Open Board remained strong, in large part as a result of superior trading methods. After all else had failed, the NYSE and Open Board leaders met to discuss a merger. One was arranged and went into effect in 1869, the birth date of the modern NYSE. Shortly thereafter the auctions were eliminated, and the specialist system was regularized and made the keystone of exchange operations, not only at the New York Stock Exchange but also at others.

A handful of small exchanges survived the Civil War era by specializing in selected groups of stocks, particularly mining issues. Four of these minor exchanges—the New York Mining and Stock Board, the American Mining Stock Board, the New York Mining Stock Exchange, and the Petroleum and Stock Board—formed alliances and in 1885 combined to create the Consolidated Stock and Petroleum Exchange, which for a time was the exchange with the largest membership in the nation. The Consolidated dealt in NYSE-listed issues, using several Big Board ticker machines to get quotations and then trading at better prices and for smaller commissions. Thus, buyers might obtain a lower quote, and sellers a higher price, at the Consolidated than at the NYSE. In addition, the Consolidated dealt in "odd lots"—purchases and sales of less than one hundred shares—and thus attracted small speculators and investors. Almost immediately the Consolidated formed alliances with the major "bucket shops" in the nation, which more often than not were betting parlors where individuals made wagers on rises or declines in the price of a stock. The brokers of the Consolidated also dealt in contracts for several commodities, petroleum in particular.

Thus, there were three major markets and exchanges in New York in the 1890's. The NYSE attracted the leaders of the industry and the seasoned securities, and was led by the major banks and trust companies of Wall Street. The outdoor market, which by then had formed a rather weak organization called the Curb Agency, traded in nonlisted securities and was dominated by immigrants and second-generation Americans—mostly East European Jews and Irish Catholics. The Consolidated contained a polyglot group, which included a large Cuban contingent and many former Confederate officers, and it traded both listed and unlisted stocks. Since the NYSE would hardly admit the immigrants or the former Confederates, the division was along social and religious, as well as business and economic, lines.

THE COMMODITY EXCHANGES

Commodity markets—places where contracts in commodities were bought and sold—existed before there were securities markets, if for no other reason than that they were needed at an earlier stage of capitalist development. There were commodity markets throughout the ancient world, and contracts were entered into at medieval trade fairs. Farmers, miners, and agents developed techniques for buying and selling paper representing actual goods, with the products to be delivered at certain places at specified times, in definite quantities, and of specific fineness. Such dealings took place in New York and other mercantile cities in the late eighteenth century, but there was no established market, much less an exchange.

Several small organizations appeared in the first half of the nineteenth century. These initial commodity markets served localities in the marketing of grain and other foodstuffs. Usually they were organized with the help of bankers, who saw the need to finance crops and assist farmers during slack seasons. The farmers understood the benefits of selling futures contracts, since they provided not only cash when needed but also an assured price for their products.

This confluence of banker and farmer interests led to the organization of the Chicago Board of Trade in 1848. Initially, only wheat futures were traded, but the organizers indicated interest in other commodities, such as lumber and corn. At first the Board of Trade was a market, with few rules and no constitution, but in 1856 a constitution was adopted, and three years later the Illinois legislature approved the document. From the time of its founding in 1862, the New York Produce Exchange dealt not only in wheat but also in most other grains, as well as in metals and petroleum. The Produce Exchange later experimented with securities trading, and at the turn of the century it threatened the NYSE in this trade. Discussions and negotiations followed, after which the Produce Exchange leaders withdrew to devote their full attention to foodstuffs and minerals.

Prior to the Civil War many cities in the South had cotton markets or exchanges, where in conjunction with local and northern banks the plantation owners sold futures contracts to mill owners, and speculators attempted to manipulate the markets. After the southern defeat several New Yorkers thought to transfer operations to the North, and in 1870 they opened the Cotton Exchange. Other commodity dealings came to be centered in New York as well—the Coffee Exchange was opened there in 1882, for example—although Chicago continued as the focus of grains. Like the others, these new exchanges were formalizations of previously existing markets, and in the postwar period many markets became exchanges while prewar exchanges were reorganized for better service of the new economic needs. This was the situation with the New Orleans Cotton Exchange, the Duluth Board of Trade, the Chamber of Commerce of Minneapolis, the Merchants' Exchange of St. Louis, the Toledo Produce Exchange, and similar organizations in other cities.

Although regionally based, some of these exchanges had national and even international scope long before the NYSE. The Chicago Board of Trade, the most powerful of all, maintained close ties with the New York banks and also worked in conjunction with leading European financial institutions. Its great power and reputation made the Board of Trade a symbol of malevolent capitalism to the leaders of agrarian America.

During the late nineteenth century many farmers' organizations charged the Board of Trade with rigging prices in such a way as to cheat the producers. Together with bankers and railroad presidents, the speculators of the "grain pit" became targets for leaders of the Populist party. Although overstated, there was some justification to this charge. There were major manipulations at the Board of Trade, although it was far more difficult to rig the price of wheat on an international scale than to corner the stock of a railroad with a million or so shares outstanding. And even while they attacked the Board of Trade, more moderate Populists conceded that it filled an important economic role. Without the ability to sell futures contracts to deliver commodities, the farmers would have been completely at the mercy of bankers. As it was, the contracts lessened the need for short-term financing while providing speculators with an exciting vehicle and brokers with profits. Still, to midwestern reformers the "grain pit" was the symbol of predatory capitalism, just as the NYSE served that function for their urban counterparts in the East.

NEW YORK AS FINANCIAL CAPITAL OF THE WORLD

When turn-of-the-century reformers spoke of the existence of a "money trust," they referred to the great investment banks. But the NYSE was looked upon as the symbol for the power of the banks. In reality it was more an instrument for the banks than a power in its own right. To consider it a "mover and shaker" would be to confuse the arena with the events and contestants. Morgan & Co., Kuhn, Loeb, and other key investment banks would underwrite the securities of the major corporations, which would then be traded on the NYSE. The banks used the exchange to help create a market for these stocks and bonds, and they looked upon the brokers as hired men. At no time was a major stock exchange figure considered a leader of the financial district. In fact, there is some doubt whether J. P. Morgan and Jacob Schiff, the two leading financiers of their day, ever set foot on the NYSE floor.

The big New York banks concentrated upon railroad securities, since this was the leading industry of the time. The Boston Stock Exchange did a good business in industrial shares—a small sector of the market—while the Philadelphia and other American exchanges increasingly became regional operations. London was, of course, the most important securities exchange in the world, just as Great Britain was the leading capitalist power of the time.

In the first decade of the twentieth century, when Boston investment banks proved incapable of providing sufficient capital for rapidly growing industrial corporations, they entered into partnerships and other combines with their New York counterparts, and leadership in industrial securities gradually moved to the NYSE. In this period too the Wall Street banks began floating loans for foreign governments, and although New York still was no match for London in this area, the challenge was being prepared.

The successful challenge came during the first years of World War I. By 1917 leadership had shifted to New York. Prior to that time NYSE securities moved in harmony with those on the London Exchange; the first question a Wall Street broker asked in the morning was "How's London?" Before the end of the war, London jobbers were asking about New York prices before opening for trading.

While solidifying its new global role, the NYSE moved to assure its position at home. The exchange confirmed its relationship with the outside brokers, who were now organized into the New York Curb Market, while demanding an investigation of the Consolidated, which it charged with being little more than a gaming room. After the NYSE gave its reluctant approval, the Curb Market went indoors in 1921, and in 1929 changed its name to the New York Curb Exchange, the forerunner of the present American Stock Exchange (Amex). State investigations of the Consolidated, along with several scandals involving its leaders, led to its demise in 1927 and to its liquidation two years later. For a while it seemed that the Chicago Stock Exchange might offer a new challenge to the domination by New York, but this did not materialize. By the mid-1920's the NYSE was the paramount marketplace for securities in the world.

The 1920's were the most illustrious decade in NYSE history. The great bull market, which began in 1923, lasted until 1929. With several minor interruptions stock prices climbed steadily, as did trading volume. Public participation was high, and stockbrokers became wealthy. To many the Wall Streeter seemed the creator of a national prosperity that would have no end.

Then came the 1929 crash, followed by a brief recovery and a major slide and economic depression. Few new corporations were able to float securities in the early 1930's, and even the more secure, established ones had difficulty finding buyers for their paper. Volume at the NYSE plummeted, and the institution and Wall Street itself took on the appearance of a ghost town. Just as they had been the symbols of the boom, so the NYSE and lesser exchanges were looked upon as the cause of the crash.

Reform of the exchanges was high on President Franklin D. Roosevelt's agenda when he took office in 1933. In 1934 Congress passed, and he signed, the Securities Exchange Act, which provided for the creation of the Securities and Exchange Commission (SEC), the first chairman of which was former stock speculator Joseph Kennedy. The exchange leadership, headed by Richard Whitney, opposed what it considered unwarranted interference in its affairs, and for the next four years it fought Kennedy and his successor, William O. Douglas. In 1938 Whitney was convicted of embezzlement and other crimes, and was sent to jail. This destroyed the last important vestige of opposition to the SEC. The exchange was reorganized under a new constitution that provided for the seating of directors who did not own seats and an administration separate from, although responsible to, the members. William McChesney Martin was elected the first paid president.

DECLINE AND REBIRTH

Investment banking was in the doldrums in the 1930's. New Deal legislation obliged the commercial banks to divest themselves of their investment affiliates—in effect, separating commercial and investment banking functions, the combination of which was considered a major source for the excesses of the 1920's. Because of this legislation and the emotional scars left by

EXCHANGES

the Great Depression, the banking community was wary regarding new underwritings. In addition, an entire generation of Americans had learned to distrust securities in general, and so volume on the NYSE and other exchanges shriveled. This meant that even solvent corporations had difficulty floating new stocks and bonds. Searching for an alternative source of funds, they turned to the Reconstruction Finance Corporation (RFC), an agency established by President Herbert Hoover in 1932, which by 1937 had become a major source of new capital. Jesse Jones, head of the RFC, became more powerful than any Wall Street figure insofar as financings were concerned, while the NYSE, the Curb Exchange, and the regional exchanges languished.

The decline of investment banking altered the power balance at the exchanges. Prior to the early 1930's the bankers had dominated the organized markets, and the commission brokers and specialists acted as their agents. Now the bankers were in eclipse, and the commission brokers lost many of their clients. By default, the specialists became the most important single force at the securities exchanges. They managed to eke out meager livings from the few trades brought to the floors, and many seemed content to be masters of a shabby house rather than servants in a mansion.

Trading picked up somewhat during World War II, as did securities prices, but this did not dispel the general feeling that recession had become the norm. Once the wartime prosperity had ended, it was believed, hard times would return, and the exchanges therefore did not expand activities in this period. But there was no new recession. Instead, almost all the economic indexes rose after a brief recession (1946–1947) and conversion to a civilian economy effort in the late 1940's. Then, with the election of Dwight D. Eisenhower as president in 1952, Wall Street and other financial districts began a new period of prosperity that, if not as dramatic as that of the 1920's, was longer-lived and stronger.

The boom placed strains upon the exchange system. Trading volume at the NYSE, which had been 208 million shares in 1940 and 377 million in 1945, rose to over 1 billion in 1961 and exceeded 2.5 billion in 1967. In 1978, volume rose to 7.2 billion shares. The American Stock Exchange and the regional exchanges shared in this prosperity and, along with the NYSE, used their earnings to modernize facilities. Mergers created the Pacific Coast Stock Exchange, the Midwest Stock Exchange, and the Philadelphia-Baltimore-Washington Stock Exchange, which, while not initially competing with the NYSE, did manage to enlarge their shares of the total trading. The American Stock Exchange embarked upon an aggressive program, seeking new listings and catering to the more speculative traders who were then coming to invest. The old over-the-counter markets, which had formerly concentrated upon government bonds and notes and those stocks not listed on either the NYSE or the Amex, underwent a great revival in the 1950's. The over-the-counter dealers found their trading methods unsatisfactory—most of the transactions were concluded by telephone—and talked of adapting the new electronic discoveries such as computers to their market. Under the leadership of the National Association of Securities Dealers, they planned even then to mount a challenge to the central exchange.

But the NYSE remained the symbol of triumphant capitalism. In 1951 Keith Funston became president, replacing the ailing Emil Schram (one of Jesse Jones's lieutenants), and almost immediately became a national celebrity. By means of a program that he called "People's Capitalism," Funston encouraged share ownership as a type of revitalized Americanism. He was not solely responsible for the increases that followed, but he did help to popularize the purchase of common stocks. The results were dramatic. In 1952 there were some 6,490,000 shareholders, and by 1970 the number had grown to 30,850,000. During this period the Dow-Jones Industrial Average rose from a low of 256.35 to a high of 842.00, and in 1972 it passed 1000. (By contrast, the average was 381.17 at the height of the 1929 bull market.)

Although the exchanges prospered, their facilities—which since the mid-1930's had been geared to the quieter, specialist-dominated kind of market—were coming under severe strains. By the time Funston stepped down in 1967, almost all the major exchanges were being obliged to rethink their methods of trading, and the brokerages were having difficulties in handling the great amount of new business. Attempts to introduce automation into the system often proved disastrous, since the old employees had little idea of how best to adapt to the new machines. Paperwork bottlenecks developed at the NYSE too, even though some of the changes there were successful. The regional exchanges had an easier time of it, so that by the early 1970's some of them had reputations for "better executions" of trades than the NYSE.

Many students of markets and exchanges believe that the key to these problems lay in nineteenth-century institutions that could not be adapted to twentieth-century requirements. For example, stock certificates originally were issued to indicate ownership at a time when trading was less hectic; the need to issue them created bottlenecks when the NYSE alone traded more than twenty million shares in some sessions. Ownership transfers might be accomplished through electronic bookkeeping, with owners receiving confirmation slips, copies of which would go to transfer agents. Yet the certificates remain, to contribute to back-office chaos.

Is there a need for so many exchanges? The regional exchanges had expanded when there were local markets for securities; the NYSE itself began as a regional exchange. But at a time when almost instantaneous communication throughout the globe is possible, do they fill any real need? Would it not make more sense to have a single national—perhaps international—exchange?

The Amex presents a special problem. This exchange originated in a decision of some brokers excluded from the NYSE to form a market which originally traded out-of-doors. Whenever the Amex raised listing standards, it was accused of attempting to fill the role of the NYSE. When the organization lowered standards so as to obtain more listings, it ran the risk of inviting gamblers and others, and in fact there was a scandal at the Amex in the early 1960's caused by just such a policy. Eventual unification of the NYSE and the Amex seemed probable by the late 1960's, but no one at either exchange made a move in that direction.

The specialist system was the most important problem. Just as the pre–Civil War auctions had proved unworkable when activity increased in the 1860's and ultimately gave way to the specialist system, so it appeared that the specialist system had been rendered obsolete by technology and the demands of heightened trading, especially by large institutions such as mutual funds, trust companies, pension funds, and banks. Given many orders for large blocks, the specialists at times abandoned their pledge to maintain orderly markets, and prices jumped erratically.

The over-the-counter houses had an answer. During the 1960's some of them increased activities in trading listed securities, using old over-the-counter techniques that involved negotiating prices, as had been the practice before the first auctions appeared. Now they expanded this practice into what came to be known as the Third Market—where listed securities were traded by nonmembers of the exchange according to over-the-counter practices. Later they developed the National Association of Securities Dealers Automatic Quotation System (NASDAQ), which went into operation in 1971. This was an electronic stock exchange, in which members were connected to one another by means of a display screen that provided information on demands from buyers and sellers, and enabled the operator to execute transactions. The traders who put their bids and asks over NASDAQ had no public obligation, and since they did not charge commissions, their prices tended to be fractionally lower than those obtainable on the exchange floor. Brokerage houses—especially those concentrating upon serving large institutions—found the Third Market a congenial place at which to trade, and over time they became divided on the question of whether to support it against the NYSE.

The NYSE retaliated with an unsuccessful attempt to influence the passage of legislation that would make the Third Market illegal. The exchange received another blow when the SEC ordered it to do away with fixed commissions, which had been one of the original reasons for founding the NYSE.

By the mid-1970's the battleground had been transferred to Congress, where several pieces of legislation affecting the exchange and market structures were being debated. The NYSE favored the establishment of a dual market-exchange system, in one part of which all the organized exchanges would be united into a single system (although retaining separate trading areas) and would be permitted to deal only in listed securities. The second part would be the over-the-counter operations, conducted over the electronic networks, which would trade in unlisted shares. The Third Market forces tended to see this as a sign of weakness and insisted that all barriers to trading be lowered. They were willing to compete with the NYSE and other exchanges for clients and business, and they were convinced that their methods would enable them to make the NYSE a relatively minor force in the market-exchange systems.

This debate began toward the end of the great bull market of the 1950's and 1960's. The combination of exchange breakdowns, the failure of several brokerage firms, an economic decline, the bankruptcy of some large corporations (especially the Penn Central), and domestic unrest brought these matters to a head. There was a major slump in 1974 during which the Dow-Jones Industrial Average fell to 570, followed by a recovery to 881 in 1975. But it appeared that the most important bear market since the 1930's had not yet ended, and the outlines of the future remained uncertain insofar as the exchange-market structure was concerned.

That there would be a continued need for some kind of structure was indisputable. The old specialist operation at the NYSE and at the regional exchanges was under strong attack and was rapidly weakening. The NYSE had already developed a system employing competitive specialist units, and further changes were contemplated.

In 1975 the exchanges and markets were united by means of a "consolidated tape," which reported all transactions in listed securities no matter where they took place. In response to prodding from Washington, the NYSE moved forward in an effort to create a truly national exchange-market system. In 1978 it introduced the Intermarket Trading System (ITS), which united several exchanges by means of computers and peripheral equipment. Representatives of brokerages on the floor of one exchange now could discover the bid and ask prices for selected securities offered elsewhere, and then place orders in the best way to benefit customers. In this way they could buy a stock at the lowest price and sell at the highest. Most observers view the ITS as a major step toward the creation of nationwide, fully integrated trading. When this happens, the financial district will be altered more basically than at any time since the early days of the New Deal.

BIBLIOGRAPHY

Clarence Barron and Joseph Martin, *The Boston Stock Exchange* (Boston, 1893), an encyclopedic work that contains sketches of prominent individuals as well as a statistical and chronological compilation; James E. Boyle, *Speculation and the Chicago Board of Trade* (Chicago, 1929), a short work that discusses major speculators and coups; John N. Brooks, *Once in Golconda: A True Drama of Wall Street, 1920–1938* (New York, 1969), the best-known work of the premier popular historian of Wall Street; Vincent Carosso, *Investment Banking in America* (Boston, 1970), the best work on the subject, and vital for an understanding of it; Henry Clews, *Fifty Years in Wall Street* (New York, 1908), a memoir of a leading investment banker, chatty and not very well organized; Cedric Cowing, *Populists, Plungers and Progressives: A Social History of Stock and Commodity Speculation, 1890–1936* (Princeton, 1965), more a series of essays than a cohesive study, but the best work in a generally ignored field; Francis Eames, *The New York Stock Exchange* (New York, 1894), a solid history by a former NYSE president.

John Galbraith, *The Great Crash, 1929* (Boston, 1955), the best-known American economist of his day, his best-known book, on the most famous Wall Street event—popular but contentious, with questionable conclusions; Joseph L. King, *History of the San Francisco Stock and Exchange Board* (San Francisco, 1910), the best work on the subject; Joseph G. Martin, *A Century of Finance: Martin's History of the Boston Stock and Money Markets* (Boston, 1898), largely statistical and biographical; Martin Mayer, *Wall Street: Men and Money* (New York, 1959), a study of the financial district at the beginning of its greatest upward movement; James Medbery, *Men and Mysteries of Wall Street* (Boston, 1870), the best source for the early period; J. Edward Meeker, *The Work of the Stock Exchange* (New York, 1922), the financial district, when it had just assumed world leadership; Margaret Myers, *The New York Money Market* (New York, 1939), a thoughtful survey of the financial district in decline; Thomas Navin and Marion Sears, "The Rise of a Market for Industrial Securities, 1887–1902," in *Business History Review*, 29, (June 1955), details the evolution of the financial district and the rise of New York; Samuel A. Nelson, *The Consolidated Stock Exchange of New York* (New York, 1907), inadequate, but the only work on the subject.

Alexander Noyes, *Forty Years of American Finance* (New York, 1909), a perceptive history by the financial editor of the *New York Times;* and *The War Period of American Finance, 1908–1925* (New York, 1926), containing a discussion of how New York replaced London as the world financial center; *The Market Place* (Boston, 1938), Noyes's memoirs; *The Philadelphia Stock Exchange* (Philadelphia, 1903), sketchy, but the only work on the history of the first American stock exchange; Wallace Rice, *The Chicago Stock Exchange* (Chicago, 1928), inadequate, but contains a decent account of the founding; Matthew H. Smith, *Bulls and Bears of New York* (Hartford, Conn., 1875), a lively memoir; Robert Sobel, *The Big Board* (New York, 1965), a history of the New York stock markets; *The Curbstone Brokers* (New York, 1970), the outdoor market in New York prior to 1921; *Amex* (New York, 1972), a history of the American Stock Exchange; *N.Y.S.E.* (New York, 1975), the New York Stock Exchange since 1935; Edmund Stedman and Alexander Easton, *The New York Stock Exchange*, vol. 1 (New York, 1905), the first volume of an uncompleted history by a famous poet who also belonged to the NYSE, an excellent and accurate work; Dana L. Thomas, *The Plungers and the Peacocks* (New York, 1967), a history of the NYSE, with stress upon dramatic incidents and individuals; Chris Welles, *The Last Days of the Club* (New York, 1975), an invaluable study of the industry today; Sheldon Zerden, *Best Books on the Stock Market* (New York, 1972), a good bibliographic guide.

[*See also* AMERICAN BUSINESS INSTITUTIONS BEFORE THE RAILROAD; ECONOMIC GROWTH; ECONOMY FROM THE REVOLUTION TO 1815; ECONOMY FROM 1815 TO 1865; ECONOMY FROM RECONSTRUCTION TO 1914; ECONOMY SINCE 1914; FINANCIAL INTERMEDIARIES; RISE AND EVOLUTION OF BIG BUSINESS; *and* SAVINGS AND INVESTMENT.]

FINANCIAL INTERMEDIARIES

George D. Green

AS SEPARATE INSTITUTIONS financial intermediaries are primarily creations of the twentieth century. Commecial banks and savings banks have existed since the time of the American Revolution, but most other intermediaries—life insurance companies, credit unions, savings and loan associations, mortgage companies, and finance companies—have experienced their great development since about 1880.

This exploration of the development of financial intermediaries begins with a brief theoretical discussion of their role in the process of finance. We can then consider some of the reasons for their expanding role in the more advanced phases of the economic development of a nation. Looking backward from this modern perspective, we may also detect the earlier existence of informal financial intermediaries. These included not only the separate specialized institutions, such as commercial banks, but also storekeepers, cotton factors, and even governments that frequently functioned as financial intermediaries.

THE PROCESS OF FINANCE

Finance essentially involves the means by which people or institutions pay for goods and services they receive. Its simplest form is internal finance, or self-finance, in which expenditures are met out of current income or accumulated savings. Internal finance creates no debt or credit; all transactions are in cash or barter. The alternative to internal finance, not surprisingly, is external finance—that is, borrowing to pay for goods and services. In this form debt and credit are created, sometimes a long chain of debts and credits.

The two primary participants in external finance are the ultimate borrower, or debtor, and the ultimate lender, or creditor. The first is a participant in the nonfinancial economy—a farmer, manufacturer, merchant, consumer, or government—whose spending exceeds income and for whom borrowing fills the gap. To match this deficit spender there must be an ultimate lender, another nonfinancial participant who saves—that is, spends less than current income. External finance, however complicated it appears in any particular transaction, always boils down to transferring current purchasing power, or current command over goods and services, from the ultimate lender to the ultimate borrower, from creditor to debtor. The saving (not-spending) of one finances the deficit spending of the other. At some later time, of course, the debt will be repaid and purchasing power will flow in the other direction, usually augmented by interest.

Transactions in external finance may be either direct or indirect. With direct finance a single claim or security is transferred from ultimate borrower to ultimate lender, although it may pass through other hands along the way. This claim or security takes different forms, depending on the borrower who issues it. Businesses issue stocks, bonds, promissory notes, mortgages, and the like. Governments typically issue bonds. The U.S. Treasury has issued "greenback" currency, gold and silver certificates, and shorter-term bonds known as Treasury bills or notes. Households issue mortgages, installment loans, and other types of consumer debts.

Indirect finance involves two steps, and the special institution that is called a financial intermediary stands between borrower and lender. First, the ultimate borrower issues an original security to the financial intermediary and obtains funds; the financial intermediary in turn raises such loanable funds by issuing a new debt claim to the ultimate lender. By "shortstopping" the original security issued by the ultimate borrower, the financial intermediary puts into circulation a new layer of its own securities.

Each type of intermediary creates its own special type of new liability, and each in turn buys a somewhat different portfolio of assets from among the original securities issued by ultimate borrowers. Savings banks and savings and loan associations, for example, purchase mainly mortgages and government bonds; they issue deposit accounts and sometimes share accounts. Recently some of them have also begun issuing draft accounts that are virtually identical to checking accounts. Credit unions buy installment loans from their members and issue share accounts and deposit accounts. Life insurance companies buy mainly corporate and government bonds (and policy loans) and issue life insurance policies as their form of new security. Pension funds buy stocks and bonds and issue pension fund claims.

In similar fashion the Social Security fund invests in federal government bonds and issues claims or entitlements to retirement and other benefits. This is made more complicated by the fact that the Social Security funds serve various purposes and are not operated according to strict actuarial principles. They are supplemented by current tax revenues and burdened by the higher benefits legislated by Congress.

Commercial banks purchase government bonds, corporate securities, consumer installment loans, and various business loans. For their new liabilities they issue mainly checking and savings accounts and certificates of deposit, although until 1935 they also issued their own bank notes. In direct finance a security may pass through several hands on its way from the issuing borrower to the ultimate lender. Such securities are often exchanged through financial markets, such as the bond, stock, commercial paper, and mortgage markets. Over the centuries specialized brokers, dealers, and agents have emerged to carry out these market transactions. Stockbrokerages, for example, help to promote and underwrite the sale of new issues of corporate securities. Once these securities are in the hands of the buyers, the ultimate lenders to the corporation, the same brokerage firms exchange these "secondhand" outstanding stocks from one person to another. Most of the daily transactions by brokerage firms on the New York Stock Exchange involve these transfers of existing shares from one holder to another; only a small portion represents new issues, new acts of borrowing by corporations. The existence of such a market increases the liquidity and salability of corporate stocks for savers and therefore provides a more economical source of financing for the issuing corporations.

The brokers and dealers who operate financial markets and facilitate the process of direct finance are not financial intermediaries. (Strictly speaking, to the extent that brokerage firms lend to their customers in the form of "brokers' loans," they do become financial intermediaries.) Operators of direct finance and the financial intermediaries of indirect finance enjoy both complementary and competitive relations. The financial intermediaries find their business made less risky because many of their assets can be readily sold through the organized markets of direct finance. On the other hand, the market agents and the intermediaries compete as channels for the funds of savers. When savers purchase stocks or bonds instead of life insurance or certificates of deposit, financial intermediaries have missed an opportunity for growth. When savers withdraw their holdings from checking or savings accounts in order to purchase stocks, bonds, or Treasury bills, such "disintermediation" may place the banks or savings and loan associations under severe liquidity pressure.

The brokers and dealers of direct finance derive their incomes from sales commissions or capital gains earned through buying and selling on their own account. Financial intermediaries earn their incomes from the difference between the interest rates obtained on their earning assets (their portfolios of stocks, bonds, mortgages, and other items) and the interest rates paid on their liabilities (their checking or savings accounts, insurance policies, pension fund claims, and so on). This interest-rate differential must provide for operating expenses—salesmen, tellers, bookkeepers, managers, rent, and utilities—as well as profit for the owners.

If financial intermediaries make their living by charging a higher interest rate to their borrowers than they pay to their depositors, why not eliminate the middleman? Why not let ultimate borrowers and lenders conduct their transactions directly? Populist farmers of the 1890's bitterly pressed this argument. They considered bankers and mortgage brokers to be "parasites" and "speculators" who made their "usurious" living by exploiting and stealing from the "honest labor" of farmers and workers.

One can answer this question by identifying the functions that financial intermediaries perform in the economy and the motives that lead borrowers and lenders voluntarily to do business with them. But first one must acknowledge that showing that they perform useful services does not fully remove the populist complaint, unless one also can show that they do so with maximum efficiency and at minimum cost to their customers and society as compared to direct methods for channeling savings into the hands of productive borrowers. Historical experience reveals numerous instances of banking monopoly or cartel behavior, of imperfections in financial markets, of fraud or mismanagement. Financial intermediaries certainly have not been perfect in competition or efficiency. But they have performed useful services for their customers and the larger society.

Many savers prefer to deal with financial intermediaries because the new securities that those institutions issue have more attractive characteristics than the original securities issued by governments or nonfinancial corporations. Savers want to hold highly liquid assets from which they can remove their funds freely and on short notice. They want some assets that can be used as money, as means of payment for consumer transactions. They may want other assets that offer insurance benefits in case of death or protection against other risks. At the same time, borrowing corporations or governments would prefer to issue very different types of securities, usually with long maturities and fixed terms of repayment. Financial intermediaries meet the needs of both parties: they purchase the types of securities that borrowers prefer to issue, and they create the very different types of claims that savers prefer to hold.

Financial intermediaries can actually lower the real costs of finance, even as compared with the case of well-developed, competitive markets for direct finance. Their diversified portfolios enable small savers to pool their funds, thereby reducing risks. By gathering up the funds of small savers, they reduce the search and transaction costs for borrowers seeking funds. Through such pooling of funds and risks, and through the large volume of their transactions, they introduce economies of scale.

By enhancing the efficiency of the financial sector, financial intermediaries can improve the allocative efficiency and accelerate the economic growth of the whole economy. Availability of their assets permits low- and middle-income consumers to adjust their lifetime cycles of spending independently of the cycles of family income. They probably raise the aggregate savings supply by spreading the use of money in the economy and by offering more attractive financial assets to domestic and foreign savers. They can improve the mobility and allocation of savings into the most productive investment opportunities.

Raymond Goldsmith's fundamental statistical research on financial intermediaries and the relationship between financial structure and economic development, for the United States and other countries, provides a sturdy foundation for an initial overview of the relative importance of finance and financial intermediaries throughout American history. The first measure of the extent of the financial development of a nation is the ratio of financial ("intangible") assets to physical assets such as land, buildings, equipment, and inventories. Goldsmith calls this the "financial interrelations ratio." It begins typically at about 25 percent in financially undeveloped countries and rises to about 1.0 or 1.25, and occasionally even 2.0, before leveling off during advanced stages of financial development. The American experience conforms to this pattern. According to Goldsmith's estimates the ratio was only 43 percent in 1860 but rose to 76 percent by 1900 and 1.0 by 1922. For most of the period since 1929 the ratio has remained between 1.2 and 1.3, except for the extraordinary financial circumstances during World War II, when it rose to a temporary peak of 1.7 because of massive war debts (see table 1).

The higher the proportion of external finance and the more layers of credit or financial intermediation involved, the higher Goldsmith's ratio will be. It was low in early nineteenth-century America because little separation had developed between consuming and producing units in the

FINANCIAL INTERMEDIARIES

TABLE 1
Financial Intermediaries and National Assets, 1800–1949
(billions of dollars)

Year	National Assets Financial	National Assets Tangible	National Assets Total	Financial Intermediation Ratio (percent)	Assets of Financial Intermediaries	Share of Financial Intermediaries in Financial Assets (percent)	Share of Financial Intermediaries in National Assets (percent)
1800	[0.6]	2.4	3.0	25	0.05	[8]	2
1860	6.5	15.0	21.5	43.3	1.2	18.5	5.6
1870	17.0	31.5	48.5	54.0	2.5	14.7	5.2
1880	26.3	45.2	71.5	58.2	4.5	17.1	6.3
1890	41.5	65.0	106.5	63.8	8.5	20.5	8.0
1900a	68.8	90.2	159.0	76.3	15.2	22.1	9.6
1900b	68.8	90.2	159.0	76.3	18.2	26.5	11.4
1912	141.0	168.0	309.0	83.9	39.4	27.9	12.8
1922	327.0	326.0	653.0	100.0	93.8	28.7	14.4
1929	555.0	427.0	982.0	130.0	152.1	27.4	15.5
1933	411.0	322.0	733.0	128.0	132.9	32.3	18.1
1939	482.0	395.0	877.0	122.0	198.5	41.2	22.6
1945	987.0	570.0	1,557.0	173.0	400.7	40.6	25.7
1949	1,135.0	881.0	2,016.0	129.0	446.8	39.4	22.2

Source: Raymond Goldsmith, *Financial Intermediaries in the American Economy Since 1900* (Princeton, 1958), pp. 57–58, 318–319, 321, 331–333.
Note: The data on financial intermediaries do not include mortgage companies, securities brokers and dealers, and investment bankers. Goldsmith describes all his estimates for 1800 as "rough guesses." The bracketed figures are interpolated calculations to fill in the missing categories.

economy. Farming, manufacturing, and much commerce were conducted by family firms with little or no resort to formal external finance. (Borrowing from family, friends, or neighbors is impossible to trace statistically and is omitted from Goldsmith's measures.) Family accounts mixed spending for production and consumption. Most savings merely transformed family labor into physical capital by clearing fields and building houses or barns. Similarly, construction materials, capital equipment, and expanded inventories usually were financed internally, out of current income. The two sectors most heavily involved in external finance in the early nineteenth century were governments (federal and state) and merchants engaged in foreign trade.

As the economy developed during the nineteenth century, structural changes increased the demand for external finance. Family-centered agriculture, for instance, required more credit to finance large plantations and rapid development of new land. Costly transportation improvements, such as canals and railroads, required massive infusions of outside funding. As small shops gave way to larger factories, manufacturers required more external finance. The Civil War occasioned a tremendous burst of borrowing by the federal government, but for the rest of the century federal debt declined steadily from $2.8 billion in 1866 to $1.3 billion in 1900. Debts of state and local governments expanded to finance veterans' benefits and improvement projects; but the panic of 1873 forced abrupt fiscal retrenchments, and debts of state and local governments declined for the rest of the century.

External finance grew after World War I at roughly the same rate as the real wealth of the nation. Within the broad leveling pattern, though, major variations occurred in particular sectors. The federal government dramatically increased its share of external financing during the two major wars; its proportion of net outstanding public and private debt varied from 1.5 percent in 1916 to 8.6 percent in 1929, 62.2 percent in 1945, 30 percent in 1958, and 18.3 percent in 1970. Corporations maintained a fairly steady share of outstanding debt, which fell from 48.9 percent in 1916 to 42.8 percent in 1970. State and local governments remained at about 6–8 percent. Farmers financed more of their capital formation internally, reducing their share of total indebtedness from 9.5 percent in 1916 to 3.2 percent in 1970. Commercial and financial debt also fell sharply in relative significance, from 24.5 percent in 1916 to 3.7 percent in 1970. Consumer and mortgage debt increased dramatically, from 9.9 percent in 1919 to 24.2 percent by 1970.

While external finance grew in importance in the nineteenth century and then leveled off, a steadily increasing part of it flowed through financial institutions. Rudimentary banks and mortgage companies have existed at least since the Middle Ages; but, in Goldsmith's judgment, such institutions did not play large roles in any national economy until the nineteenth century. France and Great Britain, "the prototypes of modern financial structure and development," did not really develop their modern financial structures before the second quarter of the nineteenth century. The rise of modern structures in the United States may have started slightly earlier, at the beginning of the century. Even though America may have been one of the leaders in financial intermediation, Goldsmith is impressed primarily with how limited such institutions were in size and impact until about the 1880's. He estimates that the total assets of financial intermediaries in 1800 equaled about 2 percent of national assets (the sum of all tangible and financial assets); by 1880 their share had risen to only 6 percent. The next decades of rapid financial development brought their share to 10–11 percent by 1900, to more than 15 percent by 1929, and to 22 percent by 1949 (see table 1).

The narrow range of institutions apparent in the nineteenth century further illustrates this limited development. Commercial banks were clearly dominant, as they nearly always are in the early stages of financial development. These banks accounted for 75–80 percent of the assets of all intermediaries through the first half of the century and held 55 percent of the assets as late as 1900. The only other significant intermediaries were savings banks and insurance companies. As the use of indirect finance accelerated after 1880, the variety of institutions increased, and the relative importance of commercial and savings banks declined. Savings and loan associations, insurance companies, and government insurance programs grew more rapidly than the older institutions. By the early 1950's all the financial intermediaries together channeled about 30 percent of the net financial flow of the entire economy, more than 50 percent of the external finance, and more than 80 percent of the external savings generated by households.

As the increased specialization and scale of businesses and government generated greater reliance on external finance, a greater variety of financial intermediaries emerged to attract the funds of savers and to channel the savings over greater distances to a wider variety of borrowers. Initially meeting only the monetary needs of the economy, they eventually provided a full spectrum of savings accounts, insurance, and retirement programs. At first financing trade and building construction, they next met the needs of railroads and large manufacturers after the Civil War, and then the expanding demands of government and consumers in the twentieth century.

BANKING AND FINANCE BEFORE THE CIVIL WAR

In the earliest stages of American development, financial intermediation often arose outside the context of formal, specialized financial institutions. None of these institutions would qualify as financial intermediaries in Raymond Goldsmith's formulation, but they performed many of the same functions. The formal intermediaries, particularly the commercial banks, formed one important link in this informal chain of credit flows.

The predominant channel of credit was the merchants. Historians have rightly called the century before 1840 the era of "merchant capitalism." American development depended heavily on exports of agricultural products and imports of manufactured goods, and wealthy merchants in coastal cities dominated both trade and finance. Through their business transactions the savings of Europe flowed into the growing young nation. They transformed trade credits from English bankers, exporters, or manufacturers into trade credits to lesser merchants who operated in the coastal cities or interior towns. At the other end of this chain of credit stood the small shopkeeper, the country storekeeper, the farmer, or the small manufacturer. Chronically short of savings, American producers wanted to sell their products for quick cash, yet pay for their purchases of supplies on slow credit. Farmers earned their incomes only once a year and used their harvest receipts to pay off a year of purchases at the local stores. Getting the farmers' crops to distant markets and processing wheat into bread, corn into whiskey or salt pork, or cotton into cloth took many months more and required external financing to cover the time between payment to the farmer and sale to the final consumer.

Only a substantial volume of credit would cover the slow transportation and seasonal sales of farm products. American merchants forwarded that credit while providing other services. In the early nineteenth century some of them began to specialize in particular commodities, such as cotton, or in particular mercantile functions, such as insurance, note brokerage, or transactions in foreign exchange. Many of the specialized commodity merchants, such as the cotton factors, continued to serve as informal financial intermediaries or as commission agents for the direct flow of external finance to the cotton planters or other producers whom they served. Other merchants invested their personal capital and helped to channel trade credits into the growing manufacturing sector, most notably the textile industry. Those merchants specializing in financial services became the first generation of private, unincorporated bankers in America.

Private bankers had played a substantial role in external finance during the colonial period, and they remained influential throughout the nineteenth century. Most early private banks emerged from merchant banking or note brokerage—that is, buying and selling currency issues, bonds, and other items on a commission basis. In the first decades of the nineteenth century some of the largest private bankers, such as Stephen Girard of Philadelphia and Jacob Barker of New York, issued bank-note currency; but beginning with Virginia in 1787 and Massachusetts in 1799, several states eventually passed legislation restricting the lucrative privilege of currency issues to their chartered banks. Private bankers continued to operate by issuing deposits and dealing in bills of exchange and letters of credit. Such leading firms as Prime, Ward and King of New York and Alexander Brown and Sons of Baltimore (with branch houses in several other cities) dominated the foreign exchange business from the 1830's to the 1880's. Other private bankers of the 1840's and 1850's, such as Corcoran and Riggs of Washington, D.C., and E. W. Clark and Company of Philadelphia, evolved toward specialization in investment banking by marketing the bonds of governments and railroads.

When banking trouble after the panic of 1837 led several midwestern states to prohibit chartered banking and bank-note currency, private bankers moved in to fill the vacuum. Some of them relied on deposit banking. Others imported the currency issues of banks in other states or issued de facto currency in the guise of insurance company drafts. The most famous example was George Smith of Chicago, whose Wisconsin Marine and Fire Insurance Company in 1852 circulated nearly $1.5 million of notes in Illinois, Iowa, and other supposedly "bankless" states. Richard Sylla has estimated that more than seven hundred private banks operated in the 1850's, representing about one-third of the banks and one-fourth of the banking capital of the country. When "free banking" laws passed the Illinois (1851) and other state legislatures, many of these private banks converted to incorporated status; others became federal "free banks" under the National Banking Act of 1863. Incorporation of these private banks completed the final step in the evolutionary transition from informal financing within general merchant firms, to increasingly specialized merchant-banking firms, to the formally chartered financial intermediaries represented in Goldsmith's data.

Governments also served occasionally as informal financial intermediaries in antebellum America. After 1830 several states helped to raise capital for canals, railroads, and other improvement projects by issuing state bonds to eastern or European savers and then using the funds to buy the stocks or bonds of the projects. In several southern states such bond sales financed land banks that in turn issued mortgages on plantations, slaves, and urban real estate. In this case the southern governments and their chartered banks provided two-stage intermediation between European savers and planter borrowers. Federal government purchases of bonds of the early transcontinental railroads followed the same pattern, as have a host of federal credit agency activities in the twentieth century.

FINANCIAL INTERMEDIARIES

Municipalities have performed similar services, ranging from investments in early railroads to the modern practices of fund-raising subsidies for industrial parks, shopping centers, stadiums, or urban renewal projects.

While merchants, country storekeepers, private bankers, and governments all served as channels for credit flows, the most pervasive and important financial intermediaries in post-colonial America were the chartered commercial banks. From the chartering of the Bank of North America at Philadelphia in 1781, banking spread quickly to all the leading urban centers. Alexander Hamilton played a leading role in founding the Bank of New York in 1784; as secretary of the Treasury he guided the federal chartering of the even more influential first Bank of the United States in 1791. By 1800 there were twenty-six commercial banks, located not only in the leading coastal cities (Boston, New York, Philadelphia, Baltimore, and Charleston) but also in lesser coastal centers (such as Salem, Massachusetts, Portsmouth, New Hampshire, Providence, Rhode Island, and Newburyport, Massachusetts) and inland trading towns (such as Albany and Hartford). By 1820 the number of chartered banks had mushroomed to three hundred. Many of them were located in small towns all across the expanding country. By 1840 there were about 900 banks, and by 1860 more than 1,500. The money supply grew in a similarly dramatic fashion, from $30 million in 1800 to about $600 million in 1860, with 80 percent of the latter amount consisting of the bank-note and deposit liabilities of chartered banks.

At first glance such a rapid expansion of the early banking system may seem excessive and inflationary, calling to mind the old textbook tales of "wildcat" banking and financial panics, which some writers of the day attributed to "speculative orgies of overbanking." But this image soon pales. In the earliest decades banks were essentially "monetizing" a barter and mercantile credit economy. After 1820 the money supply grew at roughly the same rate as population and national income. The rapid expansion of banking was certainly not inflationary, since wholesale prices in 1860 were nearly 30 percent lower than in 1800. In fact, the demand for money had grown even faster than the increase in the supply the banks had of it.

Although the long-term growth of banking and money supply does not fit the old stereotypes of "wildcat" banking and financial panics, one cannot dismiss those themes entirely. A small minority of banks, concentrated in booming frontier areas, did approach the "wildcat" stereotype of high-risk loans and grossly inadequate cash reserves. Even in these areas bank failures resulted more from inexperienced management and overoptimistic expansion than from deliberate fraud. While the growth of banking served real needs and contributed to the growth of the economy, nationwide banking crises contributed to periodic instability, disrupted growth, bankruptcies, and hardship. Paul Trescott has succinctly outlined the American dilemma of banking policy:

> . . . how to reconcile their responsibilities toward credit with their responsibilities toward money. The former dictated liberality; the latter, conservatism. The clash between the two made itself felt most painfully with respect to the *liquidity* of the individual bank—its ability to pay depositors (and in times past, banknote holders) in cash on demand. . . . Throughout American banking history, emphasis has shifted from one to the other and back again. Efforts to improve the monetary functions of the banks stressed the need to keep bank money convertible into cash and to adapt the quantity of bank money to the state of the economic system as a whole. These efforts frequently involved restrictions on bank credit, either in amount or in kind. This restrictive process was likely, in turn, to cause a steady increase in unsatisfied credit needs, which might produce a new banking policy oriented more toward credit expansion—but with greater risk of monetary disturbance. Implicitly, this oscillation reflected the fact that each responsibility was too important to be subordinated to the other [*Financing American Enterprise*, pp. 10–11].

Concern for "sound money" had been strong in America since the colonial era of land banking and sometimes inflationary paper money issues. The vast majority of the populace believed that true money consisted of specie—that is, gold or silver coins. Other forms of money, particularly government paper money issues or bank-note currency, were acceptable specie substitutes to the extent that they were "as good as gold." In fact the national money supply included a great variety of foreign coins, most of them with nominal value well above their metallic content, and an even greater variety of bank notes and deposits. Coinage issued by American mints did not exceed the value of foreign coins in circulation until the 1850's. Individual bank notes might circulate at par with specie in their local area but were accepted by distant merchants or bankers only at a percentage discount. This discount reflected the transaction costs of returning them to their source for redemption as well as the risk that the issuing institution would not honor them. "Bank-note detector" magazines appeared in the 1820's and 1830's to help merchants and bankers determine which bank notes were acceptable and at what rates of discount. Again, the criterion of value was the likelihood that any given bank note was convertible into specie.

Bankers themselves and the governments that chartered or regulated them tried a great variety of measures to assure the "soundness" of the currency. Most states eventually limited note issues to incorporated banks and then indirectly controlled the currency supply by limiting the number of charters and the amount of currency that each bank could issue relative to its chartered capital. Such charter limits on the note issues of individual banks hardly guided the aggregate money supply, because legislators were haphazard in the creation of new banks and had no control over bank failures.

One of the more successful organized efforts by bankers to assure a "sound" currency was the Suffolk Banking System initiated by several Boston banks in 1819. The city banks forced their country bank neighbors to redeem the country bank notes regularly in specie or through bankers' balances maintained in the Boston banks. In addition to providing New England with a specie-based currency, the Suffolk scheme enabled the cartel of Boston banks to reduce the circulating currency of their country rivals and to expand their own note issues. The plan also represented an early form of regional clearing-house association.

The most powerful agents for enforcing the convertibility of bank notes before the Civil War were the first and second banks of the United States, chartered in 1791–1811 and 1816–1836, respectively. With branch offices in several states and a steady inflow of funds arising from their services as fiscal agents for the federal government, the two federally chartered banks could limit the circulation of state-bank currency by returning their notes for redemption in specie. This restraining power was used most consciously and effectively by the Second Bank of the United States, under Nicholas Biddle, between 1825 and 1836. By having each branch issue its own drafts as currency, Biddle soon dominated the domestic and foreign exchange business in the nation. He probably contributed to a more stable monetary system and less costly interregional transactions, but his expansion at the expense of powerful state banks led to political opposition and to President Andrew Jackson's veto of the recharter of the bank in 1832.

State legislatures tried a great variety of strategies to assure a "sound" currency convertible at par into specie. New York established the Safety Fund plan in 1829 for the insurance of bank notes (and of deposits, until an 1842 amendment) through a fund based on assessments against capital. The Safety Fund initiated the first program of periodic bank examinations and operated successfully for a dozen years, until a flurry of bank failures in 1842 exhausted the funds and required a state subsidy to pay off the notes of the failed banks. The New York plan represents a predecessor of the Federal Deposit Insurance Corporation. Several states tried to assure a specie-based currency by outlawing the issue of small-denomination bank notes, usually under ten dollars, and by imposing severe legal penalties, such as charter forfeiture or penalty interest charges, on banks that suspended specie payments on bank notes. While these legal approaches restrained or punished the excesses of some individual banks, they could not prevent systemwide lapses of specie convertibility during financial panics.

The most effective legislative measures to promote a specie-based money supply were the requirements of fractional specie reserves behind bank issues of currency or deposits. These reserve requirements evolved from earlier requirements that bank capital be paid in specie. Initially reserves applied only to bank notes; but beginning with the Louisiana Bank Act of 1842, they were generally extended to cover deposits as well. Early reserve requirements functioned very differently from those now enforced under the Federal Reserve system. They were intended to protect the holders of bank notes and deposits against loss in the case of bank failure; and, until at least the 1930's, reserve ratios were not used to control the aggregate money supply.

The pursuit of "sound money" moved beyond specie reserve requirements to concern about other bank assets. Until about the 1840's regulators focused on bank solvency. Most restrictions were directed at "speculative" loans or "accommodation" loans granted to bank directors or employees, or to others who might be perceived as high-risk borrowers. Some bankers and legislators argued that bank liabilities could be better protected by backing bank loans with tangible collateral, especially land or real estate, rather than with the "good name" of merchants or bank employees borrowing on "accommodation." Only gradually did banking theorists and practitioners distinguish between bank solvency (the ability to pay off all liabilities if given ample time) and bank liquidity (the ability to pay out funds promptly on short-term liabilities).

Once the liquidity of bank assets became the primary concern, the attack on "accommodation" loans evolved into a preference for strictly "commercial" loans, backed either by the collateral of goods on their way to market or by manufacturers' inventories. Such commercial loans, or "real bills," were believed to be automatically self-liquidating: when the goods reached market, the merchant would sell them and pay off his bank loan from the proceeds. The Louisiana Bank Act of 1842 was again an early expression of this doctrine. It required one-third specie and two-thirds commercial paper of less than ninety days' maturity behind all bank notes and deposits. The commercial-loan theory of sound banking came to dominate bank regulation in the years after the Civil War and was finally embodied in the Federal Reserve Act of 1913, only to become practically obsolete in World War I and theoretically obsolete during the depression of the 1930's.

The prolonged financial crisis following the panic of 1837 brought forth two seemingly antithetical "sound money" movements: the prohibition of note-issue banking in the 1840's and "free banking" in the 1850's. Iowa agrarians and many others reacted to the wave of bank failures after 1837 by denouncing all banking as a "mad, untamable beast" and a "withering and blighting curse." The solution would be to outlaw banking and return to "hard money." By 1852 chartered banking was prohibited in Illinois, Iowa, Wisconsin, Florida, Arkansas, Texas, California, and the Minnesota and Oregon territories. In addition Indiana and Missouri had replaced capitalistic banking with systems of state-operated branch-banking monopoly.

To the dismay of hard-money advocates, prohibition of chartered banking did not necessarily assure a pure specie circulation. Private bankers, insurance companies, and banks in adjacent states insisted on supplying paper currency as well as bank loans, and both seemed to fill popular demands. Ironically, these illicit money issues circulating in the "bankless" states were far less readily convertible into specie than were the bank notes of chartered banks in other states.

When the prohibition of paper currency proved unattainable and the hunger for easier credit grew stronger in the expanding economy of the 1850's, many former "antibank" agrarians turned to "free banking" as an alternative. Under a general bank-chartering law anybody could establish a bank as long as certain rules about minimum capital, number of directors, regular banking offices and hours, and other practices were followed. Such open access to banking privileges would end the "monopoly" features that supposedly had resulted from chartering banks by individual special laws. The assurance of a "sound" currency would depend on backing the note issues of the free banks with an equivalent value of government bonds placed in the hands of the state auditor or other government official. If the bank failed to redeem its notes (or deposits, in the few laws that covered them too), the official could sell the bonds and reimburse noteholders from the proceeds.

The free-banking plan originated in New York, which passed its act in 1838 (Michigan copied an early draft of the New York bill and passed its law first, in 1837). The idea grew in visibility and appeal during the troubled 1840's and was adopted in thirteen additional states during the next decade. In leading commercial states such as New York and Louisiana, the free banks operated quite successfully. In a number of midwestern states promoters created virtual "wildcat" banks under the same laws, and the rate of bank failures often ran above 50 percent within a few years. In these states the bond collateral for note issues often replaced specie reserves. The bank notes might ultimately be secure in the event of bank failure, assuming that the bonds had not depreciated in value, but they were less likely to be convertible into specie on demand. Clearly the distinction between bank solvency and bank liquidity still was not fully recognized.

For most Americans in the nineteenth century, recurring financial panics provided the most compelling evidence of the breakdown of "sound money" principles. Panics swept the nation in 1819, 1837–1839, 1857, 1873, and 1893, and citizens frequently blamed them on fraud, speculation, or mismanagement by individual bankers. Bankers certainly played a part in the financial panics, but the problem was beyond their individual comprehension or control and was built into the structure of the system. The chief source of vulnerability was the fractional reserve backing for bank notes and deposits. Specie was the chief component of bank reserves, but it was also the form of money preferred by the public and the ultimate medium for settlement of international accounts. There were good reasons for the emergence of this fractional reserve system. Individual bankers wanted to keep little idle specie and the maximum proportion of earning assets. Society wanted to supplement its limited specie supply with other compatible forms of money for domestic circulation. But the system left the money supply vulnerable to fluctuations from several sources. Shifts in the national balance of payments could drain specie to foreign countries. Such a drain to Britain after 1836 helped to precipitate the crisis of 1837.

Bankers tended to lower their reserve holdings in times of economic expansion, thereby increasing the money supply for a given specie reserve base, and to raise their desired reserve ratios in times of financial pressure. Likewise, in times of uncertainty and pressure the banking public tried to raise its ratio of specie to bank money holdings. This scramble for specie and liquidity by both bankers and the general public was doomed to failure, for there simply was not enough specie to go around. Pursuing it would only destroy other forms of money through bank failures or contractions and would force debtors into bankruptcy.

During financial panics bankers and their defenders chose to suspend specie convertibility for their notes and deposits in order to end the spiral of contraction and bankruptcy. By suspending specie payments the bankers could ease the pressure on their borrowers and give themselves time to rebuild reserves and liquidity. Suspension did not mean that the banks were permanently closed, although some critics sought exactly that result. Bank notes and deposits continued in circulation, usually at some trading discount relative to specie, and bankers could make or renew loans. The bankers often formed cartels or sought state regulation during periods of suspension, in order to assure that none of them exploited the absence of specie restraints to overexpand, and that all banks cooperated in rebuilding reserves and preparing for the eventual resumption of specie payments. Predictably some of the weaker banks closed their doors, but vigilant cartels and state surveillance could prevent them from dragging the stronger banks down with them.

Discussions of banking policy in nineteenth-century America concentrated more on "sound money" than on "easy credit"; yet, as Trescott claims, the demand for expanding bank credit could not be ignored. As the dominant financial intermediaries, banks made major contributions to financing economic expansion throughout the economy. Rapid monetary expansion between 1800 and 1860 was compatible with noninflationary economic growth; the money supply was multiplied by forty while gross national product grew to eighteen times its initial level and prices declined. More direct evidence of the contribution of banks to real economic growth can be found in their asset portfolios, which reveal what sectors of the economy received their flows of credit. While bankers were unable "to melt down property into money," as some Americans expected them to do, they certainly helped channel savings to finance the building of real property.

The primary recipients of bank loans, especially in the larger cities, were the merchants. Through such commercial loans the banks indirectly financed the production and movement to market of agricultural and manufactured goods, as the merchants extended credits to the producers. In rural areas the bankers often participated directly in lending to farmers or planters on mortgage or personal security. In New England they provided important external financing to the burgeoning textile manufacturers and to many other industries.

During the boom years of the 1830's and 1840's, when internal improvements projects flourished, several states experimented with "improvement banks," which were chartered corporations the money-issue powers and anticipated banking profits of which would finance construction of their assigned "improvement." With nearly all their assets tied up in one construction project, these banks generally suffered from extreme illiquidity and most of them failed in times of financial stringency. Other banks managed to provide more limited and sounder aid to transportation projects by purchasing canal or railroad bonds or making business loans to construction or operating companies; but the large transportation projects probably received proportionately smaller financial support from banks than did commerce, agriculture, or even manufacturing.

EMERGENCE OF NATIONAL MONEY AND CAPITAL MARKETS, 1863–1913

The National Banking Act of 1863 has often been seen as inaugurating a dramatically new era in financial history. In this view national bank charters with strict standards replaced a multitude of weaker state charters and permitted the establishment of a "uniform national currency." In fact, there was much continuity with pre–Civil War banking developments, and many postwar innovations came into existence to overcome restrictions on the national banks that limited their capacity to respond to credit demands. As time passed, it became apparent that the National Banking Act, despite its provision of a "uniform national currency," had not solved the problems of "sound money" and "easy credit." The banking system still subjected the economy to periodic financial panics, which led critics to complain of "inelastic currency" and "pyramiding" of bankers' reserves in New York City. Meanwhile, credit-hungry farmers and businessmen in the South and Midwest railed against withdrawal of credit by Wall Street, through the tempting payment of interest on bankers' balances, and the resulting higher interest rates in their regions. Several restrictive features of the national banking system seemed to them to limit its usefulness as a provider of credit. These complaints against the National Banking Act led to most of the proposals for reform that later became embodied in the Federal Reserve Act of 1913 and other financial legislation of the early twentieth century.

The fiscal crisis of the federal government during the Civil War provided the immediate stimulus for the new banking law. Troubled by the difficulties of selling federal bonds and the inflationary dangers of inconvertible Treasury "greenbacks," Lincoln's secretary of the Treasury, Salmon P. Chase, sought to create a market for the bonds by requiring new federally chartered banks to purchase them as collateral for their national currency issues. Chase also expected the new currency to displace the diverse and sometimes unreliable bank-note issues of the 1,500 state banks. When the original act of 1863 and its 1864 amendments did not attract enough state bankers to federal charters, Chase persuaded Congress in 1865 to impose a prohibitive 10 percent tax on state bank-note issues. By the end of 1866 more than 1,600 banks had taken out federal charters, and only about 200 remained in operation under state charters.

In its banking provisions the National Banking Act basically transferred the "free banking" provisions of New York, Louisiana, and other states to a new federal chartering act. Its chief innovation was the creation of a standard currency design for all bank notes to be issued by these nationally chartered banks, and the related provision that each national bank would redeem at par the bank notes of all its counterparts.

The Second Bank of the United States had tried on two occasions to establish such a national currency. It failed in 1816–1819 because fixed interregional exchange rates (par money values) would have required severe deflation of western land and commodity prices to match eastern price levels, in order to end both the imbalance of regional payments and the persistent flow of currency from interior to coastal cities. Nicholas Biddle was more successful in the second attempt during the 1820's because he began in a situation of roughly equal regional prices and balanced currency flows with bank transactions in domestic bills of exchange. The National Banking Act succeeded for essentially similar reasons: improved transportation and competition had limited regional price divergences, and bills of exchange and interbank deposits and loans had helped to equilibriate interregional payments.

The uniform national currency did not really solve the "sound money" problems: regional variations in currency supply, seasonal pressures on bank reserves, and periodic financial panics still reverberated throughout the system. One defect was the shortage of the new currency in the South and Midwest. The original act limited total national bank-note issues to $300 million; when the rush of charters in 1866 reached that limit, mostly from banks in the Northeast, the law prevented creating new charters in the interior. Even though the limit on note issues was raised in 1870 and eliminated in 1875, the high prices of federal bonds discouraged bankers from buying them to back currency issues. The high minimum capital requirement ($50,000) and virtual prohibition of loans on real estate collateral also discouraged the formation of national banks in the rural South and Midwest.

Critics also complained that the reserve requirements of the National Banking Act and the payment of interest on interbank deposit balances caused the "pyramiding" of reserves in central reserve cities, especially in New York. This "drainage" of bankers' funds from the interior supposedly reduced the allocation of bank credit in rural areas and encouraged "speculative" use of the funds as New York bankers lent them in the "call loan" market to stock and bond dealers and their customers.

From the bankers' perspective, bankers' balances in New York provided an efficient mechanism for receiving or collecting funds at a distant point. This liquid "secondary reserve" asset could earn good interest on surplus loanable funds between seasons of peak local credit demand. Correspondent-banking relationships offered an opportunity to diversify heavy portfolios of loans to local farmers and merchants, all of whom might default if the crop failed or its price fell drastically, with commercial paper, call loans, or other urban investments. Despite the image of "Wall Street monopoly," correspondent banking in New York was intensely competitive, to the extent that the reserve city bankers were unable to maintain even the customary collection fees for clearing out-of-town checks.

When the country bankers reduced their New York balances in the fall, in order to finance movement of the crops to market, the resulting pressure on New York bankers and the stock market always pushed interest rates to a seasonal peak, occasionally triggered the dreaded financial panic, and started a suspension of specie payments that spread from New York to the rest of the nation. The regional and seasonal "inelasticity" of the currency came to be considered the chief structural defect of the banking system.

In retrospect, this criticism of "pyramiding" reserves and "inelastic currency" appears misguided. It was not the concentration of reserves in New York that caused the trouble, but the lack of a "lender of last resort," a central bank or bankers' clearinghouse with the capacity to create additional reserves in a period of seasonal stress or a liquidity crisis. The midwestern critics who complained about the "drainage" of their funds to Wall Street did not recognize the connection between such seasonal cash flows and the other trade and capital flows in an interregional balance of payments. They also did not perceive the key role of New York as financial intermediary for the nation, balancing the eastward flow of short-term funds (the "drainage" of bankers' reserves) with the westward flow of long-term funds invested, for example, in farm mortgages or in the stocks and bonds of railroads and manufacturers.

The desire for an elastic currency gained support from the "real bills" doctrine of strictly commercial banking, which dominated banking theory and guided "sound money" policy from 1880 to World War I. This doctrine promised that if bankers would only restrict themselves to lending on collateral of "real bills" (nonrenewable, short-term commercial loans to finance commodities in transit or storage), the currency supply would automatically expand and contract "elastically" to meet "the needs of commerce, industry and agriculture." Unfortunately, this respectable doctrine was fallacious. First, it confused "currency" with "money" and overlooked the increasing role of checking-deposit money, which already accounted for a majority of bank transactions by 1880. Second, even merchants could default on their loans in a time of falling commodity prices or liquidity crisis. Third, such an "elastic" money supply, by expanding money and credit in the booms and shrinking them in recession periods of "slow trade," would only aggravate the cyclical instability of the economy.

Perhaps it is just as well, then, that bankers widely violated the "real bills" guidelines. Approximately half of their commercial loans were renewed routinely at maturity, providing a de facto long-term credit to finance their customers' working capital. Bankers also made many non-commercial loans—unsecured "accommodation" loans or loans against collateral of stocks and bonds or real estate. National banks in some rural states even found loopholes in the prohibition against real estate loans and made some 7–10 percent of their loans on mortgages.

It is ironic that bankers became most committed to a fallacious commercial-banking doctrine for the sake of "sound money" just at the time merchants were losing their financial grip on the economy and the demands for "easy credit" came increasingly from other sectors. High sales, prices, and profits during the Civil War enabled some manufacturers to wean themselves from dependence on credit supplied by their merchant distributors or suppliers. After the war manufacturers increasingly supplemented internal financing from retained profits with working-capital loans from banks and other financial intermediaries. The formation of large, vertically integrated corporations that combined production and marketing functions also reduced the demand for external financing of working capital. Meanwhile the manufacturers' growing demand for long-term capital would be met by nonbank intermediaries, notably life insurance companies, and by expanding access to stock and bond markets.

The National Banking Act imposed three restrictions that aroused sharp complaints from advocates of "easy credit." The high minimum capital requirement ($50,000) discouraged chartering of national banks in small towns and rural areas. The virtual prohibition against initiating loans on real estate collateral especially limited credit to farmers. Beginning in the 1890's, bankers and economists joined a chorus of complaint against the prohibition of branch banking, both within a single state and across state lines. Branches, they argued, could safely provide banking services in small towns where independent banks might be unprofitable, and interstate branching would provide the large banks and nationwide mobility of capital needed to serve the giant manufacturers. Critics of all three restrictions pointed to the uneven geographical distribution of national banks and the regional differentials in interest rates as evidence of restriction and inequity.

Between 1870 and 1914 regional differences in short-term interest rates diminished dramatically as regional money markets dealing in short-term debts gradually merged into one national market. Differences as high as 4 percent in 1870 narrowed to less than 1 percent after 1905. Partial relaxation of the restrictions in the National Banking Act came too late to contribute much to the change. Minimum capital was reduced to $25,000 in 1900, and restrictions on farm mortgage loans were removed in 1913. But the larger banking system had circumvented these restrictions decades earlier. Private and state-chartered banks did not die out under the National Banking Act, as Secretary Chase had expected, but grew quite successfully, especially after 1880, by issuing checking and savings deposits and filling the market gaps created by the restrictions against mortgage loans and small-town banking. The lack of branch banking was effectively compensated for by expansion of the correspondent-banking system. Further contribution to integration of the money market came from the development of a national market network in commercial paper, which was sold to both individuals and banks.

Interest-rate differentials narrowed in the market for long-term capital during the same period, with rapid convergence between 1870 and 1885 and gradual narrowing thereafter. A major contribution came from the mortgage banks and brokerage houses that channeled eastern funds into midwestern mortgages in the 1870's and 1880's. The failure of many of these firms in the agricultural depression of the 1890's may help to explain the slower convergence of interest rates. The emergence of large life insurance companies in the 1880's also helped to mobilize capital funds nationally. In the 1890's the New York Stock Exchange and investment bankers such as J. P. Morgan extended their business beyond government bonds and railroad securities to create a national market for the stocks and bonds issued by manufacturing firms. Both improvement of the markets for direct finance and development of new financial intermediaries thus contributed to the growth of the national market in finance. By World War I only the South and the Pacific Coast states remained somewhat outside this integrated market.

Although the Federal Reserve Act of 1913 was a landmark in the slow development of American central-banking and monetary policy, it had remarkably little impact on the structure of banking or financial intermediation. In its attempts to resolve the historic tension between "sound money" and "easy credit," the act embodied the fallacious commercial loan doctrine. One obvious concession to "easy credit" was the substitution of twelve regional reserve banks for one central bank. Representatives from the West and South believed that the decentralized regional structure would prevent Wall Street domination and would permit the bankers of the interior to maintain the lower interest rates and easier credit so appealing to the farmers and businessmen of their regions. But the convergence of national money and capital markets that had been lowering their interest rates toward those of other regions would now deny them the autonomy of an independent regional credit policy.

DIVERSITY AND INSTABILITY IN THE TWENTIETH CENTURY

The growth of new financial institutions in the last half of the nineteenth century contributed to the integration of the national capital market and enhanced the volume and mobility of savings available to finance investment projects. At midcentury commercial banks probably held nearly 80 percent of the assets of all financial intermediaries; by 1900 they remained dominant but their share had fallen to 53 percent (see tables 2 and 3). The growth of mutual savings banks, mortgage companies, life insurance companies, and personal trust departments accounted for most of the decline.

Mutual savings banks had emerged early in the nineteenth century, modeled on European institutions that encouraged saving among the poor and laboring classes. Even though many of these early institutions maintained a commitment to the philanthropic tradition, they also accepted a significant volume of deposits from small businessmen and the middle class. Located primarily in the northeastern states, they experienced earlier and more gradual growth than other nonbank intermediaries. Roughly tripling their total deposits each decade from 1840 to 1870, they grew much more slowly thereafter, averaging only about 65 percent growth per decade from 1870 to 1920 and even lower rates after 1920. They reached their peak share of total intermediation (13 percent) in 1900 and have receded steadily since then, to about 4 percent in 1975. Early in the nineteenth century mutual savings banks mobilized added savings to purchase government bonds that helped to finance the Erie Canal and other projects. Since the 1840's their resources have overwhelmingly gone into building mortgages.

Savings and loan associations, quite similar to mutual savings banks in their allocation of funds to mortgages, have experienced their most significant growth in the twentieth century, particularly during the construction booms of the 1920's and the years since World War II. Their share of total intermediation ranged from 2 to 5 percent earlier in the century but had risen to about 10 percent in 1975.

In 1850 insurance meant mainly fire and marine insurance. Life insurance companies proliferated in England in the eighteenth century and a few small companies had formed in America, beginning in 1812 with the Pennsylvania Company for Insurance on Lives and Granting Annuities and the Massachusetts Hospital Life Insurance Company in 1823. A wave of mutual insurance companies emerged in the 1840's, but the industry began its period of major growth and consolidation in the late 1860's. The financial crisis and depression after 1873 interrupted this growth as many newer companies failed and the volume of insurance in force shrank. By the 1880's the largest companies spearheaded renewed growth. Equitable, Mutual of New York, and New York Life developed through the sale of tontine insurance with accumulating dividends, while Prudential, Metropolitan, and John Hancock grew through the sale of industrial insurance in the form of small policies to the working classes.

As these large companies increased their total insurance in force into the billion-dollar range, their attention shifted increasingly to the profitable investment of their accumulating reserves. By the time of the New York investigation and regulatory legislation of 1905–1906, the executives of the top insurance companies had moved from the periphery to the inner circle of financial capitalism. Since then their share of intermediation has remained fairly constant at 10–15 percent.

Personal trust companies or the trust departments of banks and insurance companies have long played an important role in administering

FINANCIAL INTERMEDIARIES

TABLE 2
Total Assets of Main Groups of Financial Intermediaries, 1900–1975
(billions of dollars)

Group	1900	1912	1922	1929	1933	1939	1945	1949	1952	1965	1975
Banking system	12.4	25.9	59.5	81.7	65.2	98.5	225.4	228.1	268.4		
Federal Reserve banks	—	—	5.3	5.5	7.0	19.0	45.1	45.6	51.9	65.5	124.7
Commercial banks	10.0	21.8	47.5	66.2	46.1	66.3	160.3	157.7	188.6	343.6	873.6
Mutual savings banks	2.4	4.0	6.6	9.9	10.8	11.9	17.0	21.5	25.2	59.1	121.1
Postal savings system	—	0	0.1	0.2	1.2	1.3	3.0	3.3	2.7		
Insurance	2.3	5.6	11.8	25.0	29.1	42.6	82.8	118.9	149.2		
Private life insurance companies	1.7	4.4	8.7	17.5	20.9	29.2	44.8	59.6	73.4	154.2	279.9
Fraternal insurance organizations	0	0.2	0.5	0.8	1.0	1.2	1.6	2.0	2.3		
Private noninsured pension funds	..	..	0.1	0.5	0.7	1.0	2.9	6.0	9.0	73.6	148.9
Federal } pension, retirement, and social security	..	..	0.1	1.0	2.1	4.6	22.6	34.3	41.0		
State and local } funds	0	0	0.1	0.5	0.8	1.7	3.0	4.9	7.5	34.1	106.0
Fire and marine insurance companies	0.4	0.8	1.6	3.1	2.2	2.8	4.2	6.6	8.7	36.5	77.4
Casualty and miscellaneous insurance companies	0.1	0.2	0.7	1.6	1.3	2.0	3.5	5.4	7.2		
Savings bank life insurance departments	—	0	0	0	0	0	0.1	0.1	0.1		
Miscellaneous financial intermediaries	0.5	1.0	1.6	15.4	13.7	22.4	47.5	49.7	71.5		
Savings and loan associations	0.5	1.0	2.8	7.4	6.2	5.4	8.6	14.5	22.5	129.6	338.4
Credit unions	..	..	0	0	0	0.2	0.4	0.8	1.5	11.0	37.0
Investment companies	..	..	0.1	3.0	1.3	1.6	2.7	3.3	6.1		
Land banks	—	—	1.0	1.9	1.9	2.4	1.2	1.0	1.2		
Government lending institutions	—	0	0.7	0.4	2.8	9.8	32.6	23.7	29.9		
Sales finance companies	..	..	..	2.1	1.0	2.3	1.1	4.8	7.7	44.7	98.4
Personal finance companies	..	..	..	0.4	0.3	0.6	0.6	1.3	2.0		
Factors	..	..	..	0.1	0.1	0.1	0.2	0.3	0.5		
Personal trust departments	3.0	7.0	18.0	30.0	25.0	35.0	45.0	50.0	60.0		
Total, standard definition	18.2	39.4	93.8	152.1	132.9	198.5	400.7	446.8	549.0		
Mortgage companies	0.2	0.4	0.6	0.8	0.4	0.4	0.2	0.5	0.6		
Securities brokers and dealers	0.6	1.0	4.0	10.0	2.5	2.0	3.0	2.7	3.5	10.3	17.2
Investment holding companies	..	..	..	4.4	1.7	1.6	2.3	2.4	3.3		
Total, broad definition	19.0	40.8	98.4	167.3	137.6	202.5	406.1	452.4	556.4		

Sources: 1900–1952—Raymond Goldsmith, *Financial Intermediaries in the American Economy Since 1900* (Princeton, 1958), pp. 73–74; 1965, 1975—Board of Governors, Federal Reserve System, *Flow of Funds Accounts, 1946–1975* (Washington, D.C., 1976), passim.

the estates of wealthy Americans. Their total assets grew rapidly in the late nineteenth century and the first three decades of the twentieth, to a peak share of 18 percent of the total assets of financial intermediaries by 1929. The majority of the funds of these trusts always has been invested in corporate stocks or bonds, but the remaining portion has shifted dramatically from real estate (40 percent in 1900) to government bonds (about 30 percent after World War II).

Since 1900 new institutions have increased the diversity and complexity of financial intermediation. Along with growing production of automobiles and other consumer durables, sales finance companies and personal finance companies have expanded to provide the neces-

FINANCIAL INTERMEDIARIES

TABLE 3
Percentage Distribution of Total Assets of Main Groups of Financial Intermediaries, 1900–1952

Group	1900	1912	1922	1929	1933	1939	1945	1949	1952
Banking System*	65.6	63.4	60.4	48.9	47.4	48.7	55.5	50.4	48.2
Federal Reserve banks	—	—	5.3	3.3	5.1	9.4	11.1	10.1	9.3
Commercial banks	52.8	53.5	48.2	39.6	33.5	32.7	39.5	34.9	33.9
Mutual savings banks	12.8	9.8	6.7	5.9	7.8	5.9	4.2	4.8	4.5
Postal savings system	—	0.1	0.1	0.1	0.9	0.7	0.7	0.7	0.5
Insurance	11.9	13.7	12.0	15.0	21.1	21.1	20.4	26.3	26.8
Private life insurance companies	9.2	10.8	8.8	10.5	15.2	14.4	11.0	13.2	13.2
Fraternal insurance organizations	0.1	0.4	0.5	0.5	0.7	0.6	0.4	0.4	0.4
Private noninsured pension funds	..	..	0.1	0.3	0.5	0.5	0.7	1.3	1.6
Federal pension, retirement, and social security funds	..	..	0.1	0.6	1.6	2.3	5.6	7.6	7.4
State and local funds	0	0	0.1	0.3	0.6	0.8	0.7	1.1	1.3
Fire and marine insurance companies	2.2	1.9	1.7	1.8	1.6	1.4	1.0	1.4	1.6
Casualty and miscellaneous insurance companies	0.4	0.6	0.7	1.0	0.9	1.0	0.9	1.2	1.3
Savings bank life insurance departments	—	0	0	0	0	0	0	0	0
Miscellaneous financial intermediaries	2.6	2.4	4.6	9.2	10.0	11.1	11.7	11.0	12.8
Savings and loan associations	2.6	2.3	2.8	4.4	4.5	2.7	2.1	3.2	4.0
Credit unions	..	..	0	0	0	0.1	0.1	0.2	0.3
Investment companies	..	..	0.1	1.8	0.9	0.8	0.7	0.7	1.1
Land banks	—	—	1.0	1.2	1.4	1.2	0.3	0.2	0.2
Government lending institutions	—	0.1	0.7	0.2	2.1	4.8	8.0	5.2	5.4
Sales finance companies	..	..	..	1.2	0.7	1.1	0.3	1.1	1.4
Personal finance companies	..	..	..	0.2	0.2	0.3	0.1	0.3	0.4
Factors	..	..	..	0.1	0.1	0.1	0.1	0.1	0.1
Personal trust departments	15.8	17.2	18.3	17.9	18.2	17.3	11.1	11.1	10.8
Total, standard definition	95.9	96.7	95.4	91.0	96.6	98.0	98.7	98.8	98.7
Mortgage companies	1.0	0.9	0.6	0.5	0.3	0.2	0	0.1	0.1
Securities brokers and dealers	3.2	2.5	4.1	6.0	1.8	1.0	0.7	0.6	0.6
Investment holding companies	..	..	..	2.6	1.3	0.8	0.6	0.5	0.6
Total, broad definition	100.0	100.0	100.0	100.0	100.0	100.0	100.0	100.0	100.0

Source: Raymond Goldsmith, *Financial Intermediaries in the American Economy Since 1900* (Princeton, 1958), pp. 75–76.

sary credits to dealers and consumers. Credit unions emerged in the Progressive era to reassert the traditional benefits of thrift as well as to participate in the increased volume of household finance. In the 1920's pension funds appeared as businesses began to finance retirement programs for their employees. These small beginnings were extended by creation of the Social Security program during the Great Depression; both private and public pension funds have expanded rapidly since World War II, accounting for nearly 20 percent of intermediation in the 1970's.

In addition to the growth of several new financial institutions, the twentieth century has seen major changes in the sectoral allocation of funds by financial intermediaries. Especially during major wars the federal government has increased its share of funds outstanding. In 1900 financial intermediaries provided only 5 percent of their loanable funds to the federal government. After massive bond purchases during World War I, this share had risen to 12 percent in 1922. Falling back to 7 percent by 1929, the federal share then rose during the depression—to 15 percent in 1933 and 28 percent in 1939—as other sectors sought to reduce their indebtedness. Federal borrowing during World War II left the intermediaries with 64 percent of their funds in government bonds by 1945; but the federal share dropped rapidly to 41 percent by 1952, as other sectors borrowed and expanded. The household sector also received an increased share of funds through expanding home mortgages and the widespread provision of consumer installment credit. The rising allocation of funds to government and families has been balanced by declining shares to agriculture, down from 10 percent in 1920 to 3 percent in 1952. Similarly, business saw its share fall from 57 percent in 1900 to 30 percent in 1952. Both of these sectors have relied relatively less on funds from financial intermediaries as they have increased their use of internal finance from retained earnings and depreciation allowances.

Since 1900 other important changes have occurred in the organizational structure of financial intermediation. Some financial institutions have experienced the failure of many small firms and the concentration and consolidation of large ones into the national oligopoly structure so characteristic of modern industry. The severe depression of the 1930's spread illiquidity and failure throughout the economy, including many of its financial institutions. As the government belatedly attempted financial rehabilitation and "reforms," the nation entered an era of increased federal regulation and a permanently expanded role for the government and its agencies as financial intermediaries.

Certain of the financial intermediaries had experienced increased concentration since the beginning of the century, most notably life insurance companies, personal trust departments, and the largest commercial banks. Other institutions, such as credit unions, savings and loan associations, savings banks, and small-town commercial banks, remained small and served primarily local markets. During the 1920's the larger commercial banks increased the scope of financial concentration by mergers, establishment of foreign branches and subsidiaries, and creation of affiliates to deal in real estate and marketing of stocks and bonds. Under the McFadden Act of 1927, several national banks established branches within their home cities.

Meanwhile, between 1921 and 1929 nearly six thousand banks suspended operations. A large fraction of them were small banks capitalized at $25,000 or less, located in small towns suffering financial distress from agricultural depression or the increased automobility of the rural population.

Contrary to popular impressions, the stock market crash of 1929 had little immediate harmful impact on commercial banks or other savings institutions. In fact, many of them received larger deposit inflows during 1930 as savers shifted to more liquid and less risky assets. The failure of many small country banks continued at roughly the same rate as before the crash. But as the emerging depression reduced the flow of incomes and personal savings, and falling incomes and prices increased the burdens of debtors and reduced the market value of bonds and other financial assets, even the larger and stronger financial intermediaries felt the pressure of illiquidity and the danger of insolvency.

The first wave of bank failures, in October–December 1930, included the Bank of United States, with $200 million in deposits. The depression spiral of incomes and prices, bankruptcies, debt defaults, and falling asset values brought other waves of bank failures in 1931 and 1932, and climaxed in the nationwide suspension of bank operations in March 1933. During that downward spiral more than eight thousand banks closed their doors, depriving their depositors of liquidity and their communities of credit flows. Savings and loan associations suffered similar illiquidity from withdrawals of savings and the inability of many of their debtors to maintain mortgage payments. Mutual savings banks suffered less because they were concentrated in slow-growing New England, had very conservative investment policies, and were perceived by savers as safe havens for funds. Life insurance companies found their mortgages and bonds severely depreciated and paid out large sums in loans or cash values to policyholders, but they suffered somewhat less because their liabilities were long-term and their customers tried desperately to maintain insurance protection by liquidating other assets first.

During the 1930's, and probably even today, many Americans blamed the stockbrokers and bankers, the "speculators and manipulators," for causing the depression. Many of the legislative "reforms" of the New Deal rested on this assumption. Certainly there were some well-publicized cases of risky investments, loans to privileged insiders, and attempts to manipulate financial markets. In retrospect most economic historians now see the financial institutions more as victims than as villains of the depression process. Most of the nation apparently shared their unfulfilled expectations of permanent growth and prosperity, which, along with high corporate earnings, propelled the stock market boom. The Federal Reserve system now receives sharp criticism, born of hindsight, for its failure to increase bank reserves and create liquidity to counteract the downward spiral of 1929–1933. Congress and presidents Herbert Hoover and Franklin D. Roosevelt generally earn equally poor marks for the lack of a strongly expansionary fiscal policy.

Although it failed to counteract the depression spiral, the government did eventually try to rescue crippled financial institutions from the worst consequences of the depression. Both Congress and many state legislatures allowed debtors to postpone or write down their debts rather than suffer bankruptcy or foreclosure on mortgages. Although these measures gave relief to debtors, they added in equal measure to the liquidity and solvency problems of the financial intermediaries and other creditors. Much more helpful were the many federal lending agencies that served as financial intermediaries, selling bonds and pumping the proceeds into the purchase of farm mortgages, home mortgages, or the stocks of distressed financial institutions.

The European financial crisis of the summer and fall of 1931 convinced President Hoover that recovery was not "just around the corner." After failure of his efforts to persuade bankers to pool their own funds to rescue failing banks, he supported congressional creation of the Reconstruction Finance Corporation (RFC) in January 1932. Essentially a resurrection of the War Finance Corporation, which had financed war production as well as farm exports in the 1920's, the RFC lent $1.4 billion to banks, savings and loan associations, and other financial institutions by March 1933, and purchased another $1 billion of bank stock by 1937. The Federal Home Loan Bank Board, established in July 1932, made a trivial contribution by lending $88 million on mortgage collateral to financial institutions.

Two groups of debtors—farmers and homeowners—especially benefited from new federal lending agencies. Farmers actually had received government-sponsored loans from land banks and intermediate credit banks since 1916. Consolidating many farm loans under the Farm Credit Administration (FCA) in 1933, the government purchased $2.1 billion of farm mortgages from farmers and financial institutions between 1933 and 1936. By the latter year FCA agencies held 40 percent of all farm mortgages. Similarly the Home Owners Loan Corporation (HOLC) held 20 percent of all home mortgages by 1936, with most of the $3.1 billion invested providing added liquidity and solvency to banks, savings and loan associations, savings banks, and mortgage companies.

The formation of the Federal Housing Administration (FHA) in 1934 to insure long-term home mortgages offered benefits to both the lending institutions and the middle-class home buyers. Since the depression years FHA has grown into a permanent subsidy program, while the crisis lending agencies (RFC, FCA, and HOLC) have preceded a long succession of other federal lending agencies not only for farmers, homeowners, and the construction industry, but also for the Lockheed Corporation, small businesses, and countless other special interests. In this fashion the share of government intermediaries, including Social Security, rose from less than 5 percent in 1929 to 10 percent in 1933, to 18 percent in 1939, and to 24 percent in 1952.

The federal government went beyond emergency measures to expand the flow of credit and to rescue debtors and financial institutions. Persuaded that the personal misdeeds and structural flaws of the financial institutions had largely caused the Great Depression, Congress attempted to "reform" the financial system. Most of the critical publicity was directed at the stock market, the brokers, dealers, and operations of which were subjected to increased regulation under the Securities Act of 1933 and the Securities Exchange Act of 1934. Some of this attack on the stock market spilled over onto the big commercial banks with securities affiliates. Attempting to restore the bankers to the "true faith" of strictly commercial banking, the Banking Act (or Glass-Steagall Act) of June 1933 required the complete divorce of commercial and investment banking. Wall Street spokesmen bitterly attacked these regulatory initiatives, complaining that such laws would disrupt the financing of business investment essential to recovery. Although the changes probably had some temporary disruptive effect, they have caused minimal long-run structural change in either banking or the brokerage industry.

Other reformers blamed the depression on "overbanking" during the 1920's and sought to reduce the risks of bank suspensions and failures. Since the mid-1920's both state and federal chartering authorities had sharply restricted the chartering of new banks. The Banking Act of 1933 included a further package of "reform" ideas: expanded branching powers for national banks, deposit insurance, prohibition of interest on checking accounts, and interest-rate ceilings on savings deposits. As financial policymaking has emerged from the intellectual shadow of depression fears and the generous faith of the New Deal generation in federal regulation, some of these 1933 "reforms" have been subjected to criticism and calls for revision.

The concern about "overbanking" led comptrollers of the currency to restrict national bank charters until James Saxon took office in 1961. As the economy expanded after World War II, this policy provided some cartel protection to the established national banks, although the chartering of nearly 1,400 new state banks between 1936 and 1955 limited the market protection in many states and helped to meet the demand for banking services in growing communities.

More controversial than chartering new banks was the movement to expand the branching powers of existing banks. Heavy failure and suspension rates among small unit banks in the 1920's and 1930's convinced many observers that branch banking was "sounder"; but the independent bankers maintained a vigorous lobbying effort against the "monopolistic" dangers of such increased competition from the branches of large city banks. Branching had grown strongly in the 1920's, mainly in state-chartered banks. The Banking Act of 1933, allowing national banks the same branching powers that each state permitted to its state-chartered banks, opened an era of slow, steady growth in branch banking from 584 banks with 2,786 branches in 1933 to 1,241 banks operating 4,721 branches in 1950. Development of large-scale data-processing operations and expanded banking services encouraged accelerated branching in the 1950's and 1960's, reaching nearly 4,000 banks with more than 21,000 branches by 1970. Where branching is legally restricted, similar results have been obtained by forming chains or groups of banks under a bank holding company. Some economists argue that nationwide branching would permit banks to provide more efficient service and greater mobility of their financial capital.

Clearly the most successful and influential reform of the Banking Act of 1933 was the insurance of bank deposits through the Federal Deposit Insurance Corporation. Its primary purpose and benefit has been not just to protect small depositors against loss, but to protect the national money supply against disruptions due to panic withdrawals of deposits or frozen deposits in suspended banks. By raising public confidence and improving the scope and standards of federal bank examinations, the law has reduced the once widespread bank failures or suspensions to a handful each year. Similar federal deposit insurance was extended to savings and loan associations in 1934 and to credit unions in 1970.

Senator Carter Glass believed that payment of competitive interest on deposits had pressured bankers into making "speculative" loans and investments, and also had attracted country bankers to hold interbank deposits instead of loans to their rural customers. He therefore included in the Banking Act of 1933 a prohibition against interest on demand deposits and a ceiling on interest rates for time and savings deposits, to be administered primarily by the Federal Reserve. For many years bankers quietly supported this cartellike price-fixing arrangement. By the 1960's these interest ceilings on savings deposits began to cause massive withdrawals, or "disintermediation," as depositors shifted to the higher rates available on Treasury bills or other assets. In the 1970's savings banks, savings and loan associations, and credit unions created interest-bearing accounts with draft, checking, or electronic payment privileges. These "near moneys" provided increased competition with bank checking accounts and caused bankers to seek loopholes, such as automatic transfers from savings accounts, to avoid the 1933 prohibition. Increasing numbers of economists have argued in recent years that the "reforms" of the 1930's should give way to at least a measure of "deregulation" in the 1980's, allowing banks and other financial intermediaries to compete more vigorously for both deposits and the full range of investment opportunities.

BIBLIOGRAPHY

Lance Davis, "Capital Immobilities and Finance Capitalism: A Study of Economic Evolution in the United States, 1820–1920," in *Explorations in Entrepreneurial History,* 1 (Fall 1963), views finance capitalists such as J. P. Morgan as temporary monopolists of mobile funds during the transition to a national and international capital market; and "The Investment Market, 1870–1914: The Evolution of a National Market," in *Journal of Economic History,* 25 (Sept. 1965), states that commercial paper and mortgage dealers reduced market imperfections and regional interest-rate differentials. Milton Friedman and Anna J. Schwartz, *A Monetary History of the United States, 1867–1960* (Princeton, 1963), concentrates on determinants and importance of changing money supply, but also has valuable details on banking laws and monetary policy decisions. Raymond W. Goldsmith, *Financial Intermediaries in the American Economy Since 1900* (Princeton, 1958), is the definitive statistical study for its period (1900–1952); see also other important theoretical and comparative developmental studies by Goldsmith.

Bray Hammond, *Banks and Politics in America From the Revolution to the Civil War* (Princeton, 1957), is a Pulitzer Prize–winning history by a Federal Reserve staff member seeking the origins of central banking half a century before its time.

John A. James, *Money and Capital Markets in Postbellum America* (Princeton, 1978), is one of several excellent studies of the period (1860–1913) before the Federal Reserve Act. Emerson W. Keyes, *A History of Savings Banks in the United States From Their Inception in 1816 Down to 1874,* 2 vols. (New York, 1876–1878), is a classic study, state by state, full of data and anecdotes. Alan L. Olmstead, *New York City Mutual Savings Banks, 1819–1861* (Chapel Hill, N.C., 1976), is a valuable study of investment decisions and social backgrounds of depositors. Fritz Redlich, *The Molding of American Banking* (New York, 1968), originally published in 2 vols. (1947–1951), is a remarkable encyclopedic study of banking theories, laws, and institutions from European origins to 1913.

J. Owen Stalson, *Marketing Life Insurance* (Cambridge, Mass., 1942), is a useful business-history survey of the life insurance industry. Paul Studenski and Herman E. Krooss, *Financial History of the United States,* 2nd ed. (New York, 1963), is a basic survey of money, banking, and public finance. Richard Sylla, "Federal Policy, Banking Market Structure, and Capital Mobilization in the United States, 1863–1913," in *Journal of Economic History,* 29 (Dec. 1969), challenges some of Davis' interpretation and emphasizes the impact of amendments to the National Bank Act; and "Forgotten Men of Money: Private Bankers in Early U.S. History," in *Journal of Economic History,* 36 (Mar. 1976), argues that the numbers and money-creating influence of private bankers before the Civil War were greater than previously acknowledged. Paul B. Trescott, *Financing American Enterprise* (New York, 1963), stresses the dilemma of "sound money" versus "easy credit" and emphasizes the contributions of banking to entrepreneurial success and economic development.

[*See also* BUSINESS CYCLES, PANICS, AND DEPRESSIONS; CENTRAL BANKING; EXCHANGES; INSURANCE; MONEY SUPPLY; *and* SAVINGS AND INVESTMENT.]

INSURANCE

Harold F. Williamson

A longing for security and attempts to find ways of avoiding or reducing the incidence of risk and uncertainty are as old as man himself. In ancient times individuals sought to avoid hazards simply by joining forces so that they faced adversity as a group. While this arrangement did not prevent misfortune from overtaking an individual, it did serve to make the misfortune of one the misfortune of all.

Modern insurance is also a way of spreading over a group a financial loss too heavy to be borne conveniently by one individual. It is essentially a device for reducing risks by applying the theory of probability to a sufficient number of exposures so as to make individual losses collectively predictable. On the basis of such estimates, insurers are able to offer an individual the opportunity of substituting a small but certain cost (premium payment) for an uncertain but possible large loss (the amount of the policy) under an arrangement whereby the few who do suffer a loss are compensated by the many who do not.

ORIGINS OF MODERN INSURANCE

Although something akin to insurance was used by the Babylonians and the Phoenicians, the first examples of anything resembling modern insurance were the marine contracts developed by the Greeks and Romans. Under these agreements a shipowner or merchant would borrow funds from a moneylender, pledging his ship or cargo as collateral. If the ship or cargo was lost, the loan was canceled; if the venture was successful, the loan was repaid with a sufficiently high rate of interest to cover both a return for the use of the capital and an additional amount ("premium") to cover the risks involved.

Early forms of life insurance were also evident in Greece and Rome with the growth of burial societies, which, in return for monthly fees, covered funeral costs of members and gave financial assistance to the families of the deceased. During the Middle Ages these functions were assumed by the guilds, which, in addition, commonly accumulated funds to protect members against the perils of fire, robbery, and "live stock mortality."

The postmedieval resurgence of the seaborne Mediterranean trade, centered in the Italian city-states during the thirteenth and fourteenth centuries, brought a renewed interest in marine insurance. By the early fifteenth century, codes of rules for the conduct of the business, strikingly similar to modern underwriting procedures, had been developed. By this time the merchant-bankers of the Italian province of Lombardy, who wrote the bulk of the policies, were well represented in England by partners or agents who had settled in the London district around Lombard Street, which was so named because of their presence there. But by the end of the fifteenth century the Italians had been forced to leave England by laws curbing the business activities of foreigners. English insurers took over the provision of insurance for the rapidly expanding British merchant marine.

Early in the seventeenth century, British insurers began meeting in London coffeehouses to discuss their work and to share information pertinent to their businesses. A shipowner or merchant interested in obtaining insurance on a vessel or cargo could come to one of these meeting places and submit his requirements in a written proposal. The proposal was usually placed on a table, and anyone wishing to participate would sign the document and indicate what portion of the total risk he would accept. The term "underwriter" originated from this custom of having insurers sign their names under a proposal.

One of the London coffeehouses that gradually became the center of marine insurance activities was operated by Edward Lloyd, who in 1696 began publishing *Lloyd's News,* which gave information about the movement of ships and other data of interest to marine underwriters. The first formal association of marine underwriters came during 1771–1772 when seventy-nine of Lloyd's Coffee House customers banded together to seek a new meeting place and appointed a committee to manage the affairs of the group. Retaining the name Lloyd's, the members in 1774 established offices in the Royal Exchange Building, where they remained until 1928, when they removed to their current location on Leadenhall Street. Never incorporated, Lloyd's has remained an organization of individuals who cooperate with fellow members in underwriting insurance policies.

The development of insurance protection against the loss of buildings and other property by fire followed many centuries after the origins of insuring marine risks. It is generally accepted that the Great Fire of London in 1666 dramatized the menace of fire and directed the attention of underwriters to the possibility of insuring fire risks. The following year Dr. Nicholas Barbon, a physician and building speculator, opened an office in London that offered to insure houses and commercial property against loss by fire. Barbon's success led others to enter the field. In 1683, for example, the Friendly Society was organized, as was the Contributors for Insuring Houses, Chambers or Rooms from Loss by Fire by Amicable Contributions (the Amicable Contributorship), later renamed the Hand-in-Hand Insurance Office. These companies, which wrote long-term policies on dwellings and commercial establishments, were the forerunners of modern fire insurance companies.

Although marine insurers would occasionally extend coverage to individuals, the first recorded bona fide life policy was written in London in 1583, on the life of William Gybbons. Sixteen individuals underwrote this policy in the amount of approximately £400 and for a period of one year. When Gybbons died just short of the twelve-month period, the insurers attempted to avoid payment on the ground that the months referred to in the contract were not calendar months but lunar months of twenty-eight days, and therefore Gybbons had died after the one-year period had expired. When the case came to trial, the court set a precedent by deciding in favor of the beneficiary.

Following the Gybbons litigation there was a growing interest in Great Britain in the concept of life insurance, with the result that life underwriting gradually became a specialized field rather than a sideline of marine insurance. Like marine insurance, these early life policies were written almost entirely by individuals, alone or as members of a syndicate, who pledged their personal resources as collateral for policies.

The earliest British life insurance association was the short-lived Society of Assurance for Widows and Orphans, founded in 1699. It introduced such modern features as the selection of risks with regard to health and age; the exclusion of such hazardous occupations as military, naval, and sea service; a grace period for payment of premiums; and the waiver of liability in case of legal execution. In 1756 the Society for the Equitable Assurance of Lives and Survivorship, the oldest life insurance company still in existence, was founded. When "Old Equitable," as it was more familiarly known, issued its first policies in 1762, life insurance as it is known today was born. Other firms followed, and by 1800 there were eight life insurance companies flourishing in England.

INSURANCE IN AMERICA BEFORE 1800

As might be expected, given the American colonists' close intellectual, family, and business ties with Great Britain, the early growth of insurance in America closely followed the development and organization of the industry in the mother country. Marine coverage, the first type of policy issued in the colonies, was handled almost entirely by local agents of British underwriters until 1721, when an "office of publik insurance on vessels, goods and merchandizes" was opened in Philadelphia. Other colonial underwriters followed, with the result that by 1760 a sizable amount of marine insurance was being underwritten in the Philadelphia, New York, and Boston equivalents of Lloyd's Coffee House. Because of limited financial resources, colonial marine underwriters were unable to insure large risks. This difficulty was not entirely overcome until after the Revolution, when the Insurance Company of North America, capitalized at $600,000—and still in existence—was incorporated in Philadelphia in 1792. Within a decade nearly a dozen other marine insurance companies had been incorporated in Philadelphia, New York, Boston, Baltimore, Charleston, and New Haven.

Since most seventeenth- and eighteenth-century American buildings were constructed of wood or had wooden roofs, there was a growing need during the colonial period for protection against the hazards of fire. The earliest attempts to meet the need resulted in the formation of volunteer fire-fighting companies; the first of these, the Union Fire Company, was founded by Benjamin Franklin in Philadelphia in 1736. It was not until 1752 that the first American fire insurance company, the Philadelphia Contributionship for the Insurance of Houses from Loss by Fire, was founded. Still in existence, the Philadelphia Contributionship was the only fire insurance company operating in America prior to 1784. During this period the company introduced two improvements on the practices of the early English companies. One involved the inspection of every building before issuing insurance on it and, if necessary, required changes to bring the property up to acceptable standards. The second set premium rates according to the degree of risk, taking into account the construction, occupancy, location, and exposure to fire hazards of the building. New entries into the industry after 1784 brought the number of domestic companies writing fire insurance to a total of fourteen by the turn of the century, including the Insurance Company of North America, which in 1796 became the first American company to offer protection against fire for properties located anywhere in the country.

There seems to have been no great demand for life insurance among the members of the predominantly agrarian colonial economy. This phenomenon led to the much-quoted comment attributed to Benjamin Franklin: "It is a strange anomaly that men should be careful to insure their houses, their ships, their merchandise and yet to neglect to insure their lives, surely the most important of all to their families and more subject to loss." The few life contracts issued by individual underwriters during these early years were short-term policies on individuals about to undertake a sea voyage or some other perilous adventure.

The first permanent American life insurance company—and the one with the longest name—was the Corporation for the Relief of Poor and Distressed Presbyterian Ministers and Distressed Widows and Children of Presbyterian Ministers. Organized in Philadelphia by the Presbyterian synod in 1759, the Fund, as it was subsequently called, employed no agents and limited its coverage to life annuities for members of the clergy or their beneficiaries. The success of this venture led to the formation a decade later of the Episcopal Corporation for Benefit of Episcopal Clergymen. In 1794 the Insurance Company of North America added life policies to its marine coverage, but after selling only a half-dozen policies during the following four years, it withdrew from the market. As of 1800 there were fewer than two hundred active life insurance policies in the United States.

AMERICAN INSURANCE SINCE 1800

Marine Insurance. The Napoleonic Wars and the War of 1812 were difficult times for American marine insurers, who were periodically subjected to heavy losses arising from the sinking, capture, or detention of American ships. This situation changed during the postwar years, as domestic insurers provided the bulk of marine insurance coverage for the United States merchant marine, which nearly quintupled between 1820 and 1860. What has sometimes been characterized as the "golden age" of American marine insurance came to an abrupt halt following the outbreak of the Civil War, when the size of the American oceangoing fleet was significantly cut by the transfer of ships to foreign registry and by losses through capture or sinking by Confederate raiders. The domestic marine insurance business continued to decline with the further reduction of American ships engaged in foreign trade during the half-century following the end of the Civil War.

The great expansion of shipping during World War I brought a dramatic increase in the demand for insurance to cover the soaring value of vessels and cargoes, as well as a tremendous increase in freight charges. The establishment of brokerage connections in New York by neutral countries and the entry of a number of fire insurance companies into the field enabled the industry to meet the need for marine insurance during the war. This expansion of underwriting capabilities proved to be a liability in the years following the war. Despite the return of many domestic companies to underwriting fire insurance and the withdrawal of foreign firms from the market, for some twenty years the excess capacity of the industry led both to intense competition and to rates that at times were dangerously low.

The situation changed abruptly with the outbreak of World War II and the accompanying need for insurance to cover a greatly expanded American merchant marine. And as in World War I, the underwriting capacity of the industry was enlarged to meet the demand.

In contrast with the period following World War I, the business of the American marine underwriters did not decline sharply after 1945. In part this was the result of action by Congress exempting the industry from antitrust laws and requiring the purchasers of United States ships to insure with domestic firms. The business was further enhanced by the growth in the size and value of such risks as huge oceangoing oil-drilling rigs, ocean liners, and oil tankers each costing $100 million or more to build. In 1976 domestic marine insurers wrote approximately 25 percent of the world total of almost $3.25 billion of marine insurance coverage generated that year. Their premium income was just over $897 million.

Inland Marine Insurance. The inland marine insurance branch of the American industry developed late in the nineteenth century, in response to a growing demand for the coverage of ships and cargoes involved in coastal and inland lake and river transportation. After 1900 protection was gradually extended to shipments by all modes of transportation—including ships, railroads, motor vehicles, and airplanes—as well as to virtually every kind of product moved in the domestic market. By the early 1920's inland marine insurance had been extended from "goods in transit" to the coverage of "all instrumentalities of transportation and communication," including bridges, tunnels, radio and television transmission facilities, electric power lines, pipelines, railroad rolling stock, wharves, and dry docks. In 1948 the premium income on inland marine insurance totaled $196 million; in 1976 it was nearly $1.4 billion.

Fire Insurance. There was a rapid growth in the number of fire insurance companies during the early decades of the nineteenth century. Because of state laws that imposed special taxes on out-of-state firms, the great majority of newcomers to the field were local firms with limited reserves, which wrote policies on properties located in relatively small geographical areas. The dangers inherent in this situation were dramatized by the fire that swept through the New York City business district in 1835, resulting in a loss to the community of approximately $18 million. Unable to meet their obligations, all but three of the twenty-six local fire insurance companies involved were forced into bankruptcy, resulting in a heavy loss to their policyholders.

Following the New York disaster, laws discriminating against out-of-state firms were relaxed, and the small firms were gradually replaced by larger companies capable of building up adequate reserves and able to spread their risks by writing insurance throughout the United States. Nonetheless, local firms made up a high proportion of the companies that flocked into the industry during the 1850's and 1860's. They contributed to the continued weakness of the industry, which was again revealed by the great Chicago fire of October 1871, which swept across an area of 2,200 acres, destroying buildings and property valued at $196 million, of which a little more than $100 million had been insured. In the final settlement less than half the total insurance claims were paid, since only 51 of the 202 companies involved were able to meet their claims in full. The unpaid balance of more than $50 million fell upon the unfortunate property owners of Chicago, who also bore the additional loss of $96 million on property not covered by insurance of any kind.

A major result of the Chicago fire was a widespread effort to strengthen state laws concerning the financial solvency of fire insurance companies. There was also a growing interest among cities in expanding and improving their fire-fighting equipment and in replacing volunteer fire fighters with professionally trained personnel supported by tax revenues. The National Board of Fire Underwriters, established in 1866, became actively concerned with such matters as agents' fees, maintaining adequate premium rates, and preventing arson. Pioneer experiments by the New England factory mutuals called attention to the importance of designing and constructing fireproof buildings and demonstrated the effectiveness of such fire-preventing or fire-retarding installations as fire doors and automatic sprinklers. During the period after 1866 members of industry also moved to standardize fire insurance contracts that over the years had become increasingly complex and cumbersome. The most significant development in this area came in 1887, when New York adopted a simplified policy contract that was soon adopted by other states.

In 1906 the city of San Francisco was hit by an earthquake and fire that killed some seven hundred people and destroyed more than 28,000 buildings. It was indicative of the financial soundness of the fire insurance industry, compared with a generation earlier, that $225 million in benefits, representing approximately 90 percent of the total covered by insurance, was paid to San Francisco property owners.

The increase in premium income from $196 million in 1910 to $3.9 billion in 1975 provides some measure of the growth of the fire insurance industry since the San Francisco fire. Much of this expansion was the result of policies introduced after 1906 that protected against damage from tornadoes, hurricanes, hail, explosives, windstorms, flooding, riots, vandalism, and even falling aircraft.

Life Insurance. Apart from a few policies issued by the Insurance Company of North America and the survivorship annuities of the two funds for ministers, the only life insurance contracts in force in the United States in 1800 had been issued by individual underwriters. The disadvantages of this situation soon became evident. Disputes over the liability of the insurers were not uncommon, as were instances where the underwriters were financially unable to pay legitimate claims.

A growing demand for life policies backed by adequate financial resources led to the organization of several well-capitalized stock companies between 1800 and 1840. The most noteworthy of these were the Pennsylvania Company for Insurance on Lives and Granting Annuities (1809), the New York Life and Trust Company (1830), and the Girard Life Insurance, Annuity and Trust Company of Philadelphia (1830). The Pennsylvania Company was the first American company to require written applications and medical examinations and to establish premiums based on the ages of applicants. The New York Life and Trust Company pioneered in the use of agents, while the Girard Company had the distinction of being the first company to let its policyholders share in the profits of the business.

Largely because of the stock companies, life insurance by the early 1840's had clearly demonstrated to a growing urban and industrial population that it could be effectively used to distribute the economic losses occasioned by death. None of these companies, however, made any vigorous attempt to promote sales, opting instead to concentrate on their trust business. This resulted in a slow growth in the volume of new policies written, as evidenced by the fact that only $4.7 million of life insurance was in force in 1840.

The situation changed drastically following the influx of a dozen or so mutual companies into the industry between 1843 and 1851. Devoted exclusively to life underwriting, these companies, wholly owned by their policyholders, began with no investment or working capital, the necessary funds for operations coming from premium payments. Thus, unlike well-capitalized stock companies, for which the volume of sales was relatively unimportant, payments by policyholders made the difference between success and failure for the mutuals.

To insure adequate premium incomes, the mutuals began at the outset to develop their marketing organizations. Agents dedicated to seeking new members with evangelical zeal were recruited in ever larger numbers. Their efforts were supplemented by newspaper and magazine advertisements and by pamphlets and brochures, all designed to acquaint prospects with the nature and benefits of life insurance, and with the fact that the profits of the mutuals were distributed to policyholders, rather than to shareholders (as was the case with stock companies).

By the mid-1840's the earlier short-term life policies calling for single premium payments had largely been replaced by long-term or whole-life contracts. Since most individuals preferred not to pay premiums that increased each year with the rise in expected mortality rates, the great majority of these policies were sold under a level-premium system that called for premium payments at a fixed rate, either for a term of years or for the life of the insured.

The adoption of the level-premium system introduced the new element of investment into the operations of life insurance companies; it also made the calculation of premium rates a more complicated process. For example, in the case of short-term fire, marine, or casualty policies, it is comparatively easy to adjust rates in such a way that income during any one year will be sufficient to cover the claims payments for that year, plus operating expenses. However, under the level-premium life insurance policies, the bulk of death claims will come due during the later years that policies are in force, so the amounts collected during the earlier years must be in excess of current needs. This "excess" income is set aside as a reserve and is invested as a guarantee that funds will be available when needed. The amount that must be collected in advance to provide adequate reserves depends in part on the interest that can be earned by companies on their investments. Accordingly, actual premium rates are based on mortality and interest assumptions that will produce adequate policy reserves, plus an allowance (called "loading") to cover contingencies and operating costs. To the extent that the actual mortality experience is better than the mortality table used to compute rates, life companies will accumulate more funds than are needed and specifically earmarked for policy reserves. These go into a surplus account and are used to pay dividends to the shareholders of stock companies or to the policyholders of mutual companies.

Between 1850 and 1900 the volume of life insurance in force in the United States rose from $96 million to nearly $7.6 billion. While the expansion of the economy was basic to this growth, much credit should go to the marketing activities of the mutual companies.

Life insurance was undoubtedly made more attractive during this period by changes in the policy contracts. At mid-century the typical policy simply provided for a single payment by the insurer if the insured died within the time period covered by the contract. Policies were declared null and void if the insured committed suicide, enlisted in the military, or traveled outside the continental United States. No provision was made for returning any part of the premiums collected if the policy was allowed to lapse or the insured outlived the contract.

Competition, legislation, and a growing sensitivity by a number of insurance companies to the needs of their policyholders subsequently led to an extensive liberalization of policy contracts. Occupational and travel restrictions were relaxed, insureds were allowed a grace period of a month or so to pay overdue premiums, policies became uncontestable after being in force for one or two years, laws were passed setting up legal reserve requirements, and nonforfeiture clauses were added that in the case of lapsed or surrendered level-premium policies called on the companies to return to the insured the value of their policy reserves in the form of cash or paid-up insurance.

The scientific basis for life insurance was also strengthened. British mortality tables, long used by the industry in the determination of premium rates and legal reserves, were superseded after 1868 by the American Experience Table, and the development of special training programs provided companies with a growing number of capable, well-trained actuaries.

Industrial life insurance, first available in England in 1854, was introduced into the United States when the Prudential Friendly Society—later renamed the Prudential Insurance Company of America—with offices in Newark, New Jersey, issued its first policies in 1875. Designed to provide insurance protection for low-income groups unable to purchase life insurance on a regular basis, industrial life policies are written in small amounts—with coverage under $1,000—and are issued without examinations to individuals of all ages. Premiums are collected by company agents on a weekly or monthly basis at the homes of the insureds. Prudential was alone in the field until 1879, when other companies, including Metropolitan and John Hancock, added industrial insurance to their established lines of ordinary life insurance. By 1880 the amount of industrial life insurance in force was just under $21 million; by 1900 it had reached almost $1.5 billion, nearly 20 percent of the total life insurance in force in that year.

The intensive competition that characterized the life insurance business during the latter half of the nineteenth century had both positive and negative effects on the industry. Many companies during this period adhered to the principles of honesty, integrity, economy, and a sense of trusteeship. Others devoted all their efforts to growth without regard for the benefits to policyholders or the financial security of their companies. Excessive commissions were paid to agents for new business, advertising expenditures were large, and the sizable assets of the companies were used to control other corporations and for the private purposes of company officials. The popularity of deferred dividend policies, which called for the payment of accrued dividends to surviving policyholders ten or twenty years after policies were issued, resulted in the accumulation of large amounts of policyholders' money that in many instances were not properly accounted for.

In 1905 the New York State legislature responded to growing public resentment against the industry by appointing a commission to investigate the affairs of life insurance companies. Named after its chairman, Senator William W. Armstrong, the commission, with Charles Evans Hughes as counsel, uncovered many abuses perpetrated by the New York life companies. As a result of the Armstrong investigation, laws were passed limiting the surplus accounts of the life companies doing business in New York State, requiring that they distribute dividends annually, restricting the size of commissions and other expenses of doing business, and regulating the nature of their investments. The findings of the Armstrong Commission affected life insurance throughout the United States, since much of the New York legislation was copied by other states. The investigation led to a housecleaning in the industry that marked the coming of age of the life insurance business. It not only strengthened state insurance supervision but also provided the legal and ethical foundation for the safe and conservative growth of life insurance.

Although the disclosures of the Armstrong investigation brought about a temporary loss of confidence in the industry and a resultant drop in sales, the growth of life insurance soon resumed. Between 1906 and 1930 the amount of life insurance in force grew from $11.8 billion to $106.4 billion as the industry successfully weathered both World War I and the 1918 influenza epidemic.

The industry was severely affected by the Great Depression; sales of new policies lagged and many old policies lapsed or were surrendered. It was not until 1937 that the amount of insurance in force was restored to the 1930 level. Since 1937 the industry has grown geometrically. By the end of 1977, 140 million individuals, two out of every three in the United States, were covered by life insurance in force that had reached the astronomical figure of $2.58 trillion.

Group life insurance, introduced in 1911, accounted for much of this expansion. Usually written without medical examination and with no restrictions on the age of applicants, group insurance originated primarily as the result of growing industrialization and rapidly became an important benefit in agreements between employers and organized labor. The attraction of this type of coverage is shown by the growth in the amount of group life insurance in force from $100 million in 1915 to $1.1 trillion in 1979, approximately 41 percent of the total life insurance in force in that year.

Accident and Health Insurance. The early growth of accident insurance in the United States was largely in response to a public demand for protection against the hazards of travel, especially by railroad and steamboat. The first American company to offer such coverage was the Travelers Insurance Company of Hartford, Connecticut. Organized in 1863, its first policies provided insurance against railway mishaps and were later extended to cover all types of accidents.

The initial success of accident insurance attracted other firms into the field, paving the way for the first ventures into sickness and disability insurance during the 1890's. By the early 1900's these policies, in addition to offering protection against virtually all types of diseases, had been extended to include surgical and hospital expense benefits.

Until 1929 disability income protection continued to be the chief attraction of accident and health insurance. With the onset of the Great Depression of the 1930's, the emphasis shifted to protection against hospital and medical expenses, partly in response to the need to help people cope with rising health care costs and partly to bring relief to hospitals faced with empty beds and dwindling revenues.

The subsequent growth of accident and health insurance has been impressive. The number of individuals with hospital insurance, for example, rose from 12.3 million to nearly 176 million between 1940 and 1976; those with surgical coverage increased from 5.3 million to 167 million; and those protected against the costs of regular medical services expanded from 3 million to 163 million. Annual premium payments during the period grew from $318 million to nearly $45 billion.

Roughly half the accident and health insurance coverage in recent years has been written by insurance companies. Most of the remainder has been provided under group insurance plans, administered in the case of hospital coverage by Blue Cross hospital associations and, in the case of medical insurance, by groups of physicians associated with Blue Shield.

Liability Insurance. Liability insurance is basically designed to cover claims by members of the public for bodily injury or property damage arising out of the business or personal activities of the insureds. Although the first policies (covering damages from boiler explosions) were sold during the late 1870's, interest in liability coverage tended to lag during the 1880's and 1890's, when only a few damage suits against individuals and business firms were taken to court. It was only as business grew and became more impersonal, and people became more claims-conscious after the turn of the century, that the demand for liability insurance began to expand.

Various types of liability policies have been developed by the industry to meet this demand. Owners', landlords', and tenants' liability policies, for example, offer protection to individuals or companies having an interest in a building, a home, or a vacant property. They cover the claims of visitors or customers who sustain bodily injury or property damage in or about the premises of the insured, as well as such off-premises accidents as those caused by employees in the demonstration or installation of household appliances. Manufacturers' and contractors' liability insurance covers damage claims by members of the public for injuries, sickness, disease, or death arising out of the business operations of the insureds. Comprehensive personal liability policies provide the broad coverage needed by the typical home dweller. In addition to protection against the ordinary hazards involved in the ownership or operation of residential property, these policies cover any type of accident sustained away from home for which the insured or any member of his family is held responsible. These include injuries attributable to pets, to the use of bicycles, lawn mowers, or power tools, to sports such as golf, hunting, or fishing, or to the accidental discharge of firearms.

Professional liability insurance is issued to individuals or firms to cover liabilities arising out of their professional activities. This type of policy was first written to indemnify practicing physicians and dentists for losses or expenses arising from damage claims for injuries resulting from malpractice (professional misconduct or a failure by the insured to use ordinary skill in the performance of a professional act). Coverage was subsequently extended to hospitals, infirmaries, sanatoriums, and nursing homes; to druggists; and to miscellaneous medical personnel, including nurses, physiotherapists, opticians, dental hygienists, and laboratory technicians. Special liability contracts have also been developed to meet the needs of attorneys, architects, engineers, and members of other nonmedical professions.

Workmen's Compensation. Workmen's compensation, a highly important type of liability insurance, had its origin in legislation adopted by the various states after 1910. On the assumption that industry, not the workers, should bear the costs of industrial accidents, the new laws disregarded the traditional notion of liability based on negligence and made employers responsible for accidents to their employees without regard to questions of fault or negligence. While employers may opt for self-insurance, the great majority have turned to insurance companies for protection. Initially limited to disability income for time lost from work, the benefits under workmen's compensation have been extended to cover medical and hospital expenses, costs of rehabilitation, or, in the case of accidental death, a lump sum or series of income payments to beneficiaries. The proportion of the United States labor force covered under workmen's compensation grew from 33 percent in the early 1930's to more than 75 percent by the mid-1970's.

Automobile Insurance. Automobile insurance grew with the expansion in the number of motor vehicles in use in the United States from a few thousand in 1900 to more than 137 million in 1976. Two types of policies have been developed to insure motorists against the hazards of motor vehicle operation. One, casualty insurance, protects policyholders from claims by others for property damage or bodily injury—including death—arising out of the ownership, maintenance, or use of an automobile, bus, or truck. The second, property damage insurance, covers the vehicle itself in the event of a loss or damage resulting from fire, theft, collision, windstorm, hail, earthquake, or explosion. A combination of inflation, more vehicles, an increasing volume of claims, and larger settlements of claims largely accounted for the growth of automobile insurance premiums from $2.6 billion in 1950 to just over $23 billion in 1976.

INSURANCE COMPANIES AS INVESTMENT INSTITUTIONS

The insurance companies of the United States have a dual function. One is to assist millions of Americans in obtaining protection against unforeseen contingencies and in providing for their old age. Second, by serving as a highly important channel through which the American people save, they make large amounts of capital funds available for investments.

As already noted, it is largely because premiums are collected in advance of the time that loss payments are due that insurance companies become custodians of large aggregations of capital. The income from the investment of these funds makes possible a substantial reduction in the cost of insurance to policyholders.

The growth in the volume of insurance savings over the years has closely paralleled the overall expansion of the industry. Between 1865 and 1900, for example, the value of the assets held by members of the industry rose from $64 million to more than $1.7 billion; by 1976 the total had reached $459 billion.

As managers and trustees of policyholders' funds, insurance companies have attempted to maximize investment yields without endangering principal by making long-term, fixed-income loans to individuals and business concerns in the private sectors of the economy. Thus, with the exception of large holdings of government securities during World War II, two outlets—mortgages and corporate bonds—have accounted for two-thirds to three-fourths of the assets acquired by the industry since the 1860's.

Within these limitations investments have in general been made in response to the shifting capital needs of the economy. For example, a high proportion of mortgage loans was made to farmers until the 1930's, when emphasis shifted to loans for the construction of urban residences, apartment houses, and office buildings. During the latter part of the nineteenth century, the emphasis among the bond holdings of the insurance companies was on railroad securities. As the public utility industry developed after 1900, investments began to flow into these securities. Since the end of World War II the bond portfolios of the insurance companies have been further expanded to include the securities of firms engaged in such diverse industrial and commercial activities as lumbering, papermaking, chemical manufacture, petroleum refining, and the construction of gas and oil pipelines, tankers, barges, toll bridges, turnpikes, and college dormitories.

It is indicative of their relative importance as financial institutions that insurance companies provided more than $29 billion—nearly 8 percent—of the total funds flowing into the capital markets from all sources in 1977. At the same time they held approximately 12 percent of the $792 billion in mortgages in the United States and almost 80 percent of the $170 billion in railroad, public utility, and industrial bonds outstanding.

BIBLIOGRAPHY

John Bainbridge, *Biography of an Idea: The Story of Mutual Fire and Casualty Insurance* (Garden City, N.Y., 1952), is a well-written account of the growth of mutual fire and casualty insurance in the United States. Sheppard B. Clough, *A Century of American Life Insurance* (New York, 1945), gives a scholarly history of the Mutual Life Insurance Company of New York. Hawthorne Daniel, *The Hartford of Hartford: An Insurance Company's Part in a Century and a Half of American History* (New York, 1960), is an excellent survey of the evolution of one of America's most prominent fire insurance companies. Edwin J. Faulkner, *Accident and Health Insurance* (New York, 1940), covers the growth of accident and health insurance in the United States in the introductory chapter. Marquis James, *Biography of a Business, 1792–1942* (New York, 1942), is a colorful history of the Insurance Company of North America founded in Philadelphia in 1792. Robert I. Mehr and Emerson Cammach, *Principles of Insurance* (Homewood, Ill., 1966), provides a brief historical sketch for each of the various types of insurance covered in this leading insurance textbook. William H. Rodda, *Inland Marine and Transportation Insurance* (Englewood Cliffs, N.J., 1958), covers the historical development of inland marine insurance exceptionally well in the introductory chapter of this book. Nicholas B. Wainwright, *A Philadelphia Story: The Philadelphia Contributorship to the Insurance of Houses from Loss by Fire* (Philadelphia, 1952), is a popular history of America's oldest fire insurance company. Harold F. Williamson and Orange A. Smalley, *Northwestern Mutual Life: A Century of Trusteeship* (Evanston, Ill., 1957), gives a detailed account of the growth and development of a leading midwestern life insurance company. William D. Winter, *Marine Insurance: Its Principles and Practices* (New York, 1929), gives an interesting survey of the growth and status of marine insurance to 1929 in the introduction to the book. Frank Worsley and Glyn Griffith, *The Romance of Lloyd's: From Coffee-House to Palace* (New York, 1932), is a colorful and somewhat romanticized history of Lloyd's of London.

[*See also* AMERICAN BUSINESS INSTITUTIONS BEFORE THE RAILROAD; AUTOMOBILE; COLONIAL ECONOMY; DOMESTIC TRADE AND REGIONAL SPECIALIZATION; ECONOMY FROM THE REVOLUTION TO 1815; ECONOMY FROM 1815 TO 1865; FOREIGN TRADE; MANUFACTURING; MEDICINE AND PUBLIC HEALTH; SAVINGS AND INVESTMENT; TRANSPORTATION; *and* URBANIZATION.]

CENTRAL BANKING

Paul Trescott

ALTHOUGH conceptions of central banking have changed over time, and although American central banking history is diverse, the following can be considered essential elements of central banking:

1. The central bank is a relatively large institution created by a national government to serve some public purpose instead of or in addition to purely private profit seeking.

2. The central bank is typically empowered to create money in the form of paper bank-note currency and in the form of checking deposits. In the twentieth century, deposits with a central bank typically serve (along with currency) as legal reserve for privately owned commercial banks. Since one dollar of legal reserve can typically support several dollars of commercial bank deposits, money issued by a central bank is often termed "high-powered money."

3. The central bank has traditionally been a major holder of international monetary reserves and an important link between the national economy and the international financial environment.

4. The central bank has typically borne substantial responsibility for assisting with governmental financial transactions: helping to manage the cash balance and payments, participating in the marketing of securities, and providing direct loans to the government.

5. Central banks have come to play an important role as regulators and supervisors of commercial banks, but this is a relatively recent development.

Central banking experience in United States history falls into two widely disparate periods. Central banking modeled somewhat after the Bank of England was performed by the first and the second banks of the United States, operating in 1791–1811 and 1816–1841, respectively. Each was a private corporation but had some degree of statutory control embodied in the charter passed by Congress. Each carried on the normal business of commercial banking, making loans and accepting deposits. Each issued bank notes that, while acceptable in payments to the government, were not legal tender in private transactions (creditors were not compelled by law to accept them in settlement of debts) but circulated in competition with the notes issued by other commercial banks. Each Bank of the United States operated branches in major cities and acted as fiscal agent for the Treasury. Each displayed some capacity to balance narrow considerations of profit maximization against a concern for maintaining the domestic and international convertibility between the dollar and its equivalent in gold and silver. Each Bank of the United States was politically unpopular and was denied an extension of its charter at the end of the original term.

Because of the "bank war" conducted against the Second Bank of the United States by President Andrew Jackson, its status as central bank actually terminated in 1833, when the government deposits were removed from it (it continued to operate under its congressional charter until 1836, and then under a Pennsylvania state charter until 1841). From 1833 to 1913 the United States had no formal central bank. Some elements of central banking were performed by the Treasury and some by city clearinghouse associations. In December 1913 the present American central banking system was created by the passage of the Owen-Glass (Federal Reserve) Act. Unlike the banks of the United States, the Federal Reserve banks were to operate as bankers' banks, not engaging in loan and deposit business with the general public but holding reserve deposits for commercial banks and making loans to them.

These reserve deposits served as the basis for a nationwide check-clearing system. The Federal Reserve banks were authorized to issue currency in the form of Federal Reserve notes, which were legal tender for public and private transactions. Unlike the first and the second banks of the United States, the Federal Reserve banks were subject to the authority of a board of federal officials. Like the two banks of the United States, the Federal Reserve system was initially conceived to defend and administer the monetary standard relating the dollar to precious metals, and to assist with Treasury cash management. Unlike the banks of the United States, the Federal Reserve banks and Federal Reserve Board were authorized to regulate the operations of commercial banks. Initially the chief public purpose in creating the Federal Reserve system was to eliminate banking panics; it was hoped that this could be done by lending distressed banks newly issued currency. It was soon apparent that extension of Federal Reserve credit by making loans or buying securities would create commercial bank reserves. Ultimately that aspect of Federal Reserve operations became the basis for modern monetary policy, whereby Federal Reserve operations serve as the dominant continuous influence on the total quantity of money in the economy.

FIRST BANK OF THE UNITED STATES

The first Bank of the United States was chartered in 1791, at the urging of Secretary of the Treasury Alexander Hamilton, as part of his comprehensive program of financial innovation. Hamilton's *Report on a National Bank,* presented to Congress in December 1790, offered two main reasons for establishing such a bank. The first was to increase the banking facilities of the country. There were at that time only three commercial banks in operation—the Bank of North America (Philadelphia, chartered 1781), the Bank of New York (1784), and the Bank of Massachusetts (Boston, 1784). Hamilton correctly argued that increasing the supply of bank credit would contribute to "the augmentation of the active or productive capital" of the economy and would aid economic growth. Hamilton recognized that as the American population shifted from relatively self-sufficient farm life to the interdependence of manufacturing and trade, money would be increasingly required as a medium of exchange.

A second motive for Hamilton's bank proposal was to aid his ambitious program to provide for the public debt. Under the Funding Act of 1790, the government had undertaken to issue new high-grade securities to holders of the diverse public debts created to finance the Revolutionary War. Hamilton proposed that these new securities be accepted in payment for stock in the Bank of the United States. The securities would be a good asset for the bank, and the prospective profitability of bank stock would make investors eager to acquire the securities (available at prices below par) as a means of buying bank stock cheaply. Both bank and funding programs were part of Hamilton's broader goal of basing the newly formed government on the political support of the well-to-do. In linking his bank proposal to support of the national debt, Hamilton followed the precedent set by the establishment of the Bank of England in 1694 as a means of helping to finance the political regime that supported the coming of William and Mary to the throne.

A third purpose was that the new bank could aid the Treasury in managing its revenue collections and disbursements. In addition, the government would need temporary loans.

Because of its connection with Hamilton's controversial public debt program, the bank proposal was strongly opposed by Thomas Jefferson and his political followers. Despite this opposition the charter (to last for twenty years) was passed by Congress in February 1791, and the bank opened for business that December. Its capitalization of $10 million was the largest of any American corporation operating during its lifetime. The government "purchased" one-fifth of the stock with funds borrowed from the bank. The charter imposed various restrictions on the bank's operations: it was not permitted to deal in commodities or real estate, or to charge more than 6 percent interest on loans, and its banknotes were to be redeemed in specie (gold and silver coin or the equivalent). But the charter did not state any social or economic objectives to be pursued by the bank.

Although Hamilton had not favored branch

operations, the bank charter authorized them, and the bank operated branches in Boston, New York, Baltimore, Washington, Norfolk, Charleston, Savannah, and New Orleans, in addition to the head office in Philadelphia. It acted as fiscal agent for the government and, although forbidden to buy government securities in the open market, made "temporary loans" to the Treasury on several occasions.

The bank operated chiefly as a conservative private business. It was profitable, and its stock typically sold above par. The stock was popular with foreign investors, and by 1809 they owned two-thirds of it (but were excluded from voting directly for directors).

The number of state-chartered banks increased substantially, with some twenty-five being formed in 1791–1800 and another sixty in 1801–1812. As the commercial banking system grew, the Bank of the United States came to play a modest regulatory role. It received a steady flow of notes and checks of other banks. By presenting these for redemption in coin, it kept the other banks from operating with inadequate cash reserves. On occasions when credit stringency might harm the economy, the bank extended credit to other banks insofar as its own specie reserves permitted.

Although some of the former political opponents of the bank, such as Albert Gallatin, became supporters, and although the bank was politically inconspicuous, a proposal to recharter it was narrowly defeated in Congress and it closed in 1811. The head office in Philadelphia was taken over by the private banking operations of Stephen Girard.

THE SECOND BANK OF THE UNITED STATES

The period 1812–1816 was one of great financial disorder attending the War of 1812. The government sustained large deficits and borrowed heavily from state-chartered banks, which greatly increased their banknote and deposit liabilities. Commodity prices rose by about 50 percent from 1811 to 1814. In 1814, when the British sailed up Chesapeake Bay and burned Washington, most banks outside New England suspended specie redemption of their liabilities. This suspension freed the banks to expand their credit with little constraint. The system of interregional payments was disrupted, and banknotes from the South and the West were substantially discounted in the Northeast.

When hostilities ceased in 1815, a movement to form a new Bank of the United States gathered momentum. As in 1790, the government was burdened with a large and disordered public debt, and its bonds were depreciated in price. If the securities could be used to subscribe to stock of a new bank, their market value could be expected to rise. Treasury officials were also eager to regain some semblance of order in the management of government funds, having suffered much from irresponsible actions by state banks employed as government depositories.

Other motives for chartering the Second Bank of the United States were very different from those operating in 1791. By 1815 the number of banks in the country was estimated at nearly 250, each issuing its own notes, and there was widespread feeling that their monetary operations required some sort of federal government control. Many political and business leaders believed that a new Bank of the United States could induce the other banks to resume specie redemptions of their notes and deposits.

Businessmen including Stephen Girard and John Jacob Astor joined with such influential political figures as John C. Calhoun and Secretary of the Treasury Alexander J. Dallas to bring about the chartering in 1816 of the Second Bank of the United States. Despite the attention to general monetary goals in the congressional debates, the charter did not specify the public purposes of the bank, except insofar as it was liable to financial penalty if it failed to redeem its own liabilities in coin. Its capital of $35 million was much larger than that of its predecessor. As in 1791, the government subscribed one-fifth of the stock with funds borrowed from the bank. A novel element was that the government was empowered to appoint one-fifth of the directors of the bank. As in 1791, subscriptions to bank stock could be made in public debt certificates, a provision that helped raise the market value of those certificates. The bank was required to pay the government a "bonus" of $1.5 million for the charter. In addition to the head office in Philadelphia, branch offices were authorized, and during most of its twenty-year lifetime more than twenty were operated. The extensive branch network gave the bank an important role in the interregional payments system but also created problems of managerial coordination.

The initial charge of the bank, to restore specie payments by the entire banking system, was not one that it was equipped to handle. The volume of the liabilities of the state banks was very large relative to their specie reserves, and the latter were subject to variations arising from international financial flows. The Bank of the United States had no coercive authority over state-chartered banks. Congress adopted the Webster resolution of 1816 (introduced by Daniel Webster), which forbade the Treasury to accept bank notes of non-specie-paying banks, but rejected a proposal to levy a penalty tax on such bank notes. Primarily, the Bank of the United States had to rely on persuasion and on the force of public opinion. Most banks nominally resumed specie payments in February 1817.

Neither the politicians, the banks, nor the business community wanted a monetary contraction, fearing adverse effects on business. But if specie resumption were to be achieved, contraction was probably necessary to reduce bank liabilities relative to specie reserves, and to improve the balance of trade by lowering commodity prices (which had already declined somewhat from their wartime peak). Banks were willing to promise specie resumption only if they were not likely to have to pay out much specie. The new Bank of the United States tried to promote resumption without contraction by expanding its own loans rapidly in 1816–1817. By the spring of 1818 its loans totaled $43 million, and about $10 million of its notes were in circulation. For the time being, the nation enjoyed a specie inflow from booming export sales and inflow of foreign capital. The expansionary policy of the bank was particularly pleasing to the management of the Baltimore branch, who used its funds extensively for private speculations. The first president of the bank, a merchant named William Jones, was a political choice poorly qualified in personality or experience.

In 1818 the international specie inflow turned into an outflow. American export sales fell sharply while domestic boom conditions kept imports high. In 1819 the Bank of England adopted a restrictive policy that reduced capital outflows to the United States. When American banks were confronted with demands for specie, many suspended specie redemptions again. Business failures and loan defaults were widespread.

The Bank of the United States was hard hit by demands for specie and by defaults on loans owed to it. Borrowing from abroad helped the bank to maintain specie payments, but its lending policy was extremely deflationary in 1818–1820. Its loans fell from $43 million in early 1818 to $31 million in September 1819; during the same period its note circulation fell from $10 million to $4 million. The bank had applied an expansionary policy while specie was flowing in and the economy was booming, but then turned to a deflationary policy that aggravated existing deflationary tendencies. Under fire both for the Baltimore scandals and for the panic, Jones resigned. His successor, Langdon Cheves, a lawyer, concentrated on restoring the liquidity and solvency of the bank without much concern for the economic needs of the country.

The role of the Bank of the United States in the panic of 1819 made it politically very unpopular. It was widely denounced as the cause of depression. Several states attempted to drive out the operations of the bank by discriminatory taxes, but such efforts were blocked by the landmark Supreme Court decision in the case of *McCulloch* v. *Maryland* (1819). John Marshall's decision upheld a broad construction of the authority granted to the federal government under the Constitution and forbade the use of state taxation to block federal programs.

Several states attempted to combat monetary deflation by establishing government-owned banks or state loan offices. Kentucky, Illinois, Tennessee, and Alabama each chartered a state bank with the primary purpose of providing relief for hard-pressed debtors. The banknotes of these banks were not redeemed in specie but were accepted in payments to the state. State laws provided that creditors must accept these notes or face long delays in collecting debts. These "relief banks" were not directly interfered with by the federal government, but the laws forcing acceptance of their notes were generally held unconstitutional.

In 1823 Nicholas Biddle became president of the Bank of the United States, after having served as a government director since 1819. Biddle, a literary man from a prominent mercantile family, became perhaps the most brilliant central banker of his day. He provided forceful leadership in the management of the bank and initiated a number of important innovations.

American central banking has always been concerned with the interregional payments system. Biddle addressed this issue by a policy under which the bank and its branches devoted a large part of their lending to purchase of "domestic exchange," mostly loan paper secured by goods produced in the interior and being shipped to the Atlantic seaboard or to Europe. The bank was a heavy lender on cotton shipments. Its western branches purchased bills of exchange payable in New York or other eastern ports. The loan documents were then forwarded to the eastern branches of the bank for collection. The credits that accumulated when such loans matured could be drawn upon by the sale of drafts by the inland branches to local people wishing to send payments east, as many of them did. Such loans were safe and liquid. Since the bank earned interest on the loans and charged a fee for the sale of drafts, this process was a good source of revenue. And in fact the bank charged less for the sale of drafts than state banks did. Not until much later did it become accepted that a check on one's own bank deposit could be used for a payment to a distant location.

Biddle was aware that the operations of the bank could be used to protect the economy against cyclical fluctuations. He had carefully watched the boom-and-bust sequence of 1816–1821 and perceived that expansion and contraction by the bank had important effects on the domestic economy and on foreign-exchange markets. Biddle articulated a modern philosophy of monetary management when he wrote, "A mixed currency is eminently useful in prudent hands but a tremendous hazard when not controlled; and the practical wisdom in managing it lies in seizing the proper moment to expand and contract it. . . ." (Redlich 1968, p. 135).

Undertaking measures of stabilization while maintaining adequate specie reserves required the ability to anticipate trouble. In early 1825, Biddle sensed the need to exercise restraint and build up the reserve position of the bank in a manner that enabled the bank to take expansionary actions later in the year, when financial stringency and specie drain arose from the collapse of a speculative boom in the English market for cotton. A similar effort at countercyclical action occurred in 1828. On several occasions the bank reduced the potential disruptive effects of government debt-retirement operations by making loans for which the collateral was securities due for redemption.

Maintaining the specie convertibility of the dollar was another central element in Biddle's policies (except in special circumstances after 1837). He followed and fully articulated the policy that loans be curtailed whenever foreign-exchange rates fell substantially. On several occasions Biddle relied on loans from abroad to provide the bank with means to meet excess demand for foreign exchange without the need for drastic curtailment of loans. He perceived that dealing in foreign exchange enhanced the potential of the bank as an economic stabilizer. He wrote:

> It belongs then to the conservative power over the circulating medium which devolves upon the Bank . . . to take an ample share in all that concerns the foreign exchanges. It may thus foresee, and either avert or diminish an approaching danger—it can thus break the force of a sudden shock, and supplying from its own accumulations or its own credits in Europe the more pressing demands, enable the State Institutions to provide for their own safety, and thus produce the necessary alteration in the state of the exchanges with the least possible pressure upon the Banks or the community [Redlich, p. 130].

Yet Biddle was also eager to expand the role of the bank in the economy. In particular he seems to have felt that increasing the note circulation of the bank would tend to curtail the note issues of the state banks, whereas the actual effect was to enable them to grow apace. During the early 1830's, when the American economy was receiving a substantial specie inflow, Biddle allowed the bank to be swept along on the tide of expansion. But by then the economic merits and shortcomings of Biddle's actions were overshadowed by political controversy. Andrew Jackson had brought to the presidency a distrust of banking operations and a jealousy of the power and independence of the bank. In 1832 Congress voted to recharter the bank, but Jackson vetoed the bill and violently denounced the bank. Its connection with the government gave it a monopoly position, he declared, that "operated as a gratuity of many millions to the stockholders." Who were these stockholders? "Foreigners . . . and . . . a few hundred of our own citizens, chiefly of the richest class." Jackson felt that the bank was designed to "make the rich richer and the potent more powerful," and that it was unconstitutional.

Jackson was triumphantly reelected in 1832. In 1833 he ordered Treasury deposits to be removed from the bank and placed with favored state-bank depositories—the "pet" banks. In response the Bank of the United States adopted a strongly contractionary policy, and financial distress was widespread in 1833–1834. Instead of closing down the operations of the bank, Biddle obtained a state charter from Pennsylvania for the head office, which became an innovative commercial banking venture, operated perhaps with a hope that a political change might restore it to its former status.

The mid-1830's was a period of boom for the American economy. One booming sector was construction of canals by state governments, generally financed by bond issues sold to foreign investors. Biddle was a major innovator in developing the practice of investment banking in such transactions. But the increasing involvement of the Bank of the United States decreased its liquidity and increased its risk in relation to bond market conditions.

The atmosphere of boom and expansion began to unravel in 1837, when specie started to flow out of the country in response to a restrictive policy undertaken by the Bank of England to protect its gold reserve. A financial crisis developed, and many American banks, including the Bank of the United States, suspended specie redemptions. In this situation Biddle launched his most innovative and risky venture. He entered the cotton market on a large scale, providing loans and in effect aiding cotton growers and merchants to hold cotton off the market sufficiently to raise the price. The policy was successful, and the crisis conditions eased in 1838. But financial stringency occurred more strongly in 1839, and this time Biddle's intervention in the cotton market was not able to withstand or reverse further price declines. The Bank of the United States sustained losses, and there was much criticism that the operation was a private speculation by insiders for personal gain.

Biddle had also come to another radical position: that the banks should not attempt to return to specie payments if such a measure would impose further contraction on already existing distress. His position brought him into conflict with financial conservatives such as Albert Gallatin, and their view prevailed. Biddle's influence in the bank was waning, and he resigned in 1839. In 1841 a factional fight among stockholders precipitated a run on the bank, and it failed.

Several bills to charter a new national bank were passed by Congress in the early 1840's, but were vetoed by President John Tyler. Thus the failure of the bank in 1841 completed the task that Jackson's veto had begun.

Jackson's attack on the Bank of the United States was irresponsible and demagogic. Yet there was something anomalous about an institution as large and powerful as the bank. True, it functioned well under Biddle, but with the same charter it had functioned badly under Jones. Nothing in the structure of the bank insured that its operations would be held accountable to the public interest. Given the condition of American political institutions, the bank was too powerful to exist either outside the government or inside it. Secretary of the Treasury Levi Woodbury captured this problem in 1834 when he wrote:

> If a National Bank of any efficient character be tolerated . . . either a great moneyed power will exist, independent, uncontrolled, and then in fact uncontrollable; or such a power will exist, with a due control by the Government, and thus enlarge greatly the present control and influence of the latter, without any increase of the present restraints on it by the people and the States [House Document 27, 23rd Congress, 2nd Session (1834), pp. 34–35].

Some scholars have argued that had the bank been rechartered, the country might have enjoyed greater monetary stability, and central banking theory and practice could have progressed steadily. This view implies that Biddle's radical post-1835 policies relating to investment banking, fixed-capital finance, cotton market manipulation, and defense of inconvertibility either would not have occurred had the bank been rechartered or were perhaps proper and beneficial central banking actions. There is a common assumption that the bank could and would have greatly reduced the banking disorders in the country after 1836, and that a continued Bank of the United States would have been far superior in 1914–1933 to the Federal Reserve system. But it is very plausible that Biddle would have undertaken many of his radical moves in the late 1830's even if the "bank war" had never occurred. Further, the instability of international finance in 1835–1841 was great, and there is no basis in the experience of the bank for believing it could have prevented serious panic, depression, and monetary disorder arising from suspension of specie payments.

CENTRAL BANKING ELEMENTS, 1840–1913

After 1840 jurisdiction in banking policy rested largely with state governments. However, many elements of central banking were at times exercised by the Treasury. In 1846, Congress adopted the Independent Treasury System, which required that government funds be held in coin or Treasury notes rather than deposited with banks. Since variations in government cash holdings could have large effects on financial markets, Treasury officials came to use their funds in a discretionary manner in an effort to relieve credit stringency. Purchase of government securities in the open market was often employed in the nineteenth century to inject government funds into the economy. Since the Treasury could not typically create currency, such actions could occur only when Treasury cash holdings were large. During business depressions, government revenues tended to fall and cash holdings usually became depleted without need for discretionary actions.

The Civil War greatly increased the monetary role of the Treasury. In 1862 greenbacks, the first legal-tender paper money under the Constitution, came into use to finance government deficits. And in 1863 and 1864 national banking legislation put the federal government into competition with the states in chartering and supervising ordinary local commercial banks. After imposition of a punitive tax on state-bank notes in 1866, the bank-note circulation came to consist entirely of notes issued by the national banks, but the Treasury had no real discretion over the quantity of bank-note circulation.

The Treasury did have some small discretion over the quantity of greenback circulation, since the amount outstanding was not always at the maximum permitted by law. Discretionary expansion of the currency was thus possible in 1872–1873, although this discretion did not differ much from that inherent in cash-balance management. More important was the option to shift Treasury funds between bank deposits and currency held in subtreasury offices.

In connection with the establishment in 1879 of specie convertibility for the greenbacks, the Treasury developed the practice of maintaining a substantial gold reserve for redeeming currency. Managing this reserve put the Treasury squarely into one leading central banking function. During the financial panic of 1893–1896, the Treasury went to extreme lengths to protect this reserve, making controversial contracts with leading bankers to obtain gold and selling large bond issues. The latter operation, which drew substantial currency out of circulation, imposed severe deflationary pressure on a depressed economy. The Gold Standard Act of 1900 separated the gold reserve from the ordinary Treasury cash balance, directed the Treasury to aim for a gold reserve of $150 million, and authorized issue of bonds to achieve this level.

During the late nineteenth century, central banking functions were also exercised by clearinghouse associations, each composed of the member banks of a city clearinghouse. The New York Clearinghouse opened in 1853, and by 1914 clearinghouses operated in more than 160 cities. These associations played an important role during financial panics. Beginning in 1857, the New York Clearinghouse issued clearinghouse loan certificates, an instrument that was originally a way of adding to bank reserves and, in later panics, became a form of emergency currency that banks could pay out to their depositors. Certificates were issued in many cities during the financial panics of 1873, 1884, 1893, 1907, and 1914.

Clearinghouse associations also took on regulatory functions associated with modern central banks, although the original intent was sometimes to reduce competition. Clearinghouse members in some cities were restricted on interest rates that they could pay on deposits and were subjected to reserve requirements beyond those required by law. Clearinghouse associations also conducted examinations of member banks.

CENTRAL BANKING

THE FEDERAL RESERVE SYSTEM, 1913–1933

Financial panics in the post–Civil War period aroused increasing public dissatisfaction with the structure of the banking system. In the wake of the panic of 1907, Congress passed the Aldrich-Vreeland Act of 1908. One provision of this law gave public approval to the principle of clearinghouse loan certificates. The law authorized the issue of emergency currency in the form of national-bank notes by groups of banks on pledge of their earning assets. The system operated successfully during the financial panic of 1914 and might have furnished an adequate method of preventing bank panics as a possible alternative to the Federal Reserve. The Aldrich-Vreeland Act also established the National Monetary Commission, which published extensive studies on monetary topics at home and abroad. On the basis of its recommendations, congressional action was undertaken that culminated in the Owen-Glass (Federal Reserve) Act of December 1913.

A major concern in the discussions was that the existing American currency was "inelastic." There was no regular means to achieve seasonal adjustment in the amount of currency or to enlarge its supply during panics. H. Parker Willis, an influential architect of the Federal Reserve Act, believed many such problems could be solved if banks would adhere to the "commercial-loan theory" of banking. Banks should, in this view, restrict themselves to short-term loans reflecting transactions in the shipment and marketing of goods already produced. (Biddle's stress on domestic exchange represented a good example.) Such loans would minimize risk and help keep banks liquid. Banks should avoid loans for fixed-capital investments and especially not lend for "speculation." A central bank that could lend newly issued currency to banks on collateral of short-term commercial loans would, in Willis' view, achieve the desired currency elasticity.

Critics also attacked the system of commercial-bank reserves. Reserves held in cash were available for the bank in question but could not easily be moved about to meet demands elsewhere. Reserves held on deposit with other banks tended to make the apparent reserves of all banks taken separately larger than the actual cash reserves of the banking system as a whole. The pyramid of interbank deposit reserves focused on New York City. The large Wall Street banks held reserve deposits for thousands of other banks and used a portion of these deposits to make call loans, repayable on the demand of the lender, on stock exchange collateral. These loans went mostly to stockbrokers and traders. The system aroused public distrust because of concentration of power in Wall Street and links to speculation in stocks. There was much support for a system to pool banking reserves in a form that would not be involved with speculation. For all its defects, the pre-1913 system of interbank relations had much economic justification and continued to exist after the coming of the Federal Reserve.

According to the 1913 law, the Federal Reserve system was established "to furnish an elastic currency, to afford means of rediscounting commercial paper, to establish a more effective supervision of banking in the United States, and for other purposes." Because of uneasiness about concentrating financial power, the organizational structure was diffuse. The law authorized the formation of as many as twelve Federal Reserve banks, and that maximum number was promptly adopted, dividing the country into twelve Federal Reserve districts. Each Federal Reserve bank would have jurisdiction over such commercial banks in its district as became members of the system. All national banks were required to become members, and state banks were encouraged to join, although few did in the early years. Each Federal Reserve bank was nominally a corporation, its stock owned by the member banks, each of which was required to subscribe in proportion to its capital. Each Federal Reserve bank was nominally subject to a nine-member board of directors, of whom six were chosen by district member banks. In practice the influence of member banks has not been large. Reserve bank presidents have, in effect, been chosen by the Federal Reserve Board in Washington, and the presidents have wielded the main influence in each bank.

The originators of the Federal Reserve system envisioned a loose federation of regional reserve banks. General governmental supervision was to be exercised by a seven-member Federal Reserve Board in Washington. Board members consisted of the secretary of the Treasury, the comptroller of the currency, and five other persons to be chosen by the president of the United States with Senate confirmation. Experience soon demonstrated that the financial economy could be treated only as a national unit. Throughout Federal Reserve history there has been some competition for power between Reserve bank presidents and the Federal Reserve Board. But the system has always been oriented toward a relatively uniform national policy.

The Federal Reserve Act of 1913 established legal reserve requirements for all member banks. These modified existing national-bank requirements by providing lower requirements for time (savings) deposits than for demand (checking) deposits. As a result, time deposits rose from relative insignificance to an important role in banking in the 1920's. In 1917, partly as a wartime measure to centralize the national gold reserve, member banks were required to maintain their entire legal reserve on deposit with Federal Reserve banks. (Earlier they could also count vault cash and deposits with other banks. In 1959–1960 they were once again permitted to count vault cash as legal reserve.)

Federal Reserve banks were authorized to issue a new form of paper currency, Federal Reserve notes. Note issue was constrained by collateral and reserve requirements, reflecting the prevailing respect for the gold standard and for the commercial-loan theory of banking. (These requirements were substantially relaxed in the 1930's and played no significant role thereafter.) It was assumed that the notes would enter the economy chiefly through the process of Federal Reserve rediscounting for member banks.

The conception of the Federal Reserve as a defense against banking panic focused largely on the power to issue currency and the provisions for loans to member banks. Central banking theory had long stressed the importance of a "lender of last resort" from which funds would always be available, no matter how severe the crisis. The Federal Reserve would stand ready to buy customers' promissory notes from member banks through a process of rediscount. To be eligible for rediscount, these notes had to be short-term, "self-liquidating" debts arising out of "real" transactions of exchange in the manner envisioned by the commercial-loan theory. Interest was charged by the Federal Reserve banks in the form of a rediscount rate that could be raised or lowered in response to economic conditions.

Concentrating on currency issue, the founders of the Federal Reserve system did not immediately perceive that Federal Reserve lending could increase member-bank reserves, and that each dollar of added reserves might support several dollars of added deposits and loans by member banks. But in practice most member borrowing was done to obtain additional reserve deposits rather than to obtain currency. The rediscount mechanism helped to adjust the supply of credit to accommodate seasonal variations in demand for loans, a problem that had received much attention before 1913. But while the rediscount system was intended to protect against panic, the demand for rediscount credit tended to swell during prosperous times and to dwindle in slumps. The rediscount system failed miserably in 1929–1933, when the volume of Federal Reserve lending fell drastically in conditions of mounting bank panic.

The reserve, currency, and discount provisions were the most important elements of the new Federal Reserve system. The Federal Reserve banks were soon cast in the role of managing the cash balance and public-debt transactions of the Treasury. Also, like the banks of the United States, the Federal Reserve undertook to facilitate the national interregional payments system. Each member bank was encouraged to clear checks through its Federal Reserve bank, and the reserve deposits served as the vehicle for those transactions. All the banks, whether members or not, were pressured by the Federal Reserve authorities to pay all checks at par. Since many smaller banks were accustomed to deriving substantial revenue by deducting "exchange" charges before paying checks coming from other banks, a bitter controversy arose. Most nonmember banks ultimately capitulated, but many hard feelings remained.

Unlike the banks of the United States, the Federal Reserve banks were bankers' banks; they did not carry on loan or deposit business with the general public. Federal Reserve banks were given the responsibility of examining member banks. Although proposals for federal deposit insurance were widespread, no federal program was undertaken until the 1930's.

The coming of World War I drastically changed the environment of Federal Reserve operation. In 1913 neither federal government expenditure nor the national debt was very large.

The war brought a huge increase in federal spending financed by issues of war bonds. The Federal Reserve undertook to aid government finance by making loans available at low interest rates for banks borrowing on collateral of government securities. The program was highly inflationary. The loans from the Federal Reserve banks swelled bank reserves and contributed to a large rise in bank loans and deposits. After the war the low-interest policy was kept in operation through 1919 to aid Treasury re-funding operations. By 1920 consumer prices had doubled from their 1914 levels.

Although Federal Reserve officials seemed unconcerned with the inflation, they were very disturbed when gold reserves began to fall in late 1919, and rapidly adopted a deflationary stance. Rediscount rates were sharply increased in early 1920 and held at high levels well into 1921. The economy underwent a very sharp recession that raised the unemployment rate to 10 percent in 1921. But price decreases absorbed a large proportion of the decrease in aggregate demand, and the episode was regarded by many as a "healthy corrective" to the wartime inflation.

The 1920–1921 depression brought a large decline in agricultural prices, which did not recover when prosperity returned to the rest of the economy in 1922 and afterward. Depressed farm prices led to a high rate of failure among small rural banks. Such banks had formed at a rapid rate after 1900, until by 1920 the country had about thirty thousand banks. Several hundred of these failed each year from 1921 to 1929, and many of the others were in a weakened condition that made them unable to withstand the economic downturn after 1929.

Federal Reserve officials successfully averted efforts of a congressional investigation in 1922 to blame their actions for the farm price distress. And throughout the 1920's they maintained the view that price stabilization was not a feasible or desirable goal for Federal Reserve operations. Insofar as a clear policy directive existed, it was probably the "rules of the game" of the international gold standard, to which major European countries had returned in the 1920's. Benjamin Strong, governor (president) of the New York Federal Reserve bank and probably the most influential figure in the system in the 1920's, told a congressional inquiry in 1928: "I still feel that everything important which is sought to be accomplished by this direction of the Congress [price stability], could be well accomplished, possibly with avoiding some misunderstanding, through a scientific application of the well-known principles of the gold standard." Strong expressed doubts about discretionary monetary management, arguing that "Where you are speaking of efforts simply to stabilize commerce, industry, agriculture, employment, and so on, without regard to the penalties of violation of the gold standard, you are talking about human judgment and the management of prices which I do not believe in at all."

Somewhat by accident, Federal Reserve officials in the early 1920's began to recognize the potential of "open-market" operations. The term refers to purchases and sales of federal government securities by Federal Reserve banks in transactions with private investors at market price. Federal Reserve officials discovered that Reserve bank purchases of securities, initially undertaken to provide some earning assets, had the effect of increasing bank reserves or aiding member banks to reduce their indebtedness to the Reserve banks. Recognition that open-market operations could have important economic effects prompted formation in 1923 of the Open-Market Investment Committee to coordinate open-market operations for the entire system (the Open-Market Investment Committee became the Open-Market Policy Committee in 1930, and the Federal Open Market Committee by the Banking Act of 1933).

The stability and prosperity of the 1920's helped raise the self-confidence and prestige of the Federal Reserve. These largely evaporated in the dismal failure of the system to deal with the economic collapse of 1929–1933. Nearly twenty years after passage of the Federal Reserve Act to end bank panics, the nation experienced the worst bank panic in history. In the four years 1930–1933, more than nine thousand banks failed. The sum of currency and bank deposits, which equaled $46 million in 1929, fell to $32 million by 1933. The value of gross national product fell by nearly half, real output declined by one-third, and the unemployment rate rose from 3 percent in 1929 to 25 percent in 1933.

There is still much controversy about the importance of monetary factors in the Great Depression, and how much better or worse things might have been under a different Federal Reserve policy. The following facts are clear:

1. The Federal Reserve had no selective means to prevent the great boom in stock prices or the stock market panic in late 1929. The government had regulated stock market margin trading during the war, but the program was discontinued in 1919.

2. Federal Reserve officials felt themselves unable to do anything about the mounting tide of bank failures after 1929. Failures were viewed as reflecting bad management; in any case, most of them involved nonmember banks.

3. Federal Reserve loans to member banks declined during the downswing. Some open-market purchases were made, but not enough to prevent member-bank reserves from declining substantially.

4. Interest rates on private bonds rose from 1929 to 1932, even though Federal Reserve officials, looking mostly at rates on government securities, believed credit was "easy." Rising bond interest rates meant falling bond prices, which lowered the value of bonds held as assets by banks and other financial institutions. For example, a bond paying $50 a year in interest would sell for $1,000 if the market interest rate was 5 percent. If the market rate rose to 6 percent, the $50 bond would fall in price sufficiently to yield its purchaser 6 percent on the amount he would pay for it (counting interest and possible capital gain).

5. The wave of bank failures led the public to make massive withdrawals of currency from the banks, depleting their reserves and lending capacity and adding to the failure rate. In December 1929, Federal Reserve credit (including loans to banks and open-market securities) totaled $1.643 billion. In April 1932 it was virtually identical, $1.694 billion. Over that period currency in circulation had increased by about $500 million and member-bank reserves had fallen $400 million. In 1931, alarmed at apparent gold withdrawals, the Federal Reserve sharply raised discount rates, and in March 1931, Reserve bank credit fell as low as $921 million.

Substantial open-market purchases in mid-1932 raised Federal Reserve credit to $2.422 billion in July. But for the following seven months, while the banking system entered its most severe distress, culminating in the bank holiday of March 1933, the Federal Reserve did nothing. In fact, Reserve bank credit in February 1933 was $2.224 billion—less than the previous July.

6. President Herbert Hoover, despairing of action from the Federal Reserve, persuaded Congress in 1932 to charter the Reconstruction Finance Corporation. This organization was to provide emergency loans to distressed borrowers, including banks—exactly what Congress had thought the original Federal Reserve Act had provided for.

7. Most of the influential people in the Federal Reserve system lacked understanding of or sympathy for expansionary actions to relieve the downswing.

In July 1930, Governor George Leslie Harrison of the New York Federal Reserve bank sent a circular letter to the other Federal Reserve banks, citing the depressed state of business and suggesting that open-market purchases might be undertaken "to facilitate a more active and stronger bond market through which capital funds may be made available for new enterprise. . . ." The responses from other governors were overwhelmingly negative. Governor John U. Calkins of San Francisco wrote:

> 1) We do not believe that the creation, promotion, or encouragement of a bond market is within the province of the Federal Reserve System, nor do we believe that any efforts which may be put forth by the System will result in such an improvement of the bond market as to favorably affect general business or foreign trade. . . .
>
> 2) We believe that to make credit progressively cheaper and more abundant may cause an unfavorable psychological reaction, rather than a favorable one.

Governor Lynn Porter Talley of Dallas urged that the New York bank "should have the fortitude to meet a period of reaction and go through an era of readjustment patiently and calmly, acting in accordance with conditions as they are found, instead of undertaking to make conditions as they are desired. . . ."

Even Harrison had no strong conviction about expansionary action. In 1932 he expressed to a congressional committee his reservations about "clogging the banks by giving them too much excess reserve. If you give them too much excess reserves when they lack confidence it is just like flooding the carburetor of an automobile."

It is ironic, then, that in its annual report for 1932, the Federal Reserve Board could solemnly state: "During 1932 the Federal Reserve System continued to pursue the policy of monetary ease which it had followed since the beginning of the depression."

Had the Federal Reserve been willing to undertake large open-market purchases of securities from 1930 on, the total supply of money and credit could have been protected from decrease. There is no way of knowing how much improvement would have been achieved in economic conditions. However, during the entire twentieth century there has been a high correlation between money and total expenditures. Had money been kept from declining after 1929, it is statistically probable that expenditures would not have declined as much as they did.

THE FEDERAL RESERVE SYSTEM, 1933–1980

The New Deal brought major changes to the financial system generally and to the Federal Reserve in particular. The most important innovation was the creation in 1933 of the Federal Deposit Insurance Corporation (FDIC). Virtually all commercial banks were brought under coverage of FDIC insurance and supervision. As a result, bank failure and currency panic virtually disappeared from the American economy. The Federal Reserve was authorized to set maximum interest rates for member-bank time deposits, and banks were forbidden to pay interest on demand deposits.

In an unprecedented move, Congress in 1935 abolished the existing Federal Reserve Board, thus dismissing its entire membership. A new seven-member agency, called the Board of Governors, was created in its place. President Franklin D. Roosevelt appointed a few of the former Federal Reserve Board members but was able also to select several new members with a more expansionary outlook. The ex officio membership of the secretary of the Treasury and the comptroller of the currency was discontinued. Statutory recognition was given in 1933 and 1935 to the Federal Open Market Committee, consisting of the seven Board of Governors members and five of the twelve Reserve bank presidents. As open-market operations came to constitute the focal point of Federal Reserve policy, this group came to be the center of policy making.

The Board of Governors was given statutory authority in 1935 to vary legal reserve requirements within limits. A year later it used this power to make drastic increases in requirements, setting off a sharp monetary setback and contributing to a severe economic recession in 1937–1938.

The Board of Governors was also given statutory authority to set minimum margins for stock-market lending. Minimum levels subsequently ranged from 40 percent upward. Minimum margins did not eliminate stock price fluctuations but did greatly reduce the likelihood of the kind of severe panic formerly encountered when a large portion of stock purchases was financed by borrowing.

The depression of the 1930's largely put an end to the gold standard and the commercial-loan theory of banking. These ceased to be significant guides to Federal Reserve policy. The government abolished gold coinage and nationalized private gold holdings in 1933. Although gold continued nominally to be required as legal reserve for Federal Reserve liabilities until 1968, this arrangement had no policy importance. After the price of gold was increased from $20.67 to $35 an ounce in 1933–1934, the United States received a large inflow of gold, which tended to raise the quantity of money and bank reserves without any need for action by the Federal Reserve. Despite the monetary growth, the economy still had 10 percent unemployment in 1941.

The coming of World War II, with massive federal deficits and the extensive manpower draft, reduced unemployment to 1 percent by 1944. The Federal Reserve, relatively inactive in the 1930's except for its reserve-requirements activity in 1936–1937, was again enlisted to aid in financing government wartime deficits. It adopted a policy of supporting the prices of government securities at very low interest rates, ranging from 0.375 percent for three-month bills to 2.5 percent on long-term bonds. Reserve banks purchased securities in the open market sufficient to keep prices from falling below support levels. Under such arrangements open-market operations could not play an independent role but served merely as a disguised printing press to help finance deficits at low rates. Reserve bank holdings of government securities increased from $2 billion in 1941 to $24 billion in 1945. Bank reserves and the money supply were greatly increased in the process. The Federal Reserve was given temporary authority to impose restrictive terms on consumer installment credit by regulating down-payment and maturity provisions. Wartime price controls helped postpone some of the inflationary results of monetary expansion, but by 1948 consumer prices were 63 percent higher than they had been in 1941.

By the Employment Act of 1946, Congress directed the government to follow policies to achieve "maximum employment, production, and purchasing power." Although the Federal Reserve was not explicitly named in the law, Federal Reserve leaders subsequently indicated that they interpreted the law as directing them to follow measures to achieve economic stabilization. Their success in this goal was mixed.

In 1947 the Federal Reserve was able to remove its support from the very low Treasury bill rate, and in the process it slowed monetary growth sufficiently to bring a halt to inflation in 1948 and even produced a slight recession in 1949. A new inflationary shock hit the economy with the outbreak of war in Korea in 1950. The Federal Reserve was still committed to support long-term bond prices, and its officials were displeased with the inflationary bond purchases required by this commitment. After controversy with President Harry Truman and the Treasury, an accord was reached in 1951, permitting the Federal Reserve to discontinue fixed-price support of government securities. The Treasury agreed to set interest rates on new issues in line with market rates. The Federal Reserve discount rate would be kept low for another two years to ease the transition.

The accord was necessary to permit open-market operations to be fully available as a stabilization instrument. By 1953 such operations were typically carried on every business day, with the actual buying and selling done by the New York Federal Reserve bank. Much of the operation consisted of "defensive" operations designed to counteract undesired disturbances to bank reserves arising from currency withdrawals, gold flows, and Treasury cash operations. Open-market operations provided Federal Reserve authorities with a potential for precision of timing and magnitude not available through other policy instruments. Open-market purchases create "high-powered money" (so called because each dollar is potentially capable of supporting several dollars of bank deposit liabilities) in the form of currency and bank reserve deposits. The annual rate of change of high-powered money is a good indicator of Federal Reserve policy.

A commitment to economic stabilization did not provide the Federal Reserve with any clear-cut criterion for policy. In particular, a wide range of discretion remained between relatively restrictive measures aimed at minimizing price increases and expansionary measures designed to minimize unemployment. The most severe problems arose in periods when prices were rising but the unemployment rate was high.

During the administration of Dwight D. Eisenhower (1953–1961), Federal Reserve policy stressed control of inflation. From the first quarter of 1953 to the first quarter of 1961, the stock of high-powered money (adjusted for changes in reserve requirements) increased by only 1.2 percent per year. Episodes of extreme restraint occurred in 1953–1954, 1957, and 1959–1960, leading to accusations of "stop-and-go." In contrast, during 1961–1969 monetary policy was much more expansionary, stressing efforts to reduce unemployment and also to aid the government in financing the Vietnam War after 1965. From the first quarter of 1961 to the first quarter of 1969, high-powered money expanded at an average rate of 4.7 percent per year.

Federal Reserve policy during most of the 1950's and 1960's was characterized as a "money-market strategy." Policy was guided by such indicators as short-term interest rates and the free-reserve positions of the commercial banks. (Free reserves equals total reserves minus required reserves minus borrowings from the Federal Reserve.) Such strategy was criticized on the grounds that the variables in focus were not valid indicators of monetary policy, and that the money-market strategy caused policy to aggravate cyclical ups and downs rather than to counter them.

Beginning with George Mitchell in 1961, a number of professional economists were appointed to the Board of Governors, the most prominent being Arthur F. Burns, who served as chairman from 1970 to 1978. As a reflection of its closer rapport with professional opinion, the Board made an important change in its policy orientation in 1970. This involved trying to maintain specified growth rates for "monetary aggregates"—measures of the quantity of money and credit. This orientation was reinforced by a joint resolution of Congress adopted in March 1975, which went far beyond precedent in indicating goals for monetary policy. It included the following passages:

> That it is the sense of Congress that the . . . Federal Reserve system . . . maintain long-run growth of the monetary and credit aggregates commensurate with the economy's long-run potential to increase production, so as to promote effectively the goals of maximum employment, stable prices, and moderate long-term interest rates.
>
> The Board of Governors shall consult with Congress at semiannual meetings . . . about the . . . objectives and plans with respect to the ranges of growth or diminution of monetary and credit aggregates in the upcoming twelve months.

Since the adoption of this resolution, the chairman has presented growth plans for major monetary aggregates to House and Senate committees each quarter.

Unfortunately, the adoption of monetary aggregates as a policy focus cannot be judged very successful. The growth rates maintained in the 1970's were consistently at a highly inflationary level, reflecting a vain effort to prevent interest rates from rising. Once the economy became adapted to rapid monetary growth and inflation, the Federal Reserve was reluctant to slow down the creation of money for fear of causing an economic recession. In 1977, chairman Burns admitted that "The monetary growth ranges established during the past 2 years have been considerably higher than they should be over the long run." Yet under Burns's successor, William Miller, monetary growth was accelerated further in 1978.

Broad outlines of monetary policy and its major effects are shown in table 1. Between 1953 and 1961, the low monetary growth rate held inflation to 1.4 percent but permitted unemployment to rise substantially. Accelerated monetary growth after 1961 sharply reduced unemployment and increased the growth rate of real output, but also produced a rise in the inflation rate to 3 percent per year. These experiences led to a belief that there existed a stable trade-off between inflation and unemployment.

By 1969 the public had come to expect continued monetary growth and attendant inflation. Economists gave increased attention to the tendency for nominal interest rates to rise point for point with the increase in inflation, and they began to question the stability of the inflation-unemployment trade-off. The step-up in monetary growth to 7.3 percent in 1969–1977 produced a great increase in the inflation rate combined with a rise in unemployment and a slowdown in the growth of real output. The interest rate on corporate Aaa bonds, which had been virtually constant around 4.5 percent in 1959–1965, rose to more than 8 percent in 1970. The period following 1970 was thus a policy-maker's nightmare, with high rates of interest, inflation, and unemployment existing side by side.

Confusion in the management of Federal Reserve policy arose partly from the difficulty of separating long-run and short-run effects of monetary expansion. In the short run, Federal Reserve expansionary measures were capable of lowering interest rates and of raising output and employment. After a lag, however, much of the impact of monetary expansion was translated into price increases, which in turn aggravated inflationary expectations and pushed interest rates up. Lagged inflation thus made it increasingly difficult to maintain satisfactory rates of employment and output growth with any given rate of monetary expansion. Thinking on monetary policy both in and out of the Federal Reserve was still burdened by a tendency to concentrate on interest rates and credit conditions, and to give inadequate attention to the growth of high-powered money as an indicator of Federal Reserve policy.

CONCLUSION

Each of the American central banks was originally established to help maintain the monetary standard relating the dollar to precious metals, and all performed this function successfully.

CENTRAL BANKING

TABLE 1
Monetary Policy and Some of Its Effects, 1953–1978

Dates for High-Powered Money	Stock of High-Powered Money (adjusted)	GNP in Current Prices	GNP in 1958 Prices (lagged two quarters)	Unemployment	Consumer Price Index (1957–1959)	Interest Rate on Corporate Aaa Bonds (lagged six quarters)
1953(qtr.1)	$48.0 bil.	$367.8 bil.	$622.4 bil.	2.7%	94.3	2.9%
1961(qtr.1)	52.8 bil.	527.2 bil.	758.7 bil.	6.8%	105.7	4.3%
1969(qtr.1)	76.6 bil.	946.9 bil.	1,083.4 bil.	3.6%	134.7	8.2%
1977(qtr.1)	137.1 bil.	1,916.8 bil.	1,343.9 bil.	6.0%	224.9	8.8%

Annual Average Percentage Rate of Change

1953–1961	1.2	4.5	2.5		1.4	
1961–1969	4.7	7.3	4.4		3.0	
1969–1977	7.3	8.8	2.7		6.3	

Sources: High-powered money adjusted for changes in reserve requirements from worksheet data of Federal Reserve Bank of St. Louis spliced into data in that bank's *Review*, July 1977, p. 27. GNP data from U.S. Department of Commerce, *The National Income and Product Accounts of the United States, 1929–1974*, 1977, pp. 19, 21, and *Federal Reserve Bulletin*, Dec., 1978, p. A52. Unemployment, prices, interest rates from current issues of *Federal Reserve Bulletin*.

This objective sometimes conflicted with the goal of economic stability, and when the conflict became severe in the 1930's, the monetary standard was essentially discarded. All central banks also contributed to improving the functioning of the internal payments system and assisting Treasury financial operations. All were aware of the problem of economic stabilization and tried to promote it. But despite the attention given to stabilization objectives in official pronouncements of the Federal Reserve system, its performance was decidedly uneven. Federal Reserve policy contributed directly to major economic downswings in 1920–1921 and 1936–1937, and was not used effectively to counter the monetary collapse of 1929–1933. Since World War II, monetary policy has been effective in preventing downswings from developing into severe depressions. But no comparable improvement occurred in policy respecting inflation. Long-run data on high-powered money and price-level behavior show clearly that expansionary monetary policies were at the root of major inflationary episodes associated with both world wars. Most disturbing was the apparent Federal Reserve commitment to a highly inflationary rate of monetary growth during the 1970's, an experience without peacetime precedent for intensity or duration. The experience shook traditional confidence that monetary expansion could lower interest rates and raise output and employment, leading to reexamination of basic economic analysis of the relationship of money to the economy.

BIBLIOGRAPHY

Surveys of American central banking experience in a context of economic and financial analysis can be found in many standard textbooks of American financial history or money and banking, such as the following: Lester V. Chandler, *The Economics of Money and Banking* (New York, 1948; 7th ed., revised with Stephen Goldfeld, 1977); Davis R. Dewey, *Financial History of the United States* (New York, 1903; 12th ed., 1934); Louis A. Rufener, *Money and Banking in the United States* (Boston, 1934; 3rd ed., 1938); Paul Studenski and Herman Krooss, *Financial History of the United States* (New York, 1952; 2nd ed., 1963); Paul B. Trescott, *Money, Banking, and Economic Welfare* (New York, 1960; 2nd ed., 1965).

The period before 1840 has been treated in a number of studies that grew out of the monetary and banking controversies around 1900. The most notable was Ralph Catterall, *The Second Bank of the United States* (Chicago, 1903; repr. 1960). Like most economic studies, this stressed the value of the bank as an instrument of conservative finance. The National Monetary Commission published studies of the two early national banks: John T. Holdsworth, *The First Bank of the United States* (Washington, D.C., 1910); and Davis R. Dewey, *The Second United States Bank* (Washington, D.C., 1910). These stressed the technical aspects of charter provisions and management. Richard Timberlake, *The Origins of Central Banking in the United States* (Cambridge and London, 1978), reviews much of American monetary history from 1790 to 1914 and stresses the ideas about the theory and practice of monetary control expressed in Congress and in the executive branch. Treasury operations receive particular attention.

The political controversy between Andrew Jackson and Nicholas Biddle has always drawn attention from political historians. A strongly pro-Jackson viewpoint was developed by Arthur M. Schlesinger, Jr., in his Pulitzer Prize–winning study *The Age of Jackson* (Boston, 1945). Schlesinger strongly criticizes Biddle and the Second Bank as centers of irresponsible power. A substantial rejoinder, with more stress on technical economic analysis, is found in numerous writings of Bray Hammond, notably his Pulitzer Prize–winning study *Banks and Politics in America, from the Revolution to the Civil War* (Princeton, 1957). Hammond's book is rich in narrative detail and personalities but also devotes much attention to the constructive role of banking in promoting the economic development of the nation. Anti-Jackson writers have often blamed his policies for the panic and depression of 1837–1843. However, a study by Peter Temin, *The Jacksonian Economy* (New York, 1969), stresses the dominant role of international financial conditions and particularly the market for American cotton. In a lengthy biography, *Nicholas Biddle: Nationalist and Public Banker, 1786–1844* (Chicago, 1959), Thomas P. Govan allows Biddle's own writings to demonstrate his intellectual brilliance and insight into economic policy. A more balanced evaluation that captures Biddle's arrogance and naiveté as well is given in the relevant chapters of Fritz Redlich, *The Molding of American Banking: Men and Ideas* (New York, 1968). Redlich's study is in a context of entrepreneurial and business history, and stresses the relationship of Biddle and his bank to both the government and the remainder of the banking system. Another judicious study, Walter B. Smith, *Economic Aspects of the Second Bank of the United States* (Cambridge, Mass., 1953), presents a detailed narrative of bank operations utilizing the abundant quantitative data available, and relates the bank to its economic environment. The books by Hammond and Redlich provide substantial discussion of both banks of the United States.

For the period when the United States had no formal central bank, a useful survey of Treasury monetary operations is provided by Esther R. Taus, *Central Banking Operations of the United States Treasury, 1789–1941* (New York, 1943; repr. 1967). The important contributions of the clearinghouse associations to central banking are detailed in Walter Spahr, *The Clearing and Collection of Checks* (New York, 1926). A work in a class by itself is Milton Friedman and Anna J. Schwartz, *A Monetary History of the United States, 1867–1960* (Princeton, 1963). This work is built around a core of original historical data on the components of the national stock of money and its principal determinants. Both this work and a companion volume by Philip Cagan, *Determinants and Effects of Changes in the Stock of Money, 1875–1960* (New York, 1965), marshal historical evidence to support the view that changes in the quantity of money have been extremely important in the determination of national money income. Controversial elements in this view are highlighted in a review by Keynesian economist James Tobin, "The Monetary Interpretation of History," in *American Economic Review*, 55 (June 1965).

The literature on the Federal Reserve system is vast. In a two-volume study entitled *The Federal Reserve System* (New York, 1930), Paul Warburg, one of the founders and early Federal Reserve Board members, presents a detailed account of the origins of the system. W. Randolph Burgess, a longtime Federal Reserve staff member, details much of the rationale for 1920's policy in *The Reserve Banks and the Money Market* (New York, 1927; 3rd ed. 1946). Comparing the first edition with the second (1936) gives a good idea of the evolution of Federal Reserve thinking. Lester V. Chandler, *Benjamin Strong, Central Banker* (Washington, D.C., 1958), is a biographical study of the first president of the New York Federal Reserve bank. In Chandler's view Strong had a vision of the Federal Reserve in a modern role as economic stabilizer; had Strong remained vigorous and influential, the Federal Reserve policies in 1929–1933 might have been more constructive. A contrary view is advanced by Elmus Wicker in *Federal Reserve Monetary Policy, 1917–1933* (New York, 1966). Wicker argues that Strong, as well as the other influential Federal Reserve officials, still held the traditional outlook of the international gold standard. The books by Wicker and by Friedman and Schwartz contain detailed narratives of Federal Reserve actions during the downswing of 1929–1933. The latter place heavy blame on Federal Reserve officials for failure to take more aggressive action for monetary expansion. They believe that had the stock of money not declined so drastically, output and employment would have decreased less. A contrary position is argued in a Keynesian frame of analysis by Peter Temin in *Did Monetary Forces Cause the Great Depression?* (New York, 1975), which answers the title question in the negative. Temin, like many Keynesians, feels that the decrease in the stock of money was primarily a passive reflection of the decrease in business activity, not a cause of that decrease.

Revived interest in monetary economics in the 1960's brought increased attention to critical evaluation of Federal Reserve policy. Materials published by the House Committee on Banking and Currency under the general title *The Federal Reserve System After Fifty Years* (Washington, D.C., 1964) contain much of historical interest. Of particular value are staff studies by Karl Brunner and Allan Meltzer entitled "Some General Features of the Federal Reserve's Approach to Policy" and "The Federal Reserve's Attachment to the Free Reserve Concept." Important changes in policy, with increased attention to monetary aggregates, are described from the inside in *Managing the Dollar* (New York, 1973) by Sherman J. Maisel, a member of the Board of Governors from 1965 to 1972.

[*See also* BUSINESS CYCLES, PANICS, AND DEPRESSIONS; ECONOMY FROM THE REVOLUTION TO 1815; ECONOMY FROM 1815 TO 1865; ECONOMY FROM RECONSTRUCTION TO 1914; ECONOMY SINCE 1914; FINANCIAL INTERMEDIARIES; GOVERNMENT MANAGEMENT OF THE ECONOMY; MONEY SUPPLY; *and* PRICES AND WAGES.]

ORGANIZED BUSINESS GROUPS

Albert K. Steigerwalt

ANYONE scanning the American business world and its environment cannot but be impressed at the array of business institutions: several hundred multibillion-dollar corporate entities, the strategies of which all lead toward sustained growth; conglomerate diversification; multinational influence; massive organizational structures (multiplant, multidivision, multifunction); continued occupation of partially monopolistic positions on both sides of markets (supply and demand); employment of thousands or hundreds of thousands of persons; and a sustained drive toward technical competence as well as innovational leadership. Nevertheless, this array can elicit deep concern about the legitimacy of huge corporations. Society is increasingly challenging their almost unlimited power.

The multicorporate structure is supported by suppliers, governments, law firms of appropriate size and stature, commercial and investment bankers, insurance companies, the mass media (television and radio networks, magazines, newspapers), and organized business groups that transcend the individual corporate entity and interact with the rest of society on behalf of their patrons. One authority has argued that the modern conglomerate or multinational corporation is the most significant social innovation since the creation of the nation-state. Whether or not this is true, the presence of such a set of institutions is awesome. Only one aspect of this phenomenon will concern us here: the emergence and development of an ancillary and client institution that, for lack of a more precise term, shall be referred to as the "organized business groups."

Several thousand of these groups and/or associations of businessmen exist, frequently playing powerful roles in ameliorating the position of their members by means of affirmative programs or in preventing deterioration when preferred positions come under attack. These organized business groups take their lead from the central fact that their members are associated with a system in which profit is the organizing and directing strategy. The interests of the members are "business interests." All business associations tend to mirror these interests.

An organized business group is an association of businessmen united to serve certain implicit or explicit purposes, and the association is sustained by methods and procedures sanctioned by the membership as well as by the larger business community. They all have some kind of formal organization and stated purposes, but the informal organization and actual purposes may differ somewhat from the formal ones. Therefore, frequently the relationships between business associations and other associations, organizations, and institutions play an important part in molding the political structure of contemporary society.

The proliferation of all sorts of associations is one of the most striking aspects of modern life. The question of their legitimacy and authority is ever present in the absence of government sanctions and in the presence of the ability of some associations to exercise coercive authority. Some further question exists as to the purely voluntary aspects of membership, inasmuch as some associations are so influential as to "command" membership. Nonmembers frequently are unable to insulate themselves from the authority and influence of the association.

Any effort to classify associations other than by broad categories such as business, labor, and religious has shortcomings. However, it appears that the population of occupational associations that are called business associations may be subjected to a more rigorous classification in terms of principal function. One classification divides all organized business groups into three separate populations:

1. The public-policy or "peak" associations, such as the National Association of Manufacturers and the United States Chamber of Commerce. These are essentially action- and program-oriented organizations designed to enhance the aggregate interests of business in society. Although not mutually exclusive, the Committee for Economic Development and the Conference Board (formerly National Industrial Conference Board) are research and study types. They rely upon the quality of their research and its essential fairness to influence public-policy actions in favor of business. They consult with educators, businessmen, and government officials, and then publish and distribute the results of their research.

2. The employers' associations concerned with labor markets, wage rates, industrial relations, labor skills, and so forth. Their interests are direct and immediate: they seek to control or influence wage rates, legislation, and other factors that affect the supply and price of labor.

3. The trade or industry association that specializes in one type of business or industry, best exemplified by the American Iron and Steel Institute or the American Petroleum Institute.

Each of these types overlaps the others to some extent, duplicating some functions, but in terms of predominant focus there is a valid means of discrimination. The associations may relate to one another in the way that the National Industrial Council, a wholly owned subsidiary of the National Association of Manufacturers, coordinates and directs the activities of local and state employers' associations.

A classification based upon geographic distinctions (local, state, and national) is inadequate. There are local chambers of commerce, state chambers of commerce, and the national chamber of commerce. They are all organizationally related and hence have no significant "type differences." Such is the case with manufacturers' and employers' associations as well. No longer are there local or regional associations of any note. The focus is almost exclusively upon the national or international level.

Another classification that deserves consideration is one based upon ideology—dominant ideas rather than dominant programs—although attitudes and behavior have an intimate relationship. This classification bifurcates the business world, establishing liberal and conservative poles; the lines of force flowing between the poles establish the common ground: antipathy to interference in labor markets by labor unions and governments.

The National Association of Manufacturers, the United States Chamber of Commerce, trade and employers' associations, and the National Federation of Independent Businesses are supposed to take the classical, fundamental, or authoritarian approach to issues confronting the business community. In this system of ideas, government plays a very limited role, markets are to be free and competitive, and all associated economics tends to find its analytical and philosophical support in the writings of the classicists. The National Federation of Independent Businesses is a variant of the classical approach to issues of public policy, because it perpetuates a deep antipathy toward "bigness" in business, and thus sets one part of business in opposition to another. As in all ideologies, there are glaring inconsistencies and ambiguities between preaching and practice. Yet this dichotomy is a helpful device in understanding the pervasive phenomenon of organized business groups in the matrix of American society.

The other division of this classification is the liberal or "managerial" position, best exemplified by the Committee for Economic Development, an organization noted for the presence in its membership of the corporate elite. It stresses the emergence of professional management in the world of the multinational corporation and the need and willingness to adapt or modify classical economic doctrine and preconceptions to the realities of the contemporary world. This point of view clearly accepts the fact of government growth and influence, and sees no return to simpler days. The proper question is not how much government should do, but what it should do and how it may be done most effectively.

ORGANIZED BUSINESS GROUPS

Although leading to different kinds of public-policy positions, the two viewpoints in the ideological classification agree on their antipathy to organized labor and to most interference in the labor market. Their views diverge in many other areas, including foreign trade. The National Association of Manufacturers tends to support a kind of protectionism rather than the free trade of Adam Smith, contrary to the position of the Committee for Economic Development. Such differences may be due to other than philosophic preconceptions; they may result from the kinds of businessmen attracted to membership in each association. The Committee for Economic Development may be composed of more sophisticated, less doctrinaire individuals, less alienated from the forces at work in the contemporary world. Members of the Committee for Economic Development are frequently called upon for government service, and do serve.

The diversity of these organized groups expresses the variety of the American business population. The full range on the national level includes the national associations of real estate boards, home builders, retailers, wholesalers, coal operators, electrical manufacturers, bankers, pharmaceutical manufacturers, manufacturing chemists, railroads, truckers, and many more. In some industries there are several associations, and most business firms hold multiple memberships, perhaps belonging to all the policy associations, one or more of the trade associations, and one or more employers' associations. Such firms are members at the national level as well as at the state and local levels. As the modern corporation conglomerates or alters its business strategy by entering new industries, the thrust toward multiple membership is accelerated.

Most members rely upon their associations for public commitments to issues affecting the company or its industry. Anonymity of the individual company is preferred, since it permits the overall organization to take the heat of attention as well as the leadership in a confrontation with legislatures, labor unions, or environmental groups. Some large corporations occasionally duplicate associational effort by taking public positions, but most do not. Even trade associations tend to restrict themselves to industry problems and to leave other types of controversies to the policy associations.

Excluded from this definition, classification, and description of organized business groups are professional associations, such as the American Institute of Certified Public Accountants, boards of trade, stock exchanges, commodity markets, and agricultural marketing cooperatives. Such groups are organized markets, marketing agents, or business concerns in their own right. The associations discussed here are only incidentally business concerns.

ORGANIZED BUSINESS GROUPS IN UNITED STATES HISTORY

Almost from the beginning of national life, the Founding Fathers and others seemed to be aware that individualism alone is not adequate to the good society. Some of them feared organizations as "factions" and were concerned for their impact upon the newly designed government process. James Madison discussed this point in *Federalist* number 10, where he wrote:

> By faction I understand a number of citizens whether amounting to a majority or minority of the whole, who are united and actuated by a common impulse of passion, or interest, adverse to the rights of other citizens, or to the permanent and aggregate interests of the community.

The term "organization" or "association" or "group" might aptly be substituted for "faction" without significantly changing the meaning. Certainly American society did not develop a unity in terms of institutions and interests, but it did clearly develop in a way that gave credence to Madison's analysis, if not to his concern. During the early nineteenth century the growth of such closely knit groups as the Masons, Mormons, and Catholics generated widespread suspicion, and in some instances led to violence.

The emergence of many factions in American society created the impression that the contemporary world, populated by numerous associations, constitutes the end product of an organizational metamorphosis so extensive as to be fairly termed "revolutionary." To some observers this is a natural evolution; while to others it is a blight upon the body politic as well as a malignant societal affliction, destructive of individual identity and conducive to alienation, that will alter the very nature of American life. Special antipathy is reserved for the emergence of the modern industrial economy after the middle of the nineteenth century.

Some see this transition as the rise of a dominant power center inaugurating the spread of the corporate organization of industry, beginning with the railroads in the late 1860's. At that time no one envisioned the world that would evolve from corporate organizations and their manifold uses, for the corporate organizational form was viewed as not adaptable to general business. But, as American business increasingly came under the sway of corporate goliaths that reinforced latent monopolistic tendencies, some people were alarmed. Such tendencies were believed to be capable of correction through reform and legislation giving the federal government regulatory power over the railroads and power to control monopoly in other industries. Progressivism, the New Freedom, the New Deal, and the Great Society repeated the reform impulse.

Corporate leviathans continued to demonstrate their adaptability and their ability to avoid the harsh restrictions of antitrust laws that seemed unable to reach oligopoly. Organized business groups were continually able to blunt legislative intent to regulate and control trade practices that contravened the mandates of competition. Conceptions of "trusteeship" and "social responsibility" emerged as techniques to make oligopoly appear benign in its neglect of rigorous rivalry for economic rewards. Some felt that American society has never faced the fact that economic power, as represented by corporate structures, could be a coercive form of social organization not subject to the usual sorts of countervailing power. What might be created thereby is a system of impersonal coercions leading to consequences unseen by even the most perceptive business leaders. The need to keep the system operating could lead to a growing intolerance of all that stands in the path of that accomplishment. More and more, such a system needs the state as its active partner, guaranteeing the welfare of the business system. In a very real sense, at this stage the state is in business.

Other points of view are somewhat less stark in their perception of the organizational transformation that overtook American life in general and the business community in particular. Yet even they exhibit a modicum of concern for the impact of such developments upon some parts of American life. The rise in the number, size, power, and diversity of organizations, especially those integral to economic organization and performance, is a natural consequence of an increase in the size and complexity of American society. In addition, these organizations have become better organized, more closely knit, and more efficient in recruiting and indoctrinating members, raising funds, and effectively pursuing their ends.

The power of the nation-state has been much affected by the rise of other power centers. The emergence of these pressure groups has substantially modified the democratic process. It is a characteristic of organizations that they tend to exacerbate the distinction between members and nonmembers, between the "in" group and the "out" group. Organizations are Janus-faced: stern-visaged toward the hostile external world and pleasant-visaged toward members. A pluralistic world dominated by organizations with such characteristics almost mandates that one find one's identity and status through organizations rather than by means of individual action. Power is now institutionalized in such organizations, and all opportunity for access to it is through organization. Furthermore, it is now more clearly perceived than ever before that organization is the only effective way to overcome hostile or negative forces in the environment.

Prior to World War I it was widely believed that political power exercised by private groups was dangerous and could only result in corruption of the democratic process. Another tradition began to take hold during that same period as the War Industries Board mobilized the economy by relying upon private groups, especially business and industrial groups, to mitigate the burden of war placed upon the government. Especially effective was the organization of rivals or competitors within an industry that, for war purposes, arrived at a consensus of reasonable goals for the industry. This experience reinforced trade associations as industry coordinators, and such coordination evolved into monopolistic modifications of competition in the postwar years. That reinforcement was amplified by governmental policies during the 1920's, especially those of Herbert Hoover as secretary of commerce and later as president. Beyond a doubt, the growth of these kinds of organizations and their patron firms created new points of economic power within society while drastically altering more traditional institutional relationships.

RELATIONS WITH GOVERNMENT

What later came to be called pressure groups were simply Madison's factions in modern guise. Such groups are not equally effective in getting their programs adopted at the local, state, or national level, but each intends to influence public policy at one or more of these levels. Associations of businessmen, like other groups, develop an ideology or a set of beliefs, ideas, and values that serve to justify the objectives of the organization. The emergence of the group basis in politics has followed naturally from the growth of an organizational society.

The large formal organization is now the repository of power that once belonged to individuals who had ready access to the seats of power. Earl Latham expressed this seminal notion when he said:

> What may be called public policy is actually the equilibrium reached in the group struggle at any given moment, and it represents a balance which contending factions or groups constantly strive to weigh in their favor.... The legislature referees the group struggle, ratifies the victories of the successful coalitions, and records the terms of surrenders, compromises, and conquests in the form of statutes.

As early as 1908 this view was being presented by Arthur Fisher Bentley, who suggested a radically new approach to the study of politics by articulating his concept of "analytical pluralism," which stressed the need to investigate the extent and consequences of the involvement of interest groups in politics. This led to a growing awareness of America as a pluralistic society. In this view, all interests are expressed through associations of like-minded people.

A manufacturer that belongs to the local manufacturers' association is reacting to the society of like-minded people in that area. So it is with members of the state and national associations of manufacturers. The influence of each of these groups tends to be restricted, but as one goes upward, the increased numbers intensify; and the power of the national association is the result of an influential confluence of lesser associations. All the evidence seems to support the conclusion that associations of economic interests, especially aggregations of corporate power, are more influential than environmental or consumer groups. Societies for the prevention of cruelty to animals, for example, have long pressed for legislation mandating humane slaughter, but the meat-packers have always been able to blunt this movement.

Another factor augmenting the power of pressure groups is the almost complete absence of party discipline in the American political system. Parties are collections of frequently divergent forces that are accommodated for the primary purpose of winning elections. Upon election, such coalitions tend to fragment; and external groups, such as trade associations, which are more cohesive and have coherent sets of objectives, can urge the adoption of their programs more effectively. Another major result is that every government agency, in its creation and subsequent development, has a constituency defined in terms of functionally oriented groups with nationwide influence.

After years of advocacy, the effort of the National Association of Manufacturers to create a federal agency to oversee business interests was rewarded in 1903 with the creation of the Department of Commerce and Labor. Despite its title, internally that department reflected business interests, not those of labor. Business interests founded the United States Chamber of Commerce in 1912, but failed in an effort to make it a quasi-governmental agency at that time. But during World War I the Chamber of Commerce was used on a voluntary basis, and the Chamber's preeminence was reinforced by Herbert Hoover's policies in the 1920's, and was made licit in 1933 by the National Recovery Administration.

Groups are frequently in adversary confrontations, and some are strong enough to veto the action of another agency or group despite the support of the other agency by its constituency. In late 1975 the combined forces of business defeated a common situs picketing bill, sought by the constituency of the Labor Department for more than twenty years. Despite prior support by President Gerald Ford, the bill was vetoed because business groups organized a campaign that brought a flood of more than six hundred thousand letters and telegrams to the White House.

Not only do business groups relate to the executive and legislative branches and processes; they are coming more and more to relate to the political process as well. Increasingly these groups seem to be committed to one party, although bargaining is occasionally attempted. Advocacy of positions by organized business groups drives them to political commitments because political decisions and outcomes are not neutral. And the party in power is in a position to assist its supporters. The increasing commitment of labor groups to the Democratic cause has led most of the powerful public-policy-activated associations, such as the the National Association of Manufacturers and the United States Chamber of Commerce, as well as many trade associations, to adopt a posture of only thinly veiled partisanship on behalf of the Republican party. All of this relates primarily to power, its acquisition, and its use.

Group power, especially that of business groups, in view of their minority position in the electorate at large, is dependent upon an appropriate balance of four elements: wealth, numbers, leadership, and access to legislative, executive, and political entities. Wealth is not exclusively what is currently available for expenditure or in the "war chest"; it is also continued access to such resources and, in a very real sense, the kinds and sources of wealth represented by the organized group. Numbers alone are only one element of power, and they are a measure only when compared with the other factors in a balanced way. Leadership is a key element related not only to the quality of the leaders but also to the time and effort that they are willing and able to devote to the cause. This clearly stresses the element of access at all levels of government, particularly at the national level. Access to lawmakers (and particularly to committee chairmen and majority and minority leaders of both houses of Congress) is essential, as is access to regulatory agency executives and the major departments in the executive branch. These avenues to influence require constant travel, which suggests regular staff contact as well as contact by the executive of the association.

Although there is currently some evidence that chairmen of congressional committees are no longer the feudal barons they once were, the seniority system for the selection and tenure of chairmen, especially in the Senate, gives continuity to such leadership and encourages organizations to cultivate long-standing relationships. Congressmen who succeed to the presidency, if only by accident, take their long-established alliances to the immense power of the chief executive.

INTERNAL STRUCTURE OF ASSOCIATIONS

When looking carefully at organized business groups, one observes that they are large organizations made up of several hundred or a few thousand members representing billions of dollars in capital investment as well as annual profits approaching a significant fraction of that sum, occupying pivotal positions through their ability to influence the economy, and led by the capable executives of the constituent member firms. Most of these organizations have a hierarchical structure dominated by an internal oligarchy composed of powerful members and strong association executives. Practically all significant organizations are headquartered in Washington, D.C., or are heavily represented there. Policymaking for the association or industry is restricted to the oligarchy.

As in business itself, the actual control, management, and manipulation of these business groups is in the hands of an oligarchic minority. It controls the mechanisms of communication, staffing, selection of candidates for office and committees, budgets, membership, and expenditures. Those who hold this power are inevitably and understandably a highly homogeneous elite in the business community. The leading businessmen in all industry know one another better and work with one another more often than they do with their own subordinates in the firms they manage. Frequently they share more with one another than they do with their own boards of directors. Oligarchic leadership tends to be self-perpetuating, and in associations that rule prevails. It would be surprising if it were otherwise. In some associations two or three member groups contribute most of the financial support because of their relative size. Their power and influence differ in kind from that of the other members, but the latter will accept this as long as power is wielded by people they can understand. When such organizations occasionally enter a period of decline, a particularly powerful and wealthy member may offer to refinance the enterprise and take control. In those cases that are known, such an offer has been declined. Oligarchy is acceptable, but an absolute ruler is not.

A specific reference to the National Association of Manufacturers may serve to illuminate these issues of association structure. Recently the association ceased to have an elected president; it now has a career president who devotes himself exclusively to the affairs of the organization and is assisted by several vice-presidents. The major elected position is chairman of the board, the titular spokesman for the organization. The board numbers about 125 elected members. This is much like a legislature, so the actual power is wielded by an executive committee of about twenty-five. The corporate oligarchy, through the executive committee of the National Association of Manufacturers, influences the major decisions of all committees and the board of directors. None of these representatives of the elite ever runs for election as chairman of the board. That honor always goes to a representative of some moderate-size firm, on more than one occasion a self-made man. Those who wield the power see no reason to seek all the glory.

All organized business groups ultimately concentrate upon matters of self-interest and undertake sustained efforts to control those external forces that are considered threatening to the progress and prosperity of business. Trade associations play this role especially well, although they are not always successful. Particularly acute is the effort of trade associations to influence prices, quality of product, and trade practices in their industry, with the strategic objective of enhancing price stability and ensuring substantial profit margins. Thus it appears that trade associations are one of several means used by businessmen in an overall strategy to influence or control the marketplace to their advantage.

All business associations are more than economic and political groupings; they are sociological groupings as well. Members tend to have similar life-styles, external evidence of a high degree of cultural conformity, and acceptance of a cohesive set of values. All the norms of the business group are not uniformly held, but deviance is the exception rather than the rule. When social cohesion is added to economic and political cohesion, the power of these groups is readily understandable.

In summary, then, the sources of power and the advantages that accrue to organized business groups are based upon several clearly identifiable factors. One of these is extensive experience in managing organizations and resources, both human and material. Another is access to or control of wealth and income, with all that this implies in terms of effective demand for certain kinds of services. Because of the latter point, as well as other kinds of dependencies, the business leader is in the position to dispense a type of patronage. In another way businessmen have assumed the role of surrogate for society, presuming in most instances that they have been deputized to perform certain quasi-public tasks and frequently clothing their self-interest with a public purpose. Witness the slogan "What is good for business is, by definition, good for the country." Finally, despite all claims to the contrary, it would appear that the relationship of business to the media, most of which are owned by business, is a distinctly advantageous one.

NATIONAL ASSOCIATION OF MANUFACTURERS

Probably the first established association to be concerned with public-policy issues was the National Association of Manufacturers (NAM), organized in 1895. From the day of organization it addressed national issues of concern to manufacturers in the United States. Until 1902, when its focus shifted abruptly, the association advocated such programs as improving foreign trade and the consular service, creation of a federal department of manufactures, more reciprocity treaties with other countries, an interoceanic canal through Nicaragua, uniform state laws, uniform commercial codes and laws governing bankruptcy, uniform freight classification, and an American merchant marine. The staff of the new association set up a foreign trade department to assist members in their quest for foreign markets, sent a representative to Washington to

ORGANIZED BUSINESS GROUPS

lobby for favorable legislation, and set up display warehouses for American manufactured goods in Shanghai and Caracas.

The association was moderately successful in its early years and had good access to presidents William McKinley and William Howard Taft as well as to key senators and representatives. It moved unilaterally to coordinate the efforts of all business associations and to assist in creating new ones, such as the United States Chamber of Commerce. It was also to spawn a host of "action" organizations as the need arose. It believed that it spoke for the manufacturing interests of the country. Most of its original objectives were met in the first ten years of its existence. Whether for this reason or for others, it changed its focus in 1902 and became a militant opponent of organized labor and all that it stood for.

At the annual meeting in 1903, the president of the NAM delivered a stinging attack on organized labor. Precisely what caused this shift is not clearly identifiable. In all probability the growing militance of organized labor, the emergence of a strong native socialism, increasing attacks upon big business by the "muckrakers," and efforts to legislate the eight-hour day as well as laws governing employee accidents and injuries in the workplace were crucial. Most of the leaders in this assault upon organized labor were in some way faced with efforts to organize their workers. They were all Middle West and middle-class, and their programs took on an evangelical fervor scarcely seen outside a prayer meeting. They spoke only in absolutes, opposing absolutely picketing, boycotting, the union shop, the eight-hour day, laws against child labor, and minimum-wage and maximum-hours legislation. They supported absolutely all management prerogatives, lockouts, yellow-dog contracts, the open shop, company unions, and the use of injunctions in labor disputes. Literature was produced in abundance and was distributed throughout the country. The NAM took the lead in controversial labor disputes, some of which involved violence and court action.

The manufacturers were convinced that the early twentieth century was an age of organization and little might be accomplished except through organization; an era when organization must counterbalance organization. Complementary action was taken to mobilize public sentiment against organized labor by establishing another organization, the Citizens' Industrial Association, with local, state, and national stature and structure. At the national level the new association was indistinguishable from the NAM. The two groups continued thus until 1907, when they jointly created the National Council for Industrial Defense, into which the citizens' group was absorbed. This became the legislative arm of the manufacturers as well as the central coordinator for almost all employer association activity in the United States. By 1913 the council had 253 national, state, and local organizations as members. Its successor, the National Industrial Council, had 275 members in 1978. The latter organization was created in 1936 with stronger centralized authority than its predecessor.

The 1903 articles of reincorporation of the NAM best express the reaction to the hostile forces the manufacturers perceived in the environment. They stated:

> The general objects and purposes for which the said corporation is formed are the promotion of the industrial interests of the United States, the betterment of relations between employer and employee, the education of the public in the principles of individual liberty and the ownership of property, the support of legislation in furtherance of those principles and opposition to legislation in derogation thereof.

One of the businessmen who served as an elected vice-president of the NAM waxed eloquent when asked to describe the businessman's mission that required organization. This individual, who was president of the Chicago Gas Trust Company, president of the Indiana Natural Gas and Oil Company, president of the Chicago Arclight and Power Company, president of the Remington-Sholes Typewriter Company, and vice-president and general manager of the Chicago Telephone Company, believed that businessmen should organize in order to "re-establish the moral basis of capitalism." He said, further:

> It were as though capitalism had no voice of its own for the press and the politicians are afraid of it. Now, at last—here in America first of all the world—you business leaders, through your great associations, are banding together . . . for the purpose of acting openly in support of big and little business, and all its lawful conse-

quences, as morally right, socially just and economically and politically invaluable; thus defending our traditional American individualism against modern European Socialism. . . . For the welfare of business, especially of big business, the product of intense individualism, necessarily means the *public* welfare. The two are absolutely inseparable.

He particularly pleased the manufacturers when he expressed what he saw to be the consequences of organization:

> What organized labor *has* so successfully done, organized business *can* certainly do! . . . labor is certainly showing us all how to exercise a political influence out of all proportion to its vote . . . far larger are the potentialities of . . . great . . . associations. They have the advantage of nation-wide membership and still greater resources, plus . . . economic weapons incomparably superior to the mere power to strike.

The manufacturers continued to pursue their objectives by various means, including support for the creation of more organizations, especially allied ones. An episode that occurred in 1912 revealed much about the manufacturers, government, and the relationship between government and organized business. The manufacturers would have liked government designation as spokesmen for American industry. However, the NAM had become so intransigent in its policies and programs toward organized labor that even a Republican president would have been ill-advised to recommend this. Nevertheless, both the government and American business sought such spokesmen.

In 1912, at a meeting in the office of Secretary of Commerce and Labor Charles Nagel, called with the support of President Taft, it was decided to create a new organization to speak for American business: a national chamber of commerce. Secretary Nagel perceived a special relationship between this organization and the government, to which he alluded when he said:

> In our government we cannot discriminate. We cannot say we will communicate with this one and not that one unless there is some authority given which will enable us to do that, and for that reason it has been suggested not only that you organize so as to have a common commercial opinion to submit to the government, but that you get the sign of authority in the form of a National Charter which will enable every officer of the government to say, "This is the recognized representative of commerce and industry in the United States."

The charter was not granted, but the United States Chamber of Commerce was created. The experiment was publicly inconspicuous and accorded perfectly with other developments of the time.

In 1916 the manufacturers cooperated with other business groups to create the National Industrial Conference Board, which was to be the research arm of organized business groups. The Conference Board, as it is now known, was designed to serve two broad purposes: to supply information to members about matters upon which businessmen should be informed, and to provide a factual background about American industry to such diverse people as professors, housewives, and day laborers. By 1920 the manufacturers were informed that the board ". . . is bringing about uniformity of thought and action among employers, woefully lacking in the past. We are thinking together."

Like all pressure groups, the manufacturers engaged in extensive lobbying in Washington and in state capitals. The election of Woodrow Wilson in 1912 brought a Democratic administration to power, one committed to reducing the tariff, amending the antitrust laws, passing a progressive income tax, legislating an eight-hour day, and ending the use of injunctions in labor disputes. This administration also created the Federal Trade Commission (1914) and the Federal Reserve System (1914). The New Freedom of Woodrow Wilson posed some threats to the status quo of business. This new environment, hostile to business, created the environment for damning exposés. The shortcomings of the NAM were presented in sensational stories sold to the New York *World* by the manufacturers' former chief lobbyist.

Given the climate of opinion at the time, the banner headlines that read "Invisible Government Exposed" precipitated a congressional investigation of lobbying by the manufacturers. Although lobbying has the protection of the First Amendment, sordid stories of bribery, inside information from committees of Congress, and other choice bits of information dealt the association a body blow. One Senate committee and three committees of the House of Representatives issued blistering reports condemning the manufacturers as "special interests" out to subvert the democratic process. A further investigation by the Commission on Industrial Relations revealed even more of the tactics used by the manufacturers to offset the power of organized labor. All of this led the NAM to curtail its activities for the next few years, but certainly not to abandon its positions or its convictions.

Although the NAM did take the lead in accident prevention and relief, as well as in the development of workmen's compensation laws, its intransigence toward organized labor and legislation sought by the advocates of labor continued unabated. The organization approved a constitutional amendment forbidding child labor in interstate commerce. The group worked against social legislation affecting the workplace, especially the cost of labor. During the 1920's the NAM led the drive to sell the "American Plan" to the country. This plan was aimed at the preservation of the "open shop" (essentially nonunion) and the abolition of the "closed shop" (union membership a condition of employment) in industrial relations. It foreshadowed the "right-to-work" laws of the 1950's. "Right-to-work" laws, which exist in about one-third of the states and are supported by section 14(b) of the Taft-Hartley Act (1947), make illegal any labor contract that provides for the establishment of a union shop (union membership is required after employment).

Despite the passage in 1914 of the Clayton Antitrust Act, which exempted labor unions from the provisions of antitrust legislation and supposedly restricted the use of injunctions in labor disputes, the manufacturers and the courts made the victory for labor a hollow one. Injunctions continued to be used both widely and effectively.

The advent of the Great Depression ended the years of "normalcy" and culminated in the New Deal. The National Industrial Recovery Act (1933) made possible the emergence of company unions, warmly supported by the manufacturers. The constitutional disabling of that act by the Supreme Court in 1935 brought about the passage of the National Labor Relations Act of 1935 (the Wagner Act), which guaranteed the right of labor to organize and bargain collectively. At that time the NAM was near rock bottom in influence and affluence. This landmark law for labor precipitated a rebirth of militance on the part of the manufacturers.

The manufacturers felt themselves to be under very heavy attack during the New Deal years, but they were challenged by the Wagner Act to begin a long and persistent campaign to amend that act out of existence. That campaign continued into the 1970's. When the law was under consideration, their general counsel testified extensively before Congress that the law would be unconstitutional, immoral, a violation of states' rights, and "unsound" public policy. NAM publications urged members to make clear their opposition to the enactment of such unjust and invalid legislation. The passage of the act led the manufacturers to realize that their defeat was caused by lack of preparation and organization.

The manufacturers began a ten-year assault, not only against the Wagner Act but also against all forces supporting a modern view of industrial relations. There was a substantial further effort to create a public view favorable to the manufacturers, one that would support repeal of the act. The new program was as extensive as any ever undertaken by any association. An employer-employee service was established to supply printed material for distribution to employees, as well as posters, films, and radio programs extolling the virtues of "free enterprise." A regular news service for daily and weekly newspapers and a cartoon series, "Uncle Abner Says," were started. Foreign-language radio programs were made available to radio stations that served ethnic communities in industrial centers. Newspaper advertisements were widely used, the public relations staff was substantially enlarged, and a "Letter to Stockholders" was made available by corporations.

By 1939 this strategy gave evidence of success. The United States Chamber of Commerce joined the fray and began to hold dinners for hundreds of congressmen in their home districts. Pressure by state manufacturers' associations on state governments began to result in laws restricting closed shops, picketing, the right to strike, and other labor union activity. In 1940 the manufacturers publicized a congressional report dealing with "labor abuses." In that same year the House Appropriations Committee stripped the National Labor Relations Board of budget funds essential for research on labor problems. Many technical staff members of the National Labor Relations Board were removed or resigned.

During World War II there was an uneasy peace between the manufacturers and organized labor. This truce ended in 1945, and the struggle began again in full force in the following year. Labor unrest, massive strikes, substantial wage demands, and attacks upon the rights of management gave the manufacturers a great opportunity to exploit the workers' cause by appealing to the public for a return to normalcy. Continued pressure began to shift support away from labor, and the Case bill supported by the manufacturers passed both houses of Congress but was vetoed in June 1946 by President Harry Truman. The effort to override the veto was unsuccessful. The manufacturers' paper headlined the article, "Case Bill Veto Assures Nation Periodic Paralysis and Truman Aligns Himself Irrevocably with C.I.O."

In 1946 the first Republican Congress in fourteen years was elected, and the manufacturers' plan went into high gear. All congressmen were given a leather-bound book, *Let's Build America,* which contained the manufacturers' legislative program. Each congressman was given one hundred copies of John Scoville's book, *Labor Monopolies or Freedom,* by an allied organization. The manufacturers went to the country with newspaper advertisements, radio programs, and magazine articles aimed at schoolteachers, clergymen, and women's clubs. Pamphlets for school use were widely supplied, and much material went to several thousand newspapers. The Taft-Hartley Act passed, but was vetoed. In 1947 the same piece of legislation passed and became law under the official name Labor-Management Relations Act. It was the manufacturers' first victory, and it included Section 14(b), protecting the "right to work" in states where such laws were on the statute books.

The Taft-Hartley Act, an amendment of the National Labor Relations Act of 1935, outlawed the closed shop and imposed strict regulations on the union shop, union welfare funds, and the collection of union dues by the employer on behalf of the union (the "checkoff" system). It also spelled out the procedures for dealing with labor disputes that threaten the national health and safety, and denied foremen the right to organize and bargain collectively. Other major provisions of the law forbade strikes by government employees and political contributions by labor unions, and mandated certain organizational and functional changes in the National Labor Relations Board.

In the 1950's the manufacturers directly entered the field of political education, offering programs designed to get corporation employees into the electoral process. The Business-Industry Political Action Committee (BIPAC) was formed in 1963, to serve as the political action arm of the national business community. It was to undertake political action and to continue the earlier programs of political education.

All efforts of organized labor to modify the Taft-Hartley Act proved fruitless. Meanwhile, the manufacturers supported legislation aimed at further modifying the Wagner Act. At the end of the 1950's another law diminishing the rights of labor was passed. The Landrum-Griffin Labor-Management Reporting and Disclosure Act or Labor Reform Act of 1959 (commonly called Landrum-Griffin) was another victory for the manufacturers.

When considered as a reinforcement of Taft-Hartley, the Landrum-Griffin Act signified the manufacturers' continued ability to offset union power by legislation. This law sought to protect union members against exploitation by their leadership through guaranteeing freedom of speech and a secret ballot, while limiting the terms of office of union leaders and requiring periodic financial reports by unions to the Department of Labor. It set stringent limits on picketing as a device to gain union recognition and prohibited secondary boycotts (organized pressure by unions to coerce third parties to labor disputes—customers or suppliers of the firm or entity against which the union has a grievance).

TRADE ASSOCIATIONS

To complete the overview of the world of organized business groups, it is necessary to examine trade associations and their role in American development. The earliest trade associations appear to be those organized in 1853 and 1854. The American Brass Association, organized in Naugatuck Valley, Connecticut, in February

1853, was an amalgamation of local associations that had been formed earlier. Its primary objective was to attain price agreements among competitors. Also, in the later 1850's efforts were made to regulate production. The organization ceased to exist in 1869. Many more trade associations were subsequently created, and the pace quickened noticeably after the monetary panic of 1873.

What was the impulse that led businessmen to interfere in the free operation of the marketplace? One could say that it was characteristic of the business community as well as part of its heritage, for these patterns of behavior can be traced back almost to the beginning of recorded history. Certainly there is sufficient evidence that such trade practices were common during the twelfth century in Western Europe. Prevailing ordinances at that time against engrossing and regrating confirm it. Adam Smith noted in his *Wealth of Nations* (1776): "People of the same trade seldom meet together, even for merriment and diversion but the conversation ends in a conspiracy against the public or in some contrivance to raise prices."

Perhaps the fundamental question here is whether we have cooperation or conspiracy. It may also be possible that there is no real distinction, for Temporary National Economic Committee Study number 18 (1940) made the distinction between collusive and noncollusive restraints of trade solely on the basis of whether the act was direct or indirect. The impulse to collude can be found very easily in American development. One example is in the correspondence of William Almy and Smith Brown, Quaker merchants in Rhode Island, who founded Almy, Brown and Slater, the first manufacturer of machine-spun cotton yarn, thus beginning the industrial revolution in the United States. In 1808 they wrote to some of their customers:

> As we were the first that undertook the business of spinning cotton yarn in this country consequently we were the first that made a price for the article, which price has, as far as we have any knowledge been adhered to by those concerned in the business. Should any vary the price, we should be very much obliged by being informed of it, and the quality of the yarn, conceiving a mutual understanding among the makers and vendors of the article would be mutually beneficial.

Written contracts designed to restrain trade by price fixing or curtailment of production were prohibited by the common law. As a result the impulse was channeled into "gentlemen's agreements" and similar devices. Such agreements were very ephemeral, so organization of trade associations was stimulated as a more permanent arrangement. Although other forms of collusion continued, trade associations proliferated as industrial development quickened. Passage of the Sherman Act in 1890 and the Clayton Act in 1914 gave evidence that there was continued confidence in competition as an economic regulator, although by 1890 it was apparent that all industry was moving in the opposite direction. Business resisted antitrust legislation at every turn. In 1918, with business support, the impact of antitrust legislation was blunted by the Webb Export (or Webb-Pomerene) Act, which permitted cartels in foreign trade. In a very real sense, what could not be accomplished through the courts in the face of the antitrust laws was accomplished through Congress under the guise of meeting foreign competition.

The passage of the Sherman Act signaled a firm public policy supporting competition, for section 1 of that act outlawed any contract, combination, or conspiracy in restraint of trade. The courts were of two minds as this law was applied to business behavior. In one instance the rule became "illegal per se" when the courts declared illegal any effort in the form of conspiracy to influence price in interstate commerce (*United States* v. *Eastern Retail Lumber Association,* 234 U.S. 600 [1914]). This applied to control of output, market sharing, and the exclusion of competitors by boycott or any other means. Under the opposite view, the courts softened the absolute mandate in 1911. The chief justice of the Supreme Court, in deciding on the dissolution of Standard Oil and the American Tobacco Company, enunciated the "rule of reason" under which the companies were found guilty of "unreasonable restraint-of-trade." From this doctrine evolved the "reasonable restraint" doctrine that was to have an exculpatory effect upon those charged in the future with violations of the antitrust laws. This doctrine of "reasonable restraint" became the license for the future proliferation of trade associations.

For this and other reasons (to be noted below), the trade association became the vehicle for organized industry in the United States. Practically every branch of industry, commerce, and finance has its association, some of which are large and powerful while others cling precariously to existence. There are thousands of these associations dedicated to promoting the interests of the membership by means of propaganda, promotion, persuasion, and pressure—political as well as economic. Their activities are highly diverse. The economic world is very different with these institutions than it would be in their absence. Such power does little to enhance the competitive process in an enterprise system that is called "free." Some practices of entities within this power group may be neutral in their impact upon competition in an industry, but most are intended to modify competition and in fact so do. In a very real sense, trade associations represent an intercorporate, intraindustry institutionalization of restrictive trade practices. Such practices are restrained only by the current level of enforcement of the antitrust laws.

Associations typically engage in practices that tend to vary from industry to industry, even from association to association in the same industry. Some of the more common activities include market surveys and commercial and industrial research. The associations promote new uses for the products of their industry. They engage in commercial arbitration, industrywide industrial relations activities, and job placement. They publish trade journals or association magazines and other materials, arrange group insurance plans, and share advertising and publicity with members. They lobby and coordinate lobbying by members on matters of concern before municipal, state, and federal legislative bodies, executive departments, and regulatory bodies.

The associations provide additional services, including the establishment of uniform cost-accounting procedures, the collection and distribution of statistics, the standardization of commercial and technical standards and practices, and the reporting of prices as well as sales. They promote the standardization of product lines and the promulgation of codes of ethics and "fair" competition. The last-mentioned item is usually a catechism of accepted and prudent trade practices rather than a code of moral behavior. Many of these services to members slip easily over the line from noncollusive into collusive acts that tend to restrain competition. Some 20 percent of the associations report uniform price markups, average prices, average-cost data, and delivered prices.

It is alleged that such services improve the performance of the market, but allegations are scarcely evidence, much less proof. In theory, at least, price reporting may be justified as improving the functioning of the market where any market has an abundance of supplier firms, practically no significant barriers (such as excessive financial requirements or technological expertise) preventing entry into the market, a demand for the product that is reasonably elastic (increasing as the price is reduced and decreasing as the price is increased), or a homogeneous product that has a very stable demand. In any kind of market except the classically competitive one, price reporting will tend to restrain competition. Any reporting plan that would minimize restraint must be open to all, buyers as well as sellers; must give anonymity to the parties reporting; must circulate no cost data; must be free of any controls or penalties on sellers; and must report only historical sales.

There are other ambiguous activities of trade associations. Statistics may merely inform members of the current state of the market, or they may facilitate curtailment of output and the tacit sharing of sales. This is particularly true of statistics pertaining to production, inventory levels, sales, shipments, and idle capacity. Standardization of industrial output and products may serve to reduce costs in an industry, but that does not prevent its being used to lessen competition in quality and variety, as well as to reduce significantly the range of choice available to consumers. Establishing uniform commercial practices (terms of sale, credit, and delivery) may also serve several purposes other than the stated one. And if any coercive power exists in the associational relationship, such advisory practices take on the force of law. Again a basic question emerges: what have we here, cooperation or conspiracy?

In the 1920's trade associations flourished. The pervasive acceptance of the "new competition" was highly touted by Arthur Jerome Eddy on the eve of World War I, when he saw in the rapidly multiplying "open-price" trade associations a new force at work in the business world. He exclaimed that "a radical change . . . is taking place in the commercial and industrial world—the change from a *competitive* to a *cooperative* basis." This view was reinforced by the extensive use of trade associations as industry contacts and coordinators by the War Industries Board during American participation in World War I. The reinforcement of the organizational propensity under government auspices accelerated when the courts began to find many activities of such associations benign. Although there are cases to the contrary, the general impression is given by the major cases in the 1920's that court approval had been obtained. (See *Maple Flooring Manufacturers' Association* v. *United States,* 268 U.S. 563 [1925] and *Cement Manufacturers' Protective Association* v. *United States,* 268 U.S. 588 [1925]).

The experience with the War Industries Board strengthened the impulse to industrial self-government, which was reinforced by governmental policies in the 1920's and 1930's. The sharp recession of 1920–1921, with its particularly heavy price declines in commodities, revived and made stronger the almost pathological resentment that businessmen feel toward price instability. Most businessmen consider such a phenomenon unnecessary, and when its ostensible cause is foreign competition, they press for protective tariffs designed to sustain prices. This also explains the struggle for legislation mandating resale price maintenance and laws forbidding any kind of price discrimination.

These forces and a few others made the 1920's a halcyon decade for organized business groups. The policy associations, such as the United States Chamber of Commerce and the NAM, led many of the trade associations into broader areas of policy concern. As a result the trade associations developed a broader set of objectives. Among these new objectives were publicly stated commitments to the following: "(1) reduce the volume of legislation that interferes with business and industry, (2) minimize and counteract political regulation of business that is hurtful, (3) discourage radicalism by labor organizations and all sorts of agitators, (4) fight for reasonable taxation by state, city and county government and (5) promote a scientific educational campaign against all socialistic and radical propaganda of whatever nature."

A broadened perspective was supported by the efforts of Herbert Hoover, first as secretary of commerce and later as president, to make the trade association movement one of the major building blocks in his plan to give the federal government a responsible role in guiding the American economy. A policy of welfare relief alone was not enough, in his view. He wanted concerted business action to assist in "regularizing" employment and investment at the level of the firm. Trade associations were to assist in this process. National planning was to mean the mobilization of the intelligence of the country, according to Hoover, as a means of creating a perspective broader than that of the individual firm and thereby permitting the intelligence gathered from the broadened viewpoint to feed back into the firm as an aid to better corporate planning. Only thereby could employment and investment be regularized and the business cycle modified. The role of trade associations was to collect statistics, disseminate them, interpret their significance, and promote uniform and improved management methods, such as budgeting simplification and standardization, throughout industry. Hoover proposed that the government focus upon production and inventory data, and avoid price reporting as such. He resisted efforts to get the Department of Commerce to take over the activities of the "open-price" associations—withholding price information from certain parties, including buyers and some sellers, while pressuring "price-cutters" within an industry.

Two other aspects of trade association activities during the 1920's continued their influential role both in business and in the larger social community. In the community at large they expended vast sums for advertising and partisan propaganda. Taking their cue from the effective use of propaganda during World War I, the advertising and public relations firms assisted in image building and creating favorable climates of opinion for association objectives. This talent was used to reinforce lobbying activities when legislation threatened the interests of the associations.

When Senator George Norris pushed legislation that would have had the government generate electric power for sale at Muscle Shoals, Alabama (embryo of the Tennessee Valley Authority), the public utilities created the National Electric Light Association (later renamed the

ORGANIZED BUSINESS GROUPS

Edison Electric Institute). This provoked a Senate effort in 1926 to investigate the public utility industry. Congress was overwhelmed with representations from the National Electric Light Association, representing 893 electric operating companies, 324 manufacturing companies, 263 associated companies, and 93 foreign companies. Added to this were representations from the Electric Railway Association, which mobilized 337 operating companies, 35 associate companies, and 423 manufacturing companies. To complete the picture, the American Gas Association joined the electric utilities with a similar array of organizational power. Huge sums of money were added to create the mass merchandising approach to defending business interests and practices against all efforts to investigate or change them.

The second aspect was the emergence and sustenance of basing-point pricing in cement, steel, corn products, malt, milk cans, crepe paper, rigid steel conduits, and bottle caps. In a basing-point system the seller selects a specific place, say Pittsburgh, from which freight charges paid by the buyer are calculated, regardless of the actual point from which the goods are shipped. By agreement or practice, all firms in an industry price from one basing point and avoid price competition based upon location, thereby establishing uniform prices from coast to coast. Buyers thus pay, in most instances, nonexistent or "phantom" freight charges. The Cement Institute and the American Iron and Steel Institute are classic examples of trade associations that coordinated and led widespread collective and systematic practices to restrict competition and to enforce price discrimination in their respective industries. They led successful legal defenses of monopolistic practices and lobbied effectively against all legislation designed to alter them. Their partisan research studies abound in the literature.

Such practices, which had originated earlier, flourished in the 1920's, despite Federal Trade Commission orders to the contrary directed at steel in 1924, and were favorably viewed by the Supreme Court. In 1948 that court again considered basing-point practices and found them in contravention of the antitrust laws. Not satisfied, the trade associations pressed for favorable legislation and gained congressional compliance in the form of legislation exempting basing-point pricing from the provisions of the law. However, President Harry Truman vetoed the law in 1950 and the practice faded.

With the onset of the Great Depression and the massive price-level deflation, unemployment and declines in real income destroyed Herbert Hoover's hopes for an economy managed by "intelligence" alone. Institutional adjustments were in order, and the electorate swept Franklin Delano Roosevelt into the presidency in 1932. Because business activity had declined drastically a number of massive programs were undertaken to stimulate recovery. One of these was for the government again to rely upon already organized business via the National Recovery Administration, established by law in 1933. It was a natural consequence of the policies of government in the 1920's, and the trade associations spearheaded a period of "industrial cooperation."

Under government auspices, and until 1935, business firms in each industry got together under the aegis of a trade association. They drew up "codes of fair competition" that fixed prices, allocated markets, restricted output, and established minimum wages and maximum hours of work. In iron and steel the codes legalized basing-point pricing and specified each of the elements in the pricing formula and their prescribed use. Sanctions against violators were in the codes and were enforced by code authorities, composed of or selected by trade associations. In three out of four cases, the code authority secretary and the trade association secretary had the same name and did business at the same address. A grand total of 874 codes were adopted and put into effect. On 27 May 1935, the Supreme Court declared the law unconstitutional. Thus ended another episode in business-government cooperation, the lesson and precedent of which would not be lost to future generations.

Losing government sponsorship led trade associations to fall back upon their arsenal of more conventional weapons, especially lobbying. With this device they pursued Congress until the Robinson-Patman Act was passed in 1936. Ostensibly to preserve competition, this law prevented discriminatory pricing except in instances where it was justified by different costs or was done "in good faith to meet competition." The trade association of the retail grocers was out to limit the power of the chain stores, but the consequence of the law was to regularize, not to outlaw, price discrimination. In addition, the retail druggists set out to preserve their margins; the result was resale price maintenance legalized in the Miller-Tydings Act in 1937. This amendment to section 1 of the Sherman Act was reinforced in 1952 to cover nonsigners of the resale price maintenance agreement between manufacturers and retailers. Only in 1975 was this law repealed. Other exceptions for antitrust were commonly achieved by legislation such as the McCarran-Ferguson Act (1945), which exempted insurance companies from federal law and returned jurisdiction over them to the states.

By the end of the 1940's, trade associations had become solidly entrenched in the business world. They remain strong, with only minor exceptions. If some have disappeared or become marginal, it is primarily due to their loss of influence as their industry conglomerated. Usually the conglomerate corporation tends to do for itself what its predecessor either feared or failed to do. One specific example is the automobile parts and equipment business, which used to focus upon original equipment business, selling directly to the manufacturer of vehicles for assembly purposes as well as for use in meeting customers' needs after purchasing the vehicles. The Automotive Parts and Equipment Manufacturers' Association disappeared in 1955 as a result of extensive diversification by members that no longer desired to serve the original equipment market or that changed their lines so much that they were no longer members of the industry. Other firms were acquired by the automobile manufacturers; for example, Electric Autolite was taken over by the Ford Motor Company. Because of the continued loss of members and the loss of identity as the independent parts industry became captive, the trade association was dissolved by its members some ten years before it completely lost its raison d'être.

The organization and development of trade associations in the automobile industry and their ultimate consolidation is certainly a microcosm of developments elsewhere in business. There is evidence that as many as forty-eight organized business associations have been formed in the automobile industry since 1899; fewer than six still exist. Because of the ephemeral nature of some, they may simply have been abortive attempts to unify interests that resisted such action at the time. Like many of the early automobile manufacturers that produced two or three cars and then failed, the early associational effort must have been at least partially promotional, with no assured market. But, as in all industries, there appeared to be a latent urge to organize some kind of entity that transcended the individual firm and was designed to bring order out of chaos.

One such entity, which lasted for only a few years, was the National Association of Automobile Manufacturers, organized 1 December 1900. It was dissolved in 1913 when its members joined with members of the Automobile Board of Trade to form a new association, the National Automobile Chamber of Commerce. The new organization had as its objectives "(1) to advance and protect the interests of the trade, (2) to procure an adjustment of freight rates, (3) to promote good roads, (4) to procure proper legislation relating to the automobile industry and (5) to take needed action regarding future shows and exhibitions." The National Association of Automobile Manufacturers lost some of its members as early as 1904, when they left to organize the Motor and Accessory Manufacturers' Association, feeling that their interests were not best served under domination by the vehicle manufacturers. The National Automobile Chamber of Commerce continued to thrive until its name was changed on 22 August 1934, to reflect its industrial character more clearly.

The Automobile Manufacturers' Association as it was then known, attempted to get an automotive code written and accepted under the provisions of the National Industrial Recovery Act. Henry Ford's intransigent refusal to join the association and cooperate with the industry prevented adoption of the code. The National Recovery Administration died, but the Automobile Manufacturers' Association continued to thrive, and under the leadership of Henry Ford II the membership was enlarged so that it finally included the Big Three (Chrysler, Ford, and General Motors) and American Motors. Thus, an industry that began with several companies grew rapidly to hundreds, eventually numbered as many as three thousand firms in the course of its history, but ended up as an oligopolistic three plus a fraction. The number of associations that speak for the manufacturers is now one.

In the present era the manufacturers' association stands face-to-face with a countervailing organization. The National Automobile Dealers Association, organized in 1917 and headquartered in Washington, D.C., is the sole spokesman for the dealers, who, on the basis of exclusive franchises, market the output of the industry. In recent years the aggressive stance of this organization has forced the manufacturers to change the terms and conditions of the franchise, thus reducing the dealers' almost total dependence upon the automobile companies. The National Automobile Dealers Association has also brought about alteration in billing dealers for cars and assessing finance charges, as well as increased compensation for dealers when satisfying the terms of the manufacturers' warranty. This association of dealers is now strong. Its numbers and small-business image give it an effective voice in Congress, the state legislatures, and city halls. Perhaps concentration of organizations and fragmentation of function in terms of organizations is a growth and development pattern for all trade associations.

ORGANIZED BUSINESS GROUPS TODAY

Despite intraindustry divisions, each of which has its association, the contemporary world would appear to have more business unity toward the nonbusiness world than might be apparent at first glance. Certain major public-policy issues seemingly have served to coalesce and unify business organizations. In other words, in the presence of disagreements over specific questions in the business world, it would appear that organized business groups are increasingly willing to present a united front on key issues that they perceive as threatening businessmen. Among these issues are antitrust legislation and its enforcement, government regulation of major industries (such as airlines, railroads, trucking, and broadcasting), the establishment of a consumer protection agency, affirmative action in the field of equal-opportunity employment laws, decontrol of natural gas prices at the wellhead, any increase in the rights of labor to strike and picket, and national economic planning. It is already evident how organized business groups plan to respond to these issues.

One organized business group, the Business Roundtable, is a recently organized spokesman for the elite of corporate business to the federal government. It is made up of several hundred corporate members, from Allis-Chalmers to Xerox. In 1975 it prevented a revised antitrust law from being sent to the floor for a vote by persuading the House Rules Committee to return it to the committee of origin for further consideration. The vote in the Rules Committee was sixteen to three for recommittal. The Business Roundtable has a multimillion-dollar budget for lobbying in Washington, with further support from member firms that send their executives to that city to attempt to persuade members of Congress. The group is composed of board chairmen and presidents of member corporations who lobby directly with Congress, usually accompanied by a plant manager or other operating executive from a congressman's home district.

The Roundtable was headed in 1978 by the chairman of the board and chief executive officer of General Electric. Its members are alert to any threatening public concern about "economic concentration," and they fear additional punitive antitrust legislation. They are constantly monitoring legislation in congressional committees. This organization is certainly in a position to coordinate and even to lead the population of business groups against any kind of legislation with which they are unwilling to cope.

Another example was the coalescence of several types of organized business groups late in 1975. The National Association of Manufacturers, the United States Chamber of Commerce, the National Right to Work Committee, and the Associated General Contractors of America, as well as numerous other associations in the construction industry, united to defeat a bill that had passed both houses of Congress and was awaiting the president's signature. They mounted a massive campaign against the "common situs" picketing bill, which would have permitted a construction union to picket an entire construction site, stopping all work until its demands were met. Some 625,000 letters and telegrams, many of them in standard form, arrived at the White House urging President Gerald Ford to veto the bill. Despite earlier assurances of support for such legislation given by the president to Secretary of Labor John Dunlop, the president vetoed the bill on 22 December 1975. Six weeks later the secretary of labor resigned, his credibility with organized labor destroyed. Subsequent efforts to revive "common situs" have been defeated. From Taft-Hartley in 1947 through Landrum-Griffin in 1959 to the currently successful effort to contain a law sought by labor since 1947, there is evidence of how effective organized business groups can be when aroused. The Taft-Hartley Act defined common situs picketing as a secondary boycott and forbade it. When the Supreme Court found that law constitutional in 1951, labor was even more determined to get legislative relief. But it failed in the face of united opposition from organized business groups.

Early in 1976 a coalition of three dozen business groups and business firms (including the United States Chamber of Commerce, the National Association of Manufacturers, General Motors, Exxon, Ford, Dow Chemical, DuPont, Radio Corporation of America, Eastman Kodak, General Electric, and International Business Machines) criticized existing government guidelines aimed at preventing discrimination in employment. This ad hoc industry group, self-identified as the Committee on Uniform Guidelines for Employee Selection, urged the adoption of a new set of guidelines that they deemed "comprehensive, accurate professionally and generally practical." Their proposal is opposed by the National Association for the Advancement of Colored People and the Equal Employment Opportunity Coordinating Council, an agency of the federal government. The Civil Rights Division of the Department of Justice, the Department of Labor, and the Civil Service Commission sided with the employers.

This issue has arisen because several decisions in the federal courts, as well as administrative precedents in governmental agencies, have substantially restricted employer reliance upon testing as a guide to employee selection and classification. Testing procedures have been shown to be prima facie a basis for unlawful discrimination in employee hiring and advancement. The proposed new guidelines would employ an appraisal of overall personnel policies in investigations of alleged discriminatory practices, but would retain testing although it has been ruled discriminatory. The decision will affect practically every employer in the United States, as well as employees and job applicants.

Concern by organized business groups with another aspect of public policy reveals their essentially conservative stance. The desire to sustain current practices, not to change anything that would alter existing relationships adversely, and to resist any revision of the perceived "rights of management" is dominant in the organized business groups. They represent institutionalized advantage and, as is characteristic of most human affairs, those with advantageous positions are not eager to surrender them. This has been clear in the past and is particularly striking in a current effort of the federal government to reduce the regulatory miasma that faces many businesses.

It is adequate to observe that federal government agencies, both executive and regulatory, are formally bureaucratic and, since the turn of the century, have been given greater scope and authority in aid of their constituents. Supposedly the federal government wants to reduce the scope and authority of some agencies because of the belief that bureaucratic regulation inhibits the kinds of economic growth necessary to accomplish the national purpose. The administration of President Gerald Ford proposed to withdraw or alter regulation of communications and transportation. Ford's specific proposals met intransigent resistance to any kind of deregulation whatever. The trade associations addressing the issue voice the need of their industry for regulation. They say "reform," if any is needed, should come very slowly. The National Association of Broadcasters and the American Trucking Associations both oppose any change at present. The truckers contend that the net result of a return to competition would be an increase in prices that would affect the consumer. Although the broadcasters want relief from regulations that increase their costs, they want no part of free competition for programs because, in their view, the cable companies that they do not control will "siphon off" programs from the airwaves over which the broadcasters have a licensed monopoly.

Again and again the behavior of organized business groups follows essentially the same pattern. Issues such as competition, regulation, taxation, labor, environment, and equal employment opportunity, which are perceived as harmful to existing institutional relationships and practices, will be vigorously challenged by business groups using a host of persuasive devices. Despite minor setbacks, organized business groups in the United States probably have had, and will continue to have, proportionally greater influence than any other identifiable group in American society.

BIBLIOGRAPHY

The literature on the general phenomenon of organized business groups in society is best represented by the following books: Kenneth Boulding, *The Organizational Revolution: A Study in the Ethics of Economic Organization* (New York, 1953), is a seminal work, particularly strong in interpretation of the role of organizations in contemporary society as well as the ethical implications of organizational behavior, with economic and business institutions extensively covered. Robert A. Brady, *Business As a System of Power* (New York, 1943), a tour de force that has withstood the test of time, gives a critical insight into major policy groups like the National Association of Manufacturers and their impact upon American life, and has not been superseded, although it is somewhat dated. Bertram M. Gross, *The Legislative Struggle* (New York, 1953), provides a superb study of the legislative process with substantial information on the role of business groups. Edward Pendelton Herring, *Group Representation Before Congress* (Baltimore, Md., 1929), is probably the first articulation of group behavior in the legislative arena. David B. Truman, *The Governmental Process: Political Interests and Public Opinion* (New York, 1958), although dated because the author did not anticipate the emergence of single issues (such as abortion) in the political arena, is probably the best single work on how the governmental process works in the context of organized groups and also provides extensive information about organized business groups. James Q. Wilson, *Political Organizations* (New York, 1973), is informative and suggestive but equivocal. Luther Harmon Zeigler, *Interest Groups in American Society* (Englewood Cliffs, N. J., 1964), is excellent and gives complete coverage, particularly of those prominent at the time of writing.

Books dealing with the specific process of lobbying—how business groups succeed in gaining preferential positions in legislative activity—are best represented by the following: Donald R. Hall, *Cooperative Lobbying: The Power of Pressure* (Tucson, Ariz., 1969), which stresses the strategic advantage of pressure groups coalescing around key issues to magnify their impact on public-policy issues, is particularly good on the National Association of Manufacturers and the Chamber of Commerce. Lewis Anthony Dexter, *How Organizations Are Represented in Washington* (Indianapolis, 1969), even though outdated, is an excellent treatment of the techniques of representation. Karl Schriftgiesser, *The Lobbyists* (Boston, 1951), is a good survey of current and past practices, although inaccurate in places.

On specific organized business groups, see the following: Clarence E. Bonnett, *Employers' Associations in the United States: A Study of Typical Associations* (New York, 1922), although seriously outdated, provides excellent coverage and has not been superseded. Robert F. Himmelberg, *The Origins of the National Recovery Administration: Business, Government, and the Trade Association Issue, 1921–1933* (New York, 1976), is an exemplary study of trade associations in the 1920's and is exceptionally informative on the influence of organized business groups on public policy. Albert K. Steigerwalt, *The National Association of Manufacturers, 1895–1914: A Study in Business Leadership* (Ann Arbor, Mich., 1964), is a documented study of the origins and early policies of a public-policy or "peak" association, stressing the forces that led to organization and subsequent events that altered the strategic objectives. Albion G. Taylor, *Labor Policies of the National Association of Manufacturers* (Urbana, Ill., 1928), focuses on one major policy of the association covering the years 1903–1927. Charles A. Pearce, *Trade Association Survey*, Temporary National Economic Committee monograph no. 18 (Washington, D.C., 1941), is a dated but invaluable scholarly appraisal of trade associations and their functions.

[*See also* ANTITRUST; AUTOMOBILE; COMPETITION; FOREIGN TRADE; GOVERNMENT MANAGEMENT OF THE ECONOMY; IMMIGRATION; LABOR ORGANIZATIONS; MARKETING; MANUFACTURING; MERGERS; MULTINATIONAL ENTERPRISE; PRICES AND WAGES; REGULATORY AGENCIES; RISE AND EVOLUTION OF BIG BUSINESS; SOCIAL WELFARE; *and* TAXATION.]

ANTITRUST

Ellis W. Hawley

IN the American setting the term "antitrust" has come to mean a set of legal activities intended to restore and maintain freedom of trade and competition. Like the exponents of classical liberalism, "antitrusters" are opposed to planned or directed economies. Yet unlike them, they hold that the competitive ideal cannot be realized through an inactive state. Systems of private power can and will develop, rendering a competitive order unworkable unless the government intervenes to sustain it. And it is this effort at maintenance of competition through government intervention, an approach that originated in and was long unique to the United States, that forms the primary subject of the present article. It will examine in particular the origins and subsequent evolution of such activities, their interaction with activities seeking to realize competing organizational ideals, and the forces shaping their varying fortunes and forms. In addition, it will offer some observations on what difference they have made and what American society might have been like without them.

THE COMING OF THE SHERMAN ACT

The remote roots of American antitrust, so most scholars agree, lie in the English common law of the fifteenth and sixteenth centuries, especially in its hostility to local "corners," government grants of monopoly, and concerted action to restrain trade. Out of these early beginnings came two forms of antimonopoly, one directed against special privilege and statist intervention, and the other against private combinations and conspiracies. And while initially the American and English doctrines on these matters were relatively close, the nineteenth century brought an increasing divergence. In England the impulse toward laissez-faire led to a new emphasis on freedom of association and sanctity of contracts, even when these were designed to restrict trade. But in the United States, a land with few government restraints and of rising entrepreneurs, the law moved even further toward sustaining freedom of trade and competition. In the American courts the older restraint-of-trade doctrine remained very much alive, partly in conspiracy actions under the criminal law but mostly in suits involving private contracts. In case after case, sometimes through the application of a "reasonableness" test and sometimes without it, contracts involving restraints of trade or efforts to monopolize were held to be against public policy, and therefore unenforceable at law.

Unenforceability, of course, did not prevent restrictive contracts from being made. But it did mean that the cartel agreements and pooling arrangements through which American businessmen were attempting to stabilize their markets were usually short-lived and difficult to sustain. The fate of those appearing in the post–Civil War years seemed to demonstrate that private controls were fragile and easily disrupted, especially in a nation where the law gave no encouragement to them. Consequently, those who joined the antimonopoly parties and movements of the 1870's were usually not advocates of government action to maintain competition. It would, they believed, maintain itself, provided an end could be put to government favoritism and transportation abuses; and it was to these problems that their remedial programs were addressed. Typically, those programs were built around railroad regulation, tariff revision, and monetary or tax reform.

The development that would change attitudes

about the general feasibility of private monopoly was the emergence in the 1880's of a new and tighter form of business combination. Suggested by the stockholders' voting trust earlier employed in corporate reorganizations, the new device was first used by the organizers of Standard Oil, initially in 1879 and more elaborately in the trust agreement of 1882. Under the latter the owners of the constituent companies in the combine transferred all properties and stocks, and hence complete working control, to a board of nine trustees, accepting in return trust certificates that entitled them to dividends but not to a voice in management. Such a combination seemed capable of achieving a much greater concentration of private power than that exercised by the earlier cartels and pools. And as other industries began to organize on the same pattern, a movement that gathered momentum from 1884 to 1889, there was a growing alarm about where the process could lead. Alongside the earlier forms of antimonopoly agitation there appeared a new antitrust movement, reflected in a literature of alarm, in state investigations of and actions against the trusts, and in numerous petitions, especially from farm and small business groups, calling for state and national legislation.

Students of the subject have disagreed about the extent of this public concern, but the weight of evidence seems to lie with those assigning it a considerable magnitude. The most thorough investigation, that by Hans Thorelli, concludes that it was serious enough to make federal action "a clear desideratum, if not an absolute necessity." And on both the state and national levels, legislators who were concerned either with the problem or with quieting public agitation began to respond with the first antitrust laws. From 1888 through 1890, some fifteen states adopted laws under which combinations in restraint of trade could be prosecuted and broken up, and at the national level the pledge of action in the Republican platform of 1888 was being translated into the measure that would become and remain the principal expression of American antitrust philosophy. In December 1889, Senator John Sherman of Ohio reintroduced a bill directed against restrictionism in tariff-protected industries. In March 1890 the bill was debated and amended in the Senate, the outcome being a decision that, as amended, it must be considered by the Judiciary Committee. And as rewritten by that committee, a process that altered the whole thrust of Sherman's measure yet left his name attached, the bill was quickly passed. The final votes were virtually unanimous, perhaps a reflection of the popularity of the bill and bipartisan support, but also an indication that congressional conservatives considered it to be a relatively innocuous concession to public sentiment.

As finally approved in July 1890, the Sherman Act brought the common-law concepts of restraint and monopolization into federal law. Declared illegal were all contracts, combinations, and conspiracies in restraint of interstate and foreign trade, and all monopolies in or attempts to monopolize such trade. Against these the government could bring both civil and criminal actions, and injured parties could sue for triple damages. Yet nowhere in the act were the meanings of "restraint" and "monopolization" spelled out. This was to be left to case law in the courts. And, as passed, the act made no provision for any new administrative mechanism to develop and enforce such law. Apparently this was to be mostly a private matter, a process that would operate through private suits with occasional government aid, gradually creating legal rules that would help competition to sustain itself. Uncontemplated as yet was any bureaucratic structure for the maintenance of competition, and consequently there were no provisions for a special prosecution agency, no special appropriations for antitrust cases, and no plans for any commercial police system to detect violators.

In the 1890's, moreover, enforcement machinery of this sort was very slow in taking shape. Neither the presidents nor the attorneys general were interested in developing and enforcing a body of antitrust law; and with the passing of the excitement over the trust device and its general abandonment as a method of organization, there was relatively little public pressure to do so. By 1900 only eighteen cases had been instituted, most of them on the initiative of district attorneys responding to local situations. In the first case to reach the Supreme Court, that involving the American Sugar Refining Company in 1895 (*United States* v. *E. C. Knight Company,* 156 U.S. 1), an unenthusiastic and weak prosecution had led to an adverse ruling that became an excuse for even greater inaction. Although cited as proof that federal authority could not reach tight combinations engaged primarily in manufacturing, the ruling had actually turned on the failure of the government to show any control or restraint of commerce. Only in labor cases was there much enthusiasm for prosecution, and initially these accounted for most of the government victories. It was not until the freight rate and cartel cases at the end of the decade that significant victories were scored against business combinations, and much of their significance was not immediately apparent.

In theory the gap might have been filled by state and private action, but in practice it was not. As the antitrust movement ebbed, it left many states still without anticombination laws; and in the twenty-five that had them, authorities were often inactive or relatively unsuccessful in the courts. Nor was private action the force that some had thought it capable of being. Although the decade following 1890 witnessed the initiation of more than twenty suits under the Sherman Act and more than sixty under state statutes or the common law, only a very few of these affected more than local rings and only two eventually developed the evidence necessary to collect triple damages. Neither private, state, nor federal action served to curb the new and larger combination movement that got under way in 1897 and was able to find substitutes for the trust device in mergers and holding companies. In industry after industry multitudes of independent firms were brought together in giant consolidations, usually under the auspices of master promoters and financiers. As the decade ended, the notion that new legal rules would help competition to sustain itself seemed a forlorn hope. Ten years under the Sherman Act and similar statutes on the state level had brought far greater concentrations of private power than had existed at the time of their passage.

ANTITRUST AND THE PROGRESSIVE MOVEMENT

Even as the new combination movement proceeded, the stage was being set for more stringent antitrust activities. In 1898, Congress responded by establishing the Industrial Commission and authorizing an extensive investigation of the labor and trust questions. In 1899 and 1900 concerned citizens discussed these problems at two highly publicized trust conferences, both meeting in Chicago. And by 1901 another antimonopoly movement was taking shape, urging new legislation, new inquiries, and new powers for the federal government. In Theodore Roosevelt, moreover, the nation had a president concerned with testing what could be done under the Sherman Act; and in three court decisions in the late 1890's antitrusters could find some basis for believing that the act did have teeth. In the *Trans-Missouri Freight Association* case in 1897 (166 U.S. 290) and in that involving the Joint Traffic Association in 1898 (171 U.S. 505), the Supreme Court had applied the law to railroads and rejected the idea of a rule of reason that would allow their traffic associations to fix rates. And in the *Addyston Pipe* case of 1899 (175 U.S. 211), it had scuttled the notion that manufacturers were outside the law and firmly established the illegality of the price-fixing cartel. Common-law precedents concerning reasonableness, it was decided, did apply; but price fixing was inherently unreasonable and therefore unlawful per se.

By 1902 it seemed possible that antitrust might be transformed into a positive policy for maintaining competition, and in the history of the institution the period 1902–1905 does constitute something of a watershed. Inaugurating the era was an announcement that the government would seek to dissolve the Northern Securities Company, a combination designed to unify control over the Northern Pacific, Great Northern, and Chicago, Burlington, and Quincy railroad systems. Shortly thereafter came the *Swift* case, against collusion and price fixing in the meat-packing industry. Once these cases were decided in favor of the government, as they were in 1904 and 1905 (193 U.S. 197, 196 U.S. 375), it was clear that the Sherman Act could be a powerful weapon against tight as well as loose combinations. During the same period, moreover, the machinery for wielding such a weapon was at last beginning to take shape. Although lack of administration support meant defeat for the more ambitious reform proposals, the congressional session of 1903 did produce measures creating the Antitrust Division of the Justice Department with a special appropriation, expediting the appeal of antitrust cases to the higher courts, and establishing the Bureau of Corporations to engage in continuous investigation.

By the end of the Roosevelt administration, antitrust had become institutionalized in the federal bureaucracy and between 1902 and 1909 had produced no fewer than forty-four cases, some against small business and labor organizations but a number against the largest industrial combines in the nation. Yet the image of Roosevelt as an antitruster is clearly a distorted and only partially valid one. Emerging also during the period was another type of progressivism, seeking not to revitalize and maintain competitive markets but to devise bureaucratic alternatives that would allegedly result in greater rationality and efficiency.

While this movement was influenced in part by a semisocialist vision of a democratic collectivism, the more influential form of it, both during the Roosevelt era and later, was a mixture of nationalism and quasi corporatism drawn from the movements for national efficiency, scientific rationalization, and business professionalism. One expression was an informal entente with such "enlightened" organizations as United States Steel and International Harvester, an entente reflected both in the investigations of the Bureau of Corporations and in cooperation to overcome the panic of 1907. Another was Roosevelt's insistence that there were "good trusts," and still another was his support of a National Civic Federation proposal that would allow the Bureau of Corporations to approve and grant immunity to agreements or combinations in the public interest. In Congress this made little headway, and in the face of much criticism the administration gradually withdrew support; but the approach involved continued to be the one that Roosevelt considered "truly progressive."

During the presidency of William Howard Taft, federal antitrust activities continued to grow. From 1910 through 1912 fifty-eight cases were instituted, several of them seeking to dissolve the giant combinations that had been put together around the turn of the century. In this respect the new administration built upon and expanded what its predecessor had started. At the same time, it proceeded to abandon that side of Roosevelt's policy that had attempted to legitimize and preserve "good trusts." Scrapping the ententes that had developed earlier, the Department of Justice started actions against United States Steel and International Harvester; and in expounding policy both Taft and Attorney General George Wickersham rejected the notion that anticompetitive arrangements could serve the public interest. To the spokesmen for the new progressivism and the new business, it seemed that Taft was engaged in irresponsible and regressive institution wrecking. And developing in response to his activities—claiming, as it emerged, to represent modernity and progress—was a considerable campaign for "modernizing" the Sherman Act that would grant special exemptions and allow public-spirited combinations to function under government control and supervision.

This was not the whole story of the period 1910–1912. Also gathering momentum were the demands for broadening the Sherman Act to reach a larger array of anticompetitive arrangements, especially the predatory practices and unfair methods that were allegedly being used to build and sustain new monopolies, crush small business, and force up the cost of living. Proposals that the law be spelled out along these lines were receiving increasing support, and strengthening them further were the Supreme Court rulings in the *Standard Oil* and *American Tobacco* cases (221 U.S. 1, 221 U.S. 106), both handed down in May 1911. In these Chief Justice Edward D. White enunciated the famous "rule of reason," ordering the companies dissolved for unduly restraining trade yet also holding that reasonable restraints having no undue effect on competition were legal. To critics this seemed to open the way to legitimation of "good trusts," and in the congressional session of 1912 a number of antitrust bills were considered, some designed to overturn the court ruling and others to strike at particular business practices or to place limits on size.

Out of the Taft era, then, came two conflicting forms of antitrust revisionism, and in the presidential campaign of 1912 these were offered to the public as the New Freedom and the New Nationalism. The goal of the former, as expounded by Woodrow Wilson and such advisers as Louis Brandeis and John Bates Clark, was a revitalized marketplace, to be achieved by ending special government privileges and by establishing expanded antitrust agencies that would put a stop to monopoly-building practices. For the most part, it was argued, monopoly power rested on special privilege and unfair practices, not upon economies of scale or the workings of natural law; hence one could have both a competitive economy and one operating at optimum efficiency. For the New Nationalists, on the other hand—for Theodore Roosevelt and such advisers as Herbert Croly, Charles Van Hise, and George Walbridge Perkins—the goal was a system in which concentrations of power and administrative controls would allegedly enhance rationality, stability, and efficiency. Optimum use of modern technology, they maintained, required organizational systems capable of wielding considerable power. In a modern economy one could no longer rely upon competitive mechanisms for guidance, safeguards, and motive power. And while they differed over the particular mechanisms to be substituted and those best qualified to direct the new systems of power, all envisioned an order in which administration would officially replace much of the effort to maintain competitive markets.

Although Wilson's position on the trusts seems to have had little to do with the outcome, it was he who won the election and the men around him who would guide antitrust revision. Following passage in 1913 of the Underwood Tariff and the Federal Reserve Act, both held forth as legislative expressions of the New Freedom, Wilson turned to the task of supplementing the Sherman Act. Despite strong opposition, legislation did move through Congress and eventually result in the Clayton and Federal Trade Commission acts of 1914. Under the former a recognition of the legality of farm and labor organizations and of certain of their practices was coupled with provisions making government-obtained decrees prima facie evidence in private suits and with specific condemnations of discriminatory pricing, interlocking directorates and shareholdings, exclusive or tying contracts, and acquisitions of the stock of one corporation by another. All of these were prohibited where their effect might be "to substantially lessen competition or tend to create a monopoly." Under the second measure, a new federal commission was given broad investigative authority, a share in antitrust enforcement, and the power to proceed against and halt "unfair methods of competition." A determination of what these were had been left to the commissioners and the courts after the administration had become convinced that statutory definition was impossible.

Ostensibly, the new measures represented a triumph for the antitrust philosophy. Yet, as implemented, they also served as vehicles for retreating from it and bringing alternatives into being. The establishment of the Federal Trade Commission, for example, had been supported not only by antitrusters but also by those with other ends in mind, some hoping to turn its rules into a form of small business protectionism, others that it would become the sponsor of an "industrial self-government" built around trade association activities curbing "unfair competition." In the early years of the agency both of these themes quickly appeared, the latter being pushed in particular by Commissioner Edward Hurley. Appearing also was a theme of business-government cooperation, especially in dealing with the recession of 1914, meeting trade challenges overseas, and mobilizing defense resources. In a search for administrative resources, the Wilsonians were taking on private partners, much as some of the New Nationalists had proposed earlier. And despite resistance from the Antitrust Division and such confirmed antitrusters as Secretary of the Navy Josephus Daniels, they were moving away from a policy of vigorous antitrust enforcement. In 1915 and 1916 only nine new cases were started, and among administration leaders there was a growing sentiment that business was reforming itself and no longer needed stringent curbs on its activities.

From 1902 to 1915, antitrust had become an established aspect of American economic policy. Following a path taken by no other industrial nation, the United States had developed a special body of law aimed at maintenance of competition, used it to brake corporate concentration and force cartel behavior underground, and institutionalized the approach in ways that were likely to ensure the continuance of some degree of enforcement. Yet from the Roosevelt administration on, these institutions and the ideals embodied in them existed in constant tension with a developing administrative science, a rising faith in managerial expertise, and growing demands for economic direction and management. While virtually no one defended "monopoly," the antitrust approach was under attack from admirers of the regulatory commission, the modern corporation, the new trade association, and the technocratic planning system. By 1915 a situation had developed that allowed such men to play a larger role in policymaking. Seemingly triumphant in 1912 and again in the legislation of 1914, the antitrust approach was now entering a long period of retreat that would not end until the late 1930's.

ANTITRUST ON THE DEFENSIVE

Speeding this retreat was the experience with economic controls and cooperative arrangements during World War I. As preparedness began in 1916, it tended to look primarily to the mobilization of administrative resources in the private sector, chiefly perhaps because public resources of this sort were still very limited. And once decisions were made to provide large-scale assistance to the Allies and to deploy a large land army in Europe—decisions creating massive demands that disrupted the normal working of market mechanisms—policy moved steadily toward giving the mobilized resources considerable power over production, allocation, and pricing decisions. Taking shape in 1917 and 1918 was a set of emergency agencies, staffed primarily by business volunteers and gradually spreading a network of administrative controls over the diversion of economic resources to war uses. Around these agencies there developed a type of administrative syndicalism, a system in which cooperating industrial associations and other private organizations shared in making and implementing policy. While such arrangements continued to be criticized by confirmed antitrusters, their emergence left little room for antitrust activities. For the duration the Federal Trade Commission served chiefly as a cost-investigation agency; and as the war progressed, the Department of Justice proceeded to grant practical antitrust immunity to any cooperative arrangements urged and fostered by the war administrators.

Out of the war experience, moreover, came a considerable movement for the permanent relaxation of antitrust activities, the argument being that much of the war machinery could be adapted to the needs of reconversion, postwar trade, and peacetime progress. In April 1918, Congress legislated antitrust exemptions for export combinations; and by the time the war ended, many businessmen were advocating legislation that would allow them to retain and expand their associational and cooperative programs. This was the central theme at business meetings late in the year; and both in and out of government numerous proposals were made for a "peace industries board" or at least some agency that could approve combinations and agreements in the public interest.

The leading war administrators showed little interest in staying in Washington to develop such programs, and even less in trying to secure the necessary legislation from a Congress in which antitrusters were still powerful. The only action taken was the establishment in February 1919 of the Industrial Board, designed to negotiate price stabilization agreements with key industries. When this collapsed, amid charges that it was fostering illegal monopolies, the movement for antitrust "modernization" subsided. Indeed, as rising living costs became a major concern, the antitrust agencies enjoyed a brief renaissance. In 1919 and 1920 the Antitrust Division started a number of actions against associational activities in the foods and building materials industries and, now taking its antitrust role seriously, the Federal Trade Commission began a parallel series of investigations and cases.

In the early 1920's such signs of life were accompanied by special laws aimed at maintaining competition among meat-packers, stockyards, and grain merchants. Yet none of this meant that the proponents of antitrust had recaptured the offensive. On the contrary, they suffered continued setbacks, and by the mid-1920's the antitrust institutions and laws had been considerably weakened. In the courts the interpretation of reasonable restraint was coming close to ending action against tight combinations. Under the ruling in the *United States Steel* case of 1920 (251 U.S. 417), no combination seemed too large to be legal, provided it did not abuse its power. Under the *International Harvester* ruling of 1927 (274 U.S. 693) price leadership received further legal sanction, and in the *Thatcher Manufacturing* case of 1926 (272 U.S. 554) the Clayton Act was held inapplicable to mergers achieved through acquisition of physical assets rather than stocks.

Meanwhile, Congress was granting legislative

exemptions to agricultural marketing cooperatives and seriously considering them for a variety of trade association programs. By 1926 the Commerce Department under Herbert Hoover had largely won its campaign to bring the antitrust agencies into line with the new age of associational and cooperative endeavors. Following the appointment in 1925 of William E. Humphrey as its chairman, the Federal Trade Commission moved toward greater cooperation with business groups, helping them in particular to devise codes of ethical practice and fair competition. Under William J. Donovan the Antitrust Division began a policy of consultation designed to help businessmen keep their plans for combination and cooperation within the bounds of existing law.

Throughout the 1920's spokesmen for various business groups, and especially for "sick" industries suffering from excess capacity and market gluts, kept trying to change the law on cartels, both by advocating legislation and by urging the courts to adopt rules of reason or doctrines that would recognize a right to economic defense. In this field, though, an initial flirtation with the desired doctrines, especially in a 1918 ruling upholding regulations imposed by the Chicago Board of Trade (246 U.S. 231), was not followed up. In the *Trenton Potteries* case of 1927 (273 U.S. 392) the Supreme Court reaffirmed the per se rule on price fixing, and in other cases the courts continued to hold that agreements to restrict production, share markets, or boycott the uncooperative were in themselves unreasonable and hence unlawful.

The only significant move toward formal approval of cartellike behavior came in cases involving statistical trade associations designed to exchange price information, purportedly to foster intelligent competition but often as an aid to market control. In the *Hardwood Lumber* case of 1921 (257 U.S. 377) the Supreme Court condemned such statistical exchanges as disguises for price fixing, but in the *Maple Flooring* (268 U.S. 563) and *Cement Institute* (268 U.S. 588) cases of 1925 it shifted ground and allowed programs the relationship of which to concerted action had not been proven. As the law stood at the end of the decade, cartel arrangements were still inherently unreasonable, and those engaging in them had either to remain underground or to seek to disguise their operations behind programs labeled educational activity, waste elimination, and ethical improvement.

Such strictures on cartels seemed to satisfy what remained of the antimonopoly tradition. Although the late 1920's witnessed another massive merger movement, again bringing numerous independent firms into larger consolidations, this aroused no general outcry comparable with that in the 1880's or early 1900's. And while antimonopolists remained active in Congress, their concerns were chiefly with the abuses of the electrical power and farm-related industries rather than with the larger combination movement. Insofar as there were demands for a general revision of the law, they were coming mostly from those who wanted to legalize cartel or quasi-cartel behavior; and as the Herbert Hoover administration began in 1929, this continued to be the case. Proposals for an agency that could approve agreements in the public interest were again being pushed by influential groups in the National Civic Federation, the American Bar Association, and the American Mining Congress. In part the new actions against trade associations in 1929 and 1930 can be traced to complaints and evidence coming from these revisionists. Such actions, they hoped, would generate support for revision and demonstrate that it was necessary.

As the nation sank into the Great Depression, pressure for antitrust action became somewhat stronger. In Congress a number of western progressives began blaming the economic debacle on the recent combination movement; and as struggles for shrinking markets intensified, the complaints emanating from small competitors and commercial buyers led to an expansion of the actions against trade associations, abandonment of the consultation policy, and the scuttling of much of the system of industrial codes administered by the Federal Trade Commission. Yet the major effect of the depression seemed to be in the opposite direction. The way to overcome it, so the argument ran, was through cooperative action on the part of economic groups and government agencies. Following the failure of programs based on voluntary cooperation and approved associational activities, strong movements developed to legalize forms of cartel action beneficial to the public and to revive the type of planning and administrative syndicalism that had existed during World War I. In the courts new efforts to expand the rule of reason finally culminated in the *Appalachian Coals* case of 1933 (288 U.S. 344), which gave legal sanction to a regional coal-marketing cartel. By 1932 much of organized business had endorsed some form of antitrust suspension, such corporate leaders as Gerard Swope and Henry Harriman had set forth widely publicized proposals for economic planning, and numerous academics and labor leaders had joined in attacking the Sherman and Clayton acts.

To the surprise of some business leaders, the movement to abolish antitrust and revive the wartime arrangements received little encouragement from President Hoover. But with the change of administrations in 1933, it quickly became a major facet of the early New Deal. In June the National Industrial Recovery Act suspended the antitrust laws for two years, bringing to fruition, it seemed, the drift of events that had been under way since 1916. From 1933 to 1935 the nation experimented with a system of government-backed cartels erected in negotiations with industrial groups and entrusted with the making and enforcement of public policy. As in the war system, some concessions were made to market preservation, supervision by public officials, and representation for labor and consumers. But for the most part, the functions once assigned to antitrust were now to be performed by a business bureaucracy operating through the new cartels and through the emergency machinery of the National Recovery Administration (NRA) that had been set up to assist and coordinate them.

Three major obstacles lay in the way of making these arrangements permanent; and, as it turned out, none of these could be overcome. In the first place, the economy did not swing into line as expected. An initial boomlet quickly gave way to a new slump; and beginning in late 1933, a growing chorus of critics claimed that the new controls were actually blocking recovery rather than fostering it. Second, the antimonopoly tradition proved more resilient than expected. In a situation where markets remained depressed while avenues of political protest remained open, it quickly became the rallying cry of the buyers of cartel products and the mavericks who were to be disciplined. Under the label of national planning, so a new wave of antimonopolists charged, the government was actually fostering a collection of rapacious and exploitative trusts; the result by 1934 was the emergence of market restorationists and public regulationists within the new bureaucracy, the development of fierce policy struggles over the powers to be exercised by private groups, and a tendency for the whole system to become increasingly incoherent and impotent. Finally, there was the difficulty of fitting such arrangements into a body of constitutional law that narrowly limited federal power and presupposed a sharp cleavage between the public and private sectors. Although legislative extension of the system seemed unlikely in 1935, it was actually the Supreme Court that applied the coup de grace. In the *Schechter* decision of May 1935 (295 U.S. 495) it held that the establishment of such controls constituted both an improper use of the federal commerce power and an unconstitutional delegation of legislative authority.

By the time of the *Schechter* decision, the initial New Deal theme of business-government cooperation had largely given way to one of attacking business power; and in the congressional sessions of 1935, 1936, and 1937 antimonopoly ideals continued to stage a comeback. The year 1935 brought special legislation to reorganize and simplify the corporate structure of the electrical power industry. The same year witnessed the beginnings of efforts to use the taxing power against excessive centralization and managerial control. And moving through Congress, pushed particularly by those who saw mass distribution as a "monopolistic" development, were measures to protect independent merchants and the older distributive methods. In 1936 the Robinson-Patman Act redefined the law against price discrimination, attempting in particular to curb the buying power of chain stores; and in 1937 the Miller-Tydings Act legalized "fair trade" contracts designed to maintain resale prices on trademarked and branded items. Increasingly, antimonopoly was becoming a winning formula in the political arena, and exerting more influence were New Dealers who saw antitrust enforcement as the best route to economic recovery. If "administered prices" could be forced down or made flexible, they were arguing, the result would be new purchasing power and fuller employment.

By 1937, then, the way seemed open for a major revival of the antitrust institutions. After years of retreat and defensive action, a process that had begun during the war era and culminated in the cartelization programs of the early New Deal, advocates of an antitrust approach were moving into the void left by the failure of the NRA and the loss of faith in business management and administrative expertise. Planners and cooperationists had been discredited, at least temporarily. Where NRA-like programs persisted, as they did in agriculture and in some of the natural resource, transportation, and "sick" industries, they had to enjoy strong industry support and have a persuasive rationale for exceptionalism. And while the new recession in 1937 would produce some further proposals for planning and cartelization, the central debate was between advocates of government retrenchment and New Dealers committed to a combination of monetary expansion and antitrust action. Once again, after a twenty-year hiatus, antitrust was to be assigned a central role in the national economic policy.

THE GREAT REVIVAL AND THE NEW ANTITRUST

Given the drift of events after 1935, it seems possible that the antitrust revival of the late New Deal might have taken shape even if recovery had continued. But clearly, one of the major propellants behind it was the new economic contraction beginning in late 1937. Forced on the defensive, the Franklin D. Roosevelt administration needed an explanation that would make its enemies primarily responsible for the setback. And in the theory of "administered prices" and a "strike of capital," as expounded by such administration spokesmen as Robert Jackson, Harold Ickes, and Leon Henderson, it quickly found one. The collapse of recovery, they insisted, was due to misuse of business power, to pricing decisions that had negated the effects of monetary expansion, and to the withholding of investment for political reasons. It was time, the president declared in April 1938, to put an end to this "private socialism" and restore a system wherein free markets would bring economic expansion.

One result was another massive inquiry into the "monopoly problem," conducted by the Temporary National Economic Committee (TNEC) and producing, over a three-year period, another set of hearings and studies resembling those of the Industrial Commission at the turn of the century. But of greater immediate impact was the revitalization of the Antitrust Division under the colorful leadership of Thurman Arnold. Reduced to a "corporal's guard" from 1933 to 1937, the division now became the mechanism through which sustained recovery was to be built. From 1938 to 1942 this central role and the success of Arnold and his lieutenants in dramatizing it were reflected in appropriations that more than quintupled, a staff that increased fourfold, and the institution of some 177 cases, a figure representing nearly half of all those begun prior to 1938. Making headlines were major cases against the oil, aluminum, automobile, and movie industries; highly publicized actions against patent abusers and medical restrictionists; and "shock-treatment" drives against collusive arrangements in the housing, foods, and transportation fields. Not since the Taft administration had antitrust been given a comparable trial, and never had there been a similar effort to make it a major tool of macroeconomic management. New at the time were staff sections charged with gathering economic intelligence, evaluating prospective cases in terms of public need, and guiding litigation accordingly.

In a few industries the new cases were aimed at structural reform. But of much greater importance was Arnold's design for regulating business conduct through consent decrees. Typically, criminal and civil suits were brought in tandem, the former being used to pressure the industry into accepting a suitable decree that could be enforced through contempt-of-court proceedings. While the remedies sought had to be couched in terms of the competitive model, the real concern tended to be with prohibiting misuses of business power and securing the investment and pricing decisions believed necessary for sustained recovery. Unlike some of the antimonopolists at the time, Arnold was never much concerned with the mere possession of economic power or the social evils of bigness per se. Large organizations and cooperative endeavors, he held, were desirable so long as they were efficient and passed along the savings to consumers; and where market compulsion did not ensure this, it could and should be secured through a system of judicial orders and commercial policing. As his critics saw it, he was creating a "negative NRA," but in Arnold's view the regulation was really analogous to the traffic controls that kept modern transportation systems functioning.

As Arnold's activities expanded, they encountered growing opposition, not only from holders of business power but also from collectivist planners, labor leaders, small business protectionists, and those charged with organizing and administering new programs of military preparedness. Yet opponents found them difficult to halt; and even as the nation moved toward and into another world war, the new antitrusters demonstrated a striking capacity for adaptation and survival. Taking the offensive, they offered antitrust action as a way to break production bottlenecks and prevent abuse of the war controls; and throughout the war they managed to keep a measure of the antitrust outlook alive, particularly in the rules governing private volunteers, advisory committees, and conflicts of interest. While agreeing to the suspension of certain cases and to grants of immunity by the War Production Board, they helped to force public-private relationships into patterns that business groups were much less anxious to perpetuate than had been the case with the arrangements of World War I.

At the end of the war the Antitrust Division remained very much alive, insisting that its activities could supplement the reconversion controls and work in tandem with the new machinery for expanding trade, maintaining maximum employment, and regulating industrial relations. Not only were the suspended cases resumed, but in the five years after the war 157 new cases were instituted. Nor was the Federal Trade Commission inactive. Although the Robinson-Patman and Wheeler-Lea acts of the 1930's had largely transformed it into a consumer and small business protection agency, its restraint-of-trade activities in the 1940's resulted in the bringing of 150 cases.

In the courts, moreover, the drift of decisional law was again toward strengthening the weapons that could be used to maintain competition. In the *Socony Vacuum Oil* case of 1940 (310 U.S. 150) the Supreme Court reestablished the per se rule on price fixing, thus rejecting the notion of a reasonable cartel as set forth in *Appalachian Coals*. In the *Pullman* ruling of 1947 (330 U.S. 806) and the *Paramount Pictures* case of 1948 (334 U.S. 131), the government won a type of structural relief that had seemed foreclosed by the rulings of the 1920's. In a new *Cement Institute* case in 1948 (333 U.S. 683) the practice of basing-point pricing was finally held illegal; and in a line of rulings beginning with the *Aluminum Company of America* case of 1945 (148 F. 2d 416) there emerged a much narrower rule of reason, under which the mere possession of monopoly power came close to being illegal.

Also emerging, in the *American Tobacco* case of 1946 (328 U.S. 781) and in several subsequent rulings, was a new law of oligopoly, one that allowed the crime of monopoly to be implied from evidence of market concentration and parallel action. In still other cases the Supreme Court struck blows at government-fostered price control and at earlier constraints on private antitrust suits. In the *Schwegmann* case of 1951 (341 U.S. 384) it ruled that resale price maintenance was legal only to the extent that it was secured by a contract, in a new railroad traffic case in 1945 (324 U.S. 439) it reapplied the Sherman Act to the rate-fixing associations encouraged by the Interstate Commerce Commission, and in the *Bigelow* case of 1946 (327 U.S. 251) it altered the rules of evidence so as to make triple-damage suits much easier to win.

Intermixed with these victories, to be sure, were some setbacks. In the *Hutcheson* case of 1941 (312 U.S. 219) the Supreme Court interpreted the labor legislation of the 1930's as granting a virtually complete exemption to labor union activity, and in Congress the *Schwegmann* and railroad traffic rulings were quickly nullified by special legislation. Yet the weapons available to antitrusters were clearly much stronger in 1952 than in 1938, and strengthening them further was the Celler-Kefauver Act of 1950, which closed the loophole opened by the *Thatcher* case and allowed action to block mergers that would substantially lessen competiton. Indeed, by the late 1940's and early 1950's the talk of a "new Sherman Act" and of per se rules on monopoly and oligopoly was producing a widespread apprehension reminiscent of the days of the Taft administration. A number of businessmen, lawyers, and economists seemed fearful that the legal shields against reckless structural reformers and neo-Populist politicians had been removed, and in a variety of articles and studies it was urged that a new rule of reason be legislated or at least adopted as an enforcement guideline. The competition to be sought, so the critics insisted, must be of the "workable" or "effective" type, as measured by tests of market performance, not the atomistic type that would destroy the progressive and dynamic elements in the American economy.

In neither the courts, the Congress, nor the administration were these suggestions formally adopted. Yet three developments in the late 1940's and early 1950's accomplished much of what the critics had in mind and allayed most of their fears. One was a resurgence of judicial conservatism, adding qualifications to the earlier rulings and making it clear that divestiture was still a remedy of last resort. Of particular importance were cases in 1954 rejecting dissolution as a monopoly remedy in the shoe machinery industry and holding that conscious parallelism was not in itself sufficient to prove conspiracy. Second, there was the growing disposition of the administration of Harry S. Truman to enlist business partners and share the tasks of administration with them, much as the Wilson administration had done after 1914. This was particularly noticeable following the recession of 1949, and with the onset of the Korean War it was soon reflected in a defense establishment again making use of private partners and in strong internal pressures against disruptive forms of antitrust action. Finally, there was the reorientation taking place within the antitrust agencies themselves. By the early 1950's the reform zeal and sense of mission that had been characteristic of the Arnold era and the immediate postwar years were rapidly ebbing, and policy was increasingly being made by those who looked upon the existing business structure as workably competitive and were loath to wield the new antitrust weapons that had become available.

This is not to say that the resources devoted to antitrust were cut back. Although there were budget cuts in 1952, the rest of the decade witnessed a gradual expansion in appropriations, staffs, and volume of litigation. Yet if the level of activity did not decline, its scope and purpose were undergoing change. The mission of antitrust, as it was now conceived, was not to make a malfunctioning economy function or to restructure a monopolistic economy; rather, it was to protect and improve a workably competitive system. The result, as Richard Hofstadter has pointed out, was the transformation of a potential reform instrument into one that functioned as part of the establishment and was rewarded accordingly. Ironically, the reforming bureaucracies forged in the great revival and used to develop the "new Sherman Act" were now perpetuating themselves by concentrating on the peripheral tasks of curbing marginal abuse and applying the rules against cartel behavior.

FROM REFORM INSTRUMENT TO VESTED INTEREST

Indicative of what was happening was the report in 1955 of the Attorney General's National Committee to Study the Antitrust Laws. Set up two years earlier and cochaired by S. Chesterfield Oppenheim, one of the most prominent advocates of a new rule of reason, the committee was widely regarded as the institutional embodiment of the new demands for "modernization." Yet its report, when filed, was essentially an endorsement of existing law and policy. Heartened, it seemed, by recent rulings and by the shifting emphasis of antitrust activity, it pronounced the status quo satisfactory, congratulated the nation for developing a maintenance of competition that helped modern business to function effectively, and suggested only minor adjustments. Insofar as there was major dissatisfaction, it came from those who felt that the promise of the "new Sherman Act" was being betrayed. Despite efforts to secure consensus, a few of the dissenting committee members expressed such concerns, and in Congress Estes Kefauver and Wright Patman denounced the report as "a gigantic brief for the non-enforcement of the antitrust laws."

In the decade that followed, this pattern changed little. Although a few congressmen and a few critics in academia continued to call for restructuring the concentrated industries and putting an end to "administered prices," the antitrust agencies showed little disposition to take on these tasks. While debate continued to swirl around the issue of small business protectionism, there was little change in the balance that had been struck between its advocates and critics. The main thrust of antitrust activity was toward mitigating behavioral problems and holding the line on cooperation and concentration—toward the type of cases, in other words, that the majority of the Attorney General's committee had thought necessary to keep a going system progressive and expansive.

The resources devoted to this type of activity kept increasing, partly because it enjoyed general approval and encountered no strong opposition, partly because the courts were basing more of their decisions on complex market analysis requiring growing inputs of money and expertise, and partly because this type of litigation tended to create an "antitrust industry" with vested interests in its continuance and expansion. Between 1956 and 1967 appropriations for the Antitrust Division increased by 121 percent; and during the same period antitrust became a highly differentiated, specialized, and bureaucratized activity, conducted by a growing array of skilled specialists in the burgeoning disciplines of antitrust law and antitrust economics. It was more dependent upon the concerns, interests, and influence of these specialists than upon mass support for a public demand for its product.

Also fostering growth was a supplementary line of cooperative activities reminiscent of those in the 1920's. In antitrust as elsewhere, "partnership" formulas were again in vogue, the assumption being that modern businessmen were strongly supportive of modernized antitrust and, if linked with the enforcement agencies through cooperative conferences and informational exchanges, would develop effective forms of self-regulation. In efforts to implement such formulas, the antitrust authorities took a variety of actions. Following Edward Howrey's appointment as chairman in 1953, the Federal Trade Commission moved rapidly toward greater use of voluntary proceedings, trade-practice conferences, and informational exchanges. At the same time the Antitrust Division sought to enlist trade association support for its activities. And in the early 1960's, despite occasional bursts of antibusiness rhetoric, the tendency was toward even greater faith in preventive self-regulation. In 1962 the FTC established the Bureau of Industry Guidance and inaugurated a new program providing formal advisory opinions. Also, the Antitrust Division, seeking similar ends, expanded its consultation and review services.

As antitrust became more technical and specialized and less adversary-oriented, it rarely generated the cheers and alarms characteristic of earlier eras. Yet "rarely" did not mean "never," and from 1956 to 1967 two areas of activity constituted exceptions to the rule. One was the discovery and prosecution of a few spectacular price-fixing conspiracies, the most prominent being that in the electrical equipment industry. In these cases the first jail terms for business defendants and the multimillion-dollar damage suits that followed generated considerable publicity and debate, as well as some revival of hope among advocates of a tougher and more aggressive antitrust. The other was the forging of stronger antimerger weapons, initially in a Clayton Act suit that severed ties between Du Pont and General Motors (353 U.S. 586), and then in cases brought under the new Celler-Kefauver Act. In the first of these to reach the Supreme Court, the *Brown Shoe* case of 1962 (370 U.S. 294), the government argued successfully that the law had established barriers against concentration as well as restraint. In a series of subsequent cases, the court went on to rule against mergers between potential as well as actual competitors, mergers that allowed entrenched firms to heighten entry barriers, and mergers involving as little as 7 percent of a market. To those concerned with checking a new merger movement, the decisions were welcome, if belated. But among those who regarded most mergers as economically beneficial, there was much talk of "populistic nonsense" and a "new crisis in antitrust."

Aside from these exceptional areas, antitrust remained relatively noncontroversial through most of the 1960's. And aside from limited administrative efforts to rationalize its activities and make them more efficient and predictable—efforts that were made chiefly during the administration of Lyndon Johnson and were reflected in an apparatus for policy planning and the publication of merger guidelines—there was little in the way of reform. The reigning assumption still was that the existing system worked, that in conjunction with other checks on business power, it was preserving a workably competitive economy capable of being "fine-tuned" by those in charge of the monetary spigots. And so long as the economy performed at a high level, there was little disposition to challenge this assumption or to question the product claims of the "antitrust industry."

ANTITRUST

CURRENT CHALLENGES AND THE HISTORICAL IMPACT

Poor economic performance could change matters. And from 1968 on, as the American economy encountered new difficulties and the trade-off between inflation and unemployment became unacceptably large, a growing body of critics began challenging both the notion of workable competitiveness and the activities that were supposed to sustain it. From a revived school of laissez-faire economists came charges that antitrust, like other forms of government interventionism, was essentially anticompetitive and subversive of free-market institutions. From new advocates of concentration and control came charges that it was essentially a charade, not only useless for disciplining a modern economy but also distinctly harmful in preventing the type of planning and controls that were actually needed. From a new group of business cooperationists came proposals for another "modernization" that would allow more self-regulation and cooperative planning. And from those who felt that genuine antitrust had never really been tried came new proposals for strengthening anticombination laws, limiting size, and using special legislation and special agencies to restructure areas of industrial concentration.

For the first time since the 1940's, moreover, these deconcentration proposals began to receive relatively serious consideration. They were endorsed by a presidential task force in 1968 and strongly urged by a consumer-oriented study group in 1971. Subsequently they were embodied in industrial reorganization bills sponsored by congressmen Emanuel Celler, Fred Harris, and Philip Hart; and in the congressional session of 1975 the Hart bill was the subject of extensive hearings. That the nation would actually place fixed limits on market shares and legislate the dismemberment of its corporate giants, as Hart proposed, seemed doubtful. But serious advocacy of such an approach was clearly much stronger in 1975 than it had been in 1965.

What seemed more likely, given the obstacles to deconcentration, laissez-faire, or national economic planning, were actions attempting to restore the credibility of the antitrust establishment. Between 1968 and 1976 its leaders and defenders were active, not only in attacking the proposed alternatives but also in launching new lines of prosecution, pushing new efforts at internal rationalization, and urging moderate reforms that would give the establishment more resources and better weapons. Receiving much publicity were limited forays into the type of structural action that had long been avoided: new cases, in particular, seeking to dissolve conglomerate mergers and to restructure such giants as International Business Machines and American Telephone and Telegraph. At the same time the FTC underwent an extensive reorganization, consolidating its antitrust functions under the new Bureau of Competition. And in Congress the antitrust agencies pushed their own legislative program and were able to translate a part of it into law. The resulting Antitrust Improvements Act of 1976 strengthened investigatory powers, required large companies to notify the government of planned mergers, and authorized state attorneys general to bring triple-damage suits on behalf of injured citizens.

Just what additional reforms would be made and whether such reform would fully restore credibility remained to be seen. But as the 1970's drew to a close, it seemed likely that American antitrust institutions would survive in forms similar to those of the 1950's and 1960's. Supporting them was not only a developed "industry" providing a livelihood for hundreds of talented and influential professionals, but also a deep-seated cultural tradition looking upon competition as the source of freedom and progress and regarding its maintenance as requiring only minimal or limited efforts. From the passage of the Sherman Act to the investigations of the TNEC to the debates of the 1970's, this tradition, although frequently under attack, had demonstrated great potency and a striking capacity for survival.

While antitrust did not have a really powerful interest-group constituency in the sense that regulatory and promotional agencies frequently did, it drew great strength from its "middle-ground" position and the disposition of conflicting groups and philosophies to accept it as an alternative to arrangements considered much more undesirable. Indeed, its very appearance can be understood partly as the compromise solution of a people who had lost faith in self-sustaining market mechanisms yet had retained a deep suspicion of centralized control; a division of power that prevented a particular managerial elite from imposing its solution; and a perennial hope that somehow the social, political, and economic benefits of a market system could be preserved. For such a people the vision of an apolitical apparatus, operating through legal and administrative technicians and aimed at fostering a neutral and scientifically determined "competition," was a vision of great appeal. It was this vision that became embodied in American antitrust.

What the historical impact of such institutions had been was a different and more difficult question. Were the peculiarities of the American economic system, generally conceded to be less concentrated and less cartelized than the systems of other industrial countries, to be attributed to the form of regulation that had developed in the American setting? And were these antitrust institutions at least partially responsible for allowing the American nation to modernize while retaining its fragmented system of multiple governments and divided powers? On both counts there were scholars who answered in the negative, some maintaining that the shape of the American economy and polity would have been much the same without antitrust, and a few arguing that the impact of antitrust, as implemented, had been the very opposite of its professed aims.

Countering such conclusions were impressive studies of how antitrust action and law had helped to mold the structure and behavior of particular industries, studies that usually conceded a degree of perversity and a significant role for other forces, yet argued convincingly that antitrust had frequently speeded up the reassertion of competitive forces, had erected barriers against European-style cartels and single-firm monopolies, had entered into corporate decision making, and by doing these things had reduced the demand for supplanting market mechanisms with bureaucratic surrogates. Although much of this was admittedly unmeasurable, it was difficult to read Simon Whitney or George Stocking or Corwin Edwards and still conclude that it had been negligible.

If there had been such an impact, though, the question remained as to whether the American people had benefited. Had their peculiar institutions made for less efficiency and less economic progress, and had they thwarted forms of regulation and control that could have done much more to realize American economic and social ideals? On these matters judgments turned even more on conflicting estimates of what might have been, estimates that could hardly be subjected to rigorous proof or disproof. Yet on two counts the cases of those who answered the questions in the affirmative seemed weak. One was the failure of recent studies to bear out their arguments about economies of scale and large-unit progressiveness. Above a certain minimum, most of these studies concluded, size was of little or no importance in determining the degree of efficiency and technical progress. If this finding weakened the economic case for trust-busting, it also meant that a policy limiting concentration and cooperation had probably not been very costly economically. The other count was the dismal record of commission regulation in those areas where it had been adopted. This was borne out in study after study, becoming something, by and large, upon which those from all quarters of the political spectrum could agree. In the face of this record it was difficult to argue that institutions limiting the amount of such regulation had been detrimental to the American people.

On balance, then, American antitrust seemed not only responsive to a peculiar pattern of cultural and political demand but also generally productive of results with benefits that outweighed their costs. What seemed far less sure, despite calls for and efforts at exportation, was the usefulness of such institutions in other cultural settings. Transplanted to Japan and Germany after World War II, they had never really taken root; and in other nations American-inspired experiments with restrictive-practices legislation had proved generally disappointing. What could not be exported was the underlying set of values and preferences that allowed American antitrust to function better than alternative approaches. And by the 1960's most of its defenders seemed willing to concede that, given other values and preferences, there were equally valid routes to effective economic and political performance. Once a uniquely American phenomenon, antitrust continued to make more sense in the American setting than anywhere else. In this setting it had demonstrated amazing staying power and might well continue to confound those who kept insisting that it was archaic and outmoded.

ANTITRUST

BIBLIOGRAPHY

Walter Adams and Horace Gray, *Monopoly in America* (New York, 1955) is a powerful indictment of American economic policy in the 1950's. D.T. Armentano, *The Myths of Antitrust* (New York, 1972), is a knowledgeable but loaded critique from a laissez-faire point of view. William Lee Baldwin, *Antitrust and the Changing Corporation* (Durham, N.C., 1961), is a policy-oriented survey of past and current economic thought on business concentration. John H. Brebbia, "The Role of Advisory Opinions and the Business Review Procedure," in *Antitrust Bulletin*, 18 (Summer 1973), is good for the business guidance programs of the antitrust agencies. Arthur R. Burns, *The Decline of Competition* (New York, 1936), is an influential study of anticompetitive developments and their implication for public policy. John D. Clark, *The Federal Trust Policy* (Baltimore, 1931), is a history and spirited defense of American antitrust institutions. Donald Dewey, *Monopoly in Economics and Law* (Chicago, 1959), is the most readable account of what economists and lawyers have thought about monopoly and public policy toward it.

Joel B. Dirlam and Alfred E. Kahn, *Fair Competition* (Ithaca, N.Y., 1954), is a good discussion and critique of the campaign for antitrust revision in the late 1940's and early 1950's. Arthur P. Dudden, "Antimonopolism, 1865–1890: The Historical Background and Intellectual Origins of the Antitrust Movement in the United States" (Ph. D. diss., University of Michigan, 1950), is an immensely informative study of the political and intellectual climate in which the first antitrust laws appeared. Corwin D. Edwards, *Maintaining Competition* (New York, 1949), is a survey of monopoly policy with recommendations for strengthening antitrust; and *Control of Cartels and Monopolies: An International Comparison* (Dobbs Ferry, N.Y., 1967), is a systematic comparison of American antitrust with restrictive-practices legislation elsewhere. Joe A. Fisher, "The Knight Case Revisited," in *The Historian*, 35 (May 1973), is a revisionist article attributing the decision to inept prosecution rather than to judicial conservatism. John J. Flynn, *Federalism and State Antitrust Regulation* (Ann Arbor, Mich., 1964), is a study of state antitrust action and the constraints placed upon it by the courts.

Sanford D. Gordon, "Attitudes Towards Trusts Prior to the Sherman Act," in *Southern Economic Journal*, 30 (Oct. 1963), is a detailed study of public reaction to trust building in the 1880's. Mark J. Green, et al., *The Closed Enterprise System* (New York, 1972), a highly critical report on antitrust enforcement by a Ralph Nader study group, is slanted but provides much inside history of the antitrust agencies. Walton Hamilton and Irene Till, *Antitrust in Action* (Washington, D.C., 1940), is a TNEC monograph on the evolution and activities of the Antitrust Division. Milton Handler, *A Study of the Construction and Enforcement of the Federal Antitrust Laws* (Washington, D.C., 1941), is a TNEC monograph offering a systematic statement of the law as of 1940. Ellis W. Hawley, *The New Deal and the Problem of Monopoly: A Study in Economic Ambivalence* (Princeton, 1966), is a study of conflicting currents in the New Deal policy toward business organization.

Robert F. Himmelberg, *The Origins of the National Recovery Administration, Business, Government, and the Trade Association Issue, 1921–1933* (New York, 1976), is the best and most complete account of the "New Era" movement for antitrust relaxation and legalized cartels. Richard Hofstadter, "What Happened to the Antitrust Movement," in Earl F. Cheit, ed., *The Business Establishment* (New York, 1964), is a famous and highly perceptive essay on the institutionalization and bureaucratization of antitrust activity. Arthur M. Johnson, "Theodore Roosevelt and the Bureau of Corporations," in *Mississippi Valley Historical Review*, 45 (Mar. 1959), is the best account of Roosevelt's policy toward business concentration; and "Antitrust Policy in Transition, 1908: Ideal and Reality," in *Mississippi Valley Historical Review*, 48 (Dec. 1961), a sequel to the above article, focuses particularly on the Hepburn Act and the reaction to it. René Joliet, *The Rule of Reason in Antitrust Law* (The Hague, 1967), is the source to consult for a concise history of the American rule of reason and a comparison of it with reasonableness tests adopted in other nations. Bryce I. Jones, "Recent Developments in Antitrust: A New Dawn," in *Quarterly Review of Economics and Business*, 5 (Spring 1965), is a good short account of antitrust developments from 1945 to 1965.

Carl Kaysen and Donald F. Turner, *Antitrust Policy: An Economic and Legal Analysis* (Cambridge, Mass., 1959), is a compound of economic analysis, legal history, and prescriptions for structural reform. Oswald Whitman Knauth, *The Policy of the United States Towards Industrial Monopoly* (New York, 1914), is an older, but still highly useful, history of antitrust legislation and litigation. Theodore P. Kovaleff, "The Antitrust Record of the Eisenhower Administration," in *The Antitrust Bulletin*, 21 (Winter 1976), is a competent summary of major developments in the field between 1953 and 1961. William Letwin, *Law and Economic Policy in America* (New York, 1965), is a detailed and authoritative history of the common-law precedents of antitrust and the evolution of federal policy to 1914. Richard W. McLaren, ed., *Antitrust Developments, 1955–1968* (Chicago, 1968), is a comprehensive statement of changes in the law, prepared as a supplement to the 1955 report of the Attorney General's Antitrust Committee. David Dale Martin, *Mergers and the Clayton Act* (Berkeley, Calif., 1959), is the most comprehensive account of antimerger policy under the Clayton and Celler-Kefauver acts.

Edward S. Mason, *Economic Concentration and the Monopoly Problem* (Cambridge, Mass., 1957), is valuable for its perceptive discussion of the literature and debates of the 1950's. Mark S. Massel, *Competition and Monopoly: Legal and Economic Issues* (Washington, D.C., 1962), a policy-oriented study exploring the interrelations of law and economics in the antitrust field, calls for improved economic analysis. Alan D. Neale, *The Antitrust Laws of the United States of America*, 2nd ed. (Cambridge, 1970), a study of American antitrust institutions, is addressed primarily to British readers. S. Chesterfield Oppenheim, "Federal Antitrust Legislation: Guideposts to a Revised National Antitrust Policy," in *Michigan Law Review*, 50 (June 1952), is a highly influential analysis calling for a rule of reason based on the concept of workable competition. Richard A. Posner, "A Statistical Study of Antitrust Enforcement," in *Journal of Law and Economics*, 13 (Oct. 1970), makes available and interprets detailed statistical data on federal, state, and private activities; and "Antitrust Policy and the Supreme Court," in *Columbia Law Review*, 75 (Mar. 1975), is an excellent summation and analysis of the new legal doctrines emerging in the 1960's.

Eugene Rostow, *Planning for Freedom: The Public Law of American Capitalism* (New Haven, 1959), a history and evaluation of modern American economic policy, has a particularly good section on the law of markets. Frederick M. Rowe, "The Evolution of the Robinson-Patman Act," in *Columbia Law Review*, 57 (Dec. 1957), is an excellent account of the origins, passage, and subsequent implementation and interpretation of the act. Charles K. Rowley, *Antitrust and Economic Efficiency* (London, 1973), contains an illuminating evaluation of antitrust as compared with other solutions to the problem of market power. George W. Stocking, *Workable Competiton and Antitrust Policy* (Nashville, Tenn., 1961), consists of essays discussing the emergence and application of the workable competition concept. George W. Stocking and Myron W. Watkins, *Monopoly and Free Enterprise* (New York, 1951), is a massive study of American industrial organization and policies shaping it. Hans B. Thorelli, *The Federal Antitrust Policy: Origination of an American Tradition* (Baltimore, Md., 1955), a monumental study of the origins, passage, and early evolution of the Sherman Act, is indispensable for understanding antitrust policy through 1903.

United States Attorney General's National Committee to Study the Antitrust Laws, *Report* (Washington, D.C., 1955), is the famous report endorsing a reasonable antitrust as part of the Eisenhower consensus. United States Library of Congress, Legislative Reference Service, *Congress and the Monopoly Problem: Fifty-six Years of Antitrust Development, 1900–1956* (Washington, D.C., 1956), is a compendium of antitrust laws and proposals, studies made, and cases litigated. Melvin I. Urofsky, *Big Steel and the Wilson Administration* (Columbus, Ohio, 1969), contains an illuminating discussion of the shifting antitrust policies of the Wilson administration. Simon N. Whitney, *Antitrust Policies: American Experience in Twenty Industries* (New York, 1958), contains case studies of antitrust action and its effects in representative industries. Robert H. Wiebe, "The House of Morgan and the Executive, 1905–1913," in *American Historical Review*, 65 (Oct. 1959), is a good account of the informal ententes developed during the Roosevelt administration and scrapped by Taft and Wickersham. Dean A. Worcester, Jr., *Monopoly, Big Business, and Welfare in the Postwar United States* (Seattle, Wash., 1967), is a revisionist work on the determinants of size and concentration, and their relationship to performance.

[*See also* BUREAUCRACY; COMPETITION; ECONOMIC THOUGHT; ENTREPRENEURSHIP; FARMERS' MOVEMENTS; GOVERNMENT MANAGEMENT OF THE ECONOMY; LAW AND POLITICAL INSTITUTIONS; MANAGEMENT; MERGERS; ORGANIZED BUSINESS GROUPS; REGULATORY AGENCIES; *and* RISE AND EVOLUTION OF BIG BUSINESS.]

REGULATORY AGENCIES

Thomas K. McCraw

THE TERM "regulatory agencies" is broad enough to encompass the entire range of public and private institutions involved in the regulation of economic activity. In its common meaning, the term pertains chiefly to that group of boards and commissions which in the states regulates public utility enterprises, and in the federal government regulates such industries as transportation and broadcasting, and such general aspects of economic life as competition and product safety.

Despite their extraordinary diversity, most regulatory agencies in the United States exhibit several common characteristics. Most commissions, whether state or federal, are appointed by the executive, are nonpartisan or bipartisan by law, and are supposedly expert in their fields. The typical regulatory statute delegates broad discretionary powers and avoids specific details. Most regulation occurs at the borderlands of politics, law, and economics, and those who have shaped its evolution have come from these three fields. Of the three, the first two have tended to overshadow the third, and considerations of politics and legal process have customarily triumphed over those of economic efficiency. Even so, the single most important context in which regulators have had to operate has been the inherent economic nature of the industries under regulation.

Historically speaking, the onset of regulation usually occurred in response to an identifiable crisis in a particular industry. To be sure, not all crises produced regulation; but regulation practically never emerged in the absence of some severe exigency that injured the industry itself, some other industry, or the consuming public.

The historical epoch during which most such crises occurred ranged roughly from the 1870's through the 1930's, with a second wave of social and environmental regulation beginning in the 1960's. Prior to the first wave, most Americans who thought about the matter probably agreed with Adam Smith that market competition was the natural and best regulator of prices and outputs. But industrialization and the rise of big business in the mid-nineteenth century suddenly made competition inadequate to meet some of the economic needs of the society. For one thing, the great virtue of the Smithian market as regulator—its ability to respond at once to changes in supply or demand—defined it as a short-range mechanism. Unassisted, the market could not promote long-run goals such as the equitable distribution of wealth and income, or the preservation of immeasurable aesthetic or ecological values. More important for the onset of regulation, competition alone could not accommodate certain profound changes in the industrial system, notably the rise of enterprises based on scale economies, with such huge fixed costs that they could not be sensibly risked to the vagaries of the classical market. The new processes of production and marketing gave rise to regulatory mechanisms, particularly in the private sector, as they changed the fundamental structure of the business system itself: thus the emergence of the oligopoly, the trade association, the rate bureau, and the price leadership phenomenon.

In the public sector, regulation first appeared for those industries that seemed distinctly out of the mainstream of the Smithian market system. Some of these industries were social overhead enterprises of critical significance to the economy as a whole, and of such an economic nature as to popularize the term "natural monopoly." Since it obviously made no sense to have multiple competing railroad lines serving thinly settled areas, or numerous systems of electrical power distribution for a single city, late nineteenth-century contemporaries began to question the efficacy of market competition as a regulator. Of what use was Adam Smith's model of numberless buyers and sellers in regulating industries with only one seller, or only a few?

Perceptions of the failure of competition derived more from experience than from theory; the normal process was trial and error. In the early days of the railroad and electric utility industries, state and city governments often attempted to regulate through the granting of charters or franchises to numerous competing groups, and occasionally to all comers. In neither industry did this kind of remedy work very well. Throughout the post–Civil War period the railroads showed an inexorable tendency toward consolidation into ever-larger systems. Even the great trunk lines, denied government permission to divide their traffic by pooling, took the alternative route to "certainty" by developing self-contained, integrated networks with exclusive feeder lines branching into the hinterlands of their major routes. Similarly, from the 1880's well into the twentieth century, competing gas and electric companies throughout urban America merged into single systems serving entire metropolitan areas, sometimes with higher costs to the consumer but usually with greatly improved service.

The reasons behind the inclination of railroads and utilities toward natural monopoly tended in turn to shape the methods of regulation selected to replace competition. The central characteristics of natural monopoly are decreasing unit costs over the whole range of possible outputs—in other words, virtually unlimited economies of scale—and a very high ratio of fixed costs to variable costs, so that a large initial investment is necessary to enter the market. These traits obviously applied to railroads, which had to purchase and develop rights-of-way, construct and maintain roadbeds and tracks, and acquire expensive locomotives and rolling stock before they could carry a single passenger or a ton of cargo. But once these facilities were in operation, they could transport numerous passengers and very heavy cargoes without much additional expense. The same characteristics may be observed for electric utilities, which had to construct generation and distribution facilities, both at tremendous cost, before they could sell a single kilowatt-hour to a customer. The waste involved in building duplicate railroad or electric facilities at very great cost constitutes the core of the natural monopoly concept. It also underlies the unusual situation in which, for certain industries, monopoly is inherently more efficient than competition. For this reason, commission regulation first emerged in part as a surrogate for the lost discipline of a market system that bore little relevance to the railroad and utility industries. At the time, few observers realized that natural monopoly was a static notion that the dynamism of industrial technology might eventually overtake.

As the economic need for regulation became apparent, lawyers searched for a legal foundation on which to base it. They located it in the doctrine of "affectation with a public interest." Derived from ancient English precedent and from nineteenth-century American riparian law, the doctrine held that such industries as railroads and utilities so impinged on the public welfare that they stood clearly apart from the normal run of enterprise. They were therefore subject to the regulatory powers of the state, even unto the prices they might charge. A corollary was that drafters of legislation often cited the "public interest" doctrine when they wrote regulatory statutes. Such phrases as "the public good" appeared in such laws as that which created the first modern regulatory agency, the Massachusetts Board of Railroad Commissioners, in 1869.

Afterward, the repetition of "public interest" and similar phrases became a distinguishing mark of both the law and the ideology of regulation. Often "public interest" purported to serve as a rudimentary guide for regulators, a general standard for them to observe in the discharge of their quasi-legislative, quasi-executive, quasi-judicial duties. Legislators' heavy reliance on "public interest"—a high-minded but vague and sometimes meaningless basis for decision—together with their avoidance of precise instructions to regulatory agencies, has produced mixed results, as might be expected. Although commissions have enjoyed a helpful freedom of action in setting their policies, they have often failed to develop clear standards of permissible business behavior or precise criteria for some of their own decisions. They have thereby opened themselves to charges of arbitrariness, caprice, and sometimes corruption.

In law the "public interest" doctrine, latitudinarian in aim, grew gradually more restrictive in impact as successive Supreme Court majorities applied it negatively, not to justify the regulation of industries within the category but to prevent the regulation of those outside it. In truth, the doctrine itself could be a semantic trap, as Justice Harlan F. Stone explained in a dissenting opinion of 1927: "To say that only those businesses affected with a public interest may be regulated is but another way of stating that all those businesses which may be regulated are affected with a public interest." Ultimately the Supreme Court overruled the restrictive thrust of the "public interest" doctrine and in effect opened the way for broader affirmative regulation under the commerce clause of the Constitution.

In the meantime "public interest," in its nonlegal but equally ambiguous common usage, continued to undergird the ideology of regulation. In some respects the very basis of public regulation has always depended on the existence of a definable public interest, however elusive the definition. The theoretically perfect regulatory agency is still conceived much as it was more than a century ago: as an apolitical, specialized, expert tribunal devoted to the pursuit of the public interest and concerned with both the complex details and the broad policy questions raised by industrialization and the partial failure of the competitive market. Few commissions, either state or federal, have quite come up to this ideal.

STATE COMMISSIONS

The first modern regulatory agencies were state commissions created to deal with the multitudinous problems associated with railroads. As organizations, the railroad corporations dwarfed all others in American life, public or private. As the first big business in the nation, they exemplified most of the problems later associated with that institution: corporate arrogance and corruption, the decline of entrepreneurial opportunity, the disproportionate division of wealth and power. Since they took the corporate form from the very beginning, and since they wielded the power of eminent domain, the early railroads required charters from the states in which they operated. They therefore were enmeshed in state politics, and from the 1830's until the 1880's regulatory activity centered in the states.

The earliest commissions were formed in New England. The most significant of these agencies was that of Massachusetts, created in 1869 and dominated during its first decade by Charles Francis Adams, Jr., descendant of two presidents and one of the leading rail experts in the nation. Adams explained in 1868, during his campaign for a commission, why a new instrumentality must supplement legislative committees, if regulation were to be effective: "Those committees are eternally fluctuating, are not peculiarly well-informed, judiciously selected, or free from bias." What was needed, wrote Adams, was a group of detached, apolitical experts organized into specialized agencies:

> Work hitherto badly done, spasmodically done, superficially done, ignorantly done, and too often corruptly done by temporary and irresponsible legislative committees, is in future to be reduced to order and science by the labors of permanent bureaus, and placed by them before legislatures for intelligent action. The movement springs up everywhere; it is confined to no one country and no one body.... [Adams, "Boston," in *North American Review*, 106 (Jan. 1868), p. 18].

Conscious of the transcendent importance of railroads in the regional and national economies, and of their anomalous position as gigantic intruders into a democratic polity, Adams preached that the interests of the corporations must somehow be harmonized with those of the general public. He especially believed that railroad policy must promote the economic growth of the state of Massachusetts. Implicitly defining the public interest as the maximizing of passenger and freight traffic, Adams sought to induce rail managers to manipulate their rates to promote economic development: low rates for raw materials such as coal and iron, recouped by slightly higher ones on manufactured items that could more easily bear the cost.

Adams consistently played down the exercise of raw power by the commission, in the belief that good sense and informed opinion would better harmonize the interests of the railroads and the public. Accordingly, his major effort went into systematic study of the "railroad problem" in all its aspects, and subsequent publication of his findings. The annual reports of the Board of Railroad Commissioners during Adams' tenure from 1869 to 1879 remain among the clearest, most insightful set of reports ever produced by any state or federal regulatory agency. They reflect his conception of the proper role of regulation: "The board of commissioners was set up as a sort of lens by means of which the otherwise scattered rays of public opinion could be concentrated to a focus and brought to bear upon a given point."

The Massachusetts agency became a national prototype of the "weak" commission, a model for many other states that wished to regulate railroads but, for one reason or another, did not wish to assume the power of setting rates and fares. In one respect the designation "weak" is deceptive, for in Massachusetts the legislature stood behind the orders of the board, took its advice, and shaped state railroad policy in accordance with its recommendations. The commission itself deliberately relied on voluntary compliance, recognizing the inherent indeterminacy and ambivalence of the relationship between the roads and the public. It all added up to a precise reversal of previous state railroad policy, which had produced very strong regulatory statutes that everyone ignored, and that therefore constituted an embarrassing impotence. The extraordinary success of the Massachusetts agency may be attributed to Adams' powers as an analyst and publicist, his historically revered name, and the diversity of the economy of the state, which did not encourage simple dichotomies of merchant versus farmer or people versus corporations. Accepting the dysfunctional role of competition as a regulator of railroads, Adams and his colleagues promoted standardization of methods and procedures, accepted consolidation as inevitable, and endeavored to show how monopoly could as easily serve the shipper and passenger as hurt them.

An alternative to the "weak" commission appeared in the early 1870's, in the states of Illinois, Wisconsin, Minnesota, and Iowa. Beginning in 1871, their legislatures passed statutes directly regulating the rates of roads operating within each state and, in three cases, creating "strong" commissions. These agencies had powers to prescribe maximum rates and to adjust the discriminatory rate structures ordinarily used by railroads. In contradistinction to their popular generic name, these "Granger laws" reflected the ire of bucolic citizens less than they did mercantile rivalries among cities that served as transshipment points for agricultural commodities, and between areas with adequate rail service and those to which the roads had not yet penetrated. More important for the overall evolution of regulatory agencies, they represented a path seriously considered but ultimately abandoned, and thus were another way station on the inexorable march toward federal regulation. For various reasons the Granger laws did not prove as effective as their proponents had hoped, and most of them were repealed within a few years of enactment, because of political counterattacks by the railroads; or because of the depression conditions of the 1870's, which drove down rates throughout the nation faster than regulatory agencies could hope to do; or because of the inflexibility inherent in the performance of the pricing functions of giant interstate corporations by small state agencies. In law the "Granger cases" (1877) established the power of public agencies to regulate, but in practice the Granger commissions failed to surpass the successes of their "weak" counterparts in the East.

The model "weak" commission, that of Massachusetts, continued to enjoy a measure of national prestige even after the departure of Adams in 1879. Such decline as its reputation did suffer occurred over a long period and reflected several tendencies common to state regulatory agencies. For one thing, after the onset of federal railroad regulation in 1887, the focus of state regulatory efforts shifted gradually to public utilities. A second problem of the Massachusetts board was its failure, after the first generation of its existence, to attract the best-quality personnel. This problem has plagued practically all regulatory agencies, and it constitutes the signal failure of the regulatory experience in America.

The shift in focus from railroads to public utilities came more rapidly in Massachusetts than in other states, but the transition there may be taken as a typical institutional evolution. Building on the railroad model of 1869, the state in

REGULATORY AGENCIES

1885 created the Board of Gas Commissioners. In 1887 this agency became the Board of Gas and Electric Light Commissioners, with general supervisory powers over the companies under its jurisdiction, but—following the railroad pattern—with no strong authority over rates. In 1909 both the original railroad board and the gas and electric commission received new powers over security issues. Four years later the railroad commission became the Public Service Commission, with additional responsibility for telephone companies, street railways, and steamships. The final step in consolidation occurred in 1919, as the state merged its railroad and utility commissions into one and named the new body the Department of Public Utilities. This agency still exists, having evolved over a century from the original three-member Board of Railroad Commissioners, with its single staff member, to a small bureaucracy of more than one hundred full-time employees housed in a government office building in downtown Boston.

Much the same pattern of institutional growth occurred in state after state as the industrial economy matured. The significant leaders in public utility regulation were New York and Wisconsin, both of which revised their commission laws in 1907 and thereby inaugurated the modern system of "rate-of-return" regulation (explained in detail below). As commissions evolved in the states, they took jurisdiction over new industries such as trucking, telephone communications, and natural gas production. Sometimes an agency created to deal with one problem, such as the Texas Railroad Commission, later spent its energies on quite another, such as the control of output by the oil wells in the state. The names of these commissions, and the industries they regulate, vary from state to state. So does the degree of regulatory authority, which ranges from general supervision to detailed pricing powers. All state commissions now have jurisdiction over gas and electric utilities, the only exceptions being Nebraska, the public power state, and South Dakota, where municipalities grant permits and set rates. The jurisdiction of most state commissions does not extend to publicly owned utilities or to rural cooperatives.

In addition, a number of other industries are regulated by state commissions, including the following:

Railroads	in 47 states
Motor buses	47
Telephone/telegraph	45
Common carrier trucks	44
Water supply	42
Contract carrier trucks	41
Petroleum pipelines	24
Steam heating	23
Taxicabs	21
Air transport	18
Sewers	18
Water carriers	18
Street railways	13
Toll roads and bridges	10
Warehouses	10
Community antenna television	10

In many states, service on commissions is a virtual sinecure, with light duties and low prestige. In others, seats on regulatory agencies are avidly sought and often go to highly qualified professionals. Most state commissions have three members, but again the range is broad, from one in Oregon to seven in South Carolina. The typical term of office is six years, with terms staggered so as to minimize turnover. In thirty-six states the governor appoints the members of regulatory agencies. In twelve others they are elected by the voters, and in two they are appointed by the state legislature. In twenty-five states the governor also appoints the chairperson; in twenty he or she is elected by the commissioners themselves and in the other five is chosen by some alternative means, such as rotation. About half the states require by law or custom that the minority party be represented on their commissions. By a very wide margin the profession most typical of state commissioners is that of attorney—a fact indicative of the past and present values and preoccupations of regulatory agencies, and significant for understanding their devotion to due process, as distinct from their economic performance.

Organizationally the commissions are as varied as the states themselves. Some are set up along functional lines, others along product division lines, and a few both functionally and divisionally (see figure 1). Some are tiny agencies that could not behave like bureaucracies even if they wished to do so. Others are large, complex organizations with major segments assigned to specialized aspects of the regulatory process.

REGULATORY AGENCIES

FIGURE 1 The Evolution of Commissions

New York Public Service Commission (700 Employees)

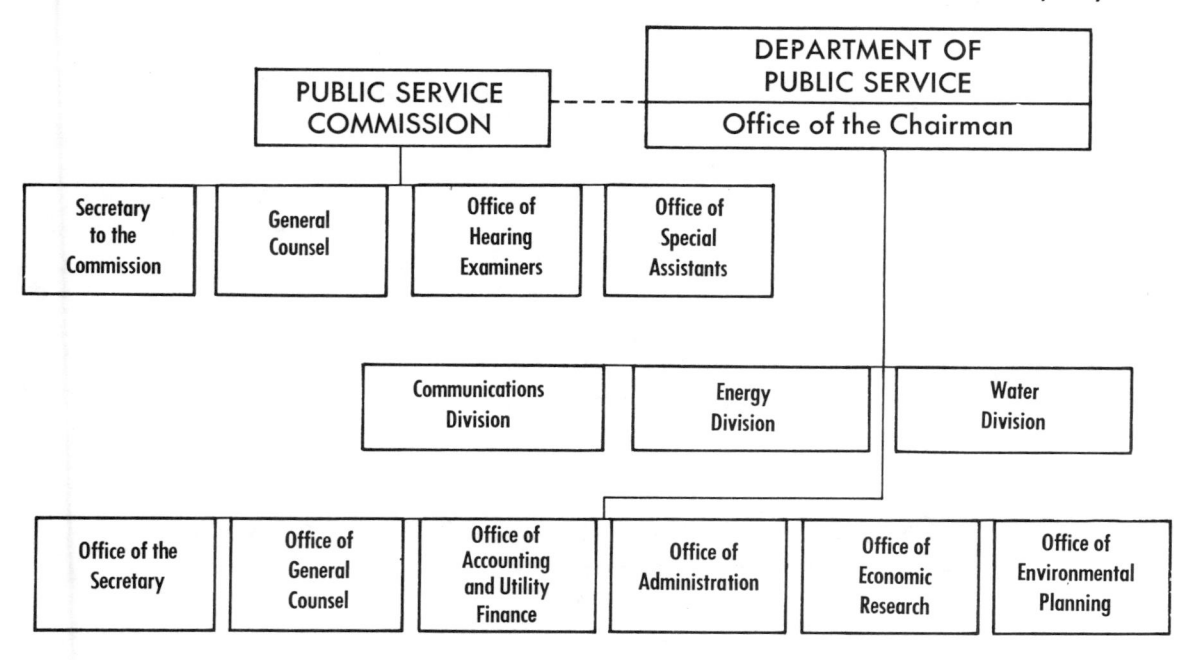

- PUBLIC SERVICE COMMISSION
- DEPARTMENT OF PUBLIC SERVICE — Office of the Chairman

Under Public Service Commission:
- Secretary to the Commission
- General Counsel
- Office of Hearing Examiners
- Office of Special Assistants

Divisions:
- Communications Division
- Energy Division
- Water Division

Offices:
- Office of the Secretary
- Office of General Counsel
- Office of Accounting and Utility Finance
- Office of Administration
- Office of Economic Research
- Office of Environmental Planning

Connecticut Public Utilities Commission (100 Employees)

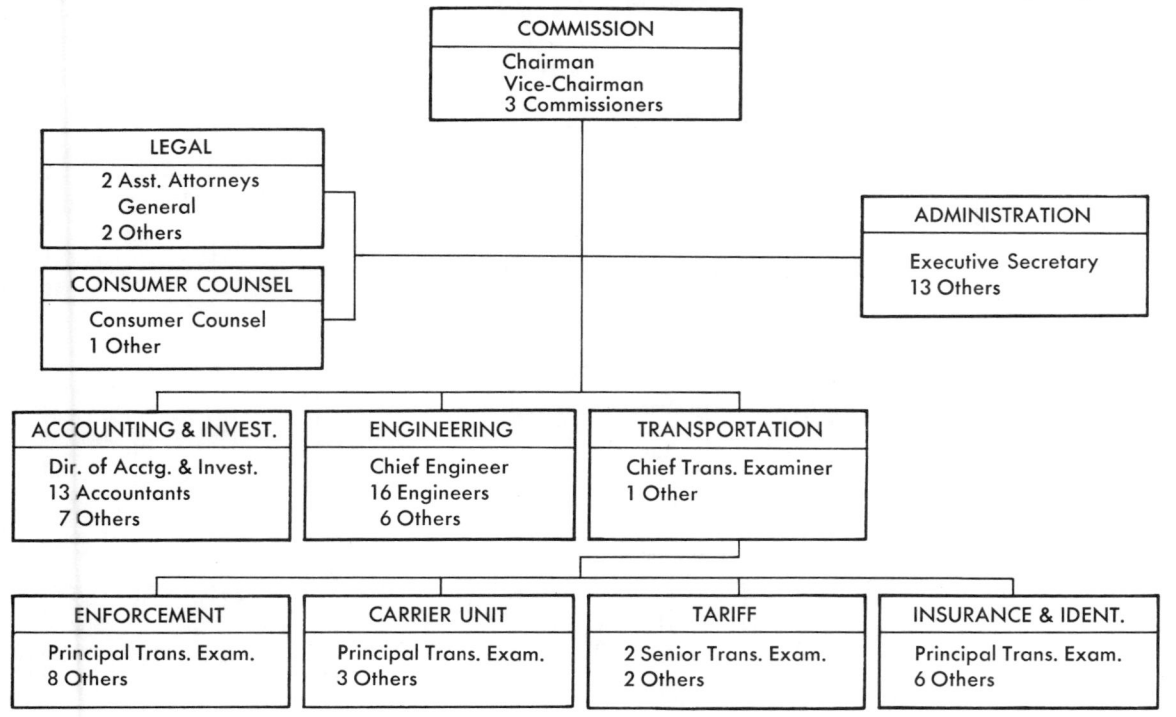

COMMISSION
Chairman
Vice-Chairman
3 Commissioners

LEGAL
2 Asst. Attorneys General
2 Others

CONSUMER COUNSEL
Consumer Counsel
1 Other

ADMINISTRATION
Executive Secretary
13 Others

ACCOUNTING & INVEST.
Dir. of Acctg. & Invest.
13 Accountants
7 Others

ENGINEERING
Chief Engineer
16 Engineers
6 Others

TRANSPORTATION
Chief Trans. Examiner
1 Other

ENFORCEMENT
Principal Trans. Exam.
8 Others

CARRIER UNIT
Principal Trans. Exam.
3 Others

TARIFF
2 Senior Trans. Exam.
2 Others

INSURANCE & IDENT.
Principal Trans. Exam.
6 Others

REGULATORY AGENCIES

FIGURE 1 *(continued)*

Texas Railroad Commission (432 Employees)

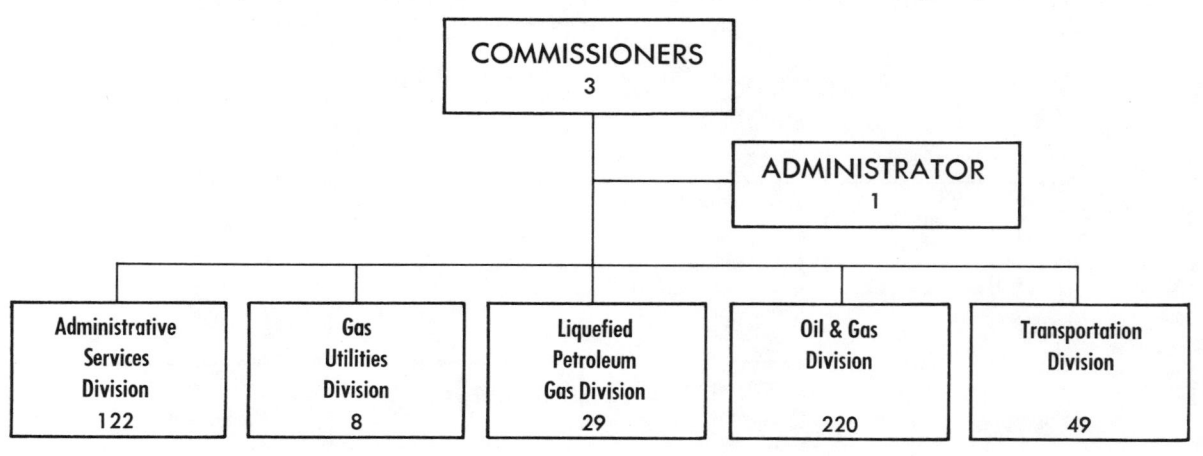

- COMMISSIONERS: 3
- ADMINISTRATOR: 1
- Administrative Services Division: 122
- Gas Utilities Division: 8
- Liquefied Petroleum Gas Division: 29
- Oil & Gas Division: 220
- Transportation Division: 49

Wisconsin Public Service Commission (150 Employees)

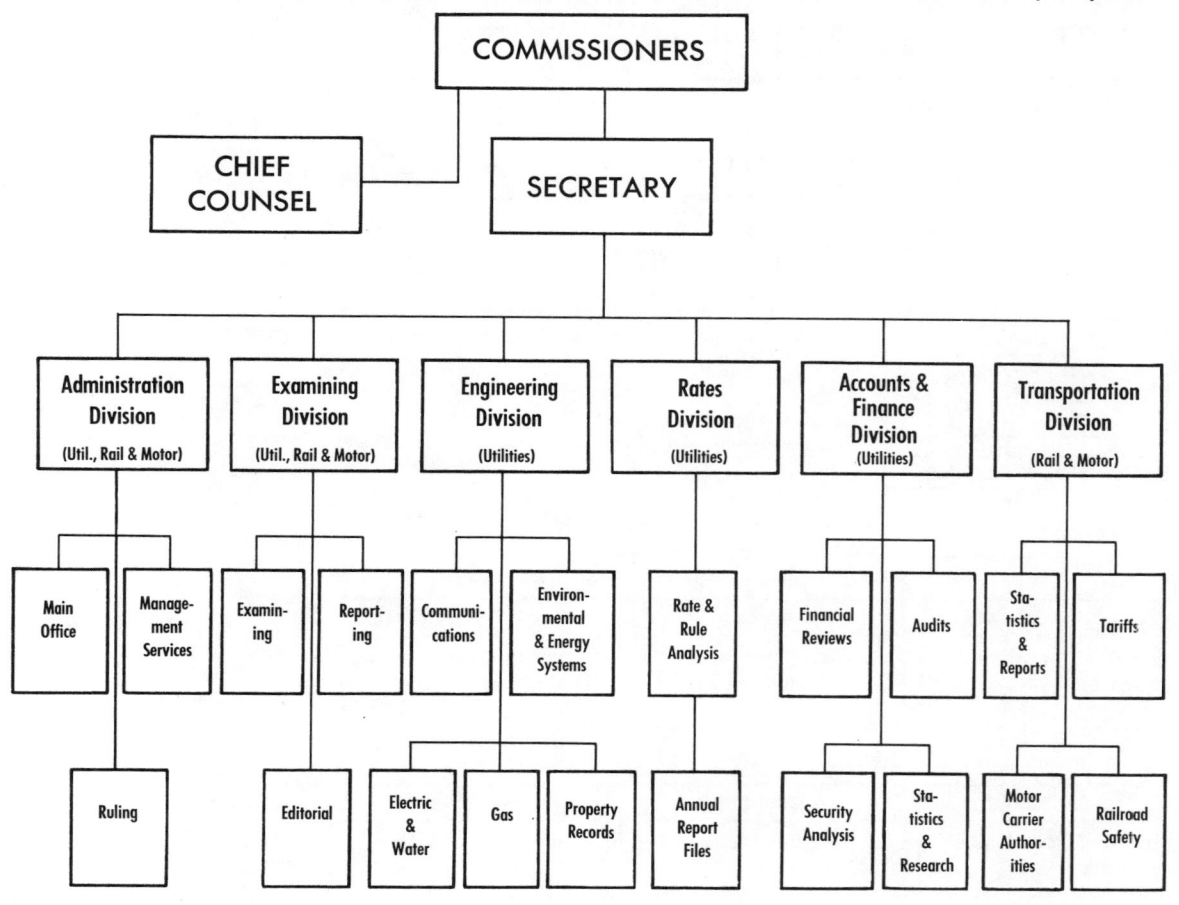

- COMMISSIONERS
- CHIEF COUNSEL
- SECRETARY
- Administration Division (Util., Rail & Motor)
  - Main Office
  - Management Services
  - Ruling
- Examining Division (Util., Rail & Motor)
  - Examining
  - Reporting
  - Editorial
- Engineering Division (Utilities)
  - Communications
  - Environmental & Energy Systems
  - Electric & Water
  - Gas
  - Property Records
- Rates Division (Utilities)
  - Rate & Rule Analysis
  - Annual Report Files
- Accounts & Finance Division (Utilities)
  - Financial Reviews
  - Audits
  - Security Analysis
  - Statistics & Research
- Transportation Division (Rail & Motor)
  - Statistics & Reports
  - Tariffs
  - Motor Carrier Authorities
  - Railroad Safety

794

REGULATORY AGENCIES

The New York Public Service Commission, for example, a pioneer in utility regulation shortly after the beginning of the twentieth century, had grown by the 1970's to a sizable bureaucracy employing some seven hundred persons and spending about $15 million annually. The chairman of the New York commission was the highest-paid state or federal regulator in the nation, with a salary in the 1970's in excess of $50,000. The functions of the agency, which in most respects other than scale are typical of state commissions, may be inferred from the following list of its professional staff members:

Inspectors and investigators	103
Engineers	57
Auditors	54
Accountants	28
Attorneys	21
Administrative staff	14
Rate analysts	13
Hearing examiners (lawyers)	13
Economists	8

RATE REGULATION

The most important aspects of state public utility regulation have to do with rates. The basic premises of the agencies, almost from the beginning, have been acceptance of the natural monopoly concept and reliance on the "rate-of-return" method. Problems with the method originated in the Supreme Court case of *Smyth* v. *Ames* (1898), in which the Union Pacific Railroad challenged a Nebraska statute that specified the maximum freight rates the corporation could charge. The court ruled that the railroad was entitled to a "reasonable" return on "the fair value of the property being used for the convenience of the public." In enunciating this "fair value" doctrine, the court inadvertently opened a Pandora's box that would plague lawyers, accountants, economists, and commissioners for the next two generations. At various times particular commissions or the Supreme Court have included in "fair value" such considerations as the original cost of the property, less depreciation (the consumer's view in periods of inflation); the cost of reproducing the same property (the view of the corporation in periods of inflation); the market value of the stocks and bonds of the corporation; and numerous other major and minor factors.

After deciding on the allowable rate base, commissions must specify the rate of return. Historically, state agencies have set allowable rates of return at some figure roughly between 5 and 8 percent of the rate base. In the 1970's the allowable percentage exceeded 10 percent, in response to rising capital costs and inflation. Although this percentage has been the subject of considerable controversy (should it equal the rate of return on other, nonutility enterprises? the cost of capital to the utility?), the major problems associated with public utility regulation have clustered around the rate base. If the percentage rate of return is to be multiplied by the rate base, then clearly the latter is quite as decisive a figure as the former. The revenue of the utility will depend as much on the rate base as on the percentage of return.

From the adjudication of *Smyth* v. *Ames* in 1898 until the ameliorating doctrine in *Federal Power Commission* v. *Hope Natural Gas Co.* (1944), and to some extent even afterward, utility commissions struggled with the "fair value" question in determining rate bases. No authoritative solution ever met with unanimous acceptance. In truth, courts and commissions might as well have attempted to make the sun stand still as to make ultimate sense of "fair value." And even if they had, the rate-of-return method would still have produced considerable mischief. At bottom, "fair return on fair value" is a cost-plus formula, vulnerable to the many problems associated with such pricing systems. Some of these problems appeared early in the history of regulation, and several of them still trouble the state commissions. Such problems include the following:

1. Temptation to pad the rate base
2. Disincentives to cut costs and therefore to efficient operation
3. Temptation to shift diminished performance from raised prices to reduced quality of service
4. Creation of a strong prejudice to emphasize capital inputs over others, in order to augment the rate base
5. "Regulatory lag," in which the typically tedious deliberations of the commission take so long that they begin to apply more to

obsolete situations than to present or future requirements
6. The problem of boundaries, in which one part of an enterprise is a natural monopoly but another is not.

These problems have promoted the rise of ingenious accounting methods within regulated industries, all calculated to maximize revenues in the face of limitations on rates of return. At worst, they have made the process of rate regulation a peculiar type of charade, serving cultural imperatives more than economic efficiency. In practice, even the rate-of-return method has in recent years been applied more or less opposite to the original theory. The procedure varies from state to state, but in essence it is as follows: the commission determines the total revenue requirements of the utility, then computes the price mix that will yield the required revenue. To do this, the commission selects a "test year," which may be an average of recent years, a projected typical year in the future, or some combination of hypothetical and actual years. The regulated firm then produces a proposed budget for the test year, showing its actual or anticipated expenses, broken down into categories required by the standardized accounting procedures of the commission. After scrutiny by the commission, the budget is adjusted according to the recommendations of the professional staff of the agency.

Full-scale rate cases are laborious proceedings that do not occur every year. In general, the regulatory process is less formal, characterized as much by negotiation and compromise as by litigation and other adversary contests. This circumstance has increased the vulnerability of commissions to charges of "capture" by the regulated interests. Historically, it is clear that "capture" has often occurred, but this result derives from other factors besides the informality of the regulatory process, among them the greater resources of the industries vis-à-vis the agencies, and above all the importance of the health of the industries to the economy.

FEDERAL REGULATION

State regulation of many industries has continued from its origins down to the present with no abatement of importance or of jurisdictional range. The movement from state to federal regulation, therefore, has been a selective one that has not occurred across the spectrum of regulated industries. As is obvious from the preceding discussion, for example, most public utilities have continued to be regulated principally by the states.

For several other industries, state regulation perforce yielded to federal. Typically the industry grew to such size or geographical extent as to render state boundaries irrelevant to its proper control. This kind of sequence illustrates once more the transcendent point that the inherent nature of an industry is often the decisive context in which regulatory agencies must operate.

As in so many other ways, the railroad industry set the pattern. In the late nineteenth century, as the "railroad problem" grew to national scope, its nature became more and more complex. In the East the problem sometimes took the form of excessive competition, with too many roads handling too little traffic. In the West and South, by contrast, it could take the form of too little competition. Whole communities complained of monopoly, as they depended on single railroad corporations for their very existence. And in all regions the railroads often exhibited tendencies toward frenzied finance, corporate arrogance, and discriminatory pricing practices that, however logically they might flow from the economics of railroading, nevertheless appeared to violate basic notions of fairness. And underlying the entire "railroad problem" was the political incongruity of a democratic society in the role of handmaiden to one of its industries.

Ultimately the railroad industry grew so powerful and vital to the national economy that continued reliance on state regulation was plainly futile. The final precipitant of federal entry into the situation was the Supreme Court decision in *Wabash, Saint Louis and Pacific Railroad Company* v. *Illinois* (1886). In it the court ruled that commerce originating or ending beyond the boundaries of a state was beyond the power of that state to regulate, even though the federal government had not otherwise provided for its regulation. This doctrine partially overturned the previous rulings of the Supreme Court in the Granger cases and it made the resort to federal regulation all but inevitable.

In 1883, Senator Shelby M. Cullom, a Republican from Illinois, had introduced a bill that provided for a federal railroad commission that would administer a general and flexible set of guidelines. The *Wabash* decision swung majority support to Cullom's bill, and the Interstate Commerce Commission was created in 1887. By that time a virtual national consensus had developed in favor of federal regulation. Merchants, farmers, passengers, politicians, and even many railroad men had become convinced, after years of trial and error with other methods, that serious federal railroad regulation was essential.

The greatest significance of the Interstate Commerce Act of 1887 lay in its creation of the prototype federal regulatory tribunal. Most of the later federal commissions were more or less patterned on the ICC in appointment and tenure of members and in relationships with the legislative, executive, and judicial branches of government (see figure 2). It is a measure of the success the ICC had in its first fifty years, or was perceived as having had, that the pattern was so often repeated in the creation of new agencies.

Federal Regulatory Agencies and Their Functions.
The Interstate Commerce Commission (ICC) began life in 1887 with several missions, not all of which were easily consistent with each other or with the inherent nature of the railroad industry. The Interstate Commerce Act forbade pooling, rebating, and—with certain important exceptions—rate discrimination between long-haul and short-haul traffic. The statute insisted that railroad rates be "just and reasonable"; and it provided a new arena, the ICC, in which determinations of reasonableness could occur. The five members of the commission were to be appointed by the president and confirmed by the Senate, for staggered terms of six (later seven) years. No more than three of the five could come from one political party, and each commissioner was to receive an annual salary of $7,500, a very large sum for 1887. This salary, greater than that of any federal judge except those on the Supreme Court, was a reflection of the importance Congress attached to the new agency.

After an auspicious beginning under its influential and distinguished first chairman, Thomas M. Cooley, the ICC encountered severe difficulties with the courts. Led by the Supreme Court, the federal judiciary restricted the powers of the agency and reduced it, by the late 1890's, to a mere collector of data. The events of the next several decades constituted a dialectical process of adjustment, involving the commission, the courts, and Congress. In response to continuing problems within the railroad industry, and problems between the ICC and the judiciary, Congress steadily added to the authority of the commission and broadened its jurisdiction. The highlights in this long process are listed below.

The Elkins Act (1903) gave teeth to the prohibition on rebating in the original Interstate Commerce Act.

The Hepburn Act (1906) gave the commission power to fix maximum rates, shifted the burden of proof in rate proceedings from the commission to the railroads, and made ICC decisions effective as soon as they were reached. It also gave the commission regulatory powers over petroleum pipelines.

The Mann-Elkins Act (1910) broadened the rate-making authority of the commission, reinforced the long-haul/short-haul rule, and created the Court of Commerce, a short-lived experiment in specialized judicial review.

The Transportation Act (Esch-Cummins Act) of 1920 empowered the commission to set minimum as well as maximum rates, to supervise the issuance of securities by carriers, and to approve the previously forbidden practice of pooling. It also instructed the ICC to undertake comprehensive studies toward a systematic and partially consolidated transportation network.

The Motor Carrier Act (1935) added the regulation of trucking to the missions of the ICC and thereby increased its work load substantially. The reasons for this measure involved the Great Depression and the ill health of the railroad industry, as well as a crisis in trucking. Unlike some common carriers, trucking did not tend toward natural monopoly, but its great flexibility permitted it to take the most profitable freights away from the railroads. The long reliance of the railroads on value-of-service rate making made the matter worse, and depression conditions necessitated action by Congress.

The Transportation Act of 1940 added domestic water carriers to the list of industries under ICC jurisdiction, continuing the trend toward regulation of all interstate transportation.

Throughout its history the ICC has remained controversial. Sometimes, as in the Progressive era (1901–1920) it has been the target of indus-

REGULATORY AGENCIES

FIGURE 2 Organizational Charts of Six Federal Regulatory Agencies

Interstate Commerce Commission

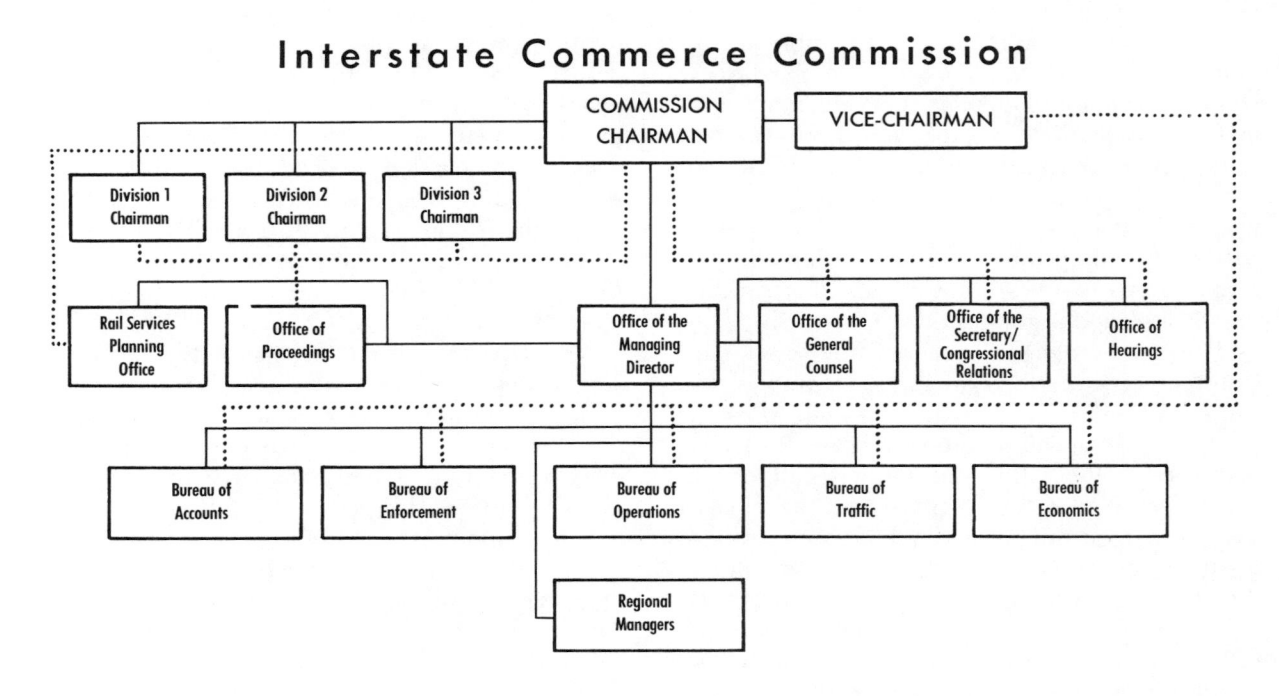

- COMMISSION CHAIRMAN
  - VICE-CHAIRMAN
  - Division 1 Chairman
  - Division 2 Chairman
  - Division 3 Chairman
  - Rail Services Planning Office
  - Office of Proceedings
  - Office of the Managing Director
  - Office of the General Counsel
  - Office of the Secretary/Congressional Relations
  - Office of Hearings

Under Office of the Managing Director:
- Bureau of Accounts
- Bureau of Enforcement
- Bureau of Operations
  - Regional Managers
- Bureau of Traffic
- Bureau of Economics

Federal Trade Commission

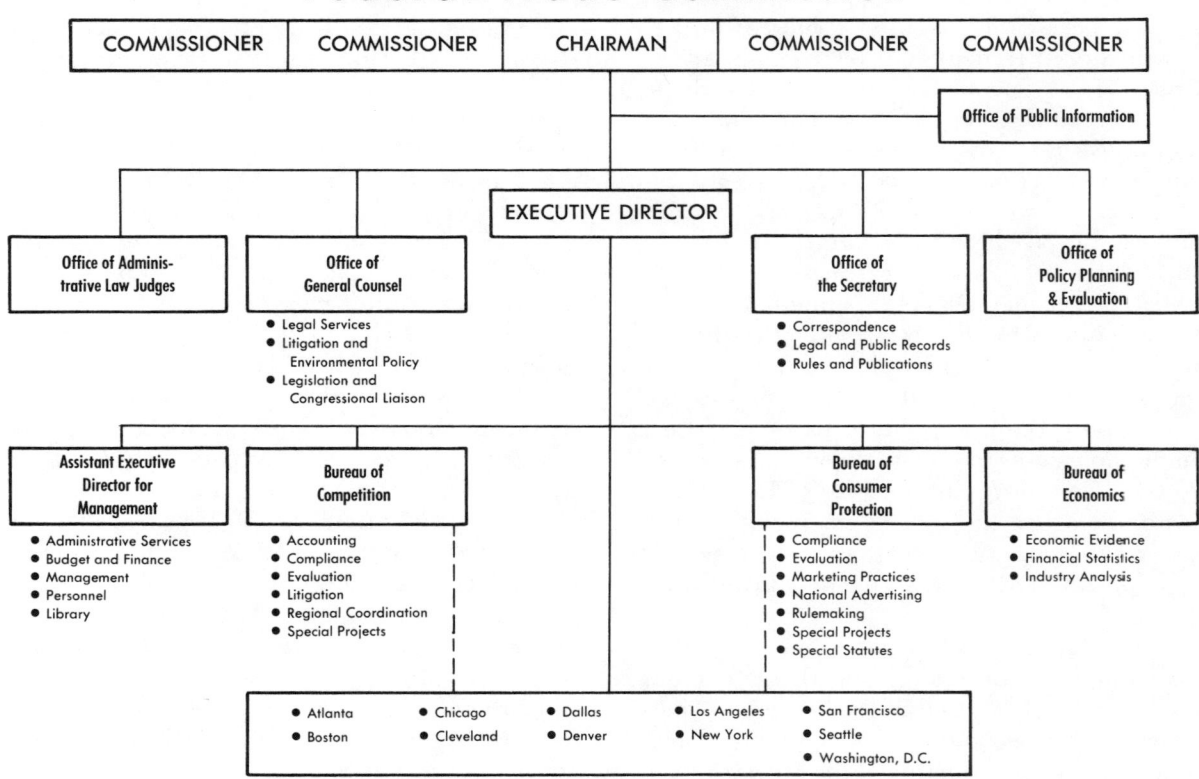

- COMMISSIONER | COMMISSIONER | CHAIRMAN | COMMISSIONER | COMMISSIONER
  - Office of Public Information
  - EXECUTIVE DIRECTOR
    - Office of Administrative Law Judges
    - Office of General Counsel
      - Legal Services
      - Litigation and Environmental Policy
      - Legislation and Congressional Liaison
    - Office of the Secretary
      - Correspondence
      - Legal and Public Records
      - Rules and Publications
    - Office of Policy Planning & Evaluation
    - Assistant Executive Director for Management
      - Administrative Services
      - Budget and Finance
      - Management
      - Personnel
      - Library
    - Bureau of Competition
      - Accounting
      - Compliance
      - Evaluation
      - Litigation
      - Regional Coordination
      - Special Projects
    - Bureau of Consumer Protection
      - Compliance
      - Evaluation
      - Marketing Practices
      - National Advertising
      - Rulemaking
      - Special Projects
      - Special Statutes
    - Bureau of Economics
      - Economic Evidence
      - Financial Statistics
      - Industry Analysis

Regional Offices: Atlanta, Boston, Chicago, Cleveland, Dallas, Denver, Los Angeles, New York, San Francisco, Seattle, Washington, D.C.

REGULATORY AGENCIES

FIGURE 2 (*continued*)

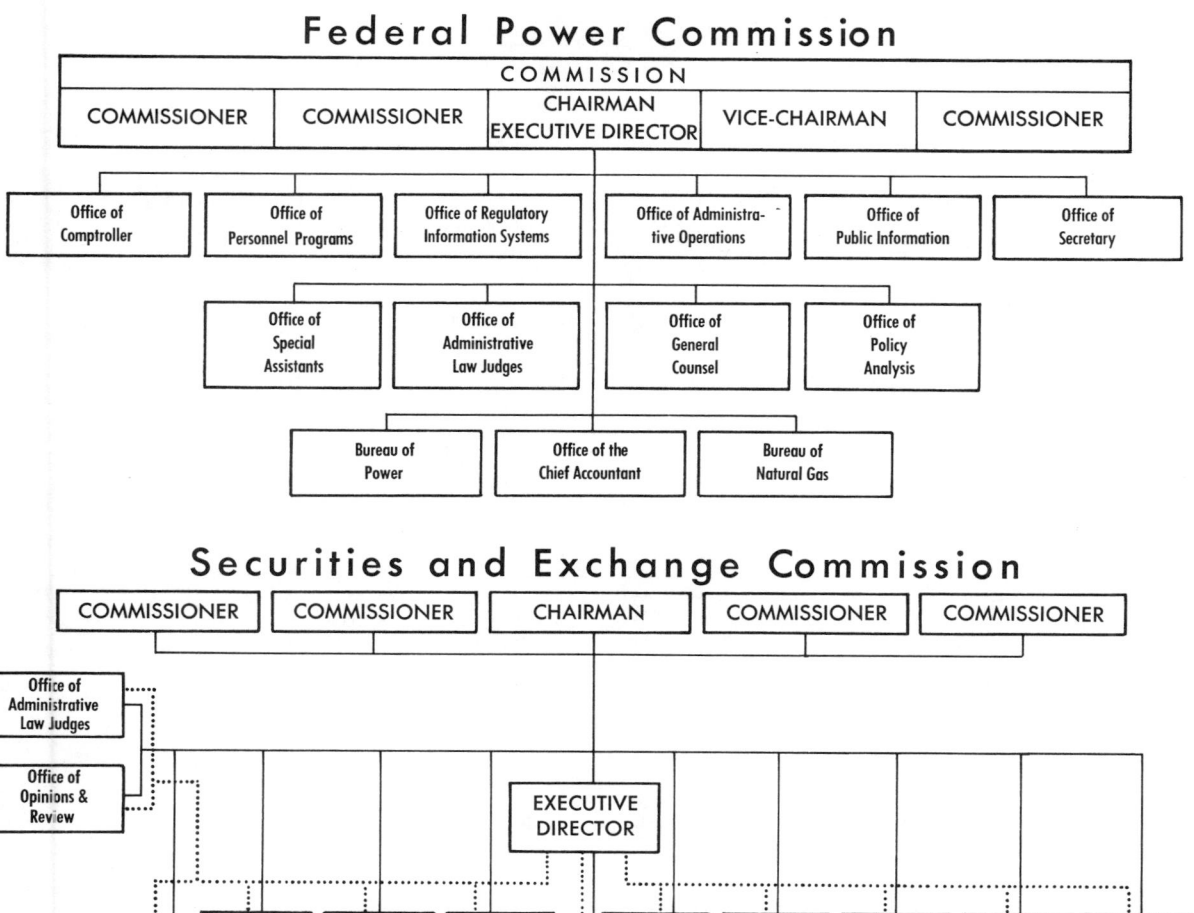

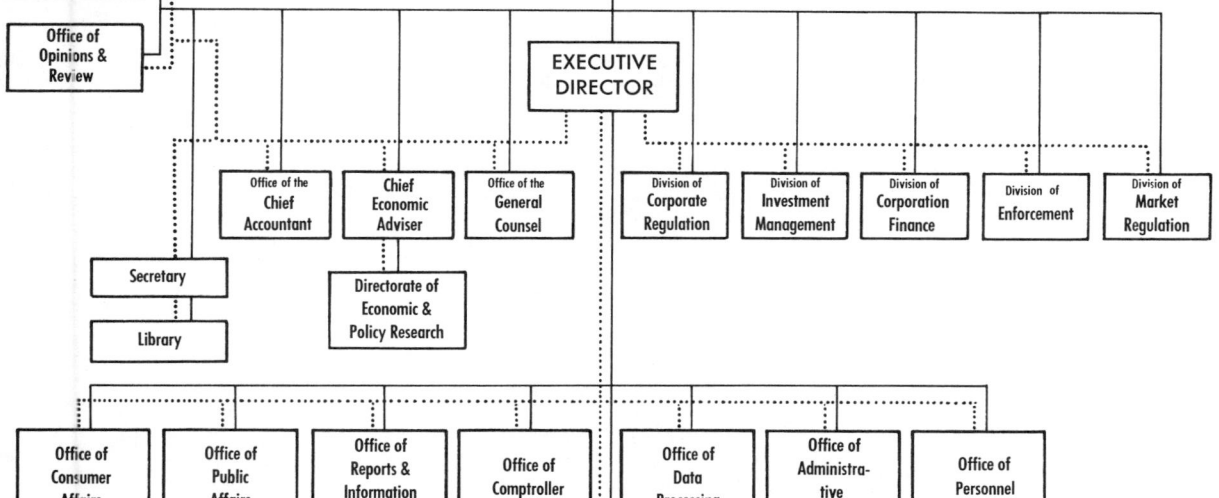

Federal Power Commission

- COMMISSION
  - COMMISSIONER
  - COMMISSIONER
  - CHAIRMAN / EXECUTIVE DIRECTOR
  - VICE-CHAIRMAN
  - COMMISSIONER

Offices reporting to the Commission:
- Office of Comptroller
- Office of Personnel Programs
- Office of Regulatory Information Systems
- Office of Administrative Operations
- Office of Public Information
- Office of Secretary

Second tier:
- Office of Special Assistants
- Office of Administrative Law Judges
- Office of General Counsel
- Office of Policy Analysis

Third tier:
- Bureau of Power
- Office of the Chief Accountant
- Bureau of Natural Gas

Securities and Exchange Commission

- COMMISSIONER
- COMMISSIONER
- CHAIRMAN
- COMMISSIONER
- COMMISSIONER

Reporting to Commission:
- Office of Administrative Law Judges
- Office of Opinions & Review

- EXECUTIVE DIRECTOR

Staff offices:
- Office of the Chief Accountant
- Chief Economic Adviser
- Office of the General Counsel
- Division of Corporate Regulation
- Division of Investment Management
- Division of Corporation Finance
- Division of Enforcement
- Division of Market Regulation

- Secretary
- Library
- Directorate of Economic & Policy Research

Administrative offices:
- Office of Consumer Affairs
- Office of Public Affairs
- Office of Reports & Information Services
- Office of Comptroller
- Office of Data Processing
- Office of Administrative Services
- Office of Personnel

REGIONAL OFFICES

New York Regional Office	Boston Regional Office	Atlanta Regional Office	Chicago Regional Office	Fort Worth Regional Office	Denver Regional Office	Los Angeles Regional Office	Seattle Regional Office	Washington, D.C. Regional Office
		Miami Branch	Cleveland Branch / Detroit Branch / St. Louis Branch	Houston Branch	Salt Lake City Branch	San Francisco Branch		Philadelphia Branch

——— LINES OF POLICY AND JUDICIAL AUTHORITY

········· LINES OF BUDGET AND MANAGEMENT AUTHORITY

REGULATORY AGENCIES

FIGURE 2 (continued)

Federal Communications Commission

COMMISSIONERS / CHAIRMAN

Reporting to Commissioners/Chairman:
- Office of Plans & Policy
- Office of Opinions & Review
- Review Board
- Office of Administrative Law Judges

OFFICE OF GENERAL COUNSEL
- Litigation and Enforcement Division
- Legislation Division
- Legal Research and Treaty Division
- Administrative Rules and Procedures Division
- Industry Equal Employment Opportunity Unit

OFFICE OF CHIEF ENGINEER
- Laboratory Division
- Research and Standards Division
- International and Operations Division
- Spectrum Allocations Staff
- Planning and Coordination Staff

OFFICE OF EXECUTIVE DIRECTOR
- Administrative Services Division
- Financial Management Division
- Data Automation Division
- Emergency Communications Division
- Management Systems Division
- Personnel Division
- Procurement Division
- Records Management Division
- Public Information Officer
- The Secretary
- Internal Review and Security Division
- Consumer Assistance Office

FIELD OPERATIONS BUREAU
- Violations Division
- Engineering Division
- Enforcement Division
- Regional Services Division
- Field Installations

BROADCAST BUREAU
- Office of Network Study
- Broadcast Facilities Division
- Hearing Division
- Complaints and Compliance Division
- License Division
- Renewal and Transfer Division
- Policy and Rules Division

CABLE TELEVISION BUREAU
- Policy Review and Development Division
- Certificates of Compliance Division
- Research Division
- Special Relief and Microwave Division
- Records and Systems Management Division

COMMON CARRIER BUREAU
- Accounting and Audits Division
- Economics Division
- Facilities and Services Division
- Hearing Division
- Mobile Services Division
- Policy and Rules Division
- Tariff Division
- International Programs Staff
- Program Evaluation Staff
- Field Offices

SAFETY AND SPECIAL RADIO SERVICES BUREAU
- Aviation and Marine Division
- Legal Advisory and Enforcement Division
- Industrial and Public Safety Rules Division
- Personal Radio Division
- Industrial and Public Safety Facilities Division
- Regional Management Staff

Civil Aeronautics Board

MEMBER | MEMBER | CHAIRMAN | VICE-CHAIRMAN | MEMBER

MANAGING DIRECTOR

- Office of Comptroller
- Office of Personnel
- Office of Facilities & Operations
- Office of Equal Employment Opportunity
- Office of Secretary
- Office of the General Counsel
- Office of Public Affairs
- Office of Consumer Advocate
- Office of Community & Congressional Relations

BUREAU OF ACCOUNTS AND STATISTICS
- Accounting and Reporting Systems Division
- Statistical Data Division
- Economic Evaluation Division
- Reports, Control and Administration Division
- Data Processing Division

BUREAU OF ECONOMICS
- Passenger and Cargo Rates Division
- Government Rates Division
- Economic Analysis Division
- Legal Division

BUREAU OF ENFORCEMENT
- Legal Division
- Investigation and Audit Division

BUREAU OF ADMINISTRATIVE JUDGES
- Administrative Law Judges

BUREAU OF INTERNATIONAL AFFAIRS
- Western Hemisphere
- Northern Europe
- Mediterranean and Africa
- Pacific and Far East
- Special Project Units

BUREAU OF OPERATING RIGHTS
- Standards Division
- Performance Monitoring and Licensing Division
- Routes Authority Division
- Supplementary Services Division
- Agreements Division
- Legal Division

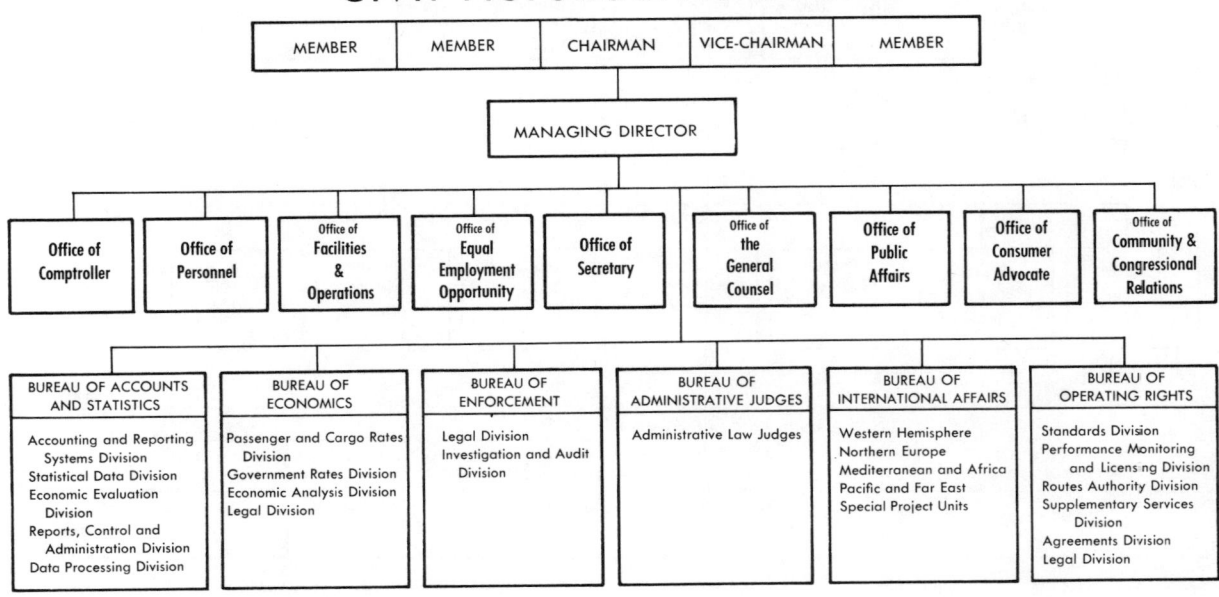

try criticism that it infringes on the prerogatives of management and wields pricing authority without responsibility for the consequences. More often, consumer groups have accused it of protecting the carriers at the expense of the general public. Sometimes critics with entirely different viewpoints have joined in blaming the ICC for the almost uninterrupted decline in rail service. But the most damning criticism of the ICC has been on the grounds of economic inefficiency. This line of argument holds that the commission has prevented competitive market forces from automatically selecting the optimal modes of moving different types of freight, and that it has thereby injected an institutional inefficiency into the national system of freight transport, at great cost to society.

The Federal Trade Commission (FTC), created in 1914, exhibits some of the characteristic patterns set by the ICC. Its five members are appointed for staggered terms, and only a bare majority may come from one political party. The commission is supposed to be "independent," that is, outside the three major branches of government but exercising some of the functions of each. On the other hand, the FTC differs from some regulatory agencies in that its jurisdiction stretches across the business establishment and is not confined to a single industry or group of industries. The original legislation was short and simple, and it left a great deal up to the agency itself. The most optimistic early promoters of the commission expected it to be a principal agent for settling the "trust" question in America, and even today the agency shares antitrust responsibilities with the Antitrust Division of the Department of Justice. Its other missions and duties include the investigation of particular industries, the regulation of advertising and branding, and the policing of "unfair methods of competition in commerce." The FTC has no pricing powers, as do state utility commissions and several federal agencies. Of the major federal commissions, it is the one most like a court in function and the one most clearly dominated by lawyers.

The recurring criticisms of the FTC, almost from the beginning, have held it to be unduly industry-minded, insufficiently aggressive in promoting competition, and too ready to expend its small resources on trivia.

The third federal regulatory commission to emerge was the Federal Power Commission (FPC; renamed Federal Energy Regulatory Agency in 1977), created by Congress in 1920 to deal with the waterpower question, a perennial problem of Progressive era politics and a part of the larger issue of conservation. Unlike the ICC and the FTC, the FPC originally had little real "independence," being composed of three cabinet officers: the secretaries of the interior, war, and agriculture. This odd administrative setup reflected the intragovernmental disputes over jurisdiction that had seemed to make such a commission desirable in the first place. After a decade of unsatisfactory experience, Congress changed the organizational form of the agency to correspond to that of other regulatory bodies; and since then the FPC has shared the characteristics of its counterparts. A reorganizing statute of 1930 also gave the commission substantial authority over interstate rates for electricity, the security issues of electric power companies, and the licensing and valuation of hydroelectric projects. Its functions thus overlap those of the state utility commissions, and the FPC has had to pay close attention to fence-mending operations and administrative coordination.

Historically, the biggest problems of the FPC have come from its extremely heavy work load and from deep cleavages within American society over energy policy. The energy debate focused on electric power and the holding companies in the 1930's and was the subject of considerable New Deal legislation. In the late 1940's the focus shifted to natural gas. Congress had given the FPC certain powers over this industry through the Natural Gas Act of 1938, but most observers believed that this act did not extend to the regulation of "field prices" for wellhead sales by hundreds of small producers. The commission, Congress, and the courts were each divided over this issue.

The resolution of the issue occurred with the Supreme Court decision in *Phillips Petroleum Company* v. *Wisconsin* (1954). After this ruling the FPC began to control the field prices of natural gas, even though most observers agreed that the industry bore little resemblance to the natural monopolies that are the most usual concerns of regulatory agencies. Economists in particular were critical of this portion of natural gas regulation. They pointed out that it tended to distort national patterns of fuel consumption, especially in periods of marked inflation, and that it upset

REGULATORY AGENCIES

the normal business growth of an important industry.

The Radio Act of 1927 created the Federal Radio Commission, which in 1934 became the Federal Communications Commission (FCC). The Radio Act was a remarkably broad delegation of power, even for a regulatory statute. Behind federal entry into broadcasting lay an almost purely technological reason: the electromagnetic spectrum can accommodate only a finite number of broadcasters, and in the absence of some authority to allocate frequencies, competing users would create electronic chaos. Ranging from local police and citizens' band operators to the affiliates of national television networks, they constitute a heterogeneous mix of applicants. The chief tool of the FCC is the licensing power over stations: it may grant, renew, or deny at its discretion.

Analysts have pointed out that this "either-or" situation hampers effective regulation. Many contend that the denial of a license is too drastic a remedy; that, like the death penalty in criminal law, it is appropriate only in the most extreme cases. For the usual situations, some more moderate means of regulation would be more suitable. The FCC has made use of the "raised eyebrow" method to meet this need, and it has very seldom resorted to the ultimate power of license denial. Indeed, many of its critics think that it has been more cooperative with the broadcasting industry than is either necessary or wise. Economists have argued that FCC restrictions on entry into the business, and particularly the inhospitable stance toward cable television, have kept the industry too small, the offerings of commercial television too narrow, and the viewers' fare too standardized and uncontroversial. The industry itself has complained that the commission has sometimes tended to use its powers of allocation to serve a censorship function not intended by the Radio Act and forbidden by the First Amendment to the Constitution. Still other critics have charged that the FCC has done a lackluster job of regulating the telephone industry, a task it inherited in 1934 from the ICC, which had had jurisdiction since 1910.

In 1934 Congress created the fifth major federal regulatory agency, the Securities and Exchange Commission (SEC). Rightly or wrongly, most Americans blamed Wall Street for the stock market crash of 1929 and the ensuing depression. The Securities Act (1933) and the Securities Exchange Act (1934) responded to this conviction and to the obvious need for regulation of stock exchange practices. Like the FCC, the SEC uses the basic tool of licensing to serve its regulatory purposes. Before a company may issue securities, it must file with the commission a set of thoroughgoing registration forms that disclose information of possible use to investors. If the registration statement is defective or misleading about either the issue or the company, the commission may hold a hearing that could result in a "stop order," which suspends the effective date of the offering. In addition the SEC promulgates numerous rules pertaining to such matters as insider trading, proxy solicitations, and the governance of exchanges. The commission also administers parts of the Public Utility Holding Company Act of 1935, the Trust Indenture Act of 1939, and Chapter X of the Bankruptcy Act.

Of all the federal commissions the SEC has probably achieved the highest reputation for effective performance. If it has not received the least criticism, then the criticism it has received has been the least persuasive. Its personnel, especially in the early years, were a cut above those of most agencies. (Its first four chairmen were Joseph P. Kennedy, James M. Landis, William O. Douglas, and Jerome Frank, an exceptionally distinguished quartet.) Moreover, the unpopularity of the securities industry during and after the Great Depression facilitated aggressive pursuit by the SEC of its mandate. Most attacks on the SEC have held that it sometimes has gone beyond the intent of Congress and involved itself in affairs that are none of its business. This line of criticism intensified after the 1960's, with respect to such matters as the responsibilities of the legal and accounting professions, and the business practices abroad of American multinational corporations.

The last created of the six federal "economic" regulatory agencies was the Civil Aeronautics Board (CAB). Its origin in 1938 points up the striking outburst of regulatory legislation during the New Deal, when aviation, securities, public-utility holding companies, natural gas, and trucking all came under federal regulation for the first time.

The principal difference between the functions of the CAB and those of the ICC, its counterpart in surface transportation, is that Congress intended commercial aviation, a struggling infant industry in 1938, to be promoted and subsidized as well as regulated. The CAB thus came into existence with a dual set of missions that sometimes ill accorded with each other. For many years it made or channeled payments to certain airlines in return for mail service or in the form of direct subsidies. At the same time the CAB, like other agencies that focus on a particular industry, wielded extraordinary powers. It controlled entry into the business of air transport, approved rates and routes, and to some extent regulated air safety, although the separate Federal Aviation Administration has principal responsibility there.

In effect the CAB operated a cartel. In so doing, it acquired the reputation of being unduly industry-minded, a result of both its promotional mission and of its historic failure to prevent air fares from rising to unnecessarily high levels.

Economists who have evaluated the performance of the CAB note that its highest priorities have often been the extension of air service to small cities that cannot support it, the promotion of technologically advanced aircraft, and the maximization of the size of the industry instead of its efficiency. These priorities, coupled with rising equipment and fuel costs in the industry, often brought the anomalous situation in which airlines did not usually show high profits and sometimes suffered net losses, but passenger and freight rates were obviously too high. The low rates charged by a few intrastate airlines beyond the reach of CAB regulation stood as a silent indictment of the performance of the board. On the other hand, since the early 1950's the quality of service in the industry has been much better than that available for other modes of travel, and in 1977 the CAB began to take decisive action to cut airline fares. In 1978, Congress sharply curtailed the CAB's authority and inaugurated an era of deregulation of the airline industry.

"Social" and "Environmental" Regulation by Federal Commissions. A new wave of federal regulatory legislation began in the 1960's and continued well into the 1970's. The new commissions that emerged from this process bore less resemblance to such older, industry-specific agencies as the ICC and CAB than they did to early state agencies for industrial safety and workmen's compensation. Each new commission cut broadly across industry lines and focused on some functional aspect of business practice: equal employment opportunity, environmental impacts, occupational safety and health, and consumer product safety. They originated less in response to some crisis in a particular industry than to changing values in American society.

The designation of this new regulation as "noneconomic" often disguised the heavy economic effects it had on business. Because the new wave of regulation is by no means spent, "social" and "environmental" regulations are clearly the types of greatest concern to business as a whole. Uncertainties are greater, the growth of the agencies is faster (see table 1), and the potential impact is virtually unlimited. It is therefore important to distinguish this new regulation conceptually from the old and not to misconstrue well-publicized campaigns for deregulation as presaging diminished concern for social justice and a clean environment. Most proposals for deregulation apply to rate regulation by older agencies such as the ICC and CAB, and not to the new commissions.

The first of the new agencies was the Equal Employment Opportunity Commission (EEOC), created to administer Title VII of the Civil Rights Act of 1964. The EEOC encourages and assists voluntary action by employers and unions in developing affirmative action programs. It is a major publisher of data on the employment status of minorities and women. It receives and evaluates written charges of discrimination made against public and private employers, and it also may initiate charges that Title VII has been violated. Ultimately it may sue in federal courts to enforce its mandate, but only after due notice and referral to affiliated state and local agencies.

The Environmental Protection Agency (EPA) was the institutional offspring of the congressional consolidation in 1970 of several existing agencies concerned with water and air quality. Its multitudinous activities are evident from the complexity of its organizational chart (see figure 3), and it has been the fastest-growing regulatory agency in American history. The EPA attempts to abate and control pollution through a combination of programs involving research, monitoring, standard setting, and enforcement. It also tries to coordinate antipollution activities by state and local governments, public and private

REGULATORY AGENCIES

TABLE 1
The Growth of Federal Regulation in America: Personnel of Selected Agencies, 1935–1977
"Economic" Regulation Agencies

	1935	1945	1960	1975
Interstate Commerce Commission (1887)	1,093	1,817	2,409	2,142
Federal Trade Commission (1914)	527	484	756	1,569
Federal Power Commission (1920)	70	723	850	1,320
Federal Communications Commission (1934)	234	1,757	1,454	2,022
Securities and Exchange Commission (1934)	153	1,249	1,000	2,150
Civil Aeronautics Board (1938)	—	385	766	713

"Social" or "Environmental" Regulation Agencies

	1970	1973	1977 (est.)
Equal Employment Opportunity Commission (1964)	780	1,739	2,377
Environmental Protection Agency (1970)	3702	8,270	9,550
Occupational Safety and Health Administration (1970)	—	1,285	2,306
Consumer Product Safety Commission (1972)	—	579	890

Source: *Budget of the U.S. Government* (Washington, D.C., various years).

groups, individuals, and educational institutions.

The Occupational Safety and Health Administration (OSHA) is not technically an "independent" commission, but a division set up within the Department of Labor in 1970. Headed by an assistant secretary of labor, OSHA develops and promulgates standards and regulations, conducts investigations and inspections to determine compliance, and issues citations and proposes penalties for noncompliance. Of all the new agencies, OSHA has confronted the most formidable enforcement tasks, since it would take an army of inspectors to visit the hundreds of thousands of American workplaces even once a year. OSHA has also had the harshest reception (EEOC being a distant second). Critics have lampooned its excessive concern with such matters as the number of rungs for ladders of given lengths and the proximity of toilets to ranch hands.

The Consumer Product Safety Commission (CPSC), established in 1972, promulgates mandatory product safety standards. It also has the authority to ban hazardous consumer products. Upon its emergence it took over responsibility for the administration of existing federal statutes, such as the Flammable Fabrics Act, the Poison Prevention Packaging Act, and the Hazardous Substances Act. The precise role of CPSC in the field of product liability is not yet clear.

The foregoing discussion of ten major agencies—six old and four relatively new—does not by any means exhaust the possible number of federal regulatory bodies that might be mentioned. Many others share some of the same administrative and functional characteristics: the Nuclear Regulatory Commission, the Commodity Futures Trading Commission, the Federal Maritime Commission, the National Highway Traffic Safety Administration, the Food and Drug Administration, and the National Labor Relations Board. All are regulatory in mission. All mix legislative, executive, and judicial functions. And all follow the administrative procedures characteristic of most commissions.

AN EVALUATION AND PERSPECTIVE

On the whole, the evolution of regulatory agencies in America suggests that regulation is an institution adaptable to many different ends and purposes. It is a flexible tool whose handle may be seized by reformers, business executives, bureaucrats, or consumers, and may be manipulated quite as easily for the particularistic goals of one of these groups as for the public interest. The functional diversity that has been the hall-

REGULATORY AGENCIES

FIGURE 3

Environmental Protection Agency

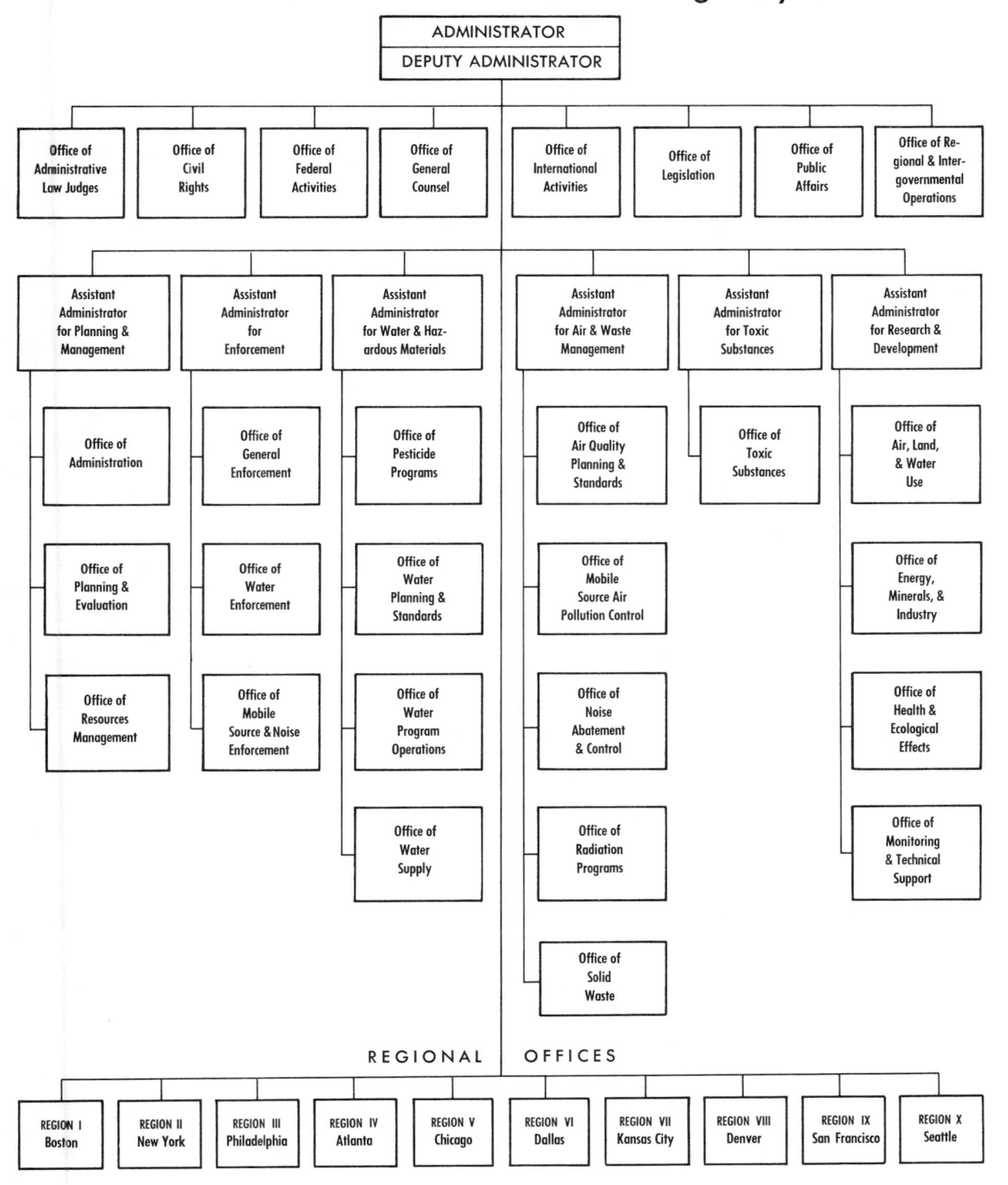

- **ADMINISTRATOR / DEPUTY ADMINISTRATOR**
  - Office of Administrative Law Judges
  - Office of Civil Rights
  - Office of Federal Activities
  - Office of General Counsel
  - Office of International Activities
  - Office of Legislation
  - Office of Public Affairs
  - Office of Regional & Intergovernmental Operations

- **Assistant Administrator for Planning & Management**
  - Office of Administration
  - Office of Planning & Evaluation
  - Office of Resources Management

- **Assistant Administrator for Enforcement**
  - Office of General Enforcement
  - Office of Water Enforcement
  - Office of Mobile Source & Noise Enforcement

- **Assistant Administrator for Water & Hazardous Materials**
  - Office of Pesticide Programs
  - Office of Water Planning & Standards
  - Office of Water Program Operations
  - Office of Water Supply

- **Assistant Administrator for Air & Waste Management**
  - Office of Air Quality Planning & Standards
  - Office of Mobile Source Air Pollution Control
  - Office of Noise Abatement & Control
  - Office of Radiation Programs
  - Office of Solid Waste

- **Assistant Administrator for Toxic Substances**
  - Office of Toxic Substances

- **Assistant Administrator for Research & Development**
  - Office of Air, Land, & Water Use
  - Office of Energy, Minerals, & Industry
  - Office of Health & Ecological Effects
  - Office of Monitoring & Technical Support

REGIONAL OFFICES

- REGION I — Boston
- REGION II — New York
- REGION III — Philadelphia
- REGION IV — Atlanta
- REGION V — Chicago
- REGION VI — Dallas
- REGION VII — Kansas City
- REGION VIII — Denver
- REGION IX — San Francisco
- REGION X — Seattle

mark of regulation derives from several variables: the industry involved, the health of the economy, the political climate. Regulation serves not only economic functions but political, legal, and cultural ones as well.

No single theory from any academic discipline will predict without error precisely which industries will be regulated and which will not. Some industries that in other national economies tend toward cartelization are in America regulated—but not all. Some regulated industries have social overhead functions and are obviously "affected with a public interest"—but not all. Some are natural monopolies, with sharply declining costs to scale—but not all. Most of the transportation industry is regulated—but not all of it.

Although most agencies originated within the context of reform politics, particularly in the Progressive and New Deal eras, their subsequent behavior often departed from the reform premises that underlay their creation. More than anything else, the inherent nature of the industries under regulation shaped the diverse experiences that the agencies encountered, the conflicting functions they performed. Some agencies, notably the FTC, sought to maximize competition in an increasingly oligopolistic economy. But others, such as the CAB and the state utility commissions, limited competition in order to promote stabilization and orderly development. That nearly every agency was perceived by the public as ideally devoted to low prices for consumers above all other functions led to numerous misapprehensions on the part of reformers, journalists, and some scholars. This was especially true for those industries in which low prices were a prelude to diminished quality of service, or even to bankruptcy.

Nearly all commissions served one function not readily apparent from the statutes detailing their duties or from the rhetoric of their advocates and opponents. This was the function of legitimization. Capitalist economies, in which the generative force of economic activity is reducible as much to self-interest as to any other single motive, need ameliorating institutions for the peace of mind of the population. In this sense, regulation, a distinctly American institution, may be seen as a bastardized form standing somewhat illogically between the flawed free market and public ownership—especially for social overhead industries like public utilities and transportation. For other industries, such as securities trading, regulation permitted the continuance of an essential element of the capitalist framework that had grown so corrupt and repugnant that it could no longer perform its function of channeling investment capital into enterprise. This too was legitimization.

So was the regulation of price discrimination in the utility and transportation industries, where the nature of the business virtually mandated different prices for different classes of customers or commodities. Without an authoritative public agency overseeing such discriminatory prices, they lacked legitimacy, as the political history of the railroad and electric utility industries shows so well.

In surveying the functional diversity of regulation, one is struck by the inescapability of controversy as the one constant in the regulatory experience. Most of the functions assigned to commissions had to be performed by some institution. But whatever agency accepted the tasks also accepted the intrinsic controversy that had made the tasks necessary in the first place. In this respect the issues common to regulatory agencies can be finally settled only when the American electorate comes to consensus on such matters as the efficacy of competition, the desirability of interindustrial harmony, and the overall worth of industrial and finance capitalism.

BIBLIOGRAPHY

Lee Benson, *Merchants, Farmers, and Railroads: Railroad Regulation and New York Politics, 1850–1887* (Cambridge, Mass., 1955), is a pioneering work that shows the complex struggle for national regulation as an intergroup conflict among different economic interests. Marver H. Bernstein, *Regulating Business by Independent Commission* (Princeton, 1955), is a synthesis of criticism against the commission form by a political scientist. Stanley P. Caine, *The Myth of a Progressive Reform: Railroad Regulation in Wisconsin 1903–1910* (Madison, Wis., 1970), argues that the industry captured even a model commission almost at the outset. Eli Winston Clemens, *Economics and Public Utilities* (New York, 1950), though dated, is an outstanding textbook, written from the institutionalist viewpoint. Robert E. Cushman, *The Independent Regulatory Commissions* (New York, 1941), is a prescriptive quasi history of exceptional breadth and of substantial scholarly influence. Henry J. Friendly, *The Federal Administrative Agencies: The Need for Better Definition of Standards* (Cambridge, Mass., 1962), presents a call for careful reform, written by a federal judge.

REGULATORY AGENCIES

E. Pendleton Herring, *Public Administration and the Public Interest* (New York, 1936), gives a shrewd, witty analysis by a political scientist. Alfred E. Kahn, *The Economics of Regulation*, 2 vols. (New York, 1970–1971), is the most thoughtful, and most difficult, of the textbooks. Louis M. Kohlmeier, Jr., *The Regulators: Watchdog Agencies and the Public Interest* (New York, 1969), presents a journalist's angry analysis of the failures of regulation. Gabriel Kolko, *The Triumph of Conservatism: A Reinterpretation of American History, 1900–1916* (New York, 1963), argues that regulators and politicians were the puppets of business; and *Railroads and Regulation, 1877–1916* (Princeton, 1965), a companion piece to the preceding item, goes into detail for one industry. James M. Landis, *The Administrative Process* (New Haven, 1938), presents a brilliant rationale for the proliferation of regulatory agencies. Paul W. MacAvoy, ed., *The Crisis of the Regulatory Commissions* (New York, 1970), is an anthology of articles and excerpts from books, generally critical of regulation on the ground of economic inefficiency. Thomas K. McCraw, "Regulation in America: A Review Article," in *Business History Review*, 49 (1975), analyzes the scholarly literature in history, economics, political science, and law.

Albro Martin, *Enterprise Denied: Origins of the Decline of American Railroads, 1897–1917* (New York, 1971), argues that the ICC infringed on the prerogatives of rail management, with disastrous results; and "The Troubled Subject of Railroad Regulation in the Gilded Age—a Reappraisal," in *Journal of American History*, 61 (September 1974), clarifies one of the most controversial periods in the historiography of regulation. George H. Miller, *Railroads and the Granger Laws* (Madison, Wis., 1971), is a model study that emphasizes the interaction of law and economics. National Association of Regulatory Utility Commissioners, *Annual Report on Utility and Carrier Regulation* (Washington, D.C., 1975, et seq.), is a compendium of information on the state commissions, prepared by their trade association.

Michael E. Parrish, *Securities Regulation and the New Deal* (New Haven, 1970), studies the origins of the SEC and its early history. Charles F. Phillips, Jr., *The Economics of Regulation: Theory and Practice in the Transportation and Public Utility Industries* (Homewood, Ill., 1965), is one of the best textbooks in the field. Richard A. Posner, "Natural Monopoly and Its Regulation," in *Stanford Law Review*, 21 (1969), presents an extended critical analysis, with a negative verdict; and "Theories of Economic Regulation," in *Bell Journal of Economics and Management Science*, 5 (1974), is an intelligent discussion by a lawyer under the influence of free market economics. Bernard Schwartz, *The Professor and the Commissions* (New York, 1959), gives a personal testament by a disillusioned idealist, especially rough on the FCC; and (ed.) *The Economic Regulation of Business and Industry: A Legislative History of U.S. Regulatory Agencies*, 5 vols. (New York, 1973), contains more than 3,600 pages of statutes and excerpts from hearings, reports, and debates in Congress. George J. Stigler, *The Citizen and the State: Essays on Regulation* (Chicago, 1975), is a brief against virtually all types of regulation, by a waggish "Chicago School" economist.

[*See also* ANTITRUST; BUREAUCRACY; COMMUNICATIONS; COMPETITION; ECONOMIC THOUGHT; GOVERNMENT MANAGEMENT OF THE ECONOMY; LAW AND POLITICAL INSTITUTIONS; MERGERS; ORGANIZED BUSINESS GROUPS; RISE AND EVOLUTION OF BIG BUSINESS; STATE AND LOCAL GOVERNMENTS; *and* TRANSPORTATION.]

GOVERNMENT MANAGEMENT OF THE ECONOMY

Byrd L. Jones

DURING the twentieth century the American government has increasingly accepted responsibility for managing the economy to achieve specific national goals such as price stability, business recovery, full employment, and growth. Local, state, and federal governments have responded to popular support for such public services as education, public safety, roads, recreation facilities, social security, health care, and national defense. In 1900, a nation of 76 million Americans produced goods and services valued at about $18.7 billion, mainly through unregulated private enterprise. In 1975, with an estimated population of 212 million, Americans achieved a gross national product of $1.5 trillion; and the government share had risen from 8 percent in 1900 to 36 percent. (In 1958 prices, output had increased from $76.9 billion in 1900 to $722.5 billion in 1970.) At present the public expects elected officials, with advice from economists, to define rules and regulations for private business and to set monetary and fiscal policies that will assure material plenty.

Within a context of American traditions and the Constitution, government management developed in response to conditions in an advanced industrial and urban society as interpreted by prevailing understandings of economic behavior. First, government curbed monopoly powers in order to protect competition. Second, some undesirable effects of industrial, banking, agricultural, and labor practices were remedied through public regulation. Then, in the 1930's, a worldwide depression and a new analysis of macroeconomic variables led to increasing federal responsibilities for recovery, full employment, and growth over the ensuing three decades. Throughout the twentieth century, new public responsibilities brought pressures for assuring honesty and efficiency through more open voter participation and appropriate management techniques.

The laissez-faire predilections of America had a powerful theoretical justification in the social welfare implications of a competitive equilibrium. Assuming that producers and consumers functioned with relevant knowledge, with decreasing marginal returns to producers (technically expressed as convexity of firm production possibility sets) and with competitive markets, then self-interest would allocate scarce resources to maximize the production of what people most wanted. In that case government would reasonably act only to establish a desired income distribution. But three major market failures have distorted efficiency and equity and thus opened the door to increasing government management. First, when increasing returns to scale lowered producer costs as output increased, market prices were indeterminate, thereby encouraging monopoly or a few dominant firms in an industry. Second, when benefits or costs could not be easily excluded from others in the market, so that prices did not reflect external effects on others, private decisions might ignore social costs or benefits that encouraged corrective action through public prohibitions, regulations, or subsidies. Third, uncertainties about the future discouraged private investors and encouraged public efforts to pool risks, acquire and disseminate

GOVERNMENT MANAGEMENT OF THE ECONOMY

new information, and achieve specific national goals through government management. Typically public action in the economic sector has responded to demonstrated failures of competitive markets resulting from some mixture of increasing returns to scale, external effects, and uncertainties.

Thus an expansion of the role of government in the economy required no revolutionary ideology or break with the past—as Alexander Hamilton had recognized much earlier. No special-interest group, partisan faction, or ideology dominated the legislative and executive decisions that created a mixed public and private economy resembling that of other industrial democracies. Usually the difficulties of forming majority coalitions among regional, ethnic, class, and special-interest groups caused the United States to adopt social welfare measures later than European countries did. Legislation has often lagged behind the best knowledge about conditions and possible remedies—a reflection of a preference for less government as well as of a tendency for voters to understate their own interest in tax-supported goods. Effective political leaders have devised humanitarian, incremental steps to end clear abuses of power or to plan improvements in economic conditions that affect most citizens.

THE PROGRESSIVE ERA, 1900–1916

By 1900 the United States, no longer having vast arable lands to settle, faced the future as an industrial and urban nation. Continued economic growth depended on intensified investment based on scientific and technological advances and on more efficient trade and management. Machines and motors replaced animal and human power on farms and in factories. Massive investments in transportation and communication networks lowered costs dramatically for commerce and for coordination of large enterprises. Economies of scale based on mass production and accumulations of specialized skills further encouraged concentration—steel in Pittsburgh, automobiles in Detroit, finance and advertising in New York. Small firms, facing increasing marginal costs and a struggle with others for profits that forced each to sell at the lowest price, no longer prevailed in major sectors of the American economy.

Those changes in industrial organization and power brought about a fundamental reversal in American politics. Prior to 1900 most Americans who sought a better society had emphasized ways to protect persons from undue government influence. President Andrew Jackson's farewell address had warned against "powerful interests" that would compound an "unjust and unequal system of taxation" with "extravagant schemes of internal improvements"—all to the disadvantage of "the farmer, the mechanic, and the laboring classes of society." Some fifty years later many farmers and laborers supported a Populist party platform of printing and coining additional money, nationalization of railroad and telegraph lines, an income tax, a federal mandate for an eight-hour day, and more direct democracy.

From 1900 to 1915 the major political parties, under the leadership of Theodore Roosevelt and Woodrow Wilson, adapted much of the Populist program to a middle-class reform movement. Motivated by humanitarian concerns unleashed by a social gospel of good works and armed with the moralistic outlook of the "clean government" movement, progressives in the Republican and Democratic parties sought to use government powers to improve society. Journalists, academics, and professional social workers traced the conditions affecting the working poor and many small entrepreneurs to abuses of power by others. Unsuspecting families purchased rotten beef and unsafe patent medicines. With special rebates from the railroads, Standard Oil undersold and destroyed its competitors. By trading small favors for votes, political bosses violated public trust in selling franchises for urban transit and allowing slum owners to profit at the expense of public health. On the basis of such evidence, a generation of leaders established public controls over many economic relationships.

Most directly, progressives enforced the Sherman Antitrust Act (1890) against blatant combinations in restraint of trade, regulated natural monopolies such as railroads and municipal water companies, and defined unfair competition through the Federal Trade Commission Act (1914) and the Clayton Act (1914). Less directly, they modified some consequences of competition for profits. States limited child labor, hours of work for women, and unsafe working conditions. Congress passed the Pure Food and Drug Act (1906) and the Volstead Act (1919) prohibiting manufacture for sale of alcoholic beverages. Overcrowded tenements encouraged cities to build parks. Conservation of natural resources gained many supporters. After the ratification of the Sixteenth Amendment in 1913, personal and corporate income taxes increased state and federal revenues.

The Federal Reserve Act (1913) established a central banking system. Bankers, borrowers, and most economists had recognized a need for some expansion and more flexibility of money and credit to aid farmers, avert panics, and perhaps stabilize purchasing power. Passage of a bill depended on a political solution for limiting the discretionary powers of a central bank. The act established twelve regional districts, made membership optional for state-chartered banks, required a 40 percent gold reserve for Federal Reserve notes, set minimum reserve requirements against deposits, and empowered a board appointed by the president to set rediscount rates. Although opponents charged that each new law threatened an end to free enterprise capitalism, most reforms aimed to limit, rather than to eliminate, business leadership and to encourage growth rather than to stifle it.

As economic decisions shifted to the public sphere, democratic procedures and effective management techniques gained support. Voter participation was strengthened through primaries, provisions for initiative, referendum, and recall in many states, as well as direct election of United States senators (1913) and women's suffrage (1920). Reformers asked experts in the social sciences to investigate conditions and to propose detailed remedies. They supported professional administrators for cities and executive agencies. After repeated demands for better management of federal spending, Congress in 1921 authorized the Bureau of the Budget in the Treasury, required the president to submit annual budget recommendations to Congress, and established the General Accounting Office to assist Congress in its oversight function.

David Kinley in his presidential address to the American Economic Association in December 1913, noted that laissez-faire had been "discredited both as a principle of political philosophy and a rule of conduct." Although some might favor socialism and others a legal limit on the size of organizations, most economists endorsed government efforts to establish conditions that would induce healthy competition. Wary of concentrated power in public or private hands, economists helped middle-class reformers devise specific, limited remedies for perceived problems. They responded to humane concerns for recent immigrants, black sharecroppers in the South, and women and children in sweatshops; but few social scientists anticipated direct action to eliminate poverty or to share power.

WORLD WAR I AND ITS AFTERMATH

During World War I, political leaders and economists saw an economic transformation as the American government purchased one-fourth of the national output and influenced the whole economy so as to guide production to meet war needs. In order to supply some thirty thousand different items for four million soldiers, President Woodrow Wilson raised expenditures per capita to twenty-five times their prewar amount. Despite waste, shortages, and price inflation, the war experience demonstrated that the government could effectively organize national output through emergency agencies and voluntary efforts. By packing typewriter ribbons in cardboard, for instance, manufacturers made 395 tons of steel available for higher-priority use. Government operation of the railroads transformed a shortage of one hundred thousand cars into a surplus of some three hundred thousand. Public crusades encouraged fuelless days and sales of savings bonds. Organized labor and management generally cooperated to boost production.

After the war the national progressive coalition splintered and collapsed. Leadership in the Democratic party suffered from exhaustion, an accumulation of frustrations affecting any group long in office, Wilson's illness, and the bruising defeat of the Treaty of Versailles in the Senate. Fears of industrial strife were fed by strikes, bombings, and the Bolshevik revolution in Russia. A resurgence of nativist agitation against blacks, Catholics, Jews, and "foreign" influences led to immigration restrictions and pietistic praise for rural and Protestant values and American individualism. Warren Harding successfully

GOVERNMENT MANAGEMENT OF THE ECONOMY

campaigned for the presidency by urging a "return to normalcy."

Still, progressive ideas continued to influence states and localities, notably New York State under Governor Alfred E. Smith. Many leaders in business and government had gained experience in and insight into the potential of large-scale organized efforts to meet national or private purposes. Natural and social scientists had enjoyed the patronage and prestige of national service. Charles W. Baker, a contemporary historian of the war effort, described it as a "revelation of the world's productive capacity" that he dared hope might be applied "for the benefit of mankind."

PROSPERITY IN THE 1920's

After a sharp decline in business from January 1920 to July 1921, the United States prospered during the rest of the decade. Prices were stable or slightly declining after 1923, in contrast to the fantastic inflationary spiral in Germany and Austria. England endured chronic unemployment because of high interest costs and trade restrictions to support the restoration of the prewar international exchange rate for the pound sterling, while favorable American trade balances encouraged investments both at home and abroad. Tax rates had remained high after the war and collections increased with prosperity, so that Secretary of the Treasury Andrew Mellon could reduce the national debt each year. President Calvin Coolidge both preached and practiced economy, and he approved federal tax cuts in 1924, 1926, and 1928. But state and local expenditures for public services rose from $678 million in 1919 to $1.9 billion in 1927.

At first glance, prosperity depended on entrepreneurial organization of mass production and national markets. Henry Ford and Thomas Edison were folk heroes. Introduced in 1913, Ford's moving assembly line helped cut labor input for a Model T from over twelve hours to one hour and thirty-three minutes. Paying high wages and reducing physical toil with machines, Ford nevertheless priced automobiles within reach of many working-class families. A mass market for cars meant profits for tire companies, gasoline stations, and highway engineers—as well as crowded beaches on Sunday. New products based on electricity reduced household chores, increased factory efficiency, and enhanced communications.

Large size made for efficiency when coordination and foresight replaced market uncertainties and transactions costs. Key sectors of production and distribution were dominated by large firms guided by salaried managers. Ford aimed to control the manufacture of motor vehicles from iron ore to local dealers. The Great Atlantic and Pacific Tea Company (A&P) applied standardization and mass-purchasing power to grow from 400 stores in 1912 to 15,500 in 1932. American Telephone and Telegraph projected future demand by studying population changes and business cycles. Du Pont and General Motors developed a structure for central management to plan and set priorities for the firm's middle-level management, which directed output and sales.

Through voluntary cooperation many small firms sought some of the advantages of size. Between 1919 and 1929, national trade associations grew from seven hundred to more than two thousand; and they had active support from Secretary of Commerce Herbert Hoover. With government involvement to prevent price fixing, trade associations agreed on standardization of sizes and equipment. Many contributed to development costs for inventions and innovations. Others shared information about sales and inventories in order to stabilize output.

Large firms or members of trade associations could extend their potential markets and lower costs through mass production, reduced externalities, and greater control over future costs; but sometimes they shifted those risks and a feeling of powerlessness to other sectors of the economy. Labor, seemingly content with higher wages and shorter hours, lost organizational strength and legal rights throughout the decade. A sample of 165 working-class families in Muncie, Indiana—presented in Robert and Helen Lynd's *Middletown* (1929)—revealed that two out of five had lost a month or more of employment during a nine-month period in 1924. After prospering from 1910 to 1914, farmers reacted to the low prices during the 1920's with a campaign for a federal program to support prices at parity with their earlier level. Despite national markets in many goods, regional differences persisted, especially the low incomes and limited industrial base of the South.

GOVERNMENT MANAGEMENT OF THE ECONOMY

Although progressive reforms had interfered with private decision making and had established new ground rules for competition, the United States basically relied on business guided by advanced techniques for large-scale organizations to achieve fair competition, efficiency, and growth. According to the Committee on Recent Economic Changes, "the distinctive character of the years from 1922 to 1929 owes less to fundamental change than to intensified activity" that reflected a "balance between the economic forces." A term commonly applied to the 1920's, "balance" indicated an awareness of the adjustments accompanying economic development, but it offered little guidance for public policies. Despite important advances in the use of index numbers and the comprehensive series of indicators of business cycles developed by Wesley C. Mitchell and the National Bureau of Economic Research, economists had no definite answer to the question of whether conditions were better or worse. Not until 1934 would Simon Kuznets and others publish current national income figures, which served as a useful measure for social welfare.

Most Americans wanted to avoid rapid inflation and periodic business depressions if actions involved only modest increases in controls and public cooperation. There were two approaches to aggregate economic change that attracted some attention from economists and public officials. Irving Fisher and other economists proposed that the government could stabilize price levels and, presumably, output through legislation to vary the quantity of money and credit. Others, under Mitchell's influence, studied business cycles with the idea of anticipating changes that led from recovery to overexpansion, a crisis, and then depression. Tentatively, the government had accepted some responsibility for stabilization during the depression of 1920–1921. Warren Harding had organized a Conference on Unemployment, which asked a committee of experts "to frame a practical program for preventing the recurrence or at least mitigating the severity of future periods of widespread unemployment."

According to Herbert Hoover's foreword to *Business Cycles and Unemployment* (1923), issued by the Committee of the President's Conference on Unemployment, slumps occurred because of "wastes, extravagance, speculation, inflation, over-expansion, and inefficiency of production developed during booms." Stabilization of output should rely on "such correct economic information as will show the signs of danger" and on more general use of that knowledge by business leaders. The report supported countercyclical action by the Federal Reserve system, dissemination of information on job openings, some unemployment insurance, and

> ... the deferment of public work and construction work of large public-service corporations to periods of depression and unemployment which, while in the nature of relief from evils already created, would tend both by their subtraction from production at the peak of the boom and addition in the valley of depression toward more even progress of business itself [Committee of the President's Conference on Unemployment 1923, p. iv].

During the stable growth and optimism that prevailed until the stock market crashed in October 1929, there seemed no immediate need to assign responsibility, authority, and guidelines to implement those recommendations.

HOOVER AND THE GREAT DEPRESSION

Expecting that panic on Wall Street would lead to bank failures and then to business declines, President Herbert Hoover proclaimed: "The fundamental business of the country, that is production and distribution of commodities, is on a sound and prosperous basis." During November and December 1929 he met with business leaders and issued reassuring statements, thereby assuming a federal role in continuing responsibility for prosperity. But he relied on local governments and voluntary cooperation among business groups to maintain crucial spending for public works, plant, and equipment. Only the federal government, through its influence over the Federal Reserve, could increase expenditures as tax revenues decreased.

Unevenly but persistently throughout 1930 the economy weakened. Railroad-car loadings, current sales, inventory estimates, and bank loans declined. Construction activity and heavy-equipment manufacturing collapsed. Mason jars for home canning sold briskly. Wholesale prices dropped, according to the Bureau of Labor Statistics index (1926 = 100), from 91.9 in October 1929 to 71.6 in March 1932, and then drifted lower over the following year to 66.5. The gross national product fell from $203.6 billion in 1929 to $141.5 billion in 1933 (1958 prices) or $103.1 billion to $55.6 billion in current prices. Although some rural banks failed, and in December 1930 the Bank of the United States in New York City closed its doors, most banks struggled to maintain liquidity by reducing their loans. International credit also grew volatile as the depression became worldwide, and in September 1931 England abandoned a fixed exchange rate with gold.

Viewing depression as an unbalanced condition resulting from previous excesses, economists and economic leaders in the administration waited for business liquidations to run their course. But depression forces continued to spread. Mitchell's view that business cycles represented cumulative processes feeding on each other seemed an apt description. Business had enjoyed high profits, expansion, and rosy expectations, and then shared losses, contraction, and pessimism. Clearly the downturn should be halted, but how? The only advice that economists generally supported was a futile petition against the Hawley-Smoot bill (1930), which raised tariffs in violation of their faith in free trade.

During 1931 and 1932 some economists and business leaders supported positive recovery measures. Many Americans were attracted to some form of planning, usually through industrial groups resembling trade associations with power to enforce prices and output decisions. Others stressed monetary expansion because the increased burden of a fixed debt during rapid deflation caused many business failures. A few urged relief and public-works expenditures, in the belief that such programs would prime the pump for recovery. Lacking an accepted measure of economic decline and an analytic framework for estimating the size of an effective program, most economists had little advice to offer.

By 1932 recovery of the American economy had become a tremendous undertaking. Gross private investment of some $14 billion was needed for reasonably full employment, leaving a shortfall of $4 billion in 1930, $8.6 billion in 1931, and some $13 billion in 1932. If federal deficits were to close that gap, expenditures would have to increase on a scale similar to the 1917 and 1918 war budgets. Instead, in 1930 the federal expenditures of $3.4 billion involved civilian purchases of goods and services of some $1.6 billion. Few engineers and planners dreamed of public-works programs costing more than $500 million a month. Governments lacked experience in planning and administering such massive programs. Likewise, federal relief seemed more abhorrent than deficits. Conventional wisdom held that depressions were a helpful purgative for the economy; that budget deficits would cause inflation, while balanced budgets in Washington would set an example of virtue for citizens; and that once the government accepted responsibility for maintaining employment, the people would lapse into slothful dependency.

President Hoover continued to find evidence of prosperity just around the corner. He came increasingly to blame the rest of the world and "the malign inheritance in Europe of the Great War." Reluctantly, in 1931 he urged federal action to ease the credit crunch and during the next year Congress authorized the Reconstruction Finance Corporation, the federal land banks, the Home Loan Bank System, and the Glass-Steagall Bank Credit Act. Shoring up lending institutions did not bring recovery; and when deficits loomed larger, Hoover adopted a negative tone toward all government actions. Again and again in 1932 he advocated tax increases and lower expenditures. "Nothing is more necessary at this time," he told Congress in May, "than balancing the budget."

The presidential election campaign of 1932 revealed some of the difficulties that arise when public preferences for economic policies are expressed indirectly and ambiguously at four-year intervals. Before the nominating convention, Prohibition was viewed as the crucial issue for a Democratic candidate. During his campaign Franklin D. Roosevelt talked about both public thrift and planning, while effectively depicting Hoover as confused and heartless. Hoover focused on the economic orthodoxy of balanced budgets. Neither candidate explained the economic situation or specific proposals in a way that enabled voters to choose among goals and programs. Nevertheless, the landslide for Roosevelt marked a new factor in American politics. Thereafter responsibility for the economy's overall performance belonged to the party in power.

ROOSEVELT AND THE NEW DEAL

The dominant theme of Roosevelt's campaign and his first administration was confidence that social and economic problems were soluble within the context of democratic and free-enterprise institutions. He applied his political skills, avoided clear-cut choices, and learned from experience. His goals were direct, humanitarian, and commonsensical. As he noted after fifteen months in office, he sought three related aims: first, relief, because democracy could not let people starve in an economy capable of producing material plenty; second, recovery, because depression destroyed the fabric of society; and third,

> ... reform and reconstruction—reform because much of our trouble today and in the past few years has been due to a lack of understanding of the elementary principles of justice and fairness by those in whom leadership in business and finance was placed—reconstruction because new conditions in our economic life as well as old but neglected conditions had to be corrected [Fireside Chat, 28 June 1934].

Acting as a broker among interest groups, Roosevelt created political conditions that ended a legislative stalemate. Something for almost everyone helped dissolve the tendency for conservative forces to combine indifference with class and regional conflicts to defeat positive legislation. Successful business leaders, their organizations, and their political allies lost power and credibility. Their rivals—other business and commercial interests, farmers, laborers, white-collar employees, the poor, the unemployed, ethnic minorities, and black Americans—welcomed most changes and voted in substantial numbers for New Deal candidates. Roosevelt called on many experts for ideas, propaganda, and an aura of scientific objectivity.

Federal relief became a big enterprise during the 1930's. In December 1934 roughly 20 million Americans received some form of public assistance. The Civil Works Administration had about 4 million persons on its rolls in February of that year. During the 1930's the Civilian Conservation Corps employed about 1.5 million young men. Between 1935 and 1941 the WPA (Works Progress Administration to 1939, thereafter Works Projects Administration) funded some eight million jobs. The parks, roads, defense installations, paintings, drama, historical research, college educations, millions of trees, and a host of other projects—all supported by relief programs—constitute a rich legacy.

Although Roosevelt tolerated deficits for humanitarian relief expenditures, and thus contributed to business recovery, those expenditures fell far short of compensating for the decline in personal consumption. Under the Social Security Act (1935) the federal government undertook a permanent role in maintaining incomes through old-age and survivors' pensions, federal support for handicapped persons unable to work, and a state-administered system of unemployment insurance. But by levying taxes before benefits were paid, the social security system impeded recovery after 1936. Subsequently the largely fixed program of social security taxes, reserves, and payments has stabilized federal fiscal impacts so that only unemployment benefits have had significant countercyclical effects.

The recovery effort of the New Deal focused on four programs, all passed in 1933—a sharp increase in federal support for credit, largely through the established Reconstruction Finance Corporation; the Public Works Administration (PWA); the Agricultural Adjustment Administration (AAA); and the National Recovery Administration (NRA). Each extended in scope, funds, and power earlier attempts by the Hoover administration, and each included characteristic reform elements. Under the New Deal the federal government vigorously used its borrowing capacity to augment private credits. Jesse Jones, chairman of the Reconstruction Finance Corporation, disbursed more than $10 billion prior to 1938, almost all in loans that were eventually repaid. New Deal programs also supported mortgages on farms and homes, while limiting the power of banks to foreclose. After 1933 credit was available for business expansion but had few takers.

Under Harold Ickes the PWA was concerned more with engineering soundness and freedom

GOVERNMENT MANAGEMENT OF THE ECONOMY

from graft than with augmenting recovery. Eventually the dams, schools, courthouses, hospitals, and other public works increased employment, government purchases, and national resources. The National Planning Board of the PWA and its successors encouraged state and regional plans for land use, river basin control and development, urban reconstruction, and public power. During the next decade experts under the directions set by Frederic A. Delano, Charles E. Merriam, and Wesley C. Mitchell produced a series of prescient studies of national needs and resources to be used in establishing priorities for public-works projects—indicating potentially valuable projects for public investment.

Public works exemplified a persistent problem in planning and implementing government management of the economy through expenditures. Congress preferred projects that were widely distributed, noncompetitive with private firms, subject to local governmental control, and capable of completion before the next election. Wise investment of public funds was difficult because large-scale works required forethought about economic developments, a weighing of external effects and tax burdens, and forceful political leadership to assure support from a variety of public and personal interests.

Major public works could reshape the economic environment and stimulate major private investments. Such plans often required a separate, quasi-independent corporation under forceful leaders who could visualize and implement changes for a whole region. For instance, the Tennessee Valley Authority under Arthur Morgan and David Lilienthal tamed a river for transportation, electric power, and better land use. Given the area's poverty and history of flooding, the valley's people participated with the leadership of the TVA to devise comprehensive plans for regional development. In contrast, Robert Moses in New York State relied on his reputation for accomplishment and on federal financial support during the 1930's for massive projects. But he built highways and bridges in preference to mass transit, leaving New York City with a colossal transportation problem based on low-density suburbs.

In agriculture Roosevelt expanded earlier proposals to restore and maintain parity prices by using an ingenious series of local and national votes to limit acreage in return for price supports. While proclaiming the virtues of competition and independence, major farm producers got production controls and price supports in an effort to balance, over several years, output and desired demand. Farmers had political power because of their geographic distribution, their independence in voting, their positive image among the American public, the relatively small cost of an effective program, and effective lobbying organizations.

Under Secretary of Agriculture Henry A. Wallace and his staff, the government helped transform agriculture into a prosperous, commercial enterprise with high productivity by extending crop loans to compensate for the vagaries of nature. Because crop loans or supports were initially financed by a tax on processors, the fiscal effect of the agricultural program contributed little to recovery. Improved international trade and general price rises raised incomes for farmers and quieted threats of a revolt against public authority. Soil conservation was encouraged by purchases of marginal lands, assistance in resettlement, payments for cover crops, flood control, and planting shelter belts of trees to protect against dust bowl conditions. Credit became easier, rural electric lines were subsidized, and better methods of farming were encouraged. The process was uneven—small farmers from Oklahoma were displaced by tractors, and many southern sharecroppers received no acreage allotments for cotton—but consistent with a long-term trend away from the family farm as an American way of life.

The most ambitious and confusing recovery program of the New Deal was the NRA. By 1933 most Americans had recognized that losses in one sector of industry led to layoffs, defaults, and price cutting, which transmitted economic problems to other sectors. Voluntary cooperation had failed, but perhaps industrial codes that included reemployment, maximum hours, minimum wages, and "fair" prices could encourage firms to expand production together. The presumed increases in wages, rents, and profits earned would provide funds to purchase the additional output—thus continuing the circulation of money at a higher level of employment. In retrospect no idea has seemed more preposterous—although no recovery program of the New Deal had more support from hardheaded business leaders.

GOVERNMENT MANAGEMENT OF THE ECONOMY

NRA director Hugh Johnson aimed at "perfect balance among all producing segments—agriculture, capital, industry, workers in industry, the services, and the segment engaged in transportation and distribution." Basically the NRA codes depended on political negotiations. Powerful individuals such as Henry Ford or John L. Lewis of the United Mine Workers could bargain hard, while consumers had no clear voice. Oligopolistic industries and strong unions could reach agreement more readily than competitive firms and unorganized workers could. Although economists in government service gathered data and sought to assess productivity of labor and fair prices, the task of national industrial planning was beyond their technical capacity. As recovery proceeded, managers chafed at any requests for information or cooperation in setting prices.

Nevertheless, many NRA codes did improve industrial conditions. Child labor and sweatshop conditions were generally eliminated. Standardization of parts and production continued. Section 7(a) of the National Industrial Recovery Act encouraged labor organizations and established precedents for the National Labor Relations Act (1935). Consumer interests in product safety and in low prices were recognized. In sum, NRA provided a trial for industrial planning to avoid destructive competition during a depression, but it could not cope with the complexity of coordinating and balancing interests during a period of recovery and growth.

For four years the New Deal sought a panacea for the depression through money and banking reform. Prices had declined unevenly, thereby distorting economic relationships and leading to a higher rate of unemployment. Roosevelt began his first term with a national banking crisis and a bank holiday. Throughout 1933 he spoke of inflation or reflation and of stabilizing the purchasing power of the dollar. He called in gold as a circulating currency, purchased more silver, talked about scrip or greenbacks, and established an insurance program for bank deposits. He spoke some of the harshest words about bankers since Andrew Jackson, and encouraged Congress to regulate and limit their activities. He appointed Marriner Eccles, a Utah banker who favored active government spending for recovery, to the Federal Reserve Board. After having substantially increased the monetary gold supply, the president fixed a price of $35 per ounce and quietly agreed to de facto stabilization with England and France in the Tripartite Agreement of 1936.

Out of the tangle of events that began in crisis and aroused heated debate, there emerged reasonable and necessary reforms of money and banking. By insuring deposits and extending the power of the Federal Reserve Board, the checking-account base for most transactions was made both more secure and more manageable. Awkward and piecemeal though they were, the decisions about gold and silver not only increased the effective reserves of precious metals but also indicated the determination to free domestic financial policies from international constraints. The relative weakness of monetary expansion measures to stimulate recovery and the small acceleration effect of rising prices convinced many observers during the next three decades not to rely on monetary means for managing the economy.

By the end of Roosevelt's first term, the relationship of government and the economy had been fundamentally altered. Expert staffs, experienced administrators, more accurate statistics, proven techniques for delegation and planning, and precedents for large-scale public works had increased the federal capability for action. By striving for recovery and testing various means, the New Deal had demonstrated weaknesses in monetary manipulations, in NRA-type industrial planning, in the possibilities for rapid expansion of public works, and in the impetus for recovery from relief expenditures. Tax reforms pushed by Secretary of the Treasury Henry Morgenthau and passed by Congress had made taxes more progressive, thereby shifting the potential burden of government programs to those more able to pay. By bringing new groups into a political coalition, the New Deal managed the economy so that it responded to new and less-business-dominated constituencies than would have been true a decade earlier.

THE KEYNESIAN REVOLUTION IN AMERICA

In September 1937, after four years of recovery, the American economy again collapsed. The recession cast doubt on capitalism and on government efforts to make competition and cooperation workable in a mixed economy. Despite low interest rates and high unemployment, industrial output plummeted 30 percent in eight months—a record rate of fall. Although economic indicators bottomed out well above their nadirs of 1932–1933 and recovered to their 1937 levels during 1939, the recession revealed important weaknesses in ad hoc recovery programs. After four years of action, many New Dealers had recalled their promises of a balanced budget, the temporary status of emergency programs, and their expectation that private enterprise, properly regulated, might stand on its own.

Public and official reaction during 1938 differed markedly from that of 1930. In January, Marriner Eccles urged a billion-dollar spending program, with the budget to be balanced "out of increased national income" during later business expansion. In April, Roosevelt asked Congress for additional appropriations of more than $2.6 billion. Expanded federal programs, together with growing defense preparations in 1939 and 1940, produced a recovery lasting into the war period, when massive deficits together with the rapid buildup of military personnel brought full employment without destroying federal credit. Throughout the expansion a growing band of economists, identified as Keynesians, supported deficit spending with an analysis of why federal management of the economy required countercyclical fiscal policies of appropriate size and timing.

Earlier economic analyses and empirical studies had suggested no positive or politically palatable means of recovery, although several economists had recommended public works and easing of credit to aid expansion. In England, John Maynard Keynes, a brilliant, iconoclastic student of Alfred Marshall, set out to restore "the practical influence of economic theory" by writing *The General Theory of Employment, Interest, and Money* (1936). Attacking the classical reasoning revealed in Jean-Baptiste Say's law that supply created its own demand—which precluded a possibility of general surpluses or excess capacity—Keynes constructed a new paradigm for considering, analyzing, and testing macroeconomic variables. In succeeding, he destroyed for his followers many of the landmarks of Marshallian economics. No longer would the highest social purpose be to maintain a competitive economy and the major empirical work be to separate industries according to increasing or decreasing returns to scale. Rather, economists would aim to maintain full employment and would investigate the determinants of aggregate demand—the consumption function, investment decisions, and various lags under dynamic conditions.

During the next twenty-five years American Keynesians produced a flood of books, articles, memos, statistical studies, and sophisticated computer models that described and analyzed the major components of changes in aggregate income over the periods of business cycles. Studies confirmed the dependent relationship of changes in consumption to changes in income. Private investment decisions, based on expectations of future earnings, shifted rapidly, without much dependence on interest rates. By simplifying the Keynesian insight that national income equaled consumption as a function of income plus investment plus government expenditures, economists could show that changes in investment or government expenditures or the relation of savings to income had a multiple impact on national income. Empirical studies supported the explanatory power of the model, which could be extended to cover growth models and applied to immediate issues of public policy.

Thus the Keynesian income-determination model—as typically presented—established guidelines for an active government policy to stabilize the private sector and assure full use of labor and capital over the long run. When aggregate demand fell short of full employment (usually because of a decline in net investment), additional federal expenditures should compensate. Deficit spending would cause a multiple expansion of national income through a chain of induced increases in private consumption. Government transfer payments for relief or income maintenance, tax cuts, or increased expenditures matched by receipts would have somewhat less powerful expansionary effects. Likewise, federal surpluses of the appropriate size could curb demand in excess of full capacity and thereby control inflation.

In America the Keynesian analysis quickly influenced policy and became embroiled in political controversies. By the fall of 1938, liberal economists associated with Harvard and Tufts universities had applied Keynesian reasoning in support of New Deal spending programs. In a seminar on fiscal policy at Harvard, Alvin Hansen fostered a creative interchange of ideas between academics and public officials. Under Executive Order 8248 (1939) Roosevelt had an official White House staff for the first time; it included Lauchlin Currie, a liberal economist who had worked with Eccles and developed many insights for monetary and fiscal controls. Keynesians established several centers of strength in Washington and effective linkages with universities and research groups such as the National Planning Association and, later, the Brookings Institution. It was a larger but intellectually more cohesive "brain trust" than had first advised Roosevelt, and eventually it dominated policy discussions.

In May 1939, Alvin Hansen, with supporting evidence from Lauchlin Currie, presented the Keynesian case to the Temporary National Economic Committee hearings on savings and investment (1940). In a letter to Senator Joseph O'Mahoney, Roosevelt had asked why "the dollars which the American people save each year are not finding their way back into productive enterprise in sufficient volume to keep our economic machine turning over at a rate required to bring about full employment." Hansen offered a lucid interpretation of consumption and investment over time that both explicated the depression and indicated some strategies for recovery. Income depended on consumption expenditures or capital investments, and "in a high saving, high investment economy such as ours, you cannot get full employment without large capital outlays, whether private or public." A mature economy required less net private investment. Thus, "A less rapidly expanding economy, in order to achieve full employment of its resources, will probably need to rely more largely in the future than in the past (1) on public investment as a supplement to private investment; and (2) on community consumption expenditures as a supplemental to private consumption expenditures" (Temporary National Economic Committee, *Investigation of Concentration of Economic Power*, no. 9 [Washington, D.C., 1940], pp. 3495–3518, 3538–3559, 3837–3859).

Through their analysis of long-run problems of secular stagnation in a mature economy, Keynesians questioned both the virtues of thrift and the established power relationships in American society. Government programs such as social security and progressive taxes enhanced social equality while tending to lower the national propensity to save. A lower rate of thrift meant less private investment required to offset those savings at full employment and a higher multiplier so that federal fiscal policies would be more effective. In light of the Keynesian analysis, large business firms posed a problem aside from their influence on prices because of their sluggish response to investment opportunities. If the economy did not usually perform adequately, then public officials would have to define specific goals in order to foster a more certain environment for both investment and the pursuit of happiness.

Keynesian economists opened major possibilities for government management of the economy through their analyses of depressions, inflations, and the potential for federal fiscal policies. They saw the weaknesses of pump-priming as a guideline for analysis and policy. They convinced some business leaders to accept countercyclical deficits, and they encouraged the New Deal to defend its spending programs on economic as well as humanitarian grounds. Economists had a model for examining relationships between the public and private sectors. In the future, policy developments need not depend on the costly lessons of another great depression. Keynesians offered a chance to plan ahead, to forecast changes in national income, and to devise specific remedies to effect those results.

GOVERNMENT PLANNING DURING WORLD WAR II

The three years before Pearl Harbor tested the versatility and usefulness of Keynesian macroeconomic analysis in determining full capacity and desired rates of saving. Early in 1940, Secretary of Commerce Harry Hopkins sent President Roosevelt an outline of fiscal policies for defense recommended by economists in his department. After deficit spending brought recovery, they wrote, "The task of fiscal policy is two fold: (1) to maintain full employment; (2) to secure as rapidly as possible that orientation of production which our defense demands." Estimating that twelve million additional workers were employable, and that the labor force would grow by three million a year, the Commerce Department economists believed that output for both defense and civilian needs could increase dramatically without danger of inflation. Keynesians in the administration successfully argued against higher taxes and price controls or rationing during this early stage of preparedness.

Detailed forecasts for national income and possible expenditures followed from a Keynesian analysis. By December 1940, Lauchlin Currie predicted in a letter to Roosevelt "that reasonably full utilization of our labor forces in 1943 would yield us a national income, with no advance in prices, of between $105 and $110 billion or from $35 to $40 billion higher than our income for 1940." During a period of rapid growth, high defense expenditures, and shortages of civilian goods, Keynesians expected an extraordinarily high rate of saving that would limit inflationary pressures. Other economists listed the military requirements for a victory program, both to encourage building the necessary plants and equipment and to detail the potential of America as the arsenal for democracy. Their work was specific and practical: how much aluminum for airframes, how much rubber for tires, how much shipping for lend-lease.

The declaration of war ended debate over the rate at which productive capacity should be expanded. Instead, economists tried to bring military orders into line with productive capacity. Only then would priorities have effect and inflation prove controllable through a pragmatic system of direct controls, rationing, higher taxes, and voluntary savings. As crucial economic decisions came to center in Washington, the debates became bureaucratic and the winners often relied on their power rather than their reasoning. But capacity limits for critical material such as steel were relatively fixed, and there were harsh penalties for producing an ineffective mix of guns and supplies for the fighting forces. When the industry study of Simon Kuznets supported the estimates of capacity based on national income potential, the War Department ordered a cutback on some contracts and extended some delivery dates.

Output in 1942 and 1943 confirmed the basic Keynesian contention, not because extraordinary deficits brought full employment and higher prices (which most Americans had expected) but because they had accurately forecast total capacity. Under Leon Henderson and Chester Bowles, the Office of Price Administration demonstrated that the economy could encourage greater production by allowing considerable excess demand without intolerable price increases. A system of priorities and subsidies, wage and price controls, and rationing could control prices and stimulate output of military goods. Not all economists were right or estimated magnitudes in a helpful fashion, but the Keynesian analysis provided a basis for predicting the national output. With forecasts, economists could learn from their mistakes.

During the war some economists applied a national income analysis to estimate postwar demand. First the Post-War Agenda Section of the National Resources Planning Board collected such studies and later the Fiscal Analysis Division of the Bureau of the Budget gathered information and responses to reconversion. Much depended on the assumptions about the length of fighting after victory in Europe and the continuation of price controls. In general, Keynesians believed that the immediate postwar months would see a continuation of excess demand. Restarting production of civilian goods would not keep pace with pent-up demand from the partly involuntary savings amassed during the war. Some economists argued for encouraging civilian production—particularly by small businesses—as soon as victory in Europe freed vital materials. Major firms and military leaders argued against any distractions from the war against Japan, in spite of the need to shift some $74 billion in military expenditures and some ten million members of the armed services into private production. Undoubtedly, rebuilding civilian output before peace would have helped maintain employment, smooth the transition, and reduce inflationary pressures as wartime savings sought an outlet.

Reconversion tested economists' skills in estimating how large the national income would have to be after the war in order to maintain full employment. In general, economists agreed, as they had after World War I, that the war had revealed a large potential. For instance, many economists in government service estimated that real per capita income at full employment in 1950 would be half again as high as in 1929, with a probability of a high rate of saving; hence, large investments, large government programs, or a series of reforms aimed at increasing the propensity to consume would be necessary. Otherwise, there would again be widespread unemployment. Other estimates reached similar conclusions, which were conservative about the potential growth but erred about the likelihood of a postwar depression.

In order to plan for a peacetime economy, government officials and other experts needed a clearer sense of national goals. Receiving little presidential leadership, preoccupied with critical tasks of managing the economy for war, and uncertain about the shape of international concerns in the future, economists could not presume that New Deal reforms would last. Recovery and military needs had been relatively clear-cut aims that left room for disagreements on means within a professional rather than a political context. Perhaps victory in World War II would lead to a rejection of liberal agendas and a depression, as had occurred in 1919–1920.

Roosevelt tentatively adopted the National Resources Planning Board list of economic rights as a start toward setting postwar goals. In his State of the Union message of January 1944, he proclaimed "a second Bill of Rights under which a new basis of security and prosperity can be established for all—regardless of station, race or creed." He included the rights to work, adequate food, shelter, medical care, and a good education. Farmers had a right to "a decent living"; entrepreneurs had a right "to trade in an atmosphere of freedom from unfair competition." Everyone should be protected from "the economic fears of old age, sickness, accident and unemployment." Later, in a campaign address, he set a goal of full employment (defined as sixty million jobs). Before that promise could be kept, Roosevelt had died. Harry Truman never developed the political power to implement a liberal program of economic rights.

In the meantime, the war had drastically, and to a degree that is scarcely recognized, changed the nature of fiscal policies in the federal government for the next twenty years. Both corporate and personal income taxes had been increased sharply and progressively. According to the consolidated cash budget, federal revenues increased from $6.8 billion in 1940 to $15.1 billion in 1942, to $47.8 billion in 1944; and in the postwar years they reached a low of $40.9 billion in 1950. Tax cuts in the postwar years were restored during the Korean War and were later reduced slightly until 1964. As a result, the federal government had a tax system that generated enormous resources, and revenues increased at a faster rate than growth of the national product.

Large federal budgets meant that unintended consequences of taxes or social security transfers or aid programs had substantial repercussions on the economy. As Keynesians noted, a balanced budget of sufficient size would have significant expansionary effects. Under pressure of emergency programs, first for relief and recovery and then for victory, the New Deal had devised a vast increase in executive powers, established a White House staff, and initiated forward planning for the economy. Those changes, as well as the tremendous fiscal impacts, were tolerated as ad hoc, emergency efforts but were not welcomed by the public or established as a permanent part of the government. Under the constitutional system Congress would have to help set goals for a peacetime economy and set down some procedures to achieve those goals.

THE EMPLOYMENT ACT OF 1946

Initially the full-employment bill introduced by Sen. James Murray had mandated a simple forecast and Keynesian fiscal program to achieve full employment. In successive stages of drafting, the bill lost its precision as a guide for fiscal policy but chartered a flexible approach to economic management in government. In its final version the Employment Act of 1946 declared:

> ... that it is the continuing policy and responsibility of the Federal Government to use all practicable means consistent with its needs and obligations and other essential considerations of national policy with the assistance and cooperation of industry, agriculture, labor, and state and local governments, to coordinate and utilize all its plans, functions, and resources for the purpose of creating and maintaining, in a manner calculated to foster and promote free competitive enterprise and the general welfare, conditions under which there will be afforded useful employment for those able, willing, and seeking to work, and to promote maximum employment, production, and purchasing power.

GOVERNMENT MANAGEMENT OF THE ECONOMY

Belatedly sanctioning the increased role of government in the economy, the Employment Act achieved three major shifts of lasting importance. First, responsibility for economic policies was placed with the federal government, on the president with advice from Congress. Second, the president had to designate the Council of Economic Advisers and report to Congress on the economy; Congress also had to select the Joint Committee on the Economic Report (later the Joint Economic Committee) to consider the president's economic report. These requirements focused responsibility for management, brought professional economists onto both congressional staffs and the president's staff, and provided for regular attention to the overall direction of the national economy. Third, the history of the Employment Act and the pressure of regular reports on goals that stressed a duty "to promote maximum employment, production, and purchasing power" meant that a macroeconomic analysis of full employment was unavoidable. As Leon Keyserling has reiterated, the vague phrases of the act "met the need for a plenary planning statute."

The implementation of the Employment Act exemplified the uneasy relationships between liberals and President Truman. He supported the bill and the goal of full employment without inflation, but he was uncomfortable with intellectual advisers, ideological liberals, and planners. Truman reacted against power grabs by others, whether by North Korea or the steel companies. Politically, he relied on liberals in Congress to support his programs and to resist the dismantling of major parts of the New Deal while his major efforts were devoted to foreign policy developments.

As first head of the Council of Economic Advisers appointed by Truman, Edwin Nourse stressed the nonpartisan role of the council in balancing interests among economic forces without resorting to planned deficits. Nourse encouraged the staff to gather data and conduct useful studies about full potential economic growth. He edited solid, unexciting reports for the president and avoided partisan controversies and the radical implications of Keyserling's emphasis on growth. After Nourse resigned, Keyserling strove as chairman to gain support for a vision of low interest rates, increasing productive capacity, and rapid growth as a cure for both inflation and unemployment.

As long as federal taxes remained high in the postwar era, the key debate occurred between those who looked first to increased public expenditures during periods of less than full employment and those who emphasized the countercyclical effects of tax revenues. According to Beardsley Ruml and the Committee for Economic Development, ideal tax rates should "balance our national budget when we have a satisfactory high level of employment and production," and should accept deficits due to lower tax receipts when business declined. For those who favored government management of the economy, the agenda of public needs at home and abroad supported the case for increasing public spending. Aid to Greece and Turkey, the Marshall Plan, and the Korean conflict created an ongoing condition of high expenditures that could not be varied for countercyclical purposes. Furthermore, many New Deal programs continued and expanded, thus achieving a high level of public investment and consumption, as Hansen and Currie had earlier recommended. Yet liberals urged higher spending for programs such as medical insurance, higher income maintenance, and urban renewal.

Truman's political weaknesses in 1948 and after 1950 limited his ability to define issues and move programs through a Congress dominated by a conservative coalition of Republicans and southern Democrats. Liberals sought a more expansive fiscal policy—medical care, flood control, public housing, hydroelectric power, peaceful uses of atomic power, foreign aid for economic development, expanded social security coverage, and higher rates of employment—though they were constrained by fears of inflation, continuing demands for defense, and opposition to high taxes and bureaucratic red tape. Perhaps the liberal agenda lacked the appeal of personal consumption during the 1950's, as Americans bought houses, cars, television sets, dishwashers, recreation equipment, and hundreds of gadgets—often paying on the installment plan.

THE EISENHOWER YEARS

The record of economic management during Dwight Eisenhower's eight years in the White

House indicates both the general acceptance of Keynesian fiscal analysis and the limitations of discretionary policy changes. Eisenhower arranged a cease-fire in Korea, reduced and stretched out defense orders, ended price and wage controls, and announced his intention to balance the budget and control inflation. At the same time, he acknowledged a federal responsibility for reasonably full employment and he would tolerate deficits for that purpose. He appointed Arthur Burns to head the Council of Economic Advisers. Neither a liberal nor an anti-Keynesian, Burns had worked with Wesley C. Mitchell and devoted his career to the study of business cycles.

When inflationary pressures from the Korean conflict gave way to a recession, Eisenhower considered using active spending programs; but before conditions justified "stirring or meddling," a recovery started in late 1954. During fiscal 1956 and 1957, his administration showed small surpluses in the new unified budget, the unexpected result of inflation, which pushed up revenues. During 1957 economic growth again faltered, although prices continued to rise. Since inflation caused by excess demand could be limited by tight credit, the declining output and growing unemployment triggered no precipitate action. In February 1958, Eisenhower asked Congress for modest increases in expenditures for an interstate highway system, for modernizing post offices, and for accelerating weapons procurement. After midyear, growth resumed, though it was insufficient to achieve full employment.

While in office, Eisenhower developed a conservative version of the public-policy implications of Keynesian macroeconomics. Growth was central—and it depended primarily on business management, which in turn reflected confidence in the future of free enterprise. With advice from Raymond Saulnier, who chaired the Council of Economic Advisers during Eisenhower's second term, and Secretary of the Treasury Robert Anderson, Eisenhower toughened his antiinflationary preachments. He urged cooperative efforts among government, labor, and business to limit price increases for their common good. Responding to Republican orthodoxy and the often-repeated promise of balanced budgets, Eisenhower strove for surpluses in his last two budgets—despite sluggish growth.

During the postwar period, tax rates and mandated programs produced an approximation of countercyclical fiscal policies. In each of the four recessions between 1948 and 1961, the federal share of national income accounts showed a deficit—largely as a result of an unanticipated decline in revenues from corporate taxes, excises, and personal income taxes. On the expenditure side, unemployment compensation and additional welfare payments cushioned the initial impact of a downturn. Taxes and insurance payments responded automatically to changes in business conditions without overreacting. Those same taxes and programs for economic security produced surpluses in years of high employment or rapid growth whenever there were no extraordinary military costs.

The forces that slowed the downward movement of output also impeded recovery. According to a study by Wilfred Lewis, the built-in fiscal effects have contributed more to stabilization of the mild postwar business cycles than discretionary changes have (see table 1). Although speeding up programs helped in 1958, as had a tax cut earlier, discretionary changes seem, in retrospect, to have destabilized almost as much as they stabilized. The tendency for surpluses to appear with recovery slowed growth and contributed to its sluggish pattern, especially noticeable in the late 1950's.

Prior to 1951 the Federal Reserve Board had supported the interest of the Treasury in stable bond prices and low charges on the debt, which had burgeoned during World War II. Afterward the Federal Reserve bought and sold government bonds in the open market and set rediscount rates so as to stabilize the economy by providing easier credit during declines and raising interest costs to curb inflation. Most economists stressed fiscal impacts on aggregate growth rather than monetary factors. Moreover, those economists who stressed the quantity of money did not approve of the timing or size of shifts in monetary stocks. Economist Milton Friedman, the leading advocate of the importance of money in stabilizing output, favored a fixed growth of the quantity of money with no discretion. Friedman opposed the step-by-step, variable-policy options posture that had prevailed, and continues to prevail, in the government management of the economy.

GOVERNMENT MANAGEMENT OF THE ECONOMY

TABLE 1
Comparison of Built-in Fiscal Stabilizers with Discretionary Policies in Postwar Recessions and Recoveries

Period	Built-in Component	Discretionary Component	Total
		Recession	
1948:4–1949:2	−3.7	−4.0	−7.7
1953:2–1954:2	−6.6	8.2	1.6
1957:3–1958:1	−8.7	−2.0	−10.7
1960:2–1961:1	−6.8	−3.2	−10.0
		Recovery	
1949:2–1950:2	6.1	6.1	12.2
1954:2–1955:2	10.4	−1.5	8.9
1958:1–1959:2	17.4	−8.8	8.6
1961	10.8	−7.4	3.4

Source: Wilfred Lewis, *Federal Fiscal Policy in the Postwar Recessions* (Washington, D.C., 1962), based on table 4 on p. 16.

THE KENNEDY-JOHNSON YEARS

During his campaign for the presidency, John F. Kennedy had promised to get the country moving again. He advocated more missiles and more conventional military capability, more private jobs, and more liberal social programs. Disliking budget deficits and concerned about his narrow electoral victory, he wanted a rapidly expanding economy that would generate revenues to support his proposals. He staffed the Council of Economic Advisers with three liberal, activist economists—Walter Heller, Kermit Gordon, and James Tobin—while continuing to call on Paul Samuelson, John Kenneth Galbraith, and others for advice. All of them shared Samuelson's belief expressed to Congress in 1956: "With proper fiscal and monetary policies, our economy can have full employment and whatever rate of capital formation and growth it wants."

During 1961 and 1962, Kennedy and his staff learned about the built-in delays of governance. Because conditions interlocked and overlapped, the president had to set priorities, marshal data and political support, and act at the opportune time in order to produce positive effects in an ever-changing political and economic situation. In addition to political and institutional barriers, Kennedy's economic advisers found considerable resistance to an active growth policy. Some people still viewed stabilization as smoothing out business cycles; others believed the problems of growth were structural and that automation was largely responsible for unemployment. Most Americans, including Kennedy himself, shared some fears of unlimited deficits and ongoing inflation.

Before the Council of Economic Advisers could gain support for growth policies, they had to establish their credibility as loyal, pragmatic advisers, reassure the business community, and clarify national goals. The council published guideposts for wage and price increases, advocated somewhat greater tolerance for inflation as a lesser problem than unemployment, and successfully supported special tax incentives for new investments. At Yale University in June 1962, President Kennedy spoke about old myths and new realities affecting the practical management of a national economy through Keynesian measures to achieve growth. In successive issues of the *Economic Report of the President* and in public testimony, the council established general acceptance for a goal of 4 percent unemployment as a reasonable measure of adequate growth.

The Council of Economic Advisers had to devise an attractive "rule of thumb" for a fiscal policy. Arthur Okun applied a sophisticated statistical analysis to show that full capacity gross national product (GNP) would grow about 3.5 percent annually. (Other estimates ranged from 2.5 percent to 4.5 percent.) Then he found that a rise in GNP of 1 percent caused a fall in unemployment of 0.33 percent. Thus, to cut unemployment from 5 percent to 4 percent in a year, real growth of 6.5 percent should be targeted. The estimated gap or forgone goods and services from unemployment was startling. According to Okun, "The United States could have produced a total of nearly $200 billion more output from 1958 to 1963, if demand had been maintained at levels consistent with a 4-percent unemployment rate" (Okun 1965, p. 22).

Those estimates brought home the "fiscal drag" of high progressive tax rates that would have produced surpluses during full employment. As Heller later noted in *New Dimensions of Political Economy,* "In a growth context, the great revenue-raising power of our Federal tax system produces a built-in average increase of $7 to $8 billion a year in federal revenue." Unless expenditures grew as rapidly (or faster, during a rapid recovery), fiscal policies would choke off growth before full employment was reached. Alternatively, there was an opportunity to cut taxes and increase federal expenditures; and from July 1960 to June 1965, some $48 billion in fiscal dividends accrued, which accounted for the $16 billion of net tax cuts and $32 billion in additional expenditures.

The clear analysis and evaluation of fiscal effects at a hypothetical full-employment level made by the Council of Economic Advisers contributed a crucial thrust for the timing, size, and distribution of the tax cut of 1964. That act cut anticipated revenues by about $11 billion, despite ongoing deficits in the unified budget accounts. A tax cut has greater popularity than an increase, and some business leaders and Secretary of the Treasury Douglas Dillon argued that it would benefit the economy primarily through enhanced incentives. Despite hundreds of compromises on tax reforms, on the timing of cuts, and on the trade-offs among beneficiaries, the tax cut could not have happened without a macroeconomic analysis of fiscal policy. When it contributed significantly to the longest uninterrupted period of growth in the twentieth century, Walter Heller could conclude that "economics has come of age in the 1960's."

Economists brought into government service a style of systematic thinking about priorities and programs to get the most from scarce resources. As fiscal policies brought rapid growth with a tolerable pace of inflation, the Council of Economic Advisers and other agencies explored population changes, internal migration, housing patterns, the effects of discrimination, education, medical care, manpower training programs, the incidence of taxes, and intergovernment relations as they affected income inequality. Economists applied refined statistical data and techniques, planned experiments, and evaluated program results. While social scientists seldom arrived at unambiguous assessments of economic developments or social welfare, they did create a growing array of indicators and guidelines for assessing the wise use of public funds.

President Lyndon B. Johnson's plans for the Great Society included a host of social programs in addition to a tax cut. While spending for national defense rose from $53.6 billion in 1964 to $80.5 billion in 1968, federal support for education and manpower development increased from $1.8 to $6.7 billion, for health and welfare increased from $26.6 to $43.5 billion, and for housing and community development outlays reached $4.0 billion. Intergovernment transfers grew both as grants in specific program categories to state or local institutions and as general revenue sharing. The progressive federal tax system avoided many inequities of local taxes. Public and private institutions have often been efficient and effective producers of public goods to meet local needs; but because neighborhoods outside the area concerned have typically shared the benefits, public agencies have tended to invest less than optimal amounts in health care, education, welfare, and recreation. Federal revenue sharing captured those external effects and averted problems from the fiscal drag without adding significantly to the bureaucracy in Washington.

In 1965, Johnson directed all major government agencies to establish a planning, programming, and budgeting system (PPBS). Program budgeting involved explicit steps for defining the objectives of an agency, considering alternatives, and identifying major problems. It allowed time for an annual cycle of review and decision, and required continuous reexamination and anticipation of future issues. PPBS asked agencies to consider probable outcomes in terms of both direct and indirect costs, and to adopt accounting procedures and reports to support the PPBS. Each year the planning staff would produce a multiyear program through such a process, and that plan would then be weighed at a higher level of administration in order to achieve overall effectiveness and coordination. This ambitious attempt to develop planning capability allowed competent staffs to raise important issues and concerns for efficiency in terms of probable outcomes and costs.

President Johnson recognized that his responsibilities for economic management exceeded his direct powers, and he sought to compensate by using professional advice and foresight. Policymaking became institutionalized on two levels. First, economic analysis and data were applied to determine policy alternatives and outcomes. Second, those alternatives were tested within a wider context of political and administrative considerations. The process began with economic forecasts prepared by staff economists from the Treasury, the Bureau of the Budget, and the Council of Economic Advisers, sometimes including the Federal Reserve Board and typically supplemented by outside experts in specific fields. The forecasters, usually at the Council of Economic Advisers, applied a formal model including both econometric equations to cover the major dynamic factors in the economy and judgmental decisions. Under various assumptions the economists predicted probable demand for goods and services in major categories and compared those estimates with the potential capacity of the economy under varying rates of growth. Any gap suggested something about anticipated unemployment or inflation as well as the size of helpful policy changes, which could then be judged in light of political considerations.

Faced with a complexity of economic analysis and data provided in a veritable stream of memorandums from his staff, Johnson did not make policy so much as oversee an organizational process for arriving at policy—while keeping final responsibility in the president's hands. Although the information and the forecasts depended on specialized knowledge and skills, the setting of public policy remained basically political. Economic policy advisers had to build coalitions among groups who differed because of their institutional viewpoints, their personal and social values, or their loyalties to others. Decisions about the national economy, including a postponement of policy changes, involved alternatives with different costs and benefits to various elements of society and with different degrees of uncertainty.

Given the costs of rapid change for producers and consumers, and the time period before benefits may accrue, the political process has some justification for its built-in delays, its redundancy of apparent vetoes, and its limitations by previous commitments and its immediate history of economic management. When retrospect has shown that actions should have been taken, the political process appears irrational. But that process has goals different from the priority setting of PPBS; it aims for a workable agreement among individuals and groups whose felt interests and needs are often incompatible. For that purpose, muddling through by quieting debates about values, by incremental changes, by allowing all groups to voice their hopes and fears, and by tolerating inefficiencies seemed helpful.

President Johnson, who had proved to be a masterful political leader during 1964–1966, lost his capacity to negotiate largely because of his commitment to escalation in Vietnam. Starting in 1965, the Council of Economic Advisers under Gardner Ackley's leadership warned that the costs of war plus domestic programs were creating inflationary pressures. They suggested increased taxes if spending could not be cut. Finally, on 3 August 1967, Johnson asked for a tax surcharge. After ten months of debate and compromises, Congress passed a temporary 10 percent increase in personal and corporate income taxes that turned a deficit of $25.3 billion in fiscal 1968 into a surplus of $3.4 billion in the next year. From Johnson's perspective, Congress had insistently debated the propriety of social programs and military costs in Southeast Asia rather than a technical bill to stabilize the economy. For various reasons—a surge in demand for automobiles, limited impact on buying plans, increases in the money supply, and contradictory cost increases created by a surtax—the measure did not slow the rate of inflation in 1968 and 1969 as had been expected.

The pressures on the Johnson administration grew: to maintain reasonably full employment without ongoing inflation, to hold together a political coalition experiencing growing defections by liberals over military ambitions in Southeast Asia, and to enlarge programs to meet the rising expectations and power of the poor, the aged, oppressed minorities, and organized labor. Many Americans concluded that the United States had limited powers both to affect world affairs and to change the quality of life. Some social scientists attacked the programs they had earlier advocated to improve cities, education, or health. Four years after the triumph of a planned tax cut in 1964, economists sensed the limitations of their influence and an onerous responsibility for mistaken growth and stabilization policies.

THE ENIGMA OF RICHARD NIXON

Elected in 1968 on a wave of criticism of many events of the 1960's (although with Democratic majorities in Congress), Richard M. Nixon, in his five and a half years as president, left an uncertain legacy of government management of the economy. Influenced by the conservative wing of the Republican party, which had rejected social welfare programs and bureaucratic regulations of business, as well as by the recent disillusionment of academic liberals with social programs, Nixon often sounded an antigovernment note more primitive than any found in Adam Smith. At the same time social unrest required solutions beyond a law-and-order campaign, and Nixon sought increased planning and management. Perhaps his economic proposals were designed primarily for their political impact. Nevertheless, many of his reforms had wide support among conservative and liberal experts.

Nixon's publicized cutbacks in the Office of Education and civil rights enforcement distracted attention from his policy initiatives. In 1969 he endorsed a welfare reform that resembled a guaranteed-income plan. He advanced proposals for population projections and planning by the federal government—a necessary first step for maintaining full employment and a high standard of living, given the available resources of the planet. In September of that year Nixon announced his New Federalism plan for sharing federal revenues with states and localities without specifying their use; and he added a line about "a coordinated system of forward planning of needs and resources." He advocated a policy-setting group to coordinate more than four hundred separate programs for alleviating urban problems. Taking a longer-range view, a presidential committee, the National Goals Research Staff, produced a rather disappointing report, *Toward Balanced Growth* (1970). Nixon also favored new initiatives for environmental controls and a bill for land-use planning that would set national standards.

Nixon recognized that a major reorganization would improve executive control over program administration. The White House staff doubled to 510 under his guidance. (Having started with 37 in 1939, it reached 283 in 1953 and then stabilized at around 250.) The Bureau of the Budget became the Office of Management and Budget (OMB) in 1971, with fewer planning and more oversight functions. As OMB director, Roy Ash replaced PPBS with a similar system of management by objectives. The Domestic Council, analogous to the National Security Council, was assigned five tasks essential for national planning: to clarify goals, to develop alternatives, to decide on policies, to coordinate programs, and to evaluate achievements. Nixon sought to regroup executive agencies along functional lines, and he won support from past and present members of the cabinet for that reorganization. Yet Congress and certain interest groups opposed the plan because it upset old relationships and access to influence.

Nixon's staff reflected the opposing forces of his administration. He appointed some of the most conservative advisers since Hoover's administration, but he retained the loyal services of professional economists, such as Arthur Burns and Herbert Stein, who could practice fiscal management for growth and full employment. Yet Nixon largely ignored the Council of Economic Advisers, which had been a model of effectiveness under Johnson. Rather than encouraging economic forecasts and open discussions of policy options, Nixon preferred the personal style and advice of individuals such as Daniel P. Moynihan, John Connally, Roy Ash, and George Schultz. Immediate political reactions and powerful personalities swayed the directions of basic long-term planning.

As American troops gradually left Vietnam and federal programs for social welfare continued, Nixon faced budget deficits, inflation, and persistent unemployment—a combination threatening political defeat in 1972. In August 1971 he invoked a temporary freeze of prices and wages that, under successive phases, lasted until the spring of 1974. Despite loopholes and halfhearted enforcement, the controls limited inflation, allowing two large deficits to stimulate full employment and high profits in time for the November election. After winning reelection by a landslide, Nixon appeared to reverse himself. He opposed some domestic-spending programs, impounded funds for others, and encouraged restrictive monetary policies. Thus, tools of economic management were used in contradictory ways, producing confusion about the overall direction of the economy. That uncertainty, coupled with persistent fears of inflation, led to the first depression in the United States since the 1930's.

Gerald Ford, elevated to the presidency through appointment to the vice-presidency and Nixon's resignation as a disgraced participant in the Watergate cover-up, spoke often about the threat of inflation as recession grew to a full-scale depression. In his previous role as minority leader in the House of Representatives, Ford had opposed federal programs for social services, and he had no experience in directing the huge operations of the federal government. His economic advisers, led by Alan Greenspan, insisted that the economy would soon improve. In the meantime, the "permanent government" of civil servants administered the existing programs and laws, and preserved a considerable degree of stability. And Congress, worried about its general loss of initiative and tired of inflation, established the Congressional Budget Office in 1974, to help coordinate and organize the size and timing of its spending programs.

CARTER AND THE LIMITS ON MANAGEMENT

As a former naval engineer, governor of Georgia, and businessman, James E. Carter entered the White House determined to streamline bureaucratic procedures for efficient administration and to curb the grandiose ambitions of the presidency. Faced with huge deficits, continuing high unemployment, and persistent inflation, the Carter administration's monetary and fiscal policies wavered. A proposal for a tax rebate soon faded away, although some personal exemptions were raised and corporate tax rates cut. Lower spending to combat inflation conflicted with Carter's promised programs for cities, welfare reform, and a comprehensive health program—as well as ongoing costs of defense. Carter's voluntary wage-price guidelines flexibly adjusted to what the market would bear or politics required. In 1978 the Council of Economic Advisers decreased its estimate of long-term growth rate from 3.5 percent to 3.0 percent, based on a slower gain in productivity. That decrease helped account for the increase of the total labor force, including many two-wage-earner households, despite sluggish growth.

Carter and the Council of Economic Advisers stressed deregulation as a way to lower prices and to reduce public dissatisfaction with governmental bureaucracy. During the 1970's, Congress had legislated environmental and health protections, starting with the Occupational Safety and Health Administration (1970), which seemed to proliferate trivial and inflexible rules. Before heading the Council of Economic Advisers, Charles Schultze had argued in *The Public Use of Private Interests* that "social intervention often fails not because it relies unnecessarily on regulation or other command-and-control devices, but because in other ways it ignores the role of properly structured economic incentives for achieving social goals" (p. 63). Yet modifying environmental protection brought protests from those who believed that conservation and clean health and air depended on prohibitions and strict requirements. A strong Federal Aviation Administration, backed by congressional legislation, allowed reductions of fares and expanded routes, which brought increased passengers and higher profits for most airlines. But in spite of obvious inefficiencies and misdirected incentives of regulation in the trucking industry, many vested interests opposed a direct application of microeconomic principles.

The conundrum of energy resources demonstrated the perplexity of economic planning and management in the 1970's. Starting with a price hike agreement among the Organization of Petroleum Exporting Countries (OPEC) in 1973, relative prices for energy continued to increase —reflecting the pressure of worldwide economic growth on a scarce resource and the failure of the United States to adjust to those new conditions. The Nixon-Ford proposal for energy independence through reliance on coal and conservation and Carter's National Energy Plan, which aimed at reversing the incentives of previous regulations for oil and natural gas, encouraging conservation, and shifting energy use to coal and nuclear power, contained some painful lessons. First, a tangle of old regulations, commitments, agreements, and rules—especially with multinational firms such as the major oil companies—makes any change unfavorable to those businesses difficult. Second, public support for a new policy usually requires some remedy that promises enhanced output or a substitute good. Third, the general impact of fiscal and monetary policies to maintain aggregate production seldom applies to specific industries or to the international power of OPEC. Fourth, the public nevertheless looks to government for some solutions—either rationing, stricter regulations, subsidies, or alternative transportation and energy.

The ambivalent responses to government management of the economy as well as to its importance were mirrored in Public Law 95-523, the Full Employment and Balanced Growth Act of 1978. Section 2(a) amended the policy declaration of the Employment Act of 1946 to include government policy and responsibility to "promote full employment and production, increased real income, balanced growth, a balanced Federal budget, adequate productivity growth, proper attention to national priorities, achievement of an improved trade balance through increased exports and improvements in the international competitiveness of agriculture, business, and industry, and reasonable price stability." In section 2(j) Congress announced its intent "to rely principally on the private sector for expansion of economic activity and creation of new jobs for a growing labor force." Further, Congress aimed "to encourage the adoption of fiscal policies that would establish the share of the gross national product accounted for by Federal outlays at the lowest level consistent with national needs and priorities." Thus the mixed economy became an explicit policy without settling the degree of reliance on government or the marketplace.

The potential force of the new legislation lay in the instructions for forward planning by the Council of Economic Advisers, the Board of Governors of the Federal Reserve, and other agencies, together with the setting of specific targets for unemployment (3 percent among those aged twenty years and older, 4 percent among those aged sixteen and older) and the rate of inflation (3 percent by the fifth year). After those goals were reached, "each succeeding Economic Report shall have the goal of achieving . . . full employment and a balanced budget" and a stable price level. The Economic Report of the President should include:

"(2)(A) annual numerical goals for employment and unemployment, production, real income, productivity, and prices for the calendar year in which the Economic Report is transmitted and for the following calendar year . . . and (B) annual numerical goals as specified in subparagraph (A) for the three successive calendar years, designated as medium term goals; (3) employment objectives for certain significant subgroups of the labor force, including youth, women, minorities, handicapped persons, veterans, and middle-aged and older persons. . . ."

This legislation authorized existing practices of active government management of the economy in light of current political mandates.

A SUMMING UP

The debate over the best guidelines for managing the economy will continue as long as large enterprises with economies of scale have some control over prices; important costs or benefits of private or public enterprises spill over to other than direct consumers; and significant uncertainties can be reduced by establishing public policies. Free-enterprise advocates have correctly foreseen that government interference strengthens demands for additional regulations or subsidies. But experience with government management has also tempered the expectations of those who foretold utopian benefits from a planned society. Although public actions have restricted private decisions in unexpected ways, they have generally increased economic security for individuals, encouraged investments in physical and human capital, and augmented meaningful options for economic development. As private and public institutions have learned to coordinate massive economic power, democratically elected officials have taken on more responsibility for guiding the economy to major national goals.

The American experience since 1900 should not lead to complacency. Issues of individual freedom and responsibility are central for a viable democracy and for an economy that relies to a considerable extent on private enterprise. Political leaders, economists, and citizens have struggled to develop a mix of private and public management to meet their immediate needs and to preserve opportunities for future development. Certainly the Keynesian revolution in American economics has had a profound impact on the public sense of government management of the economy as a limited, defined, and practical way to assure an economic environment that allows individuals to plan for their own wellbeing. As technology and management skills have allowed private and public institutions to coordinate massive economic power, there has to be a corresponding increase in responsibility to use that power for major social goals.

Economists and social scientists have sharpened their tools of analysis, enlarged their data base, and refined guidelines for policy decisions. With computers, economists have devised sophisticated models that include many endogenous variables. These large-scale models and major research efforts, such as the Studies in Government Finance issued by the Brookings Institution, have helped to develop the separation of the budget effects into automatic and discretionary components, ideas of full-employment surplus, and even more complex considerations for guiding federal budget making. Tied to an explicit Keynesian model of macroeconomic relationships, the policy recommendations encouraged both prediction and evaluation of performance. Effective policy rules characteristically combined several public goals—such as growth, full employment, price stability, and income redistribution—that represent an approximation to a social welfare function.

Gradually the American government has developed functional institutions for economic planning and management. Regulatory agencies such as the Interstate Commerce Commission, the Federal Trade Commission, the Securities and Exchange Commission, and a host of temporary boards and administrations have implemented specific guidelines more or less well, but without a national oversight function. The Federal Reserve system has been given more power and a clearer mandate for its central banking functions. The Bureau of the Budget, which became the Office of Management and Budget in 1970, has attempted to control federal spending to reflect national priorities. Regular cabinet departments such as the Treasury and Commerce have added professional economists and developed statistical and analytical capacity. Since 1946 the Council of Economic Advisers functioning directly under the president has become the focus of planning for major national objectives. The Budget Control Act (1974) created a committee in the House and in the Senate to oversee general appropriation levels, and it staffed a Congressional Budget Office to provide independent advice on fiscal and monetary policies.

In light of the loose connections between individual self-interest and changes in public policy, the deeper question may be whether the political system is responsive to class interests. Recent evidence suggests that executive actions have stimulated economic upswings during election years. More important, advanced industrial nations have faced a trade-off between inflation and unemployment, with significant differences for class interests. Rapid growth with high employment has yielded a more equal distribution of income. By contrast, business profits have been greatest under conditions of high though declining unemployment and high interest rates designed to limit inflation. Evidence since 1945 indicates that left-leaning governments (Democratic administrations in the United States) have achieved somewhat lower unemployment rates, often accompanied by higher rates of inflation. Although the differences are modest, they indicate that policy variables have made a difference and that voters have probably recognized their personal interests in public management of the economy.

Americans have characteristically resolved major class differences by seeking greater abundance. The frontier, technological developments, and a managed growth have allowed new groups to enjoy greater prosperity without taking something away from others. The 1964 tax cut exemplified the predilection for promising something for everyone. American prosperity has allowed political leaders to build reform coalitions around new power blocs, but those possibilities have narrowed as most groups except the very poor (including many minority Americans) have gained a political voice. Furthermore, prospects for economic growth have faded in light of limitations on resources, the growing costs of environmental degradation, and worldwide increases in population.

The decline of options for greater equality through abundance rather than through redistribution are troublesome, because the general effect of government management has been to increase both economic and political equality. As Alexis de Tocqueville noted, a high degree of equality of condition can create a sense of common interests and participation among all classes. As Keynes and Hansen later pointed out, a high level of average incomes with extensive public services can encourage a high propensity to consume that is appropriate for a mature economy. Yet as Charles Lindblom has warned, powerful corporations that produce and distribute the mass of goods and services have disproportionate power in dealing with a democratic voice for public goods and services. Since no political or economic system can avoid the basic management tasks of a powerful industrial economy, the responsibility for making the American system of mixed public and private decision making serve the immediate and future needs of the people remains a challenge.

BIBLIOGRAPHY

Sidney Alexander, Gerhard Colm, et al., *Economics and the Policy Maker* (Washington, D.C., 1959), consists of essays tracing the impact of economic analysis on private and public managers. Albert Ando, E. Cary Brown, and Ann F. Friedlaender, eds., *Studies in Economic Stabilization* (Washington, D.C., 1968), contains econometric studies of specific programs and countries. Stephen K. Bailey, *Congress Makes a Law: The Story Behind the Employment Act of 1946* (New York, 1950), is an excellent account of legislative process and the ideas underlying positive planning. Charles W. Baker, *Government Control and Operation of Industry in Great Britain and the United States During the World War* (New York, 1921), presents a fascinating contemporary account of the potential for planning. Alan S. Blinder, Robert M. Solow, et al., *The Economics of Public Finance* (Washington, D.C., 1974), should be consulted especially for Blinder and Solow's essay "Analytical Foundations of Fiscal Policy," which provides an excellent summary of the current state of knowledge. Alfred Chandler, *The Visible Hand: The Managerial Revolution in American Business* (Cambridge, 1977), indicates important aspects of nonmarket decision making in the private sector. Committee of the President's Conference on Unemployment, *Business Cycles and Unemployment* (New York, 1923), offers useful insights into pre-Keynesian proposals for stabilization. Committee on Recent Economic Changes of the President's Conference on Unemployment, *Recent Economic Changes in the United States*, 2 vols. (New York, 1929), an examination of the 1920's, exemplifies early efforts to monitor economic indicators.

Council of Economic Advisers, *The Economic Report of the President* (Washington, D.C., 1947–   )—published annually, these reports together with the budget messages have become the American economic plan. Louis Fisher, *Presidential Spending Power* (Princeton, 1975), gives detailed insights into current problems in monitoring actual spending by executive agencies. Edward Flash, *Economic Advice and Presidential Leadership* (New York, 1965), analyzes interactions between the Council of Economic Advisers and three presidents. John Kenneth Galbraith, *Economics and the Public Purpose* (Boston, 1973), literately presents the current liberal agenda for reform and reconstruction. Richard V. Gilbert, George Hildebrand, et al., *An Economic Program for American Democracy* (New York, 1938), contains liberal Keynesian economists' advice to the New Deal. Robert Aaron Gordon, *Economic Instability and Growth: The American Record* (New York, 1974), briefly summarizes factors causing change in the twentieth century. Otis L. Graham, *Toward a Planned Society: From Roosevelt to Nixon* (New York, 1976), records hesitant progress toward comprehensive planning.

Alonzo L. Hamby, *Beyond the New Deal: Harry S. Truman and American Liberalism* (New York, 1973), is a solid account of Truman's inability to gain Roosevelt's economic bill of rights. Alvin H. Hansen, *Full Recovery or Stagnation?* (New York, 1938), is an early analysis by an influential Keynesian adviser. Seymour E. Harris, ed., *The New Economics: Keynes' Influence on Theory and Public Policy* (New York, 1947), presents rich samples from many of the leading Keynesian economists. Ellis W. Hawley, *The New Deal and the Problem of Monopoly* (Princeton, 1966), is a subtle study of ambiguous reactions to large-scale organizations during the 1930's. Walter W. Heller, *New Dimensions of Political Economy* (New York, 1967), details Kennedy-Johnson policies; by the head of the Council of Economic Advisers. Lewis H. Kimmel, *Federal Budget and Fiscal Policy, 1789–1958* (Washington, D.C., 1959), is a comprehensive history of ideas and practices. David Kinley, "The Renewed Extension of Government Control of Economic Life," in *American Economic Review*, Supplement 4 (1914). Robert Lekachman, *The Age of Keynes* (New York, 1968), is a bold account of ideas and their growing impact on American policies.

Wilfred Lewis, *Federal Fiscal Policy in the Postwar Recessions* (Washington, D.C., 1962), discusses automatic stabilizers that influenced policy changes. Charles E. Lindblom, *Politics and Markets* (New York, 1977) offers a major international comparison of relations between markets and public authority. Lloyd Metzler, Evsey Domar, et al., *Income, Employment and Public Policy: Essays in Honor of Alvin H. Hansen* (New York, 1948), includes many examples of liberal Keynesian positions after World War II. Stanley Moses, ed., *Planning for Full Employment* (Philadelphia, 1975), contains selected current criticism of slack employment under the Employment Act of 1946. Arthur Okun, ed., *The Battle Against Unemployment* (New York, 1965), consists of essays indicating economic thinking during the Kennedy-Johnson years. David J. Ott and Attiat F. Ott, *Federal Budget Policy*, rev. ed. (Washington, D.C., 1969), summarizes federal budgets and procedures. Joseph A. Pechman, *Federal Tax Policy*, rev. ed. (Washington, D.C., 1971), gives a substantive account of tax laws. Edmund S. Phelps, ed., *The Goal of Economic Growth.* (New York, 1962), contains

GOVERNMENT MANAGEMENT OF THE ECONOMY

essays indicating economic criticisms of slow-growth policies of the Eisenhower years.

Lawrence C. Pierce, *The Politics of Fiscal Policy Formation* (Pacific Palisades, Calif. 1971), details the pressures, procedures, and product of the Council of Economic Advisers under Johnson and the passage of the surtax. Alice M. Rivlin, *Systematic Thinking for Social Action* (Washington, D.C., 1971), is a useful demonstration of the method and impact of economic thinking on public programs. Charles L. Schultze, *The Politics and Economics of Public Spending* (Washington, D.C., 1968), seeks to combine the vigor of economic analysis with the political need to establish consensus; *The Public Use of Private Interests* (Washington, D.C., 1977), argues for maximum use of incentives and markets in public regulatory activities. Herbert Stein, *The Fiscal Revolution in America* (Chicago, 1969), is an excellent, detailed account of changing thought and policies in America, with particular attention to monetary policies. James Tobin, *The New Economics, One Decade Older* (Princeton, 1974), presents a fascinating retrospective view of changes in economic thinking after the experience of the 1964 tax cut, by a leading practitioner. Aaron Wildavsky, *The Politics of the Budgetary Process* (Boston, 1964), presents a convincing defense of the usefulness of incremental, piecemeal attention to budget items with consultation among interest groups.

[*See also* ANTITRUST; CENTRAL BANKING; COSTS OF ECONOMIC GROWTH; ECONOMIC THOUGHT; ECONOMY SINCE 1914; LAW AND POLITICAL INSTITUTIONS; MEDICINE AND PUBLIC HEALTH; MILITARY-INDUSTRIAL COMPLEX; REGULATORY AGENCIES; STATE AND LOCAL GOVERNMENTS; *and* SOCIAL WELFARE.]

MANAGEMENT

James P. Baughman

ANY history of management must start with the multiple meanings of the word itself. Definitions are crucial, since the term and its derivatives have both philosophical and vocational connotations. They refer to ideas and systems of thought as well as to actions and systems of work. There is, for example, a commonly held set of values or gestalt called "managerial." There is also a purportedly coherent set of concepts and skills that supposedly can be codified, taught, learned, applied, practiced, and improved upon. And there are individuals and groups commonly called "managers" who presumably exhibit the gestalt and apply it to earn their livelihood by drawing from and contributing to the managerial stock of knowledge. We all claim to be able to recognize and appreciate "good management" when we experience it, but we are less certain as to its constituent parts and how they are perpetuated. We must be more certain before milestones or turning points in the history of management can be recorded. And when limited to the history of management in the United States, we must be even more cautious, because no single country has had a monopoly on the subject—"Yankee ingenuity" notwithstanding.

Lists of the values and behavioral characteristics of management and managers are doomed to incompleteness. There is, rather, general agreement on the following elements. Management and managers venerate efficiency, productivity, innovation, and leadership. Somehow outputs are to be made to grow faster than inputs. Somehow the processes of work and the quality of work products are to be improved. Somehow the work of others is to be multiplied. Management itself is clearly an input, not an outcome. It is conscious and purposive. It is not risk-averse. It is not solitary. Managers are rarely found outside groups or organizations. It is a human, and not a mechanical, activity. Good management cannot be patented. It is universal in the sense that its philosophy and skills can be transferred from situation to situation with little diminution of effect; it is not idiosyncratic to an individual or specific to time or place. But management is debatable. There are schools of thought, and there are fads. There is rarely one best way. Finally, management is a job, and successful practitioners expect just compensation when their job is well done.

But what do managers actually do? What is the nature of managerial work? Until recently, the most widely accepted definition was one published in France by Henri Fayol. In his *Administration industrielle et générale: Prévoyance, organisation, commandement, coordination, contrôle* (published as an article in 1916, as a book in 1925, and first translated into English in 1930), Fayol said that managers plan, organize, command, coordinate, and control. His most ardent disciple, Luther Gulick, expanded the list in the 1930's and added an acronym, POSDCORB, for what he believed were the seven basic managerial activities: planning, organizing, staffing, directing, coordinating, reporting, and budgeting.

According to Henry Mintzberg, "POSDCORB took hold and lives on. It continues to dominate the writings on managerial work to the present day" (*The Nature of Managerial Work*, p. 9). It also has dominated most historical scholarship on management thought and action. Mintzberg, while studying only managers of the 1960's and 1970's, offers an alternative formulation of the nature of managerial work. He defines the manager as

... that person in charge of a formal organization or one of its subunits. He is vested with formal authority over his organizational unit, and this leads to his two basic purposes. First, the manager must ensure that his organization produces its specific goods or services efficiently. He must design, and maintain the stability of, its basic operations, and he must adapt it in a controlled way to its changing environment. Second, the manager must ensure that his organization serves the ends of those persons who control it.... He must interpret their particular preferences and combine these to produce statements of organizational preference that can guide its decision-making. Because of his formal authority the manager must serve two other basic purposes as well. He must act as the key communication link between his organization and its environment, and he must assume responsibility for the operations of his organization's status system [pp. 166–167].

Mintzberg goes on to identify ten interrelated roles performed by all managers through which these basic purposes are made operational—three interpersonal roles: figurehead, leader, and liaison; three informational roles: monitor, disseminator, and spokesman; and four decisional roles: entrepreneur, disturbance handler, resource allocator, and negotiator.

To summarize, the manager must design the work of his organization, monitor its internal and external environment, initiate change when desirable, and renew stability when faced with a disturbance. The manager must lead his subordinates to work effectively for the organization, and he must provide them with special information, some of which he gains through the network of contacts that he develops. In addition, the manager must perform a number of "housekeeping" duties, including informing outsiders, serving as figurehead, and leading major negotiations [pp. 169–170].

So now we know how to recognize a manager when we see one—today or in the past. But whether one accepts Fayol, Mintzberg, some combination, or some alternative, there are still problems in knowing which managers are central to the history of management. Searching for "firsts" is fun but, in the end, frustrating as we discover little new under the sun. Surely the faceless builders of the seven wonders of the ancient world used POSDCORB in more than rudimentary form. Try to build a pyramid the size of the Great Pyramid of Khufu —then or now—without planning, organizing, staffing, directing, coordinating, reporting, or budgeting. And almost any great leader of the past would meet Mintzberg's specifications for a manager. Case studies of successful managers and successful enterprises are important, but most prove only that clever men or women rise to meet almost any occasion, or that necessity is, indeed, either the mother or the father of invention.

The question in the history of management more fundamental than "who," "when," "where," or "what" is "how." How is management improved? By what processes? How does a manager find out what he or she needs to know? On-the-job training? Trial and error? Read a book? Hire an expert? Go to school? Suppose he or she finds a better way. What to do, then? Monopolize it for oneself or share it? Share it for nothing or for a price? Share it in person or through an intermediary? To answer these questions, the historian must be alert to those "few isolated examples of conscious thought on management and the attempts to systematize it" (Pollard 1968, p. 292). The historian's tasks in these instances are not only to highlight the breakthroughs but also to account for their origins in more than situational terms, and to characterize the means of their further dissemination and propagation.

In the history of management in the United States, one finds the usual pragmatic continuum of on-the-job learning by doing. The list of self-made managers seems endless. But their stories properly belong to other sections of this *Encyclopedia* that are concerned with invention and big business—particularly with the "coming of the large vertically integrated, centralized, functionally departmentalized industrial organization" (Chandler 1959, p. 25). The concern here will be with five intense American movements to synthesize and propagate principles of management that are generally applicable: systematic management; scientific management; the movement to establish professional schools of management; the interrelated movements of industrial psychology, industrial sociology, and human relations; and management science.

MANAGEMENT

PRECURSORS

To put these basically American movements in perspective, their European inheritance should be briefly noted. In a careful study of the origins of modern management in Great Britain, Sidney Pollard notes the "absence of any attempt to generalize or rationalize the experiences of industrial management into a management science or at least a management technology in the period of the industrial revolution" (p. 291). He also notes that "a managerial class as such was slow to develop and even by 1830 could hardly be said to be in existence, though well-defined classes of managers had emerged in various specific industries." There were, of course, exceptions: the ironworks of Matthew Boulton and James Watt in Soho; the cotton mills of Robert Owen in Manchester and New Lanark; Benjamin Gott's woolen mills in Leeds; William Brown's flax mill in Dundee. Pollard ranks the conscious, problem-solving abilities of these men "with the best practices of the twentieth century" (p. 293). But because their ideas were not published, "as far as we know, the management pioneers were isolated and their ideas without great influence" (p. 295).

A published management literature began in the 1830's with treatises on cotton manufacturing, coal mining, ironmaking, engineering, railroads, and accounting. "All of these were mainly concerned with technical knowledge and codification of manufacturing practices; but all equally codified some managerial experiences also" (Pollard 1968, p. 295). The outstanding example was Charles Babbage's *On the Economy of Machinery and Manufactures,* which was published in England in 1832. This work was an immediate best-seller and went through four editions in three years. The 1832 London edition was pirated that same year in the United States, and a serialized version began in the New York *Mechanics Magazine* in 1833.

Babbage based his work on ten years of visiting European factories in search of "principles of generalization." With the benefit of hindsight, it is easy to read too much into Babbage, but there is no doubt that his work was "generations ahead of its time" (Pollard 1968, p. 295). Building upon Adam Smith's preoccupation with the benefits of a division of labor, Babbage emphasized visual and statistical data gathering and time-and-motion studies to achieve optimal specialization of tasks. He anticipated what would now be called production-line balancing to coordinate flows of materials with the sequential activities of men and machines. He concerned himself with cost accounting, bonus and incentive systems, and methods for determining a "fair day's work." He advocated standardized forms for reporting of managerial information and speculated on the optimal size of firms, economies of scale in production, and the merits and demerits of centralized control. His book was a repository of "best practice" as it then existed and a catechism of intriguing but unresolved speculations.

"All this, however important in itself, does not add up to a technology, still less to a science which could be taught or even summarized in textbooks" (Pollard 1968, pp. 295–296). In the United States the public literature was even more sparse.

> The first real management publications during this era were few in number, and these were published almost exclusively in engineering journals. A list of these early publications on management prepared by the New York Public Library in 1917, for instance, showed no American titles to 1881; eleven titles in the seventeen years from 1881 to 1897; and six titles in the three years from 1897 to 1899 [George 1968, pp. 79–80].

Thus, while some publications were available, and visitors and immigrants found a ready market in the United States for European ideas and methods, the "systematic management" movement that peaked between 1875 and 1900 was primarily a pragmatic and spontaneous American development. Its prime movers were manufacturing executives and engineers, but its origins lay with a group of American railroad managers of the 1840's and 1850's, notably Benjamin H. Latrobe, chief engineer of the Baltimore and Ohio; Daniel C. McCallum, general superintendent of the New York and Erie; and J. Edgar Thomson, president of the Pennsylvania.

American railroads were "the first to face the challenge of handling efficiently large amounts of men, money, and materials within a single business unit" (Chandler 1965, p. 29). This size and complexity bred innovation in managerial organization and control. Men like Latrobe, McCallum, and Thomson formalized general principles to an unprecedented degree: functional departmentalization; definition of lines of authority, responsibility, and communication; development of information flows and reporting procedures; delegation of authority; distinctions between line and staff functions; central office duties; and standardized accounting. They published their principles in manuals that were copied by railroad after railroad. Their ideas were also read outside of the railroad community and adapted where analogous situations arose in commerce and industry.

SYSTEMATIC MANAGEMENT

By the 1870's the ideas of Babbage, Latrobe, McCallum, and Thomson were fascinating an increasing number of manufacturing executives and engineers whose enterprises were reaching a scale and complexity previously experienced only by the railroads. And with comparable growth came comparable problems. But there was more self-consciousness in their solution and a much greater compulsion to generalize publicly. Leaders in what soon became known as the movement for "systematic management" were Capt. Henry Metcalfe of the U.S. Army Ordnance Department, stationed at the Frankford Arsenal, and Henry Robinson Towne, president of the Yale Lock Manufacturing Company.

The basic accusation made by Metcalfe and Towne

> . . . was that, as a result of their very success and growth, American firms had reached a point at which internal operations had become increasingly chaotic, confused, and wasteful. As this condition was both undesirable and in need of prompt correction . . . some way was needed to put "method" into the management of firms to avoid confusion and waste, to promote coordination, and to reestablish effective control by top management [Litterer 1963, p. 54].

The search for "method" and "system" resolved itself into a search for standardized operating procedures that would simultaneously simplify the range of decisions required of lower-level managers and that would free top management from as much routine as possible. Systematic management was, in brief, concerned "with finding ways to carry out the regular or routine activities of management . . . operations rather than . . . planning and developing . . . with the development of administrative systems to guide the steady-state portion of managerial activities" (Litterer 1963, p. 71). The goals were for repetitive management tasks to be carried out through standardized procedures, and for repetitively occurring problems to have preestablished solutions.

Systematic management addressed what were perceived as a breakdown of coordination among subordinates and a breakdown in control relationships between top and lower levels of management. Production and inventory control systems received particular attention, and standardized procedures were developed for coordinating and reporting the flow of orders from the time they entered the factory through the sales department to the time finished products left the factory via the shipping department. Cost accounting became a mania. Procedures were developed to separate fixed costs from variable costs, to account for overhead, and to identify costs with their incremental origins in the production process—thereby transforming costs from what had previously been historical artifacts into day-to-day variables that could be controlled. Much attention was also given to the comparative merits of wages based on hours worked versus wages based on output—both as cost-minimizing techniques and as incentives for worker productivity.

The intent of systematic management was to increase efficiency through system, to ease the job of lower-level managers with standardized decision rules, and to blend the workers into the organization effectively by specifying exactly what was and what was not expected of them. The dark side of systematic management was that as decision rules became increasingly specific, ever smaller areas of discretion were left to the lower-ranking members of the organization. The cost of system was often reduction in worker autonomy and in the decision-making prerogatives of junior managers. But Metcalfe and Towne were widely read and avidly imitated. Indeed, Towne's paper "The Engineer as an Economist," delivered to the American Society of Mechanical Engineers in 1886, pleaded for "the recognition of a science of management with its own literature, journals, and associations." He got much more than he bargained for. His paper "probably inspired Frederick W. Taylor to devote his life's work to scientific management" (George 1968, p. 80) and the world was never the same again.

SCIENTIFIC MANAGEMENT

Frederick Winslow Taylor (1856–1915) came from a well-to-do Philadelphia family and attended Phillips Exeter Academy with the intention of entering Harvard. Even though he passed the entrance examinations with distinction, poor eyesight and a desire to build up his health changed his plans. At eighteen he learned the trades of machinist and patternmaker, and at twenty-two was employed by the Midvale Steel Company as a common laborer. He rapidly progressed to time clerk, journeyman machinist, lathe operator, gang boss, and foreman of the machine shop. At thirty-one he became chief engineer of the entire works. He had also been studying at night and by correspondence and, in 1883, earned a diploma in mechanical engineering from the Stevens Institute of Technology.

Taylor was a driven man with a "frenzy for order" and efficiency (Haber 1964, p. 5)—and there was much at Midvale that offended him. He was particularly upset with the low productivity of the large work force despite what he considered fair pay. In Taylor's day there were two ways to pay a worker: for a specified period of time—by the day or the hour, for example; or for the amount of work done within that time period. Babbage, Metcalfe, and Towne had advocated the "piece rate," because they felt workers would pace themselves to earn more money and thereby increase output. Taylor agreed in theory but had not found it so in real life. He fumed at the tendency of workers to sink to the lowest common denominator of their work group, regardless of capabilities (he called this phenomenon "soldiering"). He was also disgusted with the typical acquiescence of management in this state of affairs. In response, he set out to design incentive systems that would maximize pay for each worker willing to do an "honest day's work." He was convinced that the result would reduce unit labor costs and increase overall productivity.

In his mission to define a "fair" or "honest" day's work, Taylor followed Babbage. In believing that monetary incentive systems were the key to increasing worker productivity, he followed Metcalfe and Towne. But the "Taylor system" far transcended its predecessors in intensity and impact: it was "a method of business therapy; it was a 'science'; and it was a social program." Taylor preferred to call it "functional management," but its more popular label became "scientific management." His exposition began with a paper to the annual meeting of the American Society of Mechanical Engineers in 1895; progressed through a stream of articles, papers, speeches, and public testimony; and was consolidated in his book *The Principles of Scientific Management,* published in 1911 (and translated into Chinese, Dutch, French, German, Italian, Russian, Spanish, and Swedish in Taylor's own lifetime).

What were these principles? What were his objectives? "Taylor fashioned his methods after the exact sciences—experiment, measurement, generalization—in the hope of discovering laws of management which, like laws of nature, would be impartial and above class prejudice. . . . He proposed a neat, understandable world in the factory, an organization of men whose acts would be planned, co-ordinated, and controlled under continuous expert direction" (Haber 1964, pp. x–xi). His objective was to develop a science for each element of a man's work to replace old rule-of-thumb methods. He wanted to find the most economical way to perform each task, considering methods, materials, tools and equipment, and working conditions. His method was to break each job down into its "elementary operations" and then to time several "first-class" workers with a stopwatch to determine the "point of maximum efficiency for the human machine." Babbage had advocated time study, but Taylor's use of the stopwatch to time a job by elements was an innovation. Before, timing had simply recorded the overall elapsed time of a task.

Time studies were only a part of Taylor's approach. He varied both the human and the mechanical elements of each task in search of optimality. It is estimated that he performed fifty thousand experiments on metal cutting alone. An early research project on shoveling is representative of the thoroughness of his approach. In 1898, after intensive experiments, he standardized the size of shovels used in the Bethlehem Steelworks for each type of material handled in the plant, as well as for the amount of work to be expected of any "first-class" shoveler using each type of shovel. He established a toolroom that issued the right shovel for each job.

A planning department was established to schedule the work each day. The men were assigned tasks as individuals rather than in gangs, and the material handled by each man was individually accounted for at the end of the day. Each worker was paid a bonus (60 percent above day wages) whenever he did the specified amount of work. If a worker persistently failed to earn the bonus, he was given individual instruction. After three and one-half years of operation, Taylor's system had increased output and reduced to 140 laborers a work force that previously fluctuated from 400 to 600. The cost of handling material had gone from $.07 to $.08 to $.03 to $.04 per ton. "After paying for all added expenses, such as planning the work, measuring the output of the workers, determining and paying bonuses each day, and maintaining the toolroom, Taylor still showed a saving during the last 6-month period at the rate of $78,000 per year" (Barnes 1968, p. 15).

"Taylorism" insisted

> ... that workers be treated individually and not *en masse*. Each was to be rewarded and punished for his particular deeds. In this way Taylor introduced individualism into the factory, but individualism in a diminished form.... The workers must "do what they are told promptly and without asking questions or making suggestions. ... it is absolutely necessary for every man in the organization to become one of a train of gear wheels" [Haber 1964, pp. 23–24].

According to Sudhir Kakar,

> To a very great extent, Taylor is responsible for the managerial philosophy that prevails today, which can be summed up as follows: To increase productivity, 1. break the work process into the smallest possible components; 2. fit jobs into structures that clearly emphasize the duties and boundaries of each job rather than its part in the total process; 3. wherever possible use individual or small group monetary incentive systems, gearing pay to the output; 4. subtract skill and responsibility from the job to make them functions of management" [*Frederick Taylor: A Study in Personality and Innovation*, pp. 189–190].

But Taylor also "attacked the cult of personality in management. Methods were primary, not particular men" (Haber 1964, p. 24). If methods, materials, tools, machines, and working conditions were scientifically analyzed, if time and motion were standardized, if operators were trained, if the proper wage incentive applied, and if the centralized planning, scheduling, and disciplinary department did its job, " 'in theory at least, the works could run smoothly even if the manager, superintendent, and their assistants outside the planning room were all to be away for a month at a time' " (Haber 1964, p. 25).

Taylor's intensity, sense of mission, and evangelism made him a prophet in his own time, and the gospel of efficiency was carried forth by such apostles as Frank B. and Lillian M. Gilbreth, Henry L. Gantt, and Harrington Emerson, and through the intellectual and political support of a host of progressives who saw in Taylorism the means of economic and bureaucratic reform. The efficiency expert entered every aspect of American life, and "research," "standardization," "planning," and "control" took on new meanings in the management vocabulary.

The Gilbreths are chiefly remembered as the charming but eccentric centerpieces of *Cheaper by the Dozen*—a loving memoir by Frank B. Carey, Jr., and Ernestine Gilbreth Carey. In their day, however, they were a formidable team. She a psychologist, and he an engineer, they pooled their talents in researching the "human factor" as the limiting element of efficiency. They ranged widely and made contributions to materials handling and work methods in the building trades, to the study of monotony and fatigue, to the theory of skill transfer, and to improving methods for handicapped workers. They developed process-charting and flow-diagramming conventions, and symbols still in use in systems analysis and computer programming. But their most dramatic contributions were in "micromotion study," a term they coined in 1912.

The Gilbreths invented "cyclegraphic" and "chronocyclegraphic" analyses to replace Taylor's stopwatch. By attaching a small electric light bulb to the hand or other part of a test worker's anatomy, and photographing with a still camera (open on bulb exposure) the path of light moving through space as the worker performed a task, they could create a permanent "cyclegraph" of the motions associated with each task. By placing an interrupter in the electric circuit, the light could be flashed on quickly and off slowly. The path of the bulb then appeared as a line of pear-shaped dots indicating the direction of movement. Also, as the worker moved fast, the dots would be widely separated; the opposite was true when motion was slow. This created a "chronocyclegraph" that made it possible "to measure accurately time, speed, acceleration, and retardation, and to show direction and the path of motion in three dimensions" (Barnes 1968, p. 18). Later, the Gilbreths employed motion-picture cameras and devices that accurately indicated time intervals on the motion picture film. These techniques anticipated more modern usage of slow motion and stop action to aid in improving methods, to demonstrate correct motions, and to assist in training new workers and designing new machines.

Henry L. Gantt's contributions were further refinements of Taylor's incentive system and the invention of the "Gantt chart." Taylor's "differential piece-rate system" paid by the piece for above-average workers but did not pay guaranteed wages for substandard performance. Gantt's "task-and-bonus wage system" paid the regular day rate plus a bonus if a worker accomplished his daily quota, but guaranteed the day rate without penalty if the quota was not met. The "daily balance chart," which plotted output against time on a bar chart, became the standard method for scheduling and costing sequential production operations until well after World War II.

Harrington Emerson, who corresponded with Taylor but was not a direct disciple, became famous for his summation of "the twelve principles of efficiency": clearly defined objectives; common sense; competent counsel by experts; discipline of self and others; justice and fairness; reliable, immediate, accurate, and permanent records; centralized planning; standards and schedules; standardized conditions; standardized operations; standardized instructions; and incentive rewards for performance.

PROFESSIONAL EDUCATION FOR MANAGEMENT

The systematic and scientific management movements paralleled a third movement of historical importance: the development of the first professional schools of management. The word "professional" meant different things to different people. To most it had behavioral connotations of leadership and ethical responsibility. To others, like Mary Parker Follett, speaking in 1925 but summarizing two decades of thought, it meant specialized training: "It means that men must prepare themselves as seriously for this profession as for any other" (Merrill 1960, p. 322). Measures should be taken, Follett argued, to organize the knowledge obtained by research and

> . . . to make it accessible to the whole managerial force. There should be opportunities for the training of executives through talks, suggested readings (including journals on management), through wisely led discussion groups and conferences, through managers' associations, foremen's associations, and the like. The organized knowledge of managerial methods which many of the higher officials possess should spread to the lower executives [Merrill 1960, p. 322].

There were, of course, many of these intermediaries already in existence when Follett spoke, notably the Society to Promote the Science of Management, (founded in 1911 and renamed the Taylor Society in 1915). There was also a growing movement to teach business methods in the schools and to establish professional schools of management at the college level.

What nineteenth-century educators called commercial subjects had a slow start at the secondary school level. Most educators did not consider them proper subjects for formal curricula and advocated their relegation to the apprenticeship system, or what is now called on-the-job training. There were itinerant teachers who specialized in these subjects, however, and small private commercial schools are known to have existed in New York, Philadelphia, Boston, Pittsburgh, and St. Louis prior to 1850. The independent business school industry began with the efforts of Henry B. Bryant and Henry D.

MANAGEMENT

Stratton, who established a chain of schools in fifty American cities between 1853 and 1863 (and whose operations survived until the mid-1970's). By 1893 the U.S. Bureau of Education recorded 115,748 students enrolled in "private commercial or business schools" and 15,220 enrolled in commercial courses given in public high schools.

Commercial education took hold in the public schools in the 1890's. In 1898 a separate commercial school was founded by the Central High School of Philadelphia. New York followed with its High School of Commerce, and Pittsburgh, Chicago, Brooklyn, and Washington were close behind. A U.S. Bureau of Education census in 1910 recorded 34 public and private normal schools (1,622 students), 540 private high schools and academies (10,191 students), 1,440 public high schools (81,249 students), and 541 commercial and business schools (134,778 students) engaged in "commercial education." Of the 233,640 students enrolled in these and other institutions, 119,665 were male and 113,975 were female. A model curriculum prepared by the Department of Business Education of the National Educational Association in 1895, and endorsed by the U.S. Commissioner of Education in 1898, consisted of mathematics (bookkeeping and arithmetic), writing (penmanship, shorthand, and typewriting), business (business practice, history of commerce, and commercial geography); English (spelling, grammar, business correspondence, composition and rhetoric, and public speaking), and civics (commercial law, civil government, and economics).

At the college level the movement was much more managerially and professionally oriented. As early as 1866, Robert C. Spencer, a Milwaukee businessman, had pleaded with the regents of the University of Wisconsin to include commercial education as part of state university curricula—but his proposals were tabled. More successful was Joseph Wharton, a financier and nickel manufacturer, who donated funds for the creation of the first collegiate school of management in 1881: the Wharton School of Finance and Commerce of the University of Pennsylvania. It was his intention to endow a two-year program for those who sought "an adequate education in the principles underlying successful civil government" and "a training suitable for those who intend to engage in business or to undertake the management of property" (Monroe 1911, vol. 1, p. 149). At first the course was superimposed upon the first two years of the regular college course. In 1895 it was enlarged to a four-year course leading to a Bachelor of Science in economics and included specialized courses in manufacturing, banking and finance, brokerage, accounting, transportation and commerce, insurance, social and civil work, law, public service, and "private secretaryship." By 1910 there were 535 students in the day program and 284 in an evening division.

The Wharton School stood alone for almost twenty years, but similar institutions gradually appeared. The Drexel Institute of Art, Science, and Industry (later the Drexel Institute of Technology), established in 1891 by Anthony Joseph Drexel, a prominent Philadelphia businessman, to encourage men and women to prepare for "industrial and commercial life," had separate departments of "science and technology" and "commerce and finance" from the start. The University of Chicago established its School of Commerce and Administration in 1898 (and was to award the first Ph.D. in business administration, in 1922). The University of California created its School of Commerce in the same year; and in 1900, New York University (with the support of the New York State Society of Certified Public Accountants) opened its School of Commerce, Accounts, and Finance. The University of Illinois introduced business courses in 1900 and consolidated them in the School of Railway Engineering and Administration in 1907. The University of Wisconsin followed suit—forty years after Spencer's proposal.

A $300,000 gift by Edward Tuck in honor of his father created the Amos Tuck School of Administration and Finance at Dartmouth College in 1900. The Tuck School first introduced the idea of graduate education for management (Wharton did not offer graduate work until 1921). The first year of the two-year Tuck program could be combined with the fourth year of regular college work, while the second year was strictly graduate in character. The degree awarded was a Master of Commercial Science. In 1908 the Harvard Graduate School of Business Administration was created by an endowment from the New York banker George F. Baker and began to offer a two-year program leading to a Master of Business Administration degree.

MANAGEMENT

Tuck and Harvard had close ties with the scientific management movement. Edwin F. Gay, a noted Harvard economist and public figure, and first dean of the new business school, was an open and enthusiastic supporter of Taylor and Taylorism. Harlow S. Person, who joined the Tuck faculty in 1902 and became dean in 1908, inaugurated his administration by organizing the Dartmouth College Conference on Scientific Management, at which all the proponents of the gospel of efficiency made major addresses. Person served as president of the Taylor Society from 1913 to 1919 and was a constructive link between the growing body of management consultants and academia.

Tuck and Harvard required full-time study "on the level with law and other learned professions," and emphasized "the severity of the entrance requirement" and elite professionalism. Their classes were small and emphasized "case discussions" based upon "individual investigation of a practical character" (Monroe 1911, vol. 1, p. 150). New York University and schools modeled after it, such as Northwestern University and Denver University (both of which opened business schools in 1908), took a different approach. In response to the needs of the large numbers of working managers located in the cities, their courses could be taken part-time and emphasized vocational subjects and practical electives—in both day and evening classes.

Whatever the tone, however, management education at the college level was firmly established. There were thirty such programs by 1911, the year John C. Duncan's *Principles of Industrial Management* (considered the first college textbook in management) was published. An accrediting agency, the American Association of Collegiate Schools of Business (AACSB), was formed in 1916. By 1975 there were over 600 college programs in the United States, of which 178 were accredited by AACSB.

HUMAN FACTORS

Commenting on these developments in a 1925 speech entitled "Management as a Profession," Follett saw "one of the hopes for business management . . . in the fact that executive leadership is capable of analysis and that men can be trained to occupy such positions." She went on to note a number of unfinished tasks for management education. The "technical side . . . has been recognized as a matter capable of being taught," but "on the personnel side, a knowledge of how to deal fairly and fruitfully with one's fellows" was still "thought to be a gift." What was needed, said Follett, was an application of "scientific methods to those problems of management which involve human relations" (Merrill 1960, pp. 311–316). It was the academic, and not the engineering, community that responded to her challenge.

Harold J. Leavitt has deftly summarized the watershed between the structural and technological approaches personified by systematic and scientific management and the "people approaches" that rose to challenge them. Postulating "organizations as multivariate systems" composed of four interacting variables—task, structure, people (actors), and technology (tools), Leavitt comments on those who advocated optimization of structure and harmonization of technology as the ways to optimize organizational performance:

> These are deductive approaches carrying out their analyses from task backward to appropriate divisions of labor and appropriate systems of authority. These early . . . approaches almost always mediated their activities through people to task. One improves task performance by clarifying and defining the jobs of people and setting up appropriate relationships among those jobs. Operationally one worried about modifying spans of control, defining nonoverlapping areas of responsibility and authority, and logically defining necessary functions.
>
> . . . They were . . . almost incredibly naive in their assumptions about human behavior. In fact, almost the only assumptions that were made were legalistic and moralistic ones: that people, having contracted to work, would then carry out the terms of their contract; that people assigned responsibility would necessarily accept that responsibility; that people when informed of the organization's goals would strive wholeheartedly to achieve those goals.
>
> The values underlying these early approaches were thus probably more authoritarian and puritanical than anything else. Order, discipline, system, and acceptance of authority seemed to be dominant values. The objective, of course, was optimal task performance, but within the constraints imposed by the hierarchy of authority ["Applied Organization Change in Industry . . . ," pp. 57–58].

MANAGEMENT

The flaw in the structural and technological approaches, of course, was that they did not discern or allow for many of the complexities of human behavior. Even after the efficiency experts had done their best, "people problems" remained. Order, discipline, system, authority, and monetary incentives certainly could be used to condition human behavior in organizations, but they could also fail to induce the degree of productive change that their advocates claimed was possible. And Taylor, in particular, did not help his cause by his persistent use of animal metaphors in describing types of workers as "racehorses," "dray horses," "songbirds," "sparrows," and "oxen."

An alternative approach that was still worker-centered came from the studies and recommendations of Hugo Münsterberg, Walter Dill Scott, and Walter V. Bingham—experimental psychologists trained in the tradition of Wilhelm Wundt's Leipzig laboratory. Münsterberg, Scott, and Bingham applied their academic discipline to managerial problems and were central to the beginnings of the movement known in the United States as industrial psychology.

Münsterberg trained in psychology at Leipzig and in medicine at Heidelberg before accepting what became a professorship in experimental psychology at Harvard in 1897. In 1910 he turned his attention to the psychological problems of industry and, by means of a questionnaire, asked several hundred corporate executives what traits they found most and least desirable in their employees. He published the results as *Psychology and Industrial Efficiency* (1913) and gave the first outline of what he hoped would become " 'a new science which is to intermediate between the modern laboratory psychology and the problems of economics: The psychological experiment is systematically to be placed at the service of commerce and industry.' " He granted the achievements of systematic and scientific management, but called them to task for " 'helpless psychological dilettantism.' " Industrial psychology could supply experiments and testing procedures that would permit managers to identify " 'those personalities which by their mental qualities are especially fit for a particular kind of economic work.' " Scientists would identify the " 'psychological levers,' " and managers would " 'indicate the points at which the psychological levers ought to be applied' " (Baritz 1960, pp. 36–37). The age of intelligence, aptitude, and achievement tests began.

Münsterberg found receptive clients. He developed selection tests for traveling salesmen of the American Tobacco Company and for conductors of the Boston Elevated Company. Walter Dill Scott, another Leipzig-trained psychologist, who joined the faculty of Northwestern University in 1901 (and was president of Northwestern from 1920 to 1939), performed similar work for American Tobacco, National Lead Company, Western Electric, Loose-Wiles Biscuit Company, and the George Batten advertising agency to reduce executive turnover. In 1915, in the Clothcraft Shops of the Joseph and Feiss Company, Scott developed tests of intelligence, dexterity, and general ability—"the first instance of a company using such tests for the selection of factory workers" (Baritz 1960, p. 38).

Walter V. Bingham, a Chicago-trained psychologist on the faculty of the Carnegie Institute of Technology, established the first college psychological consulting service for industry (the Division of Applied Psychology) in 1915, and Scott formed a similar but private enterprise in 1919 called the Scott Company. In addition to selection testing, Scott specialized in the development of advertising built as much on principles of persuasion as on the older belief that information was sufficient to sell a product. These ideas were published in two pioneering studies: *Theory of Advertising* (1903) and *The Psychology of Advertising* (1908).

World War I brought industrial psychologists to prominence because the War and Navy departments accepted the principle of testing for selection and assignment for the millions of inductees. Scott, for example, organized and directed a program of personnel evaluation that covered 1,727,000 army officers and men. Psychological testing became a rage, but before it entirely swept the field, it was challenged by questions and research findings from a new group calling themselves industrial sociologists rather than industrial psychologists. Their laboratory was centered in the Hawthorne Works of the Western Electric Company (the supply affiliate of the American Telephone and Telegraph Company) on the West Side of Chicago. From 1924 to 1947, Hawthorne became "the single most important social science research project ever conducted in industry.... The Hawthorne research eventually modified permanently the nature and direction of industrial personnel work and became standard material for students of industrial sociology and human relations" (Baritz 1960, p. 77).

The Hawthorne studies began simply enough. The National Research Council was interested generally in the relationship between product quality, safety, and productivity and the physical conditions of work (such as temperature, humidity, and lighting). A team of engineers from the Massachusetts Institute of Technology was retained to study the relationship between industrial illumination and industrial efficiency; the Hawthorne Works was selected as the research site. Experiments conducted between 1924 and 1927 were unable to establish a significant relationship. The matter might have been dropped, but the researchers and the managers involved were fascinated by the fact that productivity had increased in the control group (which was not given the benefit of better illumination) as well as in the test group (which was). Why?

A second series of experiments was conducted in 1927 and 1928. Six women, whose previous work records in the plant were well known, were segregated in a test room and set to work assembling relays under various experimentally imposed changes in temperature, humidity, lighting, and noise. Their work schedules, hours, rest periods, and wage systems were systematically varied.

The results were startling: production seemed to increase independently of the experimentally imposed changes, and even under the worst conditions, when output would momentarily decline, output never declined to the levels it had been at when the experiments first began. There were definite correlations observed between improved physical conditions, better methods of work, rest pauses, and the duration of the workday and output. Pay systems seemed to make some difference, but not to the extent assumed in scientific management. Relief from monotony, relief from fatigue, and monetary incentives were too simple to explain the productivity increases observed.

The first stunning conclusion of Hawthorne became increasingly obvious: that the effects of variables like fatigue, monotony, or pay could be determined only in connection with the interpersonal relations of the women while at work and their personal situations off the job. For example, rest pauses were not important just to counter fatigue and monotony. They apparently also organized the personal time and thoughts and the interpersonal relationships of the workers more effectively, and the effects of this had as much to do with productivity as did physical stamina or dexterity.

The key finding of the "relay-assembly test room" phase of Hawthorne was that the women had responded to the process of work and experimentation by forming a task-oriented group; and since they were deeply involved and frequently consulted, they developed a sense of participation and behaved as a collective and interdependent social unit—a conscious group. But what did this mean?

It was late in the relay-assembly test room phase that Elton Mayo became involved in the Hawthorne studies. He was to become its centerpiece, its interpreter, and, in the process, the prime mover of industrial sociology. An Australian trained at Adelaide, Mayo had worked as a research associate in industry at the University of Pennsylvania before joining the faculty of the Harvard Graduate School of Business Administration in 1926 and accepting promotion to a professorship in 1929.

Mayo turned the Hawthorne studies toward considerations of the effects of groups upon individuals and the effects of individuals upon groups. More specifically, in 1931 he, Fritz J. Roethlisberger, the anthropologist W. Lloyd Warner, and associates began to observe and interpret the influences upon productivity of worker groups in the bank-wiring room at Hawthorne.

Mayo and his associates discovered a worker group of startling subtlety: it disciplined its members and suppressed deviant behavior; it was supportive of individual differences and concerns; it protected its members individually and itself collectively from outside interference and control. They discovered that there was a substantial fraction of the output of the group that group norms regulated regardless of outside incentives. They also discovered that worker performance on the job was more related to group dynamics than to the capacity of the individual worker. This, of course, challenged the psychologists' assumptions that individual ability and individual performance were closely related.

If that was not the case, then what was the use of testing?

Mayo's work, published as *The Human Problems of an Industrial Civilization* (1933), and that of his colleagues Fritz Roethlisberger and William J. Dickson, in *Management and the Worker* (1934), validated once more the clinical approach to the study and improvement of management, but broadened the subject matter of investigation to the "total situation" in which the informal organizations of workers and managers interact with the formality of the work to be performed. They focused on the individual embedded in groups and upon the process of change itself. Chester I. Barnard, an AT&T executive with forty years' experience, added his voice.

Barnard was not directly involved in Hawthorne, but he was in close contact with Mayo and others at Harvard. He spoke for and to the general manager in *The Functions of the Executive*, published in 1938 and reprinted eighteen times over the next thirty years. He attempted to synthesize a comprehensive theory of cooperative behavior in formal organizations and identified the executive's principal function and objective as the "effective" management of human resources. Barnard's emphasis on "effectiveness" rather than on "efficiency" was not idle. It expressed his conviction that individuals and organizations, in doing the best they can, should aspire to workable and useful, rather than optimal and elegant, solutions. He anticipated the later observation of Herbert A. Simon that "human beings ... *satisfice* because they have not the wits to *maximize*" (Simon 1976, p. xxiv). The industrial sociologists thus began the formalization of the study of "human relations" called for by Follett and began a stream of "people approaches." The "people approaches try to change the organizational world by changing the behavior of actors in the organization" (Leavitt 1964, p. 63).

The permutations of the "people approaches" have been phenomenal since the 1930's. For example, in 1962 the U.S. Office of Naval Research, the Carnegie Institute of Technology, the Ford Foundation, and the University of Pittsburgh cosponsored a fifteen-day conference on "new perspectives in organization research" and invited participants from "business and industrial administration, economics, mathematics, political science, psychology, social psychology, sociology, and statistics" (Cooper, Leavitt, and Shelly 1964, p. 39). The twenty-three papers presented for extensive discussion referred to 617 separate articles and books considered relevant. By 1976 even a typical introductory textbook on "managerial process and organizational behavior" discussed the work of 889 authors.

Some idea of the current topics considered basic in the "people approaches" to management is gained from a partial list of the subject headings of another survey text: accountability, adjustment, authority, individual behavior, organizational behavior, bureaucracy, centralization, change, communication, complexes, conflict, conformity, control, cooperation, creativity, decentralization, delegation, dependence, organizational development, discipline, education, ego, emotions, environment, exchange, functions, groups, heredity, human relations, id, independence, interdependence, individual, inferences, information systems, innovation, interaction, interorganizational behavior, intraorganizational behavior, interpersonal behavior, language, leadership, learning, logic, management, motivation, needs, neuroses, norms, objectives, organization, perception, personality, planning, policies, power, problem-solving procedures, process, productivity, professionalization, psychological mechanisms, psychoses, rationality, renewal, response, responsibility, roles, self, span, specialization, symbiosis, synergy, system, and viability (Hicks 1972, pp. 509–513).

MANAGEMENT SCIENCE

Management science was a "war baby." The scale and complexity of World War II put unprecedented demands upon the state of the art of problem solving. In research and development, the scientific method was put to the test of utility as never before. In personnel, millions had to be selected, classified, trained, assigned, and cared for. In logistics and transportation, there were massive challenges in budgeting, procurement, scheduling, production, allocation, routing, distribution, supply, storage, maintenance, and replacement. In operations, strategic and tactical decision making constantly pursued effective organization, deployment, and maneuverability of available resources. In intelligence, as in all of the other military functions, the tasks of gathering, processing, and interpreting data were immense; the need for decision making under uncertainty was certain; and the utility of probabilistic assessments, "what if" analyses, and contingency plans was obvious. These needs spawned a set of new approaches to military problem solving that were interchangeably called "operational research," "operations research," or "operations analysis." When many of the same concepts and techniques were applied to business problems after the war, the approach tended to be called "management science" or "decision analysis."

Management science is heavily dependent upon concepts and problem-solving methods borrowed from the physical sciences and mathematics. It is decision-oriented and relies upon symbolic expression and formal mathematical models to formulate and solve problems. Its appraisals rest primarily on economic effectiveness criteria, and it makes extensive use of electronic computers to increase the speed and scale of data processing.

Russell L. Ackoff, a management science pioneer, has stated the "general form" of the operations research (or management science) model as

$$E = f(x_i, y_j)$$

> where E is the measure of the system's effectiveness (or ineffectiveness), x_i is the set of controllable variables, and y_j is the set of uncontrollable variables. For example, in a production problem E may be the total cost of production, one of the controllable variables may be the size of the production, and one of the uncontrollable variables may be customers' demand. The operations research problem is to find those values of the variables represented by x_i which will maximize effectiveness E (or minimize ineffectiveness) ["A Survey of Applications of Operations Research," p. 9].

Stated in this way, management science models can be deterministic, stochastic, or heuristic. Each approach has its strengths and weaknesses in dealing with complexity, variability, and uncertainty.

Deterministic models can be applied to various managerial problems where the values of the relevant uncontrollable variables are known with certainty. They are particularly useful in solving problems in which "a group of limited resources must be shared among a number of competing demands, and all decisions are 'interlocking' because they all have to be made under the common set of fixed limits" (Henderson and Schlaifer 1954, p. 151). Problems of allocation, distribution, location, and routing come immediately to mind. Some simple examples arise in the blending of fluids or the mixing of ingredients. More complex examples can be found in determining the shortest or least-cost route through a network of fixed points (such as planning a deliveryman's or a salesman's route, finding the shipping pattern that will minimize freight costs among dozens of supply points and hundreds of customers, or scheduling workers, materials, and machines for optimal productivity in a plant). Many questions of where to produce, where to purchase, where to sell, or where to store can then be answered.

Mathematical programming techniques are used in these cases

> . . . to reduce the whole procedure to a simple, definite routine. There is a rule for finding a program to start with, there is a rule for finding the successive changes that will increase the profits or lower the costs, and there is a rule for following through all the repercussions of each change. What is more, it is *absolutely certain* that if these rules are followed, they will lead to the best possible program; and it will be perfectly clear when the best possible program has been found. It is because the procedure follows definite rules that it can be taught to clerical personnel or handed over to automatic computers [Henderson and Schlaifer, p. 152].

A family of deterministic models has been developed to aid in decision making under conditions of certainty; that is, when the decision maker "has access to all information that would be relevant to a particular problem, and he can accurately predict the outcome of each alternative action available to him" (Johnson and Siskin 1976, p. 40). The more typical management problem, however, is rife with uncertainty. More often than not, the manager must "make decisions when any one of several different outcomes could possibly occur following the selection of a particular course of action." To make matters worse, one cannot always specify all possible outcomes of a given decision; or, while it may be possible to specify all outcomes, perhaps the relative likelihood that each will occur is unknown. Finally, the manager's tolerance of risk may change as he moves through the decision process. The management scientist seeks to capture these uncertainties in stochastic models—models that incorporate elements of chance or probability—and particularly in stochastic models that incorporate adjustments for risk into the decision process being modeled.

Stochastic models of managerial processes often combine graphics with mathematics in formulating and solving problems. PERT, CPM, and decision trees are representative historical landmarks.

PERT (Program Evaluation and Review Technique) and CPM (Critical Path Method) address the problems that concerned Gantt. The difficulty in using Gantt charts is that they do not always show interrelationships among various activities: "Thus, it is not possible to deduce from a Gantt chart that activity X must be complete before activity Y can be started, or that a delay between activity Y and activity Z is permissible but not essential" (Lockyer 1969, pp. 2–5). PERT was developed in 1957–1958 by members of the U.S. Navy Special Projects Office as part of the fleet ballistic missile program and rapidly spread to industry, where it is commonly used to schedule large, complex, nonrepetitive jobs, such as construction of a structure.

PERT represents a project graphically by a network diagram of "activities" and "events." An activity is a task the completion time of which is probabilistically estimated. An event is non-time-consuming and signals either the beginning or the end of an activity. Activities and events are interconnected by arrows that indicate their flow and arrange them sequentially or simultaneously, depending upon their relationship to each other and to the completion of the project as a whole. (Flow-charting of this sort was, of course, pioneered by the Gilbreths.) Combinations of mathematical programming and "dynamic programming" are used to "solve" the network (the technique originated in 1952 by Richard Bellman of the RAND Corporation to solve problems in which time plays an essential role and in which the sequence of decisions is vital). Typical PERT solutions include earliest and latest times for each event, permissible slack time, the probabilities of achieving specified completion times, and the "critical path" (or "least-time" path) through the project.

CPM was developed at Du Pont in 1958–1959 and added cost to the PERT-type analysis of time. Probabilistic cost estimates are assigned to each activity and, when combined with PERT, permit analyses of alternative time-cost paths through the project. CPM is used for repetitive jobs and, over time, cost and time estimates tend to become more real and less uncertain.

Decision trees are used by almost all management scientists to portray the decision process step by step. They offer a graphic representation of a multiperiod decision process, with each decision point offering only two mutually exclusive alternatives. They incorporate probabilistic estimates of the "expected value" of each action so that the decision maker can exercise his risk preference at each "branch" before choosing one alternative "payoff" or the other. As he moves through the tree, he follows his personal utility function to a "good" decision overall.

Deterministic and stochastic modeling have had broad application in management since the 1950's. They are used, for example, to assign equipment and personnel, in scheduling, in input-output analyses, in inventory control, to determine economic lot sizes, to develop maintenance and replacement routines, to allocate scarce resources against competing demands, to solve queuing and waiting-time problems, in advertising effectiveness studies, in analysis of brand switching, in capital budgeting, in credit scoring, in actuarial calculations, in production-flow smoothing, in risk assessment, in problems involving the time value of money, in portfolio selection, and in the design of management information systems. The modeling and computational needs of management scientists have also interacted fruitfully with the evolution of applied mathematics and statistics to improve the state of the art of sampling, statistical inference, forecasting, probability theory, programming, and the like.

The frontier of management science is heuristic modeling—exploratory problem-solving models that utilize self-educating "feedback" to improve their performance and utility. These models depend heavily on game theory as developed by John von Neumann and Oskar Morgenstern, general systems theory as expounded by Ludwig von Bertalanffy, feedback theories from Norbert Wiener's cybernetics, and contributions to information theory by Claude E. Shannon and Warren Weaver. They permit "gaming" situations in which "players" can explore such competitive problems as bidding, purchasing, contract negotiations, interpersonal values, or collective bargaining. They also permit simplified computer-based simulations of virtually every management decision process.

Management games have been especially useful in management education.

> The first business simulation game involved five teams of managers, each of whom directed the economic activity of a facsimile firm that was competing in a simulated consumer market with other firms. The possible economic activity was defined by a group of operation researchers in an economic model which was programmed to be manipulated by an IBM 650 computer. The computer program generated automatically accounting-like reports for each firm to observe the results of its decisions. The accounting reports and the understandability of the original model allowed the authors to involve experienced businessmen in simulated techniques not heretofore possible. The participants had the available information, felt they could control the operation of their firm, and were able to function in the simulated decision-making environment in a natural fashion [McKenney 1967, p. 6].

From this first game, devised by Richard Bellman and associates at the RAND Corporation in 1956–1957, the idea spread rapidly. By 1957 the University of California at Los Angeles had introduced a business game into its MBA program. The University of Washington version was in place by 1958. The University of California at Berkeley, Stanford University, San Diego State University, and the University of Southern California were "on-line" with teaching games by 1959. Harvard followed in 1961. By the 1970's there were several hundred games of varying complexity in use in business and academia that conformed to the specifications for "reality" suggested above by McKenney.

Simulation models had the same origins but increasingly advocated their "interactive" utility. If a management process or system or an enterprise could be accurately modeled, then "what if" analysis could be taken to a new plane of sophistication. Current systems could be described. Hypothetical systems could be explored. Improved systems could be designed. Crucial management problems, such as choice of investment policies or selection of facilities, could be simulated for exploration of alternatives. Capital markets, the stock market, individual firms, or entire industries could be modeled. An early and persistent advocate, Jay W. Forrester of the Massachusetts Institute of Technology, spoke of the origins of simulation:

> The goal is "enterprise design," to create more successful management policies and organizational structures.
>
> Industrial dynamics now becomes possible as a result of four foundations developed during the last twenty years. The theory of information-feedback systems gives us a basis for understanding the goal-seeking, self-correcting interplay between the parts of a business system. Investigation of the nature of decision making in the context of modern military tactics forms a basis for understanding the place of decision making in industry. The experimental model approach to the design of complex engineering and military systems can be applied to social systems. The digital computer has become a practical, economical tool for the vast amount of computation required [*Industrial Dynamics*, p. vii].

As to the philosophy and objectives of simulation, Forrester continues:

> The approach is one of building models of companies and industries to determine how information and policy create the character of the organization. The "management laboratory" now becomes possible. The first step is to identify the problems and goals of the organization. The second is to formulate a model that shows the interrelationships of the significant factors. Such a model is a systematic way to express our wealth of descriptive knowledge about industrial activity. The model tells us how the behavior of the system results from the interactions of its component parts. These interactions are often more important than the pieces taken separately. Finally, proposed changes can be tried in the model and the best of them used as a guide to better management.

Thus the study and practice of management continues to evolve with the "people approaches" at one extreme and management science at the other. The manager remains where he or she has always been—in the middle, between human beings and machines, with harmony and effectiveness the goals. Can what the manager really does for a living be modeled and then simulated? If so, is the manager doomed to extinction through automation of his or her function? Probably not. Management is sure to remain the same human enigma that puzzled Babbage, Taylor, and Mayo. The real impact of "science" on the performance of such an intensely human role remains to be seen.

BIBLIOGRAPHY

Russell L. Ackoff, "The Development of Operations Research as a Science," in *Operations Research*, 4 (June 1956), is a retrospective view of the first ten years of management science in the United States by a key participant; and "A Survey of Applications of Operations Research," in *Proceedings of the Conference on Case Studies in Operations Research* (Cleveland, 1956), pp. 9–17, is an early summary of work in management science, reprinted in Shuchman, op. cit., pp. 135–144. American Association of Collegiate Schools of Business, *The American Association of Collegiate Schools of Business, 1916–1966* (Homewood, Ill., 1966), is an introduction to the evolution of college business curricula. Frank Baker, ed., *Organizational Systems: General Systems Approaches to Complex Organizations* (Homewood, Ill., 1973), has a good historical section. Loren Baritz, *The Servants of Power: A History of the Use of Social Science in American Industry* (Middletown, Conn., 1960), is excellent on industrial psychology movement, Mayo, and the Hawthorne studies. Chester I. Barnard, *The Functions of the Executive: Thirtieth Anniversary Edition* (Cambridge, Mass., 1968), is a classic of the human relations school, republished with an excellent historical introduction by Kenneth R. Andrews.

Ralph M. Barnes, *Motion and Time Study: Design and Measurement of Work*, 6th ed. (New York, 1968), is a basic text with good historical sections, first published in 1937. James P. Baughman, ed., *The History of American Management: Selections from the Business History Review* (Englewood Cliffs, N.J., 1969), contains nine articles on systematic management, the evolution of business organizations, business-government relationships, and the professionalization of leadership. Alfred D. Chandler, Jr., "The Beginnings of 'Big Business' in American Industry," in *Business History Review*, 33 (Spring 1959), reprinted in Baughman, op. cit., pp. 1–28, is the standard introduction to the history of the large, vertically integrated, centralized, functionally departmentalized industrial organization; and "The Railroads: Pioneers in Modern Corporate Management," in *Business History Review*, 39 (Spring 1965), reprinted in Baughman, op. cit., pp. 29–52, details the contributions of Latrobe, McCallum, and Thomson. William W. Cooper, Harold J. Leavitt, and Maynard W. Shelly II, *New Perspectives in Organization Research* (New York, 1964), twenty-three papers and commentary from a landmark conference on the "people approaches." Ernest Dale, *The Great Organizers* (New York, 1960), is excellent on applications of systematic management in large corporations like Du Pont, General Motors, and Westinghouse.

Alan C. Filley, Robert J. House, and Steven Kerr, *Managerial Process and Organizational Behavior*, 2nd ed. (Glenview, Ill., 1976), is a survey text reviewing the vast literature on the subject. Jay W. Forrester, *Industrial Dynamics* (Cambridge, Mass., 1961), is a pioneer attempt to model industries. Claude S. George, Jr., *The History of Management Thought* (Englewood Cliffs, N.J., 1968), is the basic introduction to the subject from the Sumerians to the present day. Samuel Haber, *Efficiency and Uplift: Scientific Management in the Progressive Era, 1890–1920* (Chicago, 1964), sets Taylor and his disciples within the context of more general economic, political, and social reform movements. Alexander Henderson and Robert Schlaifer, "Mathematical Programming: Better Information for Better Decision Making," in *Harvard Business Review*, 32 (May–June 1954), reprinted in Shuchman, op. cit., pp. 149–198, is one of the first expositions for the businessman by pioneer management scientists. Herbert G. Hicks, *The Management of Organizations: A Systems and Human Resources Approach*, 2nd ed. (New York, 1972), is an introduction to the basic literature of behavioral science as applied to management.

Rodney D. Johnson and Bernard R. Siskin, *Quantitative Techniques for Business Decisions* (Englewood Cliffs, N.J., 1976), an introductory text. Sudhir Kakar, *Frederick Taylor: A Study in Personality and Innovation* (Cambridge, Mass., 1970), is an intriguing psychohistorical biography. Harold J. Leavitt, "Applied Organization Change in Industry: Structural, Technical, and Human Approaches," in Cooper, Leavitt, and Shelly, op. cit., pp. 55–71, has good conceptual distinctions made among approaches to organizational change. Joseph A. Litterer, "Systematic Management: Design for Organizational Recoupling in American Manufacturing Firms," in *Business History Review*, 37 (Winter 1963), reprinted in Baughman, op. cit., pp. 53–74, details the work of Metcalfe and Towne with references to other articles by this author on related topics. K. G. Lockyer, *An Introduction to Critical Path Analysis*, 3rd ed. (London, 1969), includes a good historical section on PERT, CPM, and related management science methods. James L. McKenney, *Simulation Gaming for Management Development* (Cambridge, Mass., 1967), is an introduction to business games with a historical preface.

Harwood F. Merrill, ed., *Classics in Management* (New York, 1960), is an excellent sampler of the writings of Owen, Babbage, Metcalfe, Towne, Taylor, Gantt, Emerson, Church, Fayol, Gilbreth, Follett, Mayo, and others. Henry Mintzberg, *The Nature of Managerial Work* (New York, 1973), is a brilliant pioneering study on what modern managers actually do. Paul Monroe, ed., *A Cyclopedia of Education*, 5 vols. (New York, 1911–1913), contains an excellent historical summary of "commercial education" and of the curricula of pioneer college business programs. Albert E. Musson and Eric Robinson, *Science and Technology in the Industrial Revolution* (Manchester, 1969), contains an excellent chapter on "training captains of industry." Mabel Newcomer, "Professionalization of Leadership in the Big Business Corporation," in *Business History Review*, 29 (March 1955), reprinted in Baughman, op. cit., pp. 244–252, is the best brief introduction to the subject. Sidney Pollard, *The Genesis of Modern Management: A Study of the Industrial Revolution in Great Britain* (Harmondsworth, England, 1968), is the basic source on the European inheritance. Abraham Shuchman, *Scientific Decision Making in Business: Readings in Operations Research for Nonmathematicians* (New York, 1963), is an excellent anthology. Herbert A. Simon, *Administrative Behavior,* 3rd ed. (New York, 1976), is a pioneering blend of behavioral and management science. Harvey M. Wagner, *Principles of Management Science: With Applications to Executive Decisions,* 2nd ed. (Englewood Cliffs, N.J., 1975), is the best general introduction to its subject.

[*See also* AMERICAN BUSINESS INSTITUTIONS BEFORE THE RAILROAD; BUREAUCRACY; EDUCATION; ENTREPRENEURSHIP; PRODUCTIVITY; RISE AND EVOLUTION OF BIG BUSINESS; SCIENCE; TECHNOLOGY; *and* WORK.]

Part V
THE AMERICAN SOCIAL FRAMEWORK

SOCIALISM

Michael Harrington

AMERICA is the only advanced industrial nation without a mass socialist movement. That historic fact can be felt in all of its immediacy on a visit to Detroit, Michigan. Canada is on the other side of the Detroit River and easily accessible, by way of a tunnel, to Windsor, Ontario. The people in Windsor have the same living standard as those in Detroit, watch the same television, work for the same giant corporations, and belong to the same international unions. Yet the Canadian workers are quite likely to vote for the New Democratic party (NDP), an affiliate of the Socialist International, and their unions endorse NDP candidates, while the American workers vote for liberals in the Democratic party, which is, like every other major institution in the nation, procapitalist.

Why is there no socialist movement in America? That question was first asked by Werner Sombart in a study published in 1906. He concluded: "All the factors that till now have prevented the development of Socialism in the United States are about to disappear or to be converted into their opposite, with the result that in the next generation Socialism in America will very probably experience the greatest possible expansion of its appeal" (*Why Is There No Socialism in the United States?*, p. 119). In fact, the socialist organizations were stronger in 1906 than they were in 1979.

One obvious explanation of this anomaly is that America is an "exceptional" society that, for unique reasons, did not undergo the same political development that took place in Europe, Australia, and Japan. And one factor in that explanation is that the American economy is different. The argument is then made that this exceptional economy was the basis of an equally exceptional social and political framework.

In what follows it will be seen that this thesis of a unique economic base in America, determining a unique social and political structure, is valuable only if used with great care and sophistication—which is not ordinarily the case. More broadly, the "base-superstructure" model of society, which is mistakenly thought to be Marxist in inspiration, is seriously flawed, since it implies that causation is linear, mechanical, and unidirectional, and it does not understand how the economy, polity, and social structure interact reciprocally.

The particular focus of the present analysis is the economic aspect of the history, theory, and practice of American socialism. At no point will I assume that there is an independent economic factor that exists in isolation from class structure, politics, and culture. I will view the organic unity of all of those factors from the vantage point of the economic, and I will regularly note the interaction of the economic and the noneconomic.

Given that methodology, the topic will be approached in three different ways: first, a survey of the political history of American socialism, with particular attention upon how it has related to the economic development of American society; second, an attempt to generalize that experience and theorize the impact of the economy upon the socialist movement; third, an examination of the way in which socialist economics has influenced the United States even though socialist politics, since about 1820, has failed to be a major force in the United States.

SOCIALISM

POLITICAL HISTORY OF AMERICAN SOCIALISM

The first phase of American socialist history covers the sixty years between 1820 and 1880. The nation was overwhelmingly agricultural, but industrialization intensified throughout the period. The central political event was, of course, the Civil War, a complex struggle that, among many other things, pitted the protectionists of the industrial North against the free traders of the plantation South. This was also the time of a peculiarly American experience that is routinely cited to explain the later weakness of socialism in the nation: the conquest of the frontier, genocide against the native Americans, and the creation of the first truly continental nation.

During those years there was no industrial proletariat of consequence. Many of the workers in the relatively small number of factories were young women who were not permanently attached to the labor force. The skilled artisans formed unions, and there were even attempts at nationwide federations (the National Labor Union and, at the very end of this first phase, the Knights of Labor). But there was no mass of factory workers concentrated in crowded cities. Therefore there was no basis for a stable, working-class-based socialist movement.

In Karl Marx's analysis such a period gives rise to "utopian" socialism, that is, to a movement with a vision of a socialist society but without the practical possibility of putting it into effect. People have begun to realize that the great political ideals of the bourgeois revolution—above all, its commitment to equality—are increasingly contradicted by the emerging economic and social inequality of the capitalist system. The masses have not yet arrived on the stage of history, and these insights are confined to individuals and sects.

In Europe the utopian socialists included François-Noël ("Gracchus") Babeuf and the Conspiracy of Equals, Count Claude-Henri de Saint-Simon ("the last gentleman and first socialist of France"), and François Marie Charles Fourier in France; Robert Owen and the followers of David Ricardo in England; and Moses Hess (who was also an early theorist of Zionism), Wilhelm Weitling, the academic "True Socialists," and the League of the Just (which became the Communist League and commissioned the *Communist Manifesto*) in Germany. Frequently the socialist group took on a quasi-religious and quite sectarian character (Weitling was thought of as a messiah; Saint-Simon dreamed of a secular religion and his followers sought a female god in the Middle East). Indeed, Marx and Friedrich Engels refused to join the Communist League until all of the rituals were removed from the structure of the organization.

In the United States the religious, sectarian character of utopian socialism was particularly pronounced. The nation had been formed, in part, by dissenting religionists, some of them from radical traditions. Land was relatively abundant, and it was possible to establish communities dedicated to Christian communism. The link between this religious, communitarian impulse and secular socialism can be seen quite clearly in Robert Owen's extraordinary visit to America in 1824.

Owen was a British industrialist who became convinced that a decent working environment would not only be socially just and offer the possibility for developing better human beings but would also increase productivity. He had initially attempted to win the British establishment to his views, and was tolerated in this effort until his atheism became public knowledge. At that point the upper classes turned on Owen and, searching for a new base, he became deeply involved in the nascent British trade union movement. America, he thought, was the perfect place to put his communitarian ideas into effect. He therefore bought a 30,000-acre farm in Indiana from a religious communitarian sect, the Rappists, who had already built three such communities. Thus the religious and secular strands of socialist inspiration came together in the 1820's—and were to do so throughout American socialist history.

When Owen came to America in 1824 to take possession of New Harmony, Indiana, he was greeted by cheering crowds. Even more extraordinary, he addressed a joint session of Congress that was attended by both the president and the president-elect. In the speech Owen stated a theme that was to be taken up by many (including Marx and Engels): America, he said, was more open to socialism than any other nation on the face of the earth. Indeed, in 1824 there was no other nation in which the political leadership would listen to an avowed socialist talk about socialism. Ironically, the very openness of American society that allowed it to greet Robert Owen and to welcome dozens of communitarian experiments may well have been one of the chief causes of socialist failure.

In the 1820's, though, that irony was far from apparent and the socialist potential was quite obvious. For example, the first labor political party in the world, the Workingmen's party, was organized, in 1829 and 1830, in Philadelphia and New York. A key figure in the New York venture was Frances Wright, one of the most extraordinary leaders of the time. She was a friend of French revolutionaries, one of the first feminists, an antiracist who established an integrated commune in Tennessee, and an activist in the New York Workingmen's party. She also believed that it was necessary to raise, and form, children apart from their families if a truly new system of motivation was to be established, a utopian attitude that hurt her politically. Still, Wright's remarkable career and the creation of the labor parties were yet another sign of the strength of the early socialist movement in America.

In the 1840's there was another burst of socialist enthusiasm, this time inspired by the ideas of Charles Fourier. Even more than Owen, Fourier defined his socialism in small-scale, communitarian terms. For him, and for most American socialists of the first phase, their ideal was a community in which everyone functioned as a family member. Through Horace Greeley and Albert Brisbane, the Fourier vogue in the 1840's made a considerable impact upon American intellectual life and led to the establishment of the most famous intentional community the nation has known: Brook Farm. In that experiment socialist theory, Unitarian faith, and, ultimately, Swedenborgian theology all played a role.

What was exceptional about the first quarter-century of socialism in America (from the early 1820's to the late 1840's) was the warm welcome it received. There were economic factors at work —the availability of land was quite important— but it is obvious that the cultural dimension was even more significant. A country that proclaimed itself "a new order of the ages" on its great seal was quite hospitable to the socialist idea. Moreover, insofar as the early American socialism had an economic theory, it was committed to small-scale communitarianism, a tradition that flourished in that innocent age but became much less relevant with the rise of capitalist industry after the Civil War and the triumph of monopoly at the end of the century.

There is one economic interpretation of this utopian socialism in America that deserves brief notice. Its author was Karl Marx. One of his followers, Hermann Kriege, had immigrated to the United States. At this point he became involved in the free land movement, a drive that culminated in the Homestead Act of 1862, which provided virtually free land to settlers. The movement, Marx commented, often spoke a dreamy rhetoric of how free land would put an end to all of the problems of capitalism and of how love was the key to the new future. Marx felt bitter toward Kriege for supporting such un-Marxist concepts. But he was quite positive about the basic movement, despite his criticisms of its rhetoric. In the United States, Marx said, the anticapitalist consciousness of working people was taking the form of a demand for small, capitalist property (a farm) for all. Objectively, Marx held (and history proved him quite right), such a perspective was bound to fail, since capitalist development would inevitably and ruthlessly overwhelm and subvert it. But subjectively, in terms of the political evolution of American socialism, it was important for American Marxists and socialists to participate in the movement. Indeed, in the *Communist Manifesto* Marx told his American followers that the free land movement should be the focus of their activities.

Marx was right on an important count. The vogue of Fourierist socialism in the 1840's passed, but the movement for free land continued and culminated in the Homestead Act, signed into law by President Abraham Lincoln. In the years before and during the Civil War, the socialists as such were not important, either as a political movement or as economic thinkers. Some of them did play a role on the Union side during the conflict, particularly the German "Forty-Eighters" who came to America after the failure of the Revolution of 1848. During the war Marx and his friends (including Albert Wedemeyer, who played a significant military role in Missouri) saw Lincoln as the hope of the Left. Indeed, Marx even mythologized that conviction, describing Lincoln as a "single-minded son of the American working class," which was hardly the case.

In the postwar years there were two socialist

tendencies of some importance. The German exiles created socialist enclaves inhabited only by those who spoke German. Engels was more than a little disgusted that his compatriots were incapable of translating their ideas into English. Moreover, many of the Germans were followers of Marx's rival, Ferdinand Lassalle. That meant, among many other things, that they believed that economic struggle—unions—could not have any appreciable effect on the position of the working class, since the capitalists would simply raise prices to compensate for any wage increase exacted from them. That was not true (prices fell throughout the nineteenth century, except during the Civil War)—but, more to the point, it isolated the German-speaking socialists almost as much as their refusal to learn English. When, for instance, a massive strike wave surged across the country in 1877, the Lassalleans told the workers that their epochal battle would make no difference, and that they must drop such struggles and organize a socialist political party instead.

The other tendency, with roots going back to Frances Wright and the early utopian movement, was most dramatically represented by Victoria Woodhull and her sister, Tennessee Claflin. They were feminists—the American women's movement had crystallized in the late 1840's among activists in the abolitionist cause who discovered that they were oppressed too—socialists, and freethinkers. When they and their friends took control of the New York branch of the International Working Men's Association (the First International), Engels was furious. American socialism, he complained, was being taken over by advocates of free love and various quack schemes. Although the movement that Engels and Marx inspired played a major role among feminists, both in America and in Europe, the inspirers were never fully liberated from the prejudices of their times.

If Engels clearly did not recognize the feminist potential in the United States, he was right on one important count: that in the 1870's, after half a century of activity in the United States, the socialists had yet to make contact with the American workers. In part, particularly in the early years of that half-century, that was because a significant factory proletariat did not exist. But in part it was because the socialists were very, very American, that is, they tended toward middle-class panaceas. Around 1880 many things in America began to change, and socialism moved toward a new phase that would culminate in the rise of the Socialist party of Eugene Victor Debs.

This was the time of industrial growth and chronic crisis, of the emergence of industrial giants. New waves of immigrants flooded into the country, to the great working-class cities of the Northeast and Middle West where they were housed in teeming, poverty-stricken neighborhoods. There were pitched battles between workers and company police (the Pinkertons, more often than not) and government troops. The strike wave of 1877 spread like a prairie fire; the workers at Homestead, Pennsylvania, defeated the steel company police, only to be routed by soldiers; there was anarchist talk, and sometimes direct action. But institutionally the greatest change, from a socialist point of view, in the last two decades of the century was the founding in 1886 of the first stable union federation in the history of the nation, the American Federation of Labor (AFL).

Many of those who organized the AFL were socialists, including Samuel Gompers, who served as its president in every year save one until his death in 1924. Gompers was a cigarmaker, and in that trade the workers used to hire someone to read to them. The books were often about the workers' movement and socialism. But there was another principle dearer to Gompers than socialism, and it was to bring him and the AFL into a momentous conflict with socialism. Gompers believed that unions must be, first and foremost, dedicated to the immediate needs of the workers.

The most successful union in America prior to the AFL was the Knights of Labor. It admitted middle-class idealists as well as workers, was sometimes less than enthusiastic about supporting strikes, and spent much time discussing schemes for reform or for utopia. Gompers was determined—quite rightly—to build an organization composed exclusively of workers and focused upon wages, hours, and working conditions. This is not to say that the early AFL was completely pragmatic. The demand for an eight-hour day and the idea of making 1 May a workers' holiday and rallying point for the demand came out of that movement.

Gompers became involved in two conflicts with socialists that had to do with the character of the labor movement. In the first a group of socialists in the AFL lobbied a ten-point platform to victory in the convention of 1895. Their program was based upon the platform of the British labor movement and included the nationalization of basic industry. When the AFL voted in favor of the motion, Gompers maneuvered so as to get full approval postponed, and in the ensuing year he was able to scuttle the idea. His motives were complex, but one important component of his thinking was the fear that if the AFL committed itself to socialist ideas, it would lose the predominantly Irish Catholic building trades, which were opposed to socialism on religious grounds. That, in turn, was an expression of one of the fundamental problems of American socialism, a difficulty that no other socialist movement had to face: the extreme heterogeneity of the American working class. Racial, ethnic, and religious divisions were often more important to workers than class solidarity, and that was to be one of the main reasons for the failure of the socialists to win the working class to their cause.

The other incident pitted Gompers against Daniel De Leon. An intense and combative intellectual, De Leon had developed his own distinctive version of Marxism. Socialism, De Leon argued, would not be organized along the parliamentary lines of the bourgeois state. Rather, people would be represented according to their place of work instead of the neighborhood in which they lived. Thus the fundamental unit of society would be the socialist industrial union, not the precinct or the voting district. And the ultimate direction of the nation would be confided not to the Congress but to the federation of socialist unions. Given this vision of the future, De Leon and his followers in the Socialist Labor party built their own unions and, in 1890, tried to get an AFL charter for their own Central Labor Federation in New York.

Gompers saw De Leon's proposal as one more attempt to politicize the unions, that is, to divert them from their basic function of fighting for wages, hours, and working conditions. He appealed to Engels to mediate the dispute, but the latter did not reply. The event was an important one in the process that was moving Gompers away from his youthful socialism. It eventually led to the doctrine of "voluntarism," a theory that dominated much of the AFL until the New Deal of Franklin D. Roosevelt. In Gompers' mature view, the workers would not rely on the (capitalist) state when they could win gains by collective union action. The government would be appealed to only in those areas where union organization was inherently unable to deal with a problem. This perspective shared some values with the leftist critique of socialism that developed in Europe under the aegis of the syndicalists, but it also had the conservative consequence of putting the labor movement officially on record as antisocialist.

Gompers' strategy did provide a basis for a socialist political party appealing to the working class. If the unions did not have a political platform, then the socialists could claim to state the political interests of the workers, which were seen as located outside the AFL. That is exactly what Debs proceeded to do.

Debs was a champion of industrial unionism, that is, of organizing all of the workers in an industry into one union instead of enrolling them in a variety of craft unions. Starting as a Democrat and a nonsocialist trade unionist, he organized the American Railway Union in 1893. In 1894 the union was involved in a bitter strike with the Pullman Company, a fight that ended with the federal government providing troops to back up the corporation. As a result of the strike, Debs was jailed, and while in prison he became a socialist. For a brief period he considered a utopian scheme to move all the socialists to a sparsely settled western state and to create a statewide showcase there. But in 1901, he supported the foundation of the Socialist party of the United States, which was to be the major socialist organization in America for the next seventy years.

In terms of the analytic framework of this article, the second period of American socialist history ended in 1933, with the emergence of the New Deal. The years between 1880 and 1933 were characterized by the attempt to build a classic, labor-based socialist party on a European model. In contrast with the utopian phase from the 1820's to the 1870's, socialism was now working within a highly capitalist, industrial, and urban framework. As might be expected, its character changed dramatically. At the same time, however, the socialists exhibited that heterogeneity that was such a key, and exceptional, characteristic of American, as contrasted with European, socialism.

For example, the Debsian socialist movement was composed of a number of quite different constituencies. In New York it was based upon the largely Jewish needle-trades unions (the International Ladies' Garment Workers and the Amalgamated Clothing Workers). In Pennsylvania and Wisconsin it had a following among the German-American working class. The northern prairies produced farmer socialists who became the basis for the Nonpartisan League (and were quite similar to the people who created the Co-operative Commonwealth Federation in Canada, the precursor of the present-day New Democratic party). In the Southwest the Debsians inherited much of the Populist strength that refused to go into the Democratic party. Indeed, the highest Socialist vote (in percentage terms) in American history occurred in Oklahoma (so did a socialist insurrection in 1917, the Green Corn Rebellion, a movement in opposition to World War I).

In the West and Northwest the socialists found support among miners, loggers, and seamen, and were sometimes associated with the anarchist-tending Industrial Workers of the World (IWW), a revolutionary competitor of the AFL. There were socialist enclaves in Texas (in the area where Lyndon Johnson was brought up) and northern Louisiana (where Huey Long probably came under socialist influence). On the Pacific Coast many of the socialists—including the novelist Jack London—were anti-Asian, terrified of what might happen if hordes of "coolies" entered the country and undercut native-born labor. And there were black socialists, notably A. Philip Randolph, who saw an integrated movement of the black and white working classes as the precondition of black liberation.

Corresponding to this human and sectional diversity, the Socialist party had a range of conceptions of socialism. There were the "sewer socialists" of Milwaukee, who defined the movement in terms of very pragmatic, and incremental, reforms. There were Marxist intellectuals, like the party leader Morris Hillquit, who tried to translate the European categories into American practice. There were Christian socialists and cooperators who continued the communitarian tradition of the earlier socialist generation. And there was a split—replicated in almost all of the European socialist parties of the period—between the socialist ultimate vision and the immediate program.

In the 1912 presidential campaign, for instance—the high point of socialist presidential activity, when Debs received 6 percent of the vote—the Socialist party campaigned for unemployment insurance, socialized medicine, the rights of unions, and other socialist reforms. Clearly, then, the socialist immediate program had a great impact on American society. It was the first political expression of the fight for what became the welfare state.

On the other side, the pro-IWW wing of the Socialist party was revolutionary to the point of indifference to such immediate demands. For instance, it did not believe in signing contracts or negotiating pensions or other benefits, since such agreements were believed to serve only to integrate the workers into the system without challenging its basic injustice. After the campaign of 1912, the various factions were often locked in furious internal battles, with Debs, who stayed out of organizational debates, refusing to join any one group (though his heart was obviously with the left wing).

But then a number of events altered the position of socialism in American society and led to the disappointment of the hope that the United States would follow the European—or, in a more sophisticated version, the British—pattern. There is scholarly dispute over the most important factors in this failure, with some dating the decline from 1912 and others from 1920. Without trying to settle this intricate argument (or even present it), some obviously important developments will simply be noted.

To begin with, Woodrow Wilson made overtures toward the AFL during his first term—he was the first president of the United States ever to attend a union convention, and he created the post of secretary of labor. During his second term his alliance with Gompers became even more marked because the AFL chief was a vociferous supporter of the war effort and tried to rally European working-class leaders to it. At this point it began to occur to Gompers and others that they did care who was in the White House, and that they might have to go beyond their policy of rewarding the friends, and punishing the enemies, of labor at the ballot box. As the unions took the first tentative steps toward the Democratic party and the welfare state, one of the preconditions of socialist success was being subverted.

Then there was the issue of the war. Most of the European socialist parties rallied to the side of their country in the conflict, thus shattering the illusion that the workers had no fatherland. The American Socialist party, though, remained true to the classic convictions of the movement and came out against the war at a St. Louis convention in 1917. The immediate impact of that action is hard to guess—Hillquit received 22 percent of the vote in the 1917 New York mayoralty race, running as an antiwar candidate—but it tended to reinforce the nativist charge that the socialists were "un-American." That suspicion was compounded later in 1917, when the American socialists, including Debs, supported the Bolshevik Revolution with great enthusiasm. And then, in a move that was strongly in keeping with the sectarian tendencies of the movement, the Communists split with the pro-Russian socialists and formed several Communist parties.

In 1919 there was a series of bitter labor struggles, most notably the great steel strike led by William Z. Foster (who later became the chairman of the Communist party and one of its most servile Stalinists). In Seattle that year there was a general strike in which the workers' committee took over effective political control of the city and people muttered about the "Seattle Soviet." All of these developments led to "red raids" and a vicious campaign of repression against radicals of every persuasion, foreign-born radicals first and foremost.

Strangely enough, one of the socialist dreams seemed to become reality in the aftermath of those setbacks. In 1924 the labor movement joined with the Socialist party in backing Robert M. La Follette's bid for the presidency. But the socialists gave more than they received in that effort, and La Follette's defeat took the steam out of the nonsocialist movement for a labor party. By 1928, when the Socialist party fielded Norman Thomas as its presidential candidate, the party had dwindled to a shadow of its Debsian self. At one point it had enrolled more than one hundred thousand members; won seats in Congress, state legislatures, and city government; and published hundreds of newspapers. Now it was reduced to a defeated remnant of about five thousand.

In 1929 the bottom dropped out of capitalism. If there were a simple relationship between politics and economics, the anticapitalists should have been the prime beneficiaries of that fact. They were not—and, in one important sense, the capitalists gained more than anyone else. So it was that the third period of American socialist history, marked by decisive (but not necessarily irreversible) defeat, took place when the system it opposed was in a shambles.

Why did the Socialist party emerge from the Great Depression with fewer members than in 1929? The main reason was the liberal reform of capitalism under Roosevelt and the New Deal; a subordinate reason was the sectarianism and tactical ineptitude of the socialists themselves. This is not to say that the Socialist party was alone in misunderstanding what was happening. The American rich, after all, viewed Roosevelt and all his works as diabolic and perhaps communistic, and thus fought tooth and nail against his programs. And it should be noted that many of the socialist criticisms of the New Deal were quite valid, a point that sometimes is obscured by the mythology of the period.

It is often forgotten that a major recession began in late 1936, and that Roosevelt campaigned that same year on a conventional, anti-Keynesian basis. Indeed, in 1939, when, as Roosevelt put it, "Dr. Win-the-War" took over from "Dr. New Deal," there were more unemployed workers than at any time since. John Maynard Keynes himself commented in an article in the *New Republic* (1940) that perhaps no peacetime capitalist government would ever undertake expenditures sufficiently massive to counteract a problem as profound as the Depression. Thus many of the criticisms made by Norman Thomas and other socialists were right on the mark.

The problem was that if Roosevelt's economic policies were a partial failure, they were also a partial success; and it was the latter fact that energized a great mass of Americans, the newly unionizing industrial workers above all. If the rich wrongly saw Roosevelt as their enemy, a good number of unionists accepted that judgment. What rules in politics, in many cases, is not what is, but what is thought to be. The New Deal was inadequate, and the socialists were right to insist on the fact; the New Deal was more adequate than anything the American working class had ever known, and it was right to act on that fact. In the process the socialists lost.

The Socialist party also made its own contributions to its defeat. In the early 1930's, the party climbed back to a membership of around twenty-five thousand and new locals were being organized across the land. But then there occurred a bitter factional struggle pitting a union-based, pro-Roosevelt right wing against a Norman Thomas center and a Marxist left wing. After a number of fights, both the left and right wings quit the party or were expelled. Thomas, one of the most decent politicians in American history, managed to conceal the enormity of the collapse of the party by the sheer force of his remarkable personality, which gave the socialists a visibility out of proportion to their numbers. But by 1939 the party had dropped to fewer than five thousand members, and was never again to rise above that figure.

Ironically, the Communists flourished while the socialists declined. Until 1935 the Communist party had been a militant ultraleft critic of Roosevelt and the New Deal. In that year Stalin decided that the Soviet Union would be protected against the Nazi threat by an alliance with the bourgeois democracies, a policy that persisted until the Hitler-Stalin pact of August 1939 and was reinstated when Hitler invaded Russia in June 1941. From 1935 to 1939 and from 1941 to 1945, it was the line of the Communist International that all of its parties—and the American party was a particularly obedient section—should make a united front with capitalist reformers like Roosevelt.

For ten years, then, with the interruption of the Hitler-Stalin pact, the Communists played a role as the left wing of the New Deal. Where socialist trade unionists, like Walter Reuther, were forced to choose between their labor loyalty, which included support of Roosevelt, and their socialist membership, which committed them to being anti-Roosevelt, the Communists could have the best of two worlds. In the name of the "dictatorship of the proletariat and the Soviet Union," they attacked the socialists from the "left," charging them with being insufficiently radical; in the name of the united front, they accused the socialists of ultraleftism, of splitting the mass movement and counterposing themselves to the unity of the working class within the Roosevelt coalition. Eventually the internal contradictions of Stalinism—the ideology of a totalitarian and antisocialist elite—and repressive law enforcement measures reduced the Communists to a sectarian shell. But during those united-front years they had created the largest organization calling itself socialist since the days of Debs.

The third period of American socialism was over within a decade: the 1930's. Everything that came afterward was epilogue, and did not alter the basic fact of socialist defeat. In recent years there have been some signs of a socialist revival in the form of the Democratic Socialist Organizing Committee, the main successor to the Socialist party, which was organized in 1973. But that development is still in process.

IMPACT OF THE ECONOMY ON THE SOCIALIST MOVEMENT

Throughout the preceding section economic factors were cited regularly. It is now time to attempt to generalize the relationship between the American economy and American socialism, always keeping in mind the complexities noted at the outset.

Economic historian Charles P. Kindleberger put it thus:

> In Europe, economic growth was to a considerable extent achieved through what is called the Lewis model of "growth with unlimited supplies of labor," hardly distinguishable from the Marxian "reserve army of the unemployed." Unlimited supplies of labor off the farm held down wages, raised profits, led to reinvestment of profits and sustained growth. In the United States, early growth came from unlimited supplies of land which furnished a good livelihood to independent farmers. When manufacture began to flourish—mainly because of the spillover of demand from affluent agriculture and only partly as a response to protectionist tariff policies—the massive infusion of [immigrant] labor sustained the process.

Ernest Mandel, a leading Marxist (Trotskyist) scholar, made much the same point:

> Marx often emphasized the case of the United States. The high wages which existed from the very beginning of this country were not a function of high labor productivity but of a chronic

shortage of wage workers as a result of the frontier. The higher productivity of American labor was not, then, the cause, but the consequence of the high wages.

So it was that the real income per capita for the working population, as Fritz Sternberg documented in 1951, rose from $767 a year in 1850 to $1,333 in 1913. Using Colin Clark's computations in *The Conditions of Economic Progress*, in the first decade of the twentieth century, manufacturing wages in the United States were slightly more than twice as high as in the United Kingdom and roughly three times higher than in France and Germany. That is in keeping with Werner Sombart's judgment that American socialism went aground on "shoals of apple pie and roast beef." But do the statistics prove the case? High wages do not necessarily immunize working people against socialism. In the years of most dramatic socialist growth in Germany—from 1890 to 1914—living standards were, on the whole, rising. The complex interrelationship of land and wages in the United States had something to do with the failure of socialism, but only because it was mediated through other aspects of American social structure.

Consider, for instance, the division of wages between native-born and immigrant workers. In 1880, 63 percent of the people in London were natives of the city and 94 percent came from either England or Wales. In the United States 78 percent of San Franciscans were foreign-born, as were 80 percent of the populations of New York and Cleveland. Therefore the relatively higher standard of living when one uses a per capita figure disguises the existence of two working classes, one of them located in sweatshops. Moreover, many of the native-born artisans, whose skills were devalued by the rise of monopoly capitalism, blamed the immigrant workers who entered the country in great numbers at that particular historic moment for keeping wages low. In short, the unevenness of the American standard of living was as fateful for the socialists as the level of the standard. Hostility within the working class, rather than *embourgeoisement*, is what needs to be stressed.

It was long assumed, in keeping with the *embourgeoisement* hypothesis, that the co-optation of the American working class took place by means of a higher rate of occupational mobility in the United States than in Europe. That notion was, and is, sometimes joined to Frederick Jackson Turner's assertion that the frontier was a decisive determinant of the uniquely American ethos. The workers, Werner Sombart said, had an "escape into freedom": ". . . the principal reason for the characteristic peaceable mood of the American workers is that many men with sound limbs and no capital or hardly any were able to turn themselves into independent farmers almost as they wished by colonizing free land" (*Why There Is No Socialism in The United States*, p. 116).

There are a number of problems with these theories. First, the American workers were not more "peaceable" than the Europeans, for American labor history is much more violent than that of the Old World. Second, as Stephan Thernstrom has pointed out, many more farmers became workers than workers became farmers. The Homestead Act, which Sombart cites, actually provided most of its benefits to railroads, either directly or indirectly. Scholars like Seymour Lipset and Reinhard Bendix have cast doubt on the marked superiority of social mobility in the United States as compared with Europe. (In some of his later research, Thernstrom has taken issue with them on this count.)

But—and here again the political power of a myth becomes important—there is considerable evidence that many Americans believed that their country provided more mobility than Europe did. The United States, Leon Samson once observed, is a country with the "socialist version of capitalism." In Europe, where capitalist classes were often imbued with feudal consciousness, workers were not regarded as being equal to aristocrats or the bourgeoisie. Indeed, the European contempt for the working class at times resembled racist attitudes in America. In the United States, in sharp contrast, there was always an egalitarian ideology, even if it rationalized a most inegalitarian reality. In Europe the working-class movement in almost every country began with a struggle for civil rights, first and foremost the right to vote. In America there was the "free gift of the ballot" to white males. The American worker was never—and is not now—the economic, social, or political equal of the American capitalist; but the American worker, in one part of his or her mind, has always half-believed the myth of equality. So it was, as Samson shrewdly observed, that Americanism served as a kind of surrogate socialism. The values that European labor had to counterpose to the established ideology formed the established ideology in America (though not, it should be emphasized again, established in social reality).

We can now turn to the question with which this article began: are the special characteristics of American capitalism the explanation for the United States being the only advanced industrial nation without a mass socialist movement? If the issue is posed in that fashion, the answer is no. Indeed, it can be argued that the analysis thus far provides some additional data for the broad thesis stated at the outset: that the economic, conceived of as a "factor" in isolation from social and cultural relationships, does not exist in reality and is not useful as an abstraction. At every point in this account of American socialism, one sees the reciprocal interaction of the economic, political, social, and cultural: abundant land and high wages operate within a framework of an extraordinarily heterogeneous (racially and ethnically) working class and of an ideology that is the "socialist version of capitalism."

But once that complexity is accepted, it can be said that the unique characteristics of the American economy were a necessary, if not a sufficient, cause of the absence of socialism in the society. Yet even that statement has to be qualified. There is, rather obviously, no mass socialist movement in the United States. There is, not so obviously, a political, organized working-class movement that stands for a distinctive program of liberal reform of capitalism and that sometimes counterposes itself in a combative fashion to corporate power. I have argued in *Socialism* (1972) that the unions constitute an invisible social democracy. The term "social democracy" has had many meanings in the course of more than a century, but one of the most recent of its connotations is ideally suited to make the point being urged here. In the European socialist movement of the 1960's and 1970's, it was commonplace to distinguish between "social democrats," who seek a more humane capitalism, and "socialists," who want to create a totally new kind of society.

Applying those definitions to American history since the politicization of the workers under the New Deal, one can say that the United States is perhaps not quite so exceptional as it might first seem. It has no socialist movement, but it does possess a mass social democracy. Moreover, as the 1970's ended, there were significant signs of structural weakness in American society that were acknowledged on both the Right and the Left, even though they were analyzed in quite different ways on various points of the spectrum. It is possible that this existing, if somewhat invisible, social democracy could become part of a new movement headed in a socialist direction. In terms of the immediate present and the past, though, I will let the judgment of this section stand on the relationship between the American economy and American socialism.

THE INFLUENCE OF SOCIALIST ECONOMICS

It is often said that if the Socialist party failed in America, socialism did not. America is a society, so the argument goes, with both capitalist and socialist elements; and one of the reasons for the existence of the latter is the history and impact of American socialism. Did not the socialists in America profoundly affect the economic thinking of the nation even though they never elected a president, or even a senator?

At first glance that might seem to be an extension of the argument just made about an invisible social democracy in the United States. In fact it is not. Unfortunately, to explain why requires that one travel rather far from the subject of American socialism. This is unfortunate because the relevant and necessary information is quite complex and can be presented here in only the most summary and sketchy form.

Whether there is "creeping" socialism in the United States, or whether there are "elements" of socialism, obviously depends on what one means by "socialism." If the word is seen as defining a number of economic policies—public ownership of the decisive means of production, socialized medicine, egalitarian tax laws—then one could properly argue that there are socialist aspects of the American economy. But that is to miss the essential that, among other things, gets back to the proposition about the interpenetration of the economic, social, political, and cultural.

Capitalist society has been socializing itself under private direction throughout its history.

SOCIALISM

The corporation is, as Marx was the first to point out, a socialized (anonymous) entrepreneur, an institution that brings together many small and medium-size capitals and fuses them into one giant capital. Even at the beginnings of the system, the government played a critical role. Consider, for instance, the importance of the railroads to the American economy, and the importance of the granting of land by the government to the railroads in that process. In the twentieth century the interaction of the government and the private corporate economy became even more pronounced as the former took the responsibility for manipulating fiscal and monetary aggregates so as to create a climate in which the latter could operate profitably. Indeed, it can be said that the most-favored beneficiaries of the welfare state are the businessmen who fought its creation.

Therefore the issue before the United States is not whether there is going to be more collectivization—more economic decisions made politically—but who is going to run the inevitably emerging collectivism, with what policies, and in what manner. Under these circumstances, to equate collectivization—or government intervention—with socialism is to embark on a profound misunderstanding. Both fascists and Stalinists nationalize property when its suits their purposes. The Brazilian economy became much more centralized under a dictatorship of generals than under the leadership of a populist president. And capitalist democacies collectivize too, although in more decorous fashion.

Socialism, then, is not collectivization, but the program for a democratic and libertarian collectivization. Stalinism, an undemocratic and totalitarian collectivization, is thus a polar opposite of socialism. But what about the American welfare state? Is it socialist, Stalinist, capitalist, or what? The answer has to be ambiguous because reality is. Historically the American welfare state was created, in large measure, as the result of a militant struggle by working people, and represents a democratization of economic life. But once American business got over its irrational hostility to this development, the welfare state also became a chief prop of the American status quo. The functioning of those reforms has allowed the system to last much longer than had it been run by reactionaries. But the reactionaries were not totally wrong to oppose this development, since the welfare state could be further, and profoundly, democratized, and might then serve as a transition to a new society.

Until now that has not happened. The welfare state has worked to stabilize and reinforce capitalism. Insofar as American socialists were the first to define, and fight for, many welfare state reforms, they, like their European comrades, had an ironic impact upon the society: they helped their enemies survive. Norman Thomas, six times the presidential candidate of the Socialist party, understood the point very well. When asked, as he often was, "Didn't the New Deal carry out the 1912 Socialist program?" he would reply, "Yes, they carried it out on a stretcher." That is, America took only from Debs's immediate program in 1912, picking only those reforms that were compatible with, and even supportive of, the system. This was not done by a conspiracy of the plutocrats. They, as has been pointed out before, hated Roosevelt. It was, rather, the consequence of a partial reform of an essentially capitalist structure that remained essentially capitalist.

This was not the case because, as some have said, the American socialists were "right wing." All wings of the European socialist movement—left, right, and center—suffered the same fate; and so, for that matter, did the most effective Western Communist party, that of Italy. Capitalism turned out to be much more structurally resilient than most socialists had thought, and could even survive the shortsightedness of the capitalists. And socialism, taken as a vision of a democratic economy truly run from the bottom up, turned out to be much more difficult to achieve than anyone, Marx and Engels included, had ever dreamed.

Interestingly, one of the two major figures in the history of American socialism, Eugene Victor Debs, was more precise on this point than almost any other socialist. Debs was no theorist, and neither was he an organization man. He was an extraordinarily decent and charismatic leader who was inspired by a vision of the great mass of people—"ordinary" people—running their own destiny. He used to tell audiences that he would not lead them into the promised land even if he could, for if he, an individual, could "lead" the people there, some other individual could lead them out of the promised land. The movement, he said over and over, had to lead itself. That point was also made with homely clarity by a member of the IWW during a violent fight with the police in the state of Washington before World War I. "Send us your leaders," the authorities demanded. "We ain't got no leaders," that worker replied.

In terms of the vision shared by Debs and that anonymous IWW militant, America today is not socialist at all, not controlled from the bottom up. It is a top-down society, whether in its corporate, its governmental, or its military structures. But the socialists contributed both the "immediate program" of 1912 and that Debsian vision; and periodically it flares up, as it did in the great struggles of the 1930's. The complex history of American socialism and its equally complex relationship to the American economy are still evolving.

BIBLIOGRAPHY

Daniel Bell, "The Background and Development of Marxian Socialism in the United States," in Donald Egbert and S. Persons, eds., *Socialism and American Life* (Princeton, N. J., 1952), argues that socialists in the United States were in, but not of, the world, and that they failed because of their unwillingness to adapt pragmatically to the political system. Harry Fleishman, *Norman Thomas: A Biography* (New York, 1964), a friendly but quite informative biography of Norman Thomas by one of his long-time associates, is a particularly good volume for an account of the relationship of the socialists to the New Deal. Michael Harrington, *Socialism* (New York, 1972), contains two chapters focused on American socialism that provide documentation for the thesis of an "invisible social democracy" presented in this article. Morris Hillquit, *History of Socialism in the United States* (5th ed.; New York, 1910), is a thoughtful discussion of early American socialist history by a leading theorist of the Socialist party. Ira Kipnis, *The American Socialist Movement, 1897–1912* (New York, 1952), suggests that the Debsian movement aborted because it made too many concessions to the conservatism of the nation; Kipnis believes that a more militant and left-wing socialism might have succeeded in America. John H. M. Laslett and Seymour Lipset, eds., *Failure of a Dream* (Garden City, N.Y., 1972), a collection of essays and excerpts from books on American socialism, is the best single volume for an introduction to the topic.

Seymour Lipset, "Why No Socialism in the United States?" in S. Bialer and S. Sluzar, eds., *Sources of Contemporary Radicalism* (New York, 1977), the most recent survey of all the scholarly literature on the topic of American socialism, is an excellent overview. Selig Perlman, *A Theory of the Labor Movement* (New York, 1928; repr. 1949), argues that American workers achieved "job consciousness" through unions, but not "class consciousness" in a political party; even though many of its interpretations are open to question, this book is a classic. Gerald Rosenblum, *Immigrant Workers: Their Impact on American Labor Radicalism* (New York, 1973), is the most recent study of a critical aspect of the history of American socialism. David Shannon, *The Socialist Party of America: A History* (Chicago, 1967), a solid scholarly survey of the most important institution ever created by the American socialist movement, is a standard reference work. Werner Sombart, *Why Is There No Socialism in the United States?* (American ed.; White Plains, N.Y., 1976), a new translation of Sombart's 1906 classic, has an introduction by C. T. Husbands and extensive notes that provide an excellent summary of the present state of opinion on the lack of socialism in America. Stephan Thernstrom, *Poverty and Progress: Social Mobility in a Nineteenth Century City* (Chicago, 1964), puts the case for doubting the notion that there actually was remarkable social mobility in the United States in the nineteenth century (in a later essay, reprinted in *Failure of a Dream*, Thernstrom revises his opinions somewhat and carries on an interesting exchange with Seymour Lipset).

[*See also* DISTRIBUTION OF INCOME AND WEALTH; LABOR ORGANIZATIONS; POVERTY; *and* SOCIAL WELFARE.]

THE COSTS OF ECONOMIC GROWTH

Alan L. Olmstead

FEW ISSUES have had more potential for causing a wholesale revaluation of historical epochs than the current concern with the environment. The 1970's marked the beginning of a stampede of social scientists to discover the abuses that parallel current problems or, in studies dealing with the relatively recent past, to detail the origins and causes of current social afflictions. The growing disenchantment with growth, especially among American youth, springs from the recognition that many of the achievements of past generations have been hollow. Growth has not brought with it "the good life," social equality, and personal contentment and happiness. On the contrary, although the 1960's witnessed a real increase in family income exceeding 30 percent, they were years of soul searching and personal anxiety. Growing numbers of Americans became alarmed that their collective actions not only were destroying the quality of life and exposing them to serious health hazards, but also were upsetting the delicate balance of nature and exhausting vital resources, thereby threatening the survival of the human race. Many critics are sincerely concerned that man's greed and shortsightedness are seriously endangering (not too distant) future generations. In place of the pictures of smoke rising from a factory smokestack that symbolized progress as late as the early 1960's there are now "Less Is More" bumper stickers.

During the 1950's and 1960's few economists bothered to dwell on the costs of growth because the benefits were seemingly so great. The main policy question was how to promote growth; the task of economic historians was to clarify the historical record and to explain why some economies failed and why others succeeded. In a nutshell, it was to discover lessons to provide better guidance in the unquenchable quest for more and more material output. Distributional issues and the social and ecological havoc left in the wake of the growing economy were sometimes given lip service but more generally ignored. Clearly, the pendulum has begun to swing in the other direction; the costs of American economic growth can no longer be hidden from view—they are ever present for all to see, smell, and touch.

FRAMEWORK FOR THE ARTICLE

The cost of American economic growth from 1869 to 1970 (in 1958 prices) was more than $21 trillion ($21,148,700,000,000). This figure was derived simply by summing gross national product for the period; and since it is known that for every dollar of output there is about one dollar of costs, a fairly good estimate of costs can be obtained. (The above assertion either can be accepted as an accounting identity or can rest on the assumption that each input in the production process is paid the value of its marginal product.) Although accurate, the above figure is in and of itself trivial. It does illustrate that the focus of interest is not all costs but, rather, a limited subset that can usefully be characterized as "illegitimate" costs. The first concern is to define this term. The second concern is to sketch out how political responses and, more generally, institutional responses can help lessen these illegitimate costs. Several qualifications are needed for the sake of clarity.

First, most discussions of the costs of economic growth in fact deal with the costs associated with "high" levels of economic output, large populations, and large urban centers. Of course all of these are the products of past

THE COSTS OF ECONOMIC GROWTH

growth; but if economic growth were to cease this instant, there would still be social costs associated with maintaining current rates of output. Much of the literature fails to make this distinction.

Second, one must bear in mind that there are few absolutes in defining "illegitimate" costs. Such costs, as is true of all costs in a market economy, are in part determined by the perceptions of individuals, which are dependent upon values and tastes, which in turn are subject to change over time. At a more physical level all costs are determined by supply and demand conditions that also are subject to change. Resources are depleted, they become scarcer, and their prices tend to rise; new technologies are invented; and legal structures change. All of these changes serve to alter the size, shape, and method of delivery of the actual (and potential) consumption package. The prices of some goods increase and the prices of others decrease in response to changing supply and demand conditions.

This is true for items that consumers normally do not recognize as economic commodities, such as clean air. So long as clean air is abundant and so long as the demand for it is small (say, because population density is low), one can reasonably expect to build a great bonfire without causing any serious harm to the environment. But an identical fire built in a crowded city already suffocating from the toxic by-products of industrial society will cause considerable discomfort for a large number of individuals. Therefore the fire imposes a high cost on them. In the first case clean air is abundant and the demand is low; in the second, clean air is scarce and the demand is high. This short digression is intended to demonstrate that, at least for most purposes, one must evaluate cases of pollution within the context of the historical milieu. One generally would be ill-advised to condemn out of hand some past scarring of the environment just because a similar action today, given current scarcities and values, would cause a public outcry.

Finally, the framework set out below is admittedly incomplete and limited. Economics as a positive science offers little help when it comes to evaluating distributional issues, and it is of even less value when it comes to making intertemporal or intergenerational evaluations. The best framework that economics has to offer, although helpful, has serious shortcomings. Moreover, what appears below is not the best framework available but is, out of necessity, a condensed and simplified version.

The Static-Allocation Problem and Marginal-Cost Pricing. In order to identify general cases of "illegitimate" resource use and come to grips with the question of what constitutes "illegitimate costs," there must be agreement on what constitutes an optimal allocation of productive capacity, goods, and services in the marketplace. Most economists start with the proposition that the distribution of resources, productive activity, and output is optimal if it is impossible to reorganize this distribution in a way that will make some people better off without making anyone else worse off. If this is not the case (that is, if workers can move from one industry to another, or if a plant can alter its output mix to produce more Hula-Hoops and fewer Barbie Dolls, or if one consumer can give up some of his or her apples in exchange for someone else's marbles and make at least one person better off without hurting anyone), then clearly the change should be made. If such a situation prevails, there is "slack" in the economy and substitutions should continue until it is no longer possible to improve anyone's lot without hurting someone else.

When no resource can command a higher price elsewhere than in its present employment, and when no exchanges occur voluntarily between people who hold stocks of commodities, then the economy is in an optimal position (there can be an infinite number of such positions). When this condition holds, the value of the last bits of any resource must be the same to all the users of that resource. If this were not the case —if, for example, an extra ton of coal is worth more to an electric company than it is worth to an iron firm—one or both firms could benefit from the trade. This, of course, violates the condition that no voluntary exchanges can occur that benefit one party without hurting another. Such trade will continue until both firms place the same value on an extra ton of coal—that is, until the marginal value of coal (or any other resource) is the same for all users.

All competitive producers also have an incentive to employ each resource at the rate at which its marginal value to the firm is just equal to the price of the resource. If this is not the case—if an extra unit of the resource is worth more to the firm than it costs (its price)—the firm clearly should buy more. If, on the other hand, an extra unit costs the firm more than it is worth (which is determined by how much it contributes to the revenue of the firm), then the firm should use less of the resource. As a firm employs less of a resource, the value to the firm of the last unit of that resource actually used will increase; and thus, eventually, its value will equal the market price. Assuming that there is a single market price for each resource, one may conclude that when the economy is at an optimum, the marginal value of each resource (technically, the value of the marginal product) to producers will be the same for all producers and will be equal to the market price of the resource.

By dividing both the marginal value of the resource and its price by the number of units of output that were produced as a result of using the last unit of the resource, one obtains the result that the marginal cost of the last unit of output equals the price of the input. Resources that are not used in accordance with this principle are being "misused" and thus, within the context of the model, can constitute the "illegitimate" costs that one is trying to identify. This is the basis for the widely touted recommendation that marginal-cost pricing be used in order to allocate resources in an efficient, socially desirable fashion.

A perfectly competitive economy tends, in theory, to move toward an optimum position; but in the real world, marred as it is by transaction costs, market imperfections, and pockets of monopoly and special privilege, there is no reason to expect that resources will be used optimally. On the contrary, both theoretical reckoning and empirical observations indicate that there has been a persistent misallocation of resources.

The simple marginal-cost pricing rule assumes that producers and consumers bear all the costs of their actions. If this is not the case—if there are external diseconomies of production or consumption, such as when a steel mill or an automobile belches noxious wastes into the air without paying for this action—then the social costs, the costs to society, of production and consumption will exceed the private costs, the costs facing the individual decision maker. Scarce resources are being used by people who treat them as free goods and do not pay for them. This does not mean that no payment is made; people who must breathe the poisoned air pay implicitly through the decrease in welfare. Because maximizing producers and consumers tend to disregard the external costs that they impose on others, there will be excess production and excess consumption of such goods.

When this situation prevails, society should try to devise a means to force producers and consumers to bear all the costs of their actions. This might be accomplished by private initiatives in the courts or by direct government intervention. Consider, for example, a factory that releases its waste products into a river and thus imposes costs on all those who live downstream. It could, at least theoretically, be determined how much of a burden an extra unit (such as one hundred gallons) of effluent imposes on others. This might be done by determining how much it costs to clean the water downstream or, somewhat less precisely, by surveying each person affected to ascertain how much money he or she would demand to compensate for the slight deterioration in water quality caused by this last unit of waste. It is essential that all costs be added up, including those incurred by sportsmen, nature lovers, and all other users of the stream. When a price tag is established, the firm can pay and continue to pollute at the same rate or it can cut back on its dumping by one hundred gallons.

The latter alternative could be accomplished by cutting production or by devising methods to clean up or recycle its wastes. If the firm cuts back, then the process must be repeated for each marginal unit of effluent. As less waste is dumped, the stream is better able to cleanse itself, less harm is imposed on others, and the price or fee to pollute declines. At the same time, the firm has exhausted easily accessible disposal alternatives and has cut back production, so that the price it is willing to pay to pollute increases. When the price it is willing to pay just equals the sum that others are willing to receive in exchange for slightly less pure water, the process stops and the stream is being used optimally. In many cases the firm will not be willing to pay the price demanded and will have to shut down altogether. Even when the firm continues to produce, it does so at a lower rate of output and emits fewer pollutants. The external costs have been internalized, and those individuals originally being damaged are now being compensated. In practice it can be very difficult to measure external costs and to work out compensation schemes, but at least there is a framework to guide one in the correct direction.

The resources that tend to be treated as having zero value and that are therefore abused (overused) generally are difficult to own or police. The atmosphere, the oceans, lakes, and rivers, and peace and quiet (the absence of noise) are not like most forms of private property. In a sense they belong to everyone, which is why they have been dubbed "common-property" resources. Since they are owned by everyone, nobody acting individually has a strong incentive, given the legal system, to protect these resources from encroachment by others and to promote their rational use over time. Indeed, the opposite is the case. Because the supply of the resource is limited, all potential users scramble to obtain as much as they can for themselves before others beat them to it. As common-property resources become scarcer, they grow more valuable and generally it is increasingly important to police or regulate their use. At the same time new technologies often emerge that reduce the cost of defending such resources. Numerous resources have evolved from common-property status to either a policed status or to private ownership. The vast American frontier is the largest-scale example, but one can also list wild game (especially fur-bearing animals) and the common fields of medieval Europe and early colonial America. Some common-property resources either met with or came precariously close to extinction before rules were established for their preservation. The frail passenger pigeon and the powerful American bison offer grim historical reminders of a saga that continues today for several species of whales and fish.

The Allocation of Resources Over Time. Problems associated with overfishing or polluting lakes and rivers are essentially examples of consuming a resource too rapidly. Not enough is being saved for the future. But how should resources be allocated over time, either between today and tomorrow or between this generation and the next? Has the actual course of American growth resulted in a squandering of the natural resources of the nation, thereby depriving future generations of their birthrights? Is it true that future generations have no voice in current consumption decisions? Has the market systematically failed to save enough resources for the next generation? If so, this failure can surely be counted among the costs of past growth.

Individuals, firms, and governments daily look to the future in making current consumption, production, and investment decisions. In a market economy the rate of exploitation of natural resources depends in part on a comparison of current prices with expectations about future prices. If some owners of a raw material suddenly change their expectations so that they now expect that in the future there will be shortages, and thus higher prices, they will hold on to at least some of the resources they had planned to sell in the current year. Doing so will increase current prices and give current users of that resource an incentive to develop substitutes or use the resource more efficiently. The point is that expectations about future prices (which of course will depend on expectations about future supplies and demands) affect the price and rate of development of raw materials today.

Here a crucial technicality must be introduced —future incomes and future desires (or, more accurately, current perceptions of future desires) are discounted. This means that owners of raw materials give lower and lower weights (in a sense they pay less and less attention) to demands perceived to be further and further in the future. They do this because a dollar of income today is worth more than the promise of a dollar a year from now. This is because a dollar received today can be invested and at the end of the year it will be worth one dollar plus the interest received. It follows that the higher the interest rate, the more a dollar today is worth relative to the promise of a dollar at some future date, because of the greater interest that one can earn in the interim. Thus the higher the interest rate (more accurately, the discount rate), the less future demands are weighted today and the more rapidly resources will be consumed. Conversely, the lower the discount rate, other things being equal, the more resources will be saved for future generations. This is the market mechanism through which current perceptions of future demands are taken into account by resource owners.

Future generations have not been ignored, but have they been adequately represented? What could go wrong to cause a gross misallocation of resources over time, which would consti-

THE COSTS OF ECONOMIC GROWTH

tute a major cost of past growth? First, it should be noted that the wishes of future generations are never expressed, just the perception of those wishes as reflected in guesses (or, more politely, estimates) of future supply and demand conditions. But such a criticism can be made of any system of allocating resources over time—the decision on what to do today cannot be made tomorrow. In addition to the obvious limitation that man is not blessed with perfect foresight, is there any reason to expect that resource owners do not give sufficient weight to future demands? In fact, a few economists including Robert Solow, Harold Barnett, and Chandler Morse (and many noneconomists) argue that regardless of the private rationality of discounting future demands, this procedure may not be correct for society as a whole. If one accepts this view that all generations should be treated equally over the very long run, then it is most likely that resources have been, and are continuing to be, used too rapidly.

On the other side of the coin there are reasons to expect that at least some resources have been used too slowly—which would also constitute a cost to growth. It can be shown that a monopolist will exhaust a natural resource more slowly than would be the case if that resource were owned by a number of firms in a competitive industry. It can also be demonstrated that monopolists in some productive process—say, making steel—will demand fewer raw materials than if the industry were more competitive. Herein lies the potential for a major revision in the interpretation of American history. Those historians who feel that Americans have consumed natural resources too rapidly, perhaps because of the existence of widespread external diseconomies, might take a far more favorable view of the more successful robber barons. Andrew Carnegie, John D. Rockefeller, J. P. Morgan, and the other captains of industry and finance who were successful in their cartelization schemes might also rank just behind the Organization of Petroleum Exporting Countries among the great conservationists of all times. The potential revision can be extended to include the absentee land speculator who has been portrayed in sinister fashion in some accounts. The fact is that the act of speculation is nothing more than holding on to a good for future use—which, of course, is what conservation is all about.

In other areas speculators devote a considerable amount of effort to predicting the future: there are futures markets in agricultural products, plywood, and basic metals, in which experts match wits in a high-powered guessing game. These specialists and the farmers and resource owners who deal in such markets have a very strong incentive to predict future needs and supplies accurately; those who do so make money, and those who do not lose it. This incentive notwithstanding, has there in fact been a systematic error in these predictions over the broad span of American history that suggests that resources have been consumed too rapidly in the past?

On this subject there is fairly reliable evidence that resource owners typically have not squandered their raw materials too rapidly. This conclusion rests in part on Barnett and Morse's observation that the relative costs of a broad spectrum of agricultural and mineral products declined secularly over the last quarter of the nineteenth century and the first half of the twentieth century, with minerals experiencing the most spectacular fall in prices. Extending these cost series to 1970 and starting with 1900 as the base year does not drastically alter the conclusion: with a few exceptions real raw-material prices do not rise at a significant rate despite a considerable increase in natural resource consumption. According to Nathan Rosenberg, an index of resource consumption (including agriculture, timber products, and minerals) rises from 17 in 1870 to 41 in 1900 and to 110 in 1954 (1947–1949 = 100). The rise in per capita consumption has not been so substantial. It has increased (in 1954 dollars) from $174 in 1870 to $221 in 1900 to $279 in 1954.

The fact that in most cases, real raw-material prices have failed to rise despite the increase in consumption means that technological changes and discoveries of new sources of supply have more than kept pace with rising demands. The major exception to this trend was forest products—a subject that will be analyzed in some detail. But even in this exceptional case the real price rise was relatively modest. Between 1900 and 1970 the real price of forest products rose about 0.50 percent per annum, which is well below the real rate of return on capital. Thus, barring unusually high rates of productivity increases, there is no clear evidence that lumbermen were personally irrational or misjudged the future so that they used up their own timber reserves too rapidly. The same argument seems to apply to other raw materials as well.

Two objections must be confronted at this point. First, is an overly shortsighted view being taken? The fact that over the course of about one century the market appeared to work does not mean that dire shortages might not be around the corner. Second, what of the exceptions—those resources that have risen in price?

Proponents of the first criticism contend that the market has systematically underestimated the gravity of the American predicament. The stock form of this statement is that the nation cannot continue to use a finite amount of resources at an increasing rate. The stock answer to this is that the rate of growth should be reduced, but that would only delay the inevitable. A zero rate of growth might be a little better, but again it would only postpone a doomsday because exhaustible resources would still be required. The only solution would be a negative rate of growth, in which all nonrenewable resources for which no substitutes were foreseen were consumed at a declining rate. Theoretically the rate of world output could be reduced to the subsistence level, but that would offer only a long, painful reprieve. The problem with almost all past predictions of resource depletion is that they have failed to envision the potential substitutes that emerged as a result of technological changes. Furthermore, they failed to recognize the increased supplies that were discovered or became economical to exploit as prices rose and as new harvesting or mining methods were developed.

Turning to the second criticism, what about the exceptions where resources have been used too rapidly? In such cases the old nemesis, common-property resources, and external diseconomies are usually lurking on the sidelines. The concepts that have been developed will now be used to analyze some of the major events in American history.

EVENTS IN AMERICAN HISTORY RECONSIDERED

Recently firms and consumers have been forced to internalize some of the most obvious external diseconomies that they generate. The Environmental Protection Agency has enforced pollution controls on producers, autos are equipped with emission control devices, and environmental impact reports have become a fact of life for the construction industry. What if such reports had been required throughout the course of American history? What if no enterprise could be inaugurated before compensating those who stood to lose by it—that is, if the perpetrators of progress had to consider the external diseconomies or spillover effects of their actions and to offer compensation to those harmed?

This would be a little unfair unless past entrepreneurs and buccaneers were also allowed to capture all the side benefits of their actions (external economies); but for illustrative purposes let us be unfair for a moment. What most Americans, even those actively involved in the environmental protection movement, do not realize is that the most apocalyptic visions offered today do not surpass the ecological calamities that recurred during the centuries of discovery, conquest, and settlement when the foundation for subsequent American economic development was being laid. Assuming that he had a crystal ball to help look into the future, what would an environmental impact report that Hernando Cortez might have filed with Emperor Charles V have contained? We find ghastly horrors equal to any conjured up in the minds of the most pessimistic modern doom mongerers.

> First, the private benefits to myself include a modest fortune sufficient to guarantee a comfortable retirement, fame, and the immeasurable satisfaction of knowing I served my King and Holy Prince. The private benefits to my gracious sponsors in the form of treasure, land, and power are enormous. Second, the social benefits to my beloved Spain and the Christian world are almost beyond calculation. Wealth, empire, and glory are to flow forth from this enterprise. The treasure secured will materially affect every Spaniard by lowering domestic taxes and increasing security and prosperity at home. Third, the private costs are substantial. Ships will be burned; rations, munitions, and horses will be spent. Many of my legion will perish; but given the opportunity for fortune and fame, this risk they gladly bear. (In more technical terms, to satisfy Your Highness, given a perfect labor market, no extra compensation need be paid to the injured and killed because the agreed-to wage implicitly accounts for the expected value of injuries.) Fourth, the issue of external costs

need not impede us. The influx of gold and silver will initiate a century of price instability, but the determination of whether this is a cost or a benefit awaits further research.

I admit that there is some possibility of contributing to the syphilitic scourge about to ravish Europe, and apologize on this account for causing undue risk to His Royal Person. Other matters about which some of my pointed-head, bleeding-heart critics have made such a to-do need not overly concern us when placed in proper perspective. Granted that the Indian nation will perish and that many, perhaps a majority, of its population will suffer a most hideous death. Being of frail blood and due to improper breeding, they will rapidly succumb to smallpox, measles, pneumonia, streptococcal infection, consumption, typhus, and divers other afflictions. Granted, others will starve as economic and social order totally collapse in the wake of the pestilence. Finally, alas, a few must perish, victims of my men's shot, swords, arrows, and interrogation. But I would implore Your Caesarean Majesty to note that the death of approximately eight million natives in the first decade of Christian rule presents no insurmountable problems. I am prepared to offer a just lump-sum compensation. I suggest we use as a proxy for determining compensation the discounted present value of the forgone money-income stream. Your Highness will recognize this as the widely accepted proxy used in personal injury cases. Since most of the Indians are involved in subsistence or near-subsistence agriculture, the discounted present value of their future net earning stream is precisely zero!

Finally, I have saved the best for last. Whereas prior to my enterprise none of the local population was blessed with the True Faith, and since one magnificent consequence of my actions will be almost universal acceptance of our Blessed Virgin Mother, in truth my venture bestows an incalculable benefit upon the natives and their descendants. In the interest of progress, I for one am willing to forgo any remuneration for this gift and further propose that those Indians above subsistence, and therefore rightly demanding more monetary compensation, be asked to extract such from their richly compensated fellows. The details of this matter can be left for the Indians to decide among themselves.

Needless to say, Charles V would have approved this report and history did march on. The epidemics, pestilence, and devastation of the native population were afflictions that invariably followed European penetration of the new continents.

Let us continue our fantasy and look at two inventions that, although separated by more than a century, irrevocably transformed the economic landscape existing when they were devised. It will be seen that the problems are almost boundless and that if in fact all external benefits and costs were accurately perceived, there is at least the possibility that some spectacular inventions might never have seen the light of day and the virtual certainty that their introduction would have been marred by political exchanges and legal disputes. What would the response have been in 1793 if Eli Whitney's patent application had been accompanied by a statement tracing out some of the probable socioeconomic consequences of the cotton gin? By vastly extending the economic domain of the slave-plantation system, this marvelous laborsaving invention helped reinforce the sectional differences that erupted sixty-seven years later. Clearly, the historical process is not so rigidly deterministic that one can state that the Civil War would not have occurred in the absence of the gin; but as history actually unfolded, it appears that this invention at least increased the probability of the holocaust that engulfed the nation.

In the case of the automobile one can be a little more assertive. What would a wise man have done, knowing that within a few decades of its invention the machine that Henry Ford popularized would claim in excess of fifty thousand lives annually and maim hundreds of thousands more, and that it would pollute cities to the point of killing trees? Would that wise man, perhaps relying on some primitive cost-benefit calculation, have put a stop to its spread? Clearly, in both these cases we have dwelt on some of the costs and ignored the enormous benefits of these inventions. But this was for a reason: the benefits were far better allocated and accounted for through the market than were the costs. When the enormity of the external costs is explicitly considered, it raises reasonable doubt as to the outcome of a cost-benefit analysis that might have been done.

These and other technological changes, along with numerous institutional innovations, lie at the heart of the growth process. They generated major disturbances that echoed through the economy as individuals and firms attempted to transform the new externalities into higher profits, wages, and rents. Within the dynamic industries, the trend was toward lower unit costs of output and a greater quantity of output. The overall effect was to release some factors of production for other uses and to displace some entirely (for instance, the tractor displaced the horse as a farming input and thereby made pasture land available for food crops), as well as to increase the total demand for inputs as the income effects of lower prices (lower unit costs in production) multiplied through the economy. Sustained economic growth is this process in perpetual motion, a constant generation and internalization of externalities such that the price mechanism is always adjusting but never adjusted.

Thus, when one talks of economic growth, one is speaking of the fact that over time, the value of the output for the economy increases at a rate greater than that of the private costs of producing that output, so that there exists a residual net social benefit. This benefit is generally imputed either to technological change (defined to encompass all the linkages discussed immediately above) or to increasing skill levels (defined as the return to human capital). That is, the whole of the residual is defined as the positive return to those inputs that are otherwise incompletely accounted for within the market structure of the economy.

On the other hand, if there exist "illegitimate costs" such that the private costs of production are less than the social costs of production, then the net residual benefit of growth imputed to these positive externalities is overstated. Put another way, the economy has not been as productive as statistics would indicate because they have not accounted for the exploitation of "free" or underpriced inputs. But even if markets had been perfect, such that there were no external diseconomies, this dynamic process still would have imposed enormous costs on some individuals. The initial efficiency criterion—that a change is unambiguously for the better if, and only if, it makes at least one person better off without hurting anyone else (allowing for compensation)—has seldom, if ever, been met.

Although many of the obvious causes of environmental and social damages are associated with common-property resources, it would be a mistake to limit this discussion to such resources.

It is almost impossible to engage in any useful economic action that does not hurt third parties or bystanders. The vast majority of such damage is accepted by the legal system as one of the costs of a dynamic society. Oliver Wendell Holmes expressed this view quite clearly:

> ... It has been the law for centuries that a man may set up a business in a country town too small to support more than one, although he expects and intends thereby to ruin someone already there, and succeeds in his intent. The reason, of course, is that the doctrine generally has been accepted that free competition is worth more to society than it costs and that on this ground the infliction of damage is privileged [Commons 1959, pp. 308–309].

The costs inflicted on a competitor or other third parties are referred to as pecuniary externalities because they are transmitted by the market mechanism. But nevertheless they are costs imposed on others—damages are done that the innovator or businessman need not consider. The history of technological change is littered with the remains of the unemployed, the dispossessed, and the financially ruined. Be they the fabled handloom weavers of the nineteenth-century textile industry, the antebellum cordwainers that John R. Commons studied in such detail, the victims of scientific management and piece rates near the turn of the century, or the small family farmers in the post–World War I era, the stories have been similar: in the backwater of the growth and modernization process were heartbreak, despair, and failure. Skilled jobs were broken into their component parts and taken over by machines or less skilled workers (often immigrants, women, or children). Many a workplace that previously had given its occupants a sense of accomplishment and allowed them to take pride in their creations was gone, and in its place emerged the modern factory and a social ideology that treated labor as just another factor of production. The gains in efficiency were obtained at a terrible cost and loss of self-respect to many of those who participated in the transition. Many skilled trades that had been enjoyable for their own sake ceased to exist, and jobs became little more than a means to an end.

To be sure, most new technologies have in the main been net blessings, lowering the cost of

THE COSTS OF ECONOMIC GROWTH

outputs to consumers and, in the more spectacular cases, creating whole new industries offering thousands of jobs. Furthermore, many of the skilled workers under an old regime managed to be absorbed into a new in equally skilled jobs or as managers. If a given change had been stopped, these individuals might well have been worse off. The intent here is not to dispute the overall desirability of most technological changes or to deny that in the long run many workers benefited from such changes; rather, it is to reiterate the obvious but too often ignored fact that most changes also unleashed significant distributional effects, and that the sterile view from afar—of the equilibrium established long after a given change first appeared—is of little comfort to those individuals wrecked and left huddled by the side of the road of progress. The hurt is just as real as if it had been caused by a nonpecuniary external diseconomy.

All aspects of life, not just the work experience, have been affected. One of the hallmarks of modern economic growth, and in some models a prerequisite for such growth, is the total collapse of traditional values and a growing discontent with the status quo. This is fine for those of us who live in the twentieth century and are imbued with "modern values"; we even applaud the change. But it is not so for those imbued with traditional values. For them it is not a comforting sight to watch much of what they hold dear—religious beliefs, customs, and family ties—defiled on the altar of progress.

On a more mundane level, the perfection of markets resulting from a transportation innovation, for instance, always meant that scores of local merchants and producers suddenly ceased to be competitive and were driven out of business. When chain stores and supermarkets killed off neighborhood shops, the small businessmen who ran them may have found jobs—even higher-paying jobs—in the new enterprises; but they paid a price in their loss of independence. One can obtain a feeling for just how widespread and rapid the attack on traditional business forms was by realizing that during the heyday of its most rapid expansion, the Great Atlantic and Pacific Tea Company (A&P) opened fifty new stores a week for the entire year of 1925. By the same token, the automobile captured much of the demand for public transportation, escalated its costs, and eventually rendered it unprofitable in many areas. Furthermore, the automobile helped extend the suburbs, which increased the dispersion of stores and homes. In this way the auto increased its own market until in many communities car ownership became a necessity—the alternative was to stay at home.

NATURAL RESOURCES, EXTERNALITIES, AND THE FIRST CONSERVATION MOVEMENT

The preceding discussions have revealed that the price of a resource relative to other factors of production has a strong bearing on utilization practices at any given time. Furthermore, expectations about future prices affect current prices and, thus, patterns of use. If people perceive a given resource to be "cheap" today and expect that its supply is so bountiful (compared with expected demand) that its relative price will not rise, they will use that resource lavishly. One would expect considerable physical, though not economic, waste of the resource in both extractive and manufacturing processes. Only when the expected relative price of the resource begins to increase would these techniques give way to less resource-intensive methods. This is precisely the way that Americans have behaved with respect to a wide range of natural resources. The history of both agriculture and lumbering certainly follows this general outline.

Natural Resources and Externalities. It is often said that colonial dirt farmers had a callous disregard for their land. They girdled, and later cut and burned, their trees, leaving the stumps to rot. They ignored advanced European farming methods designed to maintain the productivity of the soil, choosing instead cropping patterns that yielded high returns per unit of labor input but were harsh on the land. When the soil wore out, they moved on.

Although it was once popular to condemn such practices as wasteful and to blame them on the farmers' ignorance, historians some time ago tempered their criticisms. They now argue that given the scarcity and high cost of labor and the abundance and cheapness of land and timber, it was probably rational for the dirt farmer to wear out his land and move on. To have done otherwise—that is, to have adopted modern techniques developed in Europe, where labor was plentiful and land was scarce—would have wasted labor and resulted in a lower income to the farmer and a lower rate of growth. Such techniques were invariably labor-intensive, and American farmers chose to waste land and conserve labor. It should be noted in a survey such as this one that although the above story is widely told, it rests on scanty qualitative observation. In fact, there is little quantitative evidence of how widespread such instances of consciously wearing out farms actually were, and there is even a lack of firm evidence that soil quality was being depleted by a large percentage of farmers.

In any case, it is known that not all farmers behaved in this fashion. Many gentlemen farmers of the day adopted labor-intensive, land-saving techniques, and they admonished their fellow dirt farmers for not doing likewise. Since both groups of farmers faced the same factor proportions, why did one group evidently conserve the land more than the other group? Differences in the education and sophistication of the two groups may be important in answering this question, but fundamental economic forces were also at work. It is perfectly conceivable that conservation could be profitable for one group and not for the other. The gentleman farmer produced primarily for the market, which meant that his land was more likely to be near cities or water transport that provided a link to local, national, or even foreign buyers. Although land was extremely abundant, land easily accessible to markets was not. High overland transport costs caused such land to be relatively valuable, and thus it was worth expending more labor to preserve its productivity.

A second distinction between the two types of farmers was also critical in influencing the decision of how much effort was made to preserve land quality. The quasi-subsistent dirt farmers did not have the wherewithal to construct expensive buildings on their property, whereas richer farmers typically had fine homes and numerous outbuildings that constituted fixed capital investments. To have run down the quality of their land would have driven down the value of their complementary capital stock, a consideration that was much less important to poorer farmers.

A final factor that might account for some poorer farmers' refusal to preserve their lands was that they may have been squatters, meaning that they neither paid for nor held legal title to the land they worked. In such instances the farmer could have a strong incentive to use up the land rapidly, as he would any common-property resource. The existence of a vast expanse of unoccupied western lands, coupled with a federal policy that transferred acreage to private owners at or below market values, depressed land prices in older regions. This relative depression of eastern land prices delayed the introduction of conservation techniques long used in western Europe.

Federal land policy also had a crucial bearing on the use of the most abundant American natural resource, the forests. As noted earlier, the real price of forest products rose over the long run at the same time that the prices of most natural resources were declining. It is thus fitting to ask if forests were being grossly misused. Were they harvested too rapidly or in a wasteful manner? If so, why? It is also important to find out how the market, new technologies, and political institutions adjusted to the rising costs of wood products.

As the edge of settlement moved westward, the standing timber was often an impediment rather than a benefit to settlers because they literally had to cut their farms out of the forests. Five-sixths of the original American forests were located in the eastern half of the nation. Thus, during most of the antebellum era, when settlement was concentrated in the densely wooded regions east of the Mississippi River, the cost of wood, already low because of its abundance, was held down because it was a by-product of farming. Americans responded to this situation by developing techniques that used wood extensively but conserved scarce labor and capital. American saws, lathes, railroads, building methods, and fireplaces were all voracious consumers of wood compared with their counterparts in Europe.

The important role that wood once played in the economy is perhaps best indicated by the fact that in 1850 it accounted for more than 90 percent of all fuel-based energy consumed in the United States. The next half-century witnessed a secular increase in the price of wood and a corresponding decrease in its importance as a host of substitutes were found to replace it in various uses. Most striking was the demise of wood as an energy source, for by 1915 it supplied less than

THE COSTS OF ECONOMIC GROWTH

10 percent of all fuel-based energy. Railroads, the single largest users of wood in the second half of the nineteenth century, were encouraged by higher prices to reduce their consumption of wood. Most important were the switch to coal as a source of fuel for locomotives, the chemical treatment of ties to increase their life, and the use of iron and steel in bridges and trestles. By these and other means, wood consumers responded to changing prices. Over the long run those industries most reliant on wood were able to substitute other products and to decrease physical waste substantially by adopting new methods.

This story of wood resources, drawn from the more detailed studies by Nathan Rosenberg (1973), Sherry Olson (1971), and Sam Schurr and Bruce Netschert (1960), is of great illustrative significance because it demonstrates the capacity of advanced economies to innovate and adopt new technologies and to create products in the face of supply constraints. But to recognize that the market adjusted in the proper direction does not imply that all was well. The adjustments were not easy, and the market mechanism worked rather poorly to regulate the production and allocation of timber products. In fact, strictly economic reasoning suggests that the forests were being used in a very wasteful fashion. Underlying this waste, which constituted a cost to growth, were two familiar sources of market failure: external diseconomies and common-property resources.

As long as settlement remained within the heavily wooded eastern states, logging tended to be conducted on a small scale and for local markets. But as settlement advanced onto the prairies of Illinois, southern Wisconsin, and Iowa, the situation began to change and wood had to be imported. The scarcity of wood in these regions was exacerbated by the rapid expansion of the railroads, which added immensely to the demand for wood. By the 1870's railroads were devouring about one-fourth of the timber cut in the United States. The source of the wood supply was also changing. By the 1850's the logging industry in the northern Great Lakes states (Michigan, Wisconsin, and Minnesota) had emerged as a major source of lumber. The geographic separation of supply and demand meant that, contrary to the eastern experience, the small operation producing from a local supply for a local market was no longer economically profitable. Instead, logging, milling, and marketing became distinct activities separated spatially and often conducted by separate firms. By 1850 logging conducted in the Pinery (the northern half of Wisconsin) reflected this new organization. Logs were rafted downriver to mills located along the Mississippi. This saved on transportation costs and meant that the mills could receive logs from several different regions within the Pinery, thereby increasing competition among loggers. The extent of the market was broadened further by the influence of the railroads in reducing transport costs.

The dynamic reorganization of the industry was not reflected in the land laws. Federal land-use laws did not distinguish timberland from agricultural land until 1878, when the Timber Cutting Act and the Timber and Stone Act were passed. Prior to these acts, entry upon the public domain to acquire timberlands for their value as timberlands was not legally recognized. As a result, timberlands were appropriated under laws designed to encourage agricultural settlement, which was not thought of as a wholly commercial use. This system encouraged fraudulent entries, because one individual could not acquire more than one 160-acre plot, which was simply too small to allow loggers to realize the scale economies inherent in the industry. Consequently the timber companies employed dummy entrymen who would obtain title to the land and then turn it over to the companies. In this fashion large tracts of land were accumulated at prices below their market value, that is, the value of their stumpage. The fact that the company titles to these lands rested on a shaky foundation probably discouraged long-term speculation, but other factors ensured that cutting would be wasteful.

Loggers often acquired lumber simply by trespass. Here again the fault lay with the land law and its lack of enforcement. The General Land Office was prohibited from selling lands for commercial use, and it could not itself engage in commercial activities on the public lands. Because lands suitable for farming tended to be surveyed first, vast tracts of virgin forest behind the line of furthest settlement remained unsurveyed. Lumbermen regularly pirated timber from unsurveyed lands, often with the connivance of local officials. Thus public-domain forests were often perceived as a common-property resource.

The effects on land and forest management were predictable because, lacking property rights in the land, lumbermen had no incentive to speculate—that is, to withhold some of the timber from the market in anticipation of higher prices in the future. On the contrary, each individual had an incentive to cut as fast as possible in order to beat others to the trees or to obtain as much as possible before the law or its enforcement was stiffened. The combined effect of timber pirating on public lands and the continued fraudulent appropriation of timberlands at near-zero cost tended to drive the price of timber down to near the actual out-of-pocket logging costs. The price of stumpage on public lands was zero, and on privately held lands the price, although positive, was surely depressed. Public policy, by failing to acknowledge vested rights in trees, contributed to an economic waste of timber. The artificially low price and the expectations of continued low prices offered little incentive for lumbermen to save trees or adopt scientific methods of forest management. Likewise, consumers of timber products had less incentive to adopt lumber-saving techniques.

The two timber acts passed in 1878 did little to improve this situation. The Timber and Stone Act allowed timberlands to be appropriated directly; but, because it retained a 160-acre limit, fraudulent entries continued to be common. The Timber Cutting Act allowed free cutting on public lands for local use. The net effect was probably to shift a greater share of logging onto the public domain, further stimulating excessively rapid depletion of the forests.

The free timber cut on public lands, although geographically limited in its availability, nonetheless competed with timber cut from private lands. This limited the upward capitalization of privately held timber in the immediate market, thereby diminishing the incentive of owners of private timber to speculate by withholding such timber from the market. Indirectly it set a limit on how high timber prices could rise in older regions that were isolated to the extent that transportation costs were a barrier. Thus the overall effect of the common-property status of "free timber" was to produce a larger supply at a lower price than would have been the case under a different set of land laws.

Intertwined with the common-property resource problems were significant external diseconomies of production that worsened the overproduction and social waste. As the preceding discussion would lead one to expect, there was considerable physical waste in logging operations. It has been estimated that the original Wisconsin forest of thirty million acres held about 200 billion board feet of sawed lumber. Production reached one billion board feet by 1869, and by the turn of the century the annual cut peaked at 3.4 billion board feet. Fifteen years later the industry was moribund in most of the state. In 1893, Bernard E. Fernow, chief of the Division of Forestry of the United States Department of Agriculture, reported, "Hardly more than thirty to forty percent of the wood in the trees that are cut down reaches the market" (Twining 1963–1964, p. 123). This percentage was undoubtedly high compared with that of earlier years. To remain competitive with "free timber" cut from the public domain, loggers held down their unit costs by removing only the highest-grade logs. They regularly left the entire tree above the first branches, because the knots in the top sections increased manufacturing costs and decreased the value of the logs. Although only parts of the best trees were removed, the logging operations often destroyed most of the trees in a tract, with much the same effect as the modern clear-cutting method: no seed trees were left in place to reestablish the forests. Large denuded tracts were left scarred and covered with great accumulations of slash, which set the stage for an ecological holocaust.

As early as 1867 a report submitted to the Wisconsin State Legislature expressed a dire concern about the external costs that lumbermen imposed on the rest of the state. Among the complaints cited were the loss of shelter, which exacerbated the seasonal extremes, thereby making agriculture a more difficult and uncertain activity; and the loss of watershed, which increased the hazard of floods and the damage from soil erosion. But as condemning as it was, the report overlooked the most serious and most immediate externality—fire. In the dry season, fires fueled by masses of slash raged uncontrolled through both forest and prairie. Much of the cutover region of Wisconsin, Michigan, and Minnesota had become an explosive tinderbox. In October 1871 the Peshtigo fire burned over

THE COSTS OF ECONOMIC GROWTH

1.28 million acres and killed more than 1,000 people trapped in its fury. In 1881 a Michigan fire burned in excess of one million acres with a toll of 138 lives; and in 1894 a fire spread through parts of Wisconsin and Minnesota, engulfing 260,000 acres and killing about 500 people. Similarly tragic fires occurred in other lumbering districts, and smaller fires plagued the forests constantly. The following description of a 1933 fire in Oregon gives some idea of the enormity of the losses from slash-fed fires.

> The net area burned over in 11 days was 267,000 acres, over two-thirds virgin timber, estimated to contain 12 billion board feet, with an estimated loss to industry, the public, labor, etc. of $350,000,000. The stumpage value alone of the timber destroyed was $20,000,000. The amount of this fine virgin timber burned was equal to the entire timber cut in the United States in 1932, or 8 or 9 times more than the entire cut of the Douglas Fir region for 1932 [U.S. Department of Agriculture 1936, p. 10].

These fires destroyed ground cover, diminished the capacity of the land to function as a watershed, exposed the soil to erosion, and destroyed the immature trees that had survived the clear-cutting. The capacity of the forest for regeneration was thus greatly reduced.

The impairment of the utility of the forests as a watershed exacerbated the tendency of rivers to flood. These unusually severe floods caused abnormal silting of the river channels, thus diminishing their suitability for commercial navigation. More important, the silting of rivers greatly shortened the expected life of the reservoirs that were the heart of the western irrigation and hydroelectric power projects. Insofar as the frequency and extent of these fires could have been minimized by better management of the slash, they must be reckoned as a price paid by society for private savings on labor costs.

Internalizing Social Costs: The First Conservation Movement. The social and physical waste of American forests gave rise to two distinct responses as the nineteenth century ended. The first, and by far the more important in terms of its impact on conserving wood, emanated from the demand side of the market. As has already been seen, the failure of the market to ration wood kept its price down and encouraged consumers to use it lavishly. As an 1885 "Report on Wood Preservation" aptly noted: "So long as wood was cheap . . . , it was cheaper to let it rot in the good old way" (Olson 1971, p. 67). But the failure of the market also accelerated the depletion of the forests, resulting in more rapid price increases as sources of supply finally stabilized. Even as serious observers were predicting that impending wood shortages would inevitably result in a national disaster, consumers were quietly substituting other products for wood. Railroads, which as late as 1909 still consumed nearly one-fourth of the timber cut annually, would by the 1960's require only 3 to 4 percent of the annual harvest (excluding pulpwood). It was this type of consumer response to rising prices that, more than anything else, accounted for the solution to the "wood problem."

There was also a response from the supply side of the market that was aimed at the glaring economic waste generated by the common-property resource problem and the more serious external diseconomies. It was out of an effort to solve these problems that the first conservation movement, associated with the works of Gifford Pinchot and Theodore Roosevelt, was born. From a primary concern with timber management in the 1890's the concerns of the movement grew to encompass social, economic, and political issues.

It must be emphasized that the mainstream of the first conservation movement never embraced the strict protectionist views held by the likes of John Muir, who believed that the forests and other natural resources should be preserved for their intrinsic beauty. On the contrary, Pinchot was openly scornful of such a nonutilitarian attitude. He and the movement he led wanted to manage resources more efficiently, in order to promote development and ensure long-run supplies. In the case of the forests, this could be achieved by practicing what he called "scientific management," meaning sustained-yield forestry, in which the annual harvest would be matched by the annual growth. To accomplish this end, Pinchot advocated specific policies that would perfect the market mechanism. Treating publicly owned timber as if it were privately owned by charging stumpage fees commensurate with the value of the timber would alleviate the common-resource problem. Taking positive steps to prevent forest fires could reduce external diseconomies.

A second major thrust of the early conservationists was to harness American rivers for better flood control, irrigation, navigation, and electric power production. Preservationists' programs, as epitomized by the founding of the National Park Service in 1916 and by efforts to remove land from commercial use, represented a secondary theme within the movement. Here there is an interesting conflict of interests, because supporters of a more rational use of waterways (generally power companies, water companies, and farmers in need of water for irrigation) often allied with the more preservationist-minded forestry groups. The water development enthusiasts were well aware of the beneficial effects that forests had on preventing erosion, silting, and flooding by retarding the melting of snow and the flow of runoff. They therefore campaigned to protect watersheds from commercial exploitation, thereby coming into direct conflict with lumbering and grazing interests. Thus many preservationist programs succeeded because they suited the commercial interests of water conservationists.

The beginnings of federal policy to create a permanent forest reserve in the public domain date back to the Payson Act of 1891. This legislation actually increased the legal availability of free timber for agriculture, mining, and manufacturing interests; but it also contained a rider allowing the president to set apart and reserve timberlands by proclamation. Under this provision President Benjamin Harrison set aside more than 13 million acres, to which President Grover Cleveland added another 25 million. These actions elicited vigorous protest from western interests that wanted access for lumbering, grazing, and mining. In 1897 the passage of the Forest Management Act granted the secretary of the interior the power to regulate the occupancy and use of the reserves, thereby opening the door for commercial penetration and scientific management of public lands. Under the presidency of Theodore Roosevelt this movement was further advanced by the transfer of all forest reserves from the Department of the Interior to the Department of Agriculture, where they came under the supervision of Gifford Pinchot, head of the Forestry Service. Roosevelt also added almost 150 million acres to the national reserves.

The supply side of the market was finally being stabilized: the establishment of the reserves meant that the supply of timberlands in private hands was nearly fixed. Pinchot's decision to administer those lands as if they were privately held meant that little timber appeared on the market for which there had not been a payment at least approximating the market value of its stumpage. The vast pool of common-property timber ceased to exist, thereby ending the incentive to cut with abandon on public lands and increasing the incentive to adopt sustained-yield practices on privately held lands. It would, of course, take time (and high enough prices) for such techniques to spread, but the course was set.

The shift in federal government policy from one of disposal to one of permanent reserves brought pressure to reduce some of the more serious external costs of the logging industry. With the new commitment to "ownership" came an interest in protecting its property from fire damage. Both before and after the institution of timber reserves, potential losses from fire damage among the large private owners increased directly as the value of their stumpage increased. But when nearby public domain was still open, any private owner who undertook the expense of fire prevention on his land received only a small return on that investment. Fire prevention on one owner's land reduced only slightly the chance that his timber would go up in smoke: fire could still spread to his land from adjacent private or public land.

No prior fire prevention efforts had been made on the public land, at least in part because it was not regarded as being "owned" by anyone; it was "free." Placing the public land under reserve gave the Department of the Interior (and later the U.S. Forest Service) an incentive to implement a fire prevention program to protect the reserved land and the timber on it. This government action made it much more profitable for private owners to undertake fire prevention measures on their land. This private willingness to invest in fire prevention was a direct result of the timber reserve movement and was accompanied by agitation to create state and local fire protection districts. State and local governments responded to this demand, and their fire prevention efforts augmented those of the federal government and private landowners. Through this form of cooperative action, inspired by the conservation movement and propelled forward by self-interest, a major reduction in external diseconomies was achieved that had effects ranging from river control to wildlife management.

THE QUALITY OF URBAN LIFE: OVERCROWDING AND POLLUTION

The problems of pollution and waste disposal have been more serious in urban areas than in the countryside. This is so because the higher the density of population and industrial activity, the greater the burden put on the ability of nature to dissipate and absorb the offensive by-products that man creates. Recent research has heightened the awareness of the health hazards (one form that the costs take) of pollution. Most notable among these hazards has been the alarming increase in cancer during recent decades. This increase is often linked to specific environmental substances. According to the Council on Environmental Quality, from 60 to 90 percent of all cancer is related to environmental factors. Airborne pollutants common to large cities have been causally linked to cancer, respiratory illnesses, and even serious neurological disorders and mental illness. Many people may be seriously impaired psychologically by environmental contaminants without having any awareness that they are being poisoned. Clearly there is still much to learn about the potential deleterious effects of various chemicals; it is likely that the social cost of specific economic activities has been grossly underestimated.

Although the current concern with pollution is in part the outgrowth of the potential threat posed by new chemicals and high levels of urbanization, the general problem is not new, nor is it even evident that it is more serious today than in bygone days. Many commentators forget, or perhaps never realized, how serious environmental problems were in the "good old days."

A direct consequence as well as a cause of past economic growth was rapid urbanization. In an age when communicable diseases accounted for most deaths, redistributing the population from a predominantly rural setting to densely packed urban areas greatly intensified health problems. A look at mortality data indicates a pronounced difference between the health of the rural and urban populations near the middle of the nineteenth century: the rural death rate was almost twenty per thousand, while the urban rate was approximately thirty per thousand, a gap that cannot be explained by rural-urban age differences. Underlying these rather innocuous figures were millions of hours of agonizing fear and pain. Besides redistributing the population from the relatively healthy to the relatively unhealthy sector, the rapid urbanization caused a deterioration in urban health. Filled by legions of foreign immigrants and rural migrants, cities were unable to maintain basic sanitary services. Water supplies were contaminated by the seepage from privies and from open gutters that served as sewers. It is estimated that in 1880 more than half of American cities had no sewage system whatsoever. More than two-thirds of the urban households relied on privies or cesspools, the contents of which had to be emptied by hand (so to speak) and transported through the streets in open carts.

The removal of human waste was only part of the story. Dairies, slaughterhouses, stockyards, and livery stables were located within the cities, and herds of animals were driven through city streets to such locations. Scavengers, most notably pigs, were a frequent sight. But the most serious and ubiquitous health hazard was the precursor to the cursed automobile—the horse. It has been estimated that, in 1900, New York City residents had an average of nearly four million pounds of horse manure a day, or in excess of one billion pounds a year, deposited on their streets and in their stables. The implications of this would hardly create pleasant thoughts in the minds of modern public health officials concerned with controlling tetanus or glanders, or of modern urbanites who have been so upset by an occasional encounter with canine droppings. Needless to say, the stench, and at least a general awareness that the contamination caused by human and animal waste created a health hazard, did not escape the notice of nineteenth- and early twentieth-century urbanites.

To the problems created by human and animal waste must be added the other by-products of the rapidly growing urban communities. Garbage and offal from homes and restaurants were thrown into the streets and left for infrequent collection. Zoning laws and constraints on industrial disposal are largely products of the twentieth century, so the foulest of industries could, and did, locate in heavily populated areas. Next to stockyards were tanneries and fertilizer plants. Paint and varnish plants, chemical plants, copper refineries, iron and steel foundries, and even explosives plants could be found in the heart of nineteenth-century cities.

Chicagoans were constantly reminded that they lived among the greatest assemblage of stockyards on earth. The city air had a distinctive pungent aroma, as did its rivers. In 1864, William McCormick described the Chicago River, which bordered his family's famous reaper factory, thus: "I don't know of any remedy for [the] stinking river. The packing of pork is great here now and the river which has been *red* with blood I fear will be worse than ever." Other observers noted that on the fetid swamps, rivers, and inlets that crisscrossed the city floated a thick layer of grease.

At about the same time that McCormick was complaining about the Chicago slaughterhouses, a group of New York City citizens was investigating the causes of environmental health hazards in their city. Their report, published in 1866, offers some graphic descriptions of the external diseconomies generated by rapid urban growth:

> The 173 slaughter houses in this city are too offensive to health and decency to be longer permitted in their present localities. These establishments are now thrust into the midst of the most crowded districts, and it is to be observed that a loathsome train of dependent nuisances is found grouped in the same neighborhood [Citizens' Association of New York 1866, pp. xciv–xcv].

Elsewhere the report noted that in one district alone, several slaughterhouses were located on streets that had no sewers:

> ... and the blood and liquid offal is conducted by drains into the street gutters. In one instance ..., the blood and liquid offal flows the distance of two blocks before it empties into the river. This, during the summer weather, undergoes decomposition, which gives rise to a very offensive odor, and certainly must exert a very injurious effect upon the health of those living in the vicinity [ibid., pp. 261–262].

In a similar fashion the report condemned almost every aspect of public hygiene in the city. The locally drawn water contained a high concentration of putrid organic matter; privies were left full for weeks, in defiance of local ordinances; grocers, oystermen, and other businessmen threw their refuse into the streets with impunity; and rains and high tides backed up flooded sewers and privies.

As incredible as it seems, refuse companies not only composted their collections within the heart of the city; they defiantly used city parks and piers for this purpose. An 1861 report revealed that one enterprising contractor had thirty thousand wagon loads of manure stored at the Battery.

The Citizens' Association study referred to above described dozens of similar operations.

> One great source of filth in the streets is connected with the manure heap ... situated between Thirty-eighth and Thirty-ninth Streets, First Avenue and East River. Large portions of the squares adjoining are also used for the same purpose. Hundreds of loads of manure are daily brought from the stables in different parts of the city; putrefaction is excited as much as possible in the constantly-increasing heap, and at the proper season the compost is shipped for use in the country. The carts which gather the material are generally small and loosely constructed. Upon them the manure is piled until no more can be retained. As the driver proceeds to headquarters, the jolting shakes off no small portion, leaving his track wherever he goes. A single cartload fouls a street just cleaned, and a constant procession of them makes cleanliness impossible [ibid., p. 285].

This "natural" recycling center flourished about three blocks from the present location of the United Nations.

It should be reemphasized that the types of problems just described were neither new nor specific to American cities. The point is that the extremely rapid nineteenth-century urbanization (which was closely tied to the growth process) greatly magnified these problems, and more and more people were affected by them.

THE COSTS OF ECONOMIC GROWTH

CONCLUSION

It is abundantly clear that the types of social costs confronting society today are neither new nor, in terms of their impact on health and life expectancy, more serious than in some past periods. The fact that the United States is more densely populated and that a greater percentage of the people live in urban areas has increased congestion costs over time. But many costs that weighed so heavily on past generations have been reduced greatly. The despicable health and sanitary conditions found in urban centers in the 1860's offer a case in point. Summary indexes of urban health, such as data on child mortality and statistics on death from selected contagious diseases, suggest that important aspects of the quality of urban life deteriorated from early in the nineteenth century until the mid-1880's. Beginning in the 1880's and 1890's one observes significant improvements in urban health resulting from the construction of municipal sewer systems and water-filtration plants. These advances came as a result of a widespread public health movement motivated by regards similar to those of the conservation movement.

Although noxious activities adversely affected material well-being, the products of such activities often were added to, rather than subtracted from, the standard measure of economic output, the gross national product. For example, expenditures by private citizens for oats to feed their horses were counted as part of the national product. Riding horses on urban streets created pollution that led to the employment of street sweepers and cartmen. All of their earnings were included in the measure of national product. The horse-caused pollution also contributed to the spread of some diseases, thus increasing the demand for doctors and morticians and further adding to national product. It is easy to see that statistical measures are less than perfect. Double-counting intermediate steps in the production process and ignoring side costs continue to be serious problems that, if solved, would reduce the measure of economic output at any point in time. (Taking account of other factors, such as leisure and improvements in working conditions, would increase the measure.) It seems reasonable that because there are more intermediate steps, and thus more potential for double-counting, in more advanced economies, proper accounting of this problem would reduce the rate of growth over time. On the other hand, it is less certain whether the relative importance of unaccounted-for external costs has increased or decreased since the turn of the twentieth century.

William Nordhaus and James Tobin (1972) have attempted to correct the national income accounts for the period 1929–1965 by considering some of the issues just raised. Their revised estimates offer at least some assurance that even after side costs of production are explicitly considered, there still has been some improvement in welfare over the period in question. It seems highly probable that this conclusion could be extended backward into the later nineteenth century, if for no other reason than the vast improvements in health and life expectancy that occurred between 1880 and 1929. Most discussions of the welfare implications of economic growth focus on annual per capita income. But if one focuses on well-being over an entire lifetime, then the increases in health and life expectancy (much of which can be attributed to economic growth) play an even more central role in the overall evaluation of the long-run costs and benefits of growth.

BIBLIOGRAPHY

Harold J. Barnett and Chandler Morse, *Scarcity and Growth: The Economics of Natural Resource Availability* (Baltimore, 1963), shows that relative raw material prices have not risen historically as one would expect if resources were a brake on growth. Otto L. Bettmann, *The Good Old Days: They Were Terrible!* (New York, 1974), is a collection of journalistic accounts describing the unpleasant aspects of nineteenth-century life. William J. Baumol, "On Taxation and the Control of Externalities," in *American Economic Review*, 62 (June 1972), develops an economic theory of externalities and the use of taxes to mitigate their effects in a market economy. Citizens' Association of New York, *Report of the Council of Hygiene and Public Health of the Citizens' Association of New York, Upon the Sanitary Condition of the City*, 2nd ed., (New York, 1866, repr. 1970), is an excellent first-hand description of sanitary conditions in New York City in the mid-1860's. Ronald H. Coase, "The Problem of Social Costs," in *Journal of Law and Economics*, 3 (Oct. 1960), is the pioneering analysis of the reciprocal nature of social costs. Barry Commoner, *The Closing Circle: Nature, Man and Technology* (New York, 1971), gives an environmentalist's critical view of technological change and growth. John R. Commons, *Legal Foundations of Capitalism* (New York, 1924, repr. Madison, Wis., 1959), is the classic exposition on the interplay between markets and the legal structure in capitalist development. Council on Environmental Quality, *The Sixth Annual Report of the Council on Environmental Quality* (Washington, D.C., 1975), is a massive study of the full range of environmental issues: topics include air, water, solid wastes, and noise pollution; energy use; land-use policy; carcinogens in the environment. David Cushman Coyle, *Conservation: An American Story of Conflict and Accomplishment* (New Brunswick, N.J., 1957), gives a brief history of the major political conflicts surrounding the conservation of land and water resources in the United States. Alfred W. Crosby, Jr., *The Columbian Exchange: Biological and Cultural Consequences of 1492* (Westport, Conn., 1972), is a lively account of the effects of the discovery of the western hemisphere, containing an excellent summary of the effects that Old World diseases had on New World populations.

J. H. Dales, *Pollution, Property and Prices* (Toronto, 1968), is a concise example of how an economist analyzes stylized pollution problems, with a pioneering analysis of establishing a market in pollution rights. Lance E. Davis, et al., *American Economic Growth* (New York, 1972), is an excellent collection of essays written by economists on American economic history: chapter 2 analyzes long-run growth patterns in the United States and discusses the conceptual problems in measuring growth. John Duffy, *A History of Public Health in New York City, 1625–1866* (New York, 1968), is the most authoritative account of public health problems and of the social responses to those problems in New York City prior to 1866. Anthony C. Fisher and Frederick M. Peterson, "The Environment in Economics: A Survey," in *Journal of Economic Literature*, 14 (March 1976), gives a summary and analysis of the recent literature by economists, with an extensive bibliography. Robert F. Fries, "The Founding of the Lumber Industry in Wisconsin," in *Wisconsin Magazine of History*, 26 (Sept. 1942), is a descriptive history of the emergence of lumbering in Wisconsin in the pre–Civil War era. Marshall I. Goldman, "Growth and Environmental Problems of Noncapitalist Nations," in *Challenge*, 16 (July/Aug. 1973), shows that noncapitalist nations have serious environmental problems. Samuel P. Hays, *Conservation and the Gospel of Efficiency: The Progressive Conservation Movement, 1890–1920* (Cambridge, Mass., 1959), a history of turn-of-the-century conservation politics emphasizing emerging conflicts in resource use, argues that the growth of the conservation movement was part of a general trend toward centralized decision making by experts; and "The Limits-to-Growth Issue: A Historical Perspective," in Chester L. Cooper, ed., *Growth in America* (Westport, Conn., 1976), contrasts the contemporary environmental movement with the earlier conservation movement, arguing that the earlier conservation was more agreeable to economic growth than are today's environmentalists. Walter W. Heller, *Economic Growth and Environmental Quality: Collision or Co-Existence?* (Morristown, N.J., 1973), an example of how an economist analyzes the costs and benefits of growth, argues that collective or public morality on growth is changing as indicated by a growing willingness to impose taxes and other curbs on polluters and concludes that with correct government policies growth can help improve environmental quality. Benjamin Horace Hibbard, *A History of the Public Land Policies* (New York, 1924; repr. Madison, Wis., 1965), is the classic history of the evolution of public-land policy in the eighteenth and nineteenth centuries. Robert Higgs, *The Transformation of the American Economy, 1965–1914: An Essay in Interpretation* (New York, 1971), contains a concise discussion of the effect of expenditures on water treatment plants on urban health.

Eric E. Lampard, "The Social Impact of the Industrial Revolution," in Melvin Krazberg and Carroll W. Pursell, Jr., eds., *Technology in Western Civilization: The Emergence of Modern Industrial Society, Earliest Times to 1900* (New York, 1967), analyzes the impact of industrialization on living conditions and social relationships, going far beyond the usual considerations of wages and diet discussed in the debate over the working-class standard of living. Ezra J. Mishan, *The Costs of Economic Growth* (New York, 1967), is the best antigrowth discussion by an economist; and "The Postwar Literature on Externalities: An Interpretative Essay," in *Journal of Economic Literature*, 9 (Mar. 1971), is a review essay with an excellent bibliography. William D. Nordhaus, "Resources as a Constraint on Growth," in *American Economic Review*, 44 (May 1974), shows that resource prices have fallen substantially relative to the costs of labor. William Nordhaus and James Tobin, "Is Growth Obsolete?" in National Bureau of Economic Research, *Economic Growth*, Fiftieth Anniversary Colloquium V, series 96 (New York, 1972), develops an alternative measure to net national product that attempts to include many of the variables discussed in this article: the new index that they call "measure of economic welfare" has been growing more slowly than net national product, but it has been growing. Mancur Olson and Hans H. Landsberg, eds., *The No-Growth Society* (New York, 1973), a well-balanced collection of essays by leading experts dealing with all aspects of the costs of economic growth, gives an excellent overview of the important issues. Sherry H. Olson, *The Depletion Myth: A History of Railroad Use of Timber* (Cambridge, Mass., 1971), is a study of how individuals and firms responded to a declining supply of timber, showing the importance of technological change and of substitution of products by resource users.

Elmo R. Richardson, *The Politics of Conservation: Crusades and Controversies, 1897–1913* (Berkeley, Calif., 1962), is a political history of conservation issues. Nathan Rosenberg, "Innovative Responses to Materials Shortages," in *American Economic Review*, 63 (May 1973), shows how wood consumers changed their behavior in the face of impending shortages, giving an excellent example of how an economy develops substitutes and new technologies when faced with supply constraints. Sam H. Schurr and Bruce C. Netschert, *Energy in the American Economy, 1850–1975: An Economic Study of its History and Prospects* (Baltimore, 1960), a compendium and analysis of energy supply and demand in American history, is an excellent source for basic data. Frank E. Smith, *The Politics of Conservation* (New York, 1966), gives a political history of the controversies and policies surrounding natural resource use in American history; and ed., *Conservation in the United States: A Documentary History. Land and Water, 1492–1900* (New York, 1971); and *Conservation in the United States: A Documentary History. Land and Water, 1900–1970* (New York, 1971), are a valuable collection of documents dealing with the history of land and water in the United States. Robert M. Solow, "The Economics of Resources or the Resources of Economics," in *American Economic Review*, 44 (May 1974), is an exceptionally lucid summary of modern economic thinking on raw material economics. Donald C. Swain, *Federal Conservation Policy, 1921–1933* (Berkeley, Calif., 1963), argues that conservation programs expanded during the period 1921–1933 and that these programs set the stage for subsequent New Deal policies.

Joel A. Tarr, "From City to Farm: Urban Wastes and the American Farmer," in *Agricultural History,* 49 (Oct. 1975), shows a rural market existed for urban sewage. Stephan Thernstrom, "Urbanization, Migration, and Social Mobility in Late Nineteenth-Century America," in Barton J. Berstein, ed., *Towards a New Past: Dissenting Essays in American History* (New York, 1968), argues that there was much geographical mobility but little upward mobility, geographical mobility retarded the growth of labor organizations and class consciousness, and skilled workers displaced by new technologies often were absorbed into the new system. Charles E. Twining, "Plunder and Progress: The Lumbering Industry in Perspective," in *Wisconsin Magazine of History,* 47 (Winter 1963–1964), describes the lumber industry in Wisconsin in the post–Civil War period and argues that competition caused wasteful logging practices. U.S. Department of Agriculture, U.S. Forest Service, *Timber Depletion, Lumber Prices, Lumber Exports, and Concentration of Timber Ownership* (Washington, D.C., 1928), examines the relation between concentration of ownership and forest depletion; *Great Forest Fires of America,* by John D. Gutherie (Washington, D.C., 1936), is a brief statistical overview of major forest fires in American history. U.S. Department of the Interior, Census Office, *Tenth Census of the United States, 1880, Report of the Social Statistics of Cities,* George E. Waring, Jr., comp., 2 vol. (Washington, D.C., 1887), is a basic source for late nineteenth-century urban data. John S. Williams, Jr., et al., *Environmental Pollution and Mental Health* (Washington, D.C., 1973), shows that pollution is a serious contributor to mental disorders. U.S. Department of Health, Education, and Welfare, *Work in America, Report of a Special Task Force to the Secretary of Health, Education, and Welfare* (Cambridge, Mass., 1973), examines the sources of satisfaction and dissatisfaction in the workplace in the contemporary United States.

[*See also* ECONOMIC GROWTH; LAND POLICIES AND SALES; LAW AND POLITICAL INSTITUTIONS; MEDICINE AND PUBLIC HEALTH; NATURAL RESOURCES AND ENERGY; SOCIAL WELFARE; URBANIZATION; *and* WESTWARD MOVEMENT.]

IMPERIALISM

William H. Becker

IMPERIALISM, states historian Richard Koebner in *Imperialism . . . 1840–1960* (1964), "is not a word for scholars." Economists and economic historians seem to have taken this conclusion to heart, for they have not studied imperialism extensively. Major textbooks in American economic history devote few pages to the subject, if they mention it at all. Standard texts in introductory and international economics rarely treat the subject.

The relative scarcity of economic work on American imperialism is the result of two general tendencies. First, imperialism is a sociological and political as much as an economic phenomenon, and in recent years economic historians have focused on economic activity, leaving out the political and social context. Second, and perhaps of more importance, American economic historians have devoted more scholarly energy to the study of the nineteenth than of the twentieth century. The dominant economic influence of the United States in the international economy has been felt most profoundly in the period since the end of World War II, a period that to date has received comparatively little scholarly attention from economic historians.

Formal studies of American imperialism have been done. For the most part, the literature is dominated by radical critics who have attempted to refine Marxist-Leninist concepts in order to apply them to the American experience. As a result non-Marxist economists and historians generally think of imperialism as a concept more appropriate to ideological debates than to dispassionate inquiry. Imperialism has taken on such pejorative connotations that it has become the "hate word" of international politics. But scholarship cannot divorce itself from issues of great public concern. Indeed, the frequency and intensity with which the word is used suggest that scholars are the most appropriate people to try to understand imperialism.

Even after one becomes accustomed to the pejorative usage of the term, serious definitional problems remain. Lenin equated capitalism with imperialism. He argued that imperialism was rooted in the structure of the international economy and in the domestic needs of the major capitalistic states. (We shall return to a full discussion of the economic interpretation of imperialism.) Lenin's definition, though, is so closed that it prevents serious study of the subject by all but the most committed Marxists.

What is necessary is a definition that both radical and nonradical students can accept, at least as a point of departure. The most neutral definition hinges on what an imperialistic relationship is. Once scholars can establish that, and examine it empirically, they can move on to a consideration of the reasons for such a relationship. At the simplest level of definition, according to Martin Wolfe in *Economic Causes of Imperialism* (1972), an imperialistic relationship implies that the sovereignty of one state is directly or indirectly limited by another country or by powerful private interests in that other country.

AMERICAN IMPERIALISTIC BEHAVIOR

Using this definition, it is clear that the United States has been an imperialistic power. The two historical periods in which it most limited the sovereignty of other states were the early part of the twentieth century and the years since the end of World War II.

After the Spanish-American War in 1898, the

IMPERIALISM

United States acquired the Philippines, Puerto Rico, and Guam. In the Philippines it set up a full-scale colonial administration, replacing that of Spain. The United States inherited a nationalistic independence movement in the Philippines, the leaders of which turned on the United States when it became clear that independence would not be granted to the Philippines. Between 1899 and 1902 the United States had to fight an increasingly bloody guerrilla war in order to establish control.

The American government turned its attention increasingly to the Caribbean once it had suppressed the Philippine nationalist movement. By 1920 the United States had sent troops into almost all of the Caribbean countries. Some interventions were minor affairs, but others were long-lived, with far-reaching implications for the nations to which troops were sent. In Nicaragua, Haiti, and the Dominican Republic the United States administered customhouses, supervised local police, and undertook public works projects. The administration of President William Howard Taft went so far as to encourage American bankers to invest in the Caribbean, in some cases to renegotiate loans held by European banks. During the presidency of Woodrow Wilson, the scale and frequency of intervention increased. Wilson openly interfered in the internal affairs of Mexico. American entry into World War I forestalled further involvement in Mexico. The enmity generated by Wilson's policies continued for generations. Direct interventions declined after the war, and the legation guard stationed in Nicaragua was finally removed in 1923. By this time the United States generally refrained from direct involvement in the Caribbean area, although the fear persisted that it might send troops.

The United States turned inward in the 1930's, in part through disillusionment over World War I and in larger part because of the troubled economic conditions of that decade. Investment and trade fell off not only with Latin America but also with other parts of the world. Direct American involvement in the affairs of the Caribbean and Latin America was much less frequent in the 1930's than it had been in the previous twenty-five years.

After World War II the United States became more active in the world, and to its radical critics it is in these postwar years that the United States became the major imperialist power. To be sure, it consciously took on the role of organizer and defender of an international capitalistic system. Immediately after the war it helped reorganize the political, economic, and social life of Japan and West Germany, bringing them back into an international capitalistic community. In 1947, American aid to Greece and Turkey limited leftist activity in those two countries. Between 1945 and 1947 the United States government aided opponents of socialist and communist candidates for office in France and Italy. Intervention became more frequent in the following years. Either directly, through the military, or covertly, through the paramilitary operations of the Central Intelligence Agency (CIA), the United States intervened in Greece, Iran, Guatemala, Indonesia, Lebanon, Laos, Cuba, the Congo (now Republic of the Congo), British Guiana (now Guyana), and the Dominican Republic. In addition, charges persisted that America had participated in the ouster in 1964 of the government of João Goulart in Brazil and in the overthrow in 1973 of the Marxist government of Salvador Allende in Chile.

American influence was felt not only because of its military power; American institutions dominated the international economic life of the postwar world. Radical critics of the United States found as much to condemn in these economic relations as in military and paramilitary interventions. The International Monetary Fund, which the United States government helped organize, was to stabilize currencies and exchange relations. The World Bank, with significant American representation and contributions, provided international investment capital. Major private American banks expanded their business worldwide, and American multinational corporations substantially increased their direct investments in Europe, Latin America, and Asia.

The American government worked directly in the international economy through aid programs. Following the war its policymakers made loans to rebuild foreign economies. Proponents of this policy argued that such assistance would limit the poverty and political instability that led to subversion and communist governments. The most important example of this assistance was the Marshall Plan, which ultimately provided $13.5 billion to Western Europe. American aid also went to countries outside Western Europe, although after the Korean War military aid surpassed nonmilitary assistance.

In both public and private ways, then, American military and economic power was brought to bear on foreign governments and peoples. In many instances the United States limited the sovereignty of other countries. This was not a matter only of public power, for the decisions of American banking and corporate leaders, as well as those of generals and diplomats, affected the public policies and the lives of ordinary people throughout the world in the postwar decades.

The amount of money lent or invested abroad was not directly related to the extent to which sovereignty might be limited. Foreign investors in developing, capital-poor countries had greater influence than investors of substantially more money had in advanced industrial nations.

Similarly, officials of the CIA and the State Department could more easily interfere in the internal politics of weak governments in Asia and Latin America than in West European countries with developed economies and well-rooted political traditions. A small country with limited aid from the United States was probably more vulnerable than a larger and more economically and politically developed country, even though the latter might have received substantial sums of American aid and large numbers of military advisers.

ECONOMIC EXPLANATIONS OF AMERICAN IMPERIALISM

Why were there such bursts of imperial behavior by the United States? To radical and Marxist critics of America, imperialism was a requirement of a mature capitalistic state. Much of the postwar scholarly work on American imperialism has been done by such critics and scholars. To understand their analyses, one must first consider the traditional Leninist interpretation of imperialism.

Lenin wrote his famous pamphlet *Imperialism, the Highest Stage of Capitalism* (1917) in order to explain World War I to the socialist faithful and to correct the "errors" he found in some socialist interpretations of imperialism. Much of his study is an attack on errant Marxists who, like "bourgeois" interpreters of imperialism, viewed it as a policy of capitalistic states rather than as a structural prerequisite for the functioning of "monopolistic capitalism." Such later Marxist interpreters as Paul Baran, Harry Magdoff, James O'Connor, and Paul Sweezy follow Lenin's lead and interpret American imperial behavior as a result of the need of capitalism to absorb an economic "surplus" or to increase the profit rate. A point not fully developed by Lenin, yet of significance to contemporary radicals, is the effect of capitalism on the poor countries in which capitalists invest. The backwardness of much of the Third World, according to Marxist interpreters, is a result of American imperialistic exploitation, whereas in the past it was a result of the formal control of the European empires.

Most recent work has focused on the post–World War II period, although some diplomatic historians, such as William Appleman Williams, have adopted a quasi-Marxist analysis to explain American expansion at the end of the nineteenth century. These students of American diplomacy maintain that the United States became interested in the world market and international politics as a result of the need to find outlets for surplus manufactures. In response to these needs the government adopted a foreign policy that sought an "open world" for American trade and investment. As a result the United States opposed revolution even in the most oppressive societies, fearing that economic opportunities would be foreclosed by radical changes in governments and social structures.

Probably the most influential of the Marxist interpretations of recent imperialism is Harry Magdoff's *The Age of Imperialism* (1969). His work has gained the attention of non-Marxist economists because he avoids traditional Leninist determinism. Trained as an economist, he set out to study the behavior of the largest American corporations by reference to the historical context in which the multinationals made their decisions.

The need of these large corporations to expand—the "logic" of capitalistic expansion—led to the imperialistic behavior of the major capitalistic states, especially the United States. The basic drive of capitalism, as Magdoff saw it, was to accumulate. To meet this need, American capitalism spread worldwide. The American multinational corporations turned to the government for assistance in promoting or protecting their investments abroad. The government brought pressure abroad through aid programs and tariffs. Diplomacy and intelligence networks were also used, Magdoff argues, to influence foreign governments that proved unwilling to cooperate with American business. And, ultimately, American military power could be brought to bear to protect the interests of the multinational corporations.

Magdoff and others, such as Paul Baran and Paul Sweezy, see American imperialistic behavior as resulting from the needs of the capitalistic system. Baran and Sweezy's *Monopoly Capital* (1968) ambitiously tried to bring Marx and Lenin up to date by interpreting the modern American economy. While not focusing primarily on imperialism, they view imperialism in much the way Magdoff does. The largest corporations would ultimately turn to the government and the military to protect their positions in the world. They preferred peaceful control of trade and investment, but when necessary they would use political pressure and military force.

An equally influential Marxist study is Baran's *The Political Economy of Growth* (1957). Whereas Magdoff searches for the roots of imperialistic behavior, Baran focuses on the effect of the multinational corporation and the American government on the Third World. He maintains that the trade and investment of the leading capitalistic countries with the less developed world are detrimental. Investing in and buying the raw materials of a less developed country can limit its economic development. Tied, at times, to a volatile world market for these products, Third World countries find their income from trade unpredictable. Foreign investment further weakens them. Foreign investors repatriate large proportions of their profits rather than reinvesting them in new industry. Equally detrimental, according to Baran, was the growth of a "comprador element" or class that benefited most from the foreign corporations investing in their countries. This class generally did not invest their savings in their own country. Many who had substantial holdings in agriculture or mineral resources often used their earnings for conspicuous consumption or for investment in a "safer" political climate abroad. Finally, debt service in these countries became a serious problem as income generated from foreign trade was used to pay the interest on a large public debt.

There is more than a little truth to these Marxist analyses of the economic relations between advanced capitalist and developing countries. More conservative students of economic development and international trade also have found cause to lament the impact of the advanced capitalistic countries on the Third World.

Nevertheless, radical interpretations have come under attack by scholars who find them one-sided and distorted. Robert Zevin prepared a lengthy essay (1972) on the roots of nineteenth-century American imperialism to test Marxist-Leninist precepts against the American experience. Using the extensive work of economic historians on the nineteenth-century American economy, he concludes that the Marxist interpretation is at best inconclusive. Fluctuations in domestic investment were more the result of changes in European economies, especially as they affected the railroad sector, than of a swelling surplus. And when he considered the period since 1945, Zevin concludes that Leninist theory was even less applicable, since the postwar years were a period of rapid domestic growth with a comparatively full use of resources. Similarly, the radical model does not work when Zevin applies it to data on trade and the movement of capital in international markets. As a percentage of gross national product (GNP), exports remained fairly steady from the 1880's to World War I. After that conflict they began a trend downward. In the years following World War II, exports represented a smaller percentage of GNP than they did in the nineteenth century. As for foreign investment, Zevin points out that the United States remained a net international debtor until World War I. Since World War II, American net claims against foreigners generally have been about 1.2 percent of national wealth.

One of the most careful critiques of the economically determined analysis of recent imperialism is Benjamin J. Cohen's *The Question of Imperialism* (1973). A student of international economics, Cohen views imperialism in a broad historical, political, economic, and sociological context. He criticizes the economically determined analysis of imperialism because radical and Marxist observers are too rigid in their discussions of the workings of the major capitalistic economies and too negative in their views of the effects of the international economy on developing countries. Cohen argues that the United

States has shown itself to be much less dominated by a capitalistic class interest than radicals believe. The government has provided many social programs that represent genuine transfers of wealth. Although many social needs are unmet, and complacency is not called for, neither is the system sinking into the hopeless stagnation that Marx and Lenin thought inevitable.

Marxist and radical interpretations, in short, try to explain too much. Magdoff maintains that without American trade with and investment in the developing world, unemployment and stagnation would surely result. Surplus capital must be disposed of, and the monopolistic advantages of major American corporations must be protected. In fact, trade with and investment in the developing parts of the world have become less important to the United States since World War II.

Foreign trade and investment are important to the advanced industrial nations. Without these ties some industries would have lower profits, their costs would be higher, and their products would be less available. Yet, as important as exports from the industrial nations might be to Third World countries (in 1974 they amounted to $101 billion), they represent less than one-third of the exports of the major industrial powers. As a proportion of the gross national products of the major countries, exports to the developing nations averaged little more than 1 percent in the 1960's. Moreover, the share of underdeveloped countries in international trade declined, from more than 30 percent to less than 20 percent, between 1950 and 1960. Since World War II trade among the advanced industrial countries has continued to increase. This is in large part because the advanced nations have similar income and demand structures, making them good customers for each other.

Since the war foreign direct investment has been similarly important, especially to the United States. But, as with trade, there has been more direct American investment in Europe and Canada than in the developing world. Moreover, the rates of investment in the advanced economies are higher than they are in those developing. Between 1960 and 1970, American direct investment in Europe almost quadrupled (from $6.69 to $24.52 billion), and in Canada it doubled (from $11.18 to $22.79 billion). The rate and magnitudes were lower in the Third World. In Latin America direct investment did not double ($8.32 to $14.76 billion). Rates of increase were higher in Asia and Africa than in Latin America, although the magnitudes were very much below those in Europe and Canada. In Asia direct investment of American firms increased from $2.48 billion in 1960 to $5.56 billion in 1970; in Africa it was $1.07 billion in 1960 and $3.48 billion in 1970.

Radicals maintain that the earnings from investments in the poorer parts of the world are increasingly important to the functioning of the world capitalist system. To be sure, these investments are profitable to the corporations that made them, and to lose such income would be disruptive. But the earnings that American firms have made on their direct investments in developing countries have fluctuated rather than grown steadily. Between 1950 and 1957 net earnings on these investments advanced from 2.3 percent to 4.6 percent. But from 1957 to 1966 they declined to 3.6 percent. Trade with and investment in the Third World appear to be less significant to the advanced countries, rather than more significant, as the radical analysts maintain.

Yet radical critics argue that such figures ignore the growing reliance of the industrial countries on the raw materials of the developing countries. In the twentieth century industrial America has sought increasing supplies of raw materials from abroad, and many American sources of supply have been in the developing world. It does not follow, though, that the United States is dependent on these sources. In almost every category of minerals and other raw materials imported from a developing country, there are sources available either at home or in an advanced economy. The developing countries may have larger supplies and lower prices; but supplies exist elsewhere, even though they may come from lower-yield mines or fields. The technology to recycle materials has advanced markedly, as have techniques to process lower-grade resources. Similarly, synthetic materials have been, and presumably will continue to be, developed that could replace imported natural products. The elimination of important supplies of raw materials and minerals from abroad would cause hardship, lower profits, slower growth, and higher prices for finished products. Disrupted oil supplies in the 1970's have had serious effects on the American economy. But there are alternatives, costly as they may be in the short run.

There is more agreement between Marxists and nonradical economists on the potential negative effects of trade and investment on developing countries than on the importance of the Third World to advanced capitalistic countries. But here again radical analyses tend to overstate the case. Although trade and investment have retarded economic growth and contributed to "backwardness," they do not necessarily do so in every developing country.

Radical critics see trade in the raw materials of the Third World as contributing to backwardness in a number of ways. Developing countries dependent on a primary export sector operate in an international economic system dominated by the major capitalistic countries, especially the United States. The chief industrial countries have higher levels of output and income. To a large extent they determine the prices of manufactured products, for which they have significant comparative advantages. Because of their substantial demand for raw materials, they influence the supply and price of products from the developing countries, especially if the export sectors of those nations depend heavily on one or a few agricultural or extractive products.

These trade relations, radicals argue, distort other patterns of economic activity. Industrialization is difficult because of the historical head start of the major capitalistic economies. Access to increasingly advanced technology becomes harder and harder, and breaking into markets dominated by the efficient and aggressive multinational corporations is equally difficult. Even though many developing economies have advantages in cheap labor and abundant raw materials, they often lack a class of skilled native managers and technicians. Mechanical skills do not develop in economies wedded to the export of primary products. And even in such countries where human capital has developed—India, for example—there is a serious problem of emigration. The technically trained find opportunities more attractive in the richer capitalistic economies, and migrate.

Nonradical economists also have seen negative effects at work. In the nineteenth century a rapidly growing export sector stimulated some of the advanced industrial countries of today. The United States, Japan, the Netherlands, Denmark, and Sweden all benefited from trade with Great Britain. In recent decades some formerly developing countries have advanced because of the demand for primary products, most notably countries with rich oil resources. In general, though, demand from the capitalistic countries today provides less stimulus than was the case in the nineteenth century. As production in the advanced countries moves away from demand for heavy-resource-based industries like textiles and steel and toward the more technology-based industries of electronics, computers, and chemicals, primary products become less important. These trends have exacerbated the exchange problems of the developing countries as they import more to be consumed by their indigenous middle classes, to improve the efficiency of agriculture, and to stimulate the growth of local industry. A relative decline in earnings from exports limits efforts to improve agriculture and stimulate industry, since it creates a shortage of foreign exchange.

As serious as the problems of the developing nations are, Marxist critics nevertheless have tended to focus almost entirely on the negative aspects of their relations with the advanced capitalistic countries. Involvement in the international economy stimulates both national income and economic activity in the developing countries. Implicit in the radical critique is the assumption that Third World economies would be developing on their own without contact with the outside world. Even in Marxist countries like Cuba, development was not possible without trade and technology from an advanced industrial country, the Soviet Union.

There are, in addition, examples of countries that have successfully diversified their economies, beginning, in the process, to overcome the historical inequality between themselves and the advanced industrial economies. Cheap labor and abundant resources have allowed Mexico, Brazil, and South Korea to begin industrial manufacture or assembly. Their textiles, shoes, and simply assembled electronic products are competitive on the world market. The income generated from these industrial sectors helps to solve foreign exchange problems and stimulates domestic demand, which is met in part by the development of indigenous industry.

The ill effects of foreign investment also have been exaggerated. This is not to suggest that radical critics of American imperialism are wrong when they call attention to some of the negative consequences of foreign investment. Investment that hinders or prevents the growth of local enterprise, especially when credits are deliberately denied or when necessary labor is wooed away, is clearly detrimental. Even if foreign investment does nothing more than replace already existing capital facilities, it is negative. Such investment does not increase the total capital stock.

But in some developing countries foreign investment adds to the net capital stock. Even if investors realize dividends and interest on these investments, the addition to capital and to the possibilities of production is to the advantage of the country. Some critics, like Baran, seem to assume that investors should not make a return on their investment. It could be argued that the real problem with investment is not that dividends and interest are paid, but that the rate of private investment in the developing countries is not high enough. Rates of foreign investment were much higher in the nineteenth century than in the twentieth. Part of the problem for the developing countries is—to turn Lenin upside down—that investment can be made more profitably in the advanced capitalistic economies.

The outflow of dividends and interest, critics maintain, only worsens the balance-of-payments problems of the developing countries. But this is not the entire story. Indeed, in the sense that net capital stock is increased by foreign investment, a developing country might, in fact, be able to produce and export more, or it might be able to build domestic industries that could help reduce demand for imports.

Thus, while Marxist critics of American imperialism have, along with more conventional economists studying trade and development, concluded that trade and investment from the advanced industrial nations can be harmful, there is a tendency to overlook some of the benefits that accrue. It could be argued, more generally, that the problem is that developing countries have become less significant in terms of trade and investment, rather than more important, to the advanced industrial countries. Investment opportunities are good for the United States in Europe and Canada. Trade with these countries, which have income and demand structures similar to those of America, makes more sense than with developing countries that lack the vast demand for consumer goods or for the highly technological products absorbed by the capital sectors of advanced countries.

Yet if the radical critique overstates the case of the economic imperative of imperialism, how does one account for the demonstrably increased imperialistic behavior of the United States at the end of the nineteenth century and especially since 1945? To answer that question a number of scholars have turned to a different intellectual tradition. Some, like Richard Barnet, look back to Joseph Schumpeter to explain imperialism in social terms. Others, like Robert W. Tucker and Benjamin S. Cohen, find their explanations in the politics of the international state system as it has evolved in the twentieth century.

SOCIAL AND POLITICAL EXPLANATIONS OF IMPERIALISM

To turn to the social and political roots of imperialism is not to deny that economic considerations have played a part in American foreign policy. But economic explanations alone are not sufficient to clarify American imperialistic behavior since World War II or at the end of the nineteenth century. To be sure, there were numerous examples of particular economic interests affecting the course of American foreign policy in the late nineteenth and early twentieth centuries. Members of the administration of Ulysses Grant —including cabinet secretaries—stood to gain from the annexation of Santo Domingo in 1870. Similarly, Secretary of State Philander Knox was a stockholder in a firm that benefited from an American-inspired change of government in Nicaragua in 1909. But to look for a particular economic interest in the background of a major foreign-policy decision is a simplistic and ultimately fruitless task.

American imperialism is as much a social and political phenomenon as an economic one. Joseph Schumpeter's significant study *Imperialism and Social Classes* (1919) provided a social-structural analysis with important insights for understanding current imperialism. Prompted by analyses that portrayed World War I as the result of capitalistic competition, Schumpeter looked to what he called "unequal social development" to find the roots of imperialism and war. He saw the aggressive tendencies of an earlier age as "atavistic" forces lingering in the modern world. Eventually the imperialistic aristocratic classes would pass from the scene, and an inherently less warlike capitalistic class would dominate society. Until that happened, imperialism and war would continue.

To Schumpeter the militaristic and expansionist tendencies of modern European societies were as old as civilization. Ancient societies developed classes having the task of defense or expansion, and imperialism became a part of the behavior of these states. In more recent times imperialism arose from the needs of the ruling classes in the emerging modern monarchies, especially that of Louis XIV in France. The French king needed war to divert, reward, and occupy an aristocracy that he wanted to subordinate. The European states that fought World War I all had remnants of the aristocratic and militaristic classes that had been dominant in an earlier age. Schumpeter argued that the capitalistic classes as a whole were opposed to war and were in significant ways a force for peace. War disrupted business, and military establishments raised taxes. He recognized that individual capitalists might benefit from and support imperialistic policies, but as a class capitalists had been prominent opponents of mercantilist policies that were designed to raise revenue for monarchs in the seventeenth and eighteenth centuries. In the nineteenth century capitalists who engaged in international trade generally feared and opposed war for the disruption it caused in international economic life.

Schumpeter's insights can be expanded to include international politics. In their analyses of imperialism, recent scholars such as David Fieldhouse emphasize the importance of the practices of the international political system more than did Schumpeter. The aristocratic and militaristic classes that Schumpeter saw as the sources of imperialistic behavior had established the traditions that defined the ways in which international politics were conducted. As profound as economic change was in the late nineteenth century, equally momentous changes had occurred in the international system in the thirty years before World War I. The European balance of power that had developed in the seventeenth and the eighteenth centuries was comparatively fluid. Alignments changed without severely upsetting the equilibrium, without giving one state sufficient power to threaten the others. Napoleon changed this forever as he swept over Europe. After his defeat the Europeans tried to return to prewar patterns of state relations. Ultimately these efforts failed; by the latter part of the century the major states were locked into increasingly rigid alliances and competition for colonies.

What had happened? Essentially, after Germany and Italy each became unified, they wanted to behave like major states. They built navies, enlarged armies, and took colonies. These policies began as matters of prestige but became issues of strategic concern to Britain, which responded by intensifying its territorial expansion. Great Britain acted to protect its possessions and trade routes, but the pride of the aristocratic classes that conducted foreign policy there and on the Continent had as much to do with these rivalries as did the economic interests of their nationals.

The United States matured as a major international power in the last decades of the nineteenth century, and by 1898 it began to behave like some of the European states, especially in Central America. American intervention in the Caribbean cannot be understood without reference to the international system at the turn of the century. By the late 1890's the major European powers had carved up almost all of Africa in a fevered scramble for colonial possessions. A growing German navy and militant foreign policy worried American policymakers, who feared that European colonial rivalries would come to Central and South America. British economic influence was already strong in parts of Latin America, especially Argentina. German trade with several Latin American nations increased markedly, causing consternation to Britain and the United States. Most troubling to the American government were European loans to and investments in Central and South America. The administrations of William McKinley and Theodore Roosevelt feared that these investments and loans might be threatened by default or disorder and that a European nation, especially Germany, might use such a crisis as a pretext for intervention and, eventually, the acquisition of bases. Foreign naval bases in the Caribbean would have been particularly threatening to the continental United States.

In this international context the McKinley administration reserved the right of the United States to intervene in newly independent Cuba in the event of serious disorder. In 1902 the Roosevelt administration responded quickly when European powers threatened to use force to make Venezuela pay its debts. The United States reorganized Venezuelan finances and administered them in order to pay off European creditors. Similar interventions occurred in Santo Domingo, Haiti, and Nicaragua. In each instance the American government sought to bring order so as to prevent foreign intervention. American strategic concern for the area increased after the United States acquired the rights for a canal across Panama in 1903.

The administration of William Howard Taft frankly tried to induce American businessmen to trade and invest in the areas in which the United States had established protectorates. After the prolonged and bloody intervention in the Philippines (1899–1902), though, the public and the Congress were not enthusiastic about further direct commitments abroad. Taft and his secretary of state, Philander Knox, believed that increased private American investment in Caribbean countries would increase American security. On the one hand, if American bankers replaced European investors, the likelihood of an economic pretext for intervention from abroad would decrease. On the other hand, genuine American economic interests in these countries would create a stake in American policy among businessmen.

Nevertheless, Taft's policies were not directed primarily at protecting or fostering specific business interests. Like Roosevelt, he emphasized that American involvement abroad would help business generally, rather than particular interests. Such assurances were necessary because of general public antipathy to foreign involvements and because American bankers and businessmen had choicer options for investment and trade than the politically unstable and economically backward nations ringing the Caribbean. Similarly, Woodrow Wilson's interventions in the Caribbean and interference in Mexican affairs were far from being prompted primarily by economic considerations. Initially critical of Taft's "dollar diplomacy," Wilson ended up continuing and expanding American involvement in the Caribbean area. His interference in Mexican affairs stemmed from an excessive concern with the internal political organization of that country, a concern that earned the United States the enmity of people of all shades of political opinion in Mexico. Wilson's ill-advised policy was aborted by American entry into World War I in 1917.

But the international political and military competition at the turn of the century is not the only explanation for American imperialism. There were internal political and bureaucratic reasons as well. A growing military bureaucracy was particularly important to American imperialistic behavior. Concern for the growth of its organization had much to do with the support of the navy for imperialistic policies. There is much self-centered bureaucratic interest in the defense by the navy of its mission as the protector of new commerce. What better reason for an expanded navy than a worldwide commerce?

The army was no less interested in seeking bureaucratic advantage. Its establishment was enlarged by the Spanish-American War, and its responsibilities increased with the occupation of Cuba and the administration of the Philippines. Both required the army to take on new tasks. Gen. Leonard Wood, who was military governor of Cuba and later governor of Moro Province in the Philippines, oversaw the construction of sanitary systems, hospitals, schools, and roads. The successes of the army in Cuba and the Philippines made it easier for Roosevelt, Taft, and Wilson to send troops into other countries. The army supported such interventions to employ its new skills and justify its expanded role.

But the military bureaucracies were not alone in contributing to American imperialism. The Department of State and, in its own way, the Department of Commerce saw their roles enhanced by greater economic activity abroad. The Department of State encouraged businessmen to expand foreign trade and, in Latin America, investment in order to build a business constituency for the foreign-policy establishment that traditionally had been without general public support. Similarly, the Department of Commerce encouraged businessmen to develop foreign business, creating a bureaucracy to serve them by World War I.

The external context of the international political system and the forces of bureaucratic growth are even more significant in the period since World War II. In a work frankly influenced by Joseph Schumpeter and Max Weber, Richard Barnet finds the roots of American imperialism fundamentally within the bureaucracies that make up the postwar national-security state. But he observes that the bureaucracy developed an ideology, shared in the 1950's and 1960's by large sections of public opinion, that supported an expansionist, ultimately imperialistic, foreign policy. After World War II the United States justified its expanding international role as helping to bring order and law to a disorganized and violent world. In 1945 the preeminence of American power would, had it existed in the nineteenth century, probably have allowed the United States to establish the kind of international order that it wanted. But modern technology, the breakup of older colonial empires, and the coming of nationalism in former colonies, as well as the increasing power of the Soviet Union, made other peoples reluctant to accept an international system set by the United States. When thwarted, when the peace and order that it sought to bring were challenged, the United States often responded with force.

In the 1950's and 1960's there was a near-ideological consensus in the United States that defined America as the peacemaker, the model of democracy, and the harbinger of prosperity. But ideology is not sufficient to explain its imperialistic foreign policy. To understand the individual decisions that led to imperialistic behavior, Barnet closely analyzes the workings of the national-security bureaucracy: the military, the intelligence services, and traditional agencies such as the State Department. The international atmosphere to which these institutions responded created bureaucratic rivalries that helped foster a perception of the world that led to imperialistic behavior abroad.

An outgrowth of World War II, these bureaucracies grew and flourished in the early years of the Cold War, becoming a seemingly permanent part of American life with the vast increase in military expenditures during the Korean War (1950–1953). Barnet sees interventionism and imperialism as a result not so much of the realities of international politics but of the peculiar perception of the world within the national-security bureaucracy. Animating the competing elements within the national-security state were the usual bureaucratic desires for growth, security, and self-aggrandizement. Born during World War II, many of these agencies developed a code of behavior that extolled toughness and efficiency. The national-security bureaucracy adopted military solutions to political problems. It turned to the efficient American economic system to meet the economic needs of a world poorer than the United States.

Along with other radical critics of American foreign policy, Barnet sees American economic interests as tied to imperialism. But his is a restrained view of the place of capitalism in imperialism. To the extent that policymakers thought of increased trade and investment abroad as a matter of enhancing American security, there was a commonality of interest and purpose between national-security managers and business executives. Fostering close bonds between the two groups were similar social and educational backgrounds. Wall Street lawyers and leaders of industry and international banking moved with ease between government bureaucracies and the private sector.

Despite fundamental similarities in background and outlook, Barnet observes that in many instances the national-security managers and multinational corporations were at odds with each other. The concern of the corporations with efficiency and profitability was at times contrary to the policies of the national-security managers. Leaders of the multinational corporations increasingly opposed the Vietnam War (1961–1975). The conflict caused inflation and an outflow of gold from the United States. For their part, national-security managers disliked the dealings that the multinationals had with countries and regimes that did not serve American security interests. To be sure, multinationals were at times served well by the interventions planned by the national-security managers. But Barnet ultimately concludes that in the future there will be more divergence than convergence between the interests of American security, as perceived by the bureaucrats in the national-security apparatus, and the leaders of the major multinational corporations.

For Barnet imperialism stems from two

sources that diverge more than they converge. Unlike Lenin, he does not equate imperialism with capitalism; rather, he envisions at least as a possibility that American capitalism could be used to provide the cheap and durable goods that the poor of the world need. Imperialism, Barnet concludes, is as much a result of the social system as of the needs of the economy. The multinational corporations are imperialistic in the sense that, given their economic power, they define the ordering of the world economy in terms of their own interests and profitability rather than in ways that the poor might define for themselves. Barnet sees in the multinational corporation and its vision of efficiency some progress over the crude exploitation of the past. But the multinationals define economic progress in their own terms; and so, with other critics, Barnet laments the negative consequences for the Third World of the policies of the multinational corporation.

CONCLUSION

"Imperialism," then, is a word for scholars, although economic historians have not given it the extensive attention they have devoted to other subjects. As scholarly as most of the works cited here are, they have all been influenced by the times in which they were written. New interpretations are beginning to appear during a period in which American power seems to have declined. Since the end of the Vietnam War, it has become clear that the American government and public do not favor a continued activist and interventionist foreign policy. Equally important in changing the international atmosphere, and the way in which Americans perceive it, has been the success of the Organization of Petroleum-Exporting Countries (OPEC) oil cartel. The United States has less resolve to force its will in the world while seeming to be more vulnerable than it was in the 1960's. New scholarly works on aspects of imperialism are already beginning to reflect these changed circumstances. Theodore Moran's *Multinational Corporations and the Politics of Dependence* (1975), for example, points out that in the 1950's and 1960's Chile was not so weak in the face of the multinational corporations as it might have appeared at the time. A similar point is made in Stephen Krasner's *Defending the National Interest* (1978), in which he finds that in the 1950's the developing countries had greater leverage in dealing with the multinational corporations than might have been obvious.

BIBLIOGRAPHY

Paul Baran, *The Political Economy of Growth*, 2nd ed. (New York, 1962), is a careful radical analysis of the effects of capitalism on developing countries. Paul Baran and Paul Sweezy, *Monopoly Capital* (New York, 1968), a major work that applies Marxist analysis to recent American economic history, focuses on domestic developments but also devotes attention to American foreign economic activity. Richard Barnet, *The Roots of War* (New York, 1973), is an excellent social, economic, and political analysis of imperialism. Benjamin J. Cohen, *The Question of Imperialism: The Political Economy of Dominance and Dependence* (New York, 1973), written by an economist with a knowledge of history and sociology, is the best book on the subject. David K. Fieldhouse, *Economics and Empire, 1830–1914* (London, 1973), a major scholarly treatment of empire that draws on the literature of several countries, portrays the imperial context in which the United States became a major power. André G. Frank, *Latin America: Underdevelopment or Revolution* (New York, 1969), an angry Marxist analysis of American economic relations with Latin America, portrays the developing countries as the victims of systematic economic exploitation.

Alan Hodgart, *The Economics of European Imperialism* (New York, 1978), is a useful brief introduction to the literature about the theoretical controversies surrounding imperialism. Richard Koebner and Helmut D. Schmidt, *Imperialism: The Story and Significance of a Political Word, 1840–1960* (Cambridge, 1964), is the intellectual history of the use of the word "imperialism." V. I. Lenin, *Imperialism, the Highest Stage of Capitalism* (New York, 1939), is one of the many editions of this classic pamphlet that has informed most radical critiques of imperialism. Harry Magdoff, *The Age of Imperialism* (New York, 1969), is probably the most widely read of the radical critiques of American imperialism. James O'Connor, "The Meaning of Economic Imperialism," in Kuang T. Fann and Donald C. Hodges, eds., *Readings in U.S. Imperialism* (Boston, 1971), is a short statement of the radical critique of the economic impact of the United States on the world. Joseph Schumpeter, *Imperialism and Social Classes* (New York, 1951), ed. Paul M. Sweezy, is one of the classic works on imperialism.

Robert W. Tucker, *The Radical Left and American Foreign Policy* (Baltimore, 1971), is an excellent analysis of the radical criticism of American foreign policy. William Appleman Williams, *The Tragedy of American Diplomacy* (New York, 1962), the most influential criticism of American foreign policy, is as much intellectual as diplomatic history; Williams sees economic considerations as fundamental to policymakers' perception of the world. Martin Wolfe, ed., *Economic Causes of Imperialism* (New York, 1972), a useful collection of excerpts from some of the major writings on imperialism, has an editor's introduction that discusses very well the issues in studying imperialism. Robert Zevin, "An Interpretation of American Imperialism," in *Journal of Economic History,* 32 (March 1972), an extended essay that makes use of recent work of economic historians to test Leninist theories of imperialism, develops a broad social-political analysis to explain imperialism.

[*See also* BUREAUCRACY; COSTS OF ECONOMIC GROWTH; FOREIGN TRADE; MULTINATIONAL ENTERPRISE; MILITARY-INDUSTRIAL COMPLEX; *and* SOCIALISM.]